D0222738

"Routledge's Leadership: Theory and Practice series is a significant addition to the current scholarship on leadership, and *The Global Obama: Crossroads of Leadership in the 21st Century*, edited by Obama biographer Dinesh Sharma and psychologist Uwe Glelen, offers penetrating observations about President Obama's leadership style as it relates to foreign policy. With contributions from scholars from all five continents, this book is a trove of information and insight."

—James MacGregor Burns, author of *Leadership*

"An extraordinary book, not only in its sheer range of views on Obama's leadership from around the world, but on the dilemmas and possibilities of American presidency in a global context."

—Sudhir Kakar, Psychoanalyst, Writer and Management Guru, Goa, India and INSEAD, France

"True leaders do not follow where the path may lead but go where there is no path and where they can leave a trail. Dinesh Sharma and his associates have exactly done that, taking a kaleidoscopic look at the enigma that is Obama—an individual who is a true leader in hope (to quote Napoleon). For anyone who wants to know more about this US president, this book will be a must."

—Manfred F. R. Kets de Vries, Distinguished Clinical Professor of Leadership and Organizational Change, The Raoul de Vitry d'Avaucourt Chaired Professor of Leadership Development, INSEAD, France

"This global report card on President Obama by a diverse group of top contributors is a comprehensive examination of "the global Obama": the promise and the performance. It is a book certain to attract attention, and deserves a wide audience. It is first-rate from start to finish."

—Michael A. Genovese, Loyola Chair of Leadership, Professor, Political Science Director, Institute for Leadership Studies, Loyola Marymount University, USA

"This book is a most riveting exploration of the strength of a President of the most powerful country in the world, to be able to bridge the gap between the races, genders, cultures, religions and the powerful and the powerless, and his ability to bring about peace in the world through nonviolent means, written by some of the most respected international scholars."

—Ela Gandhi, Politician, Peace Activist and Director, Gandhi Development Trust, and Former Member of Parliament, South Africa

"There have been attempts, through collections of essays, to portray Obama as a global leader—the first international President since Thomas Jefferson. This collection is the first to really accomplish this difficult task. Indeed, most of the essays in this volume take a big step forward. They describe how Obama changed America's image abroad and the specific ways and locations in which this was done. How can one ask for more? The book is far more than a study of the 44th President."

—Lawrence J. Friedman, Mind, Brain and Behavior Initiative, Harvard University, and Professor Emeritus of History, Indiana University, USA

"*The Global Obama* presents a sophisticated progress report on the worldwide impact of the Obama presidency. Anyone seeking to understand how both Obama and America are perceived and judged internationally will find the answer in this book."

—Robert A. LeVine, Professor Emeritus of Anthropology and Education, Harvard University, USA

"An invaluable resource and wonderful read. This exploration of Barack Obama's impact on the international stage and his relationship to lands beyond American shores commands the attention of readers seeking to understand the importance and complexity of presidential leadership in the modern world."

—**George Goethals, Professor, E. Claiborne Robins Distinguished Professorship in Leadership Studies, University of Richmond, USA**

"*The Global Obama: Crossroads of Leadership in the 21st Century* is an enlightening book on Barack Obama's presidency leading up to his current term. In this exceptional book, edited by distinguished scholars Dinesh Sharma and Uwe P. Gielen, a number of outstanding contributors from around the world share their perspectives on Obama's leadership, struggles, and accomplishments, as viewed globally. This book is unique in its diverse and comprehensive international view of Obama's role as president of the United States. Each chapter provides a new context for understanding Obama as both an international leader as well as an individual with his own history. *The Global Obama* is not only an essential book for those interested in contemporary political psychology; I highly recommend it for both students and professionals, as well as for those who share a commitment to understanding greater issues of leadership and globalization in our ever-changing society."

—**Florence L. Denmark, Ph.D. Robert Scott Pace Distinguished Research Professor of Psychology, Former President of the American Psychological Association**

"The Global Obama is a commendable experiment in applying almost the entire spectrum of social science knowledge to a single case of global leadership. The result is kaleidoscopic perspective on leadership in its most complex manifestation. Thought provoking."

—**Jagdeep S. Chhokar, Professor Emeritus of Management and Organisational Behaviour, Indian Institute of Management, Ahmedabad**

"A seminal exploration of Barack Obama's international standing, a collaborative collage painting a complex picture of the President as a Peace Prize planetary citizen, compassionate humanitarian, militaristic expansionist and Teflon diplomat with incomparable oratory skills. Bravo!"

—**Kam Williams, Syndicated Critic, AALBC.com**

"Dr. Sharma was welcomed for his previous book tour throughout EU and North America. I look forward to his new and insightful book "The Global Obama: Crossroads of Leadership in the 21st Century" (co-editor Uwe P. Gielen), a very timely read within the context of our present global challenges."

—**Ken Sherman, International Vice Chair, and Former International Chair, Democrats Abroad**

THE GLOBAL OBAMA

The Global Obama examines the president's image in five continents and more than twenty countries. It is the first book to look at Barack Obama's presidency and analyze how Obama and America are viewed by publics, governments and political commentators around the world. The author of *Barack Obama in Hawai'i and Indonesia: The Making of a Global President* (Top 10 Black History Book) scaled the globe to gather opinions—cultural, historical and political analyses—about Obama's leadership style. Writers, journalists, psychologists, consultants and social scientists present their views on Obama's leadership, popularity, and many of the global challenges that still remain unresolved. As a progress report, this is the first book that tries to grasp "the Obama phenomenon" in totality, as perceived by populations around the world with special focus on America's leadership in the 21st century.

Dinesh Sharma is the author of *Barack Obama in Hawai'i and Indonesia: The Making of a Global President,* which was rated as the Top 10 Black History Book for 2012 by the American Library Association. He is a regular columnist for *Asia Times Online, The Global Intelligence,* and a contributor to *Al Jazeera English, Eastern Eye, News Blaze* and many other news websites. Currently, he is an Associate Research Professor (Hon.) at the Institute for Global Cultural Studies, SUNY-Binghamton, Senior Fellow at the Institute for International and Cross-Cultural Psychology, New York, and a Host and Producer at Princeton TV. He has been a visiting professor and lecturer throughout EU, Asia and Africa. He has consulted in the healthcare industry for almost ten years for Fortune 500 clients, while he authored or edited six books and hundreds of peer-reviewed, scientific as well as journalistic articles. His other books or monographs include: *Psychoanalysis, Culture and Religion* (2014); *Human Technogenesis: Cultural Pathways through the Information Age* (2004); *Childhood, Family and Sociocultural Change in India* (2003); *Socioemotional Development Across Cultures* (1998). He earned a Master's degree in Clinical Psychology from Loyola University and a Doctorate in Human Development and Psychology from Harvard University.

Uwe P. Gielen is the Founder and Executive Director of the Institute for International and Cross-Cultural Psychology at St. Francis College, New York. He is the editor of some 20 books including (with Roy Moodley and Rosa Wu) *Handbook of Counseling and Psychotherapy in an International Context* (2013) and (with Michael Stevens) *Toward a Global Psychology: Theory, Research, Intervention, and Pedagogy* (2007). He earned a Master's degree in Psychology from Wake Forest University and a Doctorate in Social Psychology from Harvard University.

LEADERSHIP: Research and Practice Series

A James MacGregor Burns Academy of Leadership Collaboration

SERIES EDITORS

Georgia Sorenson, Ph.D., is a Research Professor in Leadership Studies, University of Maryland and Founder of the James MacGregor Burns Academy of Leadership and the International Leadership Association.

Ronald E. Riggio, Ph.D., is the Henry R. Kravis Professor of Leadership and Organizational Psychology and former Director of the Kravis Leadership Institute at Claremont McKenna College.

Scott T. Allison and George R. Goethals
Heroic Leadership: An Influence Taxonomy of 100 Exceptional Individuals

Michelle C. Bligh and Ronald E. Riggio (Eds.)
Exploring Distance in Leader-Follower Relationships: When Near Is Far and Far Is Near

Michael A. Genovese
Building Tomorrow's Leaders Today: Developing Polymath Leaders for a Changing World

Michael A. Genovese and Janie Steckenrider (Eds.)
Women as Political Leaders: Studies in Gender and Governing

Jon P. Howell
Snapshots of Great Leadership

Aneil Mishra and Karen E. Mishra
Becoming a Trustworthy Leader: Psychology and Practice

Ronald E. Riggio and Sherylle J. Tan (Eds.)
Leader Interpersonal and Influence Skills: The Soft Skills of Leadership

Dinesh Sharma and Uwe P. Gielen (Eds.)
The Global Obama: Crossroads of Leadership in the 21st Century

THE GLOBAL OBAMA

Crossroads of Leadership
in the 21st Century

Edited by
Dinesh Sharma and Uwe P. Gielen

Routledge
Taylor & Francis Group

NEW YORK AND LONDON

First published 2014
by Routledge
711 Third Avenue, New York, NY 10017

and by Routledge
27 Church Road, Hove, East Sussex BN3 2FA

Routledge is an imprint of the Taylor & Francis Group, an informa business

© 2014 Taylor & Francis

The right of the editors to be identified as the authors of the editorial material, and of the authors for their individual chapters, has been asserted in accordance with sections 77 and 78 of the Copyright, Designs and Patents Act 1988.

All rights reserved. No part of this book may be reprinted or reproduced or utilized in any form or by any electronic, mechanical, or other means, now known or hereafter invented, including photocopying and recording, or in any information storage or retrieval system, without permission in writing from the publishers.

Trademark notice: Product or corporate names may be trademarks or registered trademarks, and are used only for identification and explanation without intent to infringe.

Library of Congress Cataloging-in-Publication Data

The global Obama : crossroads of leadership in the 21st
century / edited by Dinesh Sharma, Uwe P. Gielen.
        pagescm. — (Leadership : research and practice)
    Includes bibliographical references and index.
  1. Obama, Barack—Influence. 2. Obama, Barack—Public opinion.
  3. United States—Foreign public opinion. 4. United States—Foreign
relations—2009– 5. Globalization—Political aspects. I. Sharma, Dinesh, 1955– author, editor
of compilation. II. Gielen, Uwe P. (Uwe Peter), 1940– author, editor of compilation.
E907.G59 2014
973.932092—dc23   2013019650

ISBN: 978-1-84872-625-3 (hbk)
ISBN: 978-1-84872-626-0 (pbk)
ISBN: 978-0-203-76193-9 (ebk)

Typeset in Minion
by Apex CoVantage, LLC.

Printed and bound in the United States of America by
Walsworth Publishing Company, Marceline, MO.

Dedicated to a few of my notable teachers:
Bob LeVine, Sudhir Kakar, and Dan McAdams
Dinesh Sharma

Dedicated to the memory of Peter Hofstätter
who first taught me social psychology through his books
Uwe P. Gielen

CONTENTS

ix

CONTENTS

ABOUT THE EDITORS

Dinesh Sharma is the author of *Barack Obama in Hawai'i and Indonesia: The Making of a Global President,* which was rated as the Top 10 Black History Book for 2012 by the American Library Association. He is a regular columnist for *Asia Times Online, The Global Intelligence,* and a contributor to *Al Jazeera English, Eastern Eye, News Blaze* and many other news websites. Currently, he is an Associate Research Professor (Hon.) at the Institute for Global Cultural Studies, SUNY-Binghamton, Senior Fellow at the Institute for International and Cross-Cultural Psychology, New York, and a Host and Producer at Princeton TV. He has been a visiting professor and lecturer throughout EU, Asia and Africa. He has consulted in the healthcare industry for almost ten years for Fortune 500 clients, while he authored or edited six books and hundreds of peer-reviewed, scientific as well as journalistic articles. His other books or monographs include: *Psychoanalysis, Culture and Religion* (2014); *Human Technogenesis: Cultural Pathways through the Information Age* (2004); *Childhood, Family and Sociocultural Change in India* (2003); *Socioemotional Development Across Cultures* (1998). He earned a Master's degree in Clinical Psychology from Loyola University and Doctorate in Human Development and Psychology from Harvard University.

Uwe P. Gielen is the founder and executive director of the Institute for International and Cross-Cultural Psychology at St. Francis College in New York. He is the editor of some twenty books including (with Roy Moodley and Rosa Wu) *Handbook of Counseling and Psychotherapy in an International Context* (2013), (with Michael Stevens) *Toward a Global Psychology: Theory, Research, Intervention, and Pedagogy* (2007), and (with Jeffrey Fish and Juris G. Draguns) *Handbook of Culture, Therapy, and Healing* (2004). He has lectured in thirty-three countries on topics related to international psychology and has served as president of the Society for Cross-Cultural Research, the International Council of Psychologists, and the International Psychology Division of the American Psychological Association. He earned a master's degree in psychology from Wake Forest University and a doctorate in social psychology from Harvard University.

ABOUT THE CONTRIBUTORS

Ramadan A. Ahmed is a professor of psychology in the College of Social Sciences, Kuwait University, Kuwait. An Egyptian citizen, Dr. Ahmed received Egypt's State Incentive Award for Social Sciences (psychology) in 1994, and in 2008 he was named Outstanding International Psychologist by the International Psychology Division of the American Psychological Association. His publications include the volume *Psychology in the Arab Countries,* which received the Egyptian Al-Ahram Prize for Distinguished Books in 1999–2000.

Rabi S. Bhagat is a professor of international management and organizational behavior at the University of Memphis. He received his Ph.D. in business administration from the University of Illinois at Urbana-Champaign, a master's degree in labor and industrial relations from the University of Illinois, and another master's degree (with honors) in industrial relations from the Xavier Institute in India. His numerous books include *Cambridge Handbook of Culture, Organizations, and Work*, *Work Stress and Coping in the Era of Globalization*, and *Managing Global Organizations: A Cultural Perspective.*

Thomas Cieslik received a doctoral degree in political science from the Catholic University, Eichstätt (Germany), and has taught in Mexico as well as in Germany. He has authored numerous articles and books on leadership within the context of globalization and is the author of *Wiedervereinigungen während und nach der Ost-West Blockkonfrontation* [*Reunions during and after the Confrontation between the East and West Blocks*] and the coauthor of *Immigration: A Documentary and Reference Guide.*

Sathasivian "Saths" Cooper is one of the best-known South African psychologists, a political activist, and a former Anti-Apartheid prisoner from Roben Island. A clinician by training, he served as the president of the 2012 International Congress of Psychology, Cape Town, South Africa, and is the current president of the International Union of Psychological Science, a kind of United Nations for psychologists.

Dovid Efune hails from Brighton, England, and is the editor of *The Algemeiner newspaper* and director of the Gershon Jacobson Foundation (GJCF). Now living in New York, he is credited with building the *The Algemeiner* into the fastest-growing Jewish newspaper in America. He received rabbinic ordination from Machon Lehoroah in Pretoria, South Africa, and Machon Ariel in Jerusalem.

Pepe Escobar is a journalist based in Thailand where he writes a column entitled "The Roving Eye" for *Asia Times Online.* He is also an analyst and correspondent for *The Real Time News Network.* His article "Get Osama Now Or Else . . . " was published by *Asia Times Online* two weeks before the terrorist attacks of September 11, 2001, wherein he reported from Afghanistan on the Al Qaeda terrorist network.

Edwin P. Hollander has been a CUNY Distinguished Professor of Psychology at Baruch College and the City University of New York Graduate Center since 1989. Now Professor Emeritus, he is teaching and supervising student research in the industrial/organizational doctoral and master's programs of the Graduate Center. He has held visiting appointments as a Fulbright Professor at Istanbul University, as an NIMH Senior Fellow at the Tavistock Institute in London, and as a faculty member at Wisconsin University, Harvard University, Oxford University, and the Institute of American Studies in Paris. He served on military duty in psychological services twice and was study director of the Committee on Ability Testing of the National Academy of Sciences.

Akis Kalaitzidis is a well-known political scientist at the University of Central Missouri. He teaches a variety of classes, including American government, the European Union, politics of post-Communist transitions, international relations, international organizations, and American foreign policy. He is the author of *Global Politics in the Dawn of the 21st Century* and coauthor of *US Foreign Policy: A Documentary and Reference Guide.*

Matthias M. Maass was born and raised in Berlin/Germany and educated in Australia, Germany, and the United States and is now based in Korea at Yonsei University in Seoul. He teaches international law at the University's Graduate School of International Studies and International Relations Theory at the Underwood International College. His numerous publications include several recent articles regarding the political situation on the Korean Peninsula, the special role of small states, and various aspects of US foreign policies.

Khalil Marrar, who received his doctoral degree in political science from Loyola University, is a well-known political scientist at the University of Central Missouri, Warrensburg, Missouri. He is the author of many articles on topics such as the Israeli-Palestinian conflict and Mideast peace processes. His book, *Arab Lobby and US Foreign Policy: The Two-State Solution*, appeared in 2009.

Mohammad Masad is assistant professor at the Department of Humanities and Social Sciences at Zayed University, Dubai. He completed his graduate studies in history in the United States and was a recipient of the Fulbright-Hays Doctoral Research Abroad Fellowship. His research interests include Islamic history, the Middle East, Medieval divination, Mediterranean cultures and societies, Palestine, Dubai and the United Arab Emirates. He also has maintained an interest in creative writing, especially poetry and fiction.

Ali Al'amin Mazrui is a Kenyan-born Pan Africanist scholar as well as one of the best-known academic and political writers on African and Islamic studies and North-South relations. Trained at Manchester University, Columbia University, and Oxford University, he is the author of well over thirty books. He currently serves as an Albert Schweitzer Professor in the humanities and as the director of the Institute of Global Cultural Studies at Binghamton University in Binghamton, New York, as well as Albert Luthuli Professor-at-Large at the University of Jos, Nigeria.

Annette S. McDevitt is on the faculty of management at the University of Memphis. She has published extensively on organization behavior in cross-cultural settings, including, most recently, *Managing Global Organizations: A Cultural Perspective* (with Rabi S. Bhagat and Harry S. Triandis). She has presented at international meetings and has traveled throughout Europe, Japan, and Egypt.

Elisa Moncarz is Professor Emerita of accounting and finance in the School of Hospitality and Tourism Management at Florida International University, where she has been a member of the faculty since 1974. A certified public accountant in New York and Florida, she has extensive auditing, tax, and Securities Exchange experience with several national and international firms including Ernst &

Young. Professor Moncarz has coauthored six books and book chapters in accounting and financial management including a book chapter in *Accounting and Finance for the International Hospitality Industry* and a textbook on accounting for the hospitality industry in 2003.

Raul Moncarz has served as vice provost of the Biscayne Bay Campus of Florida International University and presently teaches in its Department of Finance and Real Estate. He specializes in Latin American economic and financial policy.

Donald Morrison is an American author and lecturer based in Paris and New York. In a long career at *TIME* magazine, he wrote and edited in every department of the weekly news magazine. He was editor of its Asian edition in Hong Kong and its European edition in London. A frequent public speaker and conference moderator, he has taught at New York University in London, Tsinghua University in Beijing, and the Institute d'études politiques (Sciences Po) in Paris.

Arturo G. Muñoz is a senior political scientist at the RAND Corporation. Prior to joining RAND, Muñoz served for twenty-nine years at the Central Intelligence Agency, both in the Directorate of Operations and in the Directorate of Intelligence. He created successful counterterrorism, counter-insurgency, and counternarcotic programs, from initial planning to full implementation in the field. As an analyst, he wrote groundbreaking intelligence assessments on insurgent movements in Latin America, which pioneered the application of anthropology to intelligence. Muñoz received a bachelor's degree in history and Spanish literature from Loyola University; an A.B.D. in anthropology from the University of California, Los Angeles; and a master's degree in anthropology and a Ph.D. in history from Stanford University.

Evgeny Osin received his PhD in Psychology from Moscow State University in 2007. He has conducted in a number of psychological surveys and developed several scales. His research interests include personal meaning, dispositional and attributional optimism, eudaimonic well-being, balanced time perspective, alienation, and social desirability. Osin is currently teaching at the Higher School of Economics, a national research university in Moscow, Russia. He is doing joint research with Ilona Boniwell at the University at East London. He has collaborated on several projects for online data collection and currently volunteers as the webmaster of Positive Psychology UK website.

Eijun Senaha is an associate professor of English literature and film studies at Hokkaido University in Japan. Having received a doctorate in English from the University of South Carolina, his expertise includes English literature and film studies, with a special focus on the representations of power relations in sex, gender, and sexuality as they include not only women's studies but also the study of masculinities and queer studies.

Mannsoo Shin is currently a professor of international business and serving as director for the Center for Asian Business at Korea University Business School. He received his BBA from Korea University, his MBA from the University of Hawai'i, and his Ph.D. from the University of Illinois at Urbana-Champaign. In addition to some sixty professional articles and chapters, he has published several books in Korean including *International Business* and *International Business Strategy of Korean Firms*.

Benjamin Shobert is the founder and managing director of consultancy Rubicon Strategy Group, which offers strategic consultation for Western corporations hoping to expand into Asia. His special areas of expertise include US–China relations, China's regional role, the China–India strategic relationship, and China's rapidly expanding role in Africa. He also serves on the Advisory Board of Indiana University's Research Center for Chinese Politics and Business.

Surat Singh, one of India's leading lawyers, practices at the Supreme Court of India and Delhi High Court. An international lawyer, he was educated at Delhi University, Oxford University, and Harvard University. With his three master's degrees in law from Delhi, Oxford University, and Harvard University and his Doctor of Laws (S.J.D.) from Harvard University, he is arguably the most highly educated lawyer of India. He was a classmate of American President Barack Obama at Harvard Law School during 1988–90.

Bharatendu N. Srivastava is received his PhD in Psychology at the Indian Institute of Technology in Kanpur, Uttar Pradesh. He is currently an assistant professor of behavior sciences at the Indian Institute of Management Calcutta (IIMC).

Gregory W. Streich earned his Ph.D. in political science from the University of Wisconsin and currently serves as professor of political science at the University of Central Missouri Warrensburg, Missouri. He is the author of many articles on topics such as justice, democratic theory, social capital, and national identity. In addition, he is the coauthor of *US Foreign Policy: A Documentary and Reference Guide*.

Cassandra R. Veney is an associate professor in the Department of Political Science at Loyola Marymount University, Los Angeles, California. Her primary research interest has been the politics of forced migration in Kenya and Tanzania. She is the author of *Forced Migration in Eastern Africa: Democratization, Structural Adjustment, and Refugees*.

Rinaldo Walcott is a Black Canadian academic, writer, and associate professor at OISE/University of Toronto in the Department of Sociology and Equity Studies in Education. Walcott's work focuses on black studies, Canadian studies, cultural studies, queer theory and gender theory, and diaspora studies. He holds the position of Canada Research Chair of Social Justice and Cultural Studies.

Paul Tiyambe Zeleza is one of the best-known Malawian historians, as well as a literary critic, novelist, short-story writer, and blogger at *The Zeleza Post*. A former president of the African Studies Association, he has most recently been named the dean of the Bellarmine College of Liberal Arts at Loyola Marymount University.

SERIES FOREWORD

Some years ago Jody Powell, former press secretary to President Carter, was ruminating aloud about the leadership tract taken by Carter and other recent US presidents. We were surprised to discover that even a president doesn't have enough 'chits' to get things done, referring to a transactional leadership approach—"horse-trading" as it is known euphemistically in Washington. "Something of a different order was required to create the kind of world we envisioned—you call it transforming leadership—but it eluded our grasp," he reflected.

Some presidents are able to surmount the rough and tumble of transactional leadership. It's not that they weren't good horse traders—they were. Think Lincoln and Franklin "Lion and Fox" Roosevelt. But great presidents, we have found, also have interiority, a will, an approach that captures others, and the moral imagination that allows something transcendent to emerge. And what they bring to the table is shaped by the role and their experience with others. Their vision and political agenda, in the view of presidential political scientist James MacGregor Burns, would be at its core "planned, articulated, systemic, measurable, enduring, and based on core public values."

As this book so eloquently reveals, Obama entered the world stage as a key actor embedded within richly constructed philosophical debates and narratives. It begins with an examination of American Exceptionalism and Obama's tacit alignment with it. Too, the president was immediately thrust into the narrative of received wisdom—on lateralism, enlightened self-interest, transformational diplomacy, and pre-emptive military strategy.

He had much to learn and much to parse, yet he came to power with a deeply considered and personal commitment to public values enshrined in the Constitution, especially free speech, rule of law, equality, and freedom.

This book offers an extraordinary panoply of the Obama presidency from scholars from Africa, the Middle East, the Pacific Rim, India, Europe, and the Americas. The authors review and reflect upon how he was perceived and judged around the world midway through his presidency. It is not easy to write about a president midstream, but at the same time it offers us, the readers, a rare opportunity to reflect together at a particular point in time—at the halfway point of a particular president's term in office.

Is this learning? Much has been said that this president is learning on the job, especially in international relations. But in this age of globalization aided by the World Wide Web and other factors, it really is much more than learning, it's cocreating. It's an iterative process in which our president influences who we are and we, global citizens, shape him. Over time, we take back our wishes and projections and he becomes more real. At the same time, the domestic and global feedback loop constantly recreates a relationship algorithm that produces his power differential and what we will allow him to do.

Some of this will come from horse trading to be sure, but as Jody Powell suggested, it really is much more than that. This book goes a long way toward our understanding of the presidential role and the person who now occupies that role and, importantly, how a new global system and perspective profoundly changes both the role and the person.

Georgia Sorenson
Ronald E. Riggio

PREFACE

This book began as a companion volume to *Barack Obama in Hawai'i and Indonesia: The Making of a Global President* (Sharma, 2012), which was rated as the Top 10 Black History Book for 2012 by the American Library Association. While researching and lecturing about the earlier book, which entailed travel throughout the United States, Europe, Africa, and Asia, there were varied and diverse perceptions about President Obama as a leader. However, the president frequently garnered higher approval ratings in most parts of the world than in the United States. What a paradox, we thought at the time. The first black president elected with great enthusiasm, loved by people around the world, yet struggling for approval for his policies at home—whether it be the healthcare initiative, the stimulus to bail out the economy, or his "leading from behind" on foreign policies.

We wanted to explore the stark contrast between Obama's popularity abroad and his suboptimal ratings at home, which puzzled almost everyone we interviewed: Why the inverse correlation between the public image at home versus abroad? You can't be a prophet in your own land, Obama suggested to the senior editor of *India Today* during his visit. Thus, the idea was hatched to publish an edited volume on "the global Obama."

As Obama himself has said, his life story spans many continents, races, cultures, and histories. It is only appropriate that we try to grasp the total Obama and not try to box him into a preconceived theory, which may capture only a part of his persona. Clearly, part of Obama's worldwide appeal is due to his international biography and global roots, but we found there is invariably a chasm between the soaring rhetoric and foreign policy due to various forces of history, culture, and political cycles. Yet, the search for great leaders who can speak to the totality of human experience is never-ending. Across the cultural divide from North-to-South and East-to-West, the romance of leadership continues.

Barack Hussein Obama's rise from his early life as a multiracial and multicultural outsider in a broken family—repeatedly changing composition and shifting residence between Hawai'i and Indonesia—to assuming the world's most powerful executive position is as improbable as it is global in its trajectory and in its implications for the evolving twenty-first century. But whereas his life story has been the subject of several good biographies, his global position as a leader has not been assessed in a sustained manner. Obama's global leadership qualities and position and how he is being perceived and judged around the world are the central and intertwined topics of this book.

Given that no one scholar, social thinker, or journalist has an expertise in all of the regions of the world we wanted to cover, we decided early on to develop the project as a collected volume, relying on a group of local scholars and observers connected with their communities. Our methodology is broadly social science based, yet also relying on the skills and knowledge of local journalists and reporters. The central theme of the book is Obama's leadership style as it is perceived around the world. With the guidance of Anne Duffy, the acquisition editor, the series in leadership with Routledge Press became a natural home for this project.

While the book was conceived several years ago, we decided to wait for the reelection outcome to fully gather our views on Obama's potential impact. His reelection clearly makes this project much more viable, although potentially in need of a follow-up in four years at the end of his second term. Thus, the questions raised in this book do not necessarily draw out a final conclusion but rather suggest working hypotheses and specific lines of inquiry to be followed up over time. These are issues we plan to revisit for future analysis. However, we have attempted to organize the debate in a concerted manner around the president's leadership style, which no other book has as yet attempted. In this way, we hope to make a significant contribution to the field on leadership research and practice and to the emerging field of political leadership within the ever-expanding context of globalization.

In this volume, an international team of contributors have raised an array of broad questions regarding the president of the United States. They have asked: What leadership qualities does this remarkably intelligent man bring to the White House? How does the world outside the United States see him, and have those perceptions shifted over time? Why are his approval ratings in many countries so much higher than those in own country? Why did an amazing 92% of the (supposedly anti-American) French, but only 53% of all American voters, and a miniscule 7% of all Pakistanis either approve of him or else favor his reelection over his Republican challenger? Is he the harbinger of a new multipolar world that is witnessing the rise of Asia and the Pacific region against the backdrop of European decline and the emergence of a post-American world? Or will the Obama presidency serve as a harbinger of the new American century, with the United States remaining as the world's singular dominant superpower? And will the Obama presidency help the American dream endure for yet another century in the face of steadily shifting geopolitical power structures around the world?

To provide answers to these vital questions, we invited a highly talented team of contributors, covering all five continents and more than twenty countries to assess Obama as a global leader in the context of his policies toward their country or region in which they reside. This team includes leadership experts, specialists in international relations, political scientists, internationally oriented psychologists and sociologists, economists, journalists, an international business consultant residing in China, a Japanese literary expert on gender roles, and others. Thus, this book is broadly multidisciplinary in nature as well as global in scope to better elucidate the multifaceted aspects of Obama's worldwide image and influence. Moreover, the experts assembled in this volume represent a broad range of political opinions and differ considerably in their assessment of the Obama administration's achievements.

Following a wide-ranging introduction and several chapters dissecting Obama's leadership qualities, the volume proceeds to analyze the president's worldwide image in five sections that cover major regions of the world: (1) Africa; (2) the Americas; (3) Western, Central, and Southern Europe; (4) the Middle East and Israel; and (5) the Asia-Pacific region. The book's final section is future oriented and focused on America's evolving Pacific Century, a century that is being inaugurated by the Hawaiian-born president with relatives residing in Indonesia, China, Africa, Canada, the United States, and elsewhere. Here, we actually rely on interviews with Obama's siblings—Maya Soetoro-Ng and Mark Obama Ndesandjo—to make the case that Obama is indeed "a global president" to help usher in an emerging global century.

By presenting an integrated overview of global perceptions by some of the leading academics and journalists in different countries, this book addresses strategic issues concerning America's future while building a global understanding of the Obama presidency that digs deeper than any opinion survey can. This volume represents a broader and a more penetrating analysis of the emerging global opinion regarding Obama as a leader.

This is the first book of its kind. No other volume has analyzed Obama's leadership within the context of globalization in different parts of the world as seen by international scholars, governments, and the general public. This book is accessible to educated readers in all fields and suitable for inclusion in different levels of undergraduate and graduate courses on global and geopolitical issues.

When Obama began his first term as the president of the United States, he did so with two ambitious goals in mind. On the international level he hoped to reposition his country in an increasingly multipolar, intertwined, and tumultuous world by adopting more multilateral and nuanced geopolitical strategies and diplomatic tactics than those employed by his predecessor. The contributors to this volume discuss how successful—or not—he has been in these efforts. However, Obama has also stated that America must put its own house in order by improving its deteriorating infrastructure, mediocre educational system at the primary and secondary school levels, general economic competitiveness, and scientific creativity. His efforts at accomplishing the second of the twin goals have met with variable success, but they are not the main focus of discussion in this book. Moreover, the volume's contributors pay limited attention to the not very successful efforts of the Obama Administration to reduce carbon dioxide emissions both at home and abroad since the US Senate has so far refused to pass binding policies on carbon emissions.

Given the global nature of this book, it might prove useful to say a word or two about the global experiences and interests of the editors. Both are immigrants now residing in the Greater New York Metropolitan Area who originally earned their doctoral degrees in culturally informed developmental and social psychology programs at Harvard University.

Dinesh Sharma, an immigrant from India and a US citizen, earned a doctorate in human development and psychology, but worked mostly with anthropologists, sociologists, and other social scientists in the Faculty of Arts and Sciences, including an arduous fieldwork in South Asia for his doctoral dissertation. He later worked in the healthcare and pharmaceutical industry as a consultant for a number of years. Recently, he has been a regular contributor to *Asia Times Online*, *The Global Intelligence*, *Al Jazeera English*, *Eastern Eye*, and *News Blaze*, among other online publications, while hosting and producing a TV show on *Princeton Community Television* and lecturing on globalization and political leadership. For his earlier book on Obama, which was widely reviewed in domestic and international press, he was invited by Democrats Abroad to lecture throughout the European Union, Africa and Asia.

Uwe P. Gielen grew up as an internal refugee in post–World War II Germany. By the age of twenty-five and traveling typically on a shoestring, he had already explored more than twenty-five countries located in Africa, Asia, Europe, and North America. In his travels, he learned to communicate via hand signals with Pashtun tribesmen from Afghanistan, listen to Farsi-German-French-speaking truck-drivers deride the Shahanshah of Iran and friend of America for his cruelties, fend off an Egyptian taxi driver who desperately wished to buy his girlfriend, stay overnight in Hindu temples in Uganda, grasp something about the threatened position of middleman minorities, and observe what kinds of lives are led by those billions who only rarely make their appearance in Western history books.

Although in his later academic career he learned to reflect more systematically on such experiences, it is the vivid memories themselves of these colorful but often rough experiences that have at times been his most persuasive, nagging, haunting, inspiring, and demanding teachers. Today he serves as the founder and executive director of the Institute for International and Cross-Cultural Psychology in New York where he maintains ties with psychologists located around the world.

Preparing this volume has been a challenging journey during which we received invaluable help from friends, colleagues, editors, and family members. Special thanks go to Ed Hollander and Anne Duffy who saw the early promise of this project and extended great feedback on the early drafts. Special thanks are due to Jennifer Ho and Jeannette Raymond, both research assistants at the Institute for International and Cross-Cultural Psychology in New York, St. Francis College, for nurturing yet another book on President Obama. We hope this book will be just as successful, if not more, than its earlier sibling.

We also want to thank Maya Soetoro-Ng and Mark Obama Ndesandjo for their input to this book. They offer a personal perspective, which makes the book a special and worthy project. We also wish to express our gratitude to Lawrence J. Friedman, Harvard University, for advice throughout the editing process and for sharing important details about the Obama campaign through the reelection cycle. Finally, we thank our respective family members—partners, spouses, and children—for their patience and support throughout the editing and writing process.

Dinesh Sharma
Uwe P. Gielen

Part I

OBAMA AS A GLOBAL LEADER

INTRODUCTION: OBAMA'S ADVENTURES IN GLOBALIZATION

Dinesh Sharma and Uwe P. Gielen

"The President is at liberty, both in law and conscience, to be as big a man as he can."
—Woodrow Wilson

"I came here purposefully to underscore that in today's global world, there is no longer anything foreign about foreign policy. More than ever before, the decisions that we make from the safety of our shores don't just ripple outward; they also create a current right here in America."
—John Kerry

"The world's greatest shortage is not of oil, clean water or food, but of moral leadership."
—Jeffrey Sachs

This book is an exploration of the global Obama, the image, the perception, and the record of the forty-fourth president of the United States of America as viewed by people around the world. The central questions we explore are the following: What does the Obama phenomenon mean around the world? What does it represent, and how is it perceived? How and why has the Obama image changed the American image abroad? Conversely, how has the American image remained static or deteriorated in countries and world regions where the United States is still fighting long-standing wars? In essence, this book is as much about the changing American image abroad as it is about the American president at the beginning of the twenty-first century.

When Obama was elected in 2008, his approval ratings around the world were extremely high, and they continue to remain high in 2013 except for the Middle Eastern Muslim world. Obama clearly does not lack vision or audacity: "When Obama was sworn into office in January 2009, he had already developed an activist vision of his foreign policy destiny. He would refurbish the United States' image abroad, especially in the Muslim world; end the wars in Iraq and Afghanistan; offer an outstretched hand to Iran; 'reset' relations with Russia as a step toward ridding the world of nuclear weapons; elicit Chinese cooperation on regional and global issues; and make peace in the Middle East. By his own account, Obama sought nothing less than to bend history's arc in the direction of justice and a more peaceful, stable world" (Indyk, Lieberthal, and O'Hanlon 2012).[1] The question remains: How has Obama's America fared abroad in the past four years? Has he reclaimed the trust and faith in American ideals and values around the world?

The Obama presidency represents a paradigmatic moment in the history of the United States and the emerging global civilization given the first African-American politician has been re-elected to the highest office and to the most powerful executive position in the world (Sharma 2011). His first election may have been driven by "the Bush fatigue," demographic changes in the US population, and new forms of social media; indeed, it can be argued that Obama is our first multiracial and Internet president within the context of newly formed social media networks and transmuted notions of race and ethnicity (Sharma 2011).[2]

In the 2012 reelection, he won against the odds—i.e., in spite of a high unemployment rate, anemic job growth, and a deeply divided electorate—where the chances of a clean victory were at best fifty–fifty: almost all of the earlier election polls fell within the margin of error. While Pew Research has shown that Obama's perceived political effectiveness and image have waxed and waned domestically, many of the surveys show he has remained a far more popular American president in most parts of the world than his predecessor (Sharma 2011). What are the reasons for this global popularity? What are the leadership attributes that define the president's personality traits?

There are many theories of leadership development. With over a century of writing and research on the topic, many have tried to understand the rise of a great leader from obscurity. From the "great man theory" to "transactional theory" and "cross-cultural theory," we try to cover a range of theoretical frameworks. We analyze the Obama presidency at the midpoint of its tenure. The president has been reelected with a significant margin, even if—as many have argued—the challenger Mitt Romney may not have been a particularly strong candidate. Furthermore, the economic challenges and the long-term foreign policy conundrums that Obama had to battle were unparalleled in breadth and scope. The reelection of the forty-fourth president speaks to his special charisma, his evolving leadership style, and the turbulent times we are living through. The big question is: How is America perceived internationally after Obama's first term—with clearly a new style of leadership—while remaining a superpower as well as the world's largely self-appointed "policeman" (with cowboyish tendencies)? We examine this question in five continents and approximately twenty countries.

Great Man of History or a Great President?

In **chapter 6**, Ali Mazrui, a legend in African studies belonging to the same generation of postcolonial intellectuals as Obama's father, Barack Obama Sr., has boldly predicted that Obama will go down as "a great man in history." He has claimed this in the sense that the Scottish writer Carlyle famously suggested, "The history of the world is but the biography of great men." However, it remains to be seen whether Obama is also a great president, as Mazrui clarified immediately, and many social observers would agree with this claim. The elevation of Obama has been completed twice over by American voters of diverse backgrounds and, at least in spirit, by people around the world. Yet, many are waiting with anticipation and considerable, though cautious, hope for "the second act" of the Obama presidency.

In his chapter on Obama in Africa, Mazrui suggests Obama is a great man because he fulfills two longstanding prophecies made by Mahatma Gandhi and Robert Kennedy, respectively. First, he fulfills the hopes enunciated by Gandhi about the rise of black consciousness in Africa, and second, he completes Kennedy's vision of the rise of African-Americans in the United States. Both prophecies have come true in Obama's election.

Mazrui muses openly, "Will he be the first president to not take America into a global conflict and war, following Gandhi's and King's precepts of non-violence?" There have been several American presidents who, as both great men and great presidents, managed to change the course of history. Will Obama be such a president? Will his second term reclaim the enthusiasm he generated in 2008, critical to his legacy as a great leader, or will he go the way of other presidents such as Jimmy Carter who could not fully rise to their inherent potential due to their outsider status and lack of experience in Washington?

Ali Mazrui suggests that Obama has most if not all of the prerequisites to be a great president, because he is a great man in history. Can the wheels of history grind out a generous verdict in Obama's favor? Is the latter condition, that is, to be "a great man in history," sufficient to enter the former category, to be "a great president?" Contributors to this volume offer differing opinions on the president's tenure in office. For instance, within Mazrui's context of African diaspora, Paul Zeleza and Cassandra Veney argue in **chapter 7** that while the president is an integral part of the deep and rich history of African immigration in America, especially through his father's immigrant journey as a student, his immigration policies toward Africans have been almost the same as those of the Bush administration policies, and that means they are rather disappointing.

Yet, many experts in this volume argue that Obama is uniquely qualified to become a great president especially if in his second term he should prove able to achieve legislative victories on behalf of the American people and his admiring masses around the world. In his first term, he achieved some landmark victories, above all the healthcare reform bill, yet he has faced stern opposition on many issues within the US Congress. In his second term, will he be able to cement his legacy as a transformational leader and reformer achieving a breakthrough with Iran on the international front and a balanced budget at home? At the start of his second term, he faced many challenges that will test his style of, and capacity for, leadership and determine his legacy. Here are a few critical global challenges in the second term that are being tracked throughout this book:

- fulfilling his campaign pledge to pull US combat troops out of Afghanistan by 2014
- controlling the use of drones in Pakistan, Yemen, and possibly elsewhere
- confronting successfully Iran's nuclear challenge
- dealing with the enduring challenges of Middle East peace, unrest, and the Syrian civil war
- focusing on Asia and rebalancing in the Pacific region
- dealing with China's economic and military rise
- weathering economic-political crises in the Eurozone (e.g., Greece, France, Germany)
- negotiating major new trade agreements with the European Union and with South Asian and Pacific countries
- supporting global effects to improve women's rights while enhancing their political economic, and social position
- reforming America's immigration system with a special focus on Latin American and Asian American immigrants
- dealing with the ongoing and long-term threat of climate change.

While the president has to deal with a Republican-controlled House again, the development and outcome of these issues and challenges will have a lasting effect on how he is perceived as a leader. In regards to the controversy surrounding the lethal use of drones in some situations, we have witnessed the president losing ground in the international press and among the people of many nations at the start of his second term, although new documentation has been released in the media seemingly justifying the use of drones. This became evident in the polls conducted by Pew Research prior to the 2012 election.[3]

Barack Obama's tenure as president of the United States has coincided with several intersecting global trends that have led to major challenges and opportunities for his leadership: the threat of radical Islam in the post–September 11 world, the rising economic-political power of China, and a trend toward American economic decline caused in part by the two long wars in Iraq and Afghanistan. Obama has weakened the terrorist elements in parts of the Islamic world significantly, as described in the chapter by Arturo Muñoz from RAND Corporation. This success, however, has left a huge shadow on his global image, especially on the Muslim street as reported by several chapter authors and surveys conducted by Pew Research. Many are openly wondering: Who is the real Obama? Is he someone who seems to have transformed himself "from dreams to drones"—a pragmatic politician who is more of a *Realpolitiker* than a transformational leader? Obama has been "bent by history" in Afghanistan, argues Muñoz in **chapter 16**, and he sees Afghanistan for what it is, "a graveyard of empires" to be handled with caution.

However, the economic rise of China during the global financial crisis triggered off by the misguided policies of Obama's predecessor has left the worldwide US image somewhat deflated. Many US allies now see China as the steadily rising economic superpower, while the US economy is only recovering slowly. A large majority of Germans, English, French, and Spanish citizens now identify China as the leading engine of economic growth, according to the Pew report. Here, in chapter 18, Benjamin Shobert, an American business consultant who works with Chinese firms, provides an invaluable analysis of Obama's image in China and the role China-bashing plays in the American political theater, unfortunately furthering negative views of both our president and of democracy. In many ways, the first-half of the twenty-first century promises to spawn a textbook match-up between the United States and China—individualism vs. collectivism, bottom-up vs. top-down change, and classical innovative capitalism vs. mercantilist state-capitalism. In reality, however, this does not need to be a zero-sum game, because both models can be winners.

Every idealization is followed by some form of disillusionment. This psychological truism applies to politics as well, where an invisible bond ties ordinary citizens or followers to an extraordinary leader. It is not surprising that after almost four years of unrelenting obstructionism from Republicans on the domestic issues, the toll of the drawdown of the wars in Iraq and Afghanistan, and the great global economic recession, the approval of President Obama around the world has come down to earth, according to the latest poll by Pew Research. In his chapter on "inclusive leadership," Edwin Hollander describes in considerable depth the challenges Obama has faced at home and abroad in maintaining legitimacy in the face of sustained and often bitter political opposition, in continuing to build a loyal following, and in trying to gain greater resonance among an increasingly diverse electorate.

It is somewhat surprising that internationally the disillusionment with Obama did not happen sooner. Today, many persons abroad have gained a somewhat more realistic view of his limited powers in office, and a better understanding of the considerable powers of persuasion he possesses as a leader. Although Obama has received more appreciation abroad than his predecessors, the overall confidence in him and in the US global presence has slipped. While traditional allies remain confident throughout Europe, Latin America, and Japan, Obama's approval has declined in part because of many of his tough policy decisions especially in the military realm.

Many Muslim populations have become predictably more critical of him, rooted in frequently intense disillusionment with his policies, as described by Ramadan Ahmed in his analysis of "Arab Images of Obama and the United States: An Egyptian Perspective," Mohammad Masad's chapter on "Great Disappointments in the Arab World during Obama's First Term," and Pepe Escobar's analysis of "Obama, Iran, and the New Great Game in Eurasia: A Journalist's Perspective." In the world of Middle Eastern Muslims, an unclenched hand of friendship is now perceived by many as an unmanned drone threatening to kill them. While milder forms of disappointment characterize overall ratings for the United States in most member states of the European Union, the US image there remains largely positive and trustworthy as also holds true in many parts of Latin America and sub-Saharan Africa. In Japan, the ratings have actually improved due to America's military guardianship role vis-à-vis China, especially in light of the recent military tensions between Japan and China. In Egypt, Jordan, and Turkey, however, US power is unpopular and not trusted. Moreover in Pakistan, approval ratings of the United States have reached a nadir.

Obama's image has also suffered in China, where confidence in the US president has declined by 24 percentage points, while the approval of his policies has dropped by 30 points. While many at home fear US economic decline, overseas people continue to worry about the role of the US military under the Obama administration. Despite the real changes the administration has brought to the country's image abroad, "there remains a widespread perception that the US acts unilaterally and does not consider the interests of other countries," according to the Pew Report (2012).

In most Muslim nations, anti-terrorism efforts are seen as nefarious and overreaching. There is nearly unanimous opposition to the way the Obama administration has executed its antiterrorism policy using the drone strikes. Pew Research reports that in seventeen of twenty countries, a majority disapprove of US drones targeting extremist groups in Pakistan, Yemen, and Somalia.

While Americans at home approve of the drone strikes—Republicans overwhelmingly so (74%), as do a majority of independents (60%) and Democrats (58%)—the view on the Muslim street and generally around the world is that they demonstrate a misuse of US power leading to the death of many innocent bystanders.

However, despite disillusionment with Obama's image and policies, he maintains a deep reservoir of support in Europe, as may be seen in the chapters by Thomas Cieslik on Germany, Donald Morrison on France, and Akis Kalaitzidis on Greece and the Eurozone. Prior to the presidential election, a very large majority in France, Germany, Britain, Spain, Italy, and the Czech Republic wished to see him reelected, as did most Brazilians and Japanese. In the Middle East, however, there was no love lost for Obama, so that a majority of Egyptians, Jordanians, and Lebanese opposed his reelection. In Israel as well, Obama's actions and intentions were frequently regarded with various degrees of skepticism although not with the deep sense of disillusionment found in Israel's neighboring countries.

In 2009, however, global expectations had been very high indeed. Many around the world thought or least hoped that Obama would be an enlightened leader who would consider their country's interests when making policy, conduct military campaigns with international approval, try to resolve the conflict between the Israelis and Palestinians fairly, and make climate change a priority. Today many around the world feel that too many of their hopes have been dashed. Obama gathers high marks, however, for addressing the global economy and the repercussions of the financial crisis in the Eurozone.

Despite some feelings of malaise about Obama's policies, the likelihood and acceptability of his reelection was seen as especially high in Canada, Europe, Japan, Korea, Brazil, and other parts of Latin America, as may be seen in the chapters by Rinaldo Walcott on Canada, Elisa and Raul Moncarz on Latin America, Matthias Maass on South Korea, and Eijun Senaha on Obama's manhood in Japan. Among the traditional allies, there was near-certainty that he would be reelected, a rather disheartening prospect for those Republican opponents who remained in tune with foreign opinions and perceptions.

The generally negative opinion against Obama in the Muslim world was reinforced by the drone strikes, where he has turned out to be more hawkish than originally perceived. This, however, proved to be an advantage in the presidential election against a candidate like Mitt Romney who sounded even more combative than Obama on foreign policy. Worldwide, many were turned off by politics in the United States and showed a decreased interest in the 2012 election.

Leadership in Action

We have many systematic theories of leadership that have been conceived and researched by social scientists. Scholars and practitioners from many fields have contributed to this interdisciplinary topic, but an appropriate analysis of Barack Obama's leadership style from a global perspective has not been undertaken. A convincing synthesis of different perspectives is clearly lacking. In this book, we hope to make a contribution to the leadership literature, specifically, on the attributes that define a successful president. Yet our specific purpose in editing this book is to try to understand Obama at this critical point in history from an international and cross-cultural angle. Demographic changes in the United States and geopolitical changes around the world make it imperative that we attempt to grasp Obama's leadership style and decipher what it portends for the United States and the world.

It is our main claim in this book that Obama was elected to help Americans transition into the twenty-first century, pushed and pulled by the demographic changes at home, globalization abroad, and his exit strategies for the two long wars overseas (Sharma 2011). This is not so much a hypothesis we test, but rather a claim we substantiate by locating Obama's image in many countries and continents around the world using ethnographic, narrative, and journalistic accounts; we present Obama's leadership-in-action in the context of on-the-ground reports. We show that Obama's approval remains high in many countries, supported by local democratic aspirations projected onto

American ideals, yet the situation in the local contexts remains very mixed and complicated due to long-standing perceptions and conflicts that are difficult to change or resolve.

Social scientists who study "authentic leadership" have found that whereas approximately 30% of the ability to lead may be inherited, the large remaining part is determined by the environment including the people one imitates and uses as models. In other words, "the life context one grows up in and later works in is much more important than heritability in predicting leadership emergence across one's career" (Avolio, Walumbwa, and Weber 2009, p. 425).[4] The cognitive analysis of leadership has also revealed that a self-concept and self-schema with moderately high levels of "self-concept unity, such as self-concept differentiation, self-concept clarity, and self-discrepancies" related to each other may have implications for leadership development across the lifecycle (ibid: 427).

Empirical evidence also suggests that charismatic and transformational leaders tend to inspire especially high levels of commitment, inspiration, and organizational ability in their followers with measurable positive outcomes. However, implementing successful leadership is a difficult matter; it involves psychological complexity, multilayered organizational structures, and consistent follow-through on one's intentions and plans. Leadership involves a complex system made up of adaptive, administrative, and enabling roles. When leadership is "viewed as a property of the whole system, as opposed to solely the property of individuals, effectiveness in leadership becomes more a product of those connections or relationships among the parts than the result of any one part of that system (such as the leader)" (O'Connor and Quinn 2004: 423).[5] This view is supported by Edwin Hollander's perceptive analysis of Obama's inclusive leadership style in **chapter 4** that focuses on the relationships between the president and different types of followers that are important to his success both at home and abroad.

There exists a growing literature on leader-member exchanges (LMX) and leader-follower relationships.[6] While the LMX research examines the mutual and beneficial exchange of ideas between leaders and their followers, the research on followership looks at the "romance of leadership," how and why followers construct an image of a leader that may be either deified or denigrated.[7] Researchers have examined the spiritual dimensions of leadership as well, where a felt lack of meaning drives people to search for extraordinary leaders in their lives, workplace, politics, and media.[8]

When discussing these leadership theories, it is important to keep the central assumption in mind that they all share: leadership is simultaneously determined by a large number of interacting factors including a person's original emotional temperament and crystallizing potential for analytical and social intelligence, the enduring effects of early childhood constellations in the family and immediate social environment, one's exposure to prevailing ideologies and sociocultural belief systems especially during the adolescent years, one's ongoing positions and roles in the larger social structures of society, specific historical circumstances, and the power of situational factors that typically both enable and constrain a president's efforts at leadership. In contrast, none of the theories advocates reductionism by focusing exclusively on one or two central determinants and characteristics of leadership.

According to Eric Coggins (2009), Obama displays the charismatic style in almost everything he does from using the bully pulpit to great oratory and masterful analysis of policy.[9] He validates the contingency theory when and if he captures the moment and tries to take the lead on an issue, such as the bailout of GM or the mission to hunt for Osama bin Laden. He displays LMX when he deals with the vice president or his cabinet. Many Chinese, however, do not share these perceptions as Benjamin Shobert reports in his chapter on how Obama is viewed in this vitally important country. For the Chinese, great oratory is much less important than administrative abilities and long-term experience. The Japanese also distrust those who are too skillful with words. Moreover, having an impulsive, though charismatic and charming, African father has not helped Obama's image either in China or in Japan.

Fred I. Greenstein, who has examined presidential leadership styles from Franklin D. Roosevelt to Obama, suggests that the forty-fourth president clearly has an excellent public communication style, vision, cognitive ability, and emotional intelligence to be an executive. Yet, it remains to be seen whether he has the organizational capacity and political skill to outmaneuver his opponents in Congress and deal effectively with the unprecedented economic and security challenges he has inherited.[10]

While these perspectives are relevant to this book, the framework we deploy most consistently is the cross-cultural leadership theory based on Project GLOBE (Global Leadership and Organizational Behavioral Effectiveness), which was first developed by Robert House in a large-scale, longitudinal study (House et al. 2004).[11] Although most of the leadership research has so far been focused on Western societies, there is a growing need for international and cross-cultural research. Obama's global biography lends itself nicely to such cross-cultural theorizing and analysis as may be seen in **chapter 3**, in which a team of authors led by Rabi S. Bhagat advances a cultural analysis of effective leadership in American society.

Based on a sample of sixty-two societies, the GLOBE study identified several key dimensions that can be universally perceived and measured across diverse cultures: charismatic/value-based, team-oriented, self-protective, participative, humane, and autonomous. Ten societal clusters based on distinct patterns among these characteristics can be discerned: Anglo, Germanic, Latin European, African, Eastern European, Middle Eastern, Southeast Asian, Confucian, Sub-Saharan Africa, Latin American, and Nordic. They are represented in this book except for two: Eastern European and Nordic.

In the American context, leadership carries specific requirements and behavioral schemas or "key leader characteristics that its people, implicitly and/or explicitly, look for and endorse in their leaders":

- to stand out, leave one's mark, get things done, and succeed
- be results-driven, exert control over one's environment, be decisive, forceful, and competitive
- work hard, be action-oriented, active, and have a sense of urgency
- willingly take risks, be creative, innovative, and flexible
- be objective, practical, factual, and pragmatic
- be experienced, seek input from others, and be informal.

Yet, when applied across cultures, there is invariably a clash in values and ideals where people expect different behavioral outcomes, strategies, and modes of interaction from a leader. The challenge is how to translate meaningful behaviors in different contexts. While mindful of these challenges, Obama has clearly been a target of some of these expectations and misperceptions.

Pragmatic Politician or Idealistic Professor?

In *The Republic*, Plato described the philosopher-king as the lover of wisdom, a natural-born leader of a city-state. Harvard historian, James Kloppenberg, in his book *Reading Obama* describes the forty-fourth president of the United States as a philosopher-president, placing Barack Obama in the esteemed company of presidents such as Thomas Jefferson, James Madison, Abraham Lincoln, and most recently Woodrow Wilson. These are indeed very big shoes to fill, but Kloppenberg claims that Obama fits these oversized clogs nicely.[12]

The roots of Obama's development as an intellectual can be traced back to his legal training, specifically to the period when, as a graduate student, Obama was elected president of the *Harvard Law Review*. He was engaged in the early debates about identity politics, race, and gender that fermented in America's law schools and public culture during the 1980s and 1990s. Here, Obama acquired certain core principles about the founding of the nation as "a deliberative republic" while studying the hermeneutics of the US constitution under the tutelage of law professors like Lawrence Tribe, Martha Minow, and Charles Fried. Almost all of them claim that Obama was a unifying force in the classroom as well as a critical thinker.

Kloppenberg has discovered that Obama's political philosophy and his style of politics owe a lot to the pragmatic tradition in American philosophy, spearheaded by William James and John Dewey and continued in the more recent works of John Rawls, Richard Rorty, Lawrence Tribe, and

Robert Putnam. Influenced by these prominent American thinkers, Obama can be considered a legal pragmatist.

Kloppenberg states, "From James and Dewey through the work of their many students, including progressives and New Dealers as well as DuBois and Park, the ideas of philosophical pragmatism have spread so broadly through American culture that it has become almost impossible to identify the direct lines of their influence. But [Tribe and Michael C. Dorf's] 'On Reading the Constitution' clearly reflects that influence. Lacking a 'mathematical algorithm of interpretation,' according to Tribe and Dorf, the best we can do is to rule out the extremes of unbounded judicial activism and the fiction of pure judicial restraint by pointing out that the constitution has changed over time."

The central idea here is that truth is not a fixed entity, but variable, in flux, and to be determined through deep dialogue and experimentation. We do not have access to "eternal truths," easily downloadable or passed down from generation to generation, the Pragmatists claimed. Instead, truths are influenced by shifting cultural, social, and historical trends and factors.

Kloppenberg claims that Obama believes this to be true about the American democracy and the constitution. Indeed, his former mentor at Harvard, Tribe, partly credited Obama for coming up with the analogy that interpreting the constitution is like a "conversation," a long drawn-out, historically contentious dialogue to be more precise.

Commenting on the book, Boston journalist Christopher Lydon stated: "If there is a problem with Barack Obama's thinking, his 'intellectual biographer' James Kloppenberg is saying on the morning after Obama's mid-term 'humbling,' it's not what he thinks, deep in the Democratic mainstream. Neither is Obama over-thinking his confounding broad assignment. Rather it may be the way he thinks, never so meticulously delineated. . . ."[13] Has Obama become Robert Frost's caricature of a liberal politician, who is "too broadminded to take his own side in a quarrel," asked Lydon. Certainly, the historian Alan Brinkley has suggested that the philosopher-president appears to be more of an idealist—highly intelligent, very inspiring, and full of hope and reconciliation—but less of a pragmatist who is able to cobble together a grand coalition.

"Overcoming the deep rifts within American society is a great and worthy goal, and Obama may one day be the person who can bridge the growing divides. But in the meantime, there is work to be done—shoring up the economy, helping the unemployed, fighting off the right—and that work does not seem likely to be achieved by the pragmatist's commitment to shared ideals and 'deliberative democracy,'" stated Brinkley.[14]

Pragmatism is not to be confused with practicality, expediency, and triangulation, which Kloppenberg regards as "vulgar pragmatism." Legal pragmatism, as practiced by James's friends, Supreme Court Justices Oliver Wendel Holmes Jr. and Louis Brandeis, is the philosophical orientation that law is an instrument for solving social problems, a product of history, society, and culture. James put it himself that ideas, to have merit, must "work" and be practical.

One can see a Gordian knot in Obama's thinking about the tension between pragmatism versus idealism that cannot be easily untangled. The same complexity runs through the works of James, Dewey, Mead, and Pierce about the related tensions between materialism and idealism or empiricism and spiritualism. As Pierce wrote, "If Materialism without Idealism is blind, Idealism without Materialism is void."

Obama writes in *The Audacity of Hope*, "It has not always been the pragmatist, the voice of reason, or the force of compromise that has created the conditions of liberty. . . . The hard, cold facts remind me that it was the unbending idealists like William Lloyd Garrison . . . Denmark Vesey . . . Frederick Douglass . . . Harriet Tubman . . . who recognized that power would concede nothing without a fight."

Thus, Kloppenberg's intellectual biography succinctly distills Obama's cognitive frames and higher-order thinking as a constitutional lawyer and a progressive activist, showing the different points of tension in Obama's own mind, where the philosopher may often be in a duel with the politician. Kloppenberg neither interviewed Obama nor felt content just to go through Obama's avowed list of influential books that shaped his thinking, including the Bible, Emerson's *Self-Reliance*,

Mahatma Gandhi's autobiography, Lincoln's Collected Works, Melville's *Moby Dick*, works of Reinhold Niebuhr, Shakespeare's tragedies, and a few others. This was just as well because Obama may have resisted and rolled over Kloppenberg's arguments or at least tried to smooth over many important interpretations that the author has packed into four dense and highly readable chapters.

As an intellectual historian, Kloppenberg relied on interviews and notes from the Harvard Law School professors to make the case that Obama is a descendant of the American pragmatic philosophers, experimenters, and tinkerers deeply rooted in the New England soil. This discovery has certainly disappointed those on the right who would like to paint Obama as an extreme leftist radical.

Conversely, there is a danger in aligning Obama exclusively with one philosophical tradition or school of thought. We may lose sight of the rest of the man, his expansive mind with all its soaring rhetoric, and the diverse, multicultural, and international strands of his identity. Here, Kloppenberg reveals that Obama was also shaped by many contemporary social and cultural theories, most importantly the writings of the historian of science Thomas Kuhn on the historicity of (scientific) paradigms as well as the cultural anthropologist Clifford Geertz's interpretations of symbolic culture in Indonesia.

What seems to be missing from this otherwise outstanding analysis are the ideas and patterns of reaction that Obama acquired in his childhood in Hawai'i and Indonesia (Sharma 2011), from outside the academe, and from his travels in Southeast Asia, Africa, and the Pacific. Kloppenberg's analysis is focused on Obama's American philosophical roots, while arguing against the anti-Obama forces that are trying obsessively to portray him as an un-American or "the other." His purview, however, does not include global and international influences.

First, we know that the civil rights movement in the United States was deeply influenced by the grassroots civil disobedience movements in India and elsewhere. Obama's keen understanding of social movements in different parts of the world shaped his own political vision. Here, the linkage between Obama and Gandhi as transmitted through the life and work of Martin Luther King Jr. is especially important.

Moreover, there exists a more immediate connection between Gandhi, King, and Obama, namely the life and work of Obama's own mother, Stanley Ann Dunham, who was an admirer of both King and Gandhi. As a cultural anthropologist, she dedicated her life to the development of rural poor in Indonesia and elsewhere through micro-lending, women's educational development, and what international development agencies nowadays call "human development" in the context of globalization (Scott 2012).[15] His mother's idealistic, unique, and powerful voice is deeply embedded in Obama's mind and soul, as he himself noted in the 2004 preface to his 1995 autobiography. She was, as he confesses there, "the single constant in my life. . . . I know that she was the kindest, most generous spirit I have ever known, and that what is best in me I owe to her" (Obama 2004: xii). Mislabeled socialism by his political adversaries, the son's enduring concern for the welfare of the poor and downtrodden comes straight from the mother. The effect of her voice was further reinforced by his experiences as a community organizer on Chicago's impoverished and crime-ridden South Side.

As a student, Obama participated in rallies against apartheid at Occidental College in California precisely because his outlook was international and global. He grasped the idea of social and economic justice on different continents in no small measure due to his parents' path-breaking lives and careers. His Luo lineage from his father's side of the family also gave him insights into the plight of African nations, where he inherited his Kenyan father's pan-African dream of unity and development together with a different sense of history, culture, and political tradition. While in his capacity as an exemplary father, Obama has refused to follow his own father's polygamous and frequently reckless lifestyle, there remains little doubt that his fledgling identity as an African-American was originally anchored in an abandoned son's search for a semi-mythical father figure whose failed life, it seems, he wants to redeem (Obama 2004).

Moreover, having grown up in Hawai'i and Indonesia, Obama has at times identified himself as the Pacific president. Obama's early socialization was deeply rooted in Hawai'i and Indonesia, with a Polynesian-Christian sensibility and the Aloha ethic toward family, society, and nature. His understanding of the culture and history of Hawai'i and the Pacific region is rooted in lived experiences.

The continuance of American power depends partly on remaining the major stable force in the Asia-Pacific region economically, politically, and militarily; this is something Obama understands better than most of his predecessors having lived near the Pearl Harbor Naval Base, the site of the previous sneak attack on America before 9/11, where more than three thousand lives were also lost.

Furthermore, his ideas about democracy and development were shaped by his early experiences in Jakarta and by the American involvement in nation-building in Southeast Asia. His pragmatic and secular stepfather was a member of the Indonesian military and later worked for American oil companies, while his more idealistic mother taught English to Indonesian businessmen. Living in Jakarta for four years during the late 1960s and beginning 1970s, Obama experienced the beginnings of a religiously inclusive and tolerant Islamic democracy in the making, now a model in some parts of the Islamic world and hopefully for the countries in the Middle East and North Africa that are undergoing an uncertain transition to cultural modernity while also being exposed to the influence of highly ideological interpretations of Islam.

These formative experiences not only gave Obama insights into abysmal poverty and the vexing problems of development, but they also shaped his vision of peace with the majority of Islamic nations as expressed in speeches delivered in Cairo, Istanbul, and Jakarta. There is no doubt that Obama is a landmark figure for his progressive policies that are so deeply rooted in progressive American pragmatism. At the same time, he is also a global figure because his thinking spans generations, races, cultures, and continents, an integrated vision of the emerging world community rooted in his family, socialization, and education. The political mind, after all, is as much shaped by life experiences as by the cultural and ideological currents of the times.

As the presidential historian Douglas Brinkley has said, Barack Obama is "our first global president," a president whose mind was shaped by globalization accelerated after the Cold War, with the Internet and social media serving as engines of transformation.[16] Obama now carries his diverse roots and international moorings to engage the rest of the world, giving new meaning to Melville's well-known saying, "You cannot spill a drop of American blood without spilling the blood of the whole world." Perhaps, Obama is a new kind of progressive American pragmatist, who as a president has to be a global pragmatist when dealing with the emerging but contentious world order.

It may be easier to grasp the general nature of Obama's foreign policy decisions once we realize that many of them are guided by four underlying beliefs:

1. He holds that the United States has been, and always will be, an indispensable nation in world affairs. This belief in "American Exceptionalism," which undergirds Obama's sense of mission, is discussed in considerable detail in chapter 2 by Gregory W. Streich and Khalil Marrar. Indeed, many of Obama's most inspired speeches depict the United States as the global champion of equality, liberty, and justice while emphasizing—or implying—that these manifest ideals should hold true for all peoples and all times. In contrast, in chapter 14, Pepe Escobar describes American Exceptionalism as an outmoded doctrine unsuitable for leadership in today's multipolar world, and for guiding the Obama administration's political strategies in Central Asia.
2. Contrary to rather widespread perceptions in the country, the United States is definitely not in decline. Given the right guidance, the American people will continue to serve as a beacon for the world.
3. President Obama believes that he *must* ensure the security of the United States and its citizens at all costs. Thus he has authorized some highly militarized policies including drone warfare, and the expanding network of spying operations both abroad and at home. In these pursuits, the Harvard-trained lawyer Obama has stretched the American constitution to its limits while ignoring international law on too many occasions.

4. The rapid economic rise of Asia—and of China in particular—requires a diplomatic, economic, and military "Pivot to Asia and the Pacific Region." The nature and implications of this rebalancing effort are discussed more fully in the book's concluding chapter.

It should be added that these four strongly held beliefs stand in remarkable contrast to the convictions and anti-Obama efforts of many conservative politicians and members of the public who suspect his patriotism, deride his supposedly vacillating policy-making, downplay the success of his anti-terrorist campaign, and may even claim that he is a foreigner, Muslim, fascist, socialist, anti-colonial hater of America, and—who knows—perhaps even the Anti-Christ himself. It should be obvious that this incoherent set of accusations is driven by negative emotions and, at times, by racial undertones rather than by any special insights into the nature of President Obama. The accusations sound convincing especially to those fearing that history will leave them behind and that the traditional America of "We-Caucasian-males-are-in-charge" is in the process of losing some of its luster and power. Given that Obama is the harbinger of an increasingly multicultural and multiracial nation, not everybody is happy about the direction in which the nation—and the wider world—are evolving.

Conciliator-in-Chief or Fierce Competitor?

One of the strongest personality traits to emerge from the many profiles that have been drawn of the president is that he is "a conciliator" at heart. Relying specifically on Dinesh Sharma's descriptions of the president's childhood and early socialization in Hawai'i and Indonesia, Kenneth Fuchsman, a psychologist and historian, argues compellingly that the president is still driven by his earlier attempts to unify his broken family, a drive now projected onto the bigger national and international stage.[17] Fuchsman also draws on other accounts of the president's family life and his first term in office by such eminent writers as Ron Susskind, Sally Jacobs, Justin Frank, and Stanley Renshon to make the case that Obama is a consensus builder at heart. Moreover, one might also argue that Obama's steady attempts to reconcile and transcend tensions between idealism and results-orientated action reflect the respective influences of his idealistic mother and the more pragmatic and masculine orientations of both his Indonesian stepfather and his (largely imagined) Luo father whose unsuccessful life trajectories he does not wish to repeat.

For many years now, Obama has been surrounded by a network of strong women that stretches from his mother and maternal grandmother who raised him to his strong and dutiful wife together with her two daughters, and ultimately to Valerie Jarrett, an influential African-American senior advisor in the White House with unmatched access to the whole Obama family. According to Becker (2012), Jarrett "is Mr. Obama's spine," and as such she has encouraged some of his boldest moves in areas such as immigration and women's issues, moves that were not always appreciated by his other, more centrist advisors or possibly even by the more cautious side of Obama himself. In these in-group struggles in the White House, a partial continuation and projection of ancient family constellations and struggles—where a cautious son is edged on by a progressive maternal voice to stiffen his spine and accomplish great humanitarian deeds rather than selling out to the (mostly male) rich and influential figures that rule the intertwined worlds of commerce and political power—the struggles Ann Dunham took on all her life are still playing out.

Fuchsman (2012) forcefully states the implications of his claim that Obama's hesitations derive in part from a son's anxious desire to unify a broken family: "While he had risen to the highest office in the land, he had not taken actions that could bring more people into the country's bounty as he had wished. By postponing presenting a jobs bill until September 2011, by compromising with Wall Street, and by extending the Bush tax cuts, President Obama had not dealt sufficiently with the financial mishaps, the economic misery it brought to millions of Americans, and the misdistribution of wealth in this country. For all his remarkable achievements, as President he too often remained the son seeking to bring everyone together rather than the decisive, intelligent leader."

The nomination of Hillary Clinton to the highest foreign policy role as secretary of state also partly followed a dynamic that played on these earlier family histories. As Sharma argues in **chapter 5**, "Obama, Hillary, and Women's Voices," Obama's mother and Hillary Clinton were part of the same of generation of women who came of age after WWII and embraced greater freedoms at home for women and racial as well as ethnic minorities. Moreover, both and were highly educated, traveled the world, and became ardent feminists and champions of women's rights.

Being older by a mere five years, Ann Dunham came to the issues of international development and women's rights by developing a career focused on the economic anthropology of Indonesia. Whereas Dunham was a proto-hippie, sandwiched between the conservative 1950s and the radical 1960s, Hillary became a lawyer and an activist; with parents who were rather conservative, she came of age with the women's rights movement. When Hillary arrived at the all-girl's college, Wellesley, Betty Friedan's *The Feminine Mystique* had just been published; some have argued this movement gave rise to "the Hillary mystique" or a passion for women's causes, something she has taken to the White House as first lady, to the US Senate, and later as secretary of state to more than one hundred countries around the world. Indeed, Hillary's popularity especially among women voters helped him win his second election.

Obama's "team of rivals" approach to building his cabinet shows a key leadership trait. Jena McGregor, a columnist for the *Washington Post*, has compiled a list of the president's leadership profiles. The words most often associated with his everyday persona include "conciliator," "aloof," "unflappable," "cool," "consensus-building," "insular," and "pragmatic." These descriptors have "become caricatures of the man currently leading the country."

The word "conciliator," perhaps, comes closest to describing the style of decision-making and natural leadership skills that Obama displayed during his first term although we may see a somewhat more assertive and uncompromising style in his second term. Of Obama's other traits Larissa MacFarquhar, writing for the *New Yorker* in 2007, said: "Obama is always disappointing people who feel that he gives too much respect or yields too much ground to the other side, rather than fighting aggressively for his principles." Writing about the Chicago days, she said, "Obama's voting record is one of the most liberal in the Senate, but he has always appealed to Republicans, perhaps because he speaks about liberal goals in conservative language," a tendency that has frustrated his progressive supporters. His "drive to compromise" is deeply rooted in his personality, it appears "instinctive, almost a tic," clearly something deeply embedded in his temperament and early socialization. It represents a cultivated strength rather than a failing or the inability to stake out his position (MacFarquhar, 2007).

The same conditions that define his "conciliatory" tendencies also make him a bit of a loner. Raised by a single mother, abandoned by the African father, experiencing a four-year interlude with an Indonesian stepfather, and educated by his grandparents, Obama grew up by himself as the first-born and only child for the first ten years, even though he was surrounded by family and friends. Thus, Scott Wilson, a *Washington Post* reporter, found that Obama had been constrained by what psychologists call his introverted traits, in a city that thrives on incestuous networks and political connections held together in part by what Chinese call *guanxi* (long-term ties based on mutual obligations, debts, and understandings) as well as by similarities in upbringing and background. "Is it possible to be America's most popular politician and not be very good at American politics," asks Wilson, who was concerned that Obama lacked the traditional people skills to win the reelection. Wilson claimed that Obama was a "political loner," who did not understand the power of retail politics, which would eventually hurt him in his bid for the reelection. It did not help that Obama came to Washington as a racial, political, and cultural outsider, a man born on America's periphery to parents separated by widely varying backgrounds and life experiences.

Similarly, Ryan Lizza has clarified that Obama has emerged as a "facilitator of change" rather than as a revolutionary or director of transformational change, as his rhetoric might suggest. "Facilitators are more like tacticians. Directors change the system. Facilitators work the system. Obama's first three years as President are the story of his realization of the limits of his office, his frustration with those constraints, and, ultimately, his education in how to successfully operate within them," states Lizza.

James Fallows, in one of the most extensive pieces in the *Atlantic*, makes a convincing case that there was indeed a gap between Obama's rhetoric and his record. Partly determined by his inexperience, his coldness (or at least emotional coolness), his complacency about his talent, and the sheer weight of the first term, Fallows argues that there was a "symbolic mismatch" between the "sweeping ambitions for political change" that Obama promised and Obama's actual record. Consequently, Fallows calls Obama "the incrementalist operator," drawing on his experience as an advisor in the Jimmy Carter team.

However, the way the president and his team eked out an electoral victory over Mitt Romney confirms the narrative Jody Kantor has presented of the underlying competitive nature of the game. While many accurately believe that the president is professorial, aloof, and cerebral, these descriptions are hardly complete because they don't capture the sheer competitive drive it takes to run for and later hold on to the executive office for a second term. Obama's powerful competitive drive is evident in everything he does publicly and privately, reveals Kantor, in her brief essay titled "Competitor-in-Chief," where the president claims he is "a better speech writer than my speechwriters," "gets competitive when he reads children's stories," and "cooks a really mean chili," and "it is very rare that I come to an event where I'm like the fifth or sixth most interesting person." Such real-life narratives complement what has been theorized here about the multidimensionality of the president's singular character, mission, and focus.

Michael Lewis, the popular author of *Moneyball* and many other books, sheds yet another refractory light on the presidential decision-making style. Obama lets Lewis in on his strategy, "You'll see I wear only gray or blue suits," Obama tells Lewis, because "I'm trying to pare down decisions. . . . You need to focus your decision-making energy. You need to routinize yourself." Obama then teaches Lewis: "Any given decision you make you'll wind up with a 30 to 40 percent chance that it isn't going to work. You have to own that . . . You can't be paralyzed by the fact that it might not work out." Lewis finds that the president is very analytical, premeditated, and studied in his day-to-day management of people, similar to earlier descriptions by *Washington Post* reporter and author Bob Woodward. More cerebral and self-contained, Obama does not seem to be interested in the type of backroom arm-twisting and horse trading that Lyndon Johnson practiced to perfection during his presidency. His skills, in turn, facilitated a number of important civil rights victories, which decades later made Obama's rise possible.

According to a study conducted by Jerry Newman at the State University of New York, more than one hundred management and business professors rated Obama has having higher levels of leadership skills over Romney: problem solving/decision making, global and diversity mindset, strategic thinking, team leadership, team skills, communication, interpersonal skills, integrity, results orientation, and self-management/adaptability.[18] Similarly, a Gallup poll found that American people rate Obama highly on many key leadership attributes: 72% noted he "is willing to make hard decisions," 66% saw him as "a strong and decisive leader," and 64% claimed "he can get things done." Yet, one of the critical attributes that may have given him an advantage over Romney was his sheer "likeability," where he led his rival 81% to 64% before the election.

While considered "willing to make difficult decisions" as well as "likeable" by his many followers, he ultimately prefers to arrive at many troublesome decisions by himself. After he has read position papers by his advisors and cabinet members and listened to their intense debates, he often retires to his third-floor hideout in the White House to ponder the pros and cons of the many international policy dilemmas he must confront. There, in the still of the night, he may review his geostrategic plans to cope with the rise of an old-yet-very-new China, mull over tactical aspects of drone warfare that can mean life or death for "terrorists" but also for innocents in the mountains of northwest Pakistan, or assess the probable consequences of diplomatic initiatives designed to improve ties with allied countries. This reflective approach to decision making has been criticized as "leading from behind" by some skeptics such as Miniter (2012), who know full well that American conservative men in particular tend to prefer a Caucasian president who leads the cavalry charge, as it were, from the front. Obama's predecessor, George Bush, exhibited some of this semi-militaristic style although it led to some very poor decision making in the economic field and to a mostly useless and very expensive war in Iraq that actually may have advanced the interests of a hostile Iran while costing some 800,000 Iraqis their lives.

One may surmise that Obama's reflective, lonely, and rather guarded style of decision making owes something to his changeable familial and cultural past. In the words of his biographer David Maraniss (2012), "Leaving and being left were the repeating themes of Barry Obama's young life." Such a meandering and disruptive early life trajectory tends to throw a child and teenage boy back upon himself, ready to defend his inner sanctuary against the relentless flow of unpredictable and difficult-to-control events and shifts occurring in his immediate and larger sociocultural surroundings. To this should be added his biracial makeup that in those days made identity conflicts during adolescence and beginning adulthood almost unavoidable.

Although Obama succeeded subsequently in anchoring his identity in an African-Christian-American family and community context, his rather introverted approach, his intellectual framework for political decision making, his difficult adaptation to the challenging life circumstances of his youth, and his nuanced "observer-and-writer-self" can be considered more acceptable in France's intellectualized political culture than in the more action-oriented, I-am-in-charge-here culture of the American heartland. Indeed, this is an argument made by Donald Morrison in his chapter entitled, "Obama's French Connection." It seems that the reflective writer—idealistic community organizer—ambitious but cautious politician Obama lacks the more extroverted approach that came so naturally and so early in life to various full-blooded and successful presidential politicians such as Lyndon Johnson and Bill Clinton who were able to wheedle political support even from of those most reluctant to give it.

Rorschach President or Unreconstructed Liberal?

Earlier in his run for office and even now to some degree, Obama draws "fantastic" or "unbelievable" projections from the masses of adoring publics and detractors. "I am like a Rorschach test," he told a *New York Times* reporter in 2007. "[E]ven if people find me disappointing ultimately, they might gain something." Obama is a shrewd enough politician to know that projections of his followers are not without base; they are rooted in certain ambiguities and anxieties Americans feel about their present and future, and he, as the high-priest, shaman, and mediator of history and culture in the early beginnings of the twenty-first century, is in a position to modulate, redirect, and permanently change the population. Is this the mark of a great leader, someone who knows his place in history, in the long succession of events and people who have preceded him in the uncertain march of human progress?

Avoiding the political trap of becoming too exclusively identified with the camp of traditional, reputedly resentful and angry African-American politicians, Obama plays on the ambiguities of "race," while only rarely mentioning the racial words in his speeches. He plays on the idea of an "exceptional" America, without bandying the term in his speeches except in a few instances. He almost takes it for granted that America will tackle any challenges it faces from China or any other rising power in the world. America is not declining, he often tells crowds of disbelievers; people who think America is declining don't know what they are talking about, he claims. Is this optimism a disguise of hope and audacity or a combination of all of these attitudes? Either way it often works to draw out the best in people, who perceive in Obama the goodness of the American people and democracy, the last best hope for mankind. But at times it may also set them up for disappointments because Obama has not always been able to redeem his explicit and implicit promises that pervade many of his speeches. These disappointments are at their most dramatic in the Arab world, as Ahmed and Masad unanimously report in their chapters reflecting, respectively, an Egyptian and a United Arab Emirates perspective.

About the hundreds of essays and biographies that have been penned about him he says, "It just encourages the narcissism that is already a congenital defect for a politician. . . . I find these essays more revealing about the author than about me." But then he follows up the exchange with, "Look, I don't want to sound too noble: The first time you're on the cover of *Time* magazine and the crowds are cheering, that's not bad, right? But one thing I've learned about myself is that the surface glitter, the vanity element of this campaign becomes less satisfying as I go along." One senses in these and similar comments Obama's psychological mindedness and emotional intelligence that can also be detected in his autobiography. Fully aware of his symbolic stimulus-value as a new kind of hybrid American he states, "I love it when I'm shaking hands on a rope line and I see little old white ladies and big burly black guys and Latino girls and all their hands are entwining. They're feeding on each other as much as on me. It's like I'm just the excuse."

David Axelrod, Obama's senior campaign manager, has agreed that his team had created an idealized image of Obama, yet in the election against Romney the American public could examine the two men against each other, rather than by themselves. "Ultimately, we're not going to be running against an idealized version of Barack Obama," Axelrod said during the campaign. "We're going to be running against a flesh-and-blood opponent, a Republican opponent who will present their own vision and bring their own record and their own ideas. . . . And then people will judge [whether] they trust [Obama's] character, who offers the greatest possibility for the future and who has their interests in the center of his vision. . . . Anyone who has spent time listening to him would understand that there is a real continuity and a real consistency to his vision and his message," Axelrod claimed.

In the reelection, it was clear that while Romney represented the archetype of a very successful American businessman, Obama represented the opposite, a unique combination of a community organizer, economic populist, and charismatic president, who was trying to rebuild America's middle class while using centuries-old progressive ideas about the public good. Whereas Romney represented the tradition of the American patricians, very much like the founders, Obama represented the plebeians and the outsiders, the mass of new immigrants still flooding the shores of this country, the working class, the poor, and those who look physically different from the established Caucasian ideal.

However, despite the clear demarcations in their public image, Obama as a candidate and president evokes all things to all people. His coalition in the 2012 election consisted of a tapestry of ethnic and demographic groups who see in him the emergence of the new America, a society that will become even more diverse in the coming years. "Obama's inability to fit neatly into any single racial designation is discomforting for some but provides solace to many others in a country where traditional racial categories are coming under significant strain. . . . So for some, Obama embodies the aspiration to an almost utopian future in which race no longer matters," Gary Younge, a Chicago-based writer has observed. He inspires similar emotions on the continent of Africa in countries like Kenya, South Africa, and Ghana and in parts of Asia and Europe. What is the source of this hope that keeps people attached to his image? Is Obama's iconography aligned with America's redemptive narrative in some uncanny ways? We take up these questions in this book from a global perspective.

Structure of the Book

In this book, we examine President Obama's global leadership using the six leadership dimensions from the well-known GLOBE study as developed by experts in organizational behavior and change: charismatic/value based; team oriented; self-protective; participative; humane oriented; and autonomous.[19] While a large number of people around the world found the president highly charismatic in 2008, the Obama mania seems to have abated in recent years. In the Middle East, the president appears to be self-protective while still appearing to be a team-player. In parts of Central and South Asia—Afghanistan and Pakistan—his humane reputation has suffered greatly due to the drone attacks.

Given Obama's pivotal role at the beginning of the twenty-first century, this volume offers the first systematic analysis of Obama's leadership within the framework of cultural globalization. Scholars from around the world present an analysis of Obama's image and currency from an international perspective. They present observations, on-the-ground reports, case studies, a literary exegesis, and ethnographies of Obama's leadership in action, not necessarily a judgment or a final analysis of Obama's personality or decision-making style. We have collected essays from around the world about the Obama presidency and how it is perceived.

Methodologically, we rely on historical and political analysis, cultural and psychological studies, and in-depth journalistic accounts, truly a mélange of interdisciplinary essays on Obama's leadership in action. As these papers were compiled at the end of the first term, Obama's leadership is a work in progress. Thus, we refrain from passing any final judgment on the policy decisions but rather suggest future directions for the most vexing problems in some of the highly troubled regions of the world.

The Obama presidency has indeed changed the image of America around the globe in a significant and perceptible manner after the years of "Bush fatigue," but have the US policies also changed significantly? Is there indeed a change in world opinion about the United States as a result of the Obama presidency? At this turning point in history, we find several potential opportunities and limitations in "the Obama world." While the Obama administration has ended the conflict in Iraq, the tensions in the Middle East continue to simmer and the ongoing climate change remains a viable long-term threat that is gradually becoming more real given the recent destructive storms and weather fluctuations.

Obama's policies have helped to improve America's standing in the world both in the near and in the more distant future, but will the Obama agenda enable Americans to prepare themselves and the country for the looming global challenges of the twenty-first century? In this context, scholars present the Obama agenda for their specific country or region, how that agenda might be implemented, and its effect on other countries in their region.

The book is divided into sections that, following an introductory part that focuses on Obama as a leader believing in American exceptionalism, cover five major regions of the world: (1) Africa; (2) the Americas; (3) Western, Central, and Southern Europe; (4) the Middle East and Israel; and (5) the Asia-Pacific Region. The editors reached out to scholars in each region representing different fields of study. For a more personal touch, we have also interviewed some of the globe-trotting siblings of Barack Obama: his half-sister Maya Soetoro-Ng, who lives in Hawai'i, and his half-brother Mark Obama, who resides in China.

Obama as a Global Leader

In **chapter 2**, titled "President Obama and American Exceptionalism: Is the United States an Indispensable Nation in a Multipolar World?" the political scientists and international relations experts Gregory Streich and Khalil Marrar examine Obama's conception of the traditional idea of American exceptionalism. They ask: What is American exceptionalism? What do Americans think it means today? Does President Obama, who certainly believes in the idea, conceive of it in a different way? Will American exceptionalism become a wishful fantasy in an emerging "post-American world"? Can the United States retain the status of an "indispensable" nation in the twenty-first century, or is the president presiding over an era of American decline accompanied by the rise of China and more generally, the BRICS countries? These far-reaching questions are central to this book.

The chapter authors ask: How has Obama's leadership been received in European, Asian, and Middle Eastern countries? What is the status and purpose of American power in an increasingly global and multipolar world? In short, Streich and Marrar argue that contrary to the opinions of his critics, President Obama does indeed believe in American exceptionalism. "But while he has expressly stated his belief that the United States is exceptional and remains the indispensable nation he simultaneously recognizes that US power does not rest solely on military superiority but on coalition-building and diplomacy in an increasingly multipolar world," argue the authors. "Leading from behind," as Obama's style has been dubbed, may be a smarter and leaner policy for a resource-strapped world; this is an issue we take up in the conclusion of the book.

In **chapter 3**, Rabi S. Bhagat, a leadership expert who has worked on the GLOBE study, together with his colleagues, Annett S. McDevitt, Mannsoo Shin, and Bharatendu N. Shrivastava, examines the evolution of Obama's leadership (i.e., the strengths as well as the weaknesses of his political philosophy) in the era of globalization. The authors situate their argument both within a cross-cultural context and within the history of the American presidency while discussing the attributes most Americans admire in a vital leader. Much has been written about the remarkable journey of the junior senator from Illinois to the most powerful political position in the world. While over twenty-seven books and monographs dealing with the life and the political and social philosophies of Barack Obama have been written, the only monograph looking at Barack Obama in a cultural context is the one by the senior editor of this volume; likewise, the present edited collection of essays deals with Obama's leadership within the context of globalization and international relations. Bhagat et al. further support this claim by presenting an analysis of leadership skills needed to advance globalization and multinational businesses together with the pursuit of American interests in a rapidly changing world.

In **chapter 4**, "Barack Obama and Inclusive Leadership in Engaging Followership," Edwin P. Hollander, a leadership expert trained in social psychology, examines leader-follower relationship dynamics. He asks, "If Obama's leading, who's following? Has he had enough credit?" Hollander's essay was triggered by an ironic, semi-prophetic report that ran in the humor publication, *The Onion*, the day after the 2008 election. It began as follows: "African-American man Barack Obama, 47, was given the least-desirable job in the entire country. . . elected president of the United States. . . [a] high-stress, low-reward position. Obama will be charged with such tasks as overhauling the nation's broken-down economy, repairing the crumbling infrastructure, and generally having to please more than 300 million Americans . . . on a daily basis . . . spending four to eight years cleaning up the messes other people left behind" (Nov. 5, 2008). In the meantime, he has cleaned up some of the "messes other people left behind," but the path forward is sure to remain a patchy one.

Hollander claims "that the president needs to be perceived as getting things done or else he will lose his credit and credibility with the public." President Obama had not shown enough drive in fighting for the most disadvantaged on issues such as poverty, economic opportunity and fairness, and particularly persisting unemployment worsened by historically high rates of home foreclosures. This huge challenge had become vital especially during the presidential election when the growing divide between the super-rich, the middle-class, and the working classes was being highly politicized. Hollander's chapter sets up the context for the debates that follow by examining Barack Obama's leadership style within the conditions he inherited and how far he has succeeded in improving them both domestically and internationally.

In **chapter 5**, "Obama, Hillary, and Women's Voices," Dinesh Sharma argues that by adopting a "team of rivals" strategy, Obama selected Hillary Clinton to head the State Department, a clever and bold move, as many saw it at the time. As secretary of state, Clinton has intertwined diplomacy with strategies to further development and democracy, making women and girls a centerpiece of American diplomacy. The infrastructure she has created will need to be developed further for lasting change to take place. "Achieving global justice depends on the ingenuity of human rights activists around the world and on the strength of U.S. foreign policy to advocate for women and girls—now and for generations to come," according to Ruth Messinger, president of the American Jewish World Service. Whether Hillary will don the mantle of leadership again remains to be seen. The global cause that she has championed for diplomacy, development, and democracy will endure, especially, as the woman-power, including half of the population of the world (3 1/2 billion), is the next emerging market opportunity.

Africa

In the section on Africa, we return to humanity's ultimate origins, but also, more directly, to those of Obama's father. In **chapter 6**, "Afro-Optimism from Mahatma Gandhi to Barack Obama: A Tale of Two Prophecies," Ali Mazrui, the doyen of African studies, recounts Mahatma Gandhi's prediction that "the torch of Satyagraha would be passed to black people" as well as Robert Kennedy's assertion in 1968 that "a Negro could be president in 40 years." Noting that both prophecies have been fulfilled, in different ways, in the intervening years, Mazrui suggests that whereas Africans are as violent as any other people, they move more easily toward forgiveness. And so Mazrui hopes that unlike so many recent American warrior-presidents, Obama will refrain from starting still another armed conflict between the United States and some other country/countries. This would perhaps justify the decision of the Nobel Prize Committee to award the Nobel Prize for Peace to him; he who is merely one among many other persons of African descent that have received this significant award.[20]

In addition, Ali Mazrui notes that Barack Obama has set a precedent not just in the United States but also in the entire Western world. No other Western country with a dominant white population has ever elected to install a black head of state. This chapter looks at the significance of this development for Africa and for black consciousness worldwide.

More specifically, **chapter 7** introduces an examination of Obama's immigration policies from the African region to the United States. In their essay, "African Diasporas, Immigration, and the Obama Administration," Malawian historian and novelist Paul Tiyambe Zeleza and his coauthor, political scientist Cassandra R. Veney, describe the significance of the Obama election within the long history of migration from the African subcontinent. Surprisingly, they find that Obama's policies toward immigrants from Africa are not very different from those of the Bush administration, despite the weight of history and the president's own background. However, the authors present a rare portrait of the longstanding relationship between the United States and sub-Saharan Africa—from the onset of slavery to the present—through the history of forced and voluntary immigration that remains central in America's history and national character.

In **chapter 21**, a commentary at the end of the book on the evolving relationship between Obama and Africa, Saths Cooper, a prominent clinical psychologist and former antiapartheid activist from South Africa, describes the limits of American power, which have clearly constrained Obama's global role and policies. Despite being the son of Africa who has inspired millions of youth to action, he has not been able to do much for the African people. Even with the rhetoric for change, Obama's leadership in Africa has been disappointing, according to many of these scholars and practitioners. They tend to view Obama's leadership through the lens of "collectivistic" and "future-oriented" thinking, even though they are "assertive" about their expectations and judgments. These patterns prove consistent with the findings of the GLOBE study on how African people, though otherwise quite diverse, tend to view leadership in general.

We should add to these comments that whereas Obama's 2013 visit to several sub-Saharan countries was successful and encouraging, it remains nevertheless true that he was playing catch-up with China, which by 2011 had displaced the United States as Africa's largest trading partner.

There remains the question of why the Obama Administration—and more generally the international community—have not done more to help solve the ongoing conflicts in the eastern Congo region, the world's foremost killing ground. Since the early 1990s, more than five million people have died from war-related causes in a region infamous for serious and protracted violations of human rights (The Enough Project, www.enoughproject.org). If Obama really does wish to bend the arc of human history in the direction of justice, he needs to spearhead a protected effort to create coordinated international leverage to resolve the deadliest conflict in post–World War II history.[21] In this context, one way ask: Why does Africa's son spend far more time attempting to deal with Middle Eastern conflicts rather than trying to put an end to the greatest human slaughter since World War II. Why are African lives so cheap?

The Americas

The essays contained in this next section examine Obama's positive image in the Americas and how it can help revive the economic and cultural relations with the rapidly developing countries of Brazil, Venezuela, Mexico, and Chile. The four pillars of the "new partnership for the Americas" are critically examined on issues such as sharing responsibility for governance, economic competitiveness, security, and sustainable development for the conservation of forest lands.[22] We also look north, toward the American–Canadian perceptions, for the sources of Canada's unflinching love and admiration of Obama.

In **chapter 8**, "Love as Distraction: Canadians, Obama, and African–Canadian Political Invisibility," Canadian sociologist Rinaldo Walcott examines how Obama is perceived with great expectations by the Canadian people based on their own sense of history and multiculturalism. He examines what he calls "cross-border seduction" by analyzing how Canadian multiculturalism and party politics have made use of questions of race and ethnicity to advance an anti-black agenda. At the same time, Walcott makes sense of the Canadian electorate's overwhelming support of and admiration for US President Barack Obama as a "participative" leader, someone who invites a "team of rivals" to join him. Placing Obama's very favorable ratings among Canadian voters alongside their electoral decision to elect one of the most conservative governments in recent memory opens up a set of Canadian contradictions about race, blackness, and multiculturalism. These, in turn, raise considerable questions about how Obama's significance or symbolic role may sometimes further the goals of global anti-black sentiments. Indeed, Walcott demonstrates how Obama's deployment by Canadian conservatives can ironically serve as an anti-black political strategy.

In **chapter 9**, "Changing Times and Economic Cycles: President Obama—The Southern Continent, Mexico and the Caribbean," professors of finance Elisa Moncarz and Raul Moncarz examine the Obama administration's renewed hope and vigor for the world in general and America's neighbors in Latin America and the Caribbean in particular. The region has seen unfinished agendas, new opportunities, and nascent democratic movements come to life. The Latin American region for example, since the start of the new millennium, has been transformed into mostly stable economies, while outdated political structures have been replaced by consolidation of democratic institutions. This chapter focuses on the Obama administration's actions and responses directed at the concerns of Mexico, the Southern hemisphere, the Caribbean, and Latin America in general since he assumed office in 2009.

There are many critical areas of shared concern between the Obama administration and the Latin American region. Important examples include trade, immigration, energy, the use of and the transnational smuggling of narcotics, border issues, and strategic partnerships with a number of countries. The chapter also takes a look at America's delicate managed interdependence with Mexico, Central America, and the Caribbean, a possible rapprochement with Cuba, and relations with the "Bolivarian" populist regimes.

Given the scale of economic troubles in the United States, international conflicts in the Middle East, and the pivot toward the Asian-Pacific region, countries in Latin America have not been at the center of Obama's vision. He is loved and admired in Latin America, from Mexico to Brazil to Colombia, for his "charismatic orientation," "team-building," and "humane orientation"; indeed many Latin Americans see him as one of their own, perceiving him as displaying high "in-group collectivism." The authors argue, however, that Obama's leadership on issues concerning Latin America has been largely dormant. Much remains to be accomplished, for instance, on such basic issues as the reform of immigration from south of the border.

Europe

In the European section, the book examines the Obama administration's complex relationships with the Eurozone by focusing, respectively, on Greece, France, and Germany. As the European Union appropriates more international responsibilities for the European governance and security apparatus, independent of the existing NATO structures, many policy experts have noted that the Obama administration has been relatively disengaged from its traditional allies. The European chapters examine the newly formed global formation of G-20 and the member states' attempts to grasp Obama's divergent vision for a new world order.[23]

In **chapter 10**, titled, "Is Obamamania Over in Europe?" the political scientist Akis Kalaitzidis suggests that whereas the global wave of good will toward the United States is waning, "Obamamania" may not be over. His chapter examines evidence from Europe, which historically has formed the closest global relationship to the United States culturally, linguistically, and politically. The latest surveys of the continent suggest that although President Obama's public approval ratings in Europe remain high, European support for US policies is nevertheless starting to decline. In particular regards to foreign and defense tactics and environmental policies, the Europeans have become increasingly aware of the fact that the Obama administration has not pursued any more radical changes than had previous administrations. He claims that considering the global financial climate, and in particular the European travails in the Eurozone, attitudes on American leadership regarding the global economy can only grow more skeptical. Furthermore, many European countries have pursued "green policies" favoring the environment in a more consistent manner than the United States has, and so they decry a lack of responsible American actions and leadership regarding this crucial problem.

The recent Greek elections have revealed a political and financial deadlock in the country together with an anti-austerity turn in many other countries of the Eurozone. As goes Greece, so goes the Euro, which might have had a significant negative impact on the US political economy. How the Obama administration handled the Greek dilemma affected not only Europe, but also to some degree the 2012 election in the United States as Wall Street felt the ripples of the Euro crisis. This chapter examines the Obama administration's handling of Greece and its crisis and how, in turn, Greeks and Europeans perceive the United States under Obama.

In **chapter 11**, "Obama's French Connection," author and journalist Donald Morrison attempts to explain the French and European fascination with Obama because he reminds them of the ideals of enlightenment and democracy, the better angels of our political beings. To the French, the high-minded Obama resembles in many ways a "black Kennedy" who, in sharp contrast to the unilateral bullying tactics of his predecessor, Bush, advocates dialogue with his European Allies. Consequently, the lucid thinker, articulate orator, and talented writer Obama would make an ideal political figure in France where such virtues are widely admired. In contrast to his sharply fluctuating approval ratings at home, Obama's continuing and pervasive popularity in European countries such as France and Germany may partially explain why he is divisive at home and why he "may have already lost America"—or at least the culturally and socially conservative parts of America that see in him an alien presence or even a strangely eloquent Anti-Christ. Such hate mongering and religious fundamentalism would merely be considered absurd in most parts of western Europe where Obama is considered a sophisticated, multicultural, and fascinating (if not always effective) harbinger of the world's future.

In **chapter 12**, "A Relationship of Hope and Misinterpretation: Germany and Obama," international relations expert Thomas Cieslik analyzes the relationship between the United States and Germany following the presidency of George W. Bush. He reflects upon the German euphoria in the government, media, and society during the election campaign when Obama visited Berlin in 2008. In addition, he evaluates Obama's policies toward Afghanistan, the war on terrorism, the Arab Spring movement, the Euro and global financial crises, the future of NATO, and both the political and economic transatlantic relations, all seen from a variety of German perspectives. His chapter also includes a special focus on the personal relation between Obama and Chancellor Merkel in the context of cooperation on global matters. Indeed, a majority of political experts state that while the relationship between Germany and the United States had deteriorated during the time of Germany's left-of-center Chancellor Schröder and Republican President George W. Bush, the German–American friendship was renewed and a new chapter was opened when Obama honored Chancellor Merkel by awarding her the Presidential Medal of Freedom, the highest American civilian honor. Obama appreciates in Merkel her task oriented, competent, and cooly pragmatic approach to their negotiations and exchanges of opinion that bears a certain resemblance to his own approach. Furthermore, this chapter reviews the disappointment of German supporters regarding Obama's sometimes hawkish decisions regarding military affairs, making extensive use of foreign intelligence operations, and human rights issues during the last four years and concludes with a discussion of the future relationship between the United States and Germany after the 2012 election.

The Middle East and Israel

During the last sixty-five years, the Middle East has rapidly evolved into what is perhaps the world's most strife-ridden and troubled area outside central-eastern Africa. So it should come as no surprise that the Obama administration's evolving relationships with countries such as Iran, many of the Arab countries, and to some degree even Israel, remain highly contentious. Most recently, the region has grappled with a wave of democratic revolutions in Tunisia, Egypt, Libya, and other neighboring nations that the Obama administration has supported to various degrees. According to many analysts, the president has followed a policy that has been to some degree antithetical to the previous Bush administration's policy agenda in the Middle East and Israel. The effect of this strategic policy initiative is examined both in theory and practice.[24]

In **chapter 13**, "Arab Images of Obama and the United States: An Egyptian Perspective," the psychologist Ramadan A. Ahmed examines a variety of cultural, historical, and psychological trends that have led to a political stalemate. The beginning of his chapter sheds light on selected historical and geopolitical characteristics of the Arab world. Then, Ahmed briefly reviews the bilateral relations between the United States and various Arab countries. In addition, the chapter examines how Arabs originally perceived the Obama administration in 2009, and the expectations that Arabs had for the president of the United States, especially after his visit to the Middle East and his highly regarded 2009 speech at Cairo University. Subsequently, the chapter traces the Obama administration's actions during the Arab uprisings (Arab Spring) and how they have been received in the Arab world. The chapter concludes by assessing the possible reasons for the hardening of the opinions of Arab citizens about Obama and how his decisions might affect the Arab community in the future. Ahmed offers several suggestions for removing some of the barriers that have led to the enduring political stalemate in the Middle East. However, in his opinion, the United States will continue to pay limited attention to Arab concerns including the rights of Palestinians until it encounters a unified Arab front—an uncertain prospect because "Arabs excel at undermining each other," thus remaining politically divided and fragmented. The intensifying political and economic crisis in Eygpt and the civil war in Syria make it unlikely that a unified Arab front will emerge in the next few years.

In **chapter 14**, "Obama, Iran, and the New Great Game in Eurasia: A Journalist's Perspective," Pepe Escobar examines the relationship between the two adversaries. As a reporter, he has been covering Iran on a continuous basis since the late 1990s, where he finds a deficit in leadership. In the Middle East and Iran, it seems clear that Obama would receive low ratings on his "charismatic" or "value-based leadership" style and his "team-building" skills thus far. Escobar tries to shed some light on the complex and tortuous Obama administration policy toward Iran. Obama apparently extended a hand of friendship to Iran when he came into office, but that was only part of the story. The Wall of Mistrust that has existed for thirty-two years remains rock solid—reinforced by the relentlessly manipulated nuclear dossier. However, according to Escobar, Iran's position at the heart of an Asian Energy Security Grid, and as a key player in what he calls "Pipelineistan," warrants the necessity of a deal with the West—to the benefit of Iranians, Westerners, and Asians alike.

In the book's concluding section, Dovid Efune, editor of *The Algemeiner*, a New York-based newspaper covering Jewish and Israel-related news, offers a critical commentary on Obama's leadership style and his relationship with Israel. In it, Efune points out some of the reasons why many Israelis entertain ambivalent feelings toward the president and doubts whether the Obama Administration has kept Israel's security concerns sufficiently in mind.

Indeed, Escobar's benign interpretation of Iranian policies and intentions as opposed to Efune's demand that the Obama administration give a carte blanche to Israel's leaders for military action against Iran, could hardly be more divergent or more representative of the prevailing political-military tensions in the region.

In **chapter 15**, "Great Disappointments in the Arab World during Obama's First Term," Mohammad Masad, an international relations expert writing from the United Arab Emirates, describes in more detail the remarkable speeches that Obama gave in Cairo and Jakarta, and then goes on to contrast these promising beginnings with the Obama administration's cautious, fluctuating, and seemingly unprincipled actions in the Middle East during the president's first term. Like Ahmed he notes Obama's battered image among the Middle Eastern Muslim populations that, according to both authors, has emerged from Obama's unfulfilled promises, vacillating policies, and his failure to induce Israel to make any concessions at all to the Palestinians. As Obama's second term starts, Masad exhorts the president to revisit his promises and policies while supporting peaceful transitions to democracy in the Arab world and dealing in a more just and effective way with the "Palestinian problem." One wonders, however, how much real hope either the chapter author or the Arab peoples possess that such developments will indeed come to pass. However, they may feel somewhat encouraged by Secretary of State, John Kerry's determined efforts to facilitate serious negotiations between Israelis and Palestinians.

Asia-Pacific Region

In contrast to the Middle East, Obama's image in the more eastern parts of Asia remains mostly positive, but somewhat contentious due to the economic, geopolitical, military, and cyber challenges and threats emanating from China and the ongoing wars in Pakistan and Afghanistan. The papers in the East Asian section examine the Asia-Pacific region in depth in the context of the Obama administration's multilateral strategy for the region. They also focus on the economic, technological, and long-term challenges posed by the rapidly evolving Chinese economy and China's increasing military strength. Likewise, they focus on the security challenges at home and abroad as these are rooted in the ongoing military and political conflicts especially in Afghanistan and Pakistan. Due to these reasons, the Obama administration has kept the Asia-Pacific region front and center in its foreign policy initiatives.[25]

In **chapter 16**, "Bent by History in Afghanistan," Arturo Muñoz from the RAND Corporation presents a penetrating view of the history of the AfPak region, which is littered with the corpses of foreign warriors stretching back to the invading army of Alexander the Great. Attempts by Western and European imperial powers, such as Great Britain, Russia, and the United States to tame the tribal land between Afghanistan and Pakistan, including the cradle of the Indus Valley Civilization, now referred to as the "AfPak channel," have repeatedly failed. In 324 B.C., Alexander the Great was seriously wounded in Multan, Pakistan, while he was attempting to make his way to the Indian subcontinent. In this context, Muñoz asks: Have the American forces been able to bend the arc of history in the AfPak region? His paper examines this issue with the latest evidence as the American military and NATO forces eagerly plan to withdraw from the region by 2014, with a specific focus on the Obama administration. Will Obama be able to bring peace and prosperity to the Afghan region that has eluded many of his predecessors? Muñoz finds that this represents a chimerical goal bound to elude the American administration and military.

In **chapter 17**, "Between Popularity and Pragmatism: South Korea's Perspectives on Obama's First Term," the international relations expert Matthias Maass explores Korean perceptions of the Obama administration since 2008. The chapter makes an effort to include the government's and foreign policy elite's perceptions, as well as the general image of the Obama White House in South Korea. Maass tracks changes in the Obama image, and subsequently investigates the perception of US foreign policy in Northeast Asia under the Obama administration. The Republic of Korea (ROK) maintains a military alliance with the United States that has stationed 30,000 troops in South Korea; Washington and Seoul have signed a free trade agreement; Washington and Seoul are partners in their efforts to deal with North Korea (DPRK). These are the core dynamics that generally shape the relationship between any South Korean and any American government; consequently, this also holds true for the Lee Myung-bak and Obama administrations. With respect to evaluating the performance of any US administration, South Korea, by and large, has a highly prioritized view of Washington's diplomacy toward South Korean security and in particular American foreign policy in the context of the so-called Six-Party-Talks that deal with North Korea's nuclear program. This aspect figures prominently in the chapter. In contrast to many European countries, South Korea saw little "Obamamania" after the election in 2008. In 2012, local Korean coverage of the primary elections was minimal, indicating that the election was covered primarily in light of policy implications for South Korea, the Six-Party-Talks, and above all the Northeast Asian security situation. In contrast, it dealt much less with the philosophical–political schism in the United States, Obama's internationalism, or his broader world view.

In **chapter 18**, "The Chinese View of President Obama," Benjamin Shobert analyzes how the Chinese view the president. As a business consultant, Shobert has seen China from both close-up and afar for almost two decades. As China rises, it creates different reactions in the United States, which in turn help to shape China's diplomatic and long-term strategic response. In his essay, Shobert discusses how the Obama administration is perceived by the Chinese government, various policy makers, and the public. He suggests alternative paths for US–China relations in the decades to come and how the Obama administration can be instrumental in shaping this critical relationship. Seen in this context, recent efforts by president Obama and the new Chinese president, Xi Jinping to create a special understanding between them—and thereby between the two countries—augur well for the future of their relationship.

In Shobert's view, most members of China's sober political and economic elite perceive Obama as a rather weak leader who is finding it difficult to navigate successfully through Washington's corridors of power. Short of experience and *guanxi* (connections and loyalties based on past favors and ongoing interdependencies), he is seen by many as a weak administrator lacking in planning or business experience. In contrast, Obama's soaring speeches leave China's aging leaders cold—for them, they mostly contain verbiage addressed to immature idealists unfamiliar with the hard realities of administering a recalcitrant society and empire. We might add that neither are China's leaders or the populace impressed by the multiracial dimensions of Obama's political success since in East Asia (e.g., China, Japan, South Korea), anti-African and anti–African-American racism remains a distinct influence. After all, many idealized and admired heroes and heroines in Chinese novels are depicted as having skin "as white as porcelain," and consequently, it should come as no surprise that the Chinese and Korean markets for skin-bleaching creams are thriving.

In **chapter 19**, "Radical Manhood and Traditional Masculinity: Japanese Acknowledgments for Literary Obama," Eijun Senaha, a Japanese professor of English and gender studies, examines the literary Obama as a way to understand both the man and the politician. Barack Obama impressed Japanese readers in 2007 with *My Dream: Autobiography of Barack Obama*, a Japanese title for his original 1995 book *Dreams from My Father: A Story of Race and Inheritance*.[26] In a getaway story, the young Obama takes the first steps of his remarkable political career with his election as the first African-American president of the *Harvard Law Review*. He succeeds in portraying himself as a man of our times to Japanese readers. The American critics had already applauded it when the book was reissued in 2004 after Obama won the Democratic nomination for a seat as the US senator from Illinois. The book sold over a million copies, and as the US presidential campaign reached a fevered pitch, it started to draw more attention worldwide. Soon thereafter, in late 2007, the Japanese translation was published exposing Japan to a literary Obama. He became a popular writer indeed. Japanese knew little about him except that he became the first African-American president of the United States. However, thanks to such an engaging protagonist who was born to represent multiculturalism, the Japanese appreciated him while learning much about postmodern US history. This chapter deals with how the Japanese have understood Obama as a unique political figure, a figure that, we might add, could never have risen to political prominence in a relatively homogenous and racially closed society such as Japan.

Conclusion

In the concluding section of the book, we present brief commentaries from the Jewish community in New York and Israel (**chapter 20**), South Africa (**chapter 21**), India (**chapter 22**), and Russia (**chapter 23**) on the Obama presidency to round out the views presented earlier. In Israel and South Africa, respectively, the commentators Dovid Efune and Saths Cooper find that Obama's leadership is lacking in substance and effectiveness. In regards to India, however, his former classmate at Harvard Law School, Surat Singh suggests that the American president can indeed serve as a model of inspired leadership: He can teach Indian politicians how to empower both themselves and their people. Based on the inspiring story of his own life, Obama's powerful lesson for Indians is said to be this: Discover your own greatness by learning and doing, and then help others to discover theirs.

In contrast to Surat Singh's admiring comments from India, however, Evgeny Osin's report from Russia strikes a more discordant chord. Noting the vast differences between Russian and American political culture, he cites survey data to suggest that many Russians hold negative opinions about the United States and feel mostly indifferent about Obama. Still, there does exist some modest evidence suggesting that the number of Russians endorsing Obama's agenda is slowly increasing. We may add here that the personal relationship between the tough Russian president, Vladmir Putin, and President Obama seems to be characterized by a considerable degree of tension. A powerful leader, Putin not only resents Obama but also sees him as a weak leader within his own country and even abroad. And so, the former Lieutenant Colonel in the KGB and spymaster has agreed to protect Edward Snowdon in the NSA affair against considerable pressures emanating from the Obama administration. What an irony!

In the final chapter (**chapter 24**), "America's Asian Century," Dinesh Sharma presents an analysis of one of the biggest foreign policy achievements of the Obama administration, namely, the Asian pivot. The State Department has enunciated that the twenty-first century will be "America's Pacific Century." The author examines this idea, policy, and strategy as a future-looking vision for America's role in the world, based on interviews with several leading thinkers, historians, and journalists, while highlighting Obama's leadership role in shaping this vision. He also examines the role Hawai'i—the place where the president was born and raised—has played as a microcosm of intertwined racial and ethnic relationships in the emergence of America as "a blended nation" that increasingly represents the ever more globalized world. The cross-fertilization between Asia and America has been going on for almost a century, now pushed to another level with the economic rise of China in the twenty-first century.

More generally, the final chapter provides a good opportunity for the reader to step back and view Obama's global ambitions and efforts within the broader contours of the emerging twenty-first century. Yes, the United States is, and will be, continuing in its position as the world's foremost power, but China has already surpassed it as the greatest trading nation on earth. Given this competitive situation, the intensifying dialogue between the United States, China, and other powerful and not-so-powerful nations is very much needed so that the twenty-first century will not turn into a mirror of the twentieth century with its disastrous armed conflicts and world wars.

When taken as a whole, the twenty-four chapters in this book form a gestalt. The reader is first introduced to a series of cross-culturally and biographically informed analyses of Obama's strengths and weaknesses as a leader—as seen through the eyes of a group of leadership experts. Subsequently, the reader is taken on an imaginary journey around the globe by a highly varied group of "travel guides" who together have lived and worked almost everywhere. They ask: What do the people in "my" country or world region see in Obama? Why do these perceptions exist and how might they have shifted over time? What historical, political, cultural, and economic factors could have contributed to these perceptions? What does the United States—not just Obama—and its global power mean to "my" people?

The reader is shown a series of on-the-ground reports of a highly complex and varied world that is changing ever more rapidly. Each ethnographic account is taken from a different political angle and from a different spot on this geopolitically shrinking earth. Taken together, this series of ethnographies underlines one stark fact: As the president of the world's foremost power, Obama must make his geostrategic decisions in a whirlpool of difficult-to-foresee and steadily shifting events that significantly constrain his decision making and simultaneously introduce a large dose of uncertainty into the process. Being the president of the United States is not for the faint of heart. It requires a generous portion of self-assurance which is free of arrogance, because the latter would sooner or later lead to myopic decision making detrimental to the moral status and interests of the United States—and frequently also to the welfare of the peoples of the world. It has happened before!

Final Thoughts

When Barack Hussein Obama was born on August 4, 1961, to his "snow white" American mother and his "pitch black" Kenyan father, Hawai'i had only been a part of the Union for two years. Moreover, twenty-two American states at that time still upheld anti-miscegenation laws that outlawed marriage (and sexual relations) between members of different races. One of the biggest international news at the time was the erection of the Berlin Wall that began nine days after Obama's birth. For many Americans, the most pressing international concern was the possibility of a world war between the free West and the non-free Soviet Empire. As a result, the so-called Third World received only marginal attention. After all, China's GDP would remain smaller than that of the Netherlands for years to come while the forces of information technology-driven globalization would not emerge for decades. Who would have thought in those days—when white males in the United States wielded undisputed political power and Kenya was at least nominally still a British colony—that Ann Dunham's token marriage with a sexy, self-assured, deep-voiced international student from the Luo tribe would produce America's first hybrid president?

Today, President Obama and his administration must operate in a radically changed global environment. By the 1990s, colonial Africa had already been transformed into a continent of fifty-four independent countries while the Soviet Empire had come to an end. The world's population has increased from 3.08 billion in 1961 to 7.1 billion in 2013. Instead of the Soviet Union, a slew of homegrown, radically anti-American movements in the Middle East and South Asia pose new dangers to the security, oil supply, and global leadership of the United States. The continent of the future is widely expected to be Asia, with China's overall economy likely to surpass that of the United States around the end of this decade when purchasing power parity is taken into account.

The Constitution of the United States offers an American president considerably more freedom of action in the international than in the domestic sphere. And so, if we wish to understand the real Obama—the man who grew up as a *hapa* in racially mixed Hawai'i and on the Muslim streets of Jakarta—it is best to see him as a unique global figure attempting to transcend national and cultural boundaries, pushing systematically for women's rights as a key global issue, and at the same time being ready to defend America's security interests by creating an extensive network of international spying operations, sending out assassination teams, and employing drones no matter what the "collateral damage" (dead civilians, women, and children) might be (Scahill 2013)[27]. It is perhaps not surprising that the highly diverse crew of contributors in this volume paint a multihued picture of the global Obama. Some see him as a transformative leader while others emphasize that his ambitious, idealistic goals are not always matched by effective action consistent with his lofty pronouncements. As Benjamin Shobert notes in chapter 18, Obama's transformative life story and rise to power have not been matched by a comparable ability to actualize his transformative vision of American society and its place in the world.

How successful have Obama and his administration been in preserving American leadership in the rapidly changing world? What do the people of the world think of him and his leadership? On the whole, the contributors report that he remains genuinely popular in sub-Saharan Africa, Latin America, Europe, and to varying degrees in a good many parts of Asia. For instance, although Obama has not done that much for Africa, most Africans continue to have positive attitudes toward him because they see him as almost one of their own—the descendent of a Kenyan father who became the first person of African descent to assume the world's most powerful executive position. Across the Atlantic Ocean in Latin America, he is widely viewed as a distinct improvement over his predecessor, George Bush, as someone who supports and understands immigrants from Latin America better while deemphasizing unilateral American economic and political dominance in the region. Many Europeans as well respond warmly to Obama's conciliatory idealism while seeing him as one who embodies the American dream in a form entirely suitable to the emerging multiracial world. In contrast, the Muslim people of the Middle East and North Africa view him as a typical American leader unsympathetic to their Islamic-political-nationalistic goals while ignoring the sufferings of the Palestinian people. Indeed, Obama's efforts in the Israeli-Palestinian conflict have been unsuccessful from the very beginning of his presidency.

But the world's future, we are told, lies above all in Asian hands, with China rapidly emerging as an economic superpower. But China, with its unsettled borders and rising military ambitions, is seen as a threat by several of its neighbors including Japan, Vietnam, India, and the Philippines. In contrast, the United States has no territorial disputes with any Asian country. And so it is that many of China's neighbors like to see an engaged and militarily superior America acting as a counterforce against some of the more unsettling Chinese claims and ambitions. Countries such as Japan and South Korean keep huddling beneath the American nuclear umbrella because they fear their big neighbor and also its erratic ally, North Korea.

The Asian pivot analyzed in the book's last chapter will prove to be a major test of Obama's leadership capabilities and his ability to engage in effective long-term global planning. It will also determine how his legacy will be judged by the peoples of the world and by future historians. As Obama's second term unfolds, the crucial relationship between the United States and China; the dangerous situation on the Korean Peninsula; the unstable political and economic conditions in Pakistan; the Iranian challenge to the United States, Israel, and some of its neighbors; and the civil war in Syria are only some of the Asian flashpoints that could derail world peace and challenge some of the Obama administration's long-term plans.

One thing is for sure: In an increasingly multipolar, economically competitive but also intertwined world in which the momentum is shifting away from ailing Europe toward Asia and the global South, and where smaller nuclear powers such as North Korea, Pakistan, and potentially Iran can threaten to create havoc, Obama's global leadership will be sorely tested. By now he has thoroughly mastered his impossible job, adjusted his initially outsized ambitions to that job's frustrating but inherent limitations, and is eager to try to achieve some of the political-moral greatness that he has been so admiring in his melancholic role model, Abraham Lincoln.

We believe it is in the world's interest to see this complex and intelligent man succeed especially in his more idealistic goals both abroad and at home during the remainder of his second term. At the same time, it seems likely that he will remain more successful on the global stage than at home where a divided and at times dysfunctional Congress is likely to waylay many of his plans no matter how well conceived they might be. The American people are well aware of this situation, with their approval ratings for the gridlocked Congress hovering around a dismal 15% in 2013. In contrast, the 2013 job approval ratings for Obama have generally fluctuated around a much more substantial—though hardly impressive—47%.[28] Indeed, the American people split neatly in half when it comes to their positive or negative assessment of Obama's achievements as a president.

On the international stage, Obama's foreign policy has for the most part been pursuing pragmatic goals rather than living up to his activist vision and the idealistic image that his worldwide audience had formed of him in the beginnings of his presidency. He has repeatedly promised that he will help to bend the long arc of history toward justice but, as several contributors to this volume have noted, he has only partially succeeded in realizing this admirable goal. And so, for the shrinking remainder of his second term, the crucial question remains: Can he live up to his own words or will international and American historians one day look back and judge him as a leader who acted more like a successful *Realpolitiker* and less like a worldwide, effective champion of justice and human progress? The clock of history is ticking, and Barack Hussein Obama, the ambitious forty-fourth President of the United States, is well aware that he may actualize some of his most cherished plans at home and abroad in his post-presidential years as a global statesman.

Notes

1. Indyk, M., Lieberthal, K., and O'Hanlon, M. 2012. "Scoring Obama's Foreign Policy: A Progressive Pragmatist Tries to Bend History," Foreign Affairs, May/June 2012, http://www.foreignaffairs.com/articles/137516/martin-indyk-kenneth-lieberthal-and-michael-e-ohanlon/scoring-obamas-foreign-policy?cid=rss-foreign_affairs_coverage_of_th-scoring_obamas_foreign_policy-000000.
2. Sharma, D. 2011. Barack Obama in Hawai'i and Indonesia: The Making of a Global President. New York: Praeger.
3. Pew Global Poll. 2012. Global Opinion of Obama Slips, http://www.pewglobal.org/2012/06/13/global-opinion-of-obama-slips-international-policies-faulted.
4. Avolio, B., Walumbwa, F., and Weber, T. J. 2009. "Leadership: Current Theories, Research, and Future Directions," Management Department Faculty Publications. Paper 37, http://digitalcommons.unl.edu/managementfacpub/37.
5. O'Connor, P. M. G, and Quinn, L. 2004. "Organizational Capacity for Leadership." In The Center for Creative Leadership Handbook of Leadership Development, ed. C. D. McCauley and E. Van Velsor, pp. 417–37. San Francisco, CA: Jossey-Bass.
6. Cogliser C. C., and Schriesheim C. A. 2000. "Exploring Work Unit Context and Leader-Member Exchange: A Multi-Level Perspective." J. Organ. Behav. 21:487–511.
7. Shamir B. 2007. "From Passive Recipients to Active Coproducers: Followers' Roles in the Leadership Process." In Follower-Centered Perspectives on Leadership: A Tribute to the Memory of James R. Meindl, ed. B. Shamir, R. Pillai, M. C. Bligh, M. Uhl-Bien, pp. ix–xxxix. Greenwich, CT: Inform. Age.
8. Fry L. W. 2003. "Toward a Theory of Spiritual Leadership." Leadersh. Q. 14:693–727.
9. Coggins, E. 2012. Five Leadership Theories applied to Barack Obama. Berlin: Grin Verlag. http://www.amazon.com/Leadership-Theories-Applied-Barack-President/dp/3640364503.
10. Greenstein, F. 2009. The Presidential Difference: Leadership Style from FDR to Barack Obama (Third Edition). New Jersey: Princeton Press.
11. House R. J. et al. (eds.). 2004. Culture, Leadership, and Organizations: The GLOBE Study of 62 Societies. Thousand Oaks, CA: Sage.
12. Kloppenberg, J. 2010. Reading Obama. New Jersey: Princeton University Press.
13. Lydon, C. 2010. "Reading Obama's Mind: Pragmatism and Its Perils." Huff Post, November 5, 2010, http://www.huffingtonpost.com/christopher-lydon/reading-obamas-mind-pragm_b_779574.html.
14. Brinkley, A. "Review of James Kloppenberg's Reading Obama." Democracy: A Journal of Ideas, Winter 2011, http://www.democracyjournal.org/19/6791.php.
15. Scott, J. 2012. A Singular Woman. New York: Random House.
16. http://usatoday30.usatoday.com/news/opinion/columnist/raasch/2009–04–07-newpolitics_N.htm.
17. Fuchsman, K. 2012. "Conciliator in Chief: Obama, His Family and His Presidency." Journal of Psychohistory, July 1.
18. Goshen, J. 2012. Obama has better leadership skills, Survey Shows, Official UB News Site. http://www.buffalo.edu/news/releases/2012/10/13771.html.
19. House, R, Hanges, P., Mansour, J., Dorfman, P., and Gupta, V. 2004. Culture, Leadership and Organization. New York: Sage.
20. US-Africa Policy: Obama Administration, http://www.state.gov/p/af/rls/rm/2010/139462.htm.
21. Hall, Aaron and Kumar, Akshaya. 2013. Coordinated International Leverage: The Missing Element from Congo's Peace Process, Enough Project, February 14, 2013, http://www.enoughproject.org.
22. Latin American and the Obama Administration: A New Partnership, Brookings Institution, Washington, D.C., http://www.brookings.edu/events/2010/0629_americas_partnership.aspx.
23. McNamara, S. 2011. How Obama's EU Policy undercuts US interests, Heritage Foundation, February 16, 2011, http://www.heritage.org/research/reports/2011/02/how-president-obamas-eu-policy-undercuts-us-interests.

24. Assessing the Obama Strategy towards the "War on Terror," Middle East Policy Council, November 11, 2010, http://www.mepc.org/articles-commentary/commentary/assessing-obama-strategy-toward-war-terror.

25. Hoagland, J. 2010. "As Obama Bets on Asia, Regional Players Hedge." Washington Post, February 16, 2010, http://www.washingtonpost.com/wp-dyn/content/article/2010/02/11/AR2010021103270.html.

26. Obama, B. My Dream: Autobiography of Barack Obama [Mai Doriimu: Baraku Obama Jiden]. Tokyo: Diamond, 2007. Dreams from My Father: A Story of Race and Inheritance. 1995. New York: Crown, 2004. All references to the text are from the English edition.

27. Scahill, J. 2013. Dirty Wars: The World Is a Battlefield. New York: Nation Books.

28. www.gallup.com/poll/151025/Obama-job-Approval-Monthly.aspx.

2

PRESIDENT OBAMA AND AMERICAN EXCEPTIONALISM: IS THE UNITED STATES AN INDISPENSABLE NATION IN A MULTIPOLAR WORLD?

Gregory W. Streich and Khalil Marrar

Introduction

Upon taking the oath of office, President Barack Obama set out to pursue a foreign policy guided less by what he saw as the unilateralism, interventionism, and militarism of the George W. Bush administration and more by multilateralism, coalition-building, and diplomacy. By the end of Bush's second term in 2008 not only was he personally unpopular around the world but his foreign policy—marked by perceptions of unilateralism, disregard for international law, disdain for coalition-building, and the abuse of human rights such as at Abu Ghraib—had lowered the global standing of the United States. Bush's domestic and global critics charged that his foreign policy was at the very least arrogant and at most a unilateral assertion of an imperialistic "hyperpower" (Chua 2007: xix). Therefore, upon entering office President Obama sought to rebuild trust between the United States and its traditional allies in Europe as well as to build trust in the Arab and Muslim World. First, he signaled a change of course by issuing executive orders to ban the use of torture and to close the detention facility at Guantánamo Bay. Second, he gave his first televised interview to Al-Arabiya, a Saudi network. And third, he traveled to the Middle East, giving a major speech at Cairo University in Egypt and to Europe where he began setting the tone for a more cooperative, diplomatic, and multilateral US foreign policy.

President Obama's pivot toward diplomacy, multilateralism, and cooperation was largely welcomed both in the United States and around the world. Public opinion polls showed that the image of US leadership improved quite quickly. Gallup found that across 116 countries the global median approval of US leadership rose from 34% under Bush in 2008 to 49% under Obama in 2009 (Ray 2013), and Pew Research found that across 21 countries surveyed the global median confidence in US leadership rose from 17% under Bush in 2008 to 71% under Obama in 2009 (Pew Global Attitudes Project 2009: 31). Additionally, Obama's call for a renewal of diplomacy and international cooperation helped him win the Nobel Peace Prize in 2009. At the same time, however, President Obama's trip to the Middle East and Europe sparked a domestic backlash against his foreign policy and, ultimately, his presidency. While many Democrats who voted for him were thrilled to move beyond the policies of the Bush era, Republican and Conservative critics argued that President Obama was conducting a "global apology tour" and was neglecting the special role that was granted to the United States by "American Exceptionalism."

This chapter examines the debates surrounding President Obama's foreign policy as it relates to American Exceptionalism. In the sections that follow, we examine the following questions: What is American Exceptionalism? How do Americans feel about American Exceptionalism? Does President Obama believe in it? Is American Exceptionalism increasingly a quaint and self-deluding idea in a "post-American world"? Does the United States remain an "indispensable" nation in an increasingly multipolar world, or is President Obama presiding over an era of American decline? How is

President Obama's leadership perceived in European, Arab, and Muslim countries? And how does Obama's foreign policy reflect his views on the status and purpose of American power in an increasingly multipolar world? In short, we shall argue that despite his critics President Obama does indeed believe in American Exceptionalism. But while he has expressly stated his belief that the United States is exceptional and remains the indispensable nation he simultaneously recognizes that US power does not rest solely on military superiority but on coalition-building and diplomacy in an increasingly multipolar world.

Part 1: What Is American Exceptionalism?

The term "American Exceptionalism" has a long and multilayered history. In general, it refers to a belief that the United States is unique because of its history, resources, ideals, people, and purpose (Huntington 1968: 7–8). More specifically, American Exceptionalism assumes the United States is unique along several dimensions. First, historically, the United States is thought to have established a new, democratic, and egalitarian nation in 1776 in contrast to the feudalistic hierarchies of Europe. Second, it is thought of as having been "blessed" with abundant land, natural resources, and the protective buffers of the Atlantic and Pacific Oceans. Third, the United States is assumed to represent political ideals such as liberty, democracy, and justice as well as economic ideals of free markets and free trade. Fourth, it is seen as an "immigrant nation" whose diverse citizens accomplish great things because of a shared commitment to hard work, "can-doism," optimism, innovation, and fair play. And fifth, the United States is thought to have a duty (perhaps even a divine mandate) to be proactive in global politics not just to defend its interests but to spread its economic and political ideals around the world.

We suggest there are modest and strong forms of American Exceptionalism. A modest view of American Exceptionalism focuses on what makes the United States distinct and unique—but not necessarily superior—compared to other countries. For example, the United States is exceptional in part because of its status as the world's biggest and strongest economic and military power. Within this modest view, however, other nations can also be "unique." By contrast, there is a more extreme version of American Exceptionalism that focuses on the singular role that only the United States can fulfill in promoting free trade, democratic institutions, and stability around the world. From this perspective, the United States has a special prerogative to define and establish various norms, laws, and regimes in areas such as trade and security. According to this view, the United States is thought to be not only unique but superior. Stephen Walt nicely summarized this form of American Exceptionalism when he wrote, "Most statements of 'American Exceptionalism' presume that America's values, political system, and history are unique and worthy of universal admiration. They also imply that the United States is both *destined and entitled* to play a distinct and positive role on the world stage" (Walt 2011, emphasis added).

Most discussions of American Exceptionalism emphasize the uniqueness of the United States and its dominant position in world politics in the post-WWII era. But the roots of American Exceptionalism can be traced back to Andrew Jackson's muscular expansionism as well as Woodrow Wilson's idealism and internationalism (Mead 2001). Indeed, Jacksonianism set the tone for the "hawkish" view of US power relying on the robust, unilateral use of military might to establish US dominance while Wilsonianism set the template for a more "dovish" view of US power based on diplomacy and international institutions, which were preferred over military strength alone. More recently, American Exceptionalism was thought to be vindicated when, after the Cold War, the United States entered a "unipolar moment" (Krauthammer 1990) in which the United States was thought to be the "indispensable nation." In 1998, then Secretary of State Madeline Albright was asked by NBC's Matt Lauer to speak to the parents of soldiers who may be sent into harm's way. She stated:

> Let me say that we are doing everything possible so that American men and women in uniform do not have to go out there again. It is the threat of the use of force and our line-up there

that is going to put force behind the diplomacy. *But if we have to use force, it is because we are America; we are the indispensable nation. We stand tall and we see further than other countries into the future, and we see the danger here to all of us.* I know that the American men and women in uniform are always prepared to sacrifice for freedom, democracy and the American way of life. (Albright 1998, emphasis added)

While diplomacy is enhanced by a strong military and a willingness to deploy it, Albright asserts an American Exceptionalism in which the United States alone has the unique ability to take the long view as well as a duty to act in defense of universal principles simultaneously with American national interests.

After 9/11, the duty to use force when necessary was taken by neo-conservatives in the Bush administration as a justification for the unilateral projection of US power and a rationalization for why the United States could ignore international norms and laws that constrained other nations. Guided by this view, the Bush administration undertook the unilateral projection of US "hard power" in such a way that it ultimately weakened US "soft power" and global standing. Obama's early statements upon entering the White House indicated that while he would maintain the United States as the foremost military power on Earth, he would seek to return to multilateralism and diplomacy as a way of enhancing US "soft power" and renewing its global standing. But we hasten to add that while Obama's foreign policy emphasizes multilateralism and diplomacy on issues that demand a multilateral solution he has not been afraid to authorize the use of military force as is evident in his troop surge in Afghanistan in 2009 and the increased use of drone attacks against terrorist suspects in Pakistan and Yemen. Indeed, and perhaps ironically, President Obama's Nobel Peace Prize Remarks included a powerful defense of just war doctrine (the speech was delivered after he had just authorized the troop surge in Afghanistan). In his remarks, Obama stated: "We must begin by acknowledging the hard truth: We will not eradicate violent conflict in our lifetimes. There will be times when nations—acting individually or in concert—will find the use of force not only necessary but morally justified" (Obama 2009c).

Part 2: US Public Opinion and American Exceptionalism

American politicians of all stripes are fond of saying that the United States is the greatest nation on Earth. And American citizens also remain strongly committed to the notion of American Exceptionalism. Indeed, a Gallup survey from 2010 found that 80% of Americans agree with the statement that due to its history and Constitution the United States has "a unique character that makes it the greatest country in the world" (Jones 2010). And because the United States is thought to be exceptional and unique, 66% of Americans agree that the United States has "a special responsibility to be the leading nation in world affairs" (Jones 2010). At the same time, however, Gallup found that while 58% of Americans believe that President Obama shares this belief in the unique and exceptional status of the United States, a surprising 37% of Americans doubt his commitment to this belief. Underneath these numbers is a significant partisan difference: 83% of Democrats and 34% of Republicans agree that President Obama believes in American Exceptionalism while 12% of Democrats and 61% of Republicans disagree (Jones 2010). Moreover, when asked if previous presidents believed in American Exceptionalism, Obama's 58% "yes" to 37% "no" lags significantly behind Presidents Reagan (86% yes to 9% no), Clinton (77% yes to 19% no), and George W. Bush (74% yes to 24% no) (Jones 2010).

The Pew Research Center has also conducted a survey on American Exceptionalism. And while the Gallup questions come closest to measuring the strong form of American Exceptionalism by asking questions with the phrases "the greatest country in the world" and "special responsibility" to lead, the Pew survey distinguishes the strong and modest forms of American Exceptionalism. Overall, Pew found that 53% of Americans agree that the United States "is one of the greatest countries in the world, along with some others" (Pew Research Center 2011), a more modest form of American

Exceptionalism in which the United States may be unique but not necessarily superior. At the same time, Pew found that 38% of Americans agreed that the United States "stands above all other countries in the world" (Pew Research Center 2011), a position that represents the strong form of American Exceptionalism that assumes the United States is unique *and* superior.

Pew also found important partisan differences: 52% of Republicans but only 33% of Democrats say that the United States "stands above all others" while 43% of Republicans and 59% of Democrats say that the United States is "one of the greatest countries, along with some others" (Pew Research Center 2011). Additionally, the Pew survey identifies different subcategories of Republicans and Democrats. Among "Staunch Conservatives" 67% believe that the United States "stands alone above all other countries" and only 32% believe it is "one of the greatest, along with some others." By contrast, among "Solid Liberals" only 19% believe that the United States "stands alone above all other countries" while 62% believe that the United States is "one of the greatest, along with some others" (Pew Research Center 2011). In short, Republicans and conservatives are more likely to believe in the strong form of American Exceptionalism while Democrats and liberals are more likely to support the modest form.

As is clear from the Gallup and Pew surveys, that while Americans embrace American Exceptionalism there remains an undercurrent of doubt about President Obama's beliefs. In the next section, we shall argue that President Obama does indeed believe in American Exceptionalism. However, he appears to embrace the modest view of American Exceptionalism that is popular with fellow Democrats and liberals—that the United States is unique, indispensable, but not necessarily "superior." And this is precisely what leads conservatives and Republicans to conclude that Obama is undermining their preferred stronger form of American Exceptionalism in which the United States is unique *and* superior.

Part 3: Obama's Views on American Exceptionalism and His Critics

Early in his Presidency Barack Obama traveled to Europe for a G-20 meeting and a NATO meeting. While on this trip, Obama made comments signaling his rejection of Bush-era policies when he admitted that the United States had acted selectively in promoting democracy, that torture had violated American ideals and values, and that the United States had often acted arrogantly on the world stage by disregarding the concerns of its allies. At the same time, he also criticized a lingering knee-jerk anti-Americanism in Europe. Such comments were part of his efforts to renew diplomatic cooperation and heal the rift that opened during the Bush years when the United States either ignored or dictated to its allies. While in Strasbourg, France, Obama held a press conference at which one of the many questions came from a reporter who asked him if, given his enthusiasm for multilateral frameworks, he believed in American Exceptionalism. Obama's answer is worth quoting at length:

> I believe in American exceptionalism, just as I suspect that the Brits believe in British exceptionalism and the Greeks believe in Greek exceptionalism. I'm enormously proud of my country and its role and history in the world. If you think about the site of this summit and what it means, I don't think America should be embarrassed to see evidence of the sacrifices of our troops, the enormous amount of resources that were put into Europe postwar, and our leadership in crafting an Alliance that ultimately led to the unification of Europe. We should take great pride in that.
>
> And if you think of our current situation, the United States remains the largest economy in the world. We have unmatched military capability. And I think that we have a core set of values that are enshrined in our Constitution, in our body of law, in our democratic practices, in our belief in free speech and equality that, though imperfect, are exceptional.
>
> Now, the fact that I am very proud of my country and I think that we've got a whole lot to offer the world does not lessen my interest in recognizing the value and wonderful qualities of

other countries, or recognizing that we're not always going to be right, or that other people may have good ideas, or that in order for us to work collectively, all parties have to compromise and that includes us.

And so I see no contradiction between believing that America has a continued extraordinary role in leading the world towards peace and prosperity and recognizing that leadership is incumbent, depends on, our ability to create partnerships because we create partnerships because we can't solve these problems alone. (Obama 2009b)

In this answer, President Obama clearly accepts the notion of American Exceptionalism: he emphasizes how the United States helped rebuild Europe after WWII, how the laws and ideals of the United States remain exceptional, how the United States remains the largest economic and military power in the world, and that the United States remains a leader on the world stage. However, his answer is nuanced and modest. For his critics, it is too modest because even while defending American Exceptionalism Obama implies that other countries also believe they are exceptional (thus suggesting that the United States is not the "exception" to the rule). Moreover, he admits that the United States is imperfect, is not always right, and that it cannot solve problems on its own but instead must learn from, cooperate, and create partnerships with other nations.

This answer would probably not be controversial if uttered by an academic (indeed, President Obama is often described as professorial). But to hear the president of the United States acknowledge the imperfections and limitations of his own country struck Obama's critics as nothing short of political blasphemy. For "true believers" of American Exceptionalism, the United States is truly exceptional and unique, is always right, never has to apologize, always leads but never follows, always teaches others but never has to learn from them, and can always act unilaterally to defend its interests instead of being constrained by international law or coalition partners' concerns. As a result, Obama's critics argued that he was conducting a "grand global apology tour" (Kirchick 2009) in which he was too deferential to foreign leaders and too soft on defending American Exceptionalism.

Contrary to his critics, President Obama *has* maintained a strong form of American Exceptionalism. In his Nobel Prize speech, he explained the importance of international institutions and treaties in bringing stability to a post–World War II world. He then added what amounted to a defense of the "American Century" that followed WWII:

Whatever mistakes we have made, the plain fact is this: The United States of America has helped underwrite global security for more than six decades with the blood of our citizens and the strength of our arms. The service and sacrifice of our men and women in uniform has promoted peace and prosperity from Germany to Korea, and enabled democracy to take hold in places like the Balkans. We have borne this burden not because we seek to impose our will. We have done so out of enlightened self-interest—because we seek a better future for our children and grandchildren, and we believe that their lives will be better if others' children and grandchildren can live in freedom and prosperity. (Obama 2009c)

A stronger defense of the American Century is hard to find.

More recently, in his May 2012 commencement address at the US Air Force Academy, Obama explicitly rejected declinism when he stated, "Let's start by putting aside the tired notion that says our influence has waned or that America is in decline" (Obama 2012). After offering examples of how the United States has always met its challenges and defied the odds, President Obama reminded the audience: "Never bet against the United States of America. And one of the reasons is that the United States has been, and will always be, the *one indispensable nation in world affairs*" (Obama 2012, emphasis added). He then pivoted to make the case for another American Century, again rejecting any notion of American decline. President Obama suggested that US strength rests on several sources of hard and soft power, ranging from its military to its economy, but also its innovation, optimism, creativity, resiliency, diplomacy, and humanitarianism. He once again defended American Exceptionalism while recognizing the emergence of other powers:

> I see an American Century because no other nation seeks the role that we play in global affairs, and no other nation can play the role that we play in global affairs. That includes shaping the global institutions of the 20th century to meet the challenges of the 21st. As President, I've made it clear the United States does not fear the rise of peaceful, responsible emerging powers—we welcome them. Because when more nations step up and contribute to peace and security, that doesn't undermine American power, it enhances it. (Obama 2012)

Even when defending American Exceptionalism, President Obama recognizes implicitly that while the United States may lead it can also enhance its power by working with partners. For Obama, this is an honest recognition of an increasingly multipolar world. But his nod to alliance-building and multilateralism as well as his view that US power does not rest solely on its economic and military might has been latched onto by President Obama's critics who continue to portray him as rejecting American Exceptionalism, turning his back on the Reaganite principle of peace through strength, muting the voice of the United States in world affairs, and choosing to follow a "roadmap to American decline" (Krauthammer 2012). President Obama's Republican challenger in the 2012 election, Mitt Romney, frequently repeated the claim that Obama began his presidency with "an apology tour" despite the fact that respected fact-checkers have ruled that such a claim is wrong and misleading (Kessler 2012). Indeed, Romney's book, titled *No Apology: The Case for American Greatness* (2010) embraces the strong version of American Exceptionalism in which US power and even aggression is essential for world peace and stability. And the Republican National Convention held in Tampa, Florida, in August 2012 reiterated the message that Republicans were the protectors of American Exceptionalism because they want to maintain or increase military spending in contrast to President Obama who they portrayed as insufficiently strong on military matters because he is willing to cut defense spending. But a strong military is only one dimension of foreign policy and security policy. And while Conservatives and Republicans have recently preferred military solutions to diplomatic crises, Obama's leadership style reflects the view that the unilateral projection of hard power is not always the wisest course of action nor is it the only source of US power.

Part 4: The Academic Debate about American Exceptionalism—Defenders and Critics

Within the first one hundred days of his presidency, the new tone and style of President Obama's foreign policy unfolded within the context of an unprecedented debate among academics, pundits, and politicians on the topic of American Exceptionalism. Some argue that American Exceptionalism is a self-evident *fact* that should be embraced and defended (Romney 2010; Kagan 2012). Others argue that it is a *myth* that US policy makers and citizens should reject or, at the very least, view as a *historical artifact* of a bygone era (Hodgson 2009; Walt 2011; Bacevich 2008, 2012). Still others argue that American Exceptionalism is a *status* that is in doubt for one of two reasons. First, US power is less pronounced because the world has become more multipolar or even nonpolar in the twenty-first century as countries like China, India, Germany, and Brazil close the gap and gain ground on the United States. But within this school of thought there is a split: some urge the United States to accept this new multipolar or even nonpolar world (Kupchan 2012; Zakaria 2008) while others call on the United States to renew its preeminent superpower status (Ikenberry 2011; Friedman and Mandelbaum 2011). And second, US power is less pronounced because President Obama is squandering the preeminent status of the United States and opting for a path of decline that will result in premature superpower suicide (Kagan 2012; Krauthammer 2009, 2012; Kirchick 2009). Within this school of thought are many neoconservatives who defended the unilateralism and unfettered projection of US power of the Bush years (some of whom were foreign policy advisors to Mitt Romney's campaign).

While the nuances of this debate cannot be examined thoroughly here, in this section we will focus on the debate surrounding the nature of American power in the twenty-first century. A pillar of that debate is the position staked out by Fareed Zakaria. In *The Post-American World*, he argues that rather than the United States being on the decline, states from Brazil to Taiwan are on the rise. American power, Zakaria maintains, has waxed and waned since the Second World War, but overall, the United States remains the preeminent authority in world affairs (Zakaria 2008: 1–2). And while America's military adventures and diplomatic errors following 9/11 have taxed the nation's economy, political system, and military prowess, its superpower position remains largely unparalleled, especially in defense matters. Challenges however, come in the form of what Joseph Nye refers to as "soft power": economics, culture, education, and the like (2004, 2011). Take education as an example. Recent results from the Program for International Student Assessment of the OECD revealed that the US students finished 17th in reading, 31st in math, and 23rd in science (while Canada finished in the top 10 in every category). And while President Obama referred to these results as a "Sputnik" moment that should jolt the United States into making the necessary educational reforms, these results are also a sign that the rest of the world has caught up to and surpassed the United States. Some look at these results as a sign of a new "American Averageism" (Rothkopf 2010). But rather than seeing this as an "attack" on American prestige, Zakaria's approach views these trends as a sign that rivalry and parity—rather than American superiority—will be the hallmark of the post-American world.

The rivalry between the United States and others around the world is nothing new. One needs to look no further back than the Cold War to see challenges to America's global position. What is new, however, is a development that led Thomas Friedman to proclaim *the world is flat*," mainly that because of economics and technology, most people around the world have potential or actual access to the same pool of ideas as a result of the World Wide Web and the diffusion of intellectual and raw capital across nations, regions, and continents (Friedman 2005). This phenomenon, taking place in several stages, has precipitated a shift not just in commerce and markets but has revolutionized the very way we think about global politics and indeed the concept of power itself. In this context, Friedman argues, rather than being dominated by a single state or trend, the world is open to change from all sorts of agents, especially the individual, regardless of national boundaries. The implication is that centralization of any strength or notions of exceptionalism involving any nation-state is at best passé and at worst fails to capture the way of the world and thus relegates those guilty of such thinking to fall behind and undermine any basis of their strength.

Resetting the debate on American Exceptionalism, realists like Stephen Walt have sought to expose the concept as a historical myth, an illusion that serves the purpose of dominating other nations but ironically blinding US leaders to the limits of their own power. Writing that "U.S. foreign policy would probably be more effective if Americans were less convinced of their own unique virtues and less eager to proclaim them," Walt calls for a "more realistic and critical assessment of America's true character and contributions" (2011: 1). Such an assessment, rather than giving cover for bad decisions, as had been the case in the first decade of the twenty-first century, would allow Americans and their policymakers a more sober reflection on their interests, the global order, and the limitations of their power to shape it to their liking. Moreover, reminiscent of Zakaria's "rise of the rest," Walt maintains that the United States remains "embedded in a competitive global system" (2011: 6). And while competition is becoming more fierce, American economic strength will continue to diminish as champions of exceptionalism continue to trumpet an old, even archaic theme that might have been true decades ago but in the present takes on a lackadaisical caricature of whatever strengths the United States does in fact maintain, especially in economic competitiveness. It is worthwhile to remember that even the most strident awe of the US economy might has given way to the lamentation of "That Used to Be Us" (Friedman and Mandelbaum 2011).

But at its heart, Walt's post-American (exceptionalism) world involves more than just economics or politics—it goes to self-image. To him, the image conjured up by exceptionalism blinds Americans to their "weak spots" and to the fact that their nation's policies have frequently been out of step with progress, from the US failure to take the lead against Apartheid to the stifling effect that its unwavering support for Israel has had on Middle East peace. Far from being an indicator of American Exceptionalism, such behavior has not only won the United States few friends, particularly in Africa and the Middle East, it has frustrated the American interest of pursuing a place on the right side of history. What true believers in American Exceptionalism have accomplished is to make the country they claim to cherish increasingly counterproductive in global affairs. This is evidenced in issues from the battle against greenhouse gasses to the war on terrorism, where the United States has failed to seize a leadership position it naturally possesses because it is both one of the biggest producers of greenhouse gasses and the recipient of the largest terrorist attack in world history. On both counts and others too cumbersome to enumerate here, the United States, according to Walt and his fellow critics of American Exceptionalism, has failed to be an exception to the rule of great power politics, pursuing its short-term interests at the expense of long-term, more universal, or principled goals.

It is against this backdrop that President Obama's defense of American Exceptionalism in which the indispensable role of the United States is framed within the context of diplomacy and multilateralism has incensed his detractors. Whether the phenomenon is the "rise of the rest," "flat world," or "the myth of American Exceptionalism," in just the first decade of the new century, Americans have been facing challenges that have forced a tempering of seemingly old ways of thinking. From the terrorist attacks of 9/11 to the financial cataclysm of 2008, Americans' problems were made worse in part by the haphazard ways in which their politicians dealt with the challenges they faced. And the launching of two military entanglements along with the policies of economic laxness have not only generated contempt for the United States from most corners of the world but also squandered away opportunities to resolve underlying problems and redirected the nation's energies. Thus, Americans find themselves in one of the toughest times in their history, with malaise and misdirection ever present. For the realities of challenges to America's unique global position to set in to the collective psyche is one thing. However, and especially for Obama's loudest critics, for the nation's highest political officer to identify such challenges, or worse to steer it through decline, is akin to sacrilege (Krauthammer 2009).

And then there is the Josef Joffe view that America is the "default power." Rather than decrying President Obama as an apologist of American decline, Joffe focuses on the relative weakness of America's competitors and extols the structural fundamentals that still make the US exceptional. In *The Default Power*, Joffe posits that while it is fashionable to bemoan decline every decade or so, the United States remains leaps and bounds ahead of its closest rivals, the "false idols" of Asia (2009). In addition to its military muscle, powerful economy, and dynamic population, America's competitive strength lies in its intellectual capital and lavish research and development budgets. But the US also has an unquantifiable quality that is the envy of all superpowers across time and space: the ability to transform itself from a loathed hegemon to a needed presence at will. This is the case, whether it is in America's commitment to defending Europe against a menacing Russia or in bringing warring nations to the negotiating table from the Middle East, to Africa, Asia, and Latin America. Whether doomsday prophets like it or not, the US remains exceptional, despite and sometimes because of the crises that it finds itself in. And in a step that defies other American exceptionalists, Joffe argues that the election of Barack Obama, rather than being a mortal blow to the exceptionalism thesis, actually strengthens it.

In short, the debate over American Exceptionalism remains as vigorous as ever. While some, like Fareed Zakaria and Stephen Walt have problematized the concept because of either the rise of the rest or as a myth, others, such as Thomas Friedman, have recanted their old argument about America being at the center of a rounded globalization in favor of a flatter world theory. Meanwhile, as American exceptionalists like Charles Krauthammer assail President Obama and the left for injury to US standing in the world, others like Joffe see the country's leadership as incapable of doing much to corrode the country's default status as the "indispensable" power. And while no one would argue with the fact that the United States remains a superpower ahead of its rivals, the debate is over the duration and extent of that superpower status, particularly given the trajectory of other global players and the damage done to America's leadership by wrongheaded policies from presidents Bush and Obama.

Part 5: Global Views of the US during the Obama Presidency

When President Barack Hussein Obama took power on January 20, 2009, he declared "to all the other peoples and governments who are watching today, from the grandest capitals to the small village where my father was born, know that America is a friend of each nation and every man, woman, and child who seeks a future of peace and dignity and that we are ready to lead once more" (Obama 2009a). As the new president uttered those words at the dawn of his tenure in office, the nation and indeed the world remained uncertain about America's role in the world. After all, the United States was gripped by two wars, an economic downturn the likes of which had not been seen since the 1930s, and pronouncements by terrorist organizations in word and in violent deed that taunted the US effort against them (particularly as Osama bin Laden, the mastermind behind the September 11 attacks, remained at large without the consummation of the "dead or alive" orders of Obama's predecessor). Adding to the troubled atmosphere of the president's inauguration was fallout from the collapse of Lehman Brothers and Washington Mutual, at the time two of the nation's largest financial institutions, and uncertainty over the effectiveness of the Toxic Assets Relief Program to stem further damage. The future of America's global leadership remained in doubt from every compartment. And although Obama professed that the United States was ready to take the helm again, many doubted whether it was able to do so given the insurmountable challenges it faced. Indeed, "war fatigue" was mounting in the United States as Americans were ready to shift their attention away from global affairs and national security to domestic economic troubles.

As Obama's presidency turned from inauguration to governance, many around the world looked with inquisitiveness and hope at the US president. As noted above, Obama enjoyed higher approval ratings in 2009 than Bush did in 2008. Moreover, a 2009 Pew survey found global public opinion reflected relatively high expectations that the United States would adopt a multilateral foreign policy that would take into account other nations' interests, seek international approval prior to using military force, be evenhanded when dealing with the Israeli/Palestinian conflict, as well as take concrete steps on climate change. However, on all of these dimensions, Pew finds that global opinion has slipped with strong majorities stating that the United States "has not" met these expectations (Pew Global Attitudes Project 2012a: 5). For example, in 2009 56% expected Obama to take strong steps against climate change but by 2012 61% agreed that Obama had not met this expectation. And in 2009 45% expected Obama to take their individual country's interests into account when making foreign policy decisions but by 2012 58% stated that he had not met this expectation. On economic matters, global opinion has shifted to the point that while in 2009 46% of global opinion agreed that the United States was the leading economic power to China's 27%, by 2012 only 36% agreed that the United States is the leading economic power to China's 42% (Pew Global Attitudes Project 2012a: 6). While these numbers could be used to bolster the case for American decline, Pew also finds that the United States remains respected around the world, especially when "soft power" is considered: the United States is admired around the world for its popular culture, ways of doing business, and scientific and technological advances.

However, in part due to strong global criticism of drone strikes, by 2012 Obama's international policies have lost support around the world. According to Pew:

> In nearly every country where trends are available, support for Obama's international policies has declined over the last three years. Even though most Europeans still endorse Obama's

policies, their enthusiasm has ebbed. Among the EU countries surveyed in both 2009 and 2012, a median of 78% approved of Obama's policies in 2009, compared with 63% now. Among Muslim nations, the median has slipped from 34% to 15%. Major declines have also taken place in China, Japan, Russia and Mexico. (Pew Global Attitudes Project 2012a: 5)

While global confidence in Obama has dipped, his 2012 ratings were higher than George Bush's ratings from 2008.

Corroborating the Pew survey findings, a Gallup survey of 116 countries also found that by the end of 2012 Obama's ratings had come down from his highs of 2009. While the global median approval of the "job performance of the leadership of the United States" has slipped from 49% in 2009 to 41% in 2012, there are important regional variations: first, among African countries, Obama's approval dropped from 85% in 2009 to 70% in 2012; second, in the Americas his median approval rating dropped from 53% in 2009 to 40% in 2012; third, in Europe Obama's median approval rating has dipped from 47% in 2009 to 36% in 2012; and fourth, in Asia Obama's median approval remained essentially stable at 38% in 2009 and 37% in 2012 (Ray 2013). This type of slippage is not uncommon for modern American presidents, but Obama set the bar very high. For instance, in his 2008 electoral victory speech, he pronounced "tonight we proved once more that the true strength of our nation comes not from the might of our arms or the scale of our wealth, but from the enduring power of our ideals: democracy, liberty, opportunity and unyielding hope" (Obama 2008).

In the years after that speech, President Obama went on to engage US forces in a surge in Afghanistan, took no overt position on the 2009 protests in Iran, violated Pakistan's sovereignty on a number of occasions, the most notable of which was the operation to kill bin Laden, failed to deliver on his promise to shut Guantánamo, sided with the Egyptian protests only when it became manifestly clear that the Hosni Mubarak regime was finished, and did rather little to stop the massacre in Syria or to curtail that country's cross border raids against its neighbor, Turkey, a NATO member. It is of little wonder then that America's image and that of Obama has been diminished in the Muslim world. In the larger world optimism about the United States shrunk for similar reasons, particularly as President Obama has taken drone strikes to new numbers and intensity (Pew Global Attitudes Project 2012a).

Drone strikes aside, what afflicted the Obama presidency most intensely, along with America's image and standing in the Arab and Muslim worlds often involved things beyond the administration's control. Take for instance the violent protests against US interests, reputedly as a result of an anti-Muslim film trailer on YouTube attacking the prophet Muhammad. Beginning with the killing of Christopher Stephens, US ambassador to Libya on September 11, 2012, and spreading around the world, the disturbances, while limited in the number of actors and demonstrators, spurred Obama's critics into action. Most notably, Mitt Romney, along with fellow conservatives, indicted the president's foreign policy for its apologetic stance, and even went as far as to deem the response to the Libya attacks "disgraceful" (Weiner 2012). While Romney may have been trying to score political points with his base, such a criticism resonates with a wider audience critical of a multilateral approach to foreign affairs. Outside the American political scene, Romney and what he stands for confirms that the United States is of two minds when it comes to its approach to others, the one exemplified by President Obama and the other by his predecessor, George Bush. To those on the receiving end of America's military might, the difference might be rhetorical and largely academic. And it is well known that despite rhetoric being a very important dimension of America's standing in the world, in the parts inhabited by Arabs and Muslims, action and strategy matter the most, as seen in Pakistan.

Despite the dip in global support for Obama and his policies, prior to his eventual re-election in 2012 President Obama remained trusted and popular in countries that are America's closest allies. A pre-election survey by the German Marshall Fund found that Obama's favorability ratings remained high in Europe: 82% of Europeans surveyed held a favorable view of Obama while 11% did not (Glueck 2012). Moreover, if Europeans had a choice in the 2012 presidential election, 75% would have voted for Obama while only 8% would have voted for Romney. And while Europeans may be critical of some of Obama's policy decisions (such as increasing drone strikes in Pakistan and allowing the National Security Agency (NSA) to eavesdrop on European allies) and failures (such as timid leadership on global warming and the Israeli-Palestinian peace process), they continue to admire him not only because he still represents the "anti-Bush" but because of his own global background (Glueck 2012).

Pew has found similar results. Despite disappointment with Obama's policies, there was considerable support—especially in Europe—for his reelection. Prior to the election Pew found that: "Roughly nine-in-ten in France (92%) and Germany (89%) would like to see him re-elected, as would large majorities in Britain (73%), Spain (71%), Italy (69%) and the Czech Republic (67%). Most Brazilians (72%) and Japanese (66%) agreed. But in the Middle East there is little enthusiasm for a second term—majorities in Egypt (76%), Jordan (73%) and Lebanon (62%) oppose Obama's re-election" (Pew Global Attitudes Project 2012a: 2). Of particular interest is the unpopularity for President Obama and the United States in countries such as Egypt, Jordan, Turkey, and Pakistan, where it is believed that the superpower plays a harmful role given its history of intervention and propping up authoritarian rulers. When asked if Obama should be reelected, only 39% of Turks, 18% of Egyptians, and 7% of Pakistanis agreed (Pew Global Attitudes Project 2012a).

Looking at Egypt, Gallup recently found that Egyptians have become less supportive of US economic aid: while 52% of Egyptians opposed economic aid from the United States in April 2011, by February 2012 82% of Egyptians opposed it. And when asked if the United States will allow countries of the region to "fashion their own future as they see fit without U.S. influence," 76% of Egyptians in December 2011 disagreed but by February 2012 83% disagreed (Mogahed 2012). Such trends present a challenge to Obama's foreign policy as the Egyptian public, as with others around the world, is taking a more skeptical view of US aid and intentions. And looking at Pakistan, Pew has found that while Pakistanis are opposed to extremists like al Qaeda and the Haqqani network, they are also losing confidence in the United States and Obama. While in 2009 13% of Pakistanis expressed confidence in Obama's leadership while 51% expressed no confidence, by 2012 only 7% expressed confidence in Obama's leadership while 60% expressed no confidence (the 2012 percentages are similar to George W. Bush's). And when asked whether the United States is a partner or the enemy, in 2009 9% called the United States a partner while 64% called the United States the enemy but by 2012 8% of Pakistanis called the United States a partner while 74% called it the enemy. Overall, asked whether they have a favorable view of the US, Pakistanis have become more negative over time to the point that in 2012 12% held a favorable view while 80% held an unfavorable view of the United States (Pew Global Attitudes Project 2012b). Indeed, much of this decline is linked to the fact that Pakistanis not only oppose US drone attacks but also view US military and economic aid as having little positive effect. One bright spot in the region for the United States and Obama is Libya. Gallup found that 75% of Libyans supported NATO efforts to help oust Gadaffi, 54% have a favorable view of the US leadership, and strong majorities of Libyans favor Western economic and transitional aid in building a new post-Gadaffi Libya (Loschky 2012).

Conclusion: Obama's Foreign Policy and US Power in a Multipolar World

In light of the analysis above, we conclude that while American Exceptionalism both as concept and reality is not without controversy or multiplicity of interpretations, President Obama, by necessity of his office and his place in history, has worked assiduously to demonstrate and advance the United States both as an exceptional power and as the indispensable nation. It might be argued that Obama's America is exceptional as any empire has been exceptional. However, this perspective must not lose sight of the fact that American power continues to hold unique qualities especially for the monumental challenges presented by the times, including the belief from within that the country is losing not only its uniqueness but also its ability to be competitive with even minor nations in moral and practical ways. It is true that the United States has failed to seize upon opportunities to make the world a better place, has fallen behind in many measures of progress, and has even been guilty of using its military for blunder as well as plunder. However, to suggest that the United States is fading or that President Obama is steering it toward an inevitable decline fails to recognize the reality of the image and actuality of power that the United States continues to possess. Even as his critics have struggled to deny him that role, President Obama, especially when compared to his predecessor, has restored a great deal of credibility to America's might as perceived around the world. In a February 2013 report, Gallup found that while 51% of Americans think Obama is respected by other world leaders (down from his high of 67% in 2009), this remains more than double the 21% who said this of President Bush in 2007 (Saad 2013). Moreover, the percentage of Americans who believe the United States is viewed favorably around the world has steadily increased under Obama from 45% in 2009 to 55% in 2013 (Saad 2013).

No doubt, Americans are now aware that the overall standing of the US around the world has been harmed by the wars in Iraq and Afghanistan. However, the winding down of these two wars, while presenting burning challenges, has allowed Obama the potential to think about other, more pressing issues. To name but one instance, the United States began recalibrating its strength in the Pacific to deal with China as a rising power, not so much to constrain the "rise of the rest," as much as to ensure that it happens in an orderly manner in the far East (Neisloss 2012).

As with military strength, the United States is bouncing back economically. While unemployment remains a pesky problem, the S&P 500, Dow Jones Industrials, and Nasdaq indexes reached four-year highs as President Obama went up for reelection. Prices of crude oil, commodities, healthcare, and other essentials remain high, but with record low interest rates and Federal Reserve stimulus policies, purchasing power remains intact. Housing prices might be depressed, and real estate markets remain stagnant, yet inflation remains subdued, avoiding the "stagflation" of the 1970s. And while a housing market rebound led every recovery since the 1930s, structural factors have not allowed it to lead the recovery this time around. In totality, the US economy is nowhere near where it was at the height of the recession. It is in recovery mode, and the Obama administration has the burden of proving that its policies will hasten the recovery in the future. And on this note, American society's exceptional qualities, a dynamic population, intellectual capital, high productivity, and social institutions, have made recovery not a delusion in the middle of the worst economic calamity since the Great Depression, but both an eventuality and a reality. In fact, just as Europe and China stagnated as they faced problems with the same qualities that made America an exceptional economic powerhouse, the United States grew, albeit at a paltry rate that is certainly related to the shrinkage of the global economy. This demonstrates the United States still occupies the "commanding heights" of world markets and commerce.

In addition to its economic preeminence, the United States remains the world's cultural and iconic powerhouse. In fact, "the rise of the rest" thesis depends on one undeniable truth: that rise and decline are measured by an American historical yardstick—Americans and people around the world aspire to a world conjured up by pop culture in the United States, with all of the glamour and glitz portrayed in America's sounds and images exuded by its music and film. Bangalore and Bollywood might have emergent economic and cultural influence, but New York and Hollywood remain the icons strived toward. Shanghai and Beijing are centers of power in their own right, but in commerce and politics, Chicago and Washington, D.C. are paramount targets of emulation. All of this is not lost on President Obama, whose primary focus has been not only the restoration of America's global credibility, but also the rejuvenation of its political and economic systems. And while his foreign policy may have disappointed many around the world, particularly in parts where American power has always been viewed with suspicion, the president's first four years in office, while troubled and worthy of much criticism, have demonstrated a keen understanding of America's role in the world of the past and of the coming century.

References

Albright, Madeline. 1998. "Transcript: Albright Interview on NBC-TV February 19," available at: http://www.fas.org/news/iraq/1998/02/19/98021907_tpo.html. [Accessed: September 14, 2012].

Bacevich, Andrew. 2008. *The Limits of Power: The End of American Exceptionalism*. New York: Metropolitan Books.

Bacevich, Andrew, ed. 2012. *The Short American Century: A Postmortem*. Cambridge, MA: Harvard University Press.

Chua, Amy. 2007. *Day of Empire: How Hyperpowers Rise to Global Dominance—And Why They Fall*. New York: Doubleday.

Friedman, Thomas L. 2005. *The World Is Flat: A Brief History of the Twenty-First Century*. New York: Farrar, Strauss and Giroux.

Friedman, Thomas L. and Michael Mandelbaum. 2011. *That Used to Be Us: How American Fell Behind in the World it Invented and How We Can Come Back*. New York: Farrar, Strauss and Giroux.

Glueck, Katie. 2012. "Mitt Romney Tanking Abroad, Europe Poll Finds," *POLITICO*, available at: http://www.politico.com/news/stories/0912/81093.html. [Accessed: September 12, 2012].

Hodgson, Godfrey. 2009. *The Myth of American Exceptionalism*. New Haven, CT: Yale University Press.

Huntington, Samuel P. 1968. *Political Order in Changing Societies*. New Haven, CT: Yale University Press.

Ikenberry, G. John. 2011. *Liberal Leviathan: The Origins, Crisis, and Transformation of the American World Order*. Princeton: Princeton University Press.

Joffe, Josef. 2009. "The Default Power: The False Prophecy of America's Decline," *Foreign Affairs* (September/October).

Jones, Jeffrey M. 2010. "Americans See U.S. as Exceptional; 37% Doubt Obama Does," available at: http://www.gallup.com/poll/145358/Americans-Exceptional-Doubt-Obama.aspx. [Accessed: August 24, 2012].

Kagan, Robert. 2012. *The World America Made*. New York: Knopf.

Kessler, Glenn. 2012. "Factchecking Mitt Romney's Acceptance Speech at the GOP Convention," *Washington Post*, available at: http://www.washingtonpost.com/blogs/fact-checker/post/fact-checking-mitt-romneys-acceptance-speech-at-the-gop-convention/2012/08/31/70c3d8de-f31f-11e1-adc6-87dfa8eff430_blog.html. [Accessed: September 12, 2012].

Kirchick, James. 2009. "Squanderer in Chief," *Los Angeles Times*, available at: http://articles.latimes.com/2009/apr/28/opinion/oe-kirchick28. [Accessed: August 26, 2012].

Krauthammer, Charles. 1990. "The Unipolar Moment," *Foreign Affairs*, 70(1), 23–33.

Krauthammer, Charles. 2009. "Decline Is a Choice: The New Liberalism and the end of American ascendancy," *The Weekly Standard*, available at: http://www.weeklystandard.com/Content/Public/Articles/000/000/017/056lfnpr.asp. [Accessed: August 15, 2012].

Krauthammer, Charles. 2012. *FOX News*, available at: http://nation.foxnews.com/president-obama/2012/01/06/krauthammer-obamas-military-reductions-roadmap-american-decline. [Accessed: August 15, 2012].

Kupchan, Charles. 2012. *No One's World: The West, the Rising Rest, and the Coming Global Turn*. New York: Oxford University Press.

Loschky, Jay. 2012. "Opinion Briefing: Libyans Eye New Relations with the West," *Gallup*, available at: http://www.gallup.com/poll/156539/Opinion-Briefing-Libyans-Eye-New-Relations-West.aspx. [Accessed: September 22, 2012].

Mead, Walter R. 2001. *Special Providence: American Foreign Policy and How It Changed the World*. New York: Knopf.

Mogahed, Dalia. 2012. "Opinion Briefing: Egyptians Skeptical of U.S. Intentions," *Gallup*, available at: http://www.gallup.com/poll/157592/opinion-briefing-egyptians-skeptical-intentions.aspx?ref=image. [Accessed: September 21, 2012].

Neisloss, Liz. 2012. "U.S. Defense Secretary Announces New Strategy with Asia," available at: http://edition.cnn.com/2012/06/02/us/panetta-asia/index.html. [Accessed: September 11, 2012].

Nye, Joseph S., Jr. 2004. "The Decline of America's Soft Power," *Foreign Affairs* (May/June).

Nye, Joseph S., Jr. 2011. *The Future of Power*. New York: Public Affairs.

Obama, Barack H. 2008. "Sen. Barack Obama's Acceptance Speech in Chicago, Ill.," available at: http://www.washingtonpost.com/wp-dyn/content/article/2008/11/05/AR2008110500013_pf.html; November 5, 2008. [Accessed: September 11, 2012].

Obama, Barack H. 2009a. The White House. "Inaugural Address," available at: http://inaugural.senate.gov/documents/record-012009-inaugural.pdf; January 20, 2009. [Accessed: September 9, 2012].

Obama, Barack. 2009b. The White House. "News Conference by President Obama," available at: http://www.whitehouse.gov/the-press-office/news-conference-president-obama-4042009. [Accessed: August 14, 2012].

Obama, Barack. 2009c. The White House. "Remarks by the President at the Acceptance of the Nobel Peace Prize," available at: http://www.whitehouse.gov/the-press-office/remarks-president-acceptance-nobel-peace-prize. [Accessed: September 15, 2012].

Obama, Barack. 2012. The White House. "Remarks Made by the President at the Air Force Academy Commencement," available at: http://www.whitehouse.gov/the-press-office/2012/05/23/remarks-president-air-force-academy-commencement. [Accessed: September 12, 2012].

Pew Global Attitudes Project. 2009. "Confidence in Obama Lifts U.S. Image Around the World: Most Muslim Publics Not So Easily Moved," available at: http://www.pewglobal.org/2009/07/23/confidence-in-obama-lifts-us-image-around-the-world/. [Accessed: September 9, 2012].

Pew Research Center. 2011. "U.S. Seen as Among the Greatest Nations, but Not Superior to All Others," available at: http://www.people-press.org/2011/06/30/u-s-seen-as-among-the-greatest-nations-but-not-superior-to-all-others/. [Accessed: August 24, 2012].

Pew Global Attitudes Project. 2012a. "Global Opinion of Obama Slips, International Policies Faulted," available at: http://www.pewglobal.org/2012/06/13/global-opinion-of-obama-slips-international-policies-faulted/, June 13, 2012. [Accessed: September 9, 2012].

Pew Global Attitudes Project. 2012b. "Pakistani Public Opinion Ever More Critical of U.S.," available at: http://www.pewglobal.org/2012/06/27/pakistani-public-opinion-ever-more-critical-of-u-s/, June 27, 2012. [Accessed: September 12, 2012].

Ray, Julie. 2013. "U.S. Leadership Earning Lower Marks Worldwide," *Gallup*, available at: http://www.gallup.com/poll/161201/leadership-earning-lower-marks-worldwide.aspx. [Accessed: July 12, 2013].

Romney, Mitt. 2010. *No Apology: The Case for American Greatness*. New York: St. Martin's Press.

Rothkopf, David. 2010. "Foreign Policy: American Averageism," *National Public Radio*, available at: http://www.npr.org/2010/12/08/131901687/foreign-policy-american-averageism. [Accessed: August 31, 2012].

Saad, Lydia. 2013. "Americans See U.S. Global Standing as Better, but Not Its Best," *Gallup*, available at: http://www.gallup.com/poll/160697/americans-global-standing-better-not-best.aspx. [Accessed: July 12, 2013].

Walt, Stephen M. 2011. "The Myth of American Exceptionalism," *Foreign Policy*, available at: http://www.foreignpolicy.com/articles/2011/10/11/the_myth_of_american_exceptionalism?page=full. [Accessed: June 21, 2012].

Weiner, Rachel. 2012. "Romney Calls Obama Administration Response to Libya Attacks 'Disgraceful,'" *Washington Post*, available at: http://www.washingtonpost.com/blogs/election-2012/wp/2012/09/12/romney-calls-obama-response-to-libya-attacks-disgraceful/. [Accessed: September 18, 2012].

Zakaria, Fareed. 2008. *The Post-American World*. New York: W. W. Norton and Company.

3

OBAMA'S LEADERSHIP IN THE ERA OF GLOBALIZATION: A CRITICAL EXAMINATION

Rabi S. Bhagat, Annette S. McDevitt, Mannsoo Shin, and Bharatendu N. Srivastava

Since 1945, the United States has been the world's dominant power. Even during the Cold War, its economy was far more advanced than, and more than twice as large as, that of the Soviet Union. Other countries in Western Europe, notably the United Kingdom, France, Germany, Spain, the Netherlands, and Italy, were developing their economies quite rapidly by bringing about rapid technological improvements with US cooperation. The baton of economic and political pre-eminence, before being passed to the United States, was held by the colonial powers of Western Europe such as Britain, France, and Germany and, to a much lesser extent, Spain, Portugal, and the Netherlands. While European countries played a major role in shaping the history of the world from the late eighteenth century until the mid-twentieth century, the American political emergence after World War II has been a major phenomenon. Along with its role as the dominant economic and political power after the war, it has also been regarded as a country that can serve as a role model for democratic nation-building around the world—particularly in the developing world.

The United States is a large country with more than 3.6 million square miles (fourth after Russia, Canada, and China) and has more than 315 million inhabitants. It is the third most populous country after China and India but has less than 5 percent of the world's population. Its vastness, natural beauty, and big cities attract visitors as well as economic investments from around the world. Its economic strength is unrivaled, and its per capita gross national product is higher than that of any other major country in the world. It has always been at the forefront of encouraging globalization and has clearly been most willing to risk its national security to combat fascism and communism in both Europe and East Asia. Many historians have observed that without an active role of the United States in global affairs, the world would be an unsafe place to inhabit. Even though there are extensive debates in the United States regarding the role of its intervention in the affairs and conflicts within and among nations of other continents, the fact remains that the United States is still the major force in shaping political, social, technological, economic, and cultural development in the world.

Enter Barack Obama—the forty-fortieth president of the United States. He was born on August 4, 1961, in Honolulu, Hawai'i. He was the product of an interracial marriage between a Kenyan student and a strong-willed Midwestern woman from Wichita, Kansas. As the junior senator from Illinois, he led the Democratic Party to victory in the presidential election on November 4, 2008, and then again on November 6, 2012. Obama is the first African-American to be nominated and elected as president of the United States, and this fact has had remarkable transformational effects in the political arena, not only in the United States, but also in other developed and developing countries of the world as well. From what we have seen, his foreign policy stance has been less concentrated on intervention and more focused on building the image of America as one of the leading global powers, but not necessarily the most dominant one.

A great deal has been written and continues to be written on the remarkable rise of this junior senator from Illinois to be occupying the most powerful political position in the free world. In our survey of the literature, we found over twenty-seven books and monographs dealing with the life and the political and social philosophies of Barack Obama. The purpose of this chapter is to examine the evolution and significance of his leadership (i.e., the strengths as well as the weaknesses of his political philosophy) in the era of globalization.

America and the Era of Globalization

Globalization is the worldwide economic and social trend of expanding business operations beyond the domestic boundaries of the countries in which they were founded. Globalization involves connecting diverse nations around the world economically, and transactions involving capital, goods, services, and people are taking place on a routine basis. The growth rate of globalization (i.e., the volume of economic transactions in monetary terms among trading nations around the world) has been increasing at a faster rate than the economic growth of the participating countries. The evolution of the World Trade Organizations during the Clinton administration has facilitated the growth of globalization in a more fundamental fashion. Countries like Brazil, Russia, India, and China have emerged in the past decade as some of the major non-Western powers in the global economy.

While the United States still retains its economic superiority, its multinational and global organizations are experiencing a great deal of competition from multinational corporations of other developed and emerging nations. It is clear that while the United States could play the role of peace-keeper after World War II and invest huge resources in protecting the flow of commerce on a worldwide scale, its capability is waning. These developments are not surprising given that scientific breakthroughs and technological changes which spur economic growth of nations have been spreading at a rapid rate in the last four decades. In the current era of globalization, it is not necessary for a nation to have a large stockpile of commodities such as coal, iron ore, petroleum, and agricultural products. What is of crucial importance is the quality of imagination and scientific inventiveness of people in a given geographical locale: for these human qualities to unfold in a systematic fashion, it is necessary for the institutions of societies to function not only efficiently and effectively but also in a noncorrupt fashion. The world is in great need of leaders who are able to command sincere admiration and respect from their followers and who can also articulate a vision of the future grounded in hope and aspiration.

Among the many contenders for the US presidential election in 2004, 2008, and 2012, Barack Obama has clearly emerged as an unusual leader in the political history of America. In this chapter, we examine his role as the leader of the free world in the era of globalization. It is too early to predict as to whether his ambitions will lead to a better and more peaceful world in the next two decades. What is clear, however, is the fact that his leadership style is clearly different than that of many of his predecessors, and scholars would be interested in examining the nature of fit and appropriateness of this style of leadership in the era of globalization. Before focusing on Obama's leadership style in the current era of globalization, we outline a history of US presidential leadership to provide a background of how US presidents have emerged from different social and political contexts.

US Presidents: A Brief Historical Perspective

No discussion of leadership in the United States can be fully understood without an adequate consideration of the historical, political, economic, and social contexts from which it emerged (Hoppe and Bhagat 2007). As a social science–based construct, leadership is deeply embedded in the context. In other words, behaviors and actions that might have been considered to construe effective leadership during the colonial era in the United States (1580–1750) may not be regarded as facets of effective leadership in the era of globalization. Some common themes may be present, but in overall terms, the emergence of leadership on the part of an individual or a group is largely dependent on the nature of the social and economic context in which they find themselves. Sheer luck and opportunity also play important roles and some cases (like the leadership case of Mahatma Gandhi in the early part of twentieth century) are also partly accidental. The history of the United States can be described in the following stages (Johnson 1997):

- First Stage: Colonial America, 1580–1750
- Second Stage: Revolutionary America, 1750–1815
- Third Stage: Democratic America, 1815–1850
- Fourth Stage: Civil War in America, 1850–1870
- Fifth Stage: Industrial America, 1870–1912
- Sixth Stage: America as a melting-pot society, 1912–1929
- Seventh Stage: Superpower America, 1929–1960
- Eighth Stage: Economic Superpower in the new millennium, 1960–present

As derived from the works of Johnson (1997), O'Toole (1993), and Wilson et al. (1996), the recurrent themes and tensions in the US society that have been the focus of US presidents are as follows:

1. Atoning for grievous past injustices ←→ Creating a just and fair society
2. Pursuing narrow self-interests ←→ Working for the common good
3. Current economic realities ←→ "City set upon a hill" (articulated by President Ronald Regan in 1984)
4. Liberty (free market and free from) ←→ Equality (equity and solidarity government)
5. Efficiency (big business, government, labor) ←→ Community ("small is beautiful")
6. Individualism ←→ Collectivism
7. Existential equality ←→ Existential inequality
8. Live to work ←→ Work to live
9. Change ←→ Stability
10. Data/Measurement ←→ Values/Morals
11. Practicality ←→ Ideas/Intellect
12. Action ←→ Reflection

Many of the contrasts, which are especially important in the era of globalization, revolve around the role of the state or federal government in the conduct of economic and social affairs of the United States, and it is in this context that we examine the evolving role of Barack Obama. The United States has always struggled with the painful issues of balancing grievous wrongs of the past such as slavery and the decimation of the Native American nations when a society primarily dedicated to the welfare of European immigrants and settlers was created. The struggle and resulting insensitivities on both sides continue to be evident in the divisive debate over affirmative action and diversity in the political arena, particularly evident in the 1950s.

Barack Obama was born in 1961 amidst great social and political upheavals in the United States. Issues of racial equality in the South, the Vietnam conflict in the domestic and international political arena, and the incipient rise of feminism characterized the nature of the campaigns at the time. During this period, it was impossible to think of an African-American or a female being a major political leader at the national level. Even at the state level, there were hardly any African-American or female leaders. A great deal has since changed in the cultural and social milieu. To be sure, Barack Obama is not a major cause of these significant social changes in the United States, but he clearly was able to recognize the signals at the turn of the Bush administration in 2007 and emerged as a solid contender to Hillary Clinton who was a senator from New York and had the full support of the most charismatic Democratic leader of the current era, i.e., her husband, Bill Clinton. In describing the fight for nomination, *The Economist* magazine (June 2008) noted that Obama's selection as the Democratic front-runner made America look ". . . its very best." Given that the US economy was in shambles at the end of the Bush administration and the most significant recession of the past seventy years began in October of 2008, it was not too difficult for Obama to assemble a team of tech-savvy campaign advisors and win the election against John McCain in November of 2008.

A Cultural Sketch of the Effective Leaders in US Society and Barack Obama

A comparative analysis of the cultural dimensions of the United States shows that it is at the apex of the Anglo segment of the country clusters studied by Hofstede since 1980 (Bhagat, Triandis, and McDevitt 2012; Hofstede 1980; House et al. 2004; Ronen and Shenkar 1985). The United States is characterized by high levels of *individualism, performance orientation, masculinity, and assertiveness.* Moderate levels of *power distance* and *uncertainty avoidance* are also persistent features of this society. Extensive empirical studies by noted cross-cultural researchers like Harry Triandis, Geert Hofstede, Kwok Leung, Peter Smith, Daphne Wesserman, Michael Bond, and others have demonstrated in unambiguous terms that Americans are highly individualistic in their thoughts and actions. They also admire leaders who show clarity of purpose in the face of diversity and ambiguities. Some of the popular sayings of presidents like Harry Truman ("Give them hell, Harry" or "The buck stops here") have penetrated the American vocabulary as they emerge from the jargon of presidential actions. The question that arises at this point in time is, "Where is Barack Obama in the contrast to the historical portrayal of highly regarded presidents in US history?" We examine this question by analyzing his standing on some of America's highly regarded values.

1. Individualism and Barack Obama

Since its foundation, Americans have believed that it is the right of each individual to pursue his or her occupation and engage in the pursuit of happiness. The value of individualism has been at the core of American struggles against foreign powers and to a great extent was responsible for the emancipation of slavery. Unquestionably, African-Americans, due to the nature of forced migration that characterized their settlement in the American South, did not have the opportunity to appreciate the value of individualism and benefit from it. While initiative, independence from community and society, and the pursuit of one's endeavors were admired in White society, African-Americans were not in the position to embrace and then demonstrate the significance of these deep-rooted values in US society. Self-actualization was expected to come from continuous self-improvement. One must not regard himself or herself as a victim of one's circumstances and should not engage in passive forms of coping, as Glazer and Moynihan (1970) so effectively demonstrated in the context of black-white differences.

Barack Obama was different from his immediate African-American predecessors such as Jesse Jackson, Andrew Young, Harold Washington, and Mayor Dinkins of New York City. He was raised in Hawai'i by his grandparents who hailed from the Midwestern city of Wichita, Kansas. He was a highly accomplished student and had the opportunity to study law at two of the best legal programs in the country, Columbia University and Harvard University. His father was Barack Hussein Obama Sr., a student from Kenya, a country under the British colonial rule at the time of his admission to the University of Hawai'i. His mother was Stanley Ann Dunham of Wichita, Kansas, who was an adventurous woman and had fallen in love with Obama Sr. who was highly active in the Kenyan independence movement from the British. There was nothing particularly exotic about the name "Obama" at the time of Barack Obama's birth on August 4, 1961. The hospital records of live birth read, "Mother's race: Caucasian; father's race: African." In Hawai'i, which had stronger melting pot characteristics in the composition of its citizens than those found in mainland United States, the word *hapa* is applied to anyone who is biracial, i.e., half one race and half another. This newest state of the United States was full with biracial or *hapa* people. Maraniss (2012) notes that while the Obama name might have stood out had Barack Obama been born in one of the large US cities like Chicago, Los Angeles, New York, or in the Southern United States, it fits unobtrusively into the ethnic cacophony of the surnames of babies born in Hawai'i. Names like Arakawa, Murai, Ikeda, Chun, Simpson, Walker, Kobayashi, and Nakane were fairly commonplace. This fact certainly played to Barack Obama's advantage in a developmental sense. He did not experience any racial slurs or distance from the Hawaiian *hapas* and the whites (*howla*). Giving a son the name of his father, Obama Sr., was an unusual practice, completely different from Kenyan tradition. One of Obama's relatives noted that Obama Sr. was imitating the traditions of white people, i.e., the Anglos from the United Kingdom and the mainland Americans.

For all of its racial diversity, including ethnic populations from the Philippines, Korea, Japan, and China (about two-thirds of its population was non-Caucasian), Hawai'i was not free from racial segregation although it was of a different type than the forms prevailing in the mainland United States. For instance, James Michener, who published his sweeping historical novel, *Hawai'i*, in 1959 left Hawai'i partly due to the discrimination he experienced purchasing a home because his wife was a Japanese-American. For all of its racial undercurrents, the summer of 1961 when Obama was born in Kapiolani Maternity and Gynecological Hospital in Hawai'i was uneventful. The genealogists who studied the racial roots of President Barack Obama characterized him as 50% Luo, 37.4% English, 4.4% German, 3.13% Irish, 3.13% Scottish, 1.56% Welsh, 0.2% Swiss, and 0.1% French (Reference?). The influence of Barack Sr. on Barry (Barack Obama) was minimal as he headed for Harvard University and then Kenya to play a more active role in the independence of Kenya from Britain. Collectively, these events probably fostered in Barack Obama a sense of independence that shielded him against the oppressive social situations confronted by average African-American youngsters growing up in the rural South or in inner-cities of the United States (Sharma, 2011). The young *hapa* child, was too young to know that he was roughly half white and half African, but to the rest of the American society, he was known as an ambitious African-American whose blood relatives were primarily white from mainstream America.

In our view, Barack Obama grew up in an era where walls of discrimination were being challenged by strong legislative actions of President Lyndon Johnson and the Civil Rights Act. He understood the plights of rural and inner-city blacks but did not play the kind of social activist roles that were played by his predecessors like Jesse Jackson, Malcolm X, Martin Luther King Jr., etc. Unlike some of the native-born African-Americans, Obama Sr. was an accomplished scholar and a Kenyan. There is no record of his converting his citizenship to the United States. Obama was raised primarily by his mother and grandmother and in three social contexts: Honolulu, Hawai'i; Jakarta, Indonesia; and Topeka, Kansas. The undercurrents of these different cultures and geographical regions made Barack Obama more individualistic in his outlook and are reflected in many of the decisions he made during his first term.

2. Performance and Masculine Orientation and Barack Obama

The motto *live to work* strongly reflects the United States' tough approach in teaching citizens on how to deal with the complex realities of life. They are also encouraged to admire things that are big and strong, cars that are fast, and tangible expressions of success (e.g., money and higher positions). In terms of characteristics of an effective leader, Americans expect their leaders to be performance-oriented, to respect and confront difficult challenges in various facets of the American life, and to go the extra mile in leading his or her fellow citizens out of the shadows of difficulties and despair. Decisiveness, even at the expense of one's political success, is highly admired. However, good working relationships, a spirit of collaboration with fellow politicians (Republicans or Democrats), and an encouraging sense of solidarity among various working committees and caucuses, while valued to some extent, are not necessarily regarded as essential characteristics of an effective leader, particularly in the twenty-first century.

Barack Obama presents a complex picture in this respect. He is widely popular among young voters, suburban and working-class women, and an overwhelming number of African-Americans and Hispanics. His decision to have Osama bin Laden killed in May 2011 was a decisive act because the likelihood of success was low. As we know from the recent movie directed by Katherine Bigelow, it was an incredibly tricky operation to attack Osama bin Laden's compound in Abbottabad in Pakistan and terminate the life of one of the most important terrorists of the twenty-first century. Had his plans failed, he could have experienced a political fate somewhat similar to that of Jimmy Carter in 1980. In certain Asian countries (India in particular), some degree of slow decision making by national leaders might be regarded as a sign of reflective thinking and, therefore, widely admired, but this is not the case in the United States. The first author, growing up in India, used to admire US presidents such as John Kennedy, Lyndon Johnson, and other political leaders including Robert Kennedy and Hugh O'Neill for their quick decision making and assertiveness.

It is possible that the economic strength and performance of the US economy in many sectors made it relatively easier for leaders like John Kennedy to articulate certain seminal ideas which are used even today, not only in the conduct of US affairs but also in other complex situations occurring in other parts of the world. Obama's standing on this important cultural dimension of assertiveness and performance orientation is different from that of his predecessors, particularly Ronald Regan and John Kennedy. Obama appears to be more congenial and charismatic. It is as if he has an inner reservoir of strength that is not easily revealed unless in extreme circumstances. It may also be the case that because Obama is the first African-American president of the United States, we, as citizens, are unable to come up with appropriate images concerning how Obama ought to look during times when he is making tough and highly risky decisions such as the operation to eliminate Osama bin Laden in May 2012. In the remaining three-and-a-half years of his second term, we are likely to see events where his assertiveness and performance orientation will become more apparent.

3. Power Distance and Barack Obama

Cross-culturally speaking, US society is found to be moderate in its emphasis for preferences among various social classes. It is by no means like the Philippines, Mexico, Venezuela, or China where the distance between the leaders and the led tends to be vast and of an uncompromising nature. However, the United States is also not similar to Sweden, Denmark, Norway, and Finland where the relationship between the citizens and the government is based on the value of egalitarianism. The homogeneity of cultural groups in these northern European societies makes it easier to maintain strong emphasis on extremely low levels of power distances and still serves as effective participants in the global marketplace. The vast heterogeneity of the US society makes it difficult to disregard the strong advantages that ensue when emphasizing the value of power distance, i.e., the under-privileged in the society should expect that their lots in life (economic and otherwise) is not as fortunate as those of the privileged. We (Bhagat, Triandis, and McDevitt 2012) do not expect a major turn in this cultural tendency in the United States. However, displaying overt acts of power distance—particularly in the public arena—is regarded improper and can often lead to career failures in the political sphere. Obama has been particularly tactful and indeed privileged in his and his family's display of privilege and power in public. This was certainly brought out in the election year of 2012. While Romney was regarded as an instrument to further the economic interests of the economic power houses of Wall Street, Obama was considered as a champion of the underprivileged of the main streets in the United States.

The Americans have a dialectic or inner contradiction in their response to those of us who were born in another country—particularly in a traditional culture that had its own proud origins. Events and activities that reveal the mechanics and undercurrents of power distance in the realm of politics are useful in traditional cultures such as China, Japan, India, Iran, Egypt, and Saudi Arabia. In some Western countries there remain ceremonial displays of royal power and charm. Britain, in particular, has been highly effective in designing a parliamentary democracy in the role of power and deemphasizing the power-based political rituals. The United States falls in between the United Kingdom and the traditional cultures mentioned above in terms of emphasizing the role of power distance–based rituals. US presidents are praised and regarded more highly than they are criticized or lampooned in political cartoons. Upon entering any of the 200 US embassies and consulates spread across 180 countries, one is likely to encounter the smiling portrait of Barack Obama as the 44th president of the United States. In his day-to-day dealings with Congress and the judiciary branches of the government, Obama is not regarded as one who is quick to pick a fight or one to use powerful (if not dirty) political techniques as opposed to Richard Nixon who became infamous after the Watergate scandal in the 1970s. One might be inclined to conclude that the US political system has come a long way during the Obama administration—i.e., the presidential bully pulpit is not likely to be used for rapid and forceful decision making and for legislative changes favored by the president and his political party.

4. *Uncertainty Avoidance and Barack Obama*

Uncertainties are prevalent characteristics within societies in the era of globalization. The most pressing uncertainties that plagued the United States in the early twenty-first century are issues related to economic challenges and hardships. Other uncertainties concerned gun violence and acts of random terrorism. Fear of job loss and unemployment has become ingrained in the working class during the past decade. Moreover, it is no longer the case that white-collar employees and those in the financial sectors are immune from the economic turbulences in the United States because of the end of the Bush presidency. In a sense, what Obama and Biden inherited was indeed a bleak economic situation characterizing almost all of the formerly productive sectors. The auto industry was on the verge of bankruptcy, creating enormous direct and indirect job losses in the Midwest and the South. The debacles in the financial sector were indeed unthinkable as may be seen in Morgenson and Rosner's work entitled *Reckless Endangerment: How Outsized Ambition, Greed, and Corruption Created the Worst Financial Crisis of All Time* (2011). The economic world promised to deliver huge amounts of uncertainties as opposed to hope for the vast majority of Americans regardless of their ethnic or cultural origins. The unemployment rate reached about 10% immediately after the November 2008 election, and the hopelessness in the job market characterized the young graduates from US universities in ways we had not seen since the 1930s. Overall, America, as the leader of the free world after World War II, began to appear weak compared to rising stars of the emergent economies such as the BRIC (Brazil, Russia, India, and China) countries. This was a new development which had mixed effects in Eastern and Western Europe. China as the possible leader of the economic order (Jacques 2009) was not acceptable to the leaders of the Western world, India (the major economic and political power in South Asia), or Japan (the major economy, though weakening, in East Asia). All of these created significant environmental uncertainties that are uncomfortable to Americans of all stripes and colors. However, the progress on this front has been significant though not dramatic. Americans have been more willing to understand the nature of the most severe recession in the US history for the past seventy years, particularly due to continuous communication from the "stay in touch" president based on his Saturday morning radio addresses. It is safe to note that while Obama has been somewhat effective in dealing with the current economic and other types of uncertainties, the pressures remain and will probably play a major role in the 2016 presidential election. All-in-all, the economic uncertainties experienced by many Americans are on the wane but not gone, and we do not foresee these uncertainties being completely rectified during Obama's second term.

Obama's Presidency and the Era of Globalization

The first and most important condition for the continued smooth functioning of the global economic order requires US engagement. The second concerns Europe's (i.e., the twenty-seven-member

European Union) desire to restore internal commerce as well as trade with other countries including emerging economies represented in organizations such as BRIC, MERCOSUR, and ASEAN. A strong commitment to domestic economic stabilization is key to bringing about prosperity in the United States, Europe, and other parts of the world. While full employment is an impossible goal to reach in the context of a dynamic global economy, sustaining welfare states at accustomed levels is proving problematic. The Europeans have experienced it in the recent crises in the PIIGS economies (Portugal, Italy, Ireland, Greece, and Spain) while Turkey, which is still to be granted membership in the European Union, continues to do better than many of the eastern European countries and the PIIGS economies.

To Obama and members of his Economic Council, this is indeed a very different global economic order. Gone are the days of vast US economic superiority enjoyed after World War II since the United States no longer has the economic resources or the political will to bring about appropriate austerity programs which might enable many of the smaller European economies to return to economic health. Along with mismanagement of resources from the International Monetary Fund (IMF) and the European Central Bank, there exist other factors which are responsible for the current economic crisis confronting a majority of the countries in the European Union. While it is not necessary for the Obama administration to launch full-scale economic recovery programs for the reconstruction of Europe as the Eisenhower administration did after World War II, it is important to discern some of the social and cultural forces at play in the world at large. Globalization per se is a major driver of economic growth and prosperity in many regions of the world, but there are other forces as well that must be understood for their positive and negative consequences. They are as follows:

- Geography: Certain parts of the world are clearly more positively disposed toward embracing the full benefits of globalization. Geographical advantages include access to important natural resources, access to coast lines and oceans—navigable rivers, proximity to other successful and emergent economies, advantageous conditions for agriculture, and exposure to rare incidences of infectious and dangerous diseases and epidemics.
- Social and Cultural Systems: Certain social systems are more conducive to modern economic growth as sustained by technological innovations and effective planning by activist national governments. Precapitalist social systems based on feudalism, serfdom, slavery, inalienable land holdings, and so forth tend to pose serious impediments in sustaining economic development and growth. In the twentieth century, the spread of communism from the Soviet Union to China, North Korea, Cuba, and some parts of Sub-Saharan Africa proved to be a major impediment for entrepreneurial endeavors and frustrated the economic initiatives of the United States and other Western European countries. Colonial rule was particularly troublesome in the majority of the African countries and even at the dawn of the twenty-first century, the continent of Africa continues to be a weak though improving participant in the global economic order.

These issues are not new and they were already recognized during the apex of European power occurring just prior to World War I. However, in the twenty-first century, and whether it is economically feasible or not, much of the burden for modernizing the world falls squarely on the shoulders of the United States as the largest global economy and by proxy on its executive branch, i.e., the president and his/her administration. Coupled with the above economic difficulties, the rise of the BRIC countries has also changed the economic landscape in ways that were not expected during the high noon of the US worldwide economic supremacy during the 1950s (Jacques 2009). Notwithstanding the damage wrought by two world wars, the US economy largely outperformed the European economies from 1870 to 1950 and thus helped to provide the foundation for the emergence of the European Union as the premier global economic—though not military—power after World War II.

In addition, because colonial expansion was not a concern of the early European settlers in North America, it did not have to concern itself with the political, moral, and economic baggage of the colonial expansion, which plagued many of the European countries.

The dollar became the world's currency, and a new constellation of global economic institutions like the IMF, the World Bank, and GATT (the General Agreement on Tariffs and Trade) provided further impetus to the US economic hegemony. And its military superiority based on air power far exceeded that of any other country after 1945. As we have suggested earlier, by the 1960s the United States supplemented Europe as the global superpower with the Soviet Union as the only political and military adversary. The concept of globalization was not fully understood or grasped by the ordinary Americans during the first three decades after World War II. However, the Americans and their allies in Western Europe and East Asia realized that the United Sates has supplanted Europe and even the Soviet Union as the undisputed leader of the free world and had the largest GDP. Its universities became magnets for the best scholars and students from all over the world and the US share of Nobel Prize winners was the highest since the war.

The situation in 2008, when Barack Obama became the US president, was starkly different. The United States had become the largest debtor nation in the world, and China was emerging as the second largest economic power in the world. And Japan, which was protected by US military and nuclear umbrella after World War II, according to the McArthur Plan was beginning to voice its subjections by noting the importance of emerging "Japan that can say no" (Ishihara 1992). Along with these developments, the emergence and then crises in the fiscal and economic aspects of European Union makes the exercise of US leadership in world affairs both problematic in the short term and probably unsustainable in the long term.

President Obama's major priority after winning his first election had been the reconstruction of the US economy as everyone would have expected. The steps undertaken by him and his economic council, headed by the former president of Harvard University, Larry Summers had to inject $784 billion into the US economy to resuscitate and save it. His administration put many programs into place—the most famous being the TARP Act of 2009. The Made in America initiative, implemented in 2009 to bring jobs back to the United States, when coupled with major reforms in the regulation of the country's financial sector and Wall Street, and bailing out the US auto industry were highly effective and helped to sustain the US role as the largest economic power in the early twenty-first century. To be sure, many problems are still on the horizon and the economic growth of the United States is unlikely to remain as steady as was the case after World War II. We live not only in the era of globalization but also in the era of Internet and rapid communication. Events and actions that take place at any part of the world are interpreted by a large number of political and social commentators from political and cultural vantage points. Unlike the supremacy of US media outside the East Block after World War II, there has been a significant growth of media in countries that are politically and culturally highly dissimilar to the United States and its Western European allies. As a result, the nature of public opinion tends to be quite divergent in this era and despite the attempts of the Western countries to come to the aid of developing and emergent nations, the leadership of the United States tends to be viewed with suspicion. This does not make the job of the Obama administration any easier, and for Barack Obama in particular with his early cultural upbringing mostly in Hawai'i and Indonesia, the situation must be not only problematic but also frustrating. We predict that the role of Obama's leadership in the current era of globalization will be characterized by a series of upheavals; sometimes he will be greatly admired for his bold decisions, such as the actions taken by navy seals to eliminate Osama bin Laden—originally the mastermind of terrorism in the world—and the bail out the US auto industry. However, his proposed solutions to the immigration issue have been clouded with political preferences and so far lack a clear focus. Maybe we are witnessing the evolution of an era when US presidents would no longer be able to maintain long-term effectiveness in providing leadership when attempting to resolve the routine and nonroutine problems that arise in various parts of the world and in both predictable and unpredictable manners.

Ambiguity and Coherence: Toward a Conclusion

Our research reveals that Barack Obama strongly believes in the American Dream—the dream that anyone who works hard can succeed. This includes everyone from factory and farm workers to business owners and Wall Street executives and from inventors to investors—indeed each one of us. He notes, "We tell people—we tell our kids—that in this country, even if you're born with nothing, work hard and you can get into the middle class. We tell them that your children will have a chance to do even better than you do. That's why immigrants from around the world historically have flocked to our shores. In America we are greater together—when everyone engages in fair play and everybody gets a fair shot and everyday does their fair share" (Remarks delivered in Poland, Ohio, July 6, 2012). Campaign promises that are being kept and are currently being worked on are as follows:

1. Obama's first priority has been to encourage the creation of more jobs in the manufacturing sector in the United States. While this promise is difficult to realize in this era of globalization, significant strides have been made with the cooperation of US industry and the national Chamber of Commerce. The current unemployment rate is about 7.3%, slightly lower than the 8.2% at the time of the second presidential election in November 2012. The second priority has been to control and contain our energy future. He believes that the best way to reduce our deficit is to do it in a balanced way asking the wealthy to pay a little bit more so that along with cuts in various entitlement programs (i.e., Social Security, Medicare) and defense spending the United States can invest significantly in STEM (science, technology, engineering, and mathematics)-related higher education. STEM is at the foundation of re-energizing America's economic future so that it can begin to reassume the pivotal leadership role in the world's economic, scientific, and military affairs.

2. In the area of world affairs, President Obama has restored to some degree America's standing across the globe by slowly ending the wars in Iraq and Afghanistan. He is drawing down troops in Afghanistan as the United States hands over security responsibilities to the Afghan military and para-military forces. The United States is on track to end its responsibility for securing the borders of Afghanistan by September 2014. With the death of the notorious leader of Al-Qaeda, Osama bin Laden, in May 2012 he has shown decisive leadership in eliminating a major symbol of the terrorist movement that started before 9/11 and shook the world on September 11, 2001. It has been his goal to strengthen US alliances around the world with permanent allies like the NATO countries as well as Israel, Turkey, and Saudi Arabia in the Middle East. With the eclipse of American economic influence from 1990 onward, it has been relatively difficult to continue to foster international coalitions to confront shared challenges such as Iran's nuclear ambitions and its threat to destroy the Jewish state, Israel.

   The political undercurrents influencing the nation states are not necessarily governed by rational considerations. Strong feelings from past historical events and conflicts, religious preferences, and economic and political ambitions are at the roots of conflicts taking place in much of the world. Obama's approach to world affairs is reflected in the following:

   > America will never retreat from the world. We will bring justice to those who harm our citizens and our friends, and we will stand with our allies. We are willing to partner with countries around the world to deepen ties of trade and investment, and science and technology, energy and development—all efforts that can spark economic growth for all our people and stabilize democratic change. But such efforts depend on a spirit of mutual interest and mutual respect. (Delivered to US military convoy in Afghanistan, December 18, 2011)

3. In dealing with the emergent economies (BRIC countries), the Obama administration recognizes that some of these societies are millennial civilizations responsible for major political and historical innovations. China, in particular, has considered itself as the Middle Kingdom for a very long

time. It invented paper making, printing, gun powder, the compass, seismological detectors, the double action piston pump, the suspension bridge, the parachute, and meritocratic civil service. In a parallel vein, the Indian civilization developed important mathematical ideas and tools such as the concepts of zero, techniques of algebra and algorithms, the square root and the cube root, together with concepts of the atom, principles of chemistry and medicine, the study of phonetics and sound waves, and major principles of mechanical and civil engineering. In addition, both of these civilizations have developed agricultural techniques that could support large urban populations for many centuries. It was during the nineteenth century that both of these large Asian countries suffered humiliation from European colonial powers. For proud, ancient civilizations this proved traumatic and it acted as a stubborn filter distorting the way they processed information and knowledge from the rest of the world, starting with the political foundation of their republics.

An analysis of some of the cultural underpinnings for the slow growth of these two large Asian countries is found in the earlier work of Nobel Laureate, Gunnar Myrdal in his *Asian Drama: An Inquiry into the Poverty of Nations*. He concluded that cultural factors, profoundly influenced by religious forces stood as obstacles to modernization in the countries of South and East Asia. Japan and South Korea were exceptions because of the strong involvement of the United States after World War II. Myrdal noted that, "attitudes, institutions, modes of living and belief systems are fundamental to the way a group of people may come to appreciate the benefits of globalization both in economic and cultural terms" (p. 2). As the citizens of these two countries began to break away from the limited circle of identification with their immediate neighbors and developed larger circles of trust with which they could conduct business and other transactions, developments began to take place in a somewhat disorganized fashion (Myrdal 1968).

The Obama administration realizes that in the twenty-first century, globalization processes cannot be sustained by "America showing the way." Given that the average self-esteem of the citizens of the developed and the developing countries does not differ a great deal (Bhagat, Triandis, and McDevitt 2012; Smith, Bond, and Kağitçibaşi 2006), it is unwise to force the habits and traditions of one country (no matter how technologically or perhaps even morally superior it may be at a given point in time) onto the existing customs and belief systems of another country. Perhaps, a better way of achieving economic growth in various geographical locales of the world is to encourage the development of a democratic process of mutual respect together with the worldwide consortia focused on alleviating challenges such as the introduction of renewable sources of energy, the spread of transmittable diseases, global terrorism, population growth and the associated shrinking of the world's physical resources, preventing major climate changes, and health of impoverished children in developing and poor countries.

In this context, cultures may be understood in terms of progress-resistant and progress-prone types. People in progress-prone cultures assume that wealth creation and economic growth are the products of human creativity and are expandable across the various class and caste lines. People in progress-resistant cultures hold to a zero-sum assumption that the economic pie is not expandable and what exists now will always continue to be that way. People in progress-prone cultures live to work and people in progress-resistant cultures work to live. People in progress-prone cultures actively seek equality of participation of both sexes in the labor force and also in the distribution of financial and related societal rewards. They tend to be more competitive and are always seeking new ways of developing innovative scientific and technological methods for improving existing operations and controlling nature to live a better life.

It is difficult to transform a progress-resistant society into a progress-prone society. The political leaders have to emphasize urbanization without sacrificing the contribution of agrarian sectors of the rural economy. Mass education, occupational specialization, growing interdependence among organizations and organizational networks across political and cultural boundaries, greater income equality, and participation in political processes are keys to making societies more progress-prone and modern.

The role of *political corruption* (Heidenheimer 1978) is of paramount importance in the spread of economic globalization that indeed does lift the living standards of the poor and impoverished populations of the world in many geographical locales. Corruption exists in organized and semi-organized ways and refers to sometimes tacit or implicit and oftentimes explicit and blatant means of securing wealth and/or power through illegal or improper means for private gains. Giving bribes to government officials in the transportation ministry of a developing country to sell aircraft at subsidized costs is a clear example of the type of corruption that helps only the government official and not the country. Widespread interest in the functioning of democracy and economic development in the West for the past twenty years has largely focused on the phenomenon of corruption. Even the wars in Afghanistan starting in 2001 and in Iraq in 2003 are marked by instances of corruption by contractors and subcontractors in the US Defense Department. The Obama administration, our research suggests, understands the foundations of such corrupt practices and showed some attempts at creating more transparent accounting systems. However, bolder acts of leadership are called for in this domain. As the United States begins to spend more resources in rebuilding its infrastructure (estimated to cost over $260 billion—PBS Radio, March 2012), it simply cannot afford to waste scarce and valuable resources due to various manipulative and corrupt practices of public and private officials of other countries.

Research shows that corrupt public bureaucrats in many parts of the world actively participate in shifting government expenditures to those areas where the possibility of collecting bribes and related illegal gains are more likely (Swarns and Kantor, 2009). Larger and more difficult engineering projects such as airports or highways and various manufacturing facilities for fertilizer, chemicals, and pharmaceutical products are delayed because of the corrupt practices that have become commonplace in many of the countries as reflected in the Corruptions Perception Index (CPI) (1998, 2012). The United States does not need to monitor the economic activities of the top noncorrupt twenty-five countries or more as reported by CPI. Denmark, Finland, Sweden, New Zealand, Iceland, Canada, Singapore, the Netherlands, Norway, and Switzerland are outstanding examples of countries where corrupt practices are minimal in terms of their influences on the conduct of important nation development activities and daily activities. However, in countries like Russia, Ecuador, Venezuela, Colombia, Indonesia, Nigeria, Tanzania, Honduras, Paraguay, and Cameroon corruption and corrupt practices in public and civil affairs are pervasive in nature and destructive in terms of their consequences such as inhibiting economic growth and nation-building.

Along with combating the virulent effects of terrorism on a global scale, we believe that the Obama administration has a special duty to the world community in providing leadership in dealing with corruption. To be sure, corrupt practices that are prevalent in a country cannot be eliminated by sheer examples from other countries. However, practices that reduce corruption and promote noncorrupt decision making can be institutionalized in countries that are high on the ratings provided by CPI (2012), and they should be encouraged by the Obama administration. It is difficult to know whether corruption and corrupt practices have increased dramatically since the end of World War II. What is evident, however, is that for globalization to proceed and spread its benefits to the countries that desperately need to grow wealth and improve their agricultural, manufacturing, and services sectors corruption needs to be sharply reduced—if not completely so in the short term but definitely in the long term (see Healy and Ramanna 2013 for details).

Conclusion

A recent article on identifying the one hundred best-performing CEOs of multinational and global corporations in the world noted that chief executives are often concerned with short-term financial results at the expense of longer-term performance. This is particularly pronounced in the case of CEOs from the US multinationals and global companies. The rationale is based on the fact that if they do not meet their quarterly or annual financial objectives, their compensation drops and their jobs are in jeopardy. Stock analysts, shareholders, and members of their own boards are likely to judge them harshly if they miss their articulated financial objectives even by a small margin. While this method of assessing the comparative performance of CEOs is practiced widely, Hansen et al. (2013) argue that some of the best CEOs are more focused on providing total shareholder return in a handsome way in the long-term. Their list shows that the top CEOs delivered a total shareholder return of 1,385% during their tenures and increased their firms' market values by $40.2 billion. Contrasting the criteria used for assessing effectiveness of CEOs with how we judge the performance of US presidents, the following is worth considering.

Unlike the CEOs who are primarily concerned with the financial health and well-being of their stockholders and members of the board, the president should be a compassionate human being genuinely concerned with strategies and methods that help everyone at each rung of the economic and social ladder. On that criterion, we are of the opinion that President Barrack Obama will be recorded as a great leader. The long-term effects of his economic policies are beginning to be recognized. Governing a large and diverse country with a population more than 315 million people and five distinct ethnic groups is not an easy task by any means, and it has been recognized in the memoir of President Richard Nixon and the biographies of Lyndon Johnson (Caro 2012), William Jefferson Clinton, and Dwight Eisenhower. Our survey revealed that a lot more has been written about Barack Obama's administration and presidency during the past 4–5 years when compared to writings about his predecessors. As we noted earlier, perhaps the United States and, to a great extent, the world at large is still fascinated by the rise of the *hapa* youngster from a not-so-privileged upbringing to the highest political office in the free world. One thing is for sure: While luck and affirmative action leading to admission in elite universities might have played some role, the fact remains that a remarkable constellation of rational and cool-headed thinking, accompanied by compassion for the average citizen, and displayed with charisma makes Obama an effective leader in this era of globalization. Our assessment is that his administration will ride the waves of economic uncertainties that characterize much of the global economy in the next few years. The average citizen may not be able to have a larger share of the economic pie than his or her parents or grandparents did. However, a path toward increased equalization of the country's wealth distribution is likely to bring about structural changes that may again push America toward the third phase of global superiority.

References

1998 Corruption Perceptions Index. 1999. *Transparency International*. Retrieved from http://archive.transparency.org/news_room/latest_news/press_releases/1998/1998_09_22_cpi.

Bhagat, R. S., Triandis, H. C., and McDevitt, A. S. 2012. *Managing the Global Organization: A Cultural Perspective*. Cheltenham, UK: Edward Elgar.

Caro, R. 2012. *Paths to Power: The Years of Lyndon Johnson*. New York: Alfred A. Knopf.

The Economist. June 15, 2008, cover story: *America at Its Best*.

Corruption Perceptions Index 2012. Retrieved from http://www.transparency.org/cpi2012/results.

Glazer, N., and Moynihan, D. P. 1970. *Beyond the Melting Pot: The Negroes, Puerto Ricans, Jews, Italians, and Irish of New York City*. Cambridge, MA: MIT Press.

Hansen, M. T., Ibarra, H., and Peyer, U. 2013. The Best Performing CEOs in the World. *Harvard Business Review*, January–February, 81–95.

Healy, P. M., and Ramanna, Z. 2013. When the Crowd Fights Corruption. *Harvard Business Review*, January–February, 122–129.

Heidenheimer, A. J. 1978. *Political Corruption: Readings in Comparative Analysis*. New Brunswick, NJ: Transaction.

Hofstede, G. 1980. *Culture's Consequences*. Beverly Hills, CA: Sage.

Hoppe, M. H., and Bhagat, R.S. 2007. Leadership in the United States of America: The Leader as Cultural Hero. In J. S. Chhokar, F. C. Brodbeck, and R. J. House (eds.), *Culture Leadership across the World: The GLOBE Book of In-Depth Studies of 25 Societies* (pp. 475–535). New York: Lawrence Erlbaum Associates.

House, R. J., Hanges, P. J., Javidan, M., Dorfman, P. W., and Gupta, V. 2004. *Culture, Leadership and Organizations: The GLOBE Study of 62 Societies*. Thousand Oaks, CA: Sage.

Ishihara, S. 1992. *The Japan that Can Say No: Why Japan Will Be First among Equals*. New York: Touchtone Books.

Jacques, M. 2009. *When China Rules the World*. New York: Penguin Press.

Johnson, P. 1997. *A History of the American People*. New York: Simon & Schuster.

Maraniss, D. 2012. *Barack Obama: The Story*. New York: Simon & Schuster.

Michener, J. 1959. *Hawai'i*. New York: Fawcett-Crest.

Morgenson, G., and Rosner, J. 2011. *Reckless Endangerment: How Outsized Ambition, Greed, and Corruption Created the Worst Financial Crisis of All Time*. New York: Times Books, Henry Holt & Company.

Myrdal, G. 1968. *The Asian Drama*. New York: Pantheon Books.

O'Toole, J. 1993. *The Executive's Compass: Business and the Good Society*. New York: Oxford University Press.

Ronen, S., and Shenkar, O. 1985. Clustering Countries on Attitudinal Dimensions: A Review and Synthesis. *Academy of Management Review*, 10, 435–454.

Sharma, D. 2011. *Barack Obama in Hawai'i and Indonesia: The Making of a Global President*. New York: Praeger.

Smith, P. B., Bond, M. H., and Kağitçibaşi, Ç. 2006. *Understanding Social Psychology across Cultures*. London: Sage.

Swarns, R. and Kantor, J. 2009. *In First Lady's Roots: A Complex Path from Slavery. New York Times*, Oct 7.

Wilson, M. S., Hoppe, M. H., and Sayles, L. R. 1996. *Managing across Cultures: A Learning Framework*. Greensboro, NC: Center for Creative Leadership.

4

BARACK OBAMA AND INCLUSIVE LEADERSHIP IN ENGAGING FOLLOWERSHIP

Edwin P. Hollander

Introductory Overview

As the first African-American president, Barack Obama overcame an immense historical legacy by his 2008 victory, despite efforts to discredit his legitimacy. In then winning a second term in 2012, midst difficult economic times and against heavily financed, dedicated foes, he showed his sustained appeal. Among his strengths was a call for economic "fairness" that made for an "inclusive leadership" togetherness theme. He promoted it further with his "We, the people" second inaugural address urging, "We must act" on our needs. These include vital infrastructure of bridges, schools, roads and more, stalled in Congress as workers are kept idle.

Obama had emphasized "one nation" as the new voice at the 2004 Democratic National Convention. After taking office in January of 2009, he had a strong record of achievements in his first two years, when Democrats controlled both houses of Congress. His subsequent proposals, including major job and transportation bills, were among those blocked early by foes elected in the 2010 Republican sweep, taking over the House of Representatives.

In the Senate, his opponents routinely stop his bills by a filibuster, called "ultimate obstruction" by the *New York Times* (2013), in which a minority requires a 60-vote majority for any bill or nomination to proceed, let alone to pass. Though fewer of Obama's later bills made it over this obstacle, among some notable early successes were child healthcare, the recovery act/stimulus, pay equity for women, affordable healthcare ("Obamacare"), finance, student loans, credit card reforms, two more women on the Supreme Court, also ending "don't ask, don't tell" for gays in the military, an executive order on the legal status of adult children of illegal immigrants, but also failed efforts to pass a bill for "gun purchases only-with-background-checks" bill.

Followership: Showing, Telling, Listening, and Responding in Inclusive Leadership

How did the promise and hope of the first two years turn into gridlock and frustration in the next ones? Can and will it change? Among multiple causes, a large share were beyond Obama's control. Still, some of his failings became evident, such as not sufficiently or consistently explaining his programs, which were readily misstated and denounced by opposition voices. This was seen in how healthcare was defamed by such fictions as "death panels" and "lost jobs." It deserved far better presentation and explanation.

This chapter explores Obama's role in this process, and its context. It emphasizes his need for inclusive leadership, and his inconsistent attempts to employ it earlier, before arriving at it later, to gain the added leverage this kind of leadership can provide. Proclaiming this in his State of the Union address (February 12, 2013), he indicated that he had mobilized a large effort called "Organize for America," to follow up his legislative agenda with grassroots action. His administration had not done it much before to overcome congressional opposition (Stein 2013), and he added, "Tweet your support of my plan to create jobs and strengthen the middle class."

President Obama needed to set goals to attain and maintain a following that had trust in and loyalty to him. The main point is ". . . to bring the country along with you, . . . Obama simply had not done that" (Kantor 2012: 116). He had to turn that around and be perceived as successful in doing what must be done, or he might have lost reelection by losing their support. Even with the many things achieved, there were others often absent, possibly within reach not necessarily by the actual or potential use of executive powers, but by negotiating with greater strength, from a base in followership.[1]

After the 2012 election, the Obama for America campaign implemented that strategy to affect legislation. Obama needed to be inclusive by showing and telling how he would fight for what concerned followers most, issues of economic recession, particularly unemployment, and historically high home foreclosures. This set of problems was increasingly crucial, especially during the presidential campaign. However, at the outset, he came determined to achieve healthcare for all as a prime goal, despite its history of past attempts that failed. But he hadn't put enough effort into gaining a public following for it, nor getting sufficiently ready to battle its foes.

For a year, he let congressional conferees trim the bill, hoping to get support from Republican senators, which never came. Still, the bill passed in March 2010, with an "individual mandate," amounting to a fee that some more well-off participants would have to pay to take part. The Supreme Court upheld both the bill and its mandate by a vote of 5 to 4 in June 2012, though resistance continues.

Among Obama's strengths was the inspiration about hoped-for change he showed in his 2008 campaign and book, *The Audacity of Hope* (Obama 2006). This urgent tone still came through for a while in his speeches, when he repeated, "We can't wait any longer," for that change, which he began talking about in 2011 and had probably better started earlier. He needed to stress the "inclusive" theme of his original 2004 convention speech about our being one nation, not just red and blue states. He had to "show the way" by dealing with shared economic improvements and rebuilding the infrastructure among goals he wanted strongly to achieve.

Unfortunately, Obama and his economic advisors had repeatedly underestimated the seriousness of the disastrous economic weakness in the country that he was handed after his 2008 election (Leonhardt 2012). He had to tell his story about what he had done and was going to do about these problems, without overpromising, such as he had seemed to do with an overly optimistic number expected in lowered unemployment. After some disappointments in opening up on these issues, he eventually became more inclusive on this, saying that ". . . the nature of this office is also to tell a story to the American people that gives them a sense of unity and purpose and optimism, especially during tough times" (Obama 2012a, b).

An example of failing to communicate inclusively about his policies was his mishandling of the Keynesian "stimulus program." The congressional budget office had rated it positively, though it was scorned by congressional Republicans and others. There were no signs on public works from these funds that said, "Your Stimulus Program at Work," only perhaps "National Recovery Act," virtually unknown by that name. Speaker Boehner was among those opposition voices who routinely said that the "stimulus has not created a single job," when actually it had funded hundreds of thousands of teachers, police, and firefighter positions. Obama failed to show the public enough to build a counter-voice to these deniers of how and why the stimulus avoided deeper losses and despair in a grim situation at the edge of a financial ditch. Further, it was recognized as far more constructive than the fraught austerity imposed in the United Kingdom and elsewhere in Europe (Stevenson 2012) and was supported and earned credit for him. Later, his executive order permitting grown children of illegal immigrants to remain and work was inclusively compassionate on a hot issue, despite charges he was too cautious, for instance, in not issuing more such orders. He apparently needed more credit, due to a lack of public awareness of these attainments.

Challenge to His Legitimacy

Obama's legitimacy was disputed from even before he took office. Any president's legitimacy is essential and depends on the public's perception of him. It is usually decided by the results of an election. In President Obama's case, however, highly vocal detractors immediately questioned whether he was born in the United States, as a candidate able to run in a presidential election. They asserted he was not a citizen even when he produced the demanded "long form" of his birth certificate, and believed, "He's not really one of us," which "discredited" his ability to be an inclusive leader legitimated by election. These so-called "birthers," though seen as a "fringe" by some, included a group of Tea Party–backed Republicans in Congress, still proclaiming that President Obama's birthplace was not the State of Hawai'i. He told his aides that, because of prejudice, some in the country were never going to accept anything he did as president (Kantor 2012: 116).

Legitimacy is not held just in having the presidential role, but in the public's response, the effect on them of laws passed, and on his appointments. At times out-distanced, his credit limited, Obama seemed to be losing, even facing up to the initial high legitimacy hurdle of whether he was born in the United States, and related assertions repeated that he was a Muslim.

Psychological researchers (Haidt 2012; Westen 2011) have found attitudes about Obama to be emotionally based and not readily amenable to change from new information. For instance, in contrast to the un-American "alien" picture of him opponents painted, Obama regularly expressed patriotism, though completely unacknowledged by the deniers, if even heard. An example was at the 2012 Air Force Academy graduation on May 23, where he pointedly stated that America "is bolder, stronger, and more respected in the world." The statement may be overdrawn insofar as there are considerable variations found around the world, but it strikes a distinctly patriotic chord nonetheless.

Detractors, including media megastars with huge audiences, continued to portray Obama as foreign, and often as a Muslim, especially after a warm response at Cairo University for an early conciliatory speech. Contentions that he was a Muslim were aimed at separating him from the nation's mainstream. His assertions that he is a Christian, never otherwise, were dismissed, even though his 1995 autobiography (Obama 1995) tells about coming to his religious faith many years ago. Still, in 2012 primary polls in the South, over a third of Republicans said he was a Muslim.

Culturally, Obama's background growing up in Hawai'i and Indonesia also raised some suspicions about his education and values. However, Sharma (2011) considered that this exposure influenced him in a multicultural, conciliatory way, as is more the norm in those places. Still, in his book on the Obama presidency, Bob Woodward (2012) found his tendency to be "insular," holding back, was a problem because of his reluctance "to choose sides," after extended discussion (Kantor 2012: 155). Dissatisfaction with this tendency was captured in columnist Maureen Dowd's (2011c) assertion that, "It's not enough to understand what everybody in the room thinks. You have to decide which ones . . . are right, and stand with them. A leader is not a mediator or an umpire. . . ." And she asks who is the real Obama? Viewed sympathetically, he may sincerely wish to mediate, but his foes won't let him, and he wants not to be seen unfairly as an "Angry Black" (Hayden 2011; Kennedy 2011). Indeed, there is justified fascination with him, though Eleanor Holmes Norton, the District of Columbia Delegate to Congress, a black leader, said in 2012 that the kind of question of "Who is the real Obama?" has rarely been asked of other presidents.

Though Obama was routinely rejected as president by his detractors, his broader legitimacy as the president was affirmed by the wide praise he received for his national healing address early in 2011, after the Tucson, Arizona, shootings. Six people were killed, including a federal judge and a nine-year-old girl. Congresswoman Gabrielle Giffords was severely wounded in the head, among many others shot. Obama's remarks not only were well received, but his overall handling of the tragedy had a 74% approval rating in a national poll. Still, foes ceaselessly directed accusations at him and raised doubts about his motives.

A famous statement of the goal of this negative stand was voiced by the Senate Republican leader, Mitch McConnell, in the fall of 2010, saying that his first priority was to stop President Obama from having a second term. That seemed evident well before (Draper 2012), in view of the "perpetual obstruction recession," frankly furthered by the so-called "Party of No" blocking Obama's jobs' initiatives and using historic numbers of Senate "filibusters," needing sixty votes to move ahead. This situation raises such questions as: How can a president effectively lead a nation when the opposition is completely antagonistic and doesn't want to follow?

International Relations

In the big picture, Obama mainly is a pragmatist, not given to Bush "interventionism," but instead favoring a "light footprint" approach internationally (Sanger 2012). Pragmatism is evident in Obama's foreign policy, seen as he helped settle the Turkish-Israeli dispute while in Israel. It is also in his approach to creating with Egyptian President Morsi a basis for containing the Hamas/Gaza-Israeli conflict, even for an interim ceasefire. Similarly, he has persistently followed the sanctions route to press Iran on its nuclear ambitions. Even with this pattern of limiting hostilities abroad, opposition voices berated Obama for what he did or did not do before, during, and after the "Arab Spring." The Afghanistan troop "surge" was faulted for being too little or too much, or now mostly seen as of dubious value.

In an early effort at public relations diplomacy, Roger Cohen (2011) recalled Obama's speech at Cairo University in June 2009, where he received a very favorable response when he said, "You must place the interests of your people and the legitimate workings of the political process above your party. Without these elements, elections alone do not make true democracy." Then ". . . somebody shouted, 'Barack Obama, we love you.'" However, his standing internationally has variably diminished, especially in the Middle East (Mak 2012). The change in views of him since was attributed to what foreign policy has perceived to favor long after his Nobel Award and speech in Cairo, with the expectations they raised.

Recent tensions in the Middle East have mainly raised anti-American feelings. Most often, presidents seen as "great" in history were wartime ones (Winter 1973), so is confidence in them inspired by being "a wartime president"? Can this be so even if made distant from constituents who oppose the war, such as was evident increasingly about the conflicts in Iraq and Afghanistan? This appeared not helpful for President Obama, inheriting two wars, unpaid for due to the "Bush tax cuts," while helping in NATO to rid Libyans of their dictator. Indeed, wartime presidents do not necessarily rise in public standing, as seen most recently for Obama, very likely in part because more constituents oppose the conflicts in Iraq and Afghanistan. As indicated, Obama's 2009 Nobel Peace Prize gained some luster for him, but also raised issues about its coming in his first year in office, thereby possibly creating unreal expectations that proved a burden to fulfill. However, he said then that he would not shrink from use of force and has not (Bergen 2012). Still, a cost to this position is that in the June 2012 international survey, US drone attacks were opposed by majorities in seventeen of twenty countries, though approved by a large majority at home (Mak 2012). There also was lingering disappointment found about expected changes from the previous administration, such as the issue of closing the prison at Guantanamo (Melvin and Mcguirk 2012). Nevertheless, given this mixed record, the bulk of informed comments on American foreign policy under Obama are positive, with citations to "many improved or repaired relationships" (O'Hanlon 2012).

The fact that international relations had appeared far less in the 2012 presidential race than in the past could indicate confirmation that Obama had been strong there. In particular, candidate Mitt Romney's thirty-nine-minute acceptance speech at the Republican Convention devoted only three minutes to foreign policy. This lack was seen as possibly acknowledging less to offer than current responses to hostilities and multiple troubles abroad. Exceptions were faulting President Obama for helping rebels in Libya, not helping them much yet in Syria, and not doing enough about Iran, notably commensurate with Israel's oft-expressed vital interests (*Wall Street Journal*, September 1, 2012). Still, David Brooks, a leading conservative columnist usually critical of him, wrote in the *New York Times* during the campaign that, "Obama has moved more aggressively both to defeat enemies and to champion democracy" (Brooks 2012).

The stellar instance of assertiveness was Obama's overseeing the operation that found and killed Osama bin Laden. It received wide approval, especially at home, but muted and short-lived from his opponents. Voices of criticism blamed him for taking credit that they gave only to "our forces." Psychologically, as the target of an unceasing campaign to discredit him, Obama always had to be presented as failing, even abroad, because it was too dissonant for detractors to accept his success. In that regard, presidential contender Romney was among those who repeated the desperate fiction that Obama "went around the world apologizing for America."

Having an unpopular war may still allow a president to extend his powers, like a monarch (Schlesinger 1973). A criticism of President Bush (Newport 2007) was his self-proclaimed role as "the decider," to do what he wanted without regard for the expectations of constituents and Congress. Indeed, it is the Congress that the US Constitution mandates as the body to declare war, but no president has requested it since Franklin Roosevelt did when Pearl Harbor was attacked by the Japanese in December 1941 (Maddow 2012). Wills (2010) said that the intent of the Bush administration to have a "unitary executive" was to keep control, often by secret security programs (Dean 2003). The Obama administration, contrary to anticipation, had shown little inclination to dismantle this set of executive practices. This was evident before recent revelations by Edward Snowden about the National Security Agency's (NSA) secret program monitoring phone numbers, and other intercepts. After Snowden fled, and was given refuge in Russia in 2013, U.S. relations with it were impaired as President Obama cancelled a Moscow Summit with President Putin. Also, contrasts with President Bush had produced disappointments about expected changes, such as closing the prison at Guantanamo (Melvin and Mcguirk 2012). However, in the larger picture, Obama's other expected contrasts with President Bush have produced disappointments about such issues as not closing the prison at Guantanamo (Melvin and Mcguirk 2012). However, in the larger picture, Obama mainly gave up Bush's "interventionism" in favor of a "light footprint" approach internationally (Sanger 2012).

Obama's popularity abroad varied by region, with much more favorability to him in Europe than in the Middle East or Asia, all reduced from earlier highs by judgments of realities overcoming expectations. Despite his bringing typically more favorable attitudes toward the United States in many places abroad, and status as a "world leader," the campaign to delegitimize Obama went on, with his party's sustaining major election losses in 2010. But 2012 elections reversed some of them to favor him.

According to authoritative reports, an assault on the American Consulate in Libya in September 2012 was purposeful and planned, involving Al Qaeda and the deaths of American Ambassador Chris Stevens and three other American staffers. In Egypt, at that time, demonstrations at the American Embassy in Cairo were seen to be more spontaneous and centered on a movie believed by some to be offending Islam, in an already incendiary environment. President Obama took a restrained position while awaiting a further report, but America's United Nations ambassador, Susan Rice, appeared on Sunday television shows soon after these events, coincident with the anniversary of 9/11. As a government spokesperson, she was given intelligence reports that proved to be faulty and led to problems for her being nominated to be secretary of state (Landler and Peters 2012). She withdrew from consideration, and Senator John Kerry of Massachusetts was nominated and confirmed in that role. Rice later was named Obama's National Security Advisor.

Addressing the opening session of the United Nations General Assembly on September 25, 2012, President Obama challenged the world leaders gathered there " . . . to confront the forces of intolerance and extremism within their own countries and permit more freedom at home." For a president

whose past appearances at the United Nations have typically been marked by outreach and conciliation, [he] appeared notably frustrated by the unwillingness of other leaders, particularly in the Arab
world, to examine critically the worst components of their own societies. "True democracy—real
freedom—is hard work," Obama said. "Those in power have to resist the temptation to crack down on
dissent. In hard economic times, countries may be tempted to rally the people around perceived enemies, at home and abroad, rather than focusing on the painstaking work of reform" (Obama 2012c).

Making and Standing up for Policies

What mattered domestically were views of Obama's economic policies. Did he stand up as a "man
of the people"? Glad as his followers were, many were disappointed after he signed the Affordable
(Health) Care Act (ACA) in 2010 that he had not forcefully trumpeted its benefits (Baker 2012a),
then pushed for action on jobs and economic recovery. Instead, he was accused of "appeasing" his
opposition, not sticking to his goals. In handling such severe economic problems, former Clinton
Labor Secretary Robert Reich critically said, ". . . little has been done since 2008 to widen the circle
of prosperity. Healthcare reform is an important step forward but it is not nearly enough. . . . Policies that generate more widely shared prosperity lead to stronger and more sustainable economic
growth—and that is good for everyone" (Reich 2010).

Contentious domestic policy issues usually dominate American politics, and there Obama had to
follow the political adage, "Better stand for something, or you're likely to fall for anything." He was
seen to fail on that late in 2010 by letting the due-to-expire-Bush-tax-cuts for highest-income levels
remain for two more years. Giving in, after eloquently opposing it, led to the mid-2011 battle about
raising the "debt ceiling." Opposition "power of No" let it be raised only if he took budget cuts in the
later sequester. The president had to agree to what Republicans wanted. Though a Democrat occupied the White House, a leading economist (Krugman 2012) wrote, ". . . this is already the economic
policy of Republican dreams." Still, Andrew Sullivan (2012) reminded readers that Obama faced
implacable foes in Congress, as compared with Reagan, ". . . who won 48 Democratic House and 37
Democratic Senate votes for his first signature policy of tax cuts; Obama got zero and three Republican votes, respectively, for a bill in the worst recession since the 1930s. Those are the fruits of polarization. Nonetheless, the administration has soldiered on since 2010, and the tally of achievements is
formidable" (p. 33). Here was another clear narrative telling of the obstructionism by Obama's foes.
It was mentioned, but not promoted enough to bring in followers. Speaker Boehner had repeatedly
asked, "Where are the jobs, Mr. President?" yet continued to block voting on Obama's Jobs Bill, alleg-
edly worth as much as a million jobs.

Successful persuasion requires clear and frequent facts about what is needed, why, and what was
done and is to be done, which Obama had often neglected to tell (Friedman 2012b). His inspirational appeals in campaigning needed to show results when governing. As a major supporter said,
in a much publicized statement, "Somehow we need to get back the president we thought we elected
in 2008" (McKibben 2011). This revealed a familiar despairing concern of his making concessions
under threat, even when his opponents would continue to deny him credit for any successes, including saving the auto industry or eliminating Osama bin Laden, and helping free Libya from Qaddafi's
rule. National pride seemed dimmed, perhaps still from the trauma of the 9/11 attacks. But even
more, the nation's economic recovery was being halted to make real his opponents' vow of keeping
Obama from a second term (Draper 2012).

A case in point was Obama's later "Jobs Bill," the first major legislation that he had sent to Congress in 2011 with "Main Street" concerns that still demanded attention. His early jobs bill and "stimulus package" had helped, though short of expectations he raised. When unemployment was still
over 8%, the new bill's provisions were picked apart by his congressional foes, and it essentially died.

Though "hemmed in by . . . a hostile Congress and tight economy . . . [he still had] some powerful
levers to pull" (Landler 2011). But it had been eighteen months before he proposed his comprehensive

"Jobs Bill." While often calling for tax fairness, he had to relent in the summer 2011 "debt limit" deal and settled for budget cuts in the 2013 sequester. Speaker Boehner boasted after that deal that he "got 98%" of what he wanted. An outraged, savvy deal maker decried Obama as "an unforgivably lousy negotiator" (Andersen 2011). Another expert saw him as uncertain, not telling a compelling story (Westen 2011). An explanation for these aspects of Obama's operating style was offered by psychoanalyst Justin Frank (2011) who said his desire to "establish consensus" was the result of re-pressed hostility to a father who abandoned him. Also, as a mixed-race child with an early problem of developing his identity, he was seen to want to avoid conflict, to rise above divisions of culture and society, politics and economics (Maraniss 2012). His evident empathic ability could be an asset. Another biographer concluded from an interview that, as president, ". . . he believed he could solve those real problems . . . seemingly irreconcilable: red and blue America, the legislative process and lofty goals. . ." (Kantor 2012: 5).

Affordable Care Act (ACA)

Obama's historic achievement, getting the ACA passed and signed in March 2010, was soon dubbed "Obamacare" by opponents. Though the name was intended with disdain, he came to accept and like it, even as it continued to be a major target of his foes. Obama might have embraced the term sooner, if not for fear of seeming boastful. However, he did fail to bring the public along sufficiently about what it provided and was not ready to challenge falsehoods about it, like the wide belief about "death panels" deciding patients' fates. Not popular by its name, once known its many provisions were liked, such as no rejection of coverage for a preexisting condition, retaining portability, and no lifetime cost ceilings. Keeping dependent children on until twenty-six was very popular, and more provisions were coming in 2014. Yet in mid-2013, only a third polled replied it was "good."

Nevertheless, surprisingly little public support was raised for the ACA (Shear 2012). It has been fought over in the courts and in Congress. Indeed, the first bill passed in January 2011 by the new Republican-led House of Representatives was to repeal it, which then failed to pass in the Democratic-led Senate, so there had been no repeal, yet, but a thirty-third attempt was made in July 2012. This was a rare maneuver, for the US Congress to try repeatedly to repeal a passed bill, supported by a president still in office. This unusual episode revealed a drastic lack of accurate information, widely understood about most of the ACA provisions, even though, as already stated, separately favored (Brown 2012). It showed too how readily the blatant distortions from an expensive negative ad campaign could challenge Obama, without counter-balancing assertions about ACA's merits. Since its passage, " . . . 235 million has been spent on ads attacking it [and] 69 million supporting it" (Baker 2012a). The *New York Times* (2012) criticized the Obama campaign for failing to counter this "mis-information," including outright lies that it is a "job-killer" and the "largest tax increase" ever.

Republican presidential candidate Mitt Romney also vowed that his first executive order would be to forbid the ACA's provisions to be implemented. Even after Obama's 2012 reelection, Speaker Boehner would not let it go as an issue. Though acknowledging on November 22 that Obamacare is "the law of the land," he added, "but it is raising costs and threatening jobs. Our goal has been, and will remain, full repeal" (Boehner 2012). His repeated assertions about its costs were directly oppo-site to the report of the Congressional Budget Office, which found it lowered the deficit. Again, the ACA had not proven to be well understood by the electorate, said Keller (2012). He faulted the weak effort to present the program, seen in the 2010 election of majorities of foes of Obama's policies. However, its constitutionality was upheld by the Supreme Court, 5 to 4, with Chief Justice Roberts's decisive vote.

To critics who blame Obama for not trying to bridge differences, the record is clearly otherwise. Among the efforts ACA involved, and their costs, in February 2010, he held a "health care summit" to speak with congressional leaders of both parties. This was one of many "outreaches" to show his bipartisanship in policymaking. David Axelrod, a presidential advisor, stated the case for it saying that the president couldn't just ". . . snap his fingers or even twist arms and make change happen." He added that, "[I]n this great democracy of ours, that's not the way it is" (Stolberg 2010). Still, the president got the crucial votes needed to pass the ACA by a great deal of persuasion, entirely among Democratic representatives, many of whom lost their seats in 2010. The process began in 2009 when two similar healthcare bills, as usual one from each house, did pass with Democrats' votes, after six months of concessions to get Senate Republican votes that were never given. A vibrant issue was a lack of a "public option," similar to government healthcare from Medicare. Its absence continued to be a sore point and tagged Obama as "leading from behind," rather than advocating his own position. In that year, he also failed to speak enough to counter the frequent misinformation about the bills' other provisions, which were diluted for expected bipartisan support. Fear-provoking allegations were not refuted soon enough, and strongly enough, but only after damage was done, not in time to be effective. This lapse was in the face of strict partisan opposition in Congress uniformly against any votes letting any of Obama's programs pass (Draper 2012).

The goal was clear even before a former opposition senator, Jim DeMint of South Carolina, new head of the conservative Heritage Foundation, said making passage of the ACA fail would be "Obama's Waterloo." It also had an "individual mandate," a provision taken from the Heritage Foundation. This provision was favored by Republicans and is in the healthcare bill signed by then Massachusetts Governor Romney. It required that health insurance coverage be bought, unless the patient is at or below a low-income level. But once the federal bill was enacted as an "Obama policy," this provision was targeted by Republicans for the legal challenge leading to the Supreme Court ruling. Furthermore, it allowed states to not take its Medicaid support, and many southern governors declined it (Barrow 2013).

Followers, Their Needs, and the Role of Imagery

A president, like any politician, has to answer the question, even if just implicit, "What have you done for us lately?" Follower needs will determine whether rewards, intangible as well as tangible, are found to be satisfactory in motivating them to follow. This emphasis on followership also reflects a shift in the focus of leadership study from assessing a leader's characteristics to looking at how the leader is seen by followers and how followers in turn respond to the leader (e.g., Riggio, Chaleff, and Lipman-Blumen 2008).

Given Obama's history, the inevitable followership questions of "Who, why, and where are they?" became particularly relevant for him as the first African-American to be elected US president. Because he then had 43% of the white vote and 39% in 2012, race continued to make news (Tavernise 2012). Moreover, the industry of denial of his legitimate election came with the historic, emotional residue of slavery, desegregation, and affirmative action (Kennedy 2011). That backdrop challenged his holding office, gaining public support, and instituting his policies.

Despite advice to exercise power, or at least have it "be feared," Obama's major approach still was to try persuasion (Nagourney 2009). This made for a discouraging picture. Leaders must continually face the reality, whether accurate or not, that their lities, actions, positions and motives are evaluated by others. It is from them that a leader must gain and maintain a following in organizations, John Gardner said.

Followers are a leader's major strategic audience, with the ability to affect choices and actions by the imagery they perceive. This is the lifeblood of politics, circulating with the implicit belief that "perception is reality." Appealing personal and policy narratives are likely to be far more effective on a following than mountains of facts, especially when amplified with a compelling theme, such as "New Deal," "Great Society," and "Morning in America" were for Presidents Roosevelt, Johnson, and Reagan. President Obama lacked such a theme with clear attractive elements and drawing support for his programs. A tryout may have been repeating "Winning the Future" in his January 25, 2011, State of the Union address.

Compared to others, Obama's administration has been seen as remarkably slow and diffuse in its use of the mass media to "sell" his programs by making plain his particular intentions in promoting them. Thomas Friedman (2012b) credited Obama as "a great orator," but, as already stated, wanted him to be ". . . explaining his achievements, [and] connecting with people on a gut level . . ." by a story that can change minds. The imagery of a continuing narrative was needed, said Robert Reich, to challenge a Republican narrative blaming problems on unions and government, and not deregulation, fraud, and vast concentrations of wealth. This narrative, he said, was vital to tell people where the country was going (2010).

Delegitimation's Effect on Presidential Performance

The "discrediting" process has affected Obama's presidency. By seeking to nullify the legitimacy of his election, it created a barrier to his gaining support for his actions. That can explain his reluctance to take on issues like gun control, known to be fractious. Doing so risked losing out on other fundamental needs at issue, such as the economy and healthcare. Similarly, Obama disappointed antiwar followers when sending more combat forces Afghanistan, possibly so as not to appear weak.

Obama did, however, remove combat forces from Iraq, honoring Bush's prior agreement with its government. In general, though, his latitude for action became crimped and he needed to prioritize to trim where he put his efforts, not least because of the political calendar, beginning with the midterm elections two years after his election for a four-year term by the national electorate. These "mid-terms" are for Congress and many state and local offices and some governorships. In all but a few of them, the Democrats, his party and indirectly himself, had big losses in 2010. In 2012, he won reelection, with more seats in the House of Representatives, and in the Senate, which remained in Democratic control.

It matters that a president is both head of state, as is a monarch, but also head of government, as is a prime minister. These roles are separable enough for a president to be liked as head of the nation, but less for policies and/or politics, as President Obama soon found in his first year in office. Though often the case with a new president, Obama began on a "high" of initial percentage favorable in the 70s. Such numbers carry "great expectations" that can produce a significant drop when unmet. Obama fell below 50% in job approval after a year in office, even with legislative gains, often painfully achieved with long, highly publicized, deal-making, against strong foes. At his second anniversary, his favorability was above 50%, but always susceptible to dropping. Former 10-year British Prime Minister Tony Blair (2012) reminisced that "You begin when you are least capable and most popular. And you end when you're least popular and most capable."

The demands of the presidency are enormous and consequences of its actions incalculable (see e.g., Burns 1984; Neustadt 1990; Tucker 1981). In one view, a new president fills what journalist Lou Cannon called "the role of a lifetime," in the subtitle of his book about Ronald Reagan. However, every president is responsible for many special roles and their implicit tasks, among which are these major ones : head of state, chief executive of government, commander-in-chief of the Armed Forces, chief diplomat, chief spokesperson of government, party leader, "national healer," "the decider," and "definer of reality."

These presidential roles are a large part of what political scientists, historians, journalists, and others have listed as making up the responsibilities of this immense position, sometimes characterized as "Leader of the Free World." All of them belong on any list, but they are also interdependent. Overlapping and merging occurs in carrying out these functions and conflicts between them arise. Among forces that intrude on them are inevitable sudden crises, an uprising abroad in a strategic place, an increase in unemployment, a physical disaster at home or elsewhere, all needing to be addressed, and often simultaneously. Furthermore, voices of contending constituencies may call for attention and prompt action in their sector of concern, instead of in others. Therefore, priorities have to be set, issues identified, solutions offered and considered, staff assigned, legislation conceived, consequences assessed, and costs evaluated, among other pressing tasks. Obama's latitude for action was limited.

An observer wrote, "He's beholden to lawmakers' whims, buffeted by global winds, as much a spectator as an agent of developments . . . learning how unscripted history ultimately is . . . [he needs to master] projecting more power than he actually wields" (Bruni 2012). Speaking as president of the University of Miami, Donna Shalala, a Clinton cabinet member, said hers and other executive power was like a tugboat captain keeping ships in line.

Race has been seen as the most likely source of deep antagonism toward Obama (Kennedy 2011). It amplifies and extends the normal differences between those who favor or reject a president, usually based on party, with pro or anti responses. Illustrative of its intensity was one southern member of Congress referring to Obama's then upcoming 2011 State of the Union address as him "spewing his venom," and another from the South shouting "You lie," during such an address.

Basic splits are also seen in reactions to appeals for change or for keeping things the same, whenever either is proposed. Resistance to change or insistence upon having it are powerful motivators. Other such stark conflicts affecting policy exist about freedom vs. responsibility, and freedom vs. security. Criticisms about his policies also has come from the liberal-moderate-ethnic followers who believe Obama failed them by not speaking out and fighting for policies he championed in campaigning (Thomas 2010), like immigration reform. He did make some headway on it by his late executive order. Also, after the Tucson shootings, Blow (2011) stated his strong disappointment that the president did not come out for more gun control. However, Obama did so after 20 children and 6 staff were killed in December 2012 by a gunman invading the Sandy Hook Elementary School in Connecticut.

Gaining and Using Credits from Followers

An approach to leader-follower dynamics is to think of followers giving credits to a leader when seen as belonging and performing well. This alters the long-time "leader-centric" focus on leader qualities that viewed them separately from how they affected followers. To help relate these, the concept of "Idiosyncrasy Credit" (IC) was put forward (Hollander 1958, 1964, 1978, 2004a). Initially, it was aimed at explaining the seeming paradox that leaders were at once loyal to a group's norms but were given latitude in their actions directed at change (see Price 2008). This is not paradoxical at all when viewed as a matter of sequence, with early competence and signs of loyalty allowing for a later initiation of change. Credits earned from followers' perceptions of these qualities, extended to the national level, can explain a president's acceptance by those who are his followers and his influence on them.

However, credits that would be earned from the electorate by their perceptions of a president's competence and loyalty to the nation were not given to him if he was branded a "foreigner," believed not legitimately elected, as Obama was by a significant minority of the populace. He was then also likely to be considered untrustworthy, with a range of negative attitudes about him and his policies. Though these attitudes were made to seem reasonably based on economic, organizational, military, or moral concerns, they have been found to be fixed in place by one's prior, emotionally based political tendencies (Westen 2007, 2011; Haidt 2012). An important result for Obama was that he had become a receptacle for the fears of some, encouraged by media figures, that he was a "socialist," "Nazi," and/or the "Anti-Christ." This assault presented greater, difficult psychological hurdles for him than simply arguing about his policies. For example, among political foes, "going negative" is a well-known device, but the terrain and content used against Obama were distinctive, and at a powerful extreme. An instance from former Speaker Newt Gingrich's presidential nomination quest was his promoting Dinesh D'Souza's charge that Obama had a "Kenyan, anti-colonial worldview." How successful a leader is viewed by followers, e.g., in making changes, depends upon such perceptions about a leader's motivations, targeted here.

Using credit without desired results makes a leader vulnerable to blame and more credit loss. It is as if followers said, "We expect good results from you. If you take an unusual course of action, we will go along and give you some latitude, but eventually you are responsible, if the outcome is failure to achieve our goals."

An important related expectation, even demand, is that once accumulated, credits will be used by a leader for needed action. Failing to do so results in losing credits because the leader who "sits" on his or her credits can be seen not fulfilling a role obligation to deal with needs. What followers do about it depends on such actions as elections provide. This is part of "transactional leadership," involving a social exchange in which the leader gives something and gets something (Homans 1974: Ch. 11). A president's ability to achieve a "fair exchange" with constituents is likeliest when seen to deserve his status (Jacobs 1970). However, followers may feel an inequity if the leader fails because of an apparent lack of effort, or from a disregard for followers interests, seen as a leader "out of touch" (Hollander 1978, 1992a, b). Followers may then experience a lack of enthusiasm, even despair and distance from the process. In this way, such leaders can create aggrieved followers, alienated, and if not protesting, then unresponsive, with loss of interest and of participation (Kelley 1988, 1992; Kellerman 2008), deadly at election time.

To avoid or limit this dysfunctional state, "inclusive leadership," to be discussed more shortly, is useful as a remedy. It offers a systematic process emphasizing relational factors to create and sustain loyalty as a leader-follower bond. It incorporates the credit concept to indicate the evaluative element in follower effects on leaders. Indeed, whether called transforming or transactional, a shared function is leader attention to follower needs, showing that the leader cares about them.

In general, credits cannot be earned when there are limiting conditions such as those posed by repeated challenges to a president's legitimacy. A basic lack is the absence of an "open system," less constrained by authority pressures, or here by opposition media campaigns that deny who and what a leader actually is and does.

For a president to accomplish the feat of keeping a following in the face of this assault requires trying through the media, at a distance, to present facts about "getting things done." These messages must relate to the needs and expectations of a diverse electorate, by no means all his followers. Some will be skeptical and even hostile. The general evaluation of a president, pro or con, is usually based on his party initially and underlies attitudes about him, his policies, and his ability to "sell" them successfully to constituencies and to Congress. This explains the need for a "continuous campaign mode" so a president can retain a following by positive views of what he does and tries to do on a timely basis, despite dedicated opposition.

Though the president is said to be the most personal of public officials (Barber 1972), the physical and psychological distance between him and his audience is usually bridged through the media, not just from his messages, but by many others about him, including on the Internet. These messages are then interpreted by individuals' identification with or rejection of the president, filtered through their primary groups (Katz and Lazarsfeld 1955). A president's loyal followers are likely to have positive perceptions of him and his policies. In presidential elections, and in midterm ones also, turning up to vote for his party's candidates can be especially critical, as well as getting others out, too. Obama had clearly reestablished enough of this "loyalty effect" to win in 2012 after not having sustained it in 2010, which is at risk again and may be countered in 2014 midterms.

Inclusive Leadership (IL), Trust, and Loyalty

The practice of "Inclusive Leadership" (IL) is directed toward "doing things with people, rather than to people." It emphasizes relations of "respect, recognition, responsiveness, and responsibility, both ways" for loyalty to occur. As its name indicates, it involves including others in the tasks of leadership, as seen when listening to them about their needs and interests (Hollander 2006, 2007, 2009: 3–5). IL is broadly aimed at maintaining a leader-follower bond. It underscores the importance of consideration of participants other than formal leaders in the leadership process and being responsive to these others, given the challenge of multiple constituencies to be served. This involves engaging followers based on three major pillars: perceived legitimacy as a source for leading; positive interpersonal evaluation; and a fair social exchange, with mutual benefits from caring and sharing. A vital practice in IL is informing followers about action, as much as doable, so they can help and share in mutual goals, without exploitation.

Our midterm postelection surveys in different places and times showed that follower loyalty was associated with a president's signs of reaching voters by expressions of inclusive leadership (Hollander 2009: 107–111). These practices in leader-follower relations are not the same as "stroking" constituents for votes, but instead openness to follower influence on leader behavior. This is aptly called "upward influence" (Hollander 2004b) and is likely to prove the value of two-way communication in achieving productive outcomes (Hollander and Offermann 1990). Listening is respectful and important in inclusive leadership relationships.

Follower perceptions of legitimacy and performance combine with evaluations of whether the leader shows the four inclusive elements of respect, recognition, responsiveness, and responsibility, which are returned in kind. They are vital to keeping trust and loyalty found in positive leader-follower relationships. Followers may then exercise checks on leader behavior from inclusion, even bringing about alterations. Former British Prime Minister Tony Blair (2010) concluded from his career, ". . . not that the power of politics is needed to liberate the people . . . but that the power of people is needed to liberate the politics" (p. 687).

As already indicated, identification with a president is significantly related to followers' perceptions of issues, voting preferences, and voter turnout. This accords with Freud's (1921) conception of shared "ego-ideal" for followers and also fits cognitive balance theory (Heider 1958). Its effects are demonstrated in our postelection surveys studying a president's "pull" in his first midterm election. The downside of this is seen in the 2010 midterm election when the Democrats were swept out of power and the Speakership of the House of Representatives returned to the Republicans, who had lost it in 2006. Obama's dealing with the economy's various difficulties then became much harder.

Economic Conditions, Wall Street, and the Banks

Despite Obama's efforts, his party's losses in the historic 2010 elections were widely believed to be influenced by bad economic conditions. However, research had shown that with sufficient loyalty to a president, especially of one's party, even in bad economic conditions, the turnout to vote and attitudes remained positive (Seaman, Hollander, and Richer 1975; Hollander 1983). But this time conditions had stayed depressed. President Obama also still faced another such unresolved conflict in the economic crisis called "Main Street vs. Wall Street," which he had hoped would improve enough by the Recovery Act (first "stimulus bill") that provided funds to create jobs in state and local governments, including teachers, police, and firemen. The positive effect in reducing unemployment was less than predicted at the outset. There was special distress, seen in the "Occupy Wall Street" movement, about TARP (Troubled Asset Relief Program) a Bush-era, federal effort to "bail out" banks and financial organizations (Barofsky 2012). Under it, they did not need to make loans nor take other actions to help create jobs so workers could rejoin the consumer economy, which stagnated when inability to buy sustained the recession.

A related crisis existed in housing foreclosures pursued by lenders, many of whom had been assisted with taxpayer funds, but resisted renegotiating mortgages. Relatively few homeowners, many of whom lost jobs, had been enabled to save their homes from takeovers, even with government programs to lower the many millions taken. The sense of despair created fell on Obama as the current president, even when the poor lending policies criticized came from the previous administration. As another president, John F. Kennedy, famously said, "Life is not fair." Nonetheless, it was Obama's task to have constituents feel satisfied with what he had done and would do for them. By fall of 2010, his favorability percentage fell, and stayed in the mid-40s into midsummer 2012. Unsurprising then was that his "pull" on voting in the midterm election of 2010 was weaker than his nearly 53% 2008 victory.

Faced with the nation's ongoing economic crises, including the debt, Obama seemed forced into conflicting positions in having to cut budgets. That probably would boost unemployment, at a time he wanted to promote spending on national investments in infrastructure, education, and science. These are vital to his promise of the country's "Winning the Future." This brought him continually in conflict about those expenditures, especially in the House of Representatives controlled by Republicans. Their position was to cut the size and cost of government and not support spending until the national debt was greatly reduced, even if then.

This was part of an ongoing philosophical battle between a conception of government as necessary to do things individuals and organizations in the private sector would not do for the general good, contrasted with a view that the marketplace will take care of those things. That reality was clear when considering the need for public safety, public health, public education, and the uniformed services, just to start. That said, benefits the government does provide are inevitably related to its leaders' actions, often by the president. This connection brings out followers to his rallies, speeches, and on Election Day. It forms part of a social contract that shows "leader-follower interdependence" by inclusive practices. These involve listening to constituents and sharing and explaining realities to them through informative communications. Presidents, and other leaders, then are rewarded with credit from followers, more likely to identify with and support them.

Typical of early, persisting discontent, Cornel West, a leading black studies professor on the radio in 2009 lamented that the president seemed to care more for bailing out bankers than helping a lot of ordinary people who are hurting. Unmentioned was the fact that the TARP bill was passed under President Bush at the urging of Treasury Secretary Henry Paulson, former CEO of Goldman Sachs, who said it would save the financial system and avoid a depression. Though TARP's returns seemed positive, banks' actions were not. As many as nineteen conspired to manipulate a critical interest rate in the "LIBOR Scandal" (Adelmann 2012). It was a huge risk-taking bet, yielding at first a $2 billion loss, undertaken by the largest, JPMorgan Chase, by hedging bank funds. Its scope and gravity made it the lead story on page 1 of the May 11 *New York Times* (Silver-Greenberg and Eavis 2012), though its CEO, Jamie Dimon called it a "tempest in a teapot," he later said it was a "stupid" mistake when apologizing at a congressional hearing. He updated the newest loss, on July 13, to $5.8, then $6.2 billion, stated in a Senate report in March 2013. On August 10th, 2013, the New York Times' (Protess & Silver-Greenberg, 2013) front-page lead article said two of JPMorgan Chase's former London employees were reported to be facing criminal fraud charges for their role in covering up the size of this huge loss. Even after this distressing revelation of speculative excess, some in banking still pointed out it was small relative to banking profits.

Before these distressingly huge speculating losses, which bankers were quick to point out were small relative to regular banking profits, Obama seemed ready to act more forcefully. High expectations were raised by his statement that "what gets people upset—and rightly so—are executives being rewarded for failure, especially when those rewards are subsidized by U.S. Taxpayers" (Obama 2009). The later "Occupy Wall Street" demonstrations against these financial sector practices were on this same theme. Still, he had been criticized because, "Obama is loath to target villains [but] . . . lets himself be bullied, and lets the bullies run wild" (Dowd 2011a). That may at least be contained because, in a "turnabout," Citicorp founder and former Dimon boss, "Sandy" Weill (2012), urged the largest banks be broken up.

Nonetheless, stunning in what it revealed, no conditions were put on the banks for billions in TARP taxpayer funds many received, thus allowing JPMorgan Chase free rein to take over other banks to become the biggest. Most held back, thereby not fulfilling the purpose of lending for businesses and others to recover. This pattern of indulging banks that were not helping was too much for many critics. In September 2011 this acutely felt need was expressed as, "Three years ago, the federal government used tens of billions in taxpayer dollars to save the banking system. Now, at this dire economic moment, the country needs the banks to return the favor" (Nocera 2011). Banks also still paid executives on down large bonuses after getting these public funds. That outraged many onlookers and in turn enraged bankers who felt picked on when called out on these actions, seen as "my profits are mine, but my losses are yours." This was another "heads I win, and tails you lose" game, with a public clamor. Yet, Obama's critics repeatedly claimed he was "anti-business," despite record corporate profits and surging stock market. Moreover, remarkably, the Justice Department had not gone after "pervasive corporate wrongdoing that gave us the financial crisis and Great Recession. . . . George W. Bush turned out to be tougher on corporate crooks than Barack Obama" (Nocera 2012).

Still, Obama expended great personal effort to save the American automobile industry. It proved a remarkable success on the basis of a loan program that had paid back, or soon will, virtually all of the funds lent to General Motors and Chrysler. Even Mitt Romney. Obama's 2012 presidential opponent, though opposed to the federal program at the time, on the campaign trail had tried taking credit for it. Ford had not needed nor asked for loans and had done very well on its own. Hundreds of thousands of jobs were saved, not just in these firms but also in the hundreds of suppliers to the auto industry nationwide. Obama's program, with admitted risks, was boldly pushed by him and his party, though denounced as a "giveaway" and "bail out" by opponents in and outside of Congress. Not a single Republican there had voted for its passage. Yet the "anti-business president" drumbeat continued, neither crediting this major success against great opposition, nor other benefits he furthered, such as his small business tax credits.

Though President Obama's Finance Reform bill passed Congress in the spring of 2010, it lacked key restraints to prevent the financial crisis from recurring. Yet he urged action in line with the discontent expressed about the banks in polls showing that more regulation of finance was favored 2 to 1 in national surveys, with big banks and their leaders particularly distrusted. But a reform bill that was described as a "loophole-ridden compromise" (Rich 2010) became law and was further diminished by Republican legislators' opposition to regulation, energized after their victory in the 2010 elections. That change-over in the lower house of Congress was facilitated by bitter resistance and antagonism from the financial sector itself, as many of its major leaders who had supported Obama in 2008 switched their funding to support his opponents in 2010. Furthermore, the ruling by the Supreme Court in the 2010 Citizens United case made possible huge sums to come into Congressional and next presidential races through "SuperPACs," without revealing their sources. Acutely evident now is the problem of economic inequality yielding political inequality. "When one person can write a check to finance your whole campaign, how inclusive will you be as an elected official to listen to competing voices?" (Friedman 2012a).

At the other end of the economic scale, Blow (2011) pointed out that poverty went unmentioned in the president's 2011 State of the Union address, only the second time since Harry Truman's 1948 address that a Democratic president had failed to mention it. Yet, an assessment by Tough (2012) considers Obama has done more for the "poor" than any other recent president, though he ". . . hasn't made a single speech devoted to poverty as president" (p. 27). This absence was attributed to Obama's projecting a picture of optimism, trumpeting unprecedented corporate profits, and a stock market "roaring back," both points aimed at boosting his reelection in 2012. Blow (2011) reported that 73% of the poor, with annual incomes of $15,000 or less voted for him in 2008, so the inference was that Obama counted on those among the poor, who are old enough to vote, to vote for him again.

The Need for Appeals through the Media

Presidents use the mass media to influence public images and do what they can to shape them to their purposes. The statement that, "An ounce of image is worth a pound of performance" is limited as followers who gain experience with a leader and come to know if their needs and expectations are addressed and whether or not hoped-for outcomes are met. If affirmative, there will likely be trust and loyalty, with solidarity of purpose, but the reverse is likely, when disappointed.

To make successful appeals requires trade-offs. Soon after President Obama announced allowing some coastal oil drilling, the April 2010 oil disaster occurred in the Gulf of Mexico. He then called a six-month halt in deep-water drilling there to investigate and find ways to avoid a repetition, but faced opposition. James Carville, a major Democratic strategist, said some drilling was important for Congress to pass his still-waiting energy program, to keep him succeeding (Harwood 2010). This accommodation, again to try broadening his base, netted expected criticism from some of them and a credit loss. The dilemma was to keep followers while seeking to draw in an enlarged following with others.

As noted earlier, a newly elected president generally benefits from the legitimation by an electorate committed to his four-year term of office. Two traditional sayings reflect this: "We only have one president at a time" and "The president is president of all the people." These represent very inclusive attitudes. But both are contradicted by using untruths and abusive terms about a president, as is more noticeable now in the mass media and on the Internet. A new president usually had a "honeymoon period," in which the public would "rally around" if the president initially had difficulties. In his first year, John F. Kennedy as an example, gained substantially in the polls after taking responsibility for the failed invasion of Cuba at the Bay of Pigs in 1961. The next year, he was more decisive, questioning the institutional positions and advice of senior officials, by showing restraint in the 1962 Cuban Missile Crisis. Again, Kennedy's ratings with the public rose. These events are linked, at times confused with one another, but reveal a president's progress in his role as leader in international military crises and public toleration.

As is evident, a follower's closeness, and identification with a president, is usually affected by party identity, and whether or not that person voted for him. The sense of his legitimacy is based also in respect for the integrity of the electoral process and the nature of the election victory. But it was severely tested in the 2000 Bush–Gore election, in which Gore won the popular vote, but the Supreme Court decided for Bush, after it stopped the recount of votes in Florida, giving its electoral college votes to him. At an earlier time, George Reedy (1973), who had been a press spokesman for Lyndon Johnson during the 1960s, asserted that ". . . a man might have only 51 percent of the votes, or even less, and still be able to make some rather sweeping changes. . . . Many Presidents have found their following has increased enormously the day after election" (p. 26). To the contrary, however, Obama faced an opposition right away saying in effect, "Not our president" (Draper 2012). The pronounced partisan split in the public's attitudes about President Obama challenges the unity view, even with his almost 53% of the 2008 vote, the highest total number of votes ever for a candidate. But as Presidential scholar Sean Wilentz (2010) saw it, after little more than a year in office, "Obama looks less like a political messiah and more a victim of unrealistic expectations raised . . . by his election campaign"(p. 34)—but also with opponents openly determined he should fail. Still, he did succeed in getting significant legislation passed, at least earlier.

Evident here too were reactions to his race, whether positive or negative. Susan Fiske and her colleagues (2009) found it was positive in the 2008 election campaign for both nonblacks and blacks who fit Obama into the "moderately warm, highly competent Black-professional" social subtype. This was in line with what he said in his book, *The Audacity of Hope* (Obama 2006: pp. 234–40) about the racial acceptance he experienced from whites in Senate campaigning. Yet, his 49% overall favorability at 18 months dropped most among whites to 41%. Before, in 2008, among whites, only 43% had voted for him, but a white Democratic presidential candidate, Walter Mondale in 1984, had the same 39% as Obama did in 2012, though he ran with Representative Geraldine Ferraro, the first woman vice presidential candidate, a likely contributing factor. Blacks in 2011 overwhelmingly still supported Obama (Harwood 2011) and continued to do so in the 2012 election.

An interesting point on religious diversity is that in a nation still mainly protestant, which has never had a presidential race without each major party having at least one protestant candidate, in 2012 Obama was the only protestant (Epstein 2012), and he won. This study found leaders of Congress to be Catholic and Mormon. The Supreme Court has six of the Catholic and three of the

Jewish faith, both vice presidential candidates were Catholic, and a Mormon was the presidential challenger.

Obama's initiatives for change also exposed a basic split when a threat was felt by those comfortable with the way things are. Rather than credit him for initiatives like healthcare reform, they created myths about it, spreading distrust and fear. Indeed, after a year in office, even campaigning about change, the public's trust in Obama fell to the 40% range across the board for his handling of the economy, healthcare, budget deficit, and terrorism. This relatively low level hurt because he was then at the same approval level as his Republican opponents. Hopes truly can inspire, but require clear statements of programs aimed at solutions, such as for the unemployment crisis. As a publisher stated, "[I]n politics, the failure of communication is invariably the fault of the communicator" (Zuckerman 2011).

Charisma, Character, and Promises

Charisma refers to a personal quality that increases emotional arousal and dedication to the arouser. It has been imputed to President Obama, at least to a degree, and with some of his followers. For his opponents, it seems more like its polar opposite, "derisma," coined from "derision" or "derisive." Has charisma helped with his programs and counteracted the criticism he received? The answer appears to be, "No, or at best only for a while." Can charisma help in bringing constituencies together, and even appeal to the uncommitted, ever fickle, middle? Possibly, but usually the charismatic appeal of the moment can be lost because of other negative features, such as the leader's overconfidence and narcissism (Howell and Avolio 1992; Howell and Shamir 2005), and for Obama, the added matter of race.

Even the major authority on charisma, sociologist Max Weber (1947), said that it is dependent upon favorable perceptions by followers who can withdraw it, ". . . if the leader is long unsuccessful " (p. 360). Peter Drucker (1988) affirmed the point that charisma should not be confused with performance. "Doing, not dash" is what matters, he said. In fact, much is in the "eye of the beholder" (Simonton 2008).

Charisma also can be thought of as having a big credit balance from your followers, usable to get things done. Because detractors do not want that to happen, they force conditions making it harder for the leader to succeed. Major detractors a president faces are opposition politicians, congressional leaders, such as committee chairs, even of one's own party, and interest group lobbies. At the other end of the scale is discontent among citizens with "power distance" and income disparities.

Responding by "inclusion," means showing concern that yields such phrases as "he cares about people like me," when a president goes to speak and listen to citizens, e.g., to remove resistance in Congress. In that respect, for too long Obama did not give enough attention to gaining and retaining followership and its needs. When he did, it often was sporadic. Such stylistic differences may not be recognized until presidents take office and show themselves in dealings with constituents, governmental officials, and institutions (Laski 1940). Obama for one has been seen as having "an astonishing faith in his own abilities" (Kantor 2012: 5). To his credit, while repeatedly seeking to persuade, he also deliberately avoided "groupthink" (Janis 1972) by wanting others' views. However, what a leader takes to be a strength may be viewed as a weakness in the eyes and reactions of others.

Kaplan and Kaiser (2006) make a case for a leader knowing when to moderate a strength, so that it is not relied on excessively to become an unrecognized weakness as losses accumulate. Thus, Wills (2010) faulted Obama for overconfidence that his speaking strength will always be persuasive. He also said that a president must use power or have others perceive the threat of it by showing a willingness to use it when necessary to achieve a goal. But former British Foreign Secretary David Owen (2007), a psychiatrist, emphasized hubris and impulsiveness in using great power, citing Lyndon Johnson's conduct of the Viet Nam War. Jack Valenti (2007), a Johnson aide, said Johnson tried listening to criticism of his military escalation, but then dismissed all alternative actions. On balance, though, Robert Caro (2012) stressed Johnson's power to get many of his "Great Society" social programs passed.

Idiosyncrasy Credit (IC) and Transforming Leadership (TF)

Associated with charisma is Burns's concept of "transforming leadership." Both can be linked with the IC concept. TF leaders, wishing to bring about change, provide benefits to followers that facilitate reaching that goal. These rewards are likely to earn credit from followers and be oriented to a change process, by defining a situation and giving direction to activity (Hollander and Julian 1969, 1970).

Followership therefore plays a supporting role in Burns's emphasis on TF leaders getting people together for higher purposes, more than garnering votes. They want to bring about change institutionally and systemically, " . . . to achieve broad human purposes and moral aspirations . . . among potential followers, bringing them to fuller consciousness of their needs . . . . The secret of transforming leadership is the capacity of leaders to have their goals clearly and firmly in mind . . . (Burns 1984: 103). Two presidential examples Burns gives are Franklin Roosevelt and Ronald Reagan. Though of very different political views in office, it is notable that Reagan said he admired Roosevelt and had voted for and supported him when he, Reagan, was a Democrat and served as head of the Screen Actors Guild, a union.

In his extension of work on TF leadership, Bass (1997) identified and measured "intellectual stimulation" and "inspiration" as two of its major qualities. These are clearly appropriate for a successful presidency, among others that characterize TF leadership (see Bass and Riggio 2006). Regarding the first, a president needs to communicate a credible "social reality" that becomes a shared understanding, usually accepted as fact-based. This "definition of the situation" is necessary for a president to sustain a standing with constituents (Obama 2012a, b).

Especially noteworthy, these evident rewards that the leader provides to followers led Burns (2007) to state, "I think my book (1978) is overly dichotomized. There is a stronger connection between transforming and transactional leadership than I led readers to believe. I think we have a spectrum. A few leaders operate wholly on the transforming side, but most work on both sides of that spectrum and combine transforming and transactional leadership" (p. viii).

Conclusion

Well into his fourth year, President Obama appeared to have lost credits with members of his 2008 base of support, including independents who voted for him before but were only "rented," as one observer put it. A major columnist took a hard look and concluded, "The leader who was once a luminescent, inspirational force is now just a guy in a really bad spot" (Dowd 2011b). Still, four days after that column appeared, Obama gave what was regarded as a very spirited address to a joint session of Congress on September 8, 2011, presenting his comprehensive "jobs bill." He had shown this ability to bounce back, and carry over the trust and loyalty, enough to reelect him. He now showed he had the followership when needed and where it counted to have allies to "pass a bill" (Shear 2012).

Action and results are essential to meet expectations about what a leader will provide. In assessing President Obama's relationship with his followers, fulfilling their expectations was especially important to the outcome of the 2012 presidential and congressional elections. "Whether in a corporation . . . or an entire nation, constituents seek four things: meaning or direction, trust in and from the leader, a sense of hope and optimism, and results" (Bennis 1999: 19).

Strong positive communications were needed and came from Obama daily. He was able to show followers that he was listening and furthering their interests by his policies. As was plain, his task was made more difficult after the 2010 elections when the opposition gained control of the House of Representatives. Thereafter, President Obama faced far more determined obstruction of his proposals in

Congress, backed by some continuously hostile media, favoring the opposition's positions. His long-standing tendency toward conciliation, reaffirmed in Remnick's (2010) biography, can be a positive to gain his objectives by understanding his foes. But realistically, his dedicated opposition would not yet credit him for what he had done. His appeal rested with those identifying with him from inclusion, a following who could feel part of what he accomplished and promised to do. He also needed to try further to warm up to members of Congress, lifting his self-restraint (Meacham 2012). This was labeled a "charm offensive" when he took twelve Republican senators out to dinner in March 2013. He paid for it personally to speak informally about issues and their views and also visited both parties' caucuses at the Capitol.

Obama often strived to appeal to "reason together" rationally, though he won before with the well-recalled inspirational appeals to "hope" and "change" in campaigning. His ability to rouse an audience by stressing such values as "opportunity" and "fairness," with emphasis on improving the predicament of the middle class, had become a regular feature of his speeches since the fall of 2011.

The economic picture in 2012 showed enough signs of improving since 2010 so that Obama's restored enthusiasm could again bring hope. "Americans who feel, rightly, that the world's order has shifted . . . want a leader whose emotional temperature validates their own sense of urgency. Obama has obviously concluded as much . . ." (Bruni 2011). He still had to overcome past laxity, with too many missed opportunities to gather and stir support. The positive and negative results of his shift from his failed and derided attempts to be above partisanship remain to be seen. Also, his intention after reelection not to negotiate with himself, without seeing the details of the adversary's position, may boost the leverage he has needed (Baker 2012b). Further, a psychologist/leadership researcher made these observations:

> Clearly, Obama was a better communicator as a candidate (in 2008 and in 2012) than as a president. Of course, this is not an Obama-specific problem. Until recent intransigence among elements within the Republican party began to define the party in a way that tended to undermine any positive messaging strategy, the Republicans over the past few decades seem to have done a better job selling their ideas, regardless of the quality of those ideas, than the Democrats, with the possible exception of Bill Clinton, have done selling theirs. Also, the Republicans have tended to appeal more to emotion and the Democrats to reason, which may partially explain the disparity in effectiveness. Certainly, one lesson the Democrats should have learned over time is that they cannot let negative attacks go unanswered, and they cannot let the opposition define the terms of the debate. If Obama had been as effective in extolling the virtues of the ACA as he and other Democrats were at negatively defining Romney, then I think the ACA would have been much more positively received. (Rumsey 2013)

Yet, race was ever consequential, variously showing up. Though southern states generally have the greatest unmet need for healthcare, their Republican governors have steadfastly refused expanded Medicaid funds from Obamacare. "A South Carolina legislator put it bluntly earlier this year. State Rep. Kris Crawford told a business journal that he supports expansion, but said electoral math is the trump card. 'It is good politics to oppose the black guy in the White House right now, especially for the Republican Party,' he said," (Barrow 2013).

Though critical of aspects of Obama's performance, social ethicist Gary Dorrien (2012a, b) considered him deserving of another term, given that Obama has "Big issues . . . to be fought over." He lists some of heaviest "still to do," as "Breaking up the megabanks, scaling back the global military empire, lifting the cap on the Social Security tax, adding tax brackets at the upper end, abolishing fee for service medicine, and building a clean energy economy. Obama has belatedly committed his presidency to tax fairness and social investment [but] it will require more fighting than he waged on anything in his first term" (Dorrien 2012b).

"More fighting" must be supported by an inclusive effort from followers, which Obama called for in "rallying" them (Stein 2013). Near the end of his State of the Union address in February 2013, now reelected, he issued his call: "I hope what I said tonight resonated with you. But remember, me saying it doesn't mean anything. To get it passed, to get it signed, to get it implemented, to get it done, that is going to require a big push from you guys" (Obama 2013).

The results are still to be seen in the latest combative round, this dealing with the "sequester." A very unpopular across-the-board-cut in many federal programs, Obama had agreed to it in 2011 under threat by the opposition that they would not raise the "debt ceiling" so the nation could pay its bills. Otherwise, it would be in default, a very serious financial possibility. At the time, the expectation was that a prior solution would be found to avoid the drastic sequester, but that never came. The prevailing government gridlock results mainly from "no-compromise" extremism, studied by Mann and Ornstein (2012), and reported by Draper (2012) as a calculated opposition position across the board.

The present impasse can be understood to be a longer-term structural impediment, with extreme opposition in the House and the filibuster's sixty-vote supermajority for any action in the Senate. Though it arose against the Obama presidency, aided by Tea Party activism, it has long-term consequences. Even if Obama's efforts at reconciliation and inclusion of followers do succeed in part, this impediment challenges policy making in our democracy for some time to come.

Note

1. A previous chapter of mine, "American Presidential Leadership," is in the Bligh-Riggio book Exploring Distance in Leader-Follower Relationships (Routledge 2013). It was drawn on here, but with far more attention, for this chapter, to President Obama's performance and his challenges. Among those providing helpful comments on drafts of this chapter, special thanks are gratefully extended to Alan E. Gross and Michael G. Rumsey.

References

Adelmann, B. 2012. "The LIBOR Scandal: Just the Tip of the Iceberg." *HuffPost*, July 26.

Andersen, K. 2011. "The Madman Theory." *New York Times*, August 6, p. A17.

Baker, P. 2012a. "For Obama, a Signature Issue that the Public Never Embraced Looms Large." *New York Times*, June 30, p. A12.

Baker, P. 2012b. "Obama's Not Giving In." *New York Times*, December 3, p. 1.

Barber, J. D. 1972. *The Presidential Character: Predicting Performance in the White House*. Englewood Cliffs, NJ: Prentice-Hall.

Barofsky, N. 2012. *Bailout*. New York: Simon & Schuster.

Barrow, B. 2013. "Obamacare Faces Near-Solid Block in the South." *HuffPost*, March 30, p. 1.

Bass, B. M. 1997. "Does the Transactional-Transformational Leadership Paradigm Transcend Organizational and National Boundaries?" *American Psychologist*, 52 (2):130–139.

Bass, B. M., and Riggio, R. E. 2006. *Transformational Leadership*, 2nd ed. Mahwah, NJ: Erlbaum.

Bennis, W. G. 1999. "The Leadership Advantage." *Leader to Leader*, 12 (Spring):18–23.

Bergen, P. 2012. "Warrior in Chief." *New York Times*, April 29, p. SR1.

Blair, T. 2010. *A Journey: My Political Life*. New York: Knopf.

Blair, T. 2012. Quoted in J. F. Burns and A. Cowell, "Back in Public Eye: Blair Testifies at Murdoch Inquiry." *New York Times*, May 29, p. A8.

Bligh, M. C. and Riggio, R. E. (Eds.) 2013. *Exploring Distance in Leader–Follower Relationships: When Far Is Near and Near Is Far*. New York: Routledge/Psychology Press/Taylor & Francis.

Blow, C. M. 2011. "Hard-Knock (Hardly Acknowledged) Life." *New York Times*, January 29, p. A23.

Boehner, J. 2012. Tweet about Obamacare reported by ABC-TV News, November 22.

Brooks, D. 2012. "Where Obama Shines." *New York Times*, July 20, p. A23.

Brown, C. B. 2012. "Mistaken Beliefs on Health Care Law." *Politico*, March 23, p. 1.

Bruni, F. 2011. "Nice Guy Finishing Last." *New York Times*, October 16, p. SR3.

Bruni, F. 2012. "Captain America?" *New York Times*, June 26, p. A23.

Burns, J.M. 1978. *Leadership*. New York: Harper & Row.

Burns, J.M. 1984. *The Power to Lead: The Crisis of the American Presidency*. New York: Simon & Schuster.

Burns, J.M. 2007. Foreword to R.A. Couto (Ed.), *Reflections on Leadership*. Lanham, MD: University Press of America, pp. v–viii.

Caro, R.A. 2012. *The Passage of Power: The Years of Lyndon Johnson*. New York: Knopf.

Cohen, R. 2011. "Mubarak Agonistes. *New York Times*, February 4, p. A23.

Dean, J. 2005. *Worse than Watergate*. Boston: Houghton-Mifflin.

Dorrien, G. 2012a. *The Obama Question: A Progressive's Perspective*. New York: Rowman & Littlefield.

Dorrien, G. 2012b. "The Obama Question: A Progressive's Perspective." *Huffpost*, June 8.

Dowd, M. 2011a. "Tempest in a Tea Party." *New York Times*, July 31, p. SR11.

Dowd, M. 2011b. "One and Done?" *New York Times*, September 4, p. SR11.

Dowd, M. 2011c. "Man in the Mirror." *New York Times*, October 5, p. A25.

Draper, R. 2012. *Do Not Ask What Good We Do*. New York: Free Press.

Drucker, P.F. 1988. "Leadership: More Doing than Dash." *Wall Street Journal*, January 6, p. 14.

Epstein, L. 2012. "Reported in a Historical Benchmark." *New York Times*, August 14, p. A 9.

Fiske, S.T., Bergsieker, H.B., Russell, A.M., and Williams, L. 2009. "Images of Black Americans: Then, 'Them,' and Now, 'Obama!'" *DuBois Review*, 6(1):1–19.

Frank, J. 2011. *Obama on the Couch*. New York: Free Press/Simon & Schuster.

Freud S. 1921/1960. *Group Psychology and the Analysis of the Ego*. New York: Bantam. (Originally published in German in 1921).

Friedman, T.L. 2012a. "Why Nations Fail." *New York Times*, April 1, p. SR13.

Friedman, T.L. 2012b. "Obama Should Seize the High Ground." *New York Times*, May 27, p. SR11.

Gardner, J.W. 1987. "Leaders and Followers." *Liberal Education*, 73(2):6–8.

Haidt, J. 2012. *The Righteous Mind: Why Good People Are Divided by Politics and Religion*. New York: Pantheon.

Harwood, J. 2010. "The Caucus." *New York Times*, April 5, p. A10.

Hayden, T. 2011. "In Decrying Obama's Centrism, Drew Westen Ignores Role of Race." *The Nation*, August.

Heider, F. 1958. *The Psychology of Interpersonal Relations*. New York: Wiley.

Hollander, E.P. 1958. "Conformity, Status, and Idiosyncrasy Credit." *Psychological Review*, 65:117–127.

Hollander, E.P. 1964. *Leaders, Groups, and Influence*. New York: Oxford University Press.

Hollander, E.P. l978. *Leadership Dynamics: A Practical Guide to Effective Relationships*. New York: Free Press/Macmillan.

Hollander, E.P. 1983. "Paradoxes of Presidential Leadership: Party, Popularity, Promise, Performance . . . and More." Invited Address to the APA Division of Personality and Social Psychology, Division 8, American Psychological Association Convention, August, Anaheim, CA.

Hollander, E.P. 1992a. "The Essential Interdependence of Leadership and Followership." *Current Directions in Psychological Science*, 1:71–75.

Hollander, E.P. 1992b. "Leadership, Followership, Self, and Others." *Leadership Quarterly*, 3(1):43–54.

Hollander, E.P. 2004a. "Idiosyncrasy Credit." In G.R. Goethals, G.J. Sorenson, and J.M. Burns (Eds.), *Encyclopedia of Leadership*. Thousand Oaks, CA: Sage, pp. 695–700.

Hollander, E.P. 2004b. "Upward Influence." In G.R. Goethals, G.J. Sorenson, and J.M. Burns (Eds.), *Encyclopedia of Leadership*. Thousand Oaks, CA: Sage, pp. 1605–1609.

Hollander, E.P. 2006. "Influence Processes in Leadership-Followership: Inclusion and the Idiosyncrasy Credit Model." In D. Hantula (Ed.), *Advances in Social and Organizational Psychology: A Tribute to Ralph Rosnow*. Mahwah, NJ: Erlbaum.

Hollander, E.P. 2007. "Relating Leadership to Active Followership." In R.A. Couto (Ed.), *Reflections on Leadership: Essays Honoring James MacGregor Burns*. Lanham, MD: University Press of America.

Hollander, E.P. 2009. *Inclusive Leadership: The Essential Leader-Follower Relationship*. New York: Routledge/Psychology Press/Taylor & Francis.

Hollander, E.P. 2013. "American Presidential Leadership: Leader Credit, Follower Inclusion, and Obama's Turn." In M.C. Bligh & R.E. Riggio (Eds.), *Exploring 'Distance' in Leader-Follower Relationships: When Far Is Near and Near Is Far*. New York: Routledge/Psychology Press/Taylor & Francis.

Hollander, E. P., and Julian, J. W. 1969. "Contemporary Trends in the Analysis of Leadership Processes." *Psychological Bulletin*, 71:387–397.

Hollander, E. P., and Julian, J. W. 1970. "Studies in Leader Legitimacy, Influence, and Innovation." In L. Berkowitz (Ed.), *Advances in Experimental Social Psychology*, Volume 5, pp. 33–69. New York: Academic Press.

Hollander, E. P., and Offermann, L. 1990. "Power and Leadership in Organizations: Relationships in Transition." *American Psychologist*, 45:179–189.

Homans, G. C. 1974. *Social Behavior: Its Elementary Forms* (Revised ed.). New York: Harcourt Brace Jovanovich.

Howell, J. M., and Avolio, B. J. 1992. "The Ethics of Charismatic Leadership: Submission or Liberation?" *Academy of Management Review*, 6(2):43–54.

Howell, J. M., and Shamir, B. 2005. "The Role of Followers in the Charismatic Leadership Process: Relationships and Their Consequences." *Academy of Management Review*, 30(1):96–112.

Jacobs, T. O. 1970. *Leadership and Exchange in Formal Organizations*. Alexandria, VA: Human Resources Research Organization.

Janis, I. L. 1972. *Victims of Groupthink: A Psychological Study of Foreign Policy Decisions and Fiascos*. Boston: Houghton Mifflin.

Kantor, J. 2012. *The Obamas*. New York: Little, Brown.

Kaplan, B., and Kaiser, R. 2006. *The Versatile Leader*. San Francisco: Pfeiffer/Wiley.

Katz, E., and Lazarsfeld, P. F. 1955. *Personal Influence*. Evanston, IL: Free Press.

Keller, B. 2012. "Five Obamacare Myths." *New York Times*, July 16, p. A17.

Kellerman, B. 1984. *The Political Presidency*. New York: Oxford University Press.

Kellerman, B. 2008. *Followership: How Followers Are Creating Change*. Boston: Harvard Business School Press.

Kelley, R. E. 1988. "In Praise of Followers." *Harvard Business Review* (November/December), 88(6):1–8.

Kelley, R. E. 1992. *The Power of Followership*. New York: Doubleday.

Kennedy, R. 2011. *The Persistence of the Color-Line: Racial Politics and the Obama Presidency*. New York: Pantheon.

Krugman, P. 2012. "The Republican Economy." *New York Times*. June 4, p. A25.

Landler, M. 2011. "A President Trying to Work the Levers He Still Possesses." *New York Times*, October 28, p. A20.

Landler, M., and Peters, J. W. 2012. "Rice Concedes Error on Libya: G.O.P. Digs In." *New York Times*, November 28, p. A1.

Laski, H. J. 1941. *The American Presidency: An Interpretation*. New York: Grosset & Dunlap.

Leonhardt, D. 2012. "Obamanomics: A Counterhistory." *New York Times*, September 30, p. SR1.

Maddow, R. 2012. *Drift*. New York: Crown.

Mak, T. 2012. "Survey: World Opinion toward Obama, U.S. Cools." *Politico*, June 14, p. 13.

Mann, T. E., and Ornstein, N. J. *It's Even Worse Than It Looks: How the American Constitutional System Collided With the New Politics of Extremism*. New York: Basic Books.

Maraniss, D. 2012. *Barack Obama: The Story*. New York: Simon & Schuster.

McKibben, B. 2011. "Quotation of the Day." *New York Times*, September 3, p. A2.

Meacham, J. 2012. "Socializing as a Political Tool." *New York Times*, November 26, p. A27.

Melvin, D., and Mcguirk, R. 2012. "Around World, Obama's Presidency a Disappointment." Associated Press, May 12.

Nagourney, A. 2009. "A Health Care Debate Lesson: Obama Plays by Washington's Rules." *New York Times*, December 26, p. A14.

Neustadt, R. 1990. *Presidential Power and Modern Presidents* (Revised edition). New York: Free Press. (Original 1960 from Wiley).

Newport, F. 2007. Report on NPR of Gallup National Poll Results on President Bush, January 20–21.

New York Times. 2012. "Editorial: Too Quiet, Again, on Health Care," July 4, p. A22.

New York Times. 2013. "Editorial: Ultimate Obstruction in the Senate," March 29, p. A24.

Nocera, J. 2011. "Banker, Can You Spare a Dime?" *New York Times*, September 10, p. A21.

Nocera, J. 2012. "The Mortgage Fraud Fraud." *New York Times*, June 2, p. A21.

Obama, B. H. 1995. *Dreams from My Father*. New York: Times Books.

Obama, B. H. 2006. *The Audacity of Hope*. New York: Three Rivers Press.

Obama, B. H. 2009. Remarks by the President on Executive Compensation. The White House, February 4.

Obama, B. H. 2012a. Interview with Charlie Rose on CBS-TV, July 15.

Obama, B. H. 2012b. Campaign Speech in New Orleans. In K. Dalton-Beninato, "Fired Up, Ready to Eat," *Huff-Post*, July 28.

Obama, B. H. 2012c. Address to the Opening Session of the United Nations General Assembly, September 25.

Obama, B. H. 2013. State of the Union Address, *HuffPost*, February 12.

O'Hanlon, M. 2012. "Obama's Solid Foreign Policy Helps U.S. Interests in Europe and Russia." *Politico*, May 3, p. 24.

Owen, D. 2007. *The Hubris Syndrome: Bush, Blair and the Intoxication of Power*. London: Politico's.

Price, T. L. 2008. *Leadership Ethics*. New York: Cambridge University Press.

Reedy, G. E. 1973. *The Presidency in Flux*. New York: Columbia University Press.

Reich, R. B. 2010. "How to End the Great Recession." *New York Times*, September 3, p. A21.

Remnick, D. 2010. *The Bridge*. New York: Knopf.

Rich, F. 2010. "Time for This Big Dog to Bite Back." *New York Times*, September 12, Week in Review, p. 11.

Riggio, R. E., Chaleff, I., and Lipman-Blumen, J. (Eds.) 2008. *The Art of Followership*. San Francisco, CA: Jossey-Bass/Wiley.

Rumsey, M. G. 2012. Personal Communication, August 15.

Sanger, D. E. 2012. "Even with a 'Lighter Footprint,' It's Hard to Sidestep the Middle East." *New York Times*, November 18, p. A12.

Schlesinger, A. M. 1973. *The Imperial Presidency*. Boston: Houghton Mifflin.

Seaman, F. J., Hollander, E. P., and Richer, L. S. 1975. "Candidate Preference and Attitudes in the 1972 Presidential Election." American Psychological Association Convention, September 1975.

Sharma, D. 2011. *Barack Obama in Hawai'i and Indonesia: The Making of a Global President*. Westport, CT: Praeger.

Shear, M. D. 2012. "Trying to Turn Obama Voters into Allies in Tax Fight." *New York Times*, November 26, p. A19.

Silver-Greenberg, J., and Eavis, P. 2012. "JPMorgan Chase Loses $2 Billion from Its Trades." *New York Times*, May 11, p. 1.

Simonton, D. K. 2008. "Presidential Greatness and Its Socio-Psychological Significance: Individual or Situation? Performance or Attribution?" In C. Hoyt, G. R. Goethals, and D. Forsyth (Eds.), *Leadership at the Crossroads: Vol. 1*, Psychology and Leadership (pp. 132–148). Westport, CT: Praeger.

Stein, S. 2013. "Obama Rallies the Troops." *HuffPost*, February 12, p. 2.

Stevenson, R. W. 2012. "Europe's Ills Reach the Heart of the Presidential Race." *New York Times*, April 28, p. A13.

Stolberg, S. G. 2010. "Gentle White House Nudges Test the Power of Persuasion." *New York Times*, February 24, p. A1.

Sullivan, A. 2012. "Welcome Back to the White House, Mr. President." *Newsweek*, October 1 and 8, pp. 30ff.

Tavernise, S. 2012. "Four Years Later, Race Is Still Issue for Some Voters." *New York Times*, May 4, p. 1.

Thomas, E. 2010. "Truth or Consequences." *Newsweek*, November 22, pp. 34–37.

Tough, P. 2012. "The Birthplace of Obama the Politician." *New York Times Magazine*, August 19, p. 26ff.

Tucker, R. C. 1981. *Politics as Leadership*. Columbia, MO: University of Missouri Press.

Valenti, J. 2007. *This Time, This Place*. New York: Harmony Books.

Wall Street Journal. 2012. "Editorial: Why Israel Doesn't Trust Obama," September 1, p. A12.

Weber, M. 1947. *The Theory of Social and Economic Organization*. (Translated and edited by T. Parsons and A. M. Henderson.) New York: Oxford University Press.

Weill, S. I. 2012. Quoted in M. de la Merced, "Deal Maker Now Doubts Megabanks." *New York Times*, July 26, p. B1.

Westen, D. 2007. *Political Brain*. New York: Perseus.

Westen, D. 2011. "What Happened to Obama?" *New York Times*, August 7, p. SR1.

Wilentz, S. 2010. "Obama's Fateful Choice." *New York Daily News*, January 17, pp. 34–35.

Wills, G. 2010. *Bomb Power: The Modern Presidency and the National Security State*. New York: Penguin.

Winter, D. G. 1973. *The Power Motive*. New York: Free Press.

Woodward, B. 2012. *The Price of Politics*. New York: Simon & Schuster.

Zuckerman, M. 2011. "Obama and the "Competency Crisis." *Wall Street Journal*, August 25, p. A15.

5

OBAMA, HILLARY AND WOMEN'S VOICES: LEGACY OF ANN DUNHAM

Dinesh Sharma

"I know she was the kindest, most generous spirit I have ever known, and that what is best in me I owe to her."

—Barack Obama (1995)

"If there is one message that echoes forth from this conference, let it be that human rights are women's rights and women's rights are human rights, once and for all."

—Hillary Clinton (1995)

"In the different voice of women lies the truth of an ethic of care, the tie between relationship and responsibility, and the origins of aggression in the failure of connection."

—Carol Gilligan (1993)

Political commentators, legal scholars, and psychologists all agree that Obama personifies the role of "the good black man," "a non-challenging bargainer" as opposed to the "threatening black man" in the American psyche.[1] Many of these scholars also claim that Obama cleverly deployed his conciliatory, listening, feminized, and empathic personality style to attract white American voters, including a majority of the women voters.[2]

In the first presidential campaign, Obama played down direct confrontation with his Republican counterpart John McCain, and his female competitors Hillary Clinton and Sarah Palin. In the reelection campaign, he avoided direct confrontation with Romney during the debates. Invariably, presenting a gentler black male persona of the professor—the Sidney Poitier–like image his mother always admired—he persuaded the American public.

Frank Cooper, a professor at Suffolk Law School, has called Obama "our first unisex president" for drawing on his feminine side, especially, in his dealings with women voters.[3] This has far-reaching implications for the dialogue on race and gender in America. Ann McGinley, a professor of law at the University of Nebraska, agrees. She has stated Obama walked the tightrope of politics, tactically deploying his "cool", listening style as part of his empathic black identity routine.

While women political candidates had to appear to be macho and put on a thick hyper-masculine performance, Obama simply could not risk appearing too masculine or too black (McGinley 2009).[4] Cooper quotes Carol Marin, a longtime Chicago broadcaster and journalist, to suggest that Obama is a harbinger of "the first female president" of the United States—both due to his style and policies.

In an editorial in the *Chicago Sun Times*, she stated: "If Bill Clinton was once considered America's first black president, Obama may one day be viewed as our first woman president. While [Hillary] Clinton, the warrior, battles on, talks about toughness, and out loud considers nuking Iran, it is Obama who is full of feminine virtues. Consensus. Conciliation. Peace, not war."[5]

Men's psychology suggests that a man's feminine side is partly a composite or a gestalt of the long-term interactions with the important women in his life. Barack Obama, of course, was raised by several strong women who sent him on his path-breaking journey, as I have argued in my earlier book (Sharma 2011).[6] The women who shaped Obama's life have been principally three, namely his mother Ann Dunham, grandmother Madelyn Dunham, and wife Michelle Robinson. The struggles of these three women have shaped Obama's self and identity and symbolically guide his actions on a daily basis.

There is evidence to suggest that this pattern holds true even today, where some of his most trusted advisors—from Valerie Jarrett in the White House, Hillary Clinton as the former secretary of state, Nancy Pelosi in Congress, Sebelius in the Health and Human Services, Napolitano as the Homeland secretary, and Susan Rice at the United Nations—are all strong women leaders. Obama's two Supreme Court appointments have also been women, Elena Kagan and Sonia Sotomayor. Recently, the role of the chairman of the Security and Exchange Commission has been given to a leading female lawyer, Mary Jo White, former district attorney of the Southern District of New York, and the General Counsel's appointment to Ann K. Small White House counsel.

Given Obama's father's absence, his relationships with important surrogate father figures—his grandfather, his Indonesian stepfather, literary mentors like Frank Marshall Davis, and his pastor Reverend Wright—have invariably been marked by disappointments. These men by his own account have never fully measured up to the ideal image of his biological father lodged in his heart and mind.[7] Thus, the women in Obama's inner world have by far had the strongest influence on shaping his destiny.

The three key women in Obama's personal narrative hail from the Midwest. Thus, Obama established his roots in the Midwest and displays the American traits that he is now well-known for—progressive idealism, pragmatism, and a steely determination. While Obama's autobiography, *Dreams from My Father*, is principally concerned with father loss and his personality before he became a politician (Obama 2004a), the later book, *The Audacity of Hope*, is dedicated to the key women in his life. It is an overtly political book focused on the fundamentals of the American dream and the Midwestern values of hard work and responsibility he acquired from his mother and grandmother (Obama 2006).[8]

Ann Dunham and Hillary Clinton: Two Parallel Lives

Obama's mother, Ann Dunham, who by all accounts appears to be the first anthropologist mother of an American president, planned to attend the Beijing conference on women in 1994. She had been a passionate supporter of women's education and literacy development. She had conducted many projects, which raised women's status in the developing world, especially in Southeast Asia, where for almost twenty years she did her dissertation research.[9] The president as a young boy had travelled with her on many occasions to villages in Indonesia.

As Elizabeth Moore revealed in her *Newsday* article in 2008,[10] and Jenny Scott has fully reported in her book, *A Singular Woman*,[11] starting in 1993 to the end of 1994, Ann Dunham was working in New York City, preparing for a major United Nations conference in Beijing, where she planned to speak about microcredits and microlending to poor women. This is the same conference where Hillary Clinton, then first lady, electrified the audience with her now well-known statement, "Human rights are women's rights, and women's rights are human rights. . . ."[12]

While Ann Dunham's colleagues wondered what effect she might have had at the Beijing conference, where Hillary ultimately advocated for women's rights to thunderous applause, she never made it to the event since she was suffering from the last stages of cancer in Hawai'i. "But Clinton did speak at the panel co-sponsored by the International Coalition on Women and Credit that Dunham-Soetoro had brought together at the U.N.'s initiative. Two years later, Clinton helped launch a campaign to extend microfinance to 100 million families, a goal the coalition pushed at Beijing—and attained two years ago," reported Moore.[13]

Historians might speculate what it meant to pick Hillary Clinton as secretary of state after a bitterly fought campaign, but there is no doubt it had a personal meaning as well for the president. His mother and Hillary Clinton were "generational sisters" of sorts, separated only by five years (Hillary being younger), both Midwesterners by birth and socialization, both ardent feminists who supported and championed women's liberation, and both travelled the world empowering women and girls.

Some of Ann Dunham's friends also noted the parallel: "I remember us saying it's such a shame that this is getting unpleasant, because they actually have this connection—they are one degree separated from one another," recalled a development expert who worked with Obama's mother.[14] Ann Dunham's colleagues in New York knew she was a pioneer, but they did not know that her work would gain yet another level of prominence because her son would go on to become president someday. They knew that she did "seminal field research and developed the standards that guided the program's rapid expansion."[15] Her work made it possible for development agencies to not cast "poor women as passive victims," so lending money to them could be seen as a viable idea.

Nancy Barry, the former president of Women's World Banking, an early microlender who hired her, has said that Ann Dunham's work unified us around a common theme. "We were very good at defining what our differences were. . . . What Ann's leadership resulted in is all of the leaders coming together and focusing . . . on what we believed in together," she told a reporter.

Friends remember Ann Dunham as a really earthy person, grounded in real-life experiences, but a woman with a larger-than-life passion for making a difference in the world. She wrote a 1,000-page doctoral thesis on village economy in Indonesia, the insights from which were used to design savings and credit products for millions of low-income rural clients at the People's Bank of Indonesia. She convinced bankers to see how reliable small-scale women entrepreneurs can be in borrowing, building, and expanding a business.

Ann Dunham wanted to move families out of poverty, yet all the while she was looking at "achieving a sea change in the way women are perceived," told Nina Nayar to a reporter.[16] She worked on an effort to convince the United Nations to convene an expert panel on lending to women with a survey on points of agreement they shared. The report from the experts became the foundation for the Beijing policy platform and for standards on lending that emerged later. "We sent it to every finance minister in the world, and every central bank governor. . . . We were a very small organization and we were really trying to leverage the resources we had as effectively as we could. Beijing was a huge opportunity for us to put microcredit on the map," described Nicola Armacost in a news story.[17]

The professional efforts made by Ann Dunham were on a separate but parallel track with the initiatives made by the Arkansas first lady, Hillary Clinton, who launched a project backed by Muhammad Yunus of Bangladesh. Both women viewed the Beijing conference as an opportunity to further microcredit projects. Microcredit "was mentioned in probably every other speech she made as first lady," Melanne Verveer has said, Clinton's former chief of staff.

At the conference, Clinton chaired the panel and gave a passionate speech. "It's called micro, but its impact on people is gigantic. . . . When we help these women to sow, we all reap," Clinton told the audience.[18] While Clinton may not have heard of Ann Dunham's work, she was influenced by it.

According to Lawrence Yanovitch, at FINCA International, who also worked with Ann Dunham, Hillary Clinton and the mother of the president "had the same values."[19] The confluence of their professional interests is self-evident. Ann Dunham's legacy has been carried on, in effect, through the work of the next generation of women, Hillary Clinton being one of the foremost proponents of the same set of causes. When the president chose her as the secretary of state, he was bound to improve the US image abroad and continue the legacy of the causes his mother had worked for all of her professional life.

Women's Development after Hillary

When Secretary of State Hillary Clinton famously declared in 1995 that "women's rights are human rights," she was not new on the international scene. She had publicly spoken about these issues many times before, but not from the perch of the first lady. Those words had a ripple effect, or the Hillary effect, and she cemented her status as a champion for women and girls around the world.

Beginning with her student days at the Yale Law School, Hillary Clinton had been an advocate for the rights of women and children. In her best-selling book, *It Takes a Village*, she had argued that it takes the whole community to raise a child, not technically untrue, but the conservatives chided her. Republicans including Bob Dole argued, instead, it really takes a loving and stable family unit to raise healthy kids in today's environment.

Clearly, Hillary has been a champion of progressive causes all of her life. At the State Department, during her tenure Clinton made women's development a central concern of American diplomacy, building on the work of two previous women secretaries of state, Madelyn Albright and Condoleeza Rice.

During a joint interview with *60 Minutes*, Obama said, "Well, the main thing is I just wanted to have a chance to publicly say thank you, because I think Hillary will go down as one of the finest secretaries of state we've had. . . . It has been a great collaboration over the last four years. . . . I'm going to miss her, wish she was sticking around but she has logged in so many miles I can't begrudge her wanting to take it easy for a little bit," he said. "But I want the country to appreciate what an extraordinary role she's played during the course of my administration. A lot of the successes we've had internationally have been because of her hard work."[20]

Among her signal achievements for women and girls are[21]:

- Equal Futures Partnership to increase women's leadership in politics
- Rights for women and girls are key ingredients for democracy, peace, and economic growth in every country
- Leading the US National Action Plan on Women, Peace, and Security
- US Strategy to Prevent and Respond to Gender-Based Violence Globally, an initiative of USAID and the State Department
- Secretarial Policy Directive on Gender, which has been instrumental in working to end child marriage.

With the transition to the new secretary of state, John Kerry, the media has been wondering whether Hillary's successor will be able to fill her big heels and carry on her developmental agenda. According to several reports, Kerry's statement on International Women's Day, promising to continue the commitment to women's development, is a good start. Will he be able to continue the mission of women's and girl's development with the same vigor and resolve? To make it a centerpiece of US foreign policy, at least two things must be followed through: strengthen the global campaign to end violence against women and girls, while pushing for greater education of girls; and increase funding for girls and women to access sexual and reproductive health services.

We know from data collected by 10×10 girl's educational campaign for the documentary film, *Girl Rising*, the statistics on girls' education are disheartening.[22]

GIRLS' EDUCATION

1. Globally, 66 million girls out of school. (UNESCO)
2. There are 33 million fewer girls than boys in primary school. (Education First)
3. A child born to a literate mother is 50% more likely to survive past the age of 5. (UNESCO)
4. Girls with 8 years of education are 4 times less likely to be married as children. (National Academies Press)
5. Educated mothers are more than twice as likely to send their children to school. (UNICEF)
6. School is not free in over 50 countries. (UNESCO)
7. A girl on planet earth has a 1 in 4 chance of being born into poverty. (The World Bank)
8. A girl with an extra year of education can earn 20% more as an adult. (The World Bank)
9. Women operate a majority of small farms and businesses in the developing world. (Focus on Five)
10. If India enrolled 1% more girls in secondary school, their GDP would rise by $5.5 billion. (CIA World Factbook) (Global Campaign for Education and RESULTS Education Fund)

SEXUAL VIOLENCE

1. There are 600 million girls in the developing world. (The World Bank)
2. 80% of all human trafficking victims are girls. (UNFPA)
3. In a single year, an estimated 150 million girls are victims of sexual violence. (UNIFEM)
4. 50% of all the sexual assaults in the world are on girls under 15. (UNFPA)
5. 75% of AIDS cases in sub-Saharan Africa—the region hardest hit by the disease—are women and girls. (UNAIDS)
6. 14 million girls under 18 will be married this year; 38 thousand today; 13 girls in the last 30 seconds. (UNFPA)
7. The #1 cause of death for girls 15–19 is childbirth. (World Health Organization)

Evidently, a lot more work has to be done, but the former Secretary Clinton has tightly bound diplomacy with development and democracy. She has made women and girls a centerpiece of American foreign policy. The infrastructure created by her will last, but not without additional efforts. "Achieving global justice depends on the ingenuity of human rights activists around the world and on the strength of U.S. foreign policy to advocate for women and girls—now and for generations to come," according to Ruth Messinger, president of the American Jewish World Service.[23]

Whether Hillary will take up the mantle again in a public way remains to be seen, as there are rumors circulating at the time of writing this book that she might be running again for the highest office in 2016. Be that as it may, the global cause that she has championed—for diplomacy, development, and democracy—will continue. As global businesses realize that women power, representing half of the population of the world (3.5 billion) is an emerging market opportunity even as the BRIC economies are fully integrated into the global economy. There is likely to be greater interest in women's welfare in the twenty-first century.[24]

As women gain more economic clout, their share of voice will increase. The injustices they have suffered at the hands or men or institutional structures for centuries will no longer be tolerated. One of the debates raging at the center of globalization studies is how to increase the share of voice for women. If democracy and development are to succeed in the developing world, they must give greater power to the other half of the population. How can a nation claim to be democratic while half of its citizens fear for their security and well-being? This is the question many have been asking in the wake of the rape crisis in India.

Many African women are asking similar questions. During a panel on "women activists and leaders" at a conference focused on Global Africa, they asked how can African women, and African Muslim women in particular, draw upon their local traditions to transform their societies from within?[25]

Many of the traditional societies embracing development programs tend to have powerful women at the center of the domestic sphere. By transforming their lives, it is possible to transform the lives of the next generation of young girls. Early education—primary and secondary schooling—offers one of the "cultural pathways"[26] through which to navigate some of the complex challenges of development, while drawing upon local role models for women's lives without disrupting the social and moral order. Thus, it is not a coincidence that many of the early postcolonial reformers, such as Mahatma Gandhi, made the campaign for the improvement of women part and parcel of the national development.[27]

Notes

1. Steele, S. (2008). A Bound Man: Why We Are Excited about Obama and Why He Can't Win. New York: Free Press. http://www.amazon.com/Bound-Man-Excited-About-Obama/dp/1416559175/ref=tmm_hrd_swatch_0?_encoding=UTF8&sr=&qid=.
2. Sharma, Dinesh. 2011. *Barack Obama in Hawai'i and Indonesia*. New York: Praeger. http://www.amazon.com/Barack-Obama-Hawai'i-Indonesia-President/dp/0313385335.

3. Cooper, F. (2008). Our First Unisex President?: Black Masculinity and Obama's Feminine Side. *Denver University Law Review, Vol. 86, p. 633, 2009.* http://papers.ssrn.com/sol3/cf_dev/AbsByAuth.cfm?per_id=109396".

4. McGinley, Ann C. 2009. "Hillary Clinton, Sarah Palin, and Michelle Obama: Performing Gender, Race, and Class on the Campaign Trail." *Scholarly Works.* Paper 171. http://scholars.law.unlv.edu/facpub/171.

5. Carol Marin. 2008. "Thanks to Hillary for Being a Winner at Heart," *CHISUNTIMES*, May 11, A17.

6. Sharma, Dinesh. 2011. *Barack Obama in Hawai'i and Indonesia.* New York: Praeger. http://www.amazon.com/Barack-Obama-Hawai'i-Indonesia-President/dp/0313385335.

7. Obama, Barack. 2004. *Dreams from my Father.* New York: Three Rivers.

8. Obama, Barack. 2006. *The Audacity of Hope.* New York: Vintage.

9. Dunham, Ann. 2009. *Surviving Against the Odds.* Durham: Duke University Press.

10. Moore, E. (2008). Obama's mother, Hillary Clinton shared a belief in microlending, Newsday, Dec 29. http://www.azcentral.com/news/election/president/articles/2008/12/29/20081229obama1229clinton.html?nclick_check=1#ixzz2eQMLsJe2.

11. Scott, J. (20121). A Singular Woman: The Untold Story of Barack Obama's Mother. Riverhead: New York. http://www.amazon.com/Singular-Woman-Untold-Barack-Obamas/dp/1594485593.

12. Tyler, P. (1995). Hillary Clinton in China documents abuse of women, NY Times, Sep 6. http://www.nytimes.com/1995/09/06/world/hillary-clinton-in-china-details-abuse-of-women.html.

13. Moore, E. (2008). Obama's mother, Hillary Clinton shared a belief in microlending, Newsday, Dec 29. http://www.azcentral.com/news/election/president/articles/2008/12/29/20081229obama1229clinton.html?nclick_check=1#ixzz2eQMLsJe2

14. Ibid. Moore, E. (2008). Obama's mother, Hillary Clinton shared a belief in microlending, Newsday, Dec 29. http://www.azcentral.com/news/election/president/articles/2008/12/29/20081229obama1229clinton.html?nclick_check=1#ixzz2eQMLsJe2

15. http://www.azcentral.com/news/election/president/articles/2008/12/29/20081229obama1229clinton.html.

16. http://www.azcentral.com/news/election/president/articles/2008/12/29/20081229obama1229clinton.html.

17. http://www.democraticunderground.com/discuss/duboard.php?az=view_all&address=132x8039336.

18. http://www.americanrhetoric.com/speeches/hillaryclintonbeijingspeech.htm.

19. http://www.azcentral.com/news/election/president/articles/2008/12/29/20081229obama1229clinton.html.

20. Ashburn, L. (2013). Obama Hillary love fest on 60 minutes, Jan 28. http://www.thedailybeast.com/articles/2013/01/28/hillary-clinton-and-barack-obama-s-lovefest-on-60-minutes.html.

21. Messinger, R. (2013). With Hillary gone, will State Department still prioritize women, Salon, Mar 8. http://www.salon.com/2013/03/08/will_state_depts_focus_on_women_leave_with_hillary/.

22. 10X10, Girl Rising. http://10x10act.org/wp-content/uploads/2011/12/GirlRising_fact_sheet_042213.pdf.

23. Messinger, R. (2013). With Hillary Gone, will State Department still prioritize women, Salon, Mar 8. http://www.salon.com/2013/03/08/will_state_depts_focus_on_women_leave_with_hillary/.

24. EY (2013). Women the next emerging market. http://www.ey.com/Publication/vwLUAssets/Women_the_next_emerging_market/$FILE/WomenTheNextEmergingMarket.pdf.

25. Mazrui, A. (2013). Global Africa, Triple Heritage and Pax Africana: Conference in Honor of Professor Mazrui. http://www2.binghamton.edu/igcs/nyasaconference/nyasa.html..

26. Sharma, D. (2004). Cultural pathways through the information age. New York: John Wiley. http://www.ncbi.nlm.nih.gov/pubmed/15552205.

27. Patel, S. (1988). Construction and Reconstruction of Woman in Gandhi Economic and Political WeeklyVol. 23, No. 8 (Feb. 20, 1988), pp. 377-387. http://www.jstor.org/discover/10.2307/4378142?uid=3739256&uid=2&uid=4&sid=21102622026347.

Part II

AFRICA

6

AFRO-OPTIMISM FROM MAHATMA GANDHI TO BARACK OBAMA: A TALE OF TWO PROPHECIES

Ali Al'amin Mazrui[1]

The term "Afro-pessimism" is now familiar in Africanist circles. It refers to the widespread tendency to expect mainly bad news from Africa. Less frequently used is the term "Afro-optimism," indicating a strong readiness to give Africa the benefit of the doubt.

Two historic prophecies in history have sought fulfillment in the struggle to elect the first black president of the United States. One Afro-optimistic prediction was made by [Mahatma] Mohandas Gandhi in 1936. He prophesied that "it may be through the Negroes that the unadulterated message of nonviolence will be delivered to the world."[2]

The second optimistic prophecy was made by Robert Kennedy in 1968, the year of his own assassination. In an interview on the Voice of America, Bobby Kennedy predicted that approximately in the year 2008 the United States would elect its first "Negro President." Both Gandhi and Robert Kennedy were speaking at a time when it was still politically correct to use the word "Negro" when referring to a black person. Kennedy's prediction was formulated as follows:

> [Things are] moving so fast in race relations a Negro could be president in 40 years. . . . There is no question about it. In the next 40 years a Negro can achieve the same position that my brother had.[3]

The election of Barack Obama to the presidency in the US general election of November 4, 2008, has fulfilled Robert Kennedy's prediction with staggering precision. Nostradamus, the sixteenth-century Renaissance astrologer, would have been jealous. But what has that got to do with Mahatma Gandhi's prediction much earlier that the torch of Satyagraha (soul force) would be passed to black people and make them the vanguard of global nonviolence?

Let us deal with the fate of Gandhi's prediction prior to the election of Barack Obama before we explore the implications of Obama's election for both prophecies.

In the Shadow of Nostradamus?

Mohandas Gandhi was born in Porbauder, India, on October 2, 1869. His early education in India was as modest as Barack Obama's early education in Indonesia a century later. But like Obama, Gandhi subsequently went to law school. Gandhi studied law in London; Obama at Harvard.

Paradoxically, Mohandas Gandhi came to spend much more time in Africa than Barack Obama has ever done. After his legal training at Harvard, Obama chose a career in the poorer neighborhoods of Chicago, Illinois. After his legal training in London, Gandhi sought clerical and legal work in South Africa. Mahatma Gandhi lived in South Africa from 1893 to 1914. It was in 1919 that he entered Indian politics, rose to lead the Indian independence movement, saw India become independent in 1947, and was assassinated by a fellow Hindu in January 1948.

It is, in fact, one of the curious things of history that, outside India itself, the torch of Gandhism came to be passed most prominently not to his fellow Asians, but to blacks both in the New World and in Africa. It is not without significance that among the first nonwhite winners of the Nobel Prize for Peace were Ralph Bunche, Chief Albert Luthuli, Martin Luther King Jr., and Archbishop Desmond Tutu.

Perhaps Gandhi himself would not have been surprised. Quite early in his life, he saw nonviolent resistance as a method that would be well-suited for the African as well as the Indian. In 1924, Gandhi said that if the black people "caught the spirit of the Indian movement their progress must be rapid."[4]

To understand his claim, one should perhaps link it up with something that was later said by his disciple, Jawaharlal Nehru. Nehru said: "Reading through history I think the agony of the African continent . . . has not been equaled anywhere."[5]

To the extent then that the black man had more to be angry about than other men, he would need greater self-discipline than others to be "passive" in his resistance. But by the same token, to the extent that the black man in the last four centuries had suffered more than any other, passive but purposeful self-sacrifice for the cause should come easier to him. And to the extent that the black man had more to forgive the rest of the world for, that forgiveness when it came should be all the more weighty. Perhaps in response to adding up these considerations, Gandhi came to the conclusion by 1936 that it was "maybe through the Negroes that the unadulterated message of non-violence will be delivered to the world."[6]

Was Mohandas playing Nostradamus, the sixteenth-century European seer who foretold the future? Would Mohandas Gandhi be more accurately vindicated than Nostradamus?

Certainly in America the torch came to be passed to Martin Luther King Jr. And in South Africa, where Gandhi first experimented with his methods, it passed to Albert Luthuli and later Desmond Tutu. In Northern Rhodesia (Zambia before independence) Kenneth Kaunda became a vigorous Gandhian—"I reject absolutely violence in any of its forms as a solution to our problems."[7]

In the Gold Coast (Ghana after independence) Nkrumah had translated *Satyagraha* into a program of "Positive Action," a program that he himself defined as non-cooperation based on the principle of absolute non-violence, as used by Gandhi in India."[8] In 1949 *The Morning Telegraph* of Accra went as far as to call Nkrumah the "Gandhi of Ghana."[9]

African conceptions of dignity now seemed very different from what was implied by that old ceremonial affirmation of young Kikuyu initiates, which Kenyatta once told us about—the glorification of the spear as "the symbol of our courageous and fighting spirit." But these new nonviolent conceptions of dignity could now also be differentiated from the submissive virtues of early missionary teachings.

Yet one question remained to be answered: Could passive resistance survive the attainment of independence? Would Gandhism retain political relevance once its immediate objective of liberation from colonialism was achieved?

It is perhaps not entirely accidental that the two most important Indian contributions to African political thought were the doctrines of nonviolence and nonalignment. In a sense, they were almost twin doctrines. Gandhi contributed passive resistance to one school of African thought; Nehru contributed nonalignment to almost all African countries. We should note how Uganda's President Milton Obote put it in his tribute to Nehru on his death. Obote said: "Nehru will be remembered as a founder of nonalignment. . . . The new nations of the world owe him a debt of gratitude in this respect."[10] However, Gandhi and Nehru both taught Africa and learnt from it. But how related are the two doctrines in their assumptions? For India itself, Gandhi's nonviolence was a method of seeking freedom, while Nehru's nonalignment came to be a method of seeking peace. And yet nonalignment was, in some ways, a translation into foreign policy of some of the moral assumptions that underlay passive resistance in the domestic struggle for India's independence. Indian philosophy refuses to see the world in stark Manichaean terms of good and evil; historically, Hinduism has tolerated and/or absorbed its rebels and competitors. There is a long-standing Indian tradition of *ahimsa* or nonviolence and the sense that Indian thought could contribute to the world; all were part and parcel of both Satyagraha and nonalignment. Then there was the problem of scarce resources, whether to fight internal or external battles. As Gandhi himself once said:

> Free India can have no enemy. For India to enter into the race for armaments is to court suicide. . . . The world is looking for something new and unique from India. . . . With the loss of India to non-violence the last hope of the world will be gone. . . .[11]

In spite of Gandhi's vision, independent India did not practice abstinence. Gandhian nonviolence was not fully translated into a foreign policy. And yet of all the countries in the world, India under Nehru came nearest to symbolizing the search for peace. For a crucial decade in the history of Africa and Asia, India was the diplomatic leader of both continents. And in the doctrine of nonalignment she bequeathed to many of the new states a provisional foreign policy for the first few experimental years of their sovereign statehood. What Nehru learnt from Suez War of 1956, Nehru taught the world.

With that policy, the wheel of global pacification had come full circle. Asia and Africa had once been colonized partly with a view to imposing peace upon them. But now nonalignment had turned the tables on old concepts like *Pax Britannica*. It was now those who were once colonized who were preaching peace to their former imperial tutors.

On the question of methods of liberation a major change took place in the ethic of African nationalism. When Ghana attained independence in 1957 without resort to an armed insurrection, Gandhism appeared to have once again been vindicated. Nkrumah, as we have noted, had been a disciple of Gandhi in his methods—and now his country was the first black colony to win independence from Britain.

Is there a paradox in Gandhi's prediction that it may be through the black people that the unadulterated message of soul force and passive resistance might be realized?[12] If Gandhi was right, this would be one more illustration of a culture that gives birth to an ethic that it does not necessarily fulfill itself.

The Nobel Committee for Peace in Oslo seems to have shared some of Gandhi's optimism about the soul force of the black people. Africans and people of African descent who have won the Nobel Prize for Peace since the middle of the twentieth century have included Ralph Bunche (1950), Albert Luthuli (1960), Martin Luther King Jr. (1964), Anwar Sadat (1978), Desmond Tutu (1984), Nelson Mandela (1993), Kofi Annan (2001), Wangari Maathai (2004), Barack H. Obama (2009), Elen Johnson Sirleaf (2011), and Leymah Gbowee (2011). Neither Mahatma Gandhi himself nor any of his compatriots in India seemed seriously to have been considered for the Nobel Prize for Peace. Was Mahatma Gandhi vindicated that the so-called "Negro" was going to be the best exemplar of soul force? Was this a case of African culture being empirically more Gandhian than Indian culture?

In reality black people have been at least as violent as anything ever perpetrated by Indians. What is distinctive about Africans is their short memory of hate.

Jomo Kenyatta was unjustly imprisoned by the British colonial authorities in 1952 over charges of founding the Mau Mau movement in Kenya. A British governor also denounced him as "a leader unto darkness and death."[13] And yet when Jomo Kenyatta was released, he not only forgave the white settlers, but turned the whole country toward a basic pro-Western orientation to which it has remained committed ever since. Kenyatta even published a book titled *Suffering Without Bitterness*.[14]

Ian Smith, the white settler leader of Rhodesia, unilaterally declared independence in 1965 and unleashed a civil war on Rhodesia. Thousands of people, mainly black, died in the country as a result of policies pursued by Ian Smith. Yet when the war ended in 1980 Ian Smith and his cohorts were *not* subjected to a Nuremberg-style trial. On the contrary, Ian Smith was himself a member of parliament in a black-ruled Zimbabwe, busy criticizing the post-Smith black leaders of Zimbabwe as incompetent and dishonest. Where else but in Africa could such tolerance occur?[15] India's memory of hate may not be as short as Africa's, but India had a Sikh for prime minister in 2008 although another Sikh once killed a Hindu prime minister, Indira Gandhi, in 1984.

The Nigerian civil war (1967–1970) was the most highly publicized civil conflict in postcolonial African history. When the war was coming to an end, many people feared that there would be a bloodbath in the defeated eastern region. The Vatican was worried that cities like Enugu and Onit-cha, strongholds of Catholicism, would be monuments of devastation and blood-letting.

None of these expectations occurred. Nigerians—seldom among the most disciplined of Africans—discovered in 1970 some remarkable resources of self-restraint. There were no triumphant reprisals against the vanquished Biafrans; there were no vengeful trials of "traitors."[16] Hindu attitudes to Muslims are not as forgiving, but India has experimented with a Muslim titular head of state nevertheless.

We have also witnessed the phenomenon of Nelson Mandela. He lost twenty-seven of the best years of his life in prison under the laws of the apartheid regime. Yet when he was released, he not only emphasized the policy of reconciliation—he often went beyond the call of duty. On one occasion before he became president, white men were fasting unto death after being convicted of terrorist offences by their own white government. Nelson Mandela went out of his way to beg them to eat and thus spare their own lives.

When Mandela became president in 1994, it was surely enough that his government would leave the architects of apartheid unmolested. Yet Nelson Mandela went out of his way to pay a social call and have tea with the unrepentant widow of Hendrik F. Verwoerd, the supreme architect of the worst forms of apartheid, who shaped the whole racist order from 1958 to 1966. Mandela was having tea with the family of Verwoerd.[17]

India as a state is often more tolerant than *Indians* as a people.

Was Mahatma Gandhi correct, after all, that his torch of soul force (Satyagraha) might find its brightest manifestations among black people? The latest test is now at hand. A black man has been elected president of the United States. Is Barack Obama likely to manifest Gandhian "soul force"? He is preceded by an American tradition that salutes warrior presidents. Being "presidential" has been equated with being ready to order military action.

The Romance of Warrior Presidents

Even before the United States became the sole superpower, the foundations were being laid for the role of the United States as the sheriff of the world. American infatuation with warrior-presidents perhaps goes back to George Washington, who was a soldier turned head of state. What developed in twentieth-century America was the tradition of head of state turned "soldier." Every presidential commander-in-chief wanted the experience of ordering at least one military action by American forces.

Certainly every American president since Franklin D. Roosevelt has engaged in some act of war or another. Roosevelt was inevitably embroiled in World War II; Harry Truman helped to initiate the Korean War; Dwight Eisenhower ended the Korean War but started planning for the Bay of Pigs operation on Cuba; John F. Kennedy unleashed the Bay of Pigs operation and helped to initiate the Vietnam War; Kennedy also triggered the high-risk confrontation over the Cuban missiles; Lyndon Johnson escalated the Vietnam war; Richard Nixon bombed Cambodia; Gerald Ford sent the Marines in a disagreement with Cambodia over a US cargo-ship, the *Mayaguez*; Jimmy Carter attempted to thwart the Iranian revolution and paid heavily for it; Ronald Reagan perpetrated acts of war in Lebanon, the Caribbean, and Libya, and in shooting down a civilian airplane in the Persian (Arabian) Gulf; George Bush Sr. invaded Panama and is most famous for Desert Storm in the Persian (Arabian) Gulf; Bill Clinton led military action against Yugoslavia over Kosovo and bombed Sudan and Afghanistan; George W. Bush inherited a decade of bombing Baghdad and subsidizing half a century of Israeli militarism against Palestinians. After September 11, the younger Bush not only initiated the understandable "war on terror" and the invasion of Afghanistan, but also added the totally unnecessary third war on Iraq.

Every American president since Franklin Roosevelt has regarded an act of war as the equivalent of a *rite of passage*. The commander-in-chief has to "act presidential." The political constituency celebrates warrior-presidents. Heads of state shoot up in popularity with an act of war. But if victory is not speedy, presidential popularity is rapidly at risk. And yet the United States hardly ever calls these engagements "acts of war." Even the war in Vietnam, which cost nearly sixty thousand American lives and millions of Vietnamese lives, was never an officially declared war by the United States.

America needs to find more humane rites of passage for its leaders. The warrior-president does not call his own military actions "JIHAD," but the rhetoric of *patriotism* used is not really different from the rhetoric of *piety*.

Terrorism is getting globalized, but the definition of an "act of war" is not universalized. Such a definition is still highly selective, depending upon the power of the perpetrator or the status of the victim. For the immediate future, it may also depend upon making sure that Usamaphobia does not degenerate into Islamophobia. Will Barack Obama resist the temptation of performing as a "warrior-president"?

In George W. Bush's first administration, Colin Powell partly vindicated Mahatma Gandhi's optimism by being the least hawkish of all the senior members of the Bush Cabinet, in spite of his disastrous performance before the United Nations Security Council in support of a war on Iraq. Colin Powell was the only real warrior on the Cabinet, but was the least militaristic. Can Barack Obama combine the appearance of warriorhood with the reality of a disguised peacemaker?

Whether America's first black president will turn out to be less militaristic than his white predecessors is partly tied to the recent history of racism in the United States.

Let us begin with what W. E. B. DuBois and Obama had in common. They were both products of intermarriage between black and white. They both carried names that betrayed their bicultural descent. Barack Obama's name betrayed his Luo ancestry on the side of his Kenyan father. William Edward Burghardt DuBois's name betrayed his French legacy. Both suffered from a crisis of identity in their earlier years. In personal visage, DuBois was much fairer in skin-color than Obama. However, over time DuBois identified himself with black identity more passionately that did Obama. Indeed, DuBois came to see himself as first and foremost an African, and he eventually naturalized as a citizen of Ghana. Obama, however, saw himself as less and less of an African, in spite of the fact that his father was born an African, and the father died as a citizen of Kenya. In terms of preferred policy, W. E. B. DuBois was a *Black Atlanticist*. He dreamt of the unification of the African diaspora in the Americas with Black Africa as a new racial Commonwealth in the world system. Barack Obama saw himself as fundamentally an American and forever a citizen of the United States.

From Warriors to Scholars

In 1895, DuBois became the first African-American to receive a Ph.D. in history from Harvard University. His predoctoral degree was from Fisk University in Nashville, Tennessee. In 1990, Obama became the first African-American to be elected president of the *Harvard Law Review* in Cambridge, Massachusetts. Obama's pre-law degree was from Columbia University in New York.

In his younger years, DuBois was often regarded as "not Negro enough," partly because he was fair skinned and partly because of his upper social class demeanor. Throughout much of his career,

Barack Obama was demeaned by some fellow African-Americans as "not black enough," more because he was brought up in a white family by his grandmother than simply because his Kansas mother was white. In later years, Obama's brilliant Harvard career earned him the political stigma of "elitist."

DuBois's vision of the proper destiny for African-Americans had two contemporary rivals. Booker T. Washington wanted African-Americans to forego for a while political power, civil liberties, and higher education in the liberal arts and the liberal professions. Booker T. Washington's "Tuskegee Machine" recommended for the black youth "industrial education" instead. Washington was at the peak of his influence from 1895 to 1910.

In contrast, DuBois's vision of education for the black youth focused on cultivating what he called "the Talented Tenth" in preparation for black entry into "modern civilization."

Another rival black vision in DuBois's era was that championed by Marcus Garvey, a Jamaican immigrant in the United States who succeeded in mobilizing many thousands of African-Americans in the 1920s to pursue private enterprise and aspire to migrate back to Africa en masse. W. E. B. DuBois and Marcus Garvey debated each other in abusive terms and even exchanged racial epithets.

In their different ways, both W. E. B. DuBois and Marcus Garvey were Black Atlanticists. But while DuBois aspired to send to Africa some members of the Talented Tenth of the black diaspora to help develop and even "civilize" Africa, Marcus Garvey believed in a kind of black Zionism. To Garvey, all African peoples in the diaspora were entitled to the right of returning to Africa. But because most of Africa was still colonized in the first half of the twentieth century, Garvey's dream was even more remote than DuBois's "Talented Tenth."

While in policy terms W. E. B. DuBois limited himself to the unity of the Black Atlantic, his own de facto concept of Global Africa included a version of Black Indian Ocean. Indeed, DuBois went to the extent of claiming that black-skinned South Asians like Tamils of India and Sri Lanka were descended from black Africans of pre-recorded history.

Barack Obama's dream of a postracial America also had rival paradigms among African-Americans. Jesse Jackson and Andrew Young believed in the integration of African-Americans into mainstream United States' culture, but they still retained and defended black race-consciousness. Jesse Jackson and Andrew Young tried to promote a *multiracial* America, while Barack Obama championed a *nonracial* America.

The third black school of thought in Barack Obama's life was that represented by his pastor for twenty years, the Reverend Jeremiah Wright of Trinity United Church of Christ. Reverend Wright's America was far from *nonracial* like Obama's dream. Nor was Wright's preferred America *multiracial* like that of Andrew Young and Jesse Jackson. Essentially, Revered Jeremiah Wright was a *racial separatist*, although the wider church to which he belonged was committed to *multiracialism* and racial integration.

However, a more fundamental shift that was taking place from the world of W. E. B. DuBois early in the twentieth century and the world of Barack Obama early in the twenty-first century was a shift from prejudice based on differences in color to prejudice based on differences in culture. It is to this massive paradigm-shift that we must now turn.

From Color Line to Culture Line

At the beginning of the twentieth century, W. E. B. DuBois, already regarded as a great African-American thinker and leader, predicted that the central problem of the twentieth century was going to be *the problem of the color line*. DuBois foresaw the century engulfed by racism, lynching, the white man's burden and what came to be subsequently known as apartheid. The twentieth century was overwhelmed by refugees on the run from racially and nationalistically instigated conflicts.[18]

Now that we are in the twenty-first century, the question has arisen whether the central problem of the twenty-first century was going to be the problem of *the culture line*. Has a transition occurred between a clash of identities (such as races) to a clash of values (such as cultural norms in conflict)? Are refugees of the twenty-first century already disproportionately *cultural* refugees?

Samuel Huntington is *not*, of course, a latter-day W.E.B. DuBois, but on the eve of the twenty-first century Huntington forecast that the twenty-first century was headed for a clash of *civilizations*.

He argued that now that the Cold War was over, future conflicts in the world would be less and less between states and ideological blocs and more between civilizations and cultural coalitions.

Huntington launched this debate with his article in FOREIGN AFFAIRS, New York, in 1993—an article that reverberated around the world. He followed this up with a major book on the same subject.[19]

While another African-American distinguished scholar at the University of Chicago, William Julius Wilson, had predicted earlier the declining significance of race,[20] because race was increasingly overshadowed by class and economics, Huntington predicted the rising salience of culture, overshadowing both race and culture. By a strange twist of destiny Pan-Africanism was in the lead from the politics of color-identity to the politics of shared cultural experience.

Was the intercultural experience of African-Americans a preparation for building bridges between civilizations?

Within the Black Atlantic, it began with the ultimate contradiction of W.E.B. DuBois. He was a man whose family name was French, whose actual physical appearance was virtually white, but whose allegiance was indisputably African. He was the reverse of William Blake's poem about the African child. For Blake (1757–1827) the child was black, but Oh good Lord, his soul was white. [*The Little Black Boy*]. For W.E.B. DuBois one could proclaim the reverse—that this man was white, but Oh good Lord, his soul was black. As we intimated earlier, DuBois's actual skin-color defied his real cultural allegiance. What the DuBois paradox taught us was that "blackness" could be a cultural identity rather than a physical appearance. As for Barack Obama, he was culturally brought up in a white home under his maternal grandmother. Even in multiracial Hawai'i he went to a school disproportionately white. For quite a while he was psychologically caught between a black skin and white culture. Was this paradox a psychological preparation for bridging civilizations?

Then there was the phenomenon of George Padmore's fascination with Marxism, alongside W.E.B. DuBois's response to historical materialism. Padmore was a black West Indian. Here were two major Pan-African thinkers who were involved in the politics of black identity and were at the same time drawn toward the ideas of an ethnic German Jew called Karl Marx. Padmore's most influential book was indeed originally titled *Pan-Africanism or Communism: The Coming Struggle in Africa*. It was an illustration of a huge ideological ambivalence between the politics of blackness, on the one hand, and the politics of class, regardless of race, on the other. The Black Atlantic was particularly exposed to the ideological winds of Western civilization. But were such black Westernizers like DuBois and Padmore destined to become bridge-builders between cultures?

On the whole, almost without realizing it, W.E.B. DuBois and George Padmore were products of the *Dual Heritage* (two converging civilizations). These Pan-Africanists were products of left-wing Western civilization, on the one hand, and left-wing Pan-Africanism, on the other. Without fully realizing it, DuBois and Padmore constituted a transition from the politics of black identity to the politics of multicultural ideologies.

Then came Kwame Nkrumah. He constituted the next stage of transition from the *dual heritage* of leftist Westernism and leftist Africanism to the new triple heritage of Africanity, Islam, and Western civilization. Kwame Nkrumah called this convergence *Consciencism*—identifying it as a synthesis of African tradition, Islamic heritage, and what Nkrumah called "Euro-Christian values." When he was very young, Barack Obama was briefly influenced by both Islam and Westernism. Was a multicultural upbringing a good counterculture to the tradition of presidential militarism?

The concept of "Global Africa" did not emerge until the 1980s. Was this concept first proclaimed in Mazrui's program 9 of his television series, *The Africans: A Triple Heritage*? Mazrui titled his concluding program "Global Africa." Mazrui promoted it as a synthesis of three civilizations—Africanity,

Islam, and Westernism. Was this a prelude to cultural globalization? Had his Kenyan father not abandoned Obama, he might have become a product of that Triple Heritage.

The concept of "Africa's Triple Heritage" came with Mazrui in the 1980s. But the fusion of three civilizations originated with Edward Blyden's *Christianity, Islam and the Negro Race* in the nineteenth century. It was then reincorporated in Kwame Nkrumah's *Consciencism* and was consummated in Mazrui's *The Africans: A Triple Heritage*. The struggle for an alliance of civilizations has continued.

A Conclusion: Between Nostradamus and Mister Obama

Michel de Nostredame, better known as Nostradamus, (1503–1566) has gone down in history as the most famous seer of the European Renaissance. His prophecies and predictions are being debated in books, articles, and television documentaries to the present day. Nostradamus is credited with having forecast aspects of the French revolution, the rise of Hitler, and even the September 11 attack on the World Trade Center in New York.

In this paper, we have placed two forecasts about black people within the tradition of Nostradamus. One was Robert F. Kennedy's prediction that the United States would elect a black president in 2008. Kennedy made this prediction in an interview on Voice of America in 1968 (the year of his own assassination). The election of Barack Obama to the presidency in 2008 has fulfilled Kennedy's prediction beyond wildest expectations. Hence, the play on words from Nostradamus to Mister Obama. Kennedy's forecast outshone the French astrologer of the sixteenth century.

The second prophecy was that made by [Mahatma] Mohandas Gandhi that the torch of Gandhi's "soul force" (nonviolent resistance) would be passed to black people. This Gandhian prophecy lacks the precision of Kennedy's forecast and is, therefore, closer to the ambiguities that have characterized the prophecies of Nostradamus.

However, in support of Gandhi's Afro-optimism about blacks as a vanguard of "soul force" is the phenomenon of Africa's short memory of hate. Africans are at least as violent as any other people, but Africans move toward forgiveness much faster than average. We have also drawn attention to Africa's impressive number of Nobel Laureates for peace since the second half of the twentieth century. Although Mahatma Gandhi himself was never awarded the Nobel Prize for Peace, some of his disciples in the black world (from Martin Luther King Jr. to Archbishop Desmond Tutu) became among the most famous Nobel Peace Laureates.

The population of India is greater than the populations of all fifty-three countries of Africa added together. But Africa has won many more Nobel Prizes than has India. Mahatma Gandhi was nominated more than once for the Nobel Peace Prize, but the influence of the British Empire in the 1930s and 1940s was still too strong to permit the award of a peace prize to a leader of an anticolonial movement like that of India.

Now the world is facing the staggering novelty of the first black president of the United States. As an American president, Barack Obama will become the most powerful black person in the history of civilization. This will not mean that Obama would be *greater* than Shaka Zulu of South Africa, or Menelik II of Ethiopia, or Usman Dan Fodio of Nigeria, or Ramses II of ancient Egypt. Obama is not yet so great, but from January 20, 2009, he would be exercising the immense leverage of the United States as a superpower. He will be more powerful than Africa's great icons added together.

But will Obama's performance eventually make him a great president? And will that greatness be in terms of "soul force" and avoidance of war?

We have indicated that every American president since Franklin D. Roosevelt has initiated either a full-scale war or at least an armed conflict. Indeed, presidents like Ronald Reagan and the two Bushes unleashed more than one war each.

The minimum test for Obama as an embodiment of Gandhi's soul force would be whether he can become the first US president since World War II to refrain from initiating any major conflict.

Of course Obama is inheriting two wars—the Iraqi War, which he would like to speedily end, and the Afghan war, which he may try to escalate. But neither war was started by Obama. Can he avoid *initiating* a military conflict with Iran, or North Korea, or Syria?

Will Obama be the first US president in seventy years to refrain from making a decision to *start* a new war? Will he avoid the temptation of equating "acting presidential" with readiness to initiate military force?

Mohandas Gandhi made his prediction about black nonviolence in 1936—when Franklin Roosevelt was president of the United States. Will Obama be the first US president since Gandhi made that prediction in 1936 to be a truly peace-loving commander-in-chief of the United States?

Gandhi's prophecy about black "soul force" hangs in the balance with the election of the most powerful black person in world history. Equipped with the power to destroy the world, would this particular black man, Barack Obama, start the process of truly saving it? There is no room for complacency, but is there still room for Afro-optimism and hope?

There are hopeful signs. These include Barack Obama's ambition to change the nature of domestic politics in the United States and transcend some of the deep divisions between parties, social classes, and generations.

Another Gandhian hope is manifested in Obama's remarkable record so far in initiating postracial politics in the United States. One measure of progress toward a postracial America is Barack Obama's own election as president.

A third hopeful sign is Barack Obama's background as a product of at least three civilizations (American, Africa, and Islam)—with a wider multiculturalism in Indonesia, when he was a child and in Hawai'i where he was born and spent much of his childhood. Obama is the first US president who is the son and grandson of Muslims on the paternal side. Indeed, he has a Swahili first name (Baraka), Muslim middle name, and African family name. Barack. Does Obama stand a chance of embodying Gandhian "soul force"? Amen.

Notes

1. An earlier version of this paper was presented under a different title as Keynote Address at the International Conference on "Engaging with a Resurgent Africa," sponsored by the Observer Research Foundation, New Delhi, India, November 20–21, 2008.
2. See *Harijan*, March 14, 1936.
3. Robert Kennedy's brother, John F. Kennedy, had broken the de-facto American taboo against electing a Roman Catholic president of the United States. Bobby thought the taboo against a black president would be broken forty years from 1968. See *The Washington Post*, May 27, 1968. The late Tim Russert reminded American television audiences in June 2008 of Robert Kennedy's prophecy.
4. *Young India*, 1924–1926 (madras: S. Ganesan, 1927), pp. 839–40. Consult also Pyarelal, "Gandhiji and the African Question," *Africa Quarterly*, Vol. II, No. 2, July–September 1962. See as well the selection from Gandhi titled "Mahatma Gandhi on Freedom in Africa," *Africa Quarterly*, Vol. I, No. 2, July–September 1961. For a more extensive discussion by Gandhi on nonviolence consult Gandhi, *Non-Violence in Peace and War* (2nd ed.), Ahmedabad: Navajivan Publishing House, 1944.
5. Jawaharlal Nehru, "Portuguese Colonialism: An Anachronism," *Africa Quarterly*, Vol. I, No. 3, October–December, 1961, p. 9. See also Nehru, "Emergent Africa," *Africa Quarterly*, Vol. I, No. I, April–June, 1961, pp. 7–9.
6. *Harijan*, March 14, 1936.
7. See Kenneth Kaunda, *Black Government*, Lusaka: United Society for Christian Literature, 1960.
8. *Autobiography*, p. 92.
9. *The Morning Telegraph*, 27, 1949.
10. See *Uganda Arqus*, May 29, 1964.
11. *Harijan*, October 14, 1939.
12. See Sudarshan Kapur, *Raising Up a Prophet: The African-American Encounter with Gandhi*, Boston: Beacon Press, 1992, pp. 89–90.

13. This was the appellation given to Kenyatta by British Governor Sir Patrick Renison, according to the Kenyan Ministry of External Affairs. http://www.mfa.go.ke/kenyatta.html. December 28, 2005.

14. Jomo Kenyatta, *Suffering without Bitterness*, Nairobi and Chicago: East African Publishing House and Northwestern University Press, 1968.

15. Relatedly, see Anthony Parsons, "From Southern Rhodesia to Zimbabwe, 1965–1985," *International Affairs*, November 1988, Vol. 9, No. 4, pp. 353–361; also see Victor De Waal, *The Politics of Reconciliation: Zimbabwe's First Decade*, London and Cape Town: Hurst and David Philip, 1981.

16. On the Biafra war, consult Herbert Ekwe-Ekwe, *The Biafra War: Nigeria and the Aftermath*, Lewiston, NY: E. Mellen Press, 1990; Peter Schwab, Ed. *Biafra*, New York, Facts on File, 1971; and Zdenek Cervenka, *The Nigerian War, 1967–1970. History of the War; Selected Bibliography and Documents*, Frankfurt: Bernard & Graefe, 1971.

17. On Mandela's meeting with Mrs. Verwoerd, see Anthony Sampson, *Mandela: The Authorized Biography*, New York: Knopf, distributed by Random House, 1999, p. 514.

18. There are more than 20 million asylum seekers, refugees, and others of concern to the UNHCR (over 5 million of whom are in Africa) according to the UNHCR website http://www.unhcr.org/cgi-bin/texis/vtx/basics/opendoc.htm?tbl=BASICS&id=3b028097c, as of January 1, 2006.

19. For the relevant article and early responses consult Samuel P. Huntington, et al., "The Clash of Civilizations: The Debate," New York: Foreign Affairs, 1993. The book-length expansion of Huntington's argument may be found in *The Clash of Civilizations and the Remaking of World Order*, New York: Simon & Schuster, 1996.

20. Consult William Julius Wilson, *The Declining Significance of Race: Blacks and Changing American Institutions*, Chicago: University of Chicago Press, 1978.

7

AFRICAN DIASPORAS, IMMIGRATION, AND THE OBAMA ADMINISTRATION

Paul Tiyambe Zeleza and Cassandra R. Veney

The record of the Obama administration on African and African diaspora immigration is built out of a long history. In trying to understand this history it is important to examine not only the role of state actors including the president and Congress, but also the attitudes of the general population, which influence and inform state policy and the activities of various political actors in the highly charged immigration debate. As African-Americans became enfranchised, their perspectives on immigration as well as the positions of their elected representatives and other political players increasingly began to count. African-American political influence ascended to unprecedented heights with the election of Barack Obama in 2008 as the country's first black president.

The dawn of the Obama administration was greeted with widespread enthusiasm among African-descended people in the United States, other parts of the diaspora, and across Africa. Four years later, what has been the performance of the Obama administration and how have its domestic and international policies affected African-descended peoples and Africa? In particular, how have immigration in general and the immigration of continental Africans and diasporan Africans fared under the Obama administration? This chapter focuses on two key issues.

First, it briefly traces the history of immigration policies in the United States and examines the attitudes of African-Americans to immigration. As is true among the general population, African-American attitudes have vacillated between support and opposition. Given the diversity of the African diaspora population in the United States, composed as it is of old and new diasporas that are divided and intersected by the complex dynamics of history, geography, nationality, race, ethnicity, class, gender, and generation, African-American responses to immigration have been equally complex, sometimes contradictory, and subject to periodic political shifts.

Second, the chapter explores the effect of the Obama administration immigration policies on African and African-descended immigrants, refugees, asylees, and asylum seekers. While the media has tended to focus on migrants from Mexico and other Latin American countries, the failure of immigration reform has affected immigrants from Africa and the African diaspora including Latin America itself. This chapter addresses laws and policies that the Obama administration inherited from the Clinton and Bush administrations such as the Patriotic Act and the treatment of Haitians who continue to be classified as economic migrants making it increasingly difficult for them to make asylum claims, the changes introduced by the Obama administration, and their effect on African and diasporan African immigrants.

African-Americans and the Changing Contours of Immigration

It cannot be overemphasized that the attitudes of African-Americans to immigration in general and the immigration of African-descended populations from the diaspora and continental Africa have always been complex, sometimes contradictory, and subject to change. At each historical moment, these attitudes reflect the prevailing composition of the African-American population, their political and socioeconomic conditions, overall American attitudes to immigration, and federal immigration policy, which often reproduces and reframes the politics of immigration at every level of American society and governance. Immigration has always been one of the most contentious issues in American politics, although the intensity of popular debate and discord over it has ebbed and flowed over time.

On the whole, as with much of the American population, African-American attitudes have veered between the restrictionist and liberalist. The accent of their position on either pole of this immigration spectrum has been conditioned by the particularity of the African-American experience. While the fears and realities of competition and displacement from immigration fuel restrictionist attitudes, African-Americans' enduring desire and struggle for inclusion and democratic citizenship often fosters support for liberal immigration policies.

The African-American community is of course not monolithic. Therefore, restrictionist and liberalist attitudes coexist and intersect, not always predictably, with the social, spatial, and ideological dynamics of class, gender, region, location, political orientation, and party affiliation. While the history of the massive and complex internal African-American migrations is well known, the scale of inflows from external migration into the demographic tapestry of the African-American population is not fully appreciated. Much has been written about the historical dynamics and multifaceted dimensions of the Great Migration between 1910 and 1970 that saw 6 million African-Americans migrate from the South to the Northeast, Midwest, and West, and the reverse New Great Migration to the "New South" that began at the turn of the 1970s (Lehman 1992; Sernett 1997; Arnesen 2002; Wilkerson 2011).

Not as much has been written about the continuous immigration from the African diaspora in the Americas to the United States before and after the abolition of slavery in 1863. As Ira Berlin (2010) has reminded us, African-American society and culture has been constituted out of four great migrations—the Atlantic slave trade, migration of enslaved Africans from the Atlantic world, the Great Migration from the South, and the more recent migrations from Africa and the Africa diaspora in the Americas and Europe.

Migrations from the Atlantic world to the United States go back to the seventeenth century when enslaved Africans were brought from the Caribbean especially the islands of Barbados, Jamaica, and Haiti. They were followed by growing numbers of free diasporan Africans who often became prominent in the African-American community. There were indeed periods when more people came from the Caribbean than from Africa through the Atlantic slave trade. After the civil war immigration from the Caribbean accelerated and included migrants from the Spanish territories of Puerto Rico and Cuba. African diaspora migrants also increasingly came from Central America, some of them offspring or offshoots of migration waves from the Caribbean to the region.

Altogether, between 1897 and 1937 more than 140,000 people of African descent from the Americas migrated to the United States and gradually became integrated into the African-American community. This is quite remarkable because this period was marked by increasingly restrictive policies against immigration for "people of color," culminating in the Immigration Act of 1924 that severely curtailed diasporan African and Asian immigration. The immigration doors reopened after the Second World War when tens of thousands of diasporan African immigrants from the Caribbean and Central and South America entered the country, followed to a smaller extent by rising waves of migrants from a decolonizing Africa.

The immigration floodgates for the diasporan Africans and Africans opened with the adoption of more liberal migration policies following the passage of the Civil Rights Act of 1964 and the Voting Rights Act of 1965 by the Johnson administration. In the 1960s, 470,000 Caribbean immigrants entered the country compared to 123,000 in the 1950s; the figure shot to 872,000 in the 1980s (Bryce-Laporte and Mortimer 1983; Foner 2001; Kasinitz 1992; Palmer 1995; Watkins-Owens 1996; Vickerman 1999; Waters 1999; Foner 2001). By 2000, there were between 2.6 and 3 million Caribbean immigrants of all races. In 2009, Afro-Caribbeans accounted for 1.7 million or 4.4% of the total

African-American population. The total black immigrant population that year was estimated at 3.3 million or 8.5% of the African-American population.

In recent decades, the African immigrant population has grown rapidly. The number of African-born immigrants rose from 35,355 in 1960 to 80,143 in 1970; 199,723 in 1980; 363,819 in 1990; 881,300 in 2000; and 1,606,914 in 2010 of whom 74.3% were classified as black. The African-born population increased its share of the total foreign-born population from 0.4% in 1960 to 0.8% in 1970, 1.4% in 1980, 1.8% in 1990, 2.8% in 2000, and 4% in 2010. The size of the African-American population varies between those who solely identify as black or African-American alone and those who identify as black or African-American in combination with other races. In 2010, the figure for the first category was 38.9 million (12.6% of the total population) and for the second 42 million (13.6% of the total population). Africans classified as black constituted 3% of the African-American population using the first figure (US Census Briefs 2011).

Altogether, the number of black immigrants in the United States rose from 816,000 (out of a total of 14,079,000) in 1980 to 1,447,000 in 1990 (out of 19,682,000) to 2,403,500 in 2000 (out of 31,133,000) and 3,267,000 in 2008–9 (out of 38,234,000) (Capps, McCabe, and Fix 2011). By the latter date, black immigrants from Africa constituted 33% of all black immigrants in the country, up from 7.8% in 1980, while the share of blacks from the Caribbean dropped from 55.5% to 52% during the same period, and that of black from other regions mostly Central and South America fell from 36.6% to 14.8%. Thus, the migration of people identified as black in the US Census is growing much faster from Africa than from other world regions. If current trends continue, by 2020 Africa will overtake the Caribbean as the largest source of the black immigrant population in the United States.

Clearly, the African-American population is constituted out of complex waves of internal and external migrations. Thus it is a diverse population, which at any point in time represents people of different historical and geographical origins. As might be expected for such a historically, spatially, socially, culturally, and politically varied community, African-American attitudes to immigration have been quite complex, frequently ambiguous, and subject to periodic shifts.

African-American sensitivity to immigration is evident from the early nineteenth century long before the abolition of slavery. According to Jeff Diamond (1998), in the first half of the nineteenth century increased immigration from Germany and later Ireland was seen as an unwelcome source of competition and displacement for free blacks from various occupational sectors in which they had established a presence. Relations between the European immigrants, who often quickly adopted American racism to bolster their occupational entry and class mobility, and African-Americans tended to be characterized by divisiveness and conflict that occasionally erupted into violence. Later in the century, the importation of unskilled labor from China elicited among African-Americans opposition to both Chinese immigration and white racism against Chinese immigrants. In the meantime, increased migration of free blacks from the Caribbean was generally welcomed for it boosted the ranks of free blacks. Indeed, many of the immigrants became professionals and political leaders in the black community.

The massive migrations to the United States between 1880 and 1920 provoked great consternation among African-Americans, which engendered strong restrictionist sentiments. Most of the 23 million immigrants came from southern and central Europe. This resulted in the decline of the overall proportion of the black population as well as significant occupational displacement. By 1910 African-Americans comprised 10.7% of the American population, down from 19% in 1810. Occupational displacement was mostly pronounced in the North where the new immigrants settled, but also crept in parts of the South that attracted some of the immigrants.

Efforts by employers to reduce wages by pitting black and immigrant white workers, superimposed on the racist regressions and violence of Jim Crow reconstruction, reinforced black antagonism to immigration. By the 1920s even progressive black leaders such as W.E.B. Dubois and A. Philip Randolph who had previously espoused liberal attitudes to immigration welcomed legislative immigration limits. While some in the black press and among African-American leaders criticized the racialized restrictions of the 1924 National Origins Act, most overlooked its shortcomings and the regime of forced deportations against Mexicans attracted to the booming agricultural economy of Texas and California.

After the Second World War, the escalating struggles for civil rights facilitated the deracialization and liberalization of immigration. The landmark civil rights legislation of the mid-1960s coincided with the passage of the Hart-Celler Act in 1965, which overturned the national immigration quota system operational since 1924. This ushered the largest wave of immigration since the late nineteenth century and a historic shift in migration to the United States from Europe to the global South led by Latin America and Asia. By 2000, the foreign-born population reached 31.1 million, up from 9.7 million in 1960 and 14.1 million in 1980. In 2000, the relative size of the foreign-born population (12.3% of the total) was comparable to the 1920s (13.3% in 1920 and 11.8% in 1930). Four-fifths of the foreign-born population in 2000 originated in Latin America (51.7%), Asia (26.4%), and Africa (2.8%), while 15.8% came from Europe and 2.7% from Northern America. In 1920, Europe accounted for 85.7% of the immigrants and for more than half until 1970 (61.7%) (Gibson and Jung 2006).

Despite this explosive growth, in the late 1970s and early 1980s what Espenshade and Hampstead (1996: 540) call neorestrictionist sentiments began to emerge, which is often attributed to "growing economic insecurity, concerns with migrants' undesirable cultural traits, and an increase in illegal immigration." Their research and that of many others has demonstrated correlations between feelings toward immigrants and economic trends; recessions and increased unemployment seem to correspond to rising anti-immigration sentiments and vice-versa. In immigration surveys, it is clear attitudes are tied to various demographic characteristics of the respondents including race and ethnicity, class and income, age and gender, ideological orientation and party affiliation, and region or location of residence, as well as the relative importance they place on America's place in the world and the symbolic politics of American identity. Proponents of group threat theory maintain that Americans who believe immigrants threaten national unity, security, and prosperity are more likely to oppose immigration (Wilson 2001), while contact theorists maintain that intimate and continuous interactions with alien groups tends to promote more positive views. In reality, as Shang Ha (2010 30) argues, "the dynamics of intergroup conflict operate at different levels of geography." Depending on the racial context, proximity in neighborhoods can engender lower levels of antagonism than racial diversity at larger county, metropolitan, or state levels.

Espenshade and Hampstead (1996: 555) found that "minority respondents, especially Asians and African Americans, desire higher levels of immigration than non-Hispanic whites. . . . On the other hand, Hispanics are not significantly more likely to want more immigrants than Anglos." An overview of public opinion surveys shows that during the 2000s the majority of Americans held positive views of immigration, favored legalization for undocumented immigrants whose numbers reached an estimated 8.5 million in 2000 rising to 12 million in 2008, and generally did not support get-tough measures on immigration enforcement. In the elections of 2006 and 2008, immigration ranked in fifth or sixth place as a priority among voters when weighed against other issues. Nevertheless, the political effect of race, immigration, and America's changing electorate is expected to grow (Frey 2008).

Robert Suro (2009: 8) observes, "On both the size of immigration flows and the basic judgment on immigrants' impact, non-Hispanic whites and blacks express similar views." He notes negative views of immigration tend to be held by those who are older, male, white, conservative, Republican, and lack a college degree. Thus the attitudes and effect of immigration on African-American well-being is more complex than often described. The widely held assumption that immigrant competition harms African-Americans economically and socio-psychologically has been contested in some studies on the effect of Hispanic immigrant population growth. According to Taylor and Schroeder (2010: 492) "sharing a location does not necessarily engender competition. For one thing, large immigrant populations can expand certain employment opportunities. For another, enclave economies can insulate immigrants and African Americans against competition from the other group." Also, "contrary to speculation in the academic and popular press, our findings provide scant evidence that local Hispanic presence or population growth is deleterious to the social psychological outlook of African Americans" (Taylor and Schroeder 2010: 502).

African-American attitudes are influenced by the origins and behavior of the immigrants as can be seen in the cases of Southeast Asian, Cuban, and Haitian refugees. Many of the Asian migrants in the 1970s were refugees from the US imperial debacle in Southeast Asia. "African-American leadership," writes Diamond (1998: 458), "which had emerged out of the principled humanitarian struggle of the Civil Rights movement, supported accepting the refugees. . . . While many blacks came increasingly to resent the Southeast Asians and what sometimes appeared preferential treatment accorded them, black leaders continued to defend a liberal asylum policy."

African-American sentiments were particularly strong on Haitian refugees, who many felt were not treated as fairly as white Cuban refugees. While Cuba has a large African population, the majority of Cuban refugees following the 1959 revolution were white. African-Americans felt little affinity with them, and some resented the added competition they brought especially in Florida for scare jobs, public services, and political power (Reitan 1999). However, African-Americans identified racially with the Haitians. The Haitian "boat people" came to embody some of the most negative stereotypes against refugees ingrained in racist prejudices against the first black republic in the Americas. The pathologized images of the Haitian refugees seemed to erase the fact that previous waves of Haitian migrants were, successively, from elite, middle-class, and lower middle-class backgrounds and had made significant contributions to their new communities of residence. Relations between African-Americans and Haitian immigrants had their tensions rooted in differences of history, language, culture, and identity (Remy 1996; Zephir 1996).

Equally complex were African-American views on the rising immigration from Latin America. Popular and political attitudes were framed by the long history of diasporan African migration from the region and the need for political solidarity among African-American and Hispanic leaders. Throughout the 1980s and 1990s the growing Congressional Black and Hispanic Caucuses worked together for comprehensive and progressive immigration legislation and reform, positions often supported by many African-American politicians especially city mayors who sought to court the growing Hispanic vote as well as major civil rights organizations such as the NAACP and the National Urban League. However, among some African-Americans, a minority to be sure, moral opposition to restrictionist and racist immigration bills was sometimes trumped by concerns for competition, both real and perceived. Competition was real for those in low-skilled service sector jobs. In the African-American press, positions both for and against immigration restrictions were widely expressed, although "the opinion pages and editorials also frequently took pro-immigration stands" (Diamond 1998: 463).

The growth of immigration from Central and South America, regions with their own complicated racial histories and regimes, brought its challenges. Not only are the immigrant populations from these regions highly racialized, but they also came into a society with a rigid binary racial boundary system. While the racial systems in the United States and Latin America differ in some of their permutations, in both blackness lies at the bottom of the racial hierarchy. For Hispanic immigrants, therefore, including those who are phenotypically black there are strong pressures to distance themselves from US blackness. This often entails distancing themselves from African-Americans.

Some light-skinned Hispanics try to reposition themselves into whiteness as various ethnic European groups did in the past, while those who can't or don't want to do so seek to blur US racial boundaries and reconstitute themselves into an alternative Latino or Hispanic racial designation. Gravitation toward whiteness is reinforced by white America's apparent preferences for Hispanics over African-Americans. Thus Hispanic distancing from blackness is facilitated by the dialectics of internal and external opinions and processes among Hispanics and non-Hispanic whites. Data from the 2003 New Immigrant Survey showed that "the majority of the sample identified as White (79 percent), with a smaller percentage identifying as non-White (7.5 percent). About 14 percent of the sample did not identify with any of the listed races" (Frank et al. 2010: 388). This has led some scholars to argue that while Hispanic immigration has modified the historic binary color line in the United States and reinforced trends toward a multiracial model, it has done little to shift the position of African-Americans in the country's racial hierarchy. Indeed, it heralds the reemergence of a new black–white color line reinscribed as black–nonblack (Marrow 2009; Bean et al. 2009).

The campaign and election of President Obama in 2008 underscored the growth of postcolonial African migrations to the United States. The son of a Kenyan father, and a self-identified African-American, in his personal and political biography he embodied the intersected histories of old and new African migrations in the country. His victory electrified the old and new diasporas in the United States, Africans on the continent, and diasporan Africans around the world. The rapid increase in African immigration from the mid-1960s owed much to the doors opened by the civil rights movement and advocacy by African-American leaders. In turn, African-American communities served as crucibles of political, social, and consumer acculturation to American society for African immigrants. For their part, the latter facilitated the expansion and refashioning of diasporan African and black identities.

An example of consumer acculturation includes a fascinating study of how new Kenyan immigrants in a large city in the South found their needs for hair care, church service, night clubs, music, and socialization into American society met through African-American consumer products and practices (Wamwara-Mbugua et al. 2008). The role of African immigrants in redefining shades of blackness while reframing racial and religious identities can be seen in the effect of West African Muslim immigrants on their African-American community in Harlem, New York City. As the former negotiate their new and old identities of being simultaneously African, Muslim, and American in their daily lives and public cultural performances, the latter are compelled to readjust "their sense of themselves . . . to rethink their idea of Africa and their relationship to it" (Abdullah 2009: 53; also see Kane 2011).

To be sure, relations between the new African immigrants and African-Americans have their fair share of tensions and conflicts. As Zeleza (2010) has argued elsewhere, depending on the social and spatial arenas in which they interact, the dynamics that mediate their interactions, and the content and processes of the interactions relations between the old and new diasporas are characterized by mutual antagonism, ambivalence, acceptance, adaptation, and assimilation. For immigrants from Africa and African diaspora, this is the broad context in which the immigration policies of Obama administration have been enacted.

The Obama Administration and Refugee and Immigration Policies

President Barack Obama inherited a number of policies, programs, and issues from the Bill Clinton and George W. Bush administrations that included immigration reform, the war on crime and drugs, and the war on terror. However, many African and African-descended people believed that somehow the president would be able to chart a different course—a course that would help and not hinder their ability to apply for refugee status, political asylum, and immigrant status. Some believed that due to his more recent immigrant background through his father who was born in Kenya, he could readily identify with them (Kimenyi 2012). That overall has not been the case for several reasons. First, most presidential candidates in recent years have campaigned on promises to either enact or overturn immigration legislation and candidate and then president Obama has not deviated from this pattern. Second, politicians and the media take these promises seriously and pass these messages on to the public without fully explaining the role of the legislative and executive branches in crafting and enacting immigration reform. Third, President Obama inherited federal immigration legislation (Immigration and Nationality Act) that sets overall immigration policy. In recent years, various states have enacted immigration legislation that can be overturned by the Supreme Court if it decides to hear a case and then rules the law or a part of it is unconstitutional. Fourth, although the president can take the responsibility to craft immigration bills, for them to be enacted into law, they must pass both houses of the legislative branch, which was virtually impossible under a Republican Senate and House that made it clear soon after his election that they would not co-operate with immigration reform legislation. Therefore, the last three years have not witnessed any new immigration laws executed by President Obama, rather, the Obama administration has worked within federal immigration laws enacted not just by the Bush administration but also by the Clinton administration. This has limited his ability to fulfill campaign promises. However these limitations are not adequately addressed by the media or his administration. However, he has executive powers that he can exercise in an attempt to circumvent federal laws and Supreme Court rulings in his efforts to enact immigration reform such as the 2012 directive that will offer a stay of deportation for some individuals who were brought to the country by their parents. Moreover, the Department of Homeland Security (DHS), which was established under the George W. Bush administration, is responsible for enforcing immigration laws (deportations, arrests, detentions, returns, and removals) regardless of President Obama's position on the laws. The following sections of the chapter are an attempt to examine and analyze immigration policies inherited by President Obama and examine the effects on Africans and the African Diaspora in the United States. In addition, it will examine policies solely adopted by the Obama administration with a particular emphasis on Haitian immigrants.

To fully understand Obama's position on immigration reform, the positions he took as a senator are worth examining. In other words, if people hoped that Obama would move in a radical direction away from the Bush administration's position on immigration, it is evident from his senate record that would not be the case. Dorsey and Diaz-Barriga (2007: 96) argue that Senator Obama was in line with the Republicans and Democrats and "that Obama's immigration platform centers on three concepts: border security, employer accountability, and earned citizenship." In other words, if one wants to understand President Obama's stance and policies toward immigration, one only needs to look at his record in the Senate. For example, Senator Obama was in favor of policies that can be characterized as militarized in their efforts to punish the undocumented immigrants and those who hired them. Hence, he favored an enhanced border patrol and sanctions against employers who hired immigrants without documentation. His position on how undocumented immigrants could adjust their status and become legal immigrants is basically the position he continues to hold, and it is touted in his executive authorization to allow undocumented immigrants who came to the United States as children to remain and obtain work authorization that will be discussed later.

As Barack Obama campaigned for the presidency, the issue of immigration was on the minds of some voters, and therefore, it had to be addressed. Again, presidential candidate Obama did not deviate far from his position in the senate. He continued to advocate "immigration reform in terms of national security, the rule of law, and fairness" (Dorsey and Diaz-Barriga 2007: 100). In other words, the pathway to citizenship would come with a cost—penalties and taxes and those who qualified would have to learn English (Aguirre 2008–09).

The above examination of Obama's position on immigration and immigration reform serves as a backdrop to what has transpired since he assumed the presidency in 2009. His fundamental position on immigration and immigration reform remains unchanged. However, there are exceptions. He was in favor of the Development Relief and Education for Alien Minors Act (DREAM Act) that would have allowed undocumented individuals who were brought to the country by their parents as children to remain in the country and avoid deportation (Vargas 2012). This would have done very little to create a path to citizenship for those African immigrants who were twenty one and older and who had not lived in the United States for less than five years (Vargas 2012). Although most African immigrants enter the United States through legal channels and therefore acquire the legal right to remain—most of the applicants have an immediate relative in the United States— "there are about 200,000 unauthorized Black Africans in the United States, out of a total unauthorized population of 11 million or more" (Capps, McCabe, and Fix 2011: 6). For example in 2010, the overwhelming percentage of African immigrants (95%) "gained permanent lawful residence . . . through family relations . . . diversity visa program . . . as refugees and asylees and over 860,000

African immigrants gained lawful permanent residence in the United States between 2001 and 2010" (McCabe 2011). Nevertheless, even if he wanted to implement immigration reform, it would have been virtually impossible given the unwillingness of the Republicans in the Senate to engage in politics over the issue, which involves compromise. The DREAM Act, which should be called a bill, dragged on in Congress for ten years even though the House of Representatives passed it in 2010. The bill never became an act after it was blocked in the Senate by a Republican-led filibuster in 2010. The sixty-required votes to end the filibuster were not forthcoming; therefore, the bill died in the Senate.

In 2012, President Obama took matters into his hands by initiating a directive that will allow those who would have been covered under the DREAM Act to escape deportation. Many Obama critics in government and the media and ordinary citizens accused the president of overstepping his presidential powers by implementing a bill that was never passed into law in an attempt to shore up the Latino vote for the presidential election in November 2012. While most of the undocumented people in the United States are from Mexico and on the surface it appears that this directive would help them, a closer examination leads one to conclude that Mexicans are not the only undocumented group in the United States and the executive action may help African and African-descended immigrants who include many from Latin, Central, and South America in the short run, but in the long run it does not provide permanent legal status (Lovett 2012). First, individuals must meet qualifications that include: "must have arrived in the U.S. before their 16th birthday, are 30 or younger, have been living here at least five years, are in school or graduated or served in the military. They also must not have a criminal record or otherwise pose a safety threat" (Caldwell 2012). As stated above, most Africans reside in the country legally because they entered the country legally—many entered as refugees, or they were granted asylum after their arrival (Capps, McCabe, and Fix 2011. Second, for those who qualify, the deportation orders would be halted for two years and work authorization would be granted for two years. Even if President Obama was reelected, individuals would have to reapply for a stay of deportation along with the work authorization every two years. Because of the backlash Republican lawmakers receive, if there is any hint of a softening of their positions on illegal immigrants from their constituents, it is unlikely that a Republican president would continue to enforce this directive if President Obama was not reelected. Third, cases will be evaluated on an individual basis. This entails a very long process during which applicants will continue to live in limbo while they wait for their cases to be cleared.

Where does this leave African and African-descended immigrants and refugees? It leaves them basically in the same position where they were under the Bush administration, and in some instances, their circumstances have worsened under President Obama in terms of lack of protection and an increase in human rights violations as immigrants both legal and illegal have been deemed criminal and the immigration system has been militarized to fall in line with the war on terror. The infrastructure put into place under Bush following the terrorist attacks of 9/11 has not been dismantled or improved to lessen the ability to violate African and African-descended immigrants' human rights. Instead, "new border security and law enforcement initiatives, heightened visa controls and screening of international travelers and would-be immigrants, the collection and storage of information in vast new interoperable databases used by law enforcement and intelligence agencies are the order of the day" (Chishti and Bergeron 2011). That infrastructure, put into place for national security, includes the DHS, the US Citizenship and Immigration Services, the US Immigration and Customs Enforcement (ICE), and the US Customs and Border Protection. County jails that house asylum seekers and those arrested for violent and nonviolent crimes have taken on new importance following 9/11 (Mittelstadt, Speaker, Meissner, and Chishti 2011). It is unfortunate that the media and politicians in the United States have portrayed immigration or rather illegal immigrants as "Mexican," and therefore, they are the concern of Mexican-Americans and those states where they reside. However, there are thousands of Africans and African-descended immigrants who reside in the United States both legally and illegally, and so policies inherited and further implemented by the Obama administration are overdue for an analysis and examination. The following sections of the chapter will attempt to accomplish this goal.

African Refugees Admitted under President Obama

Africans admitted to the United States as refugees have been a fairly recent phenomenon that began in the 1980s as thousands of people fled the civil war and drought in Ethiopia. Other refugees followed in the 1980s and 1990s from Somalia, Liberia, Sierra Leone, and Sudan. Although the continent is one of the world's largest refugee-producing arenas, the numbers of refugees admitted to the United States remains rather small. It is the president and Congress that set the admission ceilings for each region (Kerwin 2011). If Africans and the African diaspora believed that those numbers would increase under President Obama, they were mistaken. First, it is the president alone who determines ceilings for each region. This is done in consultation with Congress that continues to wield the power of the purse in terms of appropriating funds for refugees' resettlement. Second, it is important to understand the refugee admissions process which is protracted and lengthy and has gotten worse after 9/11 with additional security screening enacted under the Bush administration. Refugees from particular countries such as Somalia have a very difficult time filing successful asylum claims as the suspicion of terrorist associations looms large over their applications. Third, "the multiple arms of the federal government, states, localities, and NGOs" make for a convoluted process as the government wants to ensure the validity of the asylum claim along with the applicant's identity (Kerwin 2011: 5). It is difficult for most African refugees to have at their disposal often in a refugee camp the necessary documentation that includes date of birth, place of birth, and education. All of this information must be checked and verified and that may take months and even years. In addition, each applicant must provide detailed documentation to support their claim of persecution if she or he is processed under the P1 category, which few Africans are.

The categories the US refugee resettlement program were not defined by President Obama. Third, the actual numbers admitted have been lower due to allegations of fraud by African applicants who applied under family reunification that resulted in the closure of the P3 program in March 2008— no new applications were accepted and those under review in Kenya, Ethiopia, and Uganda had to undergo DNA testing (US Department of State 2009). It was not the case that Africa was signaled out, applications for all regions and nationalities were no longer accepted. However, other nationalities had a better chance of admissions because they could qualify under P1 and P2 processing. Most Africans are processed under the P3 program as "fewer than five percent of P3 cases are processed outside of Africa" (US Department of State 2009). Furthermore, not all African countries qualified for this program. For example, in 2009, only Burundi, Central African Republic, Democratic Republic of Congo, Eritrea, Ethiopia, Somalia, Sudan, and Zimbabwe were included (US Department of State 2009). The question should be asked why so many Africans are admitted under Priority 3 (P3) guidelines and not Priority 1 (P1) or Priority 2 (P2). This is because P1 processing is done for individual applicants who are referred by the US embassies, the United Nations High Commissioner for Refugees (UNHCR), or nongovernmental organizations. P2 admissions are done for refugees who are of special interest to the United States and are recognized as groups—the Lost Boys of Sudan, the Somali Bantu. Again, these groups are recognized by the US Department of State in consultation with the UNHCR, other US government departments, and nongovernmental organizations (US Department of State 2009). The suspension of P3 refugee processing occurred before President Obama was elected. The Department of State through its Bureau of Population, Migration and Refugees (PRM) "published proposed rules that would change its procedures for processing P3 applicants, including mandatory DNA testing to prove claimed family relationships" (Esbenshade 2010: 4).

This should have caused immediate alarm if these rules only applied to Africans. As Esbenshade (2010: 4) argues "how family relationships are proved" needs to be examined to determine if and under what circumstances they should apply to African applicants who may and do form family relationships that do not correspond with American ones generally and refugee realities in particular. There are many instances where unaccompanied minors are "adopted" by African refugees, especially in refugee camps for many reasons. Often during flight, children get separated from their parents and families in haste to escape civil war and other violence. They are often taken in by other refugee families and become their children in every way, although they are not legally adopted in a way that is acceptable for P3 admissions. In addition, many African parents have lost their children either during conflict, on the journey as they seek sanctuary in a second country or even after they find sanctuary in a refugee camp. Some of these refugees "adopt" children to replace the ones they have lost (Veney 2007). Furthermore, many African communities do not base kinship on blood ties. According to the PRM, these children do not meet the definition of a derivative relation and should not qualify for family reunification. Most African refugees qualify for resettlement to the United States under P3 admissions or family reunification. This means that "already settled refugees who are 18 or older—called "anchors"—can request that their immediate refugee relatives (parents, spouses, and unmarried children under 21) be considered for refugee admission. The immediate relative is the "primary applicant" in the P3 cases and is allowed to include his or her spouse and children under 21, who are the "derivative" beneficiaries. While the primary applicant must establish a refugee claim, the derivatives are joining in the application and do not need to show persecution" (Esbenshade 2010: 5).

The inability to take advantage of P3 refugee admissions has had adverse effects on the refugees in the United States and their family members in Africa, and the establishment of required deoxyribonucleic acid (DNA) testing under a pilot project in 2008 has not helped matters (Jordan 2008). It was the State Department's contention that too many cases for family reunification in East Africa, mainly Kenya were fraudulent. Therefore, the reliance on documentation to support cases such as birth and marriage certificates along with adoption papers, baptismal and school records, and testimony from the anchor relative in the United States and the applicant in Kenya was not sufficient enough to make the case for family bonds (US Citizenship and Immigration Services n.d.). Under the guise of protecting national security and fighting the war on terrorism, Somali and Ethiopian applicants were initially examined as the US government feared persons with ties to Al Qaeda would enter the country as refugees (US Citizenship and Immigration Services n.d.). After high levels of fraud were detected, the programs expanded to include Ethiopia, Liberia, Uganda, Ghana, Guinea, Gambia, and Côte d'Ivoire (US Department of State 2009). The actual number of fraudulent cases is in dispute because even when people refused to submit to DNA testing or they did not show up for their interview, these cases were considered fraudulent. In other words, a case can consist of several family members, but if one person refuses to take the test or does not appear for the interview, the entire case is considered fraudulent. This makes the program appear as if it is targeting Africans, and their ability to be processed for admissions appears to be undermined as only the derivatives were tested. It makes one wonder why the relationships between anchor relatives in the United States and the primary applicants in Africa were not tested.

Finally, the number of African refugees admitted is often lower than the ceiling due to the numbers who are unable to be processed in a timely manner, which has been made worse by the suspension of P3 processing. Nevertheless, the ceiling set for all African refugee admissions is extremely low and has actually decreased since Obama became president. Again, the president alone does not determine refugee admissions; it is done in conjunction with Congress, and it is unlikely that during a very anti-immigrant climate President Obama could have convinced Congress to raise the number for African refugees. During Bush's first four years in office, the allocation for African refugees was 20,000 (FY 2001), 22,000 (FY 2002), 20,000 (FY 2003), and 30,000 (FY 2004). The overall refugee ceiling under Bush was 80,000 in FY 2001 and 70,000 for FY 2001–2005. The refugee admission ceiling for Africa under Obama was 12,000 (FY 2009), 15,500 (FY 2010), 15,000 (FY 2011), and 12,000 (FY 2012). It is important to note that the "2011 ceiling is almost 25 percent lower than the average for the previous decade (2000–2010)" (Esbenshade 2010: 7). From FY 2009–2011, the total refugee ceiling was 80,000 and it was reduced to 76,000 for FY 2012. Moreover, it is important to point out that the actual number of arrivals does not increase even when the ceiling is increased because cases in the previous year's pipeline are folded into the new admissions numbers. For example, out of the 15,000 refugees allocated for Africa in FY 2011, 7,685 were actually admitted—a majority of them came from four countries—Eritrea (2,032), Somalia (3,161), Democratic Republic of Congo (977), and Ethiopia (560) (US Department of State, January 31, 2012). In addition, FY 2012 has an admissions number of 12,000 refugees; however, 8,500 of that number is from the previous year. This means that the possibility of getting 12,000 "new" refugees is null and void because only 3,500 are really "new" refugees. Furthermore, legislation that President Obama inherited during the post-9/11 era serves to restrict the number of African and African-descended refugees and immigrants—mainly the US Patriot Act, which makes it more difficult for those suspected of terrorist activity to be admitted. Also the REAL ID raises the bar for individuals who are seeking asylum to prove that they have a fear of persecution based on their membership in a racial, religious, nationality or social group or when due to their political opinion they fear persecution (Kerwin 2011). Asylum seekers are now placed in detention as if they have committed a criminal offense while they wait for their cases to be adjudicated.

Haitian Immigrants and the Obama Administration

As stated earlier, the Obama administration inherited immigration policies from the Clinton and Bush administrations, but it is important to point out that immigration policies did not automatically became harsher after 9/11. They had begun to get harsher in 1996 under Clinton because this was when the government began to arrest and detain people regardless of their immigration status (Venters, McNeely, and Keller 2009). According to Human Rights First (2010) "of particular concern are policies that mandate on-going detention, without so much as a hearing, of certain nonviolent offenders, lawful permanent residents, and individuals who committed offenses decades ago. ICE also detains many people even after court rulings in their favor; people granted refugee status who fail to do proper paperwork." In other words, legal immigrants, undocumented persons, and asylum seekers under the Illegal Immigration Reform and Immigrant Responsibility Act and Antiterrorism and Effective Death Penalty Act signed into law by Clinton are also criminalized, and therefore, they can be rounded up, detained, and finally deported under expedited removal proceedings (Veney 2009). The criminal justice system and not civil law is now responsible for legal and undocumented immigrants as if they were the same as rapists, murders, kidnapers, and armed robbers. In sum, after 1996 only citizens are really safe from immigration detentions and deportations. One group of African-descended immigrants will be highlighted in this section—Haitians.

There has been ongoing debate over how the US government treats Cubans and Haitians in their attempts to enter the country leaving some Haitians and their advocates to believe the policies are biased and racist. Until recently, most Cubans who attempted to enter the country were admitted because they fled from a communist state. Haitians, however, were classified as economic migrants who did not meet the definition of refugee. Therefore, when a boatload or boatloads of Haitians are sighted by the US Coast Guard, they are often interdicted and sent back to Haiti after interviews reveal that they do not have a well-founded fear of persecution. From 2009–2011, 3,826 Haitians have been interdicted and repatriated to Haiti whereas 1,609 have been returned to Cuba, 35 from China, and with all of the alarm surrounding undocumented Mexicans only 204 were interdicted and returned during this period. Haitians were granted a reprieve by being eligible for Temporary Protected Status after the devastating earthquake in 2010. Haitians who had entered the country at the time of the earthquake (January 12, 2010) could apply (after paying a fee) for Temporary Protected Status (TPS) for eighteen months. TPS is a designated category determined by Congress and can be used at the president's discretion by his attorney general (Kerwin 2011). For those Haitians who had criminal records, they were still considered deportable (Immigration Policy Center 2010). It did very little to help this population in the long run. They still remained undocumented. What seemed like a very callous approach by the Obama administration following the earthquake was the continuation of the policy to interdict and repatriate Haitians who attempted to enter the country eight days after the earthquake (Kerwin 2011). The Obama administration was urged not only to halt this practice but also to create a program similar to the one created for Cubans that would allow family members in Haiti to join their families in the United States. These are people who have been approved by the DHS but still must wait for years to be reunited with their relatives (Forester 2012). We know that federal laws limit the power that the president has in enacting new immigration reforms and policies, and some Republican Congressional members have made it clear that they will not support any legislation that he wants to pass. However, he was not obstructed by Congress unlike his efforts to pass the DREAM Act—Republicans and Democrats urged the president to adopt a program for Haitians similar to the one for Cubans. He simply refused to institute a similar program for Haitians that the Bush administration did for Cubans in 2007. President Obama has the power to assist Haitian asylum seekers by abolishing the "shout test," which only applies to Haitians who seek to enter the country by sea. This policy was passed down to the president, but he does not have to continue using it—he is not bound by federal immigration laws to enact the policy. This policy means that if Haitian asylum seekers do not physically and verbally resist repatriation, their cases will not be considered. This is against international laws that the United States is a signatory to such as the 1951 UN Convention Relating to the Status of Refugees and its 1967 Protocol. The United States is required to allow asylum seeker entry into the country to make their claim for asylum (Veney 2006).

This chapter has attempted to demonstrate that the pattern of migrations for Africans and the African diaspora to the United States has been complex. The historic African diaspora's attitude toward immigration in general and African and African diasporan immigration in particular has varied over time depending on the perceived advantages and disadvantages that the new migrants offered. What is clear from this chapter is that as the historic African diaspora gained civil rights through their efforts and legislative acts, a political space was opened for the extension of immigration opportunities for African and African-descended populations. Therefore, the expectations thrust upon President Obama to advocate fairer and more open immigration policies were expected regardless of the role played by Congress, which as of late has been cold and hostile toward immigrants, especially the undocumented. In addition, states and even local governments have attempted to implement restrictive immigration policies. This chapter has demonstrated that on one hand President Obama's powers to influence immigration policies are limited due to federal legislation that he cannot overturn. On the other hand, he has some powers such as the use of executive orders to stay deportations, grant work authorization, extend TPS, and allow asylum seekers to enter the country. His record on exercising these powers in ways that would help African and African-descended immigrants is mixed, especially concerning Haitians.

In conclusion, President Obama's recent trip in late June to early July 2013 to three countries in Africa—Senegal, South Africa, and Tanzania—reinforces the argument that an American president who has a Kenyan father will not necessarily or automatically advance a progressive African agenda whether it is predicated on fair immigration policies, economic growth, development, or stronger ties between Africa and its diaspora. President Obama missed the opportunity to identify with and strengthen US–Africa relations on a couple of fronts. First, the president waited until his second administration to visit the continent. To some, his actions were the equivalent of too little too late especially in light of the many visits by Chinese officials in recent years. It is worth noting that soon after Chinese president Xi Jinping assumed the presidency, he visited three African countries. In other words, unlike President Obama, he signaled to African leaders and Africans that Africa–China relations are central to the country's economic, diplomatic, political, and cultural relations. This gives Africans and their leaders the impression that Africa–China relations are just as important as China's relations to the United States, Europe, Latin America, and any other region. However, the lateness of Obama's visit and its brevity (June 27–July 2) leave the impression that Africa is an afterthought. The entire continent of Africa is not as important as a single country such as Israel.

Second, President Obama, regardless of the reason, did not visit Kenya—the country where his father was born. He chose rather to visit the neighboring country of Tanzania. Clearly, the Kenyan government, politicians, and nationals found this offensive. President Obama would have gained a lot of support and goodwill in Kenya, East Africa, Africa, and with Africans and African-descended people throughout the diaspora if he had visited his father's homeland. His refusal to do so gives the impression that he deliberately distances himself from Kenya in particular and Africa in general. The reason provided by the Obama administration for not visiting Kenya was the indictments by the International Criminal Court of the recently elected president Uhuru Kenyatta and other officials for their alleged involvement in political violence surrounding the results of the 2007 presidential elections. This appears to run counter to the very bedrock of the American judicial system—one is assumed innocent until proven guilty.

The last point relates to the first point in terms of the timing of his visit particularly to South Africa. By the time President Obama visited South Africa, former president Nelson Mandela was in ill health and was hospitalized preventing a one-on-one visit. Therefore, and rightly so, the South Africans at all levels were focused on their beloved leader's well being. Whatever the importance and significance of the visit, it was overshadowed by the world's attention on Mandela. Instead of a personal visit with Mandela, we saw President Obama visiting Mandela's former jail cell at Robben Island. The opportunity for these two important leaders for Africans and its diaspora to meet will probably never occur again. Finally, at the end of his quick trip to Tanzania, former president George W. Bush joined him to show respect for those who lost their lives in the 1998 terrorist attacks against the US embassy in Dar es Salaam. This should have been President Obama's solo moment to indicate his connections to Africa and his convictions to Africa as the current president and as an African-descended president.

References

Abdullah, Z. 2009. "African 'Soul Brothers' in the 'Hood: Immigration, Islam, and the Black Encounter," *Anthropological Quarterly* 82, 1: 37–62.

Aguirre, A., Jr. 2008–09. "Immigration on the Public Mind: Immigration Reform in the Obama Administration," *Social Justice* 35, 4: 4–11.

Arnesen, E. 2002. *Black Protest and the Great Migration: A Brief History with Documents*. Bedford: St. Martin's Press.

Bean, F. D., C. Feliciano, J. Lee, and J. Van Hook. 2009. "The New U.S. Immigrants: How Do They Affect Our Understanding of the African-American Experience." *The ANNALS of the American Academy of Political and Social Science* 621, 1: 202–220.

Berlin, Ira. 2010. *The Making of African America: The Four Great Migrations*. New York: Penguin Books.

Bruno, A. 2012. *Refugee Admissions and Refugee Policy*. Washington, DC: Congressional Research Service. Available at www.fas.org/sgp/crs/misc/RL31269.pdf.

Bryce-Laporte, R., and D. Mortimer, eds. 1983. *Caribbean Immigrants to the United States*, 2nd ed. Washington, DC: Smithsonian Institution.

Caldwell, A. A. 2012. "AP Exclusive: Internal Documents Show Obama Deportation Proposal Could Cost More than $585M," *The Washington Post*. http://www.washingtonpost.com/politics/ap-exclusive-internal-documents.

Capps, R., K. McCabe, and M. Fix. 2011. *New Streams: Black African Migration to the United States*. Washington, DC: Policy Migration Institute. http://www.migrationpolicy.org.pubs/AfricanMigrationUS.pdf.

Chishti, M. and C. Bergeron. 2011. "Post-9/11 Policies Dramatically Alter US Immigration Landscape." http://www.migrationinformation.org/USfocus/display.cfm.

Diamond, J. 1998. "African-American Attitudes towards United States Immigration Policy." International Migration Review 32, 2: 451–470.

Dorsey, M. E. and M. Diaz-Barriga. 2007. "Senator Barack Obama and Immigration Reform." *Journal of Black Studies* 38, 1: 90–104.

Esbenshade, J. 2010. "An Assessment of DNA Testing for African Refugees," Immigration Policy Center: Washington, DC. http://www.immigrationpolicy.org/assessment-dna-testing-african-refugees.

Espenshade, T. J., and K. Hampstead. 1996. "Contemporary American Attitudes Toward U.S. Immigration." *International Migration Review* 30, 2: 535–570.

Foner, N. ed. 2001. *Islands in the City: West Indian Migration to New York*. Berkeley: University of California Press.

Forester, Steven. 2012. "Even after Obama's Immigration Policy Change, Haitian Families' Dreams Deferred." *The Grio*. http://thegrio.com/2012/06/18/even-after-obamas-immigration-policy.

Frank, R., I. R. Akresh, and B. Lu. 2010. "Latino Immigrants and the U.S. Racial Order: How and Where Do They Fit In?" *American Sociological Review* 75, 3: 378–401.

Frey, W. H. 2008. *Race, Immigration and America's Changing Electorate*. Washington, DC: The Brookings Institution. http://www.psc.isr.umich.edu/pubs/pdf/rr08-635.pdf.

Gibson, C. and K. Jung. 2006. *Historical Census Statistics on the Foreign-Born Population of the United States: 1850–2000*. Washington, DC: US Census Bureau. http://www.census.gov/population/www/documentation/twps0081/twps0081.html.

Ha, S. E. 2010. "The Consequences of Multiracial Contexts on Public Attitudes Toward Immigration," *Political Research Quarterly* 63, 1: 29–42.

Human Rights First. 2010. "A System Designed to Fail Haitians," http://www.humanrightsfirst.org/our-work-refugee-programs-Haitian-Refugees.

Immigration Policy Center. 2010. "Granting Refuge: Temporary Protected Status for Haitians in the United States," http://www.immigrationpolicy.org.

Jordan, M. 2008. "Refugee Program Halted as DNA Tests Show Fraud," *The Wall Street Journal*, http://online.wsj.com/article/SB12191919647430755373.html.

Kane, O. 2011. *The Homeland Is the Arena: Religion, Transnationalism, and the Integration of Senegalese Immigrants in America*. New York: Oxford University Press.

Kasinitz, P. 1992. *Caribbean New York: Black Immigrants and the Politics of Race*. Ithaca, NY: Cornell University Press.

Kerwin, D. M. 2011. *The Faltering US Refugee Protection System: Legal and Policy Responses to Refugees, Asylum Seekers, and Others in Need of Protection*. Washington, DC: Migration Policy Institute. http://www.migrationpolicy.org/pubs/refugeesprotection-2011.pdf.

Kimenyi, M. S. 2012. "Africa: Understanding U.S.–Africa Relations During Obama's Presidency." http://allafrica.com/stories/201202271612.htm1.

Lemann, N. 1992. *The Promised Land: The Great Black Migration and How It Changed America*. New York: Vintage Books.

Lovett, I. 2012. "For Many Immigrants, Policy Offers Joy and Relief." *The New York Times*. http://www.newyorktimes.com/2012/06/17/us/for-many-immigrants-obamas-policy.

Marrow, H. B. 2009. "New Immigrant Destinations and the American Color Line." *Ethnic and Racial Studies* 32, 6: 1037–1057.

McCabe, K. 2011. "African Immigrants in the United States." *Migration Information Sources*. http://www.migrationinformation.org/USFocus/display.cfm.

Mittelstadt, M., B. Speaker, D. Meissner, and M. Chishti. 2011. *Through the Prism of National Security: Major Immigration Policy and Program Changes in the Decade Since 9/11*. Washington, DC: Migration Policy Institute. http://www.migrationpolicy.org.pubs/FS23_Post_9–11.

Palmer, R. 1995. *Pilgrims from the Sun: West Indian Migration to America*. New York: Twayne Publishers.

Reitan, R. 1999. *The Rise and Decline of an Alliance: Cuba and African American Leaders in the 1960s*. East Lansing: Michigan State University Press.

Remy, G. M. 1996. "Haitian Immigrants and African American Relations: Ethnic Dilemmas in a Racially-Stratified Society," *Trotter Review* 10, 1: 13–16.

Sernett, M. 1997. *Bound for the Promised Land: African Americans' Religion and the Great Migration*. Durham, NC: Duke University Press.

Suro, R. 2009. *America's Views of Immigration: The Evidence from Public Opinion Surveys*. Washington, DC: Migration Policy Institute. http://www.migrationpolicy.org/pubs/TCM-USPublicOpinion.pdf.

Taylor, M. C., and M. B. Schroeder. 2010. "The Impact of Hispanic Population Growth on the Outlook of African Americans," *Social Science Research* 39: 491–505.

US Census Briefs. 2011. *The Black Population 2010*. http://www.census.gov/prod/cen2010/briefs/c2010br-06.pdf.

US Citizenship and Immigration Services. n.d. "Expanding DNA Testing in the Immigration Process—Senior Policy Council Options Paper." http://www.eff.org//uscis_DNA_Senior_Policy_Council_Optonal_Paper.pdf.

US Department of State. 2012. "FY11 Refugee Admissions Statistics," US Department of State, Bureau of Population, Refugees, and Migration. http://www.state.gov/j/prm/releases/statistics/184843.htm.

US Department of State. 2009. "Fraud in the Refugee Reunification (Priority Three) Program," US Department of State, Bureau of Population, Refugees, and Migration. http://www.state.gov/j/prm/releases/factsheets/2009/181066.htm.

Vargas, J. A. 2012. "Not Legal Not Leaving," *Time* (June): 34–42.

Veney, C. R. 2009. "The Effects of Immigration and Refugee Policies on Africans in the United States: From the Civil Rights Movement to the War on Terrorism." In Isidore Opkewho and Nkiru Nzegwu, eds., *The New African Diaspora: Assessing the Pains and Gains of Exile*. Bloomington and Indianapolis: Indiana University Press: 196–214.

Veney, C. R. 2007. *Forced Migration in Eastern Africa: Democratization, Structural Adjustment and Refugees*. New York: Palgrave-Macmillan.

Venters, H. D., J. McNeely, and A. S. Keller. 2009. "HIV Screening and Care of Immigration Detainees," *Health and Human Rights*, 11, 2: 89–100.

Vickerman, M. 1999. *Crosscurrents: West Indian Immigrants and Race*. New York: Oxford University Press.

Wamwara-Mbugua, L., T. Wakiuru, B. Cornwell, and G. Boller. 2008. "Triple Acculturation: The Role of African Americans in the Consumer Acculturation of Kenyan Immigrants," *Journal of Business Research* 61: 83–90.

Waters, M. 1999. *Black Identities: West Indian Immigrant Dreams and American Realities*. Cambridge, MA: Harvard University Press.

Watkins-Owens, I. 1996. *Blood Relations: Caribbean Immigrants and the Harlem Community, 1900–1930*. Bloomington: Indiana University Press.

Wilkerson, I. 2011. *The Warmth of Other Suns: The Epic Story of America's Great Migration*. New York: Vintage.

Wilson, T. C. 2001. "Americans' Views on Immigration Policy: Testing the Role of Threatened Groups Interests," *Sociological Perspectives* 44, 4: 485–501.

Zeleza, P. T. 2010. "Diaspora Dialogues: Engagements between Africa and Its Diasporas," In Isidore Opkewho and Nkiru Nzegwu, eds. *The New African Diaspora: Assessing the Pains and Gains of Exile*. Bloomington and Indianapolis: Indiana University Press: 31–60.

Zephir, F. 1996. *Haitian Immigrants in Black America: A Sociological and Sociolinguistic Portrait*. Westport, CT: Bergin.

Part III

THE AMERICAS

8

LOVE AS DISTRACTION: CANADIANS, OBAMA, AND AFRICAN-CANADIAN POLITICAL INVISIBILITY

Rinaldo Walcott

Introduction

There is a Facebook page called "Canadians for Obama." The page is an extremely interesting example of what some conservative and right-wing critics of President Obama have termed his celebrity. The Canadians for Obama Facebook page is an amalgamation of photos, quotes, and comments which celebrate him, his family, and even his policies as a signally important moment in US history that Canadians can be proud, celebratory, of. Let me be clear: this is not a page produced by ex-pat US citizens in Canada; it is a page produced by self-identified Canadians. Indeed the existence of this page opens up a truly tantalizing question about Canadians' seeming love for President Obama: It is a love that has not seemed to wane since his first presidential campaign and now into the beginning of his second term reelection. Canadians seem to love Obama in a very strong way.

Why do Canadians seem to like President Barack Obama so much? What does it mean that Canadians seem to be more committed to him as a leader of the United States than to any of his challengers during the last two elections? What is Canada's national fascination with the first African-American president of the United States? How might a black or African-Canadian make sense of this fascination? Is there anything significant for African-Canadians in terms of Canada's likability and fascination with President Obama? Does President Obama's likability in Canada affect the prospects for black or African-Canadian political figures? In this essay I will not be able to answer all of these questions, but I hope to provide enough insight into them from the position of a black Canadian who is a keen observer of both Canadian and US politics. What I hope to do is to demonstrate the ways in which President Obama provides and highlights a number of paradoxes and contradictions in the Canadian political landscape and system, but most importantly, I hope to demonstrate that these paradoxes and contradictions have a long linage in Canadian mythologies touching upon their difference from Americans. The perceived difference I speak of is one that concerns racism as a defining factor of US society but one that is supposedly rare in Canadian society. Indeed, Canadians strong belief that racism and its effects in Canada both historically and contemporarily are radically different than it is in the United States has been a steady underlying feature of Canada's global mythology. Canadians are too smart and one might even say too pragmatic to deny that racism exists in Canada. Instead, what the Canadian mythology concerning racism and its structuring presence in the nation does is to obscure the history of trans-Atlantic slavery in Canada, thus assigning slavery entirely to the United States from where the most brutal forms of racism then flow. Once slavery is obscured, the question of racism becomes more one of individual experiences rather than representing the deep structure of the nation's culture in which very specific bodies are significantly excluded.

But before we can go any further, it is crucially important to note that my own invocation of the term *Canadian* refers to a troubled term. By this, I mean that I both invoke a notion of Canadian that is meant to signal what might be termed *Anglophone* and *Francophone* white Canadians, often referred to as the founding nations and also the post–World War II notion of a multicultural

Canadian citizenry that exceeds the earlier idea of an Anglophone and Francophone Canada, but never fully displaces it as a founding myth (Haque 2012). Central to the founding myth is a significant displacement of Aboriginal or First Nations peoples. What is particularly confounding is that the national mythology does not understand Aboriginal displacement through the lens of racism but rather through the lens of a notion of colonization in which racism and its structural effects appears to be absent. Indeed, in contemporary Canada Aboriginal and First Nations peoples have been ambivalently reincorporated into the national story through two important recourses: 1. An acknowledgement of their original presence on the land and 2. A significant push to bring those communities with resources, oil, minerals, and so on into late capitalism. I will claim that such distinctions are important for the ways in which the likability of President Obama might begin to make sense in Canada. In particular, I will be suggesting that the post–World War II reconstitution of Canada as a multicultural nation provides some insight into why Obama is so loved by the Canadian nation. What I mean by this is that the likability of Obama can never be fully separated from Canada's national consciousness as a multicultural nation. A multicultural nation that I would suggest makes use of culture as a metonym for race. Thus, Obama comes to symbolize a Canadian desire for a certain kind of racial integration that in Canada we would call cultural change. I am also suggesting that the love of Obama is a projection of Canadian desires that they can own, even if they themselves cannot produce figures like him in their political sphere. As I said at the outset of this essay, it is fundamentally about paradoxes and contradictions and that the radical invisibility of black or African-Canadian politicians in the context of Canadians' love for Obama is in stark contrast to the American situation.

It is important to note that the likability of Barack Obama in Canada is a real and sustained phenomenon that has lasted from his first presidential campaign right into his reelection. For example, in the last US election cycle, an Angus Reid survey found that Canadians preferred Obama by a seven-to-one margin. Seventy-two percent of Canadians reportedly said they would vote for Obama, while 10% said Romney and 18% reported being unsure (Bolen 2012). Other opinion polls have reported even more lopsided numbers. These figures suggest a quite substantial number of Canadians see something in Obama that many of them for example do not see in current Prime Minister Stephen Harper. A recent poll by Environics and reported in the *Globe and Mail* found that only 16% of Canadians trusted Prime Minister Stephen Harper and he was near the bottom of all leaders in the Americas (November 18, 2012). In poll after poll, Canadians have overwhelmingly endorsed Obama's presidency even when his decisions went against his campaign promises. So how do we make sense of those kinds of numbers? Can they really tell us anything significant about how Canadians actually feel about politicians, race, and even leadership? While I am not prepared to dismiss the numbers, it seems important to me to think about the ways in which race works in the Canadian context. As well, it is necessary to point out that Canada's multicultural mythology provides a rhetoric of it being a place where race does not matter, as Cecil Foster has termed it (2005).

Like much of the advanced western and especially North Atlantic world, Canadians tend to think of their nation as a white nation, that is a nation founded out of the historical movement and settlement of Europeans in the Americas. This kind of founding myth, which I earlier marked as Anglophone and Francophone, remains despite or in spite of newer myths of a multicultural reordering of Canadian society. It is a multicultural reordering that is premised on a post–World War II migratory politics and logic and it fundamentally denies the presence of the very groups marked as "ethnic" and "multicultural" prior to 1945. The very foundation of formal multiculturalism then is premised on a significant delusion. Thus, one of the paradoxes is that while the state, and even in everyday life, Canadians might draw on multicultural policies, narratives, discourses and even forms of representation to produce a progressive, antiracist nation in which racism is something that we work hard to overcome, at base the primary understanding of the nation is founded in European enlightenment understandings of the world. Indeed, this became very clear in the post-9/11 public debates in Canada concerning Muslims, liberty, and civilization. And it became even clearer in the now (in)famous Toronto 18 case in which a group of mainly young Muslims either born in Canada or having in migrated very early in life were accused and mostly convicted of plotting to commit acts of terrorism (Teotonio 2010). I enumerate these incidences because their evidence provides the backdrop to what I would have to now term the complicated love that Canadians hold for President Obama.

Multicultural Gazes

One look at President Obama and most Canadians would imagine him to be someone that would be easily sighted in one of our major cities or even a neighbor, definitely a workmate—that is a familiar-looking figure. What I mean is that in large cities like Toronto, Montreal, and Vancouver, but increasingly also in cities like Calgary, Edmonton, and Saskatoon, the multiracial makeup of Canada is immediately present and evident. Canadian demographics have been transformed through an immigration policy that has sought to unify families, admitted significant amounts of refugees from a range of places (often accompanied by great public debate and racist accusations), and also used investment in the country to produce a population of "immigrants" whose main contribution has been the ongoing cementing of Canadian capitalism given the shrinking of the founding demographic groups (e.g., white Anglophones and Francophones). Thus, for many Canadians Obama looks just like one of us and could be one of us.

Additionally, President Obama's family configuration speaks to one of the central myths of Canadian society. Indeed, one might argue that while the term "postracial" was not coined in Canada, the attitude it attempts to characterize might well have already taken hold in certain regions of Canada's political class. Indeed, in the postmulticultural Canada the question of race has come to carry a kind of taint to it in which Canadian politicians hardly ever consider questions of race as a constitutive element of their own makeup. Indeed, I can think of no recent public discussions by any Canadian political party about their almost all-white leaderships (I shall return to this below). So returning to Obama's family, what makes his family fit the Canadian unspoken postracial myth is significantly heightened by the fact that his half-sister is married to a Chinese-Canadian. Maya-Soeoro-Ng and Charles Ng's marriage fits neatly into a Canadian discourse of cross-cultural and cross-racial marriages, as well as mixed-raced families, often now understood as one of the successful outcomes of Canadian multicultural policy. The idea of the multicultural and multiracial family has been given much attention in Canada in recent years, helping to produce a rhetoric around it as a signal of a racially and culturally progressive nation.

Furthermore, in the 2006 census it was reported that about 4% of all couples in Canada are in mixed unions of some sort (common law or married/gay and straight) (Milan, Maheux, and Chui 2010). These couples tend to be younger, highly educated, and born in Canada and to live in metropolitan areas of the country (Milan, Maheux, and Chui 2010). While the empirical evidence supports some changes in how Canadians are organizing their intimate lives, it can still be a bit of a stretch to assume that such organization has a significant effect on the political public sphere. However, the point remains that Canadians now seem to think that such is the case and that it makes them/us singularly different from many other places in the North Atlantic western world. It is precisely such claims and assumptions I hope to unpack. But suffice to say that with such sturdy claims Canadians see Canada in Obama or at least an image of Canada that they believe is representative of where their nation has moved to. Obama personally and symbolically provides Canadians the evidence of the correctness of their multicultural policies and desires. To gaze at Obama is to see Canada, not the United States. Obama's presence only brings the United States into view in so far as it reminds Canadians that our historical past does not contain the kinds of racial dreadfulness that the United States' historical past contains and in some ways perpetuates. In a strange sense then Obama's election and reelection justifies Canada's multiculturalism and reminds us that its racial order has never been that of the United States. Strange, yes it is.

How Visible Is the Black or African-Canadian Politician in Canada?

On October 25, 2010, the city of Calgary swore in its first nonwhite mayor. Naheed Nenshi, a South Asian Canadian became the city's thirty-sixth mayor and the first Muslim to hold such a position in Canada. Nenshi's campaign made great use of social media to galvanize support, and thus he was immediately figured as a kind of Canadian Obama figure. What made the comparison even more salient was the claim that Nenshi was an underdog in the race and that Calgary is where a significant part of the country's political right is centered, if not its heartland. Therefore, it was supposedly not ready for a nonwhite person holding such office. Indeed, Nenshi's win vaulted Calgary into the realm of progressive cities and produced a host of news reports about its changing status as a big city flushed with oil money and confidence. What is most significant, however, is that Nenshi's win helped to further cement the discourse of postracial attitudes in postmulticultural Canada. However, under closer scrutiny Nenshi's win opens up more avenues for the questioning of Canada's political class than it actually solves or demonstrates a genuine postracial political landscape.

More specifically, Canada's love affair with Obama only seems to demonstrate more pointedly what the nation lacks in relationship to black or African-Canadian politicians, and one might even argue the entire black populace of the country. Importantly, African-Canadians and Aboriginal peoples are Canada's poorest and least represented in federal politics. While it is true that a number of African-Canadians hold political office, there is no African-Canadian politician with any significant national profile. And, while Nenshi might be invoked as some kind of symbol of racial progress and does indeed muster a certain kind of national attention, he is still not a national political figure of significant weight. Indeed, given the ways in which Canada's postmulticultural political settlement works, it is necessary to ask about specific "racial groups." So where do black and African politicians rate in the national landscape?

Before I give some sense of how black and African-Canadian politicians are positioned in the nation-state, it is necessary to highlight the significance of their absence through the unspokenness of whiteness. Whiteness continues to frame the national public sphere precisely because it is the unspoken in the public sphere. Now well-reported, and in the aftermath of his great flameout, Michael Ignatieff's return home to take a prominent place in national political life is an example of how racial whiteness shapes the political public sphere in Canada. Michael Ignatieff, a career journalist, novelist, and professor at the Harvard Kennedy School of Government, was seduced and invited back to Canada to lead one of the major political parties—the Liberal Party of Canada. His leadership of the party was not a very successful one, but I believe his invitation was very much understood in light of Obama's emergence as the potential for a certain kind of cerebral and intellectual leader. It is precisely his introduction back to the country that marks a certain kind of political unconscious of the white Canadian nation-state in which black and African-Canadians and one could say other nonwhite Canadians remain unimaginable in major roles like finance minister, foreign affairs minister, and prime minister of Canada.

What is particularly striking about the attempts to launch Ignatieff's career as a politician and his return to lead the party is how they exposed the blatant manner in which his selection appeared to be driven by a white leadership who could not think outside the box about mentoring and indeed positioning nonwhite Canadians as national leaders. The parliamentary system of which Canada is a part and the manner in which political parties choose their leaders makes it almost impossible for an insurgent candidate to emerge at a convention and win the leadership of the party. Importantly, the leader of the party is also, once elected, the prime minister. Therefore to an observer of Canadian politics it is crystal clear that there are presently no nonwhite Canadians in any of the national parties that can muster the internal support in their party to emerge as its national leader and a potential prime minster. Given Canada's changed demographics, this is a significant example of the ongoing ways in which racial whitenesss frames and structures the Canadian political public sphere.

There are few black or African-Canadian politicians in either Canada's House of Parliament or its Senate. Among those in both houses, none of them are national figures. To make such a claim is not to diminish their accomplishments but rather to point to the ways in which racial whiteness continues to be the foundation of Canada's political system and its political class. Additionally, a brief scan of the leadership of Canada's major political parties will find almost no black or African-Canadian politicians holding influential office in them. It is precisely these kinds of contradictions and paradoxes that makes Canada's love affair with Obama a curious and unsettling thing. The profound invisibility of black and/or African-Canadian politicians induced Senator Donald Oliver, a conservative, to remind Canadians of slavery in the country and to issue a call for blacks to rise up.

"In Parliament is there racism? In the Senate, in the House of Commons, in the library of Parliament are there barriers? There certainly are. In the past, I have met with the clerk of the Senate, with the clerk of the House of Commons and with the head of the library of Parliament and have had very candid and frank talks with them about the barriers that exist" (*National Post*, June 27, 2011, http://news.nationalpost.com/2011/06/27/).

Senator Oliver is among the very small number of black or African-Canadians in Canada's national political institutions. His form of black conservatism is informed by the struggle against racism both in his home province of Nova Scotia and nationally. However, it is crucial to note that while national news might cover such comments by Senator Oliver it would be quite over-blown to even suggest that he is a national political figure.

It is equally crucial to note that the kinds of invisibility I am documenting here do not only exist in governmental institutions. In the extra-governmental institutions like for example the media the crisis of invisibility is even more deeply evident. In terms of political commentators and/or pundits the political landscape is almost entirely white. On any given day, for example, on the national twenty-four-hour news channels CBC or CTV, national political conversations, analysis, and debate are entirely engaged in and practiced by all-white faces. Canada's demographic diversity only shows up in such moments when the topic is deemed to merit a representative "racial" or "cultural" insider—that is deemed to be of interest to a specific "ethnic" group. It is such circumstances that produce the contradictions concerning Obama's likeability, because at the national level in Canada it would appear that the political elites and the political class have given very little thought to the (ethnic and other) invisibilities in their own realm. Indeed, the only way to make sense of his likeability is that a certain kind of desire exists among nonwhite Canadians that his accomplishment is a projection of their future possibilities. As I suggested above, for white Canadians, Obama's presidency represents a perverse inversion of the United States actually accomplishing something they believe they had already achieved but without the evidence to show it.

One might begin to suggest that the profound circumstances surrounding antiblack racism in Canada makes the love affair with Obama a paradox and contradiction. However, I would add that in the Canadian popular imaginary multicultural discourse and its representative practices always create a place for exceptionalism. It is precisely because Obama represents such exceptionalism and his exceptionalism is not one of rejection of the colonial nation-state but rather a significant belief in its rightness and possibilities that he can be so loved by Canadians. One might even suggest that Obama represents and helps to placate a certain kind of Canadian fear of what the nonwhite others might do should they ever seize power in the postcolonial multicultural state. It is precisely struggles over the meaning of the state and the national imaginary that multicultural policies were enacted to disrupt. Therefore, Obama can be so vociferously loved by Canadians as an example or symbol of how those once excluded from "the racial state," as Goldberg (2002) names, it can become not only its defender but one of its most prized articulators.

References

Bolen, M. 2012. "Obama Romney Poll," *Huff Post Canada*, October 31. http://www.huffingtonpost.ca/2012/10/31/obama-romney-canada-poll_n_2049167.html.

Foster, C. 2005. *Where Race Does Not Matter: The New Spirit of Modernity*. Penguin Canada.

Goldberg, T. 2002. *The Racial State*. London: Blackwell.

Haque, E. 2012. *Multiculturalism in a Bilingual Framework*. Toronto: University of Toronto Press.

LeBlanc, D. (2012). Harper among least trusted leaders, poll finds, Globe and Mail, Nov 12, 2012. http://www.theglobeandmail.com/news/politics/harper-among-least-trusted-leaders-poll-shows/article5187774/

Milan, A., H. Maheux, and T. Chui. 2010. "A Portrait of Couples in Mixed Unions." Statistics Canada. http://www.statcan.gc.ca/pub/11-008-x/2010001/article/11143-eng.htm.

National Post. 2011. Daily Archives, June 27. http://news.nationalpost.com/2011/06/27/.

Teotonio, I. 2010. "The Toronto 18." *Toronto Star*. http://www3.thestar.com/static/toronto18/index.html.

9

CHANGING TIMES AND ECONOMIC CYCLES: PRESIDENT OBAMA—THE SOUTHERN CONTINENT, MEXICO, AND THE CARIBBEAN

Elisa Moncarz and Raul Moncarz

Introduction

Since the beginning of the twenty-first century, Latin America has gone through very significant changes within its external and internal environments. After overhauling and modernizing its financial and capital markets, as well as becoming more market oriented, a number of its economies seemed ready to become part of the world economy. Between 2004 and 2012, the area known as Latin America has recorded its best economic performance in nearly half a century, fueled primarily by its agricultural and industrial commodities as well as by a global lust for its natural resources, especially from China. Trade and investment ties have been diversified. Regionally, its international reserves have tripled since 2002, and foreign borrowing as a percentage of GDP is down to around 20% from 44% in 2002.[1] Countries such as Brazil, Colombia, Chile, Mexico, and Peru have earned investment-grade ratings.

It is important to note that for countries like Mexico, the Obama administration took on importance even at its outset. Its planned emergency effort to quarantine itself from challenges as a result of circumstances in Mexico and to devise a more effective partnership in order to help deal with Mexico's deepening crisis of governance was well on its way.[2] According to Lowenthal, cooperation between the United States and the Western Hemisphere had been strengthening in the post–cold war years of the early 1990s; it slowed down in the late 1990s and also at the outset of the new millennium. Some Latin Americans resented Washington's perceived inattentiveness to their countries and rejected some of the US global policies, especially the invasion of Iraq, the intervention in Afghanistan, and the meddling in Honduran affairs. At the same time, Venezuela's Hugo Chavez took advantage of this ill feeling toward the United States by pursuing an even more aggressive public policy that ensured economic support to Latin America. This he did by subsidizing the sale of much-needed petroleum to Central America and by infusing dollars to receptive neighbors. Venezuela's public policy also included close cooperation with Cuba, Ecuador, Nicaragua, Brazil, Bolivia, and Argentina.

As of 2012, the United States relies on Latin America as the primary destination for its exports, and trade with the region will soon create more than 2 million jobs in the United States according to the Obama administration. Latin America has also emerged as a leader in alternative energies, security, and emergency response. In 2012, the United States exported more than three times as much to Latin America as it did to China. In 2010, the president said US exports to Brazil supported more than 250,000 US jobs.

Among the many critical issues still present even after the president's many trips to the region are trade and immigration (very important issues for many States of the Union); energy; narcotics; border security; strategic partnership with Brazil; managed interdependence with Mexico, Central America, and the Caribbean; rapprochement with Cuba; and relations with the "Bolivarian" populist regimes.[3] In spite of the many far-reaching issues, President Obama is constrained by a US Congress that insists on protective quotas and high tariffs for agricultural products.[4]

The World Crisis of 2008

According to Sweig,[5] reality proved very different from expectations when the world financial crisis of 2008 came to the region. Even though between 2004 and 2008 the region had registered the best economic performance in nearly half a century—fueled primarily by a global drive for its natural resources as well as agricultural and industrial commodities—the effect was no less severe.

With a stronger financial sector and a solid macro sector, many thought that the effects of the 2008 crisis would be different from previous ones. Yet whatever sense of relative security existed has long disappeared as strong spillover effects from financial markets in the West have proven dominant. A lower rate of growth and exports has weakened the economies, leading many countries' robust trade surpluses to contract significantly. Capital stock and financial markets too have weakened across the hemisphere. Accordingly, the region lost at least 40% of its financial wealth in 2008. As a result, key infrastructure and industrial expansion projects have been slowed or placed on hold.[6]

The Obama administration has not specifically addressed how it is going to create and direct the issue of mid- to long-term economic productivity as it continues to emphasize short run issues such as joblessness, healthcare reform, and others.

President Obama's Visits to Latin America in 2009 and 2012

During President Obama's first months in office, his administration took a very active interest in Latin America and the Caribbean because even though the new administration saw no urgent issues for the United States, some of the countries—especially Mexico—are proving increasingly important to the future of the United States.

In his first extensive trip to Latin America since assuming office in 2009, President Obama spoke in conciliatory terms acknowledging that many of the countries in the area are becoming important economic and political entities in the global arena and deserving of being called partners.[7] On the campaign trail in 2008, the president promised to build better relations with his American neighbors. Although the financial meltdown and ongoing strife in the Middle East had the administration focused elsewhere, they still had an interest in the region.

According to O'Grady,[8] the president unfortunately discredited his trip even before it began by peddling it as a trade mission to create jobs and to boost the US economy. In 2012, as was the case in 2009, President Obama found a region with increasing confidence in its own future, diversified in its relationships, and seeking to amplify and strengthen its ties with the United States.

Trade

While Latin America reaches out for trade with Asia and the European Union, Washington hesitates. The American point of view is that politics do not allow for better relations as well as the perennial excuse of Labor Unions and Tea Party protectionist interests. However, President Obama has been instrumental in ratifying free trade agreements with Colombia (approved in April of 2011) and Panama as well as Peru to deepen commercial ties throughout the region. According to José Perez Jones,[9] the Colombian free trade agreement means 6,400 new jobs and more than $500 million in export sales annually just for the state of Florida.

Admittedly, US agricultural–protectionism is widespread and unlikely to diminish any time soon. In fact, the prospects are that it will be a major source of discord in US–Latin American relations for years to come. Subsidies, tariffs, and quotas sharply restrict sales of many Latin American products to the United States, and Latin American countries are also raising trade barriers despite continued talk to "connect the Americas."[10]

While the president was in Brazil in 2009, a treaty on trade and economic cooperation was signed that calls for the creation of a commission that will study ways to boost trade as well as agreements and memoranda of understanding on issues ranging from open skies, cooperation on biofuels and climate change, to the productive exploration of outer space and agreements to cooperate on safety and security for major sporting events, such as the upcoming Olympics in 2016.[11]

President Rousseff asserted in 2009 that, "If we want to build a relationship in depth, it's necessary, frankly to deal with our contradictions." Brazil wants more fairness and balanced trade relations, yet must deal with US barriers against its ethanol, orange juice, and airplanes. The 54-cent-per-gallon tariff on Brazilian ethanol in particular has recently been cut, and its subsidies on cotton, which have been ruled illegal by the World Trade Organization in a case brought by Brazil, must all be addressed.

The Obama administration's approach to trade policy has been confusing, at best. It rejects protectionism, but it has accepted a "buy American" provision in the economic stimulus legislation. It has also talked about energy cooperation with Brazil but has not yet made any concrete proposals on the very positive effects of cooperation.

Adding to the confusion, the White House and Congressional Republicans were for many months in a political standoff, finally resolved in 2011, over passage of trade agreements with South Korea, Colombia, Peru, and Panama. This dispute, largely over federal assistance to trade-displaced workers, reflects broader tensions over spending (the program provides training money and other benefits for workers whose jobs shift outside the United States as a result of trade pacts. The program costs about $800 million annually.)[12]

Brazil's President Rouseff's April 2012 visit to the United States was an attempt to expand the ties between the two nations. Trade with Brazil, which in 2012 surpassed that with Britain, is thriving.

However, these trade patterns disguise tension; the United States does not have a trade agreement with Brazil, despite reaching such agreements with eleven other countries in Latin America.[13]

Most Asian and Latin American economies have gained a degree of sovereignty. Others no longer depend on US-influenced international financial organizations like the International Monetary Fund (IMF) and World Bank by securing commercial loans. Most have diversified their trading and investment partners and deepened regional ties. In some countries such as Brazil, Argentina, Chile, and Peru, China has replaced the United States as the principal trading partner. Most countries no longer look to the United States to aid or stimulate their growth, preferring instead to work out joint ventures with multinational corporations frequently based outside of North America.

The free trade area of the Americas has fallen apart. In the Latin American context, US policy makers have often appeared to believe that free trade alone would alleviate poverty and reduce inequality. It is wrongly assumed that the region's still-stratified societies possessed the institutional capacity, political will, and outlines of a basic social contract necessary to endure the dislocations of free trade while at the same time taking advantage of market openings. The US trade agenda is weakening under the weight of high expectations. Collectively, the combined effects of the collapse of the Doha round and the emergence of the G-20 and other groups together with the global financial crisis of 2008, not to mention growing reservations about free trade among the US public watching manufacturing jobs leave for abroad, have effectively torpedoed the idea of trade as the answer to all problems informing US–Latin American relations for almost the past twenty years.[14]

On a more positive note, the US Congress did not extend the 54-cents-per-gallon tariff levied against imported ethanol, which has opened the US market for Brazilian and other imports. Concurrently, the US Congress refused to extend the complementary production tax credit of 46 cents per gallon, which has been provided to US producers for three decades. These changes complement the tariff elimination enacted by Brazil in 2010. All of a sudden, there is a hemispheric free market for ethanol.[15]

Immigration

Unfortunately the politics of immigration make the issue much tougher. A quick resolution is unlikely. Still, Mr. Obama can use his executive power to diminish the numbers of deportations for noncriminals. Thus far, the immigration debate is tenuous at best. President Obama's early promise that comprehensive immigration reform would be a first-year priority gave way to a more limited commitment only to begin consultation on this issue in 2010.

Given the power of gangs in the Mexican countryside, the country that has long defended the rights of its citizens in the United States, illegal or not, has been unable to defend the rights of Central American migrants that cross Mexico illegally in their journey northward. Kidnapping Central American and Mexican immigrants is one of the latest rackets of Mexican organized crime groups, which are expanding beyond drugs into pirated DVDs, illegal alcohol sales, and business extortion.[16]

A Changing Scenario for All

Broadly, there are two views from which to look at the recent US–Latin America relationship. A favored view of many experts is for the United States to have a shared global outlook to serve as the basis for a common agenda. However, according to Sweig,[17] since 1989's democracy promotion, counternarcotics and trade liberalization have constituted the central part of US priorities in Latin America. This combination is no longer adequate.

It is recognized that domestic politics in the United States often drive, and pervert, US policies toward the region. Between organized labor, the farm lobby and the energy industry, a socially and environmentally sustainable liberalization of trade and energy cooperation will remain more the province of domestic political actors than Washington's foreign-policy experts. A reality is that the Americas and the Caribbean are stuck with each other, and so new policies, new alliances and better accommodations will have to be crafted in an increasingly diverse scenario where both problems and positive outcomes necessarily matter for all parties involved.

As Henry Kissinger[18] writes about China (but which we can also extrapolate to Latin America), "I am aware that the cultural, historic and strategic gaps in perception will pose formidable challenges for even the best-intentioned and most far-sighted leadership on both sides. On the other hand, were history confined to the mechanical repetition of the past, no transformation would ever have occurred. Every great achievement was a vision before it became a reality." Noting the above, the Obama administration in a surprise move said on August 17, 2011, that the federal authorities will review the deportation cases of 300,000 illegal immigrants and might allow many to stay in the United States. Under the plan, authorities will review individually all cases of immigrants now in deportation proceedings. Those who have not committed crimes and who are not considered a threat to public safety will have a chance to stay in the United States and later apply for a work permit.[19]

The Image

The region's view of the United States has improved according to the Chilean polling firm Latino-barometro. The survey showed that 73% of Chileans believe the United States is either a "positive" or "very positive" force in Latin America.

That's compared to 47% in 2007. Across Latin America, 57% of those surveyed saw the United States as a positive influence, according to the poll.[20] In April of 2012 ahead of the president's trip to the Summit of the Americas, Gallup reports some very different figures showing that only 24% of the Latin-American respondents in April of 2012 believed Obama will strengthen ties between the two Americas. On the Gallup poll in 2009, by contrast, that number was 43%.[21]

Latin Americans in the United States

The number of inhabitants from Central and South America and the Caribbean in the United States in 2011 now tops 50 million, comprising 16% of the US population. By 2060, they will likely be one-third of the population in the United States.[22]

We need to get away from misconceptions and generalizations while railing about Latin Americans in the United States. The unprecedented 43% growth in the Latin American population in the United States in the last decade did not primarily come from immigration. The largest factor in that increase was childbirth; "compared to 2000 the Latin American birth rate increased by 14 percent while both the U.S. population and black birth rates declined 2 percent," according to a Bloomberg analysis of census statistics.

Nearly three in four Latin Americans in the United States are citizens,[23] not interlopers taking something from America and its way of life. A new report out by the US Department of Labor notes that Latin Americans comprise 15% of the labor force, almost equal their proportion of the entire population. Furthermore, Latin American men have the highest workforce participation rate of any group.[24]

Because of their age and work habits, Latin Americans are the *worker bees* of the nation and will continue to be in the future. They are also highly entrepreneurial. Latin American owned companies grew by 43.7% between 2002 and 2007, compared to 14.5% among other groups. As a relatively young population, they will comprise a larger proportion of the working population, especially as elder Americans retire.

Another factor to consider is the political and social impact that this group has made in the United States. Mexicans, Cubans, Central Americans, Venezuelans, Colombians, Haitians, Dominicans, and Brazilians as well as Puerto Ricans and others have established communities now in every state of the Union over successive generations, making for a sustained cultural and demographic transformation.[25] Still what distinguishes these groups from those of Europe and Asia before them is the ease of staying connected to families and cultures left behind, whether through remittances, technology, or the influence of language and communications.

One in ten Mexican citizens lives in the United States. Include their American-born descendants and you have about 33 million people or around a tenth of the US population. In 2011 the Mexican economy grew faster than Brazil's, and it was predicted to do so again in 2012.[26]

Latin America Today

According to Bitar,[27] Latin America has acquired an economic dimension and an institutional solidity that will continue to be consolidated. As has been true in the past, US policies toward Latin America are likely to be shaped in great measure by evolving domestic concerns and by broader international pressures. That is the nature of US policy affecting Latin America no matter who occupies the White House, for Latin America is often affected by the residual effect and unintended consequences of decisions taken for other reasons.

Many South American countries have experienced positive growth rates in their economies. In other words, they are not as dependent on the US markets as they have been historically. The reason for the new found change is that commodities have become much more of a global market, while China, India, and others have become bigger players.[28]

Recent US Preoccupation

Brazil has taken on an increasingly firm role in Latin America.[29] The US and Brazil have different positions on Cuba, Venezuela, Nicaragua, Ecuador, Honduras, and Paraguay. In this instance, it is Washington that stands alone in its refusal to end its diplomatic and economic isolation of Cuba. Both countries, however, now appear willing to tolerate the differences in views, and new flare-ups over Cuba seem unlikely. Brazil has been far less accommodating in its policy toward Honduras. The US–Brazilian disagreement has sustained a divisive standoff in hemispheric relations.[30] However, as the United States seeks durable security partnerships, Brazil is a natural ally in the region. American and Brazilian soldiers have worked together in Haiti, where Brazil commands the United Nations Stabilization Mission.[31]

Latin American Initiatives by President Obama

Among the new initiatives unveiled before Obama's trip to the region were the following: plans to use social media and online networks to encourage collaboration among students, scientists, and entrepreneurs throughout the region and plans to expand foreign exchange programs to allow 100,000 US and 100,000 Latin American students to learn about each other's cultures.[32] At the 2012 Summit of the Americas, the attending countries accepted plans to expand broadband access in the region, electricity integration projects, and the student exchange programs.

The Narcotics Challenge

On the security front, President Obama said the United States is working with Chile, Colombia, and Mexico so that those nations can share with Central America their expertise in fighting drug traffickers and criminal gangs. At the same time the president acknowledged the United States' part in the drug trade. The United States increased funds for national drug education and treatment programs by $10 billion in 2011, even as authorities continue cracking down on guns being shipped to Central America and Mexico. The seriousness of the issue has recently been translated into citizen's security initiatives[33] as well as a national and regional effort to challenge the threat. Furthermore, the administration has continued and even extended militaristic counternarcotics policies in the Americas. The funding for plan Colombia was an estimated $672 million in 2009, and Obama's expansion of the Merida initiative, the regional security partnership, started with Mexico in 2007. Under Obama, funding for the Mexican initiative almost doubled in 2009 to $830 million making it the largest US foreign aid program. According to professor Reiss,[34] the drug war has failed to achieve even its stated goals of a net decrease in illicit drug production and trafficking, in spite of the increased cost in human life, government's credibility, and physical assets. Rarely discussed is the drug wars' great success in achieving unstated goals such as extending global US military control and extending the reach of the legal US drug economy, which often depends on raw materials and consumer markets in the very same nations participating in the drug control effort.

According to Sweig,[35] aggressive counternarcotics programs focused on eradication and interdiction continue to absorb the lion's share of all US assistance to Latin America. Resources for alternative and viable rural development remain sadly lacking. Although the statistics from year to year at times show a decline in the acreage of coca-growing land, the disheartening reality is that after more than twenty years and billions of dollars spent annually (over $8.5 billion between 2000 and 2008) more coca is cultivated in the Andean region than ever before, while street prices are lower and the quality more stable. Given these circumstances, it seems that the war on drugs has been a failure and that it's time for a new estimate that directly addresses both demand as well as other dimensions of the industry, such as arms trafficking and exploitation of illicit financial networks that keep it thriving.

The April 2012 Summit of the Americas took steps forward in directing the Organization of American States (OAS) to begin a thorough review of drug control policy in the region. "We emphasized the possibility of exploring alternatives with consumer countries,"[36] said the president of Mexico. The OAS review will seek to analyze alternatives long brought forth by a number of countries. President Obama reiterated his opposition to decriminalization, but said it was appropriate to discuss the issues.[37] Leonard Pitts summarized the argument in a very clear way: "Drug legalization is not the answer? O.K. Mr. President, fair enough. What is?"[38]

Inter-American Relations

On the topic of Cuba, the president said that no other US administration in decades had made more changes in its Cuba policy, "but Cuban authorities must take some meaningful actions to respect the basic rights of its own people," he said, "not because the U.S. insists upon it, but because the people of Cuba deserve it." Worthy of mention are the Obama administration's fine distinctions and case-by-case treatment of the various populist and potentially populist regimes: Venezuela, Bolivia, Ecuador, and Nicaragua, as well as El Salvador and Paraguay. Accordingly, the Obama administration recognizes social and economic inequities as the root cause of many of the region's problems, calling for special and deferential attention to Brazil, and a clear preference for multilateral approaches.[39] All of these initiatives seem to be broad in scope but short on detail.

The issue of small weapons is another situation that remains a challenge. After the Obama administration acknowledged the need to regulate if not prohibit, the export of small weapons from the United States to Mexico, the president himself suggested that this goal was unrealistic because of domestic politics.[40]

If we add the immigration and trade issues, it becomes clear that the timing has not been right to tackle some of these issues, or it illustrates the continuing power of key interest groups and their access to the highly porous process of US foreign policymaking, particularly on routine issues that do not involve high-priority national security concerns.[41]

Another View and Recent Events

In addition, according to the North American Congress on Latin American report on the Americas,[42] what Latin America needs is not change that would enhance US interests but a healthy dose of social justice. The region suffers from considerable inequality in Bolivia, according to the United Nations Development Program (UNDP); the ratio of income received by the richest 10% of the population to the poorest 10% is 168 to 1, making it the most income-unequal country in the world. Ten Latin American countries are among the next 15 on the UNDP's rankings, vying for second place among the "most unequal." Inequality among countries is also immense. According to LatinFocus, about 70% of the region's GDP is produced by just two countries—Brazil and Mexico. And IMF data show that gross domestic product per capita respectively in Chile, Argentina, Uruguay, and Venezuela are more than double that of most countries of the Caribbean and Central America.

Military

According to Professor Petras,[43] Obama's militarization of US policy toward Latin America in general, and toward Venezuela, Bolivia, Cuba, Ecuador, and Nicaragua in particular, is part of his global policy of armed confrontation against any country that refuses to submit to US domination. It has to be also noted that in 2009 the Obama administration first opposed and then backed a military coup in Honduras, ousting the democratically elected government of President Zelaya, a Chavez ally and replacing it and supporting another government favored by Washington.

Latin America perceives the US military aggression toward a number of countries in the region as a first step southward toward their countries.

That, and the drive for greater political independence and more diversified markets, has weakened Washington's diplomatic and political attempts to keep their former grip on the area.[44]

Foreign Policy

Obama's continuing policy to isolate Cuba and Venezuela has been disregarded by Latin American countries, while the effort to revive free trade agreements was also rejected. With the failing of diplomatic initiatives, other strategies were followed such as the US backed coup in 2002 in Venezuela and the 2008 effort in Bolivia, which were defeated by mass popular mobilizations and the support of the military for the current governments. This has also been the case in Argentina, Brazil, Ecuador, and Paraguay, where postneoliberal regimes, backed by industrial mining, and agro-export elites and popular classes, were able to maintain the existing governments.[45]

The effects of the US policies of tension and the "war of attrition" are hard to measure, but the White House policy based on greater militarization and virtually no new economic initiative has been a failure. It has encouraged the larger Latin American countries to increase regional integration, as witnessed by the custom and tariff agreements taken at the MERCOSUR meetings. While the United States is hesitant, Latin America has moved toward a new regional political organization that excludes the United States.

For the last ten years, The US policy has either ignored or mildly chastised Chavez for his policies and activities. At a minimum, denunciation of Venezuelan–Iranian activities and Chavez's meddling in Colombia and elsewhere are critical to gain international support for US policies. While regime changes in Venezuela may be difficult, Chavez's illness, growing discontent, economic difficulties, and possible rifts in the Chavista regime may offer policies to undermine the government.[46] However, "Gallup studies suggest that people in many Latin American countries do not believe Obama has strengthened the mutually beneficial relationships he pledged to pursue at the 2009 Summit of the Americas," the report reads. "Obama will need to convince a highly skeptical audience that the U.S. is serious about its key commitments to Latin America."[47]

The Obama administration has been influential in the passage of the Colombia and Panama trade agreements, engaged in building the Trans-Pacific Partnership (TPP), and supported the resolution of US–Mexico trucking disputes, generating promise for the future.[48]

The 2012 Summit of the Americas agreed on three concrete areas, including a US proposed plan to expand broadband access in the region, electricity integration projects, and large-scale student exchanges.[49] However, the Summit underscored the fact that President Obama, while pledging a new relationship with the United States to doubtful Central and South American and Caribbean neighbors, had little success in bridging significant policy differences that have divided the region for decades.[50]

Obama's 2012 Reelection and Latin America

The 2012 reelection of President Barack Obama will continue to affect Latin America's social, political, and economic outlook particularly if the administration advances its plans to create a TPP. If successful, the TPP is poised to become the world's largest economic bloc. The Obama plan, though focused on Asia, would also include some Pacific Rim, Latin American countries, such as Mexico, Peru, and Chile.[51]

According to Enrique Peña Gómez, Mexico's newly elected president, it is a mistake to limit the region's mutual interests merely to a bilateral relationship of drug interdiction and security concerns. The United States and the region's mutual interests are too vast and complex to be restricted to such a myopic view.[52] Mexico is rising again, and the new Obama administration should look very carefully at the new scenario. Undervaluing trade and overemphasizing the negatives of immigration have led to bad policies that need to be remedied.[53] Mexico remains the largest source of immigrants to the United States. Some leading analysts detect new momentum toward immigration reform after 71% of Hispanic voters favored Obama in the 2012 election. This successful alignment makes a very strong case for comprehensive immigration law reform.

On the political side of the equation, according to Oppenheimer,[54] the November 6, 2012, passage of pro-marijuana legalization amendments in the states of Colorado and Washington will put pressure on the Obama administration to accept starting formal talks with Latin American countries that want either to legalize some drugs or to seek other alternatives to the war on drugs.

Regarding Cuba, the fact that a surprisingly large number (47%) of Cuban voters in Florida voted for Obama in the 2012 election may encourage the White House to further relax travel and licensing restrictions to the island. Lifting the entire US embargo is unlikely, because that decision would have to be made by Congress.[55]

A new reality for Latin America and the Caribbean is that the United States presently holds Asian countries such as Burma, Cambodia, and even China to a lower standard of democracy and human rights than their Western Hemisphere counterparts. It may not be fair, but that's the way it's going to be.[56]

A pressing issue in the near term is how Latin America feels toward the United States in terms of its great power and influence in the region. Since Obama's reelection in November 2012, the Administration and the new Secretary of State, John Kerry, have been trying to improve relations with the ALBA counties (Brazil, Argentina, Cuba, Venezuela, Ecuador, Bolivia, and Nicaragua). Despite this renewed American effort, fast-changing events and variables have led the ALBA participants and other countries to an important crossroad.

Edward Snowden, the former National Security Agency contractor who acknowledged giving journalists secret documents, remains at large and the US government's efforts to pursue him have become a great *controversy* around the world.[57] Furthermore citing classified NSA documents, Brazil's *O Globo* newspaper[58] has reported that the United States was spying on Colombia, Mexico, Brazil, and other friends and foes alike, threatening to open and widen challenges for the Obama administration as it tries to diminish the fallout of Edward Snowden's revelations and his asylum request in a Latin American country.[59]

Snowden's request for asylum in Latin America clearly upsets the Obama administration. In Venezuela's case as well as other countries in the region, the United States has become vulnerable in the war of public opinion. After July 2, the presidents of Venezuela and Ecuador seemed to decide that the Snowden fiasco gave them an out—in other words, international political cover for jilting the new outreach between a number of ALBA countries and Washington. Despite the Snowden imbroglio, the Obama administration and Latin America are on a negotiating course that should bring more growth and well-being to the region.

More fertile grounds for cooperation may be less glamorous; however, important issues like energy policy, education, and intellectual property rights still need to be broached.

Concluding Remarks

While the United States continued its movement away from Latin America, other countries were growing economically. It has become easier for a number of countries in the region to diversify and expand their trade, investments, diplomatic, and in some cases security-related ties to such nations as Spain, China, India, Russia, and Iran.

Despite the absence of bold concrete proposals, the optics of Obama's 2009 trip to the region accompanied by his family and a well-thought-out itinerary, created very positive feelings abroad. As President Obama stated in Brazil, "a better foundation has been laid for enhancing greater cooperation between the U.S. and the countries visited for decades to come." The April 2012 Summit of the Americas ended with a political standoff on whether Cuba's totalitarian leaders should be invited to the next meeting and with disagreements about the Falkland (Malvinas) islands. However, having stayed nearly three days in Cartagena made Obama the first US president to spend this much time in Colombia.

It is also a fact that in today's Latin America the region's macroeconomic management is in contrast to the situation in the United States and Europe, which have found themselves with inadequate regulation, the near collapse of their financial systems, very large deficits and huge debts. Still it is important to note the progress made on democracy and the efforts to deal with the region's vast inequalities.

In terms of the immigration outlook, a good place to make an unequivocal commitment to improve the US immigration system would be to change the status of Salvadorians and Hondurans in the United States from temporary protected to citizens with full rights. In August of 2011 the Obama administration changed its policy toward illegal immigrants especially those who have not committed crimes and who are not considered a threat to public safety. This shift serves to help counter growing discontent among Hispanic voters and immigration advocacy groups about recent record deportations, audit of businesses that have pushed undocumented workers underground, and the lack of progress toward accomplishing some changes in the immigration system under Obama. The recent US (2012) election showed the growing demographic bonds that connect Latin America with the United States and the need for immigration reform to become a reality.

The region has been transformed to stable economies, and consolidated democratic institutions are replacing outdated political and economic models. If Brazil is seeking renewed ties with the United States, it is a welcome development for the entire hemisphere. Latin America possesses today greater autonomy to engage in global affairs. The United States and currently the freshly minted Obama administration have tried to balance the new world realities as they apply to different countries in the Latin American region.

The basic approach is one of achieving a necessary balance with the existing and future challenges. However, no country in Latin America has challenged the national-security interests of the United States as Venezuela has.

Another line of thinking asserts that Latin America perceives US military aggression toward a number of countries as a "blueprint" to eventually also attack their countries. That and the drive for greater political independence and more diversified markets have weakened Washington's diplomatic and political attempts to isolate a number of countries in the region.

There are many layers to the regional as well as individual country relationships with the United States. Presently, there are important conflicting interests and advocacy groups in the United States. There are also diverse and competing interests within the executive branch and Congress, as well as among and within the countries of Latin America and the Caribbean. How policies and relationships develop will depend, as in the past, largely on the push and pull of these different actors in a series of overlapping and interlocking bargaining processes, within themselves and among the United States and the countries of the region.

On the positive side, prior to the Cartagena summit, the Obama administration had been favorable to allowing the passage of the Colombian and Panamanian trade agreements. Furthermore, the resolution of the US–Mexico trucking dispute, as well as the cutting of the ethanol tariff creating for all practical purposes a hemispheric free market in ethanol, have generated promising impetus.

One result of the 2012 Cartagena Summit was to direct the OAS to name a group of experts to study the drug issue and whether current policies are effective. President Obama made clear that he did not believe it would prove more effective than the law enforcement approach funded by the United States. In 2012, pledging a new relationship with the US guarded southern neighbors brought little success in bridging significant policy differences that had divided the region for some time now.

Brazil, Chile, Peru, Colombia, Trinidad and Tobago, and Argentina are becoming stronger economically and politically. Brazil and Venezuela have emerged in their own right, asserting themselves on the global stage and establishing new regional and subregional institutions that explicitly exclude the United States and Canada.

President Obama's November 2012 reelection suggests that a shift of emphasis should occur from the war on drugs to improved trade and foreign investments. Other possible areas for Washington policy change toward the region are Cuba and their trade relations.

In terms of social policy and decision making, fertile grounds for cooperation, though less glamorous however still important, are issues such as energy policy, education, and intellectual property rights. The management of these issues is also important to a more harmonious future in the region. Finally, one key element in the relationship between the United States and Latin America is how they go about seeking and developing strategic partnerships or alliances. What such partnerships or alliances would mean in principle and practice and whether they will genuinely serve everyone's interests are worthwhile topics for further contemplation and discussion.

We would like to thank Scott Kass, Roger Moncarz, and Dwight Nimblett for their excellent research, assistance, and advice.

Notes

1. Sweig, Julia E. The Hemispheric Divide. The National Interest 100, March–April 2009: 48(9).
2. Lowenthal, Abraham F. Fresh Start or False Start? The American Interest, Winter (January/February 2010), p.110.
3. Ibid., p. 111.
4. Ibid., p. 116.
5. Sweig, op cit.
6. Moncarz, Raul. The Obama Administration and Latin America: A "New Partnership for the Americas" Global Economy Journal, Vol. 10, No. 1, 2010, Article 5.
7. Wyss, Jim, Mimi Whitfield, and Tim Johnson. Obama Latin America Trip Gets Praise. The Miami Herald, March 23, 2011, p.10A.
8. O'Grady, Mary Anastasia. Why Obama Went to Brazil. The Wall Street Journal. March 21, 2011, p. A15.
9. Perez-Jones, Jose. Colombia Trade Pact Won for South Florida. The Miami Herald. March 20, 2011, p. 5L.
10. Oppenheimer, Andres. Latin American Countries Are Raising Trade Barriers Despite Vows to "Connect the Americas." The Miami Herald, April 16, 2012, p. A1.
11. Whitefield, Mimi and Vinod Sreeharsha. Lybia Intrude in Brazil Visit. The Miami Herald. March 20, 2011, p. 17A.
12. Williamson, Elizabeth. Trade Pact Tied to Worker Aid. The Wall Street Journal. May 17, 2011, p. A2.
13. Romero, Simon and Jack Calmes. Brazil and U.S. Accentuate the Positive. The New York Times, April 10, 2012, p. A10.
14. Sweig, The National Interest, 49.
15. Mathews, John. The End of the U.S. Ethanol Tariff. The Globalist, January 12, 2012.
16. Casey, Nicholas. Migrants Fall Prey to Mexican Gangs on Way to the U.S. The Wall Street Journal, July 19, 2011, p. A11.
17. Sweig, Julia E. The Hemispheric Divide. The National Interest, March–April 2009, pp.48–49.
18. Kissinger, Henry. The China Challenge. The Wall Street Journal, May 14–15, 2011, p. C2.
19. This Week. The Wall Street Journal, August 20, 2011, p. A5.
20. Wyss, Jim. In Chile, Obama Reaches out to Region. The Miami Herald, March 23, 2011, p. 13A.
21. Christy, Patrick. Latin America Loses Faith in Obama. The Weekly Standard, http://www.ws.com, April 12, 2012.
22. Sanchez, Mary. As Latinos Go, so Goes the Nation. The Miami Herald, April 5, 2011, p. 13A.
23. Lowenthal, Abraham F. Fresh Start or False Start?, p. 116.
24. Sanchez, Ibid. p. 13A.
25. Sweig, Julia E. The Hemispheric Divide. The National Interest, March–April 2009, p. 49.
26. The Economist, The Rise of Mexico, November 23, 2012.
27. Bitar, Sergio. Obama's Visit to Latin America: A View from the South, Inter-American Dialogue, March 2011, p. 3.
28. Moncarz, Raul. The Obama Administration and Latin America: A "New Partnership for the Americas." Global Economic Journal, Vol. 10, No. 1, 2010, Article 5.
29. Hakim, Peter. Why the US and Brazil Can't Get Along: A Story of Turf, Ideology, and Interests. Foreign Affairs Latinoameica, March 1, 2011, p. 2.
30. Ibid.
31. Menendez, Robert. Brazil Is Our Natural Ally in the Region. The Miami Herald, April 6, 2012, p. 17A.
32. Wyss, Jim. In Chile, Obama Reaches out to Region. The Miami Herald, March 23, 2011, p. 13A.
33. Farnsworth, Eric. Fiddling While Central America Burns. The Miami Herald., July 12, 2011, p.11A.
34. Ibid., p. 28.
35. Sweig, op.cit., 49.
36. Brodzinsky, Sibylla. Summit's Future in Doubt without Cuba. The Miami Herald, April 16, 2012, p.2A.
37. Calmes, Jackie., and W. Neuman. Americas Meeting Ends With Discord Over Cuba. The New York Times, April 16, 2012.
38. Pitts, Leonard., Jr. If Not Legalization, then What? The Miami Herald, April 18, 2012, p. 13A.
39. Lowenthal, Abraham F. Fresh Start or False Start? Latin Landscapes, Winter, 2o1o, p. 114.
40. Ibid., p. 115.
41. Ibid.
42. NACLA, Not Just Change, but Justice: Taking on Policy in the Obama Era. p. 14.

43. Petras, James. The U.S. Empire Strikes back at Venezuela—and Falls. The ccpa Monitor, November 2010, p. 32.
44. Ibid., p. 33.
45. Wilson, Scott. Obama Concludes Summit of the Americas on the Defensive about Inviting Cuba, The Washington Post, April 15, 2012.
46. Suchlicki, Jaime. Chavez, Cancer and Cuba: The Implications for U.S. Policy. The Miami Herald, July 17, 2011.
47. Christie, Paul. Op.cit., April 12, 2012.
48. McLarty III, Thomas F. and Nelson W. Cunningham. U.S. Poised to Build on Its Successes, The Miami Herald, April 13, 2002, p. 19A.
49. Oppenheimer, Andres. Colombia Is Regional Summit's Winner. The Miami Herald, April 15, 2012.
50. Wilson, Scott. Obama Concludes Summit of the Americas on the Defensive about Inviting Cuba, The Washington Post, April 15, 2012.
51. Oppenheimer, Andres. Obama's Latin America Policy May Change Slightly. The Miami Herald, November 10, 2012, p. 2.
52. Pena Nieto, Enrique. A Mexican Partner in Prosperity. The Washington Post, November 25, 2012, p. A19.
53. The Economist, The Rise of Mexico, November 24, 2012.
54. Oppenheimer, Andres. Obama's Latin America Policy May Change Slightly. The Miami Herald, November 10, 2012, p. 2.
55. Oppenheimer, op,cit. The Miami Herald.
56. Bosworth, James. For Messages Obama Is Sending Latin America for His Trip through Asia. The Christian Science Monitor, November 19, 2012, p. 2.
57. Ehrefreund, Max. Search for NSA Leaker Edward Snowden Reveals Tensions with Bolivia, Latin America. Washington Post, July 5, 2013.
58. Kinzer, Stephen R. Latin America Is Ready to Defy the United States over Snowden and Other Issues. The Guardian, June25, 2013.
59. Wyss, Jim. Americans Riled over Report of NSA Spying. The Miami Herald, July 10, 2013.

Part IV

EUROPE

10

IS OBAMAMANIA OVER IN EUROPE?

Akis Kalaitzidis

The global wave of good will toward the United States is waning, but is the phenomenon that has been titled "Obamamania" over? This chapter will examine evidence from Europe, historically the closest global region to the United States both culturally and politically. The latest surveys of the continent suggest that although President Obama's approval rating in Europe remains high, those same surveys reveal that European support for US policies is starting to decline. In particular, the Europeans have been waking up to the fact the Obama administration did not pursue radical changes with past administration policies in foreign and defense policies as well as the environment. It is my contention here that considering the global financial climate, and in particular the European travails in the Eurozone, attitudes on the continent can only get more skeptical of American leadership regarding the global economy.

Introduction

On July 24, 2008, a huge crowd of a hundred thousand people gathered in Berlin to hear the Democratic nominee for US president, Barack Obama, speak on the future of US foreign policy. This speech was a feather in the candidate's cap and capped what was, by all accounts, a very successful foreign tour.[1] Candidate Obama was visiting Europe, meeting with leaders and speaking to European publics to silence critics at home, especially his opponent John McCain, who charged him with inexperience in the field of foreign policy. It was love at first sight. Tired of the divisive foreign policies of the Bush administration from 2000 to 2008, Europeans clamored for a fresh perspective, and candidate Obama seemed to have it all. Obama's popularity in Europe led the press to coin a term to describe this phenomenon: "Obamamania."[2]

With such an intense interest in and high approval rating for candidate Obama in 2008, people were bound to be a bit disappointed when the dust settled and he became president of the United States. Yet looking at Europe today, President Obama remains hugely popular and well accepted even in countries with traditional anti-American views. It seems that Obamamania may have faded, but his appeal has generally held as a public figure in the continent of Europe. Although initially hugely popular, the president was bound to disappoint his fans on the continent considering that the United States and its European allies view the world in such different terms on several issues such as the war in Afghanistan, which involves both American and NATO coalition forces (the vast majority of them European) as well as trade and environmental issues. In addition to these long-term disagreements, a catastrophic global financial crisis started in the United States and very quickly engulfed the entire world and most importantly the European Union, which operating in a single currency market, the Euro, has been unable to head off complete collapse once and for all, and it lingers year after year on the verge of collapse. Most interesting, however, is that despite this global calamity and the normal "national interest" disagreements between the United States and Europe the president's image did not suffer much and he is still very popular among Europeans.

This chapter will examine the effect on the popularity of the United States of both the issues that divided the United States and its European allies as well as the effect of the European crisis on the image of the US president abroad. It will examine in particular the effect of the crisis and use the case of Greece, a traditional outlier in terms of approval ratings for US presidents, to argue that despite a small decline in approval for president Obama his image is still very strong on the continent.

The Things that Divide Us

Europeans were severely divided during the Bush administration (2000 to 2008) primarily due to the 2003 invasion of Iraq and the subsequent civil war. The US image suffered enormously with half of the European Union countries, but President Bush was able to get solid support from the newer members of the European Union, especially Eastern European countries that seemed to be attracted to the United States after having spent decades in the shadow of the Soviet Union and harboring strong anti-Russian feelings. Natural allies in terms of foreign policy and the plans of the Bush administration to establish a defense shield against ballistic missiles purportedly coming from Iran or North Korea, Poland and the Czech Republic among others rushed to sign agreements with the United States and join the fight in Iraq while facing strong opposition from European public opinion. The ineptitude of the handling of postinvasion Iraq, the brutal civil war, and the coalition's personnel losses on the ground hampered the initial buoyancy of joining the United States in a Middle Eastern adventure while on the rest of the continent the unpopular war solidified public opinion and the position of the Franco-German alliance for caution. This generated much ill-will toward the Bush administration that also affected public opinion toward the United States as a whole.

As candidate Obama came to the fore promising to reverse much of US foreign policy regarding the War on Terror by closing the Guantánamo Bay prison and ending the war in Iraq, naturally the crowds in Europe were elated. And when candidate Obama became President Obama, let us not forget that one of his first executive orders was to order the closing of Guantánamo Bay prison. And when he received the Nobel Peace Prize on October 9, 2009,[3] this was taken as a strong indication of how much Europe supported his foreign policy views and valued the future of his presidency as much as an indirect criticism of President Bush's hawkish and unilateral policies in the Middle East. Obama's critics insisted, very accurately, that the president had not accomplished much as the leader of the world's only remaining superpower to deserve such an award because even his first executive order to close the Guantánamo Bay prison was floundering in the US Senate and was never approved, and that this award was presented more in the hope some of the promises he made would materialize rather than the actual accomplishments of the young president.[4] Meanwhile, his views on nuclear nonproliferation and his dismissing the nuclear shield

Table 10.1 Percentage in Favor of US-Led War on Terrorism[*]

	Summer 2003	*May 2003*	*March 2004*
US	89%	–	81%
Britain	69%	63%	63%
France	75%	60%	50%
Germany	70%	60%	55%
Russia	73%	51%	73%
Turkey	30%	22%	37%
Pakistan	73%	16%	16%
Jordan	13%	2%	12%
Morocco	–	9%	28%

* Pew Global Attitudes Project in http://www.pewglobal.org/2004/03/16/a-year-after-iraq-war/

bases in Poland and the Czech Republic brought high-toned accusations of betrayal from the Polish president, not what someone would call an image improving move with the "older" part of Europe.[5]

In addition to his foreign policy goals, the expectation was that President Obama would act to close the enormous gap that divided Europe and America regarding climate change. The Europeans have asserted themselves as lead negotiators when it comes to environmental issues, and the United States under previous administrations was constantly on the defensive, refusing to go along with global climate initiatives such as the Kyoto protocol. In the Republican administration of George W. Bush, Kyoto was a dirty word and it became a matter of pride to resist any changes in carbon emission standards. Candidate Obama seemed serious about reversing this course, but it was not to be. In the lead time toward the Copenhagen Summit in 2010, the Obama administration followed the paths of previous administrations and was nicknamed "the foot-dragger-in-chief."[6] To avoid being blamed for the collapsing negotiations and in the face of what was deemed a very generous offer by the Europeans, the Obama administration asked that the final result be applied equally to developing countries knowing full well that they would reject the proposal not only because most of them do not come near the environmental footprint of the United States but also because they considered the proposal highly unjust. Thus, one commentator observed that "one of the unfortunate lessons from Copenhagen is that even an Obama-led United States cannot be counted on as a reliable partner."[7]

Naturally, the first four years of the Obama presidency saw his approval rating is Europe slip, but was it the end of Obamamania? The divisions over foreign policy in the Middle East, US criticism about European reluctance to spend more on defense and thus lighten the American load, the rise of China and the BRICS, and the disagreement over environmental issues all played a role in the dip in the US president's appeal among Europeans, but his numbers did not bottom out. As seen in the following report from the PEW global attitudes project[8] the president's approval rating suffered but only slightly and according to the *New York Times*, his star is about to shine again in Europe.[9]

In the end, it has come down to one major crisis rather than a whole host of smaller peripheral disagreements, a crisis that started in the United States in 2008 and continues to the present day unabated. The global financial crisis threatened the unity of the Eurozone as well as Obama's chances to be reelected, and for that reason the president's handling of the economy is foremost in the minds of people on both sides of the Atlantic.

Table 10.2 Confidence in US President and Opinion of the US, 2012[*]

	Confidence in the US President	Opinion of the US
Germany	87%	80%
France	86%	74%
Britain	80%	60%
Italy	73%	74%
Spain	61%	58%
Poland	50%	69%
Russia	36%	–
Greece	30%	35%
Turkey	24%	15%
Jordan	22%	12%
Pakistan	7%	12%

* Pew Global attitudes Project in http://www.pewglobal.org/2012/06/13/global-opinion-of-obama-slips-international-policies-faulted/

The Financial Crisis

Both the Bush and the Obama administrations had to deal with the worst financial crisis in the world since the Great Depression.[10] The problem with global capital movements in this globalized world is that they no longer obey borders, as we witnessed in the 1996 East Asian financial crisis. Capital will flee from places that seem increasingly risky, especially nonsovereign capital, investments held by private owners. In the case of the 2007–2012 crisis the ball started rolling in the United States where a mixture of deregulation, Wall Street greed, and bad economic practices ended a lengthy housing bubble that had developed in more than one country. According to the Financial Crisis Inquiry Commission findings, otherwise known as the Levin-Coburn report, the crisis was the result of "high risk, complex financial products; undisclosed conflicts of interest; the failure of regulators, the credit ratings agencies, and the market itself to reign in the excesses of Wall Street."[11] This financial crisis saw major banking houses of the twentieth century collapse and sold in a fire sale for pennies to the dollar, unemployment hit ten percentage points in the United States and persist at that level well after the crisis was contained in the United States, and a very unpopular and largely unprecedented fiscal stimulus which included much-maligned institutional bailouts and cash transfers. Both presidents Bush and Obama were severely criticized for bailing out the banking industry, the industry at the heart of the problem, but it fell to the latter to move the US economy out of a severe recession bequeathed to him by his predecessor. Meanwhile, in Europe the major figures of the continent's elite were increasingly worried about the situation in the United States and rallied in their universalist tones, and it seemed with such a crisis of free market capitalism that Europe would be called to stabilize the global economy. Nearly all of Europe's major figures such as Angela Merkel, the German chancellor, Christine Lagard, then the French finance minister, Nikolas Sarkozy, and even Silvio Berlusconi all supported Bush's handling of the crisis, i.e., the bailouts, and talked of the importance of the European Union for the global economy.[12]

Unfortunately for everyone involved, it quickly became apparent that the old dictum about the United States catching a cold while the entire world catches pneumonia[13] was by a large measure true. When on January 7, 2009, Germany attempted to auction 6 billion Euro of ten-year bonds they failed to reach a 100% rate in the sale, and by January 9 the Standard and Poor rating agency downgraded most of the smaller EU countries' outlooks (Bastasin 2012: 88). Naturally the most important economy of Europe, one that had a highly liquid bond market, one that was trustworthy for all investors having to take a failure in the bond markets was worrying to investors. Coupled with the uneasiness of private money in the global financial system that had become increasingly nervous over the US housing crisis, this produced a run on the smaller economies of the European Union who because they were using the Euro were considered so far safe environments in which to invest (Bastasin 2012: 89). Many of the smaller economies, Ireland, Greece, Portugal, and eventually Spain, the ones that are now referred to pejoratively as PIGS, had used the money in different ways and not all had the same problems but the reaction of private investors was the same and markets collapsed.

The Causes of the Crisis for Europe

The causes of the crisis for Europe are very complex but primarily, as I have argued in the previous section, have to do with the loss of confidence for smaller European countries, which by 2010 were watching their bond ratings cut down to junk status by AAA. The Economist Intelligence Unit argued that the crisis in the European Union is economic as much as it is political because the expectation of the market was that these countries would have to restructure their economies and while they were about to do this their interests rates on their long-term sovereign debt increased by the day, reaching levels that were not serviceable any longer (Economist Intelligence Unit 2011: 4).

In addition to global panic and private investor psychology, there were real problems with each of the European economies under water at this time. The Spanish government, the largest of the PIGS, was facing a real-estate bubble similar in nature to that in the US, financed by cheap money flowing into the country during the previous decade. The Spanish banks overextended themselves, creating enormous real-estate portfolios that in the crisis were dwindling fast along with their reserves. In Ireland, the fastest growing economy in the world in the 1990s, the housing bubble had reached hysteria levels and banks were all but happy to finance real-estate development, which then had to be assumed by the taxpayer to save the country from economic catastrophe. Meanwhile in Greece the cheap credit financed better terms for public employees and increased the commitment of the country's treasury to retirees while the country was deindustrializing due to uneven trade imbalances with its European partners.

Another major reason why the crisis in the United States became a crisis in Europe is the uneven trade between countries in which Germany became the world's leading exporter by taking advantage of its European Union partners' markets and its financial well-being due to cheap credit, thus driving the competition out of business. Countries like Greece, deindustrialized mostly by increasing the cost of labor in their country and pricing themselves out of competition, took in German corporate giants for over a decade, and when the crisis hit they had to service the debt they incurred with dwindling revenues and increasing interest rates. The trade imbalances, in addition, meant highly indebted households in southern Europe who for the first time had seen the line of credit extend to everyone cheaply and banks actively recruiting people to hold their credit cards. Household debt, trade imbalances with their Northern European Union partners and fiscal irresponsibility were the reasons Greece is in trouble, argued Paul Krugman, Nobel Laureate in economics, in his weekly column for the *New York Times*.[14] His partner Thomas Friedman agreed: "In Europe, hyperconnectedness both exposed just how uncompetitive some of their economies were, but also how interdependent they had become. It was a deadly combination. When countries with different cultures become this interconnected and interdependent—they share the same currency but not the same work ethics, retirement ages or budget discipline—you end up with German savers seething at Greek workers, and vice versa."[15]

At its core, however, this crisis is political. It is a crisis that was perpetuated through a rather new currency, a structure that was not ready for such demands on it and politicians with ethnocentric views who were attempting to solve a problem that is inherently global. Edwin Truman in his testimony before the US House Committee on Financial Services Subcommittee on International Monetary Policy and Subcommittee on Domestic Monetary Policy and Technology explained, "Because the European Union did not have mechanisms in place either to enforce responsible fiscal management or to support fiscal adjustment and because EU leaders delayed for months before cobbling together a mechanism to provide some measure of financial assistance, Europe is now undergoing a massive process of fiscal retrenchment."[16] The European leadership ultimately failed to curb the crisis by failing to chart a common course, something not unusual in European Union circles, but most importantly it became a game of politicians attempting to put one over on the other, all of which further endangered the Eurozone. The most active politician with the greatest of all visions was Nicholas Sarkozy who advocated no less than the complete overhaul of the international financial system and its restructuring with a European core. Sarkozy's plan was predictably lukewarmly received in Washington, DC, by President Bush, was more warmly received by Prime Minister Gordon Brown of the United Kingdom considering the importance of the financial industry for his country, but was opposed by the German Chancellor Angela Merkel who saw it as no less than a coup within the European Union (Bastasin 2012). According to Bastasin, "As the Germans see it, the thrust coming from Paris marks the beginning of a conflict over which model is to dominate Europe in the future, that of social market economy, which keeps government out of the business of running companies to the greatest extent possible or the French model of a government-controlled economy" (Bastasin 2012: 65). In his efforts to bring about the change in the global financial system and relocate power to the European Union, which one assumes would presumably be located in Paris rather than Brussels, the French president extended a helping hand to ailing countries such as Portugal and Greece, visiting with the embattled leaders and taking them into his confidences with promises of financial help, and actively sought out the prime minister of the United Kingdom breaking with a long-standing tradition of the Berlin-Paris axis. This was a highly dangerous game to play, one that ended up being detrimental to the European economy and to the ailing smaller economies. The reaction of the Germans to the demands of the French that Europe create Euro-bonds administered by the European Central bank, for example, is indicative that not only his wish was rejected but the European Central Bank stuck to a highly neoliberal line of action regarding the greatest of all ailing countries in the Eurozone, Greece. As the Spiegel reported, "During a meeting with parliamentarians from the Free Democratic Party (FDP), her junior coalition partner, she [Angela Merkel] said there would be no full debt sharing 'as long as I live.' SPIEGEL online was told that several FDP lawmakers responded by saying: 'We wish you a long life.'"[17]

Greece: Political Tragedy's Child

Greece went from one of the fastest growing economies of Europe in 2000 to Europe's financial problem child within a decade. It is the ultimate highlight of the global crisis that started unraveling in 2007, a cautionary tale of how to avoid behaving in the global market. The roots of the problem are as much economic as they are political, in line with what was happening in Europe at the time. Greece, a third-wave democracy (Huntington 1991), had a peaceful transition to socialist rule the same year as it was admitted to the European Union in 1981. Transition to socialist rule meant that people who were traditionally excluded politically from the decision-making centers of power would now be occupying them. Politically, it meant Greece had matured. Economically, however, it spelled disaster considering the Socialist Party of Greece went on to implement an agenda that was heavily influenced by its founder's ideology and political baggage (Papandreou 1973) and was completely unrealistic in regards to the economic capacity of the country. The debt ballooned while the Socialists oversaw a turnover and the explosion of the public sector while implementing great social programs in education, healthcare, and pension schemes creating a middle class out of thin air (Bastasin 2012).

The behavior of the socialists was not unusual; it mirrored changes in socialist France under President Francoise Mitterrand and Spain under socialist Prime Minister Felipe Gonzales. In the Greek case, however, nobody put the brake on the state excesses or was able to steer the country away from its destructive course. The enormously beneficial terms of employment for the Greek state could not be rescinded even at the height of the crisis. Even when the Socialists attempted to reign in the excess they were unsuccessful at stemming its flow. Almost thirty years later, it was time to pay the proverbial piper, and in a last ditch effort to stem the tide the conservative government of Kostandinos Karamanlis, whose uncle by the same name had successfully negotiated the terms of Greek entry into the EU, told the country that it was time for sacrifices and belt tightening, knowing full well that the Greek deficit spiraled out of control and that his government was in cahoots with major financial institutions such as American behemoth Goldman Sachs that was cooking the books. His opponent, socialist leader and scion of the Papandreou dynasty in Greek politics claimed that he could do it by deficit spending, which he argued would stimulate the economy and increase revenues that would then offset the negative effect on the deficit. Within a week of his inauguration as Greece's prime minister, he knew there was no way his plan could be implemented but that he in fact was ruling a country facing financial collapse. The only solution would be to go the way of fiscal belt tightening with an austerity package that was needed to keep the country solvent (Verde 2011).

Greece became the poster child for what was wrong with Europe and was the country that came close to being the first one to exit the Eurozone with all the possible catastrophic consequences that this move would entail. In their effort to reestablish legitimacy and financial rigor, global financial ratings houses rushed to reduce Greek sovereign debt to "junk status," otherwise known as BB+ rating, fearing the default of the country, and the global markets shivered in the thought of a Greek exit from the Euro. The Greek government entered negotiations with the European Union and the

International Monetary Fund for an initial loan of 45 billion Euros, a rather small sum initially but the European leaders blinked and the damage was done. Europe panicked when the financial crisis hit a country that represented at best 2% of the Eurozone gross domestic product (Bastasin 2012), and the markets responded by making it impossible for the Greeks to find available funds to service its debt and stay solvent. Thus the country required a bailout, something the German leadership had vowed not to ever allow.

As the time came close for Greece to be bailed out, considering the terrible financial situation it was in, it found herself the victim of political divisions at the highest level of global finance, the unwillingness of the European Central Bank to understand the problems of Greece and to offer help, and the ideological opposition, verging on racism, to bailing out the "lazy Greeks." The former European Central Bank president Jean Claude Trichet was against not only a Greek default to begin with, considering the effect on the Eurozone and on private banks holding Greek debt but also the International Monetary Fund involvement, which would give the Obama administration a way to dictate economic policy in Europe. He was also strongly predisposed to use traditional neoliberal economic practices to solve a problem of liquidity (Quiggin 2012a). In addition to this, the German public played a massive role in pushing its leadership against the Greek bailout and Chancellor Merkel to the brink of letting Greece withdraw from the Euro. As highlighted by Bastasin, "The new German economic doctrine—centered on painful reforms, a rudimentary concept of stability in terms of monetary restraint, and skepticism about the virtue of state expenditures—became sort of civil religion. A daily prayer was sung from minarets of some of the press against the archetype of non-German vices: Greece. And there's never a shortage of ayatollahs when orthodoxy gains popularity" (Bastasin 2012: 179).

Finally, though, the crisis reached its apex and contagion was a very real possibility, and thus Greece was given a very structured 110 billion Euro bailout that required very painful adjustments. The Greek government collapsed, and European Central Bank Vice President Loukas Papademos became care-taker prime minister until elections were held in May 2012. Meanwhile, the German chancellor lost yet another election in Rhine Westphalia while her nemesis French president Nicholas Sarkozy was ousted in the national election of 2012. The crisis was declared over by *The Economist*,[18] while the new European Central Bank president, Mario Draghi, vowed to do "whatever it takes" to support ailing European economies even if that meant buying sovereign debt (Quiggin 2012b).

Conclusion: Obama's Star Remains High on the Continent

The Obama administration moves in Europe have been rewarded with near universal support by the populations and significant support from European capitals. His approval ratings remain very high, and even in Greece, a holdout country with a high percentage of anti-Americanism, he is seen as a president who supported them. Obama's willingness to meet with embattled Prime Minister George Papandreou may have lost him favor with the left in Greece, which in any event remains very suspicious of American involvement in European affairs for political reasons going back to the Greek dictatorship. Moreover, Vice President Joe Biden's visit to Greece has not gone unnoticed in Athenian circles. With the acute crisis over (Frieda 2012), Obama received accolades from colleagues internationally and his fate remains intricately dependent on the events in Europe.[19]

Bibliography

Bastasin, Carlo. 2012. Saving Europe: How National Politics Nearly Destroyed the Euro. Washington, DC: Brookings Institution Press.

Dela Posta, P. and Talani L. eds. 2011 Europe and the Financial Crisis. London: Palgrave /MacMillan.

Economist Intelligence Unit. 2011. State of the Union: Can the Eurozone Survive Its Debt Crisis? London: The Economist.

Ferguson, N. Niall Ferguson on How Europe Could Cost Obama the election. The Daily Beast. http://www.thedailybeast.com/newsweek/2012/06/10/niall-ferguson-on-how-europe-could-cost-obama-the-election.html.

Frieda, Gene. 2012. Is Europe's Financial Crisis Over? Project Syndicate publication. http://www.project-syndicate.org/.

Heisburg, Fracois. 2012. In the Shadow of the Euro Crisis. Survival: Global Politics and Strategy, 54:4, 25–32.

Huntington, Samuel. 1991. The Third Wave: Democratization in the Late Twentieth Century. University of Oklahoma Press.

Kalaitzidis, Akis. 2011. Europe's Greece: A Giant in the Making. NY: Palgrave/McMillan.

Kupchan, Charles. 2012 Centrifugal Europe. Survival: Global Politics and Strategy, 54:1, 111–118.

Papandreou, Andreas. 1973. Democracy at Gunpoint: The Greek Front. New York: Pelican Books.

Quiggin, John. 2012a. Are Eurobonds Inevitable? The National Interest, August 1.

Quiggin, John. 2012b. Blame the European Central Bank. The National Interest, July 3, 2012.

Schinasi, Garry and Truman, E. 2010 Reform of the Global Financial Architecture. Peterson Institute for International Economics, Working Paper Series 10–14, September 2010.

Verde, Antimo. 2011. The Greek Debt Crisis: Causes, Policy Responses and Consequences, in Dela Posta, P., and Talani, L. (eds.). Europe and the Financial Crisis. London: Palgrave/MacMillan.

Notes

1. Peter Walker and Elana Schor, "Crowds Gather in Berlin to Hear Obama's Foreign Policy Speech," The Guardian, July 24, 2008.
2. Lisa Lerer, "Obama Mania Verges on Obsession," The Politico, February 20, 2008, http://www.politico.com/news/stories/0208/8605.html.
3. CNN "Nobel Peace Prize is a Call to Action," http://articles.cnn.com/2009-10-09/world/nobel.peace.prize_1_norwegian-nobel-committee-international-diplomacy-and-cooperation-nuclear-weapons?_s=PM:WORLD.
4. Reuters "Obama Peace Prize has some Americans Asking Why?" http://www.reuters.com/article/2009/10/09/us-nobel-peace-usa-sb-idUKTRE5983AM20091009.
5. Rebecca Heinrichs, "Polish President Blasts Obama on Missile Defense," http://blog.heritage.org/2012/08/08/polish-president-blasts-obama-on-missile-defense.
6. Steve Hill, "Europe's Post Copenhagen View of Obama," The New York Times, http://www.nytimes.com/2010/01/14/opinion/14iht-edhill.html.
7. Ibid.
8. http://www.pewglobal.org/2012/06/13/global-opinion-of-obama-slips-international-policies-faulted.
9. Judy Dempsey, "Obama or Romney, Europe Is in for Disappointment," The New York Times, July 9, 2012, http://www.nytimes.com/2012/07/10/world/europe/10iht-letter10.html.
10. http://yaleglobal.yale.edu/content/global-economic-crisis. Also see Bastasin, Carlo. Saving Europe: How National Politics Nearly Destroyed the Euro. Washington DC: Brookings Institution Press, pp. 26–30.
11. http://fcic.law.stanford.edu/report.
12. Carlo Bastasin. Saving Europe: How National Politics Nearly Destroyed the Euro. Washington DC: Brookings Institution Press, pp. 18–24.
13. http://www.businessmirror.com.ph/home/companies/32633-economic-pneumonia.
14. Paul Krugman, "Eurozone Problems," The New York Times, January 20, 2012.
15. Thomas Friedman, "Two Worlds Cracking Up," The New York Times, June 12, 2012.
16. http://www.iie.com/publications/testimony/testimony.cfm?ResearchID=1580.
17. http://www.spiegel.de/international/europe/chancellor-merkel-vows-no-euro-bonds-as-long-as-she-lives-a-841163.html.
18. http://www.economist.com/node/21564603.
19. Judy Dempsey, "Europe and Obama," International Herald Tribune, July 9, 2012.

11

OBAMA'S FRENCH CONNECTION

Donald Morrison

Angela Merkel was not pleased. The 2008 American presidential election was only four months away, and the German chancellor had just received word that one of the candidates, Barack Obama, wanted to hold a rally in Berlin. Worse, he wanted to speak in front of the Brandenburg Gate, a site of particular significance for Germans. For more than 300 years, the gate has stood as a symbolic point of entry to central Berlin. The ornate sculpture of a four-horse chariot crowning the structure was hauled off to Paris by French soldiers in 1809 after the Napoleonic wars. Prussian troops brought it back in 1871 after the Franco-Prussian War. Nazi partisans marched through the gate upon taking power in 1933, and East Germans streamed through it in 1989 for their first glimpse of the West after the fall of the Berlin Wall.

Why did Obama want to visit Berlin? After all, the city is more than 3,000 miles from the United States and holds only a few thousand American voters. Didn't Obama—a first-term Democratic senator who spoke no German and was locked in a fierce election campaign—have more pressing duties back home? Merkel knew the answers, which no doubt deepened her irritation. Obama, then only forty-six years old, was clearly hoping to benefit from comparisons to another young American: John F. Kennedy, whose 1963 speech in Berlin has become one of the century's most memorable rhetorical feats. Kennedy, also forty-six at the time, came to what was then West Berlin as the youngest man ever elected US president. He spoke only a few minutes before a crowd of half a million people, but his closing words echo through the ages: "All free men, wherever they live, are citizens of Berlin, and, therefore, as a free man, I take pride in the words, *Ich bin ein Berliner.*" When Kennedy delivered those last four words, the crowd went wild. Germans got the message that the United States would stand behind them in the face of Soviet expansionism, and Kennedy gained a permanent place in their hearts.

Contrary to popular myth, Kennedy did not speak at the Brandenburg Gate, but about two miles away, in front of West Berlin's city hall. It was another American president, Ronald Reagan, who put the Brandenburg Gate back on the map for Americans. On June 12, 1987, as the Cold War was reaching its dénouement, Reagan stood before the gate, gestured toward the ugly concrete barrier alongside it, and directed a challenge to his Soviet counterpart: "Mr. Gorbachev, tear down this wall." The crowd went wild. The wall fell two years later.

Obama's request put Merkel in a difficult position. Opinion polls showed that the candidate was far from certain to win the election. He had relatively little experience in national politics, and he was black—a serious electoral handicap. In the meantime, Merkel had to deal with the current president, George W. Bush, with whom she had a workable if sometimes strained relationship. (She had never quite gotten over her fright when Bush tried to give her an unsolicited back rub at the 2006 summit of G-8 industrial nations in St. Petersburg.) German news media reported that Bush, who was barred from running for another term and supported his fellow Republican John McCain in the election, was pressuring her to prevent Obama from speaking.

Merkel did not need Bush to persuade her. McCain had visited Germany many times during his own long career in the US Senate, and his politics were closer to Merkel's center-right views than those of Obama, one of the Senate's more left-leaning members. Merkel was especially uncomfortable with

Obama's presumptuous choice of venue. Through a spokesman, she pronounced it inappropriate "to bring an election campaign being fought not in Germany but in the United States to the Brandenburg Gate. No German candidate would think of using [Washington's] National Mall or Red Square in Moscow for rallies."

And so it was that the world outside America got its first close look at Barack Hussein Obama—not in front of the Brandenburg Gate, but three kilometers away at a place Merkel considered more "appropriate": Berlin's Siegessäule (Victory Column), a monument to nineteenth-century Prussian military successes. On July 24, 2008, before a crowd of at least 200,000 people, Obama unleashed the charm and eloquence that would soon make him Europe's favorite American.

He strode to the podium with athletic grace as the late-afternoon sun began to bathe the nearby summer foliage in the clear light of a German Renaissance painting. He began by suggesting a subtle reference to his race. "I know that I don't look like the Americans who've previously spoken in this great city," he said. Obama reminded his listeners of the Berlin airlift, the Marshall Plan, and other milestones of German-American amity, and then warned of new challenges: terrorism, nuclear proliferation, drug abuse, climate change. No one nation was powerful enough to take on all of these challenges, he said, so transatlantic unity was more necessary than ever. True, there were genuine differences between Europe and the United States, "but the burdens of global citizenship continue to bind us together." The road ahead will be long, Obama concluded, his voice rising, but "we are heirs to a struggle for freedom. We are a people of improbable hope. With an eye toward the future, with resolve in our hearts, let us remember this history, and answer our destiny, and remake the world once again." The crowd went wild.

The speech contained no enduring *Ich bin ein Berliner* lines. Nor any specific details of how Obama might manage the US–European relationship, which after nearly eight years of Bush's tone-deaf unilateralism could use a good back rub. Nonetheless, Obama scored a triumph—not so much in the eyes of voters back home, but in the imaginations of Europeans. The crowd went wild because Obama touched some nerve deep in the heart of a world that had long been yearning for an American politician in the style of John F. Kennedy, a leader who embodied the best of American ideals and their own.

Not since the foreshortened days of Kennedy had the world outside the United States been so enthusiastic about an American presidential candidate. In one typical 2008 opinion poll, 76% of Germans said they wanted Obama to win. In another, 78% of French reported that they would vote for him if they could. To them, and to Europeans generally, Obama embodied qualities they felt were missing in his predecessor: intelligence, articulateness, a preference for dialogue over bluster. Barthélemy Courmont, a researcher at France's Institute for International and Strategic Relations, summed up that view: "Obama represents an America that rejects inequalities, faces the future, accepts its place as the premier global power while not imposing its own views, and is strongly engaged in the resolution of major international challenges. This is the America Europeans have been waiting for."

When Obama was elected a few months later, with 53% of the vote to 47% for McCain, Europe largely believed that change had arrived. The United States, continental commentators said, had finally overcome its legacy of slavery, racism, and bigotry. Political leaders throughout Europe declared they now had a partner they could work with. Even Angela Merkel, long past her doubts about Obama, congratulated him on his election victory and warmly invited him back. "The next time you come to Germany," she said, "you can speak at any gate you want."

Of course, foreign leaders customarily congratulate each other after winning office. But the warmth of the messages that greeted Obama set new standards. President Hu Jintao telephoned the American president-elect to say he looked forward to "a new high" in the volatile China–US relationship. Even Mahmoud Ahmadinejad sent cordial best wishes, the first time an Iranian president had congratulated his US counterpart-to-be since 1979.

Nowhere was the euphoria greater than in France, a country whose love-hate relationship with the United States dates back at least to their twinned revolutions in the late eighteenth century.

Anti-Americanism has long been a staple of the French left (which vilifies Hollywood and McDonald's as tools of American cultural hegemony), just as anti-French sentiment has long animated the American right. (Remember "freedom fries"?) In the months after Obama's election, however, I found it more pleasant than usual to be an American in Paris, where I have lived for the past decade. Strangers on the street would offer congratulations. (Do I really look *that* American?) I found myself the center of attention at French dinner parties. (What is Obama really like?) Friends who disliked France's pro-US President Nicolas Sarkozy stopped calling him "Sarko l'Américain" as a term of disdain. To be "Américain" was cool. Enthused celebrity philosopher Bernard-Henri Levy, one of the first of his countrymen to predict, in 2005, that Obama would become president, said: "We French have the confused feeling that he is the living resurrection of the two greatest heroes, in our eyes, of modern America: Martin Luther King and John Kennedy."

So enthusiastic were the French about Obama that Olivier Abbou, a French director and screenwriter, turned out a new film whose title, *Yes We Can!*, was borrowed from Obama's 2008 campaign slogan. The amiable road comedy is about two unemployed Parisian losers who decide to kidnap Obama's paternal grandmother in Kenya and hold her for ransom. Shown on the Franco-German television channel Arte in 2012, the movie sank with nary a trace—though its trailer lives on at http://www.youtube.com/watch?v=H60qS_ZNaso&feature=relmfu.

Obama's European popularity did not sink with his election victory. Eight months later, a poll conducted in twenty countries by WorldPublicOpinion.org found him to be the most popular national leader on the planet. In a 2009 Trans-Atlantic Trends study, 77% of European Union respondents backed Obama's handling of international affairs, compared with only 19% who had thought the same of George W. Bush. In Germany, where Obama enjoyed an astounding 2009 approval rating of 92% (vs. 12% for Bush), he was widely referred to as "The Black Kennedy," the title of a best-selling book by *Tagesspiegel*'s Washington correspondent Christoph von Marschall—and a reminder that Kennedy's 1963 Berlin speech had left its mark. A Pew Research poll found that 90% of Germans had "a lot or some" confidence in Obama, as did 87% of French, 84% of Britons, and 69% of Spaniards. By June 2012, his Pew numbers had barely budged.

Outside Europe, the story was largely the same. In a 2009 poll by China's *Global Times*, Chinese Internet users named Obama the world's second-most powerful person, after Hu Jintao. The Pew survey put Obama's presidential job-approval rating in China at 55%, unusually high for an American president. His Pew approval ratings were even better in Japan, South Korea, Kenya, and Nigeria. Indeed, Obama scored higher among Europeans, Asians, and Africans in the survey than he did among Americans.

Therein lay a problem. Soon after Obama began his four-year term as president, he found himself virtually rejected by his own country. While his popularity soared overseas, at home it was in tatters. After barely eight months on the job, Obama's approval rating among his fellow citizens had dropped below 45%, down from nearly 70% when he first took office. In other words, one in four Americans had changed his or her mind about him since the election. That was a president's most precipitous popularity loss in recent history.

Indeed, more Americans disapproved of the job Obama was doing than approved of it. That disappointment was reflected in the Democrats' 2010 midterm election disaster, the worst showing by a governing party in seventy years. Even Obama's role in the May 2011 killing of Osama bin Laden was able to improve the president's domestic approval ratings only fleetingly. Within months, they were back in the 40% doldrums. In Paris, I went from accepting congratulations for Obama to apologizing for him.

More ominously, Obama's first year in office saw a steady rise in the percentage of Americans who thought the country was on the "wrong track." A sour, antigovernment pessimism took root among the roughly half of Americans who call themselves Republicans. These partisans questioned not just Obama's policies but also his patriotism and even his paternity. A majority of Republicans in some surveys believed that Obama was a Muslim, a Marxist, a socialist, a fascist, or a terrorist, and many thought that he was all of those. Some even insisted that he had been groomed from youth by shadowy foreign powers to bring America to ruin, a theme developed in several of the many anti-Obama books that began to appear.

More than two years into his presidency, one in four Americans—and nearly half of Republicans—believed that Obama was born overseas and was thus not qualified under the Constitution to be president. Even the April 2011 release of his official "long form" birth certificate, showing definitively that he was born in the United States, failed to convince many of the doubters. A survey by the Public Religion Research Institute showed that the percentage of Americans who believed Obama to be a Muslim actually increased, from 12% to 16%, during his first term. A 2010 Harris poll found that more than a third of Republicans felt Obama was "doing many of the things that Hitler did." And nearly one-quarter in that survey believed that the forty-fourth president of the United States may be the Antichrist. So intense was the anti-Obama feeling that an alarming number of people wanted to kill him. Secret Service officials reported more threats of violence against the president than for any of his predecessors since the service began keeping records in the nineteenth century.

The rise of the Tea Party movement reflected a growing frustration among many Americans that their government and their new president had grown profligate, distant, and out of touch with their concerns. Those complaints were certainly reflected in the 2010 midterm elections, which swept a small army of Tea Party–backed candidates into Congress. Shortly afterward a new populist movement, Occupy Wall Street, attacked Obama from the left for favoring moneyed interests.

Thus, Obama found himself facing a newly energized Republican opposition, dissatisfaction among his own Democrats, a stumbling economic recovery, and a widening budget deficit. Meanwhile, populist revolutions were threatening US-backed rulers in Egypt, Tunisia, Libya, and elsewhere. Iran and North Korea were plunging ahead with their nuclear programs, a newly confident China was challenging US economic and diplomatic power, and US troops were still fighting in Iraq and Afghanistan. The euphoria of Obama's historic election victory seemed a distant memory.

That fall from grace came as a shock to Europeans. Why, they wondered, was Obama so little appreciated by his fellow citizens despite having accomplished so much in his first years in office, from reforming American healthcare to rescuing the global financial system? What, Europeans asked, had one of the most exciting US statesmen in recent memory done to alienate his own people?

To be sure, much of Obama's misfortune was the result of impossibly high expectations: no matter how well he performed as president, the hype that preceded him would never be fulfilled. Nearly every president suffers a decline in domestic popularity as the heady excitement of the election campaign gives way to the quiet frustrations of governing. Besides, world leaders often look better overseas than they do at home. As Bernard-Henri Levy reminded me during a 2011 conversation, "It's even true of [Nicolas] Sarkozy. He's more popular in the US than he is in France." Indeed, a 2009 survey by WorldPublicOpinion.org gave the French president a 46% approval rating in the United States, six points higher than his score in France. Three years later, I wrote an article for Le Monde suggesting only half-facetiously that, because Obama and Sarkozy were more popular in each other's countries than in their own, they should swap jobs. Sarkozy, at least, should have listened. Within months, he had lost his bid for reelection.

But Obama also compounded his problems through tactical missteps, a failure to set the right priorities, misplaced trust in the good will of his adversaries, and—oddly for a president whose eloquence was so evident—an inability to communicate his intentions and triumphs to the American public.

Much has been written about Obama's shortcomings, and they were ventilated thoroughly during and after the 2012 election campaign. So I will not dwell on the subject, except to note that Obama's perceived missteps in the United States had little effect on his popularity in Europe. Six months before the 2012 election, Obama's European approval ratings in the Pew Research poll were virtually unchanged from four years earlier. In France, 92% of respondents said they would like to see him reelected, exactly the same figure as in 2008. His popularity also remained stable in Britain

(73%), Spain (71%), and Italy (69%). Support for Obama's policies received similarly high marks, with more than seven in ten respondents in Germany, France, Britain, the Czech Republic, and Italy expressing confidence that Obama would do the right thing in world affairs.

Obama's popularity was substantially higher among Europeans than that of their own leaders. In France, President Sarkozy's approval rating was stuck in the 30% range for the waning months of his presidency. His successor, François Hollande, started out around 60% after his May 2012 election victory but had sunk to less than half that level a year later, according to Ipsos and other pollsters. In Britain, Prime Minister David Cameron came in at a mere 33% in a Comres poll taken shortly after the successful 2012 London Olympics, which had been expected to give his Conservatives a lift in the polls. (David Milliband, leader of the opposition Labour party, scored 44%.) The longest-serving head of a major European government, Germany's Angela Merkel, fared somewhat better. A survey by *Stern* magazine found that if Germans could choose their leaders directly, 49% would vote for Merkel. Still, that was forty percentage points behind Obama's Pew Research approval rating in Germany.

Among American expatriates living in Europe (unofficial estimates put their number at upward of 1 million), Obama was also immensely popular. No pertinent polling numbers exist, but most Americans residing in Europe are registered Democrats. Thus, Obama was widely thought to be a heavy favorite among expats over John McCain in 2008 and Mitt Romney in 2012. In terms of fund-raising, preliminary figures in mid-2012 showed Obama substantially ahead of Romney, a reversal of the situation in the United States. (Candidates can accept foreign money only from Americans living abroad.) In Britain, for instance, Obama had collected $246,000 to Romney's $219,000. In France, Obama had received $110,000 to Romney's $2,500. And this was before a fundraiser in Geneva at which Hollywood's George Clooney helped Obama harvest an estimated $15 million.

Why was Obama so popular in Europe? One reason is that, like foreigners elsewhere, Europeans tend to ignore the daily cut-and-thrust of the Washington political scene, a sausage factory that can diminish the stature of any US president in the eyes of those who do pay attention. Consider the battle over healthcare reform. Obama wisely decided to let Congress work out the details, thus avoiding a mistake Bill Clinton had made on the same subject. Clinton, with his wife, Hillary, taking a lead role, produced a health plan virtually in secret and then presented it as a fait accompli to Congress. The legislators, who consider lawmaking to be their province, were so indignant that they let the plan die a lonely death. Yet Obama's decision to involve Congress drew him into a morass of horse trading and sail trimming that diminished both his approval ratings and his image of high-mindedness. Not to Europeans, however. They saw only the end result, which seemed like a vast improvement in America's notoriously inefficient health system—and thus a major triumph for Obama.

Another reason for Obama's enduring popularity in Europe is that he quickly rebuilt relations with America's European allies, ties that had been strained by the unilateralism of George W. Bush. Of course, almost anything Obama did would likely be considered by Europeans as an improvement over Bush, one of their least favorite American presidents in memory. In a 2005 Pew Research Center survey, strong majorities in Britain, France, Germany, Spain, and the Netherlands said that Bush's 2004 reelection led them to have a less favorable opinion of the United States.

A relationship that needed considerable repairing was the one with France. President Jacques Chirac's opposition to Bush's invasion of Iraq had angered many Americans (hence "freedom fries"). For their part, many French felt that they were being unfairly snubbed after a vast outpouring of sympathy for the United States following the September 11, 2001, attacks. After all, as my Paris friends often reminded me, that tragedy inspired the French daily *Le Monde* to editorialize, "We are all Americans," a declaration that met virtually no rebuttal. Obama had little trouble healing that sense of abandonment. When France's president visited Washington in 2011, Obama told journalists, "We don't have a stronger friend and stronger ally than Nicolas Sarkozy and the French people." The French were clearly delighted, though US conservatives, a notoriously anglophile bunch, complained that Obama's formulation denigrated America's "special relationship" with Britain.

The French, and Europeans generally, were also gratified at Obama's reduction of troop levels in Iraq and Afghanistan, the elimination of Osama bin Laden, and especially the US willingness to let European allies—notably France—play a leading role in the ouster of Libyan dictator Muammar Gaddafi. True, not all of Obama's foreign initiatives went well. Early attempts to improve relations with Iran, North Korea, and Russia came to nought, and Obama was unable to move the Israeli–Palestinian dialogue forward. Still, viewed from Europe, Obama appeared to be a more subtle and effective steward of the US brand overseas than his immediate predecessor.

If so, it was not because Obama showed any special interest in Europe. On the contrary, he signaled early in his presidency that he would shift the focus of America foreign policy away from Europe and "pivot" toward Asia. That seemed a reasonable evolution: a 2011 Transatlantic Trends poll indicated that most Americans consider Asia to be more important to their country than Europe. Observed Richard Gowan, a policy fellow at the European Council on Foreign Relations: "Obama's vision of international engagement rests on working with rising powers like China and India, rather than palling around with old European friends."

Accordingly, Obama kept his European appearances rare and low-key. (One exception: a tumultuous 2011 visit to his mother's ancestral village in Ireland. "My name is Barack Obama, of the Moneygall Obamas, and I've come home to find the apostrophe we lost somewhere along the way," he quipped to a jubilant crowd.) During Obama's one-day trip to France for the sixty-fifth anniversary of the 1944 Allied landings in Normandy, then President Sarkozy almost had to beg for a face-to-face meeting. On an earlier visit, Obama had declined an invitation to dine with Sarkozy and his pop-star wife, Carla Bruni, choosing instead to spend a quiet evening with his family at a Paris bistro. Overall, the Obamas and the Sarkozy-Brunis got along well, though not without some mutual incomprehension. As journalist Jonathan Alter wrote in *The Promise: President Obama, Year One*, Bruni confided to Michelle Obama when they first met in 2008 that she and Sarkozy had once kept a head of state waiting while they had sex. Bruni asked if the Obamas had ever done something similar. Michelle laughed nervously and said no.

One curious feature of Obama's popularity is that it remained relatively high in Europe during his second term, even as support there for US foreign policy declined. Disappointed by American reliance on drone strikes and electronic surveillance, as well as US inaction on such problems as climate change and the conflict in Syria, only 64% of Europeans told Pew Research in 2013 that they viewed the United States favorably, down from 78% in 2009. But on the eve of his June 2013 visit to Europe for a G-8 summit, 88% of Germans said they had confidence in Obama to do the right thing in world affairs—nearly the same level as in 2009. Nonetheless, it was clear that the euphoria accompanying his first term had dissipated. When Obama appeared at an outdoor rally in Berlin after the summit—this time at the Brandenburg Gate—only 4,500 people showed up.

The American president built no close transatlantic friendships equivalent to the personal bond between Ronald Reagan and Britain's Margaret Thatcher or between Bill Clinton and Tony Blair. Obama did not seek to have his Democrats forge a transatlantic "third way" (between socialism and capitalism) with their social-democratic counterparts, as did Clinton with Blair. Indeed, Obama had a decidedly un-European resistance to ideology: He surrounded himself with pragmatists, chose his policies from both sides of the left-right ledger, and even denounced ideology as irrelevant to the lives of Americans. If Europeans found his behavior toward them inconsistent, there was a reason. "He is not doctrinaire," Bob Woodward, the journalist of Watergate fame, told me on a visit to Paris. "He's a lawyer, which is both a blessing and a curse. He balances interests and views, modifies his behavior and moves on."

Mutual incomprehension is an old theme in transatlantic relations, as readers of Alexis de Tocqueville, Henry James, and Mark Twain can attest. Many French still believe that Richard Nixon was cruelly underappreciated in his own country, that Ronald Reagan was laughably over-rated, and that Bill Clinton was unfairly impeached by Congress for pecadillos that would, if anything, have enhanced his standing in France.

If Europeans are confused by the decline in Obama's popularity in the United States, they are mystified by the attendant upheavals in American political culture. Viewed from Europe, the United States—for decades a self-designated beacon of stability and civic virtue—was becoming a seething cauldron of petty self-interest and strident partisanship. The country seemed to be devolving into two feuding camps—Republican and Democratic, red and blue—with vastly dissimilar goals, values and even versions of reality. After nearly two-and-a-half centuries of success, the American experiment appeared to be in danger of running aground.

That experiment was, in a sense, founded in Europe—on Enlightenment ideals of freedom, democracy, and justice. In fact, those ideals were put into practice by the new nation a few years *before* they began to reshape the old monarchies of Europe. America's 1776 Declaration of Independence borrows heavily from Enlightenment themes—parts of it could have been written by Jean-Jacques Rousseau or John Locke. The 1789 US Constitution incorporates Locke's and the Baron de Montesquieu's ideas about separation of governmental powers, as well as the French Enlightenment's deist-influenced belief in the separation of church and state. And just as the American Revolution was inspired by French ideas, the US success at installing those notions helped to inspire France's Revolution a decade later.

But Enlightenment luminaries would no doubt be astonished by the turn America has taken in the past decade or so. Much has been written about the growing polarization of US politics, so it suffices to note that current-day Europeans are troubled by a growing role of money in American elections, recent attempts to breach the wall between church and state, and a coarsening of public discourse.

France has not been immune to such currents, but it seems tranquil in comparison to the United States. The 2012 French presidential campaign was conducted with considerably more restraint and propriety than the one unfolding almost simultaneously in the United States. President Sarkozy and his leading challenger, Socialist François Hollande, largely confined their discourse to the fine points of taxation, immigration, and the social safety net. The French press, with its usual delicacy, mostly ignored the personal lives of the front-runners, despite a rich menu of colorful spouses, unmarried partners, and other targets on offer. Obama and the United States were rarely mentioned.

Europe, however, was a constant presence in the 2012 US election campaign. For Obama, the European financial crisis threatened to derail the US economic recovery and with it his reelection prospects. For Romney, Europe served as a negative example of what Obama wanted to do to the United States. Romney accused Obama of seeking "European solutions" to such problems as healthcare and the economy, warning that the president's policies would turn America into "another Greece." Of course, Romney's critics noted that he and his fellow Republicans favored the kind of austerity policies that were aggravating Europe's economic problems, but that did not stop the GOP from trying to tie Obama to European socialism. "Conservatives have finally figured out their critique of President Obama's agenda," wrote *Slate*'s Jacob Weisberg, "and it's a familiar one: He wants to make us French."

Anti-European sentiment has a long history in the United States, which did after all have to fight a European country for its independence. George Washington in his famous farewell address warned against "entangling alliances" with the Old Continent. American isolationists in the twentieth century tried to keep the United States out of what they called "Europe's wars." More recently, anti-Europeanism flourished in the United States after France and other continental governments declined to support the 2003 US invasion of Iraq. Historian Timothy Garton Ash, writing in the Hoover Institution's *Digest*, described the then-prevailing stereotype: "Europeans are wimps. They are weak, petulant, hypocritical, disunited, duplicitous, sometimes anti-Semitic, and often anti-American appeasers. . . . They spend their euros on wine, holidays, and bloated welfare states instead of on defense. Then they jeer from the sidelines while the United States does the hard and dirty business of keeping the world safe for Europeans."

In that context, saying that Obama wanted to make the United States more like Europe was a serious allegation. There is a tiny speck of truth in it. Obama did, temporarily and partially, nationalize some automotive and financial companies in his attempt to prevent another Great Depression. He increased regulation of the financial, health, and energy industries. He raised taxes on the rich, and he railed against income inequality. Though Obama's agenda was too modest to be described as either socialist or European, Republican primary contender Newt Gingrich dismissed it as "the boldest effort to create a European socialist government we have seen."

The problem is that most Americans have only a hazy comprehension of Europe or socialism, both of which they dislike nonetheless. To them, Europe is a benighted realm of higher taxes, lower growth, persistent unemployment, economic inflexibility, obstructive trade unions, rigid bureaucracies, intrusive regulation, and weak entrepreneurship. (Oddly, Europe's successful health, education, and transportation systems are never part of the package.) The European way, these Americans fear, diminishes individual initiative, promotes economic sclerosis and encourages decadence. Many Europeans, of course, see the United States as a benighted realm of violence, inequality, crumbling infrastructure, and pitiful public services. The food is awful, too. But Americans have long valued their relatively low taxes, their minimalist government, and their ability to order the same Big Mac from sea to shining sea. That Obama would impose some foreign-made alternative did not seem likely.

Nor did he try especially hard. He resisted calls from fellow Democrats for full nationalization of failing firms during the financial crisis. His reforms in health, energy, and even education were largely market-based. And he proposed cutting back some Democratic sacred cows, like Social Security and Medicare, in the name of debt reduction. But that has not stopped his opponents from using Europe as a model of what's wrong with Obama's presidency. Political analyst Dick Morris suggested that the new president had received his Nobel Prize as a reward for attempting to reduce America's competitive advantage over slow-growing Europe. The conservative blogosphere lit up in alarm over an Obama adviser's call for a 10% value-added tax to pay for healthcare reform. The United States is one of the few major industrial countries without a value-added tax—which American conservatives consistently labeled as "European-style," even though most value-added tax jurisdictions are outside Europe.

Mitt Romney in particular found much to dislike about the continent. Here he is in a 2007 verdict on the trend toward civil unions: "In France, for instance, I'm told that marriage is now frequently contracted in seven-year terms where either party may move on when their term is up. How shallow and how different from the Europe of the past." Romney himself spent two years in France as a young Mormon missionary. He is the rare American politician who can speak French. That skill was a liability for John Kerry, the 2004 Democratic presidential candidate, whose fortunes plummeted when a Republican politician alleged that he "looked French."

Obama visibly does not share that handicap, though a large and growing proportion of the French population—estimated at 5% to 10%—can trace their origins to the country's former African colonies. Nonetheless, the issue of race may help to explain Obama's popularity among non-Americans. To them, his election was proof the United States had finally completed the work of Abraham Lincoln and exorcised a disgraceful history of slavery and racial bigotry. "Obama's election is the ratification of the American dream," a South Korean cabinet minister told a visiting American (as reported by Jonathan Alter). "If a first-generation minority can become president of the most powerful nation on earth, anything is possible."

That view was especially strong in France, which abolished slavery twenty years before the United States and is so color-blind, at least officially, that the government does not even collect racial data (which is why France's figures on minorities have to be estimated). The day after Obama's inauguration, Rama Yada, the Senegal-born human rights minister, said that Obama's electoral victory marked "the end of one world and the start of another" and a challenge to France's elite to let the new generation in. "This morning we all want to be American, to channel a small part of the American dream playing out before our eyes."

Beyond race, Obama is seen to embody a number of personal qualities that Europeans, much more than Americans, value in a national leader. He is educated, articulate, and, of particular importance, literary. In France, a politician cannot expect to succeed unless he or she has written a sufficiently impressive number of books, the denser the better. Thus, Charles de Gaulle is revered not only as a wartime hero and exemplary president, but also for writing graceful volumes on modern French history. His successors Georges Pompidou, Valery Giscard d'Estaing, and François Mitterrand were all accomplished authors, and even the less obviously literary Nicolas Sarkozy has written and coauthored a half-dozen books. As for Obama, his two elegant memoirs, *Dreams from My Father* and the *Audacity of Hope*, both best sellers in France, place him firmly in the tradition of French author-politicians.

Obama also possesses several more basic qualities that please Europeans, especially the French. One is a certain personal elegance—a physical grace that coincides with the French respect for poise, taste, and aesthetic excellence. Some of my Parisian friends note with approval that Obama is tall, certainly compared with Nicolas Sarkozy, for whom a lack of height seemed almost a character defect. French like their presidents tall (*viz.* De Gaulle, Pompidou, and Giscard). They also value a certain dignity in the head of state, a quality many found lacking in George W. Bush and, especially, Sarkozy. The former French president was faulted by many of his countrymen for consorting with billionaires and celebrities in a lifestyle derided in the press as "bling-bling." Also for making certain overheated public comments, notably his characterization of unruly minority youths as "scum." In France, where the civility of language is valued and business letters are models of extravagant politeness, calling someone "scum" is not considered appropriate behavior for a president. And certainly not an excess the French would expect from Obama.[1]

In fact, Obama's appeal to the French and other Europeans has as much to do with their self-perceived role as America's tutor in comportment and civic character. Having invented democracy, sort of, they feel a responsibility to mentor their American cousins on the topic. Europeans well know what flawed individuals politicians can be, the world over, and they have seen their share in recent years. But like many Americans, they yearn for something better. In Obama, in his inspiring journey to the White House and in his soaring rhetorical appeals to humankind's better angels, they saw something appealing: a transformative figure who exhorts the world to rise above its petty enmities, ancient prejudices, and bad habits.

Obama's strength, and also his weakness, is that people expect so much of him. Europeans certainly do. Having come from the continent that gave the world some of its most inspiring ideas and ideals, they have not given up on them. Though they are, in most cases, separated from Obama by language, culture, race, and an ocean, they cannot help but see something of themselves in him: the flaws, the mistakes, the aspirations. In the prologue to *The Audacity of Hope*, Obama wrote: "I serve as a blank screen on which people of vastly different political stripes project their own views." In other words, Barack Obama is a mirror in which Europeans sees themselves. Their better selves.

Note

1. For a complete view of the French romance for Obama, read Morrison's "Comment Obama a perdu l'amérique (How Obama Lost America)", Paris: Denoel, 2012.

12

A RELATIONSHIP OF HOPE AND MISINTERPRETATION: GERMANY AND OBAMA

Thomas Cieslik

Introduction

"Germans would re-elect Obama again!" On the one hand, this headline was surprising after the disappointing presidency[1] of Obama, but on the other hand, it reflected the German desire (*Sehnsucht*) for a better world in their typical social-romantic idealism.

Despite the disillusion of Obama's performance as a global "peace president," Germans would have reelected the US president if they could. According to the poll "ARD Deutschlandtrend" of the well-recognized institute "Infratest dimap," 86% of the Germans would have voted for Obama and only 7% for the Republican candidate Mitt Romney.[2] Furthermore, 75% appear satisfied with his work, which means that this figure is even higher than that of the popular German Chancellor Angela Merkel (61%).[3]

This chapter analyzes the relationship between the United States and Germany after the presidency of George W. Bush in its historical context. It reflects the German euphoria in government, media, and society during the election campaign with Obama's visit in Berlin in 2008, and it evaluates Obama's policies toward Afghanistan, the war on terrorism, and the global financial crisis. In addition, the article has a special focus on the personal relation between President Obama and Chancellor Merkel in the cooperation of global matters.

There can be no doubt that the relationship between Germany and the United States deteriorated during the time of German Chancellor Gerhard Schröder and US President George W. Bush when Germany rejected to support the United States in the war against Iraq. The German–American friendship, however, was stronger than personal vanities and disputes. Indeed, when Obama honored Merkel with awarding her the Presidential Medal of Freedom, the highest American civilian honor, in June 2011, a new chapter of mutual comprehension and cooperation was opened. Eventually, a debate about the future relationship between the United States and Germany after 2012 concludes this article.

"Obamania" in Germany

The Victory Column (*Siegessäule*) is one of the most popular tourist attractions in Berlin. It was inaugurated in 1873 commemorating the Prussian victory in the Danish-Prussian War in 1864, which was the first step in the foundation of the German Empire in 1871. Nowadays, tourist guides recall at this location the famous speech of Barack Obama on July 24, 2008, when he presented his political program during his presidential election campaign. In his speech, he reviewed the importance of the divided city of Berlin during the Cold War as a pillar of freedom where Germans and Americans learned to work together after the Second World War. He mentioned the famous airlift and quoted former mayor Ernst Reuter when he called during the blockade: "People of the world—look at Berlin!" The international solidarity helped the Berlin people to overcome their isolation. The fall of the Berlin Wall brought new hope, freedom, democracy, and market economy around the world. Obama mentioned the new challenges brought on after the terrorist attacks of September 11, 2001, criticizing indirectly the unilateral policy of his predecessor George W. Bush and appealing for a new partnership between Americans and Europeans that would permit them to protect their common security and humanity. Furthermore, he referred indirectly in his speech to President Roland Reagan who asked on June 12, 1987, in front of the Brandenburg Gate: "Mr. Gorbachev, tear down this wall!" According to Obama, "Now the walls between races and tribes; natives and immigrants; Christian and Muslim and Jew . . . are the walls we must down." This emphasis on creating a world of global citizenship elated the Germans. And he concluded his statement in a way that reminded everyone President John F. Kennedy's famous solidarity speech for freedom when he declared on June 26, 1963: "*Ich bin ein Berliner!*" During this moment, Obama spoke not only to the people of the German capital, Germany, or Europe, but also to all people of the global society as the next president of the last superpower in the world that would fight consistently for regaining new trust, legitimacy and loyalty:

> Those are the aspirations that joined the fates of all nations in this city. Those aspirations are bigger than anything that drives us apart. It is because of those aspirations that the airlift began. It is because of those aspirations that all free people—everywhere—became citizens of Berlin. It is in pursuit of those aspirations that a new generation—our generation—must make our mark on history. People of Berlin—and people of the world—the scale of our challenge is great. The road ahead will be long. But I come before you to say that we are heirs to a struggle for freedom. We are a people of improbable hope. Let us build on our common history, and seize our common destiny, and once again engage in that noble struggle to bring justice and peace to our world.[4]

More than 200,000 people cheered him enthusiastically. It seemed that with his messages a new chapter of a better relationship between the United States and Germany had been opened. Since there was only one international speech in his campaign, the German mass media celebrated the presidential election as an all-embracing global TV-event. The leading German magazine *Der Spiegel* wrote: "Obamania in Berlin: An American Idol in Germany."[5] Two years later, the German author and journalist Rudolf Freiherr von Waldenfels published a book that reflected accurately the mood at that time *The Black Messias: Barack Obama and the Dangerous Desire for Political Redemption*.[6] The Germans placed all of their concerns onto Obama believing he could solve the global problems and would change politics as a whole: "Germans will hail him as a magician with the ability to transform a gloomy world into a brighter place."[7] At that time, only a few and independent German journalists could provide nuanas to the glorious picture of Obama. Karl Feldmeyer, former correspondent of the German daily paper *Frankfurter Allgemeine Zeitung*, wrote in his blog that Obama's requests for more German support in the war on terrorism were lost among the most naïve members of the audience. It wanted to listen to visions, not to real challenges.[8] And there can be no doubt, that Obama consciously selected the German stage as being perfect for his appearance as the upcoming "global president." The exaggerated jubilance in Berlin transmitted beautiful pictures into the American households. The Germans are still struggling among themselves with their role in Europe. On the one hand, they desire more leadership according to their growing economic and political importance and position in the world, but on the other hand, they reject all power of leadership due to their historical experiences with National-socialism, chauvinism, and militarism in the Second World War. Their point of view saw things only in black and white: George W. Bush was the evil one, and Barack Obama the good and holy one. The *Spiegel* wrote:

> In this respect, George W. Bush was a godsend for Germans and their complex inventory of emotions. Never before had they been able to complain so openly about the Americans' hubris and arrogance and then feel so vindicated afterwards. The Texan Bush embodies everything the Germans criticize about America: the small-minded and swaggering demeanor of a Southerner.

Obama is far closer to the Germans. In fact, he seems almost European: not some Texas cowboy, but a Harvard graduate from an urban environment, and not a "straight shooter" but a man who emphasizes dialogue and mutual understanding.[9]

In the election of Obama, the Germans developed a new projection from the American to the "German dream," where immigrants could achieve high positions in state and economy. After the struggle for gender equality including setting quotas for political parties, state institutions, or in a board of shareholder companies—with or without legal foundations—the demand for race equality led to a renewal of the political debate about integration and assimilation. Foreigner's associations and left-wing organisations successfully demanded a focus on more affirmative actions in the German system. Chancellor Merkel advocated in the National Action Plan for Integration a minimum quota regulation for immigrants or people with migration background (that definition includes also Germans whose parents have been foreigners) in public services.[10]

Furthermore, German media asked which immigrant will be the first chancellor? Around 7 million foreigners live in Germany, among them some 1.6 million from Turkey, which comprise the largest community of foreigners.[11] The first minister of Turkish descent in a German land was Aygül Özkan. In April 2010, she was appointed minister for social affairs in Lower Saxony. Nowadays, the prime minister of this land is David James McAllister who holds two citizenships: a German and a British one. Additionally, the vice chancellor of the Federal Republic of Germany since May 2011 is Philipp Rösler. He is the chairman of the Liberal Party, minister of economics, and originally from Vietnam. He was adopted by German parents from a Catholic orphanage during the Vietnam War when he was nine months old.

German Results of the Pew Global Attitudes Project and the Transatlantic Trends

Initially, the "Obamania" helped to reconstruct a positive image of the United States. In 1999/2000, 78% of the Germans had a favorable opinion, but it crashed during the Iraq War in 2004 to reach a mere 38% and received its lowest point in 2007 with 30%. After the election of Obama it rose to 64% and changed to 52% in 2012. The Pew Research Center has ascertained the opinion of nations on American Foreign Policy.[12] In general, Germany still has a positive attitude toward the United States although the decline during the two terms of George W. Bush's presidency could not be recovered completely. In this rank, Germany has among other European states the most critical position on US foreign policy, except for Greece (35%). Though many nation states around the globe have rejected the unilateral foreign policy of the United States, Germany still has a better opinion. After all, 43% said the United States took into account the interests of Germany "a great deal" or "a fair amount" (e.g., United Kingdom 35%, Italy 27%, and Spain 17%). However, this issue has also shifted dramatically from its original 56% in the last years. Like other European countries, the German support for American antiterrorism policies was low at the end of the Bush presidency (42% in 2007). In 2012, it approached around 60%. But a crucial point is the approval of the tactics of the United States in fighting terrorism. In almost all nations polled, the majority disapproved drone missile strikes, including Germany at 59%. In terms of evaluating the leading actors of US foreign policy, the research study indicated that the Germans expressed the highest rate of confidence in Europe in the politics of President Obama (87%) and US Secretary of State Hillary Clinton (69%). By comparison to this continuous highest approval rating in the surveys of the last years, in 2008 only 14% had supported President George W. Bush.

In general, Germans tend to be skeptical. This attitude is strongly underlined in the comparative assessment of American economic power. China is considered as the news world's economic leader. In 2008, 25% of Germans said the United States would be the leader; in 2012, only 13% believed so. In comparison, China's position improved dramatically from 30% to 62%. Nevertheless, the Germans approved Obama's handling of global economic problems (61%) along with other Western European people. But they have been disappointed about his politics on multilateralism, his security policy in the Middle East, as well as his policy approaches to fighting the climate change. In all categories, the respondents judged Obama in 2012 worse than in 2008. For Germans, his politics in taking serious steps on climate change have been a disaster (down from 76% to 23% in 2008). However, regarding confidence in global leaders, Obama has kept his position as a more popular president in Europe and Germany (87%) than in his own country (61%), and even more than the German chancellor (77%).

In spite of the disappointment in Obama's economic policies, a vast majority (89%) of Germans would reelect him as president. His rival Romney received generally bad reviews in the German press. Most Germans rejected his conservative positions on abortion, the death penalty, homosexuality, the welfare state, or taxes. German journalists picked up the arguments of the Obama supporters. They characterized Romney as a frigid capitalist, a hedge funds manager who paid less taxes than a nurse, or a puppet of the Tea Party movement. Besides, his membership in the Church of Jesus Christ of Latter-Day Saints seemed suspicious because the Mormons are considered as a sect that permits polygamy. Therefore, even Chancellor Angela Merkel avoided a meeting with Romney. Romney's team had prepared a visit to Germany during his journey to Great Britain, Israel, and Poland during the summer of 2012. Merkel's counselors feared that Romney's bad image would damage her reputation, although Merkel was, contrary to her good personal relations with George W. Bush, uneasy about Obama's way of making politics, his waywardness, and his informality.[13] Pleasurably, the German press diffused his *faux pas*: for instance, in Poland when his press advisor insulted Polish journalists, when his remarks on security at the Olympic Games offended British Prime Minister David Cameron, or finally when he stated that he would not worry about those 47% of the Americans who live off the welfare state.

Beyond politics and the economy, the American people continue to receive positive ratings, indicating that 63% of the Germans like them. This survey has also identified that American ideas about democracy are still popular in Germany (45%). Besides, American popular culture in the form of music and movies enjoys unchangeable approval ratings: in 2002 around 66% and in 2012 even 67%. And especially young people between 18 and 29 years old like that the American cultural influence is spreading in Germany (41%), although older people (50+ years) dislike it (16%). In comparison with other nations, this tremendous oldest-youngest gap could have its reasons in growing conservative attitudes toward new cultural trends in the so-called 1968-generation, which was shaped through its experiences during the era of the anti–Vietnam War movements.

A further indicator for measuring the German and European attitude toward the United States has been published by the Transatlantic Trends.[14] This project by the German Marshall Fund of the United States and the Compagnia di San Paolo is an annual survey of US and European public opinion. It started in 2002 as "World Views." Generally speaking, the results of this study do not differ fundamentally from the Pew Research survey. On the one hand, 52% of European Union citizens (60% of Germans) desired a United States that would exert stronger leadership in world affairs; on the other hand, 63% of Americans wanted a European Union that would take more responsibilities and leadership in global matters. Within the European Union, 86% of Germans expressed the most support for European Union leadership. Moreover, a vast majority shared the opinion that the United States and Europe share common interests that would permit them to cooperate on international issues.[15] Finally, the results of this survey support the trend that the election of Obama has helped to consolidate the transatlantic relations.

Explaining the Euphoria on Obama

Though an American president has less constitutional power relative to Congress than any European chancellor or prime minister, Obama epitomized the power with his insignia of the *Air Force One* and the *Nuclear Codes Biscuit*. "For Barack Obama, however, the contrast between his aura and reality has been more flashy than for his predecessors. Through his charismatic uniqueness as the first

Black man at the top of the state he was able to enhance the myth of the president in new dimensions."[16] German journalist Christoph von Marschall published in 2007 an astonishing book about Obama, calling him the "black Kennedy,"[17] and presenting him to the German audience as the new hope for America and the World.

After the Second World War and the division of Germany, the United States became its most important ally. The quick economic recovery of West Germany through the Marshall Plan was in the interest of the United States since it stabilized its sphere of influence against Soviet expansionism. President John F. Kennedy became the idol of an entire generation when he visited Berlin after the construction of the Wall. President George Bush Sr. was the first president who recognized a possible German reunification among the four Allies in fall 1989. For Germany, integration into the West and NATO-membership have been the cornerstones of effective transatlantic relations. Chancellor Gerhard Schröder's statement that Germany declared "unconditional solidarity" with the United States after the terror attacks of September 11, 2001, followed the logical assumption of mutual cooperation within Western civilization. Although Germany rejected President George W. Bush's policy on Iraq, it supported the US financially and militarily from the beginning of Operation Enduring Freedom in the war on terrorism together with the International Security Assistance Force. Currently, some 5,300 German soldiers are serving in Afghanistan.

The traditional links between the two countries were founded through the influence of German immigrants into the United States. Hence the mutual exchange in science, culture, and economy has been steadily growing. The list of famous German immigrants in the United States is long. German Americans or "Deutschamerikaner" comprise about 50 million people (17.0%) of the US population, and form the largest ancestral group ahead of Irish-Americans. It is well known that three US presidents were of clear German descent: Richard Milhous Nixon (1969–1974) (Nixon's maternal ancestors were Germans who anglicized *Melhausen* to Milhous), Dwight Eisenhower (1953–1961) (original family name Eisenhauer), and Herbert Hoover (1929–1933) (original family name Huber).

But even Obama has some rather remote German roots.[18] The great-grandfather in the fifth generation of his mother Ann Dunham was Christian Gutknecht. The tobacco preparer was born in 1722 in Bischweiler, a small village in the Alsace that nowadays belongs to France. He was married to Maria Magdalena Grünholtz, immigrated to Philadelphia in 1749, and died as Christian Good-(k)night in 1795 in Germantown (Pennsylvania).

Obama, however, did not emphasize his European roots during his election campaign. But his visit to Berlin in 2008 helped to restrengthen the transatlantic relationship as a key for multilateral cooperation in the war on terrorism.

From the German perspective, Obama has been designated as a president onto whom all desires and sympathies were projected that had not found a home in Germany. He has been considered as a new type of politician whose election slogans "Yes, we can!" and "Change!" animated Germans to believe in the will to rule and to transform and permanently improve society into a better place. They characterized him as a charismatic leader that could convince and inspire citizens to build up a better community. He has perfectly personified the American dream, where the melting pot of hundreds of nations had formed into a prosperous society emphasizing cultural sovereignty and social-moral clams.

"The American Dream has become a global phenomenon. In many ways, this American idea now stands for an aspiration that can be shared even by people outside the United States with no intention or opportunity to migrate to that country. Even if the same opportunities available in the United States are not offered in their home countries, the fact that the idea of unhindered progress exists somewhere may serve as an inspiration."[19]

Germans identified Obama as a politician that would also fit in their own society that is characterized by the struggle of creating a new identity after the reunification in 1990 and the permanent task of successfully integrating immigrants into the community. Moreover, German society is characterized by the search for more economic and social justice. The Germans believe that they live in a deeply unfair society separating the rich from the poor,[20] though Germany has an expanded social welfare state with some of the highest social welfare benefits (around 31% of the gross domestic product for all social benefits).[21] And of course, it does not display the extremes in income distribution like the United States. The GINI-Index for Germany is 0.30 (ranking 15th among 31 OECD-countries) and for the United States is 0.38 (rank 27).[22]

Assessing Obama's Politics

In general, most Germans have always supported a Democratic Party candidate for the American presidency. However, from the point of national interests, a Republican president has served the German interests better, for example when Ronald Reagan initiated the arms race in the 1980s that led to the collapse of the Soviet Union or when George Bush Sr. convinced the Allies to accept the German reunification. Political scientist from the University of Bonn, Thomas Speckmann, has argued that the rhetoric of Republicans were rougher and more aggressive thus irritating the Germans; Democrats, however, would discourse in a more European style including many promises regarding social benefits.[23] But Obama's advice in the Euro crisis was not really helpful for the German fiscal policy. Opposing Merkel's austerity politics, he suggested that Germans should help to stimulate the recovery of the European economy even with deficit spending.[24]

After the election in 2008, German mass media drew a positive picture of Obama as a passionate president who has been fighting with his social programs, especially in the health sector, against resistance coming from the Republicans, rightwing extremists, and racists. Furthermore, German journalists have also reported with some rancor about the political, social, economic, and cultural decline of the United States. In this context, they sometimes labeled his Republican opponents or the Tea Party movement as extremist, weird, dumb, Christian fundamentalist, or bullheaded. They depicted an America that moved far away from the common values of Western civilization. They played with such prejudices and finally drafted Obama's role as that of the lone warrior for the Good and the Poor and against the Republicans' superiority: Obama—the "Feel Good-President" of the Germans![25]

German authors pointed out the polarized society, the bias of the two-party system, and the mutually aggressive rhetoric in politics and media that left the impression of a country in the process of being deeply split.[26] Obviously, this scenario was lopsided and exaggerated. It helped some authors like von Marschall to sell their books, but it did not keep attention on the US election compared to four years previously. According to the Pew Research Study, German public interest in the election process has decreased from 56% (in 2008) to 36% (in 2012).

Reviewing Obama's performance during the four years of his presidency suggests it should be judged somewhere between modest success and disappointment.[27] He decreased the rate of the United States' economic decline with the American Recovery and Reinvestment Act of $800 billion, saving the financial and automobile sectors like GM and Chrysler. However, he struggled to reverse the economic depression. Poverty has increased; in 2008 only 31 million people received food stamps but four years later it was around 46 million. The debt of the US is still high with $16 trillion. The rate of unemployment was 7.8% in September 2012.[28] Ostentatiously, German press reported in detail about the unemployment rate. No president had been reelected when the unemployment rate was higher than the benchmark of 8%.

Journalist Matthias Rüb from the prestigious "Frankfurter Allgemeine Zeitung" stated that Obama's main success in his security policy was the killing of Osama bin Laden, but that did not finish the war on terrorism.[29] Furthermore, his meaningful speech in Cairo (June 4, 2009) on the "New Beginning" between America and the Muslim World as well as his discourse in Prague (April 5, 2009) on disarmament have become mere words in the course of his presidency. Because of the military intervention in Libya and Obama's hesitant policies during the turbulent developments of the so-called Arab Spring, the United States could not move the peace-building process forward in the Middle East. A fundamental shift in the relations between the United States and Russia did not occur, either. Obviously, his foreign policy did continue the Bush doctrine. While he kept Secretary of Defense Robert Gates, he completed the withdrawal of troops from Iraq and promised to end the Afghanistan occupation by 2014 although he temporarily raised troops by around 30,000 temporarily. He made decisions on his own, sometimes hesitantly, sometimes with courage, and consequently when he declared on February 1, 2011, that the transformation process in Egypt should start immediately, the German journalists Martin Klingst and Jan Ross evaluated his efforts as heroic, not as cowardly. They declared the finiteness of the political power of the United States, while taking into account the consequences of the overstretched empire in regards to military and economic power, and convincing partners to share the burdens of keeping the world safe from extremism. In this context, his speech at West Point[30] is a good document to review this approach.

Human rights activists have been disappointed about the failure to close the prison camp in Guantánamo. He signed the National Defence Authorization Act 2012 authorizing the government to detain persons suspected of involvement in terrorism for an unlimited period.[31]

Very late, he backed same-sex marriage. He could realize neither his promises to help change the (il)-legal situation of immigrants nor his climate policy. German publicity lauded his success in establishing a new healthcare law. German supporters of Obama indicated correctly that the president lost much of his ability to lead due to the loss of the Democratic majority in the House of Representatives after the midterm elections. Sociologist Peter Lösche evaluated the general disappointment as a consequence of the growing lack of knowledge in German society about America and the American political system. The relations between the two countries have become less emotional than in the past.[32] In conclusion: After his first term, German media offered the excuse that the public expected too much from him and drew a picture of a man who was fighting for his policy, that he was attempting to recover lost trust and to convince the American people that only he could lead the country out of the economic misery. Two weeks before the election the leading German weekly paper *Die Zeit* offered the following headline about Obama: "Trotz allem: Ein Held" ["In spite of everything: A hero"].[33] And Christoph von Marschall added, Obama came back not as a Messiah but a "cool mechanist of power."[34]

The Reestablishing of Good German-American Relations

During the presidency of Obama, good relations between Germany and the United States have been reestablished. However, the Pacific orientation of the president, his criticisms of the development of the Euro crisis, and his restrained position of the future of transatlantic relations have given the impression that Germany did not play an important role in the US vision for global matters.

A review of the bilateral political relations clearly demonstrate the asymmetry. During the eight years of their presidencies, President Bill Clinton and President George W. Bush each visited Germany five times, Obama only twice in four years. On April 3–4, 2009, President Obama attended the Strasbourg-Kehl summit of the North Atlantic Treaty Organization, commemorating the sixtieth anniversary of its founding. Furthermore, on June 5, 2009, he visited the Buchenwald Concentration Camp and the Landstuhl Regional Medical Center and had a meeting with Chancellor Merkel in Dresden.[35] But this short trip was only embedded between two major events: his speech in Cairo to the Muslim World and his participation at the sixty-fifth anniversary of D-Day on the Normandy beaches. In contrast, Chancellor Merkel officially visited the United States seven times during the first term of Obama's presidency:

- June 26, 2009, Meeting with President Obama in Washington, DC
- September 24–25, 2009, G-20 Pittsburgh Summit on Financial Markets and the World Economy
- November 2–3, 2009, Speech before the US Congress, Washington, DC[36]
- April 12–15, 2010, State Visit in Washington, DC, Los Angeles and San Francisco with Participation at the Nuclear Security Summit
- September 20–21, 2010, Participation at the United Nations Summit on the Millennium Development Goals

- June 7–8, 2011, Meeting with President Obama while being awarded with the Presidential Medal of Freedom
- May 18–20, 2012, G-8 Summit in Camp David and NATO-Summit in Chicago

There can be no doubt that Merkel's award of the Presidential Medal of Freedom was the diplomatic highlight of the German–American relations in the last decade. President Obama complimented her for what she had achieved when she gained freedom.[37] Former Chancellor Helmut Kohl was the last German who received this honor. Moreover, Merkel was invited to give a speech to the Congress. Only Chancellor Konrad Adenauer had been given the opportunity to address the Senate and the House of Representatives in 1957. In this way, Obama hoped to bind Merkel closer to his political agenda: "the administration is giving added weight to the importance of its friendships in Europe."[38] However, the tension between Obama and Merkel could not be covered completely. They disagreed in summer 2011 over the military campaign in Libya, the restoration of the global economy, the Euro recovery through Euro-bonds, and the admission of Turkey into the European Union.[39] After Schröder's earlier disagreement with American unilateral foreign policy, Washington has remained skeptical about German foreign policy. Germany's abstention from the 2011 Libya War, its quick phase-out, and military contributions to American military such as that in Afghanistan underline this attitude.[40]

Apart from diplomacy, the United States and Europe have failed to enhance economic ties. In May 1998 both announced in London a Transatlantic Economic Partnership to boost the foundation of a free trade area. With the beginning of the German presidency of the European Union and chairing the G-8 in January 2007, German Chancellor Angela Merkel presented the idea of the Transatlantic Free Trade Agreement (TAFTA) to foster economic ties beyond removing more trade barriers. Merkel promoted the plan of joint financial market regulations, stock exchange rules, intellectual property rights, and mutual recognition of technical standards for the Northern hemisphere as a counterweight to emerging markets like China and India, for example. Moreover, the plan proposed that both the United States and the European Union could serve as forerunners for the introduction of new global market rules and promote the idea of a liberal economy in times of the paralysis of the World Trade Organisation Round in Doha. Furthermore, the integration of the United States and the European Union could enhance political ties in the promotion of democracy, human rights, and international security as opposed to international terrorism and drug trafficking. In 1994, the United States had signed with Canada and Mexico the North Atlantic Free Trade Agreement. Merkel and Bush agreed to adopt a framework for transatlantic economic integration, which would lay a long-term foundation for building a stronger and more integrated transatlantic economy, in particular by fostering cooperation to reduce regulatory burdens and accelerating work on key "lighthouse projects." They signed an agreement on the foundation of the Transatlantic Economic Council, which created initiatives like the TransAtlantic Business Dialogue and the Innovation Action Partnership. However, mutual nontariff barriers are still an obstacle in deepening the economic ties. The realization of TAFTA would stimulate economic change. Germany is already the sixth largest export market for the United States. "In 2010, U.S. goods and services exports to Germany rose to $73.5 billion. German goods and services exports to the United States in 2010 were $113.7 billion. German exports to the United States are larger than German exports to China and India combined."[41] And vice versa, the United States is the largest source of foreign direct investment in the European Union. The total stock of US Federal Deposit Insurance in Germany reached more than $116 billion in 2010.[42]

Obama's Second Term: The Future of German–American Relations

The German press cheered after the reelection with Obama. "Yes, he can again!" were the headlines of some German newspapers and online magazines. For most German politicians, candidate Romney was a "black box." German Minister of Defense Thomas de Maizière was helpless about the foreign policy strategy of Romney relating to Afghanistan. He feared that a vacuum of power in the White House could endanger German positions in that region.[43]

Philip D. Murphy, US ambassador in Germany, felt certain during the election night in Berlin that Obama would visit the German capital in the second term of his presidency. "During his visit as a Senator he had an extraordinary experience in Berlin," stated the ambassador.[44] Instantaneously after his reelection, Chancellor Merkel invited him to travel again to Germany. Vice Chancellor and Minister of Economics Philipp Rösler hoped that the United States and Europe could agree to a free trade agreement that would reduce tariffs, permit companies to participate in public competitions in federal states, and liberalize fundamentally the trade in the agriculture sector.[45]

But it seems likely that German hopes and expectations are too high again. In the election campaign, Germany and Europe were not part of the debate. The debt crisis in the United States might reduce the American military presence in Germany. US Secretary of Defense Leon Panetta said in January 2012 that two of the four brigades in Europe would leave. The downsizing of the US force would affect the 170th Infantry Brigade in Baumholder (Palatinate) and the 172nd Infantry Brigade in Grafenwöhr (Bavaria), each with some 3,800 troops, by 2013.

The gradual military withdrawal from the continent might provoke a lack of security in Europe with its challenges in the Mediterranean Sea, Northern Africa, and the Middle East. Germany along with its European allies might invest more recourses in their military capabilities to secure peace in the region. Facing the Euro crisis and the paralysis of European integration and institutional reforms, this new responsibility would not become a high priority for Europeans politicians.

German Foreign Minister Guido Westerwelle emphasized that Germany has acted together with Obama.[46] According to Westerwelle, budget consolidation, economic growth, finding political solutions in Syria, Mali, and Iran are the common challenges. From his point of view, Europe and the United States are the closest partners of trade and democratic values, and therefore the construction of a transatlantic free trade area would secure the future of this alliance in the world with its newly rising powers.[47]

And it seems that again history repeats itself. The euphoria after Obama's first election, when Westerwelle for example spoke of a magic moment for democracy (Sternstunde der Demokratie),[48] has been repeated after his second election. Only a few authors warned that Europe should not be too apathetic toward American problems. For example, Josef Braml from the German Council on Foreign Relations (Deutsche Gesellschaft für Auswärtige Politik)[49] identified the American asymmetry in a realistic manner: the economic asymmetry would hinder the United States to be a fully successful player in global politics. Ulfried Weißer argued that the stability of the American identity and prosperity could be fragmented while comparing it to the Soviet Union at the end of its disintegration process after the collapse of the communist ideology.[50] And Hubert Wetzel alerted his readers that any American decline would affect Europe dramatically. The United States helped twice to overcome war and chaos in the twentieth century. It guaranteed peace and stability in Europe, whereas a Chinese twenty-first century, for example, would not be better for Europe.[51] Friedrich Merz, former prominent Christian-Democrat parliamentarian and Chairman of the "Atlantic Bridge," is right when he said: "America has become more introvert and more self-centered. . . . This means that we must make an effort to be viewed in America as a continent and as a country of political and economic relevance."[52]

But a "Western world" that does not speak with one voice in managing the global challenges of Islamic fundamentalism and terrorism, authoritarian capitalism and the destruction and exploitation of environmental resources will not be able to fortify democracy, the rule of law, and civil liberties for their own sake and for Europe's security. Sharing and protecting the common values in a world that has become more instable since the end of the Cold War is the new duty of the governments of both the United States and the European states including Germany.

Finally, both Germany and Europe must fight for America's solidarity and cooperation. Despite its current economic troubles, the United States still has enormous economic and natural resources, strong beliefs in the nation, and positive demographic trends. Obama knows that a "social-democratic" Europe is not a model for America. Together with the Republicans he will try to restrengthen America's power by focusing efforts on *nation-building* in his own country. Therefore, Germans and Europeans must attract the attention of Obama in order to rediscover the meaning of the alliance as held true during the Cold War. Obama himself argued in his first interview with a German newspaper that "our relationship with Europe is the cornerstone of our engagement with the world and a catalyst for global action. Germany is at the center of Europe, and the cooperation between the United States and Germany is central to everything we hope to accomplish in the world."[53] A "lonely" superpower could not by itself defend the traditional Western values in a world where authoritarianism is rising again in many parts around the globe. If Germans and Europeans do not achieve this, the warning of the political scientist Helga Haftendorn might become reality:

> With the Pax Americana gone, no commanding force or overarching structure will shape global agenda and mediate competition and conflict. Given the structural asymmetries between Europe and America, it is unlikely they will unite to cope jointly with new challenges. Rather, each will seek to adapt according to its own needs. America will try to retain as much of its power as it can, and Europe needs to muster its resolve to overcome nationalist habits and become a dynamic actor on the global stage.[54]

Notes

1. Reymer Klüver: Changed? Obama 2012, Aus Politik und Zeitgeschichte, 51–52/2011, December 19, 2011, pp. 3–7.
2. Infratest dimap (ed.): ARD-DeutschlandTREND, September 2012, http://www.tagesschau.de/inland/deutschlandtrend1572.pdf, p. 25, access: October 3, 2012.
3. Ibid., pp. 8–9.
4. Barack Obama's Remarks at Berlin's Victory Column, July 24, 2008, http://www.cfr.org/us-election-2008/barack-obamas-remarks-berlins-victory-column/p16853, access: October 1, 2012.
5. Spiegel-Staff: Obamania in Berlin: An American Idol in Germany, July 21, 2008, http://www.spiegel.de/international/world/obamania-in-berlin-an-american-idol-in-germany-a-567148.html, access: October 1, 2012.
6. Rudolf Freiherr von Waldenfels: *Der schwarze Messias: Barack Obama und die gefährliche Sehnsucht nach politischer Erlösung*, Gütersloh 2010.
7. Spiegel-Staff: Obamania in Berlin: An American Idol in Germany, July 21, 2008, http://www.spiegel.de/international/world/obamania-in-berlin-an-american-idol-in-germany-a-567148.html, access: October 1, 2012.
8. Karl Feldmeyer: Obama und die Sehnsucht nach der heilen Welt, July 2008, http://karlfeldmeyer.de/?p=45, access: October 3, 2012.
9. Spiegel-Staff: Obamania in Berlin: An American Idol in Germany, July 21, 2008, http://www.spiegel.de/international/world/obamania-in-berlin-an-american-idol-in-germany-a-567148.html, access: October 1, 2012.
10. Nationaler Aktionsplan Integration, Focus, January 31, 2012, http://www.focus.de/politik/weitere-meldungen/nationaler-aktionsplan-integration-merkel-fuer-hoehere-migranten-quote-im-oeffentlichen-dienst_aid_709168.html, access: September 30, 2012.
11. Ausländerzentralregister, Statistisches Bundesamt, December 31, 2011, https://www.destatis.de/DE/ZahlenFakten/GesellschaftStaat/Bevoelkerung/MigrationIntegration/AuslaendischeBevoelkerung/Tabellen/StaatsangehoerigkeitJahre.html, access: October 10, 2012.
12. Pew Research Center: Global Attitudes Projects, Global Opinion of Obama Slips, International Policies Faulted, Drone Strikes Widely Opposed, June 13, 2012, http://www.pewglobal.org/2012/06/13/global-opinion-of-obama-slips-international-policies-faulted/, access: September 30, 2012.
13. Robin Alexander: Wie Merkel einen Besuch von Romney abwimmelte, Die Welt, 14. October 2012.
14. German Marshall Fund of the United States et. al. (ed.): Transatlantic Trends 2012, http://trends.gmfus.org/files/2012/09/TT-2012-Key-Findings-Report.pdf, access: November 1, 2012.
15. Ibid., p. 9.
16. Martin Klingst, Jan Ross: Die coole Macht, Die Zeit, October 11, 2012, pp. 2–3. My own translation.
17. Christoph von Marschall: Barack Obama. *Der schwarze Kennedy*, Zürich 2007. His further publications on Obama: *Michelle Obama. Ein amerikanischer Traum*, Zürich 2009; *Der neue Obama. Was von der zweiten Amtszeit zu erwarten ist*, Zürich 2012; *Was ist mit den Amis los? Warum sie an Barack Obama hassen, was wir lieben*, Freiburg 2012.

18. William Addams Reitwiesner (compiled): Ancestry of Barack Obama, http://www.wargs.com/political/obama.html, access: September 30, 2012.

19. Matthias Maass: A "Global Event" with global stakeholders: Obama's Election and the "Idea" of America, in: Matthias Maass (ed.): The World Views of the U.S. Presidential Election: 2008, New York, Palgrave/Macmillan: New York 2009, pp. 253–261, p. 260.

20. The majority of the Germans evaluate the tax system (82%), the income distribution (81%), the retirement and pension system (73%), the healthcare system (73%), and family policy (65%) as unfair. TNS Emnid, 2012, http://de.statista.com/statistik/daten/studie/1606/umfrage/ungerechtigkeit-in-deutschland/, access: October 1, 2012.

21. Bundesministerium für Soziales und Arbeit: Sozialbudget 2011, 2012, http://www.sozialpolitik-aktuell.de/tl_files/sozialpolitik-aktuell/_Politikfelder/Finanzierung/Datensammlung/PDF-Dateien/abbII1a.pdf, access: October 5, 2012.

22. Bertelsmann Stiftung: Soziale Gerechtigkeit in der OECD. Wo steht Deutschland? Sustainable Governnace Indicators 2011, http://www.bertelsmann-stiftung.de/bst/de/media/xcms_bst_dms_33013_33014_2.pdf, access: October 5, 2012.

23. Thomas Speckmann: Republikaner besser für die Deutschen, August 24, 2012, http://www.merkur-online.de/nachrichten/politik/republikanische-us-praesidentenbesser-deutschen-zr-2473031.html, access: October 1, 2012.

24. Amy Gardner: Obama Effort to Contain European Debt Crisis Takes on Greater Urgency, June 17, 2012, http://www.washingtonpost.com/politics/obama-effort-to-contain-european-debt-crisis-takes-on-greater-urgency/2012/06/17/gJQAPEiKjV_story.html, access: October 10, 2012.

25. Jan Fleischhauer: Unsere Obama-Liebe ist infantil, Spiegel Online, November 8, 2012, http://www.spiegel.de/politik/deutschland/fleischhauer-kolumne-die-seltsame-liebe-der-deutschen-zu-obama-a-866075.html, access: November 9, 2012.

26. Christoph von Marschall: Divided States of America, Das Parlament, October 8, 2012, p. 1.

27. Kurt Kister: Warum Obama eine Enttäuschung ist, Die Süddeutsche, November 23, 2011. See also: Sebastian Fischer: Obamas Präsidenten-Bilanz: Versprochen! Gebrochen?, Spiegel Online, September 4, 2012, http://www.spiegel.de/politik/ausland/obama-bilanz-gebrochene-und-gehaltene-versprechen-des-us-präsidenten-a-845204.html, access: October 1, 2012.

28. Bureau of Labor Statistics, http://www.tradingeconomics.com/united-states/unemployment-rate, access: October 10, 2012.

29. Matthias Rüb: Zwist statt Wandel, Das Parlament, October 8, 2012, p. 4.

30. Barack Obama: Speech to West Point 2010 Cadets, May 22, 2010, http://www.cbsnews.com/2100-201_162-6509577.html, access: October 1, 2012.

31. Yassin Musharbash: Obamas Anti-Terror-Gesetz empört Bürgerrechtler, January 4, 2012, http://www.spiegel.de/politik/ausland/guantanamo-obamas-anti-terror-gesetz-empoert-buergerrechtler-a-807132.html, access: October 1, 2012.

32. Peter Lösche, Anja Ostermann (ed.): *Die Ära Obama. Erste Amtszeit,* Bundeszentrale für politische Bildung, Bonn 2012, p. 24.

33. Die Zeit, October 11, 2012, p. 1.

34. Christoph von Marschall: Der neue Obama, Der Tagesspiegel, September 2, 2012.

35. Barack Obama, Angela Merkel: Remarks, June 5, 2009, http://germany.usembassy.gov/dresd_remarks.html, access: September 30, 2012.

36. November 3, 2009, http://www.bundesregierung.de/Content/EN/Reden/2009/2009-11-03-merkel-usa-kongress.html.

37. Karin Schlottmann: Lob an Kanzlerin „Mörkel" für ein offenes Gespräch, Sächsische Zeitung, June 6, 2009, http://www.sz-online.de/special/obama-in-dresden/artikel.asp?id=2175082, access: September 15, 2012. Mary K. Bruce June 7, 2011: Obama Awards Merkel the Medal of Freedom, http://abcnews.go.com/blogs/politics/2011/06/obama-awards-merkel-the-medal-of-freedom/, access: September 30, 2012.

38. Alan Greenblatt: President Obama Embraces Troubled German Ally, NPR, June 7, 2011, http://www.npr.org/2011/06/07/137011509/president-obama-embraces-troubled-german-ally, access: October 3, 2012.

39. Scott Wilson, Howard Schneider: Obama, Merkel Disagree on Libya, Economics. But They're Working on It, The Washington Post, June 8, 2012.

40. Gregor Peter Schmitz: Außen Ehre, innen Lehre, Spiegel Online, June 6, 2011, http://www.spiegel.de/politik/ausland/0,1518,766784,00.html, access: October 1, 2012.

41. The White House: Fact Sheet: U.S.-German Bilateral Economic Ties, June 7, 2011, http://www.whitehouse.gov/the-press-office/2011/06/07/fact-sheet-us-german-bilateral-economic-ties, access : October 10, 2012.

42. Ibid.

43. Severin Weiland: Berlin rästelt über Romney, Spiegel Online, November 1, 2012, http://www.spiegel.de/politik/deutschland/romney-und-die-auswirkungen-auf-die-deutsche-aussenpolitik-a-864310.html, access: November 2, 2012.

44. News-Ticker: Barack Obama bleibt im Weißen Haus, November 6, 2001, http://www.morgenpost.de/politik/us-wahl/article110683814/Barack-Obama-bleibt-im-Weissen-Haus.html, access: November 9, 2011.

45. Burkhard Ewert: Interview mit Philipp Rösler, Neue Osnabrücker Zeitung, November 9, 2012, http://www.noz.de/deutschland-und-welt/politik/67823738/vizekanzler-und-bundeswirtschaftsminister-philipp-roesler-im-interview-natuerlich-trete-ich-an, access: November 9, 2012.

46. Karsten Kammholz: Wir haben mit Obama an einem Strang gezogen, Die Welt, November 7, 2012, http://www.welt.de/politik/wahl/us-wahl-2012/article110766852/Wir-haben-mit-Obama-an-einem-Strang-gezogen.html, access: November 8, 2012.

47. Guido Westerwelle: Worauf wir gemeinsam bauen, Frankfurter Rundschau, November 3, 2012, p. 10.

48. Daniel Brössler: Europäische Euphorie, Süddeutsche Zeitung, November 6, 2008, p. 5.

49. Josef Braml: *Der amerikanische Patient,* München 2012.

50. Ulfried Weißer: *USA—Niedergang und Krise,* 2nd ed., Berlin 2012.

51. Hubert Wetzel: Wählerische Weltmacht, Süddeutsche Zeitung, October 20, 2012, p. 4.

52. Friedrich Merz: A Community of Values, Jewish Voice from Germany, Autumn 2012.

53. Christoph von Marschall: Obama on Merkel: "We Don't Always Agree on Everything," http://www.tagesspiegel.de/weltspiegel/in-english/interview-obama-on-merkel-we-dont-always-agree-on-everything-seite-3/4253564-3.html, access: November 8, 2012.

54. Helga Haftendorn: Transatlantic Stress, IP, Spring 2008, pp. 68–73, p. 73.

Part V

THE MIDDLE EAST AND ISRAEL

13

ARAB IMAGES OF OBAMA AND THE UNITED STATES: AN EGYPTIAN PERSPECTIVE

Ramadan A. Ahmed

Historical and Geopolitical Background

The Arab region has a population of over 330 million people. It includes twenty-two countries in regions as geographically disparate as North Africa and the Middle East, while stretching from the Atlantic Ocean to Central Asia, from the Black to the Mediterranean Seas, and all the way down to the Horn of Africa. Lying at the crossroads where Europe, Asia, and Africa meet, this territory hosts a vast realm of enormous historical and cultural complexity. The earliest civilizations rose from the Mesopotamian Plain and stretched from the Tigris and Euphrates Rivers to the banks of the Nile. Here walked the religious prophets Moses, Jesus, and Mohammed, whose teachings continue to be followed by hundreds of millions of people around the world. The twentieth and twenty-first centuries have seen the most bitter and dangerous conflicts occur in these areas; today, these areas continue to provoke extensive, armed confrontations (Ahmed 2010).

Historical Review of the Relationship between the United States and the Arab World

The relationship between the United States and the Arab world dates back to more than a century ago. Mark Twain and his associates documented their 1867 journey to the Middle East, and his writings created the first impressions of this region that prevail today. Following Twain's book *Innocents Abroad*, Americans have derived their information through channels such as CNN, the *New York Times*, and *Times* magazine, but these have done little to change their attitudes toward the Arab and Muslim worlds. Before the Second World War, the United States had focused on establishing and maintaining a normal, bilateral relationship with minimal intervention. However, the United States grew increasingly interested in Middle Eastern oil resources, especially in the Gulf region and Saudi Arabia (Little 2009). Until September 11, 2001, a pronounced unilateral tendency dominated and shaped the US actions and attitudes toward other countries, particularly the Arab nations (Thebat and Al-Enany 2007: 61). By the end of September 2002, the Bush administration had adopted a policy of preemption instead of containment. It aimed at asserting and expanding American dominance and influence around the globe (Thebat and Al-Enany 2007: 17). It reflected Theodore Roosevelt's belief a century ago that "Americanizing the world is our destiny and our fate" (cited by Galal 2010: 70). The American (and British, French, and German) media, TV, and film industries have issued misleading portrayals of this region in the last five or six decades. Arabs were, and still are, presented in America as ignorant, unreasonable, and dangerous. Such a negative image of Arabs has played a role in increasing negative attitudes against Arabs among the Americans. In addition, some writings, e.g., B. Lewis's "Roots of Muslim Rage," S. Huntington's "Clash of Civilizations," (Huntington 2009), and slogans such as "The Muslims are coming" (Esposito 2009: 473–530) intimidated the Western world and led them to believe in the existence of an Islamic threat.

Tessler and Corstange (2002) presented empirical data from Egypt, Palestine (West Bank and Gaza), Jordan, Lebanon, Morocco, Algeria, Kuwait, and Turkey on how Americans and Arabs view each other at the grassroots. They tested the extent to which contrasting civilizations agree on this perception. While we have much information and knowledge about what government officials and public intellectuals say, it is particularly germane to understand the attitudes of "ordinary" men and women. Results agree with the results of previous surveys. The data show a strong dislike of American foreign policy and strong positive attitudes toward American society and culture, toward American education and forms of government, and toward the American people.

The Hosni Mubarak era in Egypt began with a cautious recalibration. Cairo attempted to restore a sense of proportion in its foreign relations, mainly by improving ties with Arab countries and befriending the Soviets once more. During that period, Mubarak tried to maintain the country's ties with the United States and Israel. In one accident, following the Sabra and Shatila massacre, he recalled the Egyptian ambassador from Tel Aviv to express his displeasure with Israeli policies. But on the whole, cooperation and coordination with the United States gathered pace, culminating in Egypt's participation in the international coalition that President George Bush Sr. put together to drive Saddam Hussein out of Kuwait in 1991. As a reward, Egypt had $7 billion of its military debts written off. However, under George Bush Jr., relations soured. Washington's persistent rhetoric of promoting democracy grated against the Egyptian regime's sensibility, but nevertheless, this model remained a lynchpin of US strategy in the region.

As of 2004, a palpable strain in relations led to the discontinuation of Mubarak's yearly visits to the United States, but this did not hinder Egyptians' continual cooperation with the United States. Egypt allowed US ships to sail through the Suez Canal during the war in Iraq. It signed the QIZ (Qualified Industrial Zone) agreement, allowing for the incorporation of Israeli components in Egyptian textiles to be exported to the United States. At the encouragement of the United States, Egypt also began exporting natural gas to Israel.

When Obama took office, many expected Egypt–US relations to improve because of Obama's vows to support the peace process, help create a Palestinian state, and end Israel's building of settlements. However, what mattered most for the Egyptian regime was Obama's more "lenient" approach to democracy. Obama's administration, like many US administrations before it, preferred stable partnerships to democratic ones. For decades and in several cases, the United States tended to keep good relations with many nondemocratic regimes in countries such as Pakistan, Yemen, Libya, Tunisia, and Iraq (before 1990 Iraqi's occupation to Kuwait), and several others.

In this context, it is interesting to examine how Arab-Americans have voted in recent US presidential elections. Arab-Americans used to vote almost equally for the Republican and Democratic parties. The Arab-Americans' political attitudes changed during George W. Bush's administration (2000–2008). In the 2008 presidential election, 67% of Arab-Americans voted for Obama and 28% voted for John McCain. A recent survey conducted by the Arab American Institute led by James Zoghby (cited in *Al-Qabas* October 2, 2012: 45) shows that 52% of Arab-Americans support Barack Obama, and 28% of them would vote for Mitt Romney. The survey indicates that Arab-Americans consider economic conditions to be the most important issue, followed by foreign policy matters and healthcare issues. Overall, they believe that President Obama will deal successfully with these three issues. The survey also reveals that the percentage of the Arab-Americans who classify themselves as Democrats decreased from 54% in 2008 to 46% in 2012. Similarly, the percentage of the Arab-Americans considering themselves a Republican has decreased from 27% in 2008 to 22% in 2012. Finally, the survey indicates that 24% of Arab-Americans consider themselves independent.

In 2009, Obama went to Cairo University to meet the Muslim world. His landmark speech promised to support democracy that Washington assumed would come, thanks to outside pressure on entrenched rulers in countries such as Egypt and Saudi Arabia (Hammond 2011).

In January of the same year, President Obama promised to turn the page in US relations with the Middle East and the Muslim world, calling for "a new way forward, based on mutual interest and mutual respect" (Hammond 2011). During his first hundred days in office, he fulfilled that promise with a number of initiatives, reaching out to Arabs and Muslims across the globe. Obama granted his first interview to the Arabic-language news channel Al Arabiya, where he introduced his Special Envoy for Middle East Peace, George Mitchell, who had been instructed to listen, "because all too often the US starts by dictating" (Ibid.). Later, Obama offered a New Year's greeting of hope and peace in a video message to the Iranian people and their government; in Ankara, Turkey, he told the Muslim world that "the United States is not, and will never be, at war with Islam" (Ibid.). And although slightly behind schedule, Obama finally delivered a much-touted speech in Egypt in which he highlighted shared interests between Americans and Muslims; he described a desired "new beginning between the United States and Muslims around the world" (Ibid.).

With the challenges posed by the global financial crisis and the historical significance of being the nation's first African-American president, Obama accomplished much in his first hundred days in office. Western media outlets such as CNN devoted special segments to analyze the president's first few months at work, while commentators and editorial pages picked apart his opening policies. Politicians, scholars, and pundits on Salon.com and in *Foreign Policy* magazine issued report cards for Obama, grading his management on both foreign and domestic issues. He passed with flying colors.

The Arabs and Muslims took a natural interest in President Obama and his Middle East outreach initiatives, comparing them to his reversals of US policies on Iraq, offshore prisons, and torture. How did Arabs and Muslims in the Middle East, that have been on the receiving end of so much previous hostile foreign policy from the United States, evaluate Obama's first hundred days in office and his historic Cairo speech?

J. Simons (2009) analyzed evaluations from three Egyptian prominent writers (F. Howeidy, S.A. Salama, and I. Eissa) regarding Obama's first hundred days in office and his Cairo address. The writers concluded that this period of time was accompanied by overwhelming failures. Obama set out to fundamentally alter the relationship between the United States and the Arab and Muslim worlds; Obama's administration extended its hand, and the president himself visited the region, directly addressing Arabs and Muslims. Many expected that a change in administration (seen positively after the much-derided previous administration), coupled with Obama's likeability and willingness to engage, would result in major changes in America's relationship with the Arab and Muslim worlds, along with their perceptions of the United States. But, while the relationship is slowly shifting, the Arab and Muslim worlds remain dissatisfied with US foreign policy.

The three Egyptian writers broached the Arab–Israeli conflict more often than they did any other topic regarding US foreign policies. The lack of US support for democracy in Egypt came in a distant second, as one writer discussed. The other two writers believed this issue to be far less important than the first. The wars in Iraq and Afghanistan were cited as sources of discontent in the Arab and Muslim worlds while, in contrast, the global financial crisis was barely touched upon. The 2008–2009 Israeli offensives in Gaza, which ended shortly before Obama took office, could explain why the three writers excessively elaborated on the Arab–Israeli conflict. This issue continues to play a prominent role in the public discourse of Egypt and the region as a whole. Polling has consistently shown that US policies toward the Arab–Israeli conflict remain a crucial factor in shaping Egyptian and Arab public opinions of the United States. It seems as though, in the wake of the Israeli offensive, these writers anticipated an official statement from Obama in support of their own views. Although he has adopted a strong stance on Israeli settlements in the West Bank, Obama has yet to satisfy these writers with substantial changes in US policy on the Arab–Israeli conflict.

Waiting in vain for a clear reversal of US foreign policy, the writers often compared Obama to his predecessor, President George W. Bush. In a January 24, 2009 article titled "Waiting for Obama," published four days after Obama was sworn into office, F. Howeidy explained that "one of the reasons for the new American president's welcome in the Arab world is that the people in our countries hate Mr. Bush to the point that they are convinced that any other person coming to the White House would be better than him" (Simons 2009). Although some Egyptians and other Arabs have expressed an affinity with Obama because of his (partially) African and Muslim background, another writer criticized those who have accepted President Obama simply because of who he is and who he is not: "Hate for George Bush was the number one reason for our love for Barack Obama, as if the story is about names and personalities, and not policies and positions." "Everything Obama said, Bush also said word for word," Howeidy explained in one article (Simons 2009). According to Howeidy, Obama's policies in the Middle East represent a change in means but not in ends. American strategic objectives will not change; rather the change occurring is in the methods of carrying them out. In this regard, Obama wants to use "soft power" whereas his predecessor would resort to harsher actions.

According to the Egyptian writers, Barack Obama's first hundred days in office and his Cairo address prove that rhetoric and public diplomacy can only do so much for America's image. In their views, it is US policy that remains the point of tension between the United States and the Arab and Muslim worlds. Indeed, Howeidy described the Cairo speech as "the same old film, but with a change in direction," stressing that "politics is not about good will" and "it is now time for deeds."

Since stepping into the White House, Obama must have realized the extent of change that was needed. The United States must alter its policy toward the Middle East, especially its relations with Israel. Because of the exceptional treatment the United States has given Israel over the years, the latter has become accustomed to getting away with anything—to act, in the words of one publication, like a spoiled brat (*Al-Ahram Weekly* January 14–20, 2010). Obama's speech in Cairo in June 2009 served as the highlight of his public relations success. Some may discount the novelty of his speech that day, citing his approach to relations between the United States and Arabs and Muslims, his alleged even-handed treatment of Israeli claims and the aspirations of the Palestinians, or the sincerity of the American president's intentions. However, Obama undoubtedly charmed his audience that afternoon. His Arab fans' expectations soared through the roof when Obama apparently promised to pressure the Israelis to freeze the building of new settlements in the West Bank in order to jump-start negotiations with Mahmoud Abbas. One wonders why these fans were excited by such a gesture, especially because the current administration went to great lengths to explain to Netanyahu that his predecessors had committed themselves to such a policy in Annapolis via Bush's roadmap. In other words, Obama was merely reiterating demands made by his predecessor. This gesture pales in comparison to George H. W. Bush's decision to withhold loan guarantees to Israel in the early 1990s, an act that compelled Yitzhak Shamir to participate in the Madrid Conference. Was the euphoria of his fans a reflection of hope or a sign of despair? Most likely, it would be the latter (*Al-Ahram Weekly* December 17–23, 2009). In fact, several analysts described Obama's speech in Cairo as a change in style of expression rather than a change in strategies (Little 2009, the translator's introduction).

One year after Barack Obama's dramatic White House victory, some analysts stated that developments in the Palestinian cause and US–Israeli relations showed significant progress in regards to promoting a negotiated settlement to the Israeli–Palestinian conflict (*Al-Ahram Weekly* June 17–23, 2010). A few month later, *Al-Ahram Weekly* (September 2–9, 2010) asked a sample of Egyptians to evaluate the US president's performance. The general opinions may be summarized as follows:

1. We do not buy into Obama's claim about US inability to pressure Israel. Washington has many cards it could play to convince Israel to abandon its policy of humiliating the Palestinian people.
2. Obama has failed to fulfill many of his foreign policy promises made during his first year in office.
3. What Obama has done so far has been disappointing in the eyes of many Arabs. He has had no successful record on foreign policy at all. Obama's decisions over the past few months tended to rely on military solutions rather than political ones, and that was what the Bush doctrine was all about.
4. Obama lost historic momentum in pushing the peace process and improving US relations with the Islamic world.

5. The United States is not ruled by one person. Obama's speeches were just propaganda to clean up the mess the Bush administration had made in the world. Nothing has happened since Obama's election to make people believe that the United States is really committed to changing its policy in the Arab world. There has been no progress in improving relations with the Muslim world since his election to the White House.

6. We do not see any difference between Bush and Obama. They are just two sides of the same coin, though Obama is the "softer" side.

7. The American people elected Obama for their own reasons: to improve their economy and healthcare. Why should we expect him to do anything for us?

8. Obama has not insulted us as Muslims, unlike Bush or Reagan.

As Hammond noted on May 19, 2011, Obama stood at a State Department lectern in Washington to address the protest movements driven by mostly peaceful, ordinary Arabs. These succeeded in removing autocrats in Tunisia and Egypt but so far have failed to bring change in Yemen, Bahrain, and Syria.

Under the title "Frustrated Hopes" (*Al-Ahram Weekly* June 3–9, 2010), G. Shahine's article stated that one year after US President Barack Obama's historic speech at Cairo University hopes of change gave way to disappointment in the Arab and Muslim worlds. People felt they had received words of reconciliation, but nothing happened on the ground to support these words. Even among the wider public, hopes had largely evaporated. A public opinion survey was conducted in May 2010 on a random sample of 1,198 Palestinian adults in the West Bank and Gaza Strip (*Al-Ahram Weekly* June 3–9, 2010). Results indicated that Palestinian hopes for Obama to bring an end to the Israeli occupation of Palestinian territory had significantly declined in recent months. According to the Israeli newspaper *Haaretz* (cited in *Al-Ahram Weekly* June 3–9, 2010), only 9.9% of Palestinians now believe that Obama's policies will increase chances of achieving a "just peace," down from 23.7% in October last year and 35.4% last June (i.e. June 2009).

However, Obama has been applauded for avoiding the use of charged terminology, such as references to "Islamo-fascism," by using phrases such as "violent extremism" instead. As a result, a survey by the US-based Gallup Center found that approval ratings for American leadership during 2009, the first year of Obama's presidency, increased by a significant margin in most Arab countries when compared to 2008, Bush's last year in the office.

The numbers rose most impressively in Tunisia (from 14% to 37%), Algeria (25% to 47%), Egypt (6% to 25%), Saudi Arabia (12% to 29%), and Syria (4% to 15%). However, ratings continued to fall in Lebanon (25% to 22%) and Palestine (13% to 7%), when Obama's rhetoric was not followed by concrete policies (*Al-Ahram Weekly* June 3–9, 2010).

These polls are not enough to preserve Obama's reputation in the Arab world. Poll results announced at a recent symposium at the Center for the Study of Islam and Democracy in Washington, DC, warned that one year following Obama's Cairo speech, "public hopes could turn into disappointment, especially with regard to Middle East peace, unless the Obama administration begins delivering on some of its Cairo promises" (Ibid.).

The polls indicated that, although there had been "some improvement in the way Muslims view the US since Obama took office," there was "still a lot of anger towards America, especially regarding the Israeli-Palestinian conflict." According to Steven Kull, director of the Center's Program on International Policy Attitudes, people in the Middle East are interested in seeing the United States "put more pressure on Israel" (Ibid.). A survey of America's image among Arab young people, conducted by Cairo University Professor M. Abdel-Fattah, similarly indicated that optimism about improving US relations with the Muslim world was giving way to frustration in the absence of concrete steps regarding Middle East policies (Ibid.).

Although some positive changes have occurred—Muslims had their concerns heard—little has changed on the ground. The administration has taken action on certain issues that Muslim-Americans are concerned about, such as problems facing Muslim charities, as part of the follow-up to Obama's Cairo speech. But many other—perhaps more pressing—issues still need to be addressed. US anti-terrorism laws have hardly changed, and the notorious US detention camp in Guantanamo Bay in Cuba has not been shut down (Ibid.).

Equally disappointing is the fact that the respect Obama expressed toward Muslims and Islamic culture from the podium of Cairo University has hardly helped the tarnished image of Islam in the United States. A recent public-opinion survey conducted among US citizens by the US-based Gallup research organization has revealed that, almost a year after Obama's speech in Cairo, Islam still elicits the most negative views compared to all other faiths (Ibid.).

According to Khaled Hroub, director of Cambridge University's Arab Media Project, "the spurt of fresh air that US-Muslim relation enjoyed after Obama's arrival in the White House is already somewhat musty and could be exhausted even before the end of his period in office and certainly after it" (Ibid.).

Arab Attitudes toward Obama as Seen in Public Opinion Polls

Although US President Barack Obama's rhetoric has lent him worldwide popularity, it has failed to defuse anti-US sentiments in the Arab and Muslim worlds (*Al-Ahram Weekly* November 22–29, 2012).

In 2011, two years after Obama's speech in Cairo, James Zogby conducted a survey to assess the attitudes of over 4,000 Arabs from six countries (Morocco, Egypt, Lebanon, Jordan, Saudi Arabia, and the United Arab Emirates) toward the United States and President Obama (*Al-Ahram Weekly* July 21–27, 2011). Results showed that favorable attitudes toward the United States had declined sharply since J. Zogby's last poll conducted after Obama's first hundred days in office in 2009. For most Arab countries, results indicated that US ratings had fallen in 2011 to levels lower than they were in 2008, the last year of the Bush administration. In Morocco, for example, positive attitudes toward the United States went from 26% in 2008 to a high of 55% in 2009. In 2011, they had fallen to 12%. The same happened in Egypt: US ratings went from 9% in 2008 to 30% in 2009, finally plummeting to 5% in 2011. Respondents clearly indicated that most Arabs perceived the continuing occupation of Palestinian lands as the main obstacle to peace and stability in the Middle East. The second dissatisfaction pertained to the American interference in the Arab world and explained why the US establishment of a no-fly zone over Libya was neither viewed favorably in most Arab countries nor seen as improving Arab attitudes toward the United States. In fact, when presented with several countries (Turkey, Iran, France, China, and the United States) and asked to evaluate whether each of them play a constructive role "in promoting peace and stability in the Arab world," eight in ten Arabs gave a negative assessment to the US role, rating it significantly lower than that played by France, Turkey, China, and, in four of six Arab countries, even lower than Iran.

The results of the 2011 poll of Arab opinion highlight the precarious position the United States occupies in the Middle East and how important it has become for American policymakers to pay attention to what Arabs are saying to Americans. Some may play at politics with critical Middle East issues and celebrate the stymie of President Obama's efforts to make peace and restore America's image in the region. But as the results of the 2011 poll show, this attitude has come at a price, one that is being paid by the entire country (Ibid.).

Hammond (2011) added that the Arab activists took a negative view of Obama because of Washington's long support for former Egyptian President Hosni Mubarak. During the unrest in Egypt, Obama appointed a special envoy to Egypt whose public comments suggested his remit was to save Mubarak, not to fulfill the popular demands for the fall of a thirty-year dictator. Arab activists believed that US financial aid boosted Mubarak's domination and stunted grassroots pressure for democracy.

The Egyptian People's Revolution inevitably affected other repressive regimes in the region (e.g., Libya, Yemen, and Syria, with other candidates such as Sudan and Algeria). Decades-long authoritarian rule has stymied political and economic development and the enjoyment of human rights in most Arab countries. The pressure for change and democratization has now become irreversible. For President Hosni Mubarak, a one-time air force pilot, the Egyptian popular uprising had reached a point of no return (*Al-Ahram Weekly* February 10–16, 2011).

Done in conjunction with Zogby International and released by the US-based Brookings Institute, "Arabs Lose Faith in Obama," an annual survey of nearly 4,000 people from six Arab countries (Egypt, Saudi Arabia, Morocco, Lebanon, Jordan, and the United Arab Emirates) shows Turkey's rise in popularity and Arabs' desire for peace with Israel increasing. Arab opinion of the United States and President Barack Obama dimmed throughout 2009 and 2010, while the popularity of Recep Tayyib Erdogan, the Turkish prime minister, skyrocketed.

The survey finds that the majority of Arabs continue to believe that peace between Israel and the Palestinians will never happen and that, unlike in past years, a larger number of Arabs are identifying themselves as Muslims rather than as Arabs or citizens of a particular country (Hill 2010). These trends could lead Arabs to identify themselves with issues and politics outside the Arab region. As a possible consequence, a weakened or lack of confidence in the West in general, and the United States in particular, may exist among Arabs.

James Zogby blames the drop in support for Obama in the Arab world on Obama's failure to exert the amount of pressure on Israel the Arab world wanted to see. But according to the poll, the Arab population does not seem to be happy with *any* of America's foreign policy positions. Respondents rated Obama's policies as the least popular, when compared with other leaders, including Iranian President Mahmoud Ahmadinejad.

Killing Osama bin Laden also contributed to the Arabs' negative views of Obama. All six Arab countries surveyed said killing bin Laden made them feel "less favorable toward the US." Moreover, in Egypt, only 2% said the al Qaeda leader's death made them view America more positively.

Most surprisingly, Obama's approval ratings had dropped even lower than President Bush's before he left office in 2008. They dropped from 26% to 12% in Morocco, 9% to 5% in Egypt, 16% to 10% in Jordan, and 22% to 12% in the United Arab Emirates (though they did improve in Saudi Arabia and tick up slightly in Lebanon).

The Arab Spring and Obama

Obama's unique background was supposed to make him a prime candidate to improve relationship between the United States and the Arab world. But by the beginning of his second term, not only had there been no progress, it appears that relations are worse than before. Obama has tried to frame a coherent response to an Arab Spring, yet improvisation has been the only American constant. His major address on the Middle East at the State Department on May 19, 2011, was eclipsed by the issue most in the region see as a sign of his country's waning power: failure to end Israel's occupation of Arab land (G. Usher, *Al-AhramWeekly,* September 2–9, 2010).

Indeed, Graham Usher in Washington (*Al-Ahram Weekly,* September 2–9, 2010: 2) and others observed that the real crisis is not between Israel and the United States, but the absence of an American policy for ending the Arab–Israeli conflict. "Will Obama be the first American president to say the US and Israeli governments have different interests in the region and different goals?"

Obama's foreign policies continue to stress the traditional assertion of American power in the face of America's weakening economic influence around the world. The religious-political-nationalistic rise of Islamic ideologies, America's dependence on oil imported from the Middle East, and the economic rise of China are perceived as main threats toward the American political, ideological, economic, and military dominance, as stated in the introduction to this volume and elsewhere (Sharma 2011; Gielen, 2012).

Uprisings that began as peaceful protests in Tunisia and Egypt nearly two years ago have spread across the Arab world, creating a new reality for countries experiencing a political awakening and far beyond. More worryingly for the United States, the Arab Spring created fresh uncertainties and pressures regarding its policies in the Middle East. At present, there is growing resentment among many Arabs who feel that their revolutions have been hijacked by forces not originally anticipated, such as the Muslim Brotherhood Group. Demonstrations in Egypt, Jordan, Bahrain, Morocco, and Kuwait in 2012 are acute symptoms of the prevailing mood in the region.

Two opposing trends are at work. The pressure from below succeeded in overthrowing the regimes in Egypt and Tunisia, and the pressure from above overthrew and led to the lynching of Libya's Muammar Gaddafi after NATO intervention. However, NATO policies continue to sustain Bahrain's minority Sunni ruling class, thanks to the entry of Saudi troops and Western military assistance.

In Syria, Bashar Al-Assad has proven much more resilient, despite serious attempts by the United States and its Arab and European allies to end his regime. The prospect of the United Nations Security Council approving a Libya-type full-scale Western-led intervention in Syria is dim at present. The Russians and the Chinese would not play ball with America, Britain, and France.

Even so, external forces can determine Syria's fate. Much depends on whether the Syrian armed forces will remain loyal to the regime. There are several signs of defection from the Syrian military, but at the moment, the military as an institution appears to be with Al-Assad. However, the United States wishes to see a change of regime in Syria. The future could turn even bloodier. The implications of radical change for the Middle East, starting from neighboring Lebanon, would be very serious indeed.

What began peacefully in the Arab world two years ago has emerged as a bloody scene. Authoritarian regimes, assisted and sustained by great powers, have long dominated the region. Although the Cold War ended and the Soviet threat ceased over two decades ago, the United States continues to pursue its grand strategy in the region with increasing, desperate vigor. The need for oil and support for Israel remain the two fundamental motivating forces of US regional policy. The Arab Spring threatens the status quo, and with it, America's interests in the Middle East. It has to be reversed.

What we see now is a counter-revolution from above, frustrating the will of the people. After Libya, the only exception is Syria. Democracy would be welcomed there, as it would be throughout the Arab world. But turmoil inspired by foreign powers is not what the region needs.

The United States has adopted a double standard of international law for friends and foes as it continues to pursue its grand strategy in the Middle East. This strategy has not learned from the calamitous legacy of America's war under the Reagan presidency in the 1980s, and more recently from George W. Bush's "war on terror." It is difficult to escape a deeper sense of foreboding as we approach the next chapter of an already bloody history.

President Obama's speech on Libya (*The Daily Beast* March 28, 2011) laid out his moral argument for saving lives in defense of democracy without boots on the grounds, an American role that has won him support in the Arab world. It is one of those twists of irony that the US-backed no-fly zone over Libya has more support in the Arab world than in the US Congress. This speech did articulate an American role that the Arabs embrace. Obama's strong moral argument stimulated certain Arab reactions. For instance, "This is the one of the rare occasions a US foreign policy in the Middle East aligns with America's backing for human rights and democracy" (*The Daily Beast* March 28, 2011: 3). However, critics questioned the cost, length, and rationale of the US military role in Libya. They wondered what it is worth to earn Arab respect and appreciation. At a time when America's alliances and interests in the region have been upended by multiple prodemocracy revolutions, perhaps it is worth a small war over Libya to win a little love in an increasingly surprising Arab world.

As the revolutionary spring unfolds in the Arab world, the United States finds itself at a new cross-road. Protest movements that swept nine Arab countries targeted diverse regimes, including pseudo-republican autocracies such as Egypt, Tunisia, Libya, and Yemen, and conventional monarchies such as Bahrain, Morocco, and Saudi Arabia. The process of long-suppressed Arab transformation is taking its inevitable course. For the United States, it poses a dilemma of navigation: between the support of what President Obama called universal rights and the protection of US interests, historically guarded by oppressive Arab regimes (*Al-Ahram Weekly* March 24–30, 2011).

The revolutions in Egypt and Tunisia were America's easier challenges. The reluctance of the military in both countries to intervene on behalf of the regimes and the dramatic change in US attitudes toward Mubarak and Bin Ali after they showed signs of vulnerability led the Obama administration to pronounce that it would side with the choice of the people. As a result, the leaders had no option but to step down (*Al-Ahram Weekly* March 24–30, 2011). In September 2011, President Obama established a special unit, under the supervision of Secretary Hillary Clinton, to monitor the Arab Spring, its currents, and its consequences (*Al-Ahram* September 10, 2011).

In a survey conducted in April 2011 (Ahmed unpublished), nearly 350 Kuwait University male and female students believed that the most accepted, powerful, and influential leaders in the world include Barack Obama, Recep Tayyib Erdogan, Nicolas Sarkozy, King Abdel-Allah, and ranking fifth, both V. Putin and K. Moon. In contrast, students perceived Al-Qaddafi, Saddam Hussein, Aly Abdel-Allah Saleh, Bashar al-Assad, and Hosni Mubarak as the worst world leaders.

In February 2012, the US president asked Congress to maintain Egypt's $1.3 billion annual military aid despite NGO furor. Obama proposed an $800 million economic aid toward the Arab Spring countries (*Reuters* February 14, 2012). The White House announced plans to offer these countries $800 million worth of economic aid, while maintaining US military aid to Egypt. The proposals are a part of Obama's budget request for the fiscal year 2013, beginning on the first of October. His requests need approval from Congress; some lawmakers want to cut overseas spending to address US budgetary shortfalls.

According to the president's budget plan, most of the economic aid for the Arab Spring countries—$770 million—would establish a new "Middle East and North Africa Incentive Fund [MENAIF]," which would provide incentives for long-term economic, political, and trade reforms to countries in transition and to countries prepared to make reforms proactively. Analysts said it was difficult to predict how much of the proposal would actually be new money. The proposal did not mention how the MENAIF would be divided between countries or offer any other details of the plan.

Egypt has long been among the top recipients of US aid, receiving about $1.6 billion annually for mostly military assistance. In the fiscal year 2012, $250 million of aid approved for Egypt was economic, $1.3 billion was military, and there was a $60 million "enterprise fund" approved by US Congress.

According to J. Norris, a former US foreign aid worker, "As presented, it is very difficult to determine if the Arab Spring fund is new wine in new bottles or old wine in new bottles" (Reuters, February14, 2012).

In January 2012, members of nongovernment organizations were arrested and detained in Egypt on the grounds of unlicensed practices during the uprisings and later events. Because of this issue, the United States has threatened to cut their aid to Egypt. The Egyptian public and authorities received these threats with displeasure. An announcement from the Supreme Council of Armed Forces "SCAF"in Egypt stated clearly that "Egypt will not accept any threats from US or elsewhere, and will not be a subject of submission" (*Al-Ahram* February 10, 2012: 1). Other sources (*Akhabar el-Youm* 2012) mentioned that the United States would be the greater loser if Washington cuts its economic and military aid to Egypt. According to those sources, the United States benefited more from helping Egypt than Egypt is gaining from it.

A recent Gallup survey (*Al-Ahram Weekly* November 22–29, 2012) found that 82% of Egyptians opposed US economic aid on the grounds that it was used as a tool on the part of the US administration to interfere in Egypt's internal affairs. A survey by Ibn Khaldoun Centre in Cairo on 2,000 Egyptian males and females from different socioeconomic backgrounds, with 63% of them were under thirty-five years of age (Annahar March 18, 2013: 1 and 22), reveals that 82% of the respondents prefer the return of the army to rule the country for a limited period of time.

The Decline of the US Influence and Barack Obama

The relative decline of US influence in the Arab region following the Arab Spring has changed the strategic environment for Israel. Israeli Defense Minister Ehud Barak clearly expressed his feelings of bitterness and concern about Israel's "national security" because of serious repercussions of a decline in the US role in the region. Barak suggested rethinking Israel's security doctrine to take into consideration this transformation. Israeli strategic experts point to some features that reflect a retreat in the US standing. Another Israeli highlighted the US inability to prop up its allied Arab regimes that contributed to achieving US–Israeli interests in the region, especially supporting the regime of ousted President Hosni Mubarak in Egypt (*Al-Ahram Weekly* June 14–20, 2012).

A manifestation of the above-mentioned US decline of influence could be noted from the demonstrations—although small—that accompanied the visit of Secretary H. Clinton to Cairo in mid-July 2012. For the first time in decades, the public could express their opinions. Ironically enough, the protesters in Cairo and Alexandria were liberal groups used to support the American role in the region, and not the followers of Islamic movements, especially the Muslim Brotherhood Group (Ibid.).

Retired general senior researcher at Israel's Institute for National Security Studies, Ron Tira, has listed signs that indicated US weakness. He pointed out how the US administration was forced to hold official talks with representatives from Islamist movements who came to power or are on their way to power in Arab Spring countries. The Americans view dialogue with Islamists as an attempt to contain some of the damage resulting from the fall or weakening of its allied regimes. Although Israel has officially recognized Islamists' power, which constitutes a serious transformation in Israel's strategic environment, the Americans have made it clear that changing this course is not an option (*Al-Ahram Weekly* June 14–20, 2012).

Another Israeli analyst believes that the blow to pro-Western military leaders in Turkey by the government of Erdogan and Washington's inability to intercede and defend them is another manifestation of US weakness. What annoys Israelis the most is that Erdogan's standing was boosted to a large extent after the outbreak of the Arab revolutions (Ibid.).

Israelis view the success of Hizbullah and its allies in forming a government in Lebanon and the agreement between Fatah and Hamas to end divisions, despite US objections, as additional signs that US importance is declining in the Middle East. An Israeli analyst emphasized that one cannot ignore the economic factors that distracted Obama's administration from focusing on the Middle East. He added that the incumbent US administration has become very sensitive to any development that could negatively affect the US economy (Ibid.). The United States is also apprehensive about China's ability to increase its influence in Southeast Asia and its attempts to dictate specific formulae in this region that threaten US economic and military interests (Ibid.).

At the same time, a retreat in the US status in the Middle East has increased Israel's isolation in the region. While some countries in the region were keen on improving relations with Israel as the best path to curry favor with Washington, a decline in US standing in the region has increased the strategic burden on Israel and reduced its ability to maneuver (Ibid.). Thus, a lowering US appeal will negatively affect Israel's strategic environment and its ability to take action against its enemies. Even more burdensome for Israel, public opinion has become an influential factor in Arab decision making after the Arab revolutions (Ibid.).

An article by Erin Cunningham published in *Global Post* (*Aljarida,* September 11, 2012: 11) reveals that while the US influence/role is decreasing in countries such as Egypt, the influence/role of China is increasing. As an indicator, results of a survey conducted by Pew Research Attitudes Project in November 2010 (released on June 13, 2012) reveal that 52% of Egyptian sample have positive attitudes toward China, whereas only 17% were positive toward the United States. Similar results have been found for samples from other Arab countries (i.e., Lebanon, Jordan, and Tunisia). Forty-eight percent from Lebanon, 45% from Tunisia, and 12% from Jordan favored the United States, whereas 59% from Lebanon, 69% from Tunisia, and 47% from Jordan expressed favorable attitudes toward China. As for the confidence in world leaders (i.e., Obama, Merkel, Ban Ki-Moon, and Putin), results of the Pew research Attitudes Project indicate that in Egypt, Obama was more popular than Merkel and Putin (29% for Obama, and 16% and 15% for Merkel and Putin, respectively), but Obama was less popular than Ban Ki-Moon (36%). For the Tunisians, Obama was more popular than the other three world leaders (28% for Obama, and 22%, 19%, and 17% for Merkel, Ban Ki-Moon, and Putin, respectively). In Jordan, Obama was found to be more popular than Putin (22% versus 17%, but less popular than Merkel (26%) and Ban Ki-Moon (43%). Finally, in Lebanon, Obama was found more popular than Merkel and Putin (39% for Obama, 30% for Merkel, and 33% for Putin), yet, 43% of Lebanese sample considered Ban Ki-Moon as more popular than Obama.

Recently, some analysts (R. Khawaji and T. Karasik cited in *Aljarida* February 17, 2013: 11) noticed a new trend in US foreign policy, especially in the Middle East. They called this new trend as "Strategic Withdrawal" accompanied with a decline of the US influence in the region. The analysts predicted that such withdrawal, and the decline of influence, will weaken the US voice and make it unable to keep the balance of power strongly required in the Middle East.

A poll published in the *Washington Post* on March 18, 2013, on the attitudes of Americans toward Israel and the Palestinians (cited in *Al-Qabas* March 19, 2013) shows that while 55% of the respondents sympathized with Israel, only 9% of them reported their sympathy with the Palestinians. It also showed that 35% of the respondents reported sympathy for both sides or they had no opinion at all.

The United States and the Uprisings in Syria

In March 2011, the uprising of Syrians began against Bashar Al-Assad's regime. The conflict turned into a civil war. The Arab League could ask the UN Security Council to act, but until now, opposition from Russia and China has prevented the world body from even criticizing Syria, an old ally of Moscow (*Reuters* January 18, 2012). Until today (November 25, 2012) nothing has changed and Russia remained the key to a political transition in Syria (*Al-Mintor* January 9, 2013). On September 25, 2012, in his speech at the sixty-seventh session of the United Nation General Assembly in New York, the Emir of Qatar stated the need for a united Arab military camp—similar to what happened in Libya in 2011 (*Al-Qabas* September 26, 2012).

This statement was not always received positively in the Arab world. Moreover, few Western powers, among them the United States, have favored any Libyan-style military action in Syria, which is situated in the heart of the conflict-prone Middle East. Bordering Lebanon, Turkey, Jordan, Iraq, and Israel, Syria's government is allied with Iran and the armed Lebanese Shi'ite Hezbollah group (Reuters January 18, 2012). Many Syrians were willing to risk bullets and torture chambers to add him to the list of recently toppled Arab leaders (Ibid.). Army deserters and other rebels have taken up arms against security forces dominated by Assad's minority *Alawite* sect, pushing *Sunni* Muslim-majority Syria to the verge of all-out civil war (Ibid.).

By October 7, 2012 (*Aljarida* October 7, 2012: 11), more than 30,000 persons had been killed, an uncountable number of Syrians had been arrested, tortured, and raped, and nearly 1 million Syrians were forced to flee to countries such as Turkey, Lebanon, Jordan, and Iraq. However, the international community has so far been unable to end the bloody conflict in Syria. This failure does not fit with the US image as the world's protector of democracy. S. Hamid, at the Brookings Institute in Doha, Qatar, described Obama's reluctance in taking actions against B. Assad to stop this bloody conflict as "aggressive hedging" (J. Goldberg, as cited in *Aljardia* October 7, 2012: 11). On February 15, 2013, US Secretary J. Kerry, in his phone call with his Saudi counterparts, estimated the number of Syrian conflict victims as 90,000 (*Al-Qabas* February 16, 2013). Some Arab analysts attributed the reluctance of the West, especially the United States, to the increasing influence of Islamists and potential terrorists among the opponents of Al-Assad's regime (Ibid.). Another Arab analyst (*Al-Qabas* March 16, 2013: 33) noticed that the world became more interested in the possibility of using chemical weapons by Al-Assad's regime rather in the increasing number of victims and refugees created by the conflict.

US Relationship with Newly Elected Arab Leaders, the Muslim Brotherhood-Islamists

Beginning in 2012, US policy toward Arab countries, especially countries that had experienced the Arab Spring uprisings, has witnessed a dramatic change. Arabs and Egyptians have noticed an extreme shift in US attitudes toward the Muslim Brotherhood group and Islamists and their leaders in countries such as Egypt and Tunisia. After decades of supporting the ousted regime of Hosni Mubarak (*Al-Ahram* February 17, 2012), the US administration received, hosted, and supported leaders of the Muslim Brotherhood group. The American standpoint toward the 2012 presidential election in Egypt remains vivid in the minds of the Egyptians. At the same time, leaders of the Muslim Brotherhood group, who strongly opposed American policy for decades, publicly announced that they would have to build a strong relationship with the United States. Several observers call this newly established US–Muslim Brotherhood group relationship a "honeymoon" and recall the same close relationship between the Americans and the Muslim Brotherhood and Islamists during the Soviet occupation of Afghanistan in the late 1970s. During that time, the Americans encouraged, supported, and used Muslim Brotherhood members and Islamists to fight the Soviets on their behalf (*Al-Ahram Al-Arabi* July 7, 2012; *Al-Ahram Weekly* August 2–8, 2012).

Twenty months after the January 25, 2011, revolution, many Egyptians continue to believe that Egypt's subservient relationship to the United States did not end under the Islamists' regime. Many Egyptians noted that the Muslim Brotherhood group, which used to protest against US policies and Israel's aggressive actions, now gives no sign of such protests. These Egyptians conclude that the United States would not have allowed an Islamist to become president of Egypt unless he would pursue policies that were reasonably friendly to US interests in the region (*Al-Ahram Weekly* November 22–29, 2012).

The Egyptian analyst E.A. Shalabi (*Al-Ahram Weekly* August 2–8, 2012) noticed that the United States has apparently shifted its position on Islamist politics and currents. Following decades of skepticism, even paranoia, US officials seem to be more at ease with the Islamists who are now in power. No longer viewed in Washington as an imminent threat to US policy in the region, Islamists are being treated, at least for now, as potential partners.

Washington has been monitoring the rise of the Islamists since 2005 when they won 88 seats in the Egyptian parliament. US officials have held meetings with the Muslim Brotherhood members and remained familiar with their views. Of course, the interest was motivated by bitter memories of the Iranian revolution, which the Americans failed to anticipate, severely underestimating the vehemence of its ideology (Ibid.).

It boils down to pragmatism. The Americans hedged their bets on the January 25 revolution as far as they could, and when it was clear that the revolution was unstoppable, they demanded Hosni Mubarak's resignation. The same happened after the revolution, for when the Islamists emerged as the dominant force, the United States did not think twice about which side to take (Ibid.).

No matter what the Americans believe, or claim to believe, when it comes to foreign policy, they often play it safe. This is why US officials had little trouble accepting the new reality that catapulted Islamists to power in Egypt. The fact that Egypt's liberals are divided and weak was factored into the new US political thinking (Ibid.). American politicians and top brass have been coming to Egypt quite frequently since the revolution. Hillary Clinton's audience with President Mohamed Morsi on July 2012 was symptomatic of Washington's interest in Egyptian politics. The Americans are especially attentive to the position of the new regime on Egypt's peace treaty with Israel. Judging by the way Secretary Clinton reacted to her meeting with Morsi; she must have heard some reassurances in this regard. Clinton, who went immediately to Israel afterward, may have relayed the comforting news to the Israelis (*Al-Ahram Weekly* August 2–8, 2012).

The current interaction between the Americans and Islamists reminds me of 1952, wrote one Egyptian analyst, when the Free Officers were the new kids on the block, and the Americans were hoping to win them over (Ibid.). At the time, the Americans were busy "containing" the Soviet Union, an effort that required the entire Middle East, if possible, to be on their side. So when the 1952 revolution broke out, the United States was quick to forge close links with the new leaders. The Free Officers, in turn, were thrilled to have Washington on their side. Who else would keep the British off their backs? But the honeymoon did not last long. The Free Officers' brand of nationalism did not sit well with American plans for the region, and Egypt started pulling back from the Americans. Initial friendship turned sour, and animosity was only a few years away (Ibid.).

Will history repeat itself? Will the United States be disappointed with the Islamists and vice versa? If the Islamists allow their doctrinal beliefs to shape their regional policies, conflict with Americans would most likely ensue. On issues such as Palestine and Iran, the Islamists of Egypt may not be able to see eye to eye with the Americans. The two may be able to keep their differences to a minimum for at least a while, but the chances of confrontation are too real to be ignored (Ibid.).

US–Iran Relationship and the Arab World

No doubt, Israel's threats against Iran are an attempt to influence the positions of the superpowers who met on June 2012 with Iranian officials. They wanted to hear Tehran's final response to their proposal about halting its nuclear program before these countries would impose unprecedented economic sanctions against Iran. Ironically, what adds to Israeli pressure on the US administration is the fact that some of Washington's Arab allies—such as the Saudis—also want the program to stop (*Al-Ahram Weekly* June 7–13, 2012). Some Arab analysts (*Al-Ahram Weekly* August 30–September 5, 2012) believe that the United States should give priority to the Palestinian–Israeli peace process as a way to solve the crisis with Iran. Other analysts (D. Makousky and D. Pollock, cited in *Aljarida* February 18, 2013: 11) believe that the United States should encourage both Palestinians and Israelis to create new forms of negotiation and communication that eventually could lead to an acceptable procedure to solve their long-lasting bitter conflict. Makousky and Pollock described the US efforts related to the Palestinian–Israeli conflict as a lot of talk and very few actions.

In early February 2013, the Iranian president visited Cairo on the occasion of attending the Islamic Summit, and ending thirty-four years of the absence of a direct relationship and contacts between Egypt and Iran. Ahmadinejad was received by his Egyptian counterpart in a friendly fashion. However, several demonstrations occurred in Cairo against this visit and the potential beginning of expanding Shiite influence in a dominant Sunna Muslim–oriented country. The Iranian president's visit to Cairo was not welcomed either by the Americans or by the leaders of Arab Gulf states, especially Saudi Arabia and the United Arab Emirates (*Al-Qabas* February 9, 2013). J. Zogby (cited in *Al-Qabas* February 28, 2013: 37) considers Obama's and Kerry's visits to the Middle East as a sign of decline of the US interest in the Palestinian issue in favor of the growing interest in Iran and Syria.

President Barack Obama as Seen by Arab and Muslim World's Caricatures

In the days following the March 5, 2012, meeting between President Barack Obama and Israeli Prime Minister Benjamin Natanyahu and Obama's address to the annual American Israel Public Affairs Committee conference, newspapers across the Arab world featured political cartoons on the anti-Semitic theme of Jewish/Israeli control of American foreign policy and the American political system. (Among these newspapers: *Al-Ahram*, *Al-Akhabar*, *Akhabar el-Youm*, *Al-Ahram al-Arabi*, and *Al-Ahram Weekly* [Egypt], *Al-Sabil* [Jordan], *Al-Watan* [Qatar], *Al-Madina* [Saudi Arabia], *Al-Mustqbal* [Lebanon], *Al-Ayyam* [Palestinian Authority], *Gulf News* and *Al-Ittihad* [UAE], *Tishrin* [Syria], and *Al-Hayat* [UK]). These cartoons depicted President Obama as a puppet or mouthpiece of Israel, or the so-called "Zionist lobby," and showed Israel and Jews controlling the ballot boxes for the upcoming US presidential election. The age-old anti-Semitic allegation of Jews manipulating and controlling governments frequently appears in caricatures and articles in newspapers across the Arab and Muslim world (*Al-Ahram Weekly* March15–21, 2012).

The Rise and Fall of Arab Presidents for Life

In May 2012, the British historian Roger Owen published a book titled *The Rise and Fall of Arab Presidents for Life* (*Al-Ahram Weekly* August 9–15, 2012). The book seeks to explain Arab presidents for life, a "peculiar" form of modern political practices. The author noted that the presidents of Libya, Egypt, Tunisia, Syria, Yemen, and Algeria seemed to have engineered constitutional settlements or amendments allowing them to remain in office for further terms and so, in effect, for as long as they wished. As a result, Muammar al-Qaddaffi ruled Libya for forty-two years and Mubarak ruled Egypt for thirty years, A. A. Saleh ruled Yemen for thirty-two years, Z. Bin Ali ruled Tunisia for twenty-three years, Assad's family has ruled Syria since the late 1960s, and Bouteflika has been ruling Algeria since the late 1990s. It is widely believed in the Arab world that these ousted dictators were not able to continue in power without the support they received from the West in general and the United States in particular.

Although the United States has long been blamed for having supported dictators in the Arab world (as a result of fearing the rise of political Islam), many secularists, leftists, and Coptic Christians in Egypt also now blame the United States for the new ascendancy of the Muslim Brotherhood in Egypt and Tunisia (*Al-Ahram Weekly* November 22–29, 2012). Many analysts agree that in countries such as Egypt and Yemen, the United States is at best hesitant regarding the revolutionary movements, if not supportive of the former autocratic regimes (Ibid.).

Lessons to Be Learned

Graham Usher wrote (*Al-Ahram Weekly* February 17–23, 2011), "The US seems not have learned any of the lessons of Egypt's revolution. . . ." At the same time, people of the world have been forced to rethink their ideas of the Arabs as a result of the Egyptian uprising, R. Baroud noted (*Al-Ahram Weekly* February 10–16, 2011). J. Zogby (Ibid.) noticed that the reaction of US politicians to the momentous events in Egypt has once again revealed their basic ignorance of the Arab world. He added that "when US politicians are forced to discuss critical Middle Eastern matters, more often than not their remarks either display an ignorance of facts, are shaped more by political needs than reality, or are just plain dumb." One lesson to be learned from the Arab Spring, especially the uprising in Egypt, is that Arab opinion matters. For too long, Arab voices have been ignored and their sensibilities or aspirations not been respected. But the Egyptian people have risen up, demanding to be heard; they have challenged other Arabs and the West to pay attention to what they are saying (*Al-Ahram Weekly* February 17–23, 2011).

When ousted President Hosni Mubarak made his last-ditch effort to save his rule, the protesters formed a throng in Tahrir Square (Ibid.). The disconnect was real. Mubarak was talking, yet he simply was not listening. He played every card at his disposal: the caring father, the patriot, the xenophobe, the reformer, and more. J. Zogby believed that Mubarak was reaching out beyond the square to those he thought might also be listening. But if his imagined and hoped-for audience was there, they were not responding. The crowd in the square was listening, and his lack of responsiveness to their concerns only served to inflame them and deepen their resolve (Ibid.). Even now, and in spite of the dramatic changes that occurred in Arab Spring countries, still Egyptians (and Tunisians, Libyans, and Yemenis as well) face the problem of not being listened to as noted by N. Hawi (*Al-Qabas*, January 23, 2013: 43).

The problem of not listening to Arab voices is not only a problem for those presidents who have fallen or those who are still at risk, but a problem for the West as well. For too long, the United States,

Great Britain, and others have ignored the concerns and sensibilities of the Arab people. Arabs have been treated as if they were pawns to be moved about on the board. While those in the West paid attention to their own needs and policies, Arabs were left to accommodate themselves to realities created for them, as the West sought to protect its own interests rather than theirs (*Al-Ahram Weekly*, February 17–23, 2011).

This is not a new phenomenon. The cavalier dismissal of Arab voices began with Lord Balfour. When a survey found Arabs overwhelmingly rejecting the European powers' plans to carve up the Arab East into British and French mandatory entities for the creation of a Jewish national home in Palestine, Balfour responded, "We do not propose even to go through the form of consulting the wishes of the present inhabitants of the country . . . Zionism, be it right or wrong, good or bad . . . is of far greater importance than the desire and prejudices of the Arabs who now inhabit that ancient land" (*Al-Ahram Weekly*, February 17–23, 2011). These statements clearly indicate that the needs and interests of Arabs have been ignored for decades.

As blatant as that rejection was, this practice of ignoring Arab concerns has persisted. Until this day, the West has often acted across the Middle East as if Arabs were objects without sensibilities or concerns. The United States invaded Iraq without understanding the effect this might have on Arab opinion. The West has continued to ignore Palestinian suffering and aspirations (recall Condoleeza Rice's dismissal of the plight and rights of Palestinian refugees with a casual remark: "bad things happen in history"). And the United States has engaged in widespread profiling and other forms of deplorable treatment of Arabs and Muslims within the country, paying no attention to the toll that these and other policies had on the legitimacy of Arab governments who were Western friends and allies (Ibid.).

Now, all of this necessitates change. When the Egyptian people organized themselves while demanding to be heard, they introduced a new and potentially transformative factor into the political equation. It will no longer be possible to operate as if Arab public opinion does not matter. It will no longer be possible to act as if policies can be imposed and blindly accepted by the people (Ibid.).

No longer will the West be able to consider only the Israeli internal debate or the consequences of its own actions on Israeli opinion in its calculations. Arabs have been inspired by Egypt and empowered to believe that their voices must be heard and respected. It will make life more complicated for Western and some Arab policymakers, but this complication is a good thing as it represents the long-awaited change (Ibid.). As US President Barack Obama stated, this is just the beginning, and after today nothing will be the same. The reality is that this transformation will not only affect Egypt; it may be bigger than any of us can imagine at present (Ibid.).

Even though the West lectures the Arabs and Muslims on the virtues of democracy and free elections, it does not necessarily imply the same desires for them. As Robert Fisk says, in the Arab world, we (the West) want law and order and stability—and we will get it. "It's the same old problem for us in the West. We mouth the word 'democracy' and we are all for fair elections—providing the Arabs vote for whom we want them to vote for" (*Al-Ahram Weekly*, January 27—February 2, 2011). This is why, in countries ranging from Palestine to Pakistan, autocrats are always chosen over democrats. This suits the West and its long-term geopolitical interests. Besides, unlike those tried and tested dictators, democrats are troublesome and ask too many inconvenient questions (Ibid.).

On the eleventh anniversary of September 11, 2001 (September 11, 2012), the US envoy to Libya and three other Americans were killed when a furious mob, angered over a movie, stormed the US consulate in Benghazi and sparked world outrage. The film was produced and released in the United States by an Israeli-American, a few immigrant Egyptian Coptic Christians, and others, mocking Islam and the Prophet Mohammed (*Kuwait Times* 2012; *Arab Times*, September 14, 2012; Alseyassah, September 13, 2012).

At the same time, deeply angered protesters railed against the insult to Islam and Prophet Mohammed in Egypt, Yemen, Tunisia, Sudan, and many other Islamic countries such as Pakistan, Afghanistan, and Indonesia. They tried to enter and attack the US embassies and consulates, accompanied by the burning of the American flag (*Alanba* September 12, 2012; *Al-Qabas* September 13, 2012;

September 15, 2012). The protesters held that depicting Prophet Mohammed in a deeply insulting, nonreligious way is simply not acceptable to Arabs and Muslims. Protesters in the Arab and Islamic countries consider the production of this movie a thinly veiled act of hatred and terror, wrapped in velvet (*Kuwait Times* September 13, 2012), while believing that the United States is responsible for such an action. The protesters' expressed their indignation over the blasphemous movie *Innocence of Muslims*, and they announced that they will continue their protests until the American government blocks the attack on the Prophet Mohammed on YouTube (*Arab Times* September 29, 2012: 1). However, as much as those images delivered a message of hate for the United States, many of the protesters insisted they did not hate the American people (*Al-Ahram Weekly,* November 22–29, 2012).

The tsunami of anger that swept many Arab and Muslim countries in reaction to the US-made anti-Islam film, September 2012, was widely seen by Western pundits as one alarming indication that anti-Americanism remains intense in many Middle Eastern countries (*Al-Ahram Weekly* November 22–29, 2012). Several conclusions could be drawn from the September 2012 events. Among them are the following:

1. The insulting movie is not the first of its kind. Several attempts have been made to insult Muslims and Arabs (such as the insulting drawings/paintings in Denmark published some years ago). One week after the release of the insulting movie, a French magazine, and a few days later another Spanish magazine published insulting articles and drawings, which mocked Islam and Prophet Mohammed.
2. The September 2012 events clearly reflect wide differences in the visions and views of both sides: the United States and the Arab/Muslim countries, while also reflecting a lack of mutual understanding. It seems that each side does not fully understand the other.
3. The September 2012 events and the reactions of both the United States and the Arab/Islamic world clearly point to the extent to which the relations between both sides are fragile. Robert Fisk has noted (cited in *Asharq Al-Awsat* September 14, 2012: 10), that "We need only a mentally disturbed person 'a maniac' who can—in a few seconds—inflame a small war in the Muslim world." One of the important questions currently preoccupying the minds of Arabs/Muslims is: "Why are Arabs/Muslims so easy to provoke?" (*Al-Qabas* September 26, 2012: 10).
4. Following the attack on the US Consulate in Benghazi, Lybia, September 11, 2012, the US embassy in Cairo issued a statement in which it condemned the insulting of Islam and Prophet Mohammed, and reiterated US respect for Islam. Later on, Washington announced that this statement was released without prior coordination with the White House (*Aljardia* September 23, 2012: 12). Related to this and as observed by several analysts (*New York Times*, *The Guardian* September 29, 2012) were the changing explanations/interpretations which were given by Washington for the attack on the US Consulate in Benghazi.
5. The September 2012 events clearly indicate the failure of both sides (United States/West and Arab/Muslim worlds) in establishing a valid and stable balance between the values strongly believed in by the United States/West and the influence and sensitivity of religious issues among Arabs and Muslims.

On the eve of his first trip to the United States, Egypt's new Islamist President Mohammed Morsi stated in his interview with David D. Kirkpatrick and Steven Erlanger from the *New York Times* (September 22, 2012) that "the United States needed to fundamentally change its approach to the Arab world, show greater respect for its values, and help build a Palestinian state, if it hoped to overcome decades of pent-up anger." He added, "It is up to Washington to repair relations with the Arab world and to revitalize the alliance with Egypt, long a cornerstone of regional stability" and "the US must respect the Arab world's history and culture, even when that conflicts with Western values."

In his speech at the sixty-seventh session of the United Nations General Assembly, New York on September 25, 2012, President Obama condemned the insulting movie and considered it as insulting not only to the Arab and Islamic worlds but also to the United States. Obama's words were—to some extent—positively received in the Arab countries (*Arab Times* September 26, 2012). He also added that no movie could justify the attack on the American facilities in Arab and Muslim countries. In their response to Obama's speech, several Arab and Muslim leaders demanded an urgent stop to any actions which are insulting Islam and Prophet Mohammed (*Annahar* 2012: 23, *Al-Qabas* September 26, 2012). Indeed, most Westerners simply do not grasp how deeply offensive remarks, cartoons, and movies insulting Prophet Mohammed are to Muslims everywhere.

Evaluation of the New Arab Islamists' Regimes

A recent published book titled *Where Will Arabs Go?* (*Alseyassah* December 3, 2012) reviewed the responses and evaluations of thirty Arab scholars to the consequences of the Arab Spring, in particular the uprisings in Egypt, Tunisia, and Libya. Two trends have emerged. The first sees the Arab revolution as having achieved significant successes due to the democratic course they followed. The second trend believes that such revolutions have failed due to the absence of strong leadership and, at the same time, due to dominance of the Islamists. Other reasons for such failure include the attempts made by the transitional authorities that are aimed at the distortion of revolutionary movements and their members/activists.

While the new Islamists leaders have made a reasonable progress/success in Tunisia and Morocco, and to a smaller extent in Libya, their Egyptian counterparts have failed to achieve similar progress. The Brotherhood and Salfi parties wrapped up the draft constitution, overriding the objections of the opposition and widespread anger over the composition of the constituent assembly, which in turn led to the withdrawal of the liberals and Egypt's three churches from the body of this assembly. The Islamist Egyptian president Mohammed Morsi, who recently received compliments from President Obama and Secretary Clinton and Israeli leaders such as S. Perez for so-called pragmatic behavior, which contributed quickly to a cease fire between Israel and Hamas in November 2012, has sweeping power, as he issued on November 22, 2012 a declaration that grants him broad powers. Morsi's decree divided the Egyptian society into protesters/opponents and supporters. According to *Financial Times* (December 1, 2012), Morsi's latest decree reflects his inability to confront the requirements of the transitional stage in Egypt. Many Egyptians believe that Morsi's constitutional decree, and his manner of dealing with the crisis as well, threatens the stability of the country and reflects the deep rift between Islamists and the opposition (*Al-Ahram* December 4, 2012). Moreover, Morsi's decree was negatively received by the United States itself, several European countries, the European Union, and several international organizations such as *Human Rights*.

For the first time in Egypt, the Constitutional Court on December 2, 2012, has suspended its work after the Islamists supporters laid siege to its premises before a hearing regarding the legality of the panel that drafted the country's new constitution (*Financial Times*, December 2, 2012).

A recent survey conducted by the Egyptian Centre for Public Opinion Research (*Basira*) on November 28 and 29, 2012 (*Al-Watan* December 7, 2012: 31) showed that while 30% of the participants supported Morsi's decree, 37% refused it, and 33% were not able to judge it or its effect on the country.

The main weakness of the opponents of the Islamists is that they do not provide an alternative route. Moreover, the opponents' command is decentralized because they are composed of disparate groups such as democrats, leftists, liberals, army rule supporters, and some of supporters of Mubarak's regime. The opponents of the Islamists in Egypt, and in other Arab Spring countries as well, were—and still are—portrayed as seeking to distort the country and standing in the way of religion because they are conspirators implementing sinister agendas (*Financial Times*, December 1, 2012).

The unstable situation, demonstrations, riots, assassinations, and unemployment, which occurred recently in most of the Arab Spring countries, led analysts to conclude that the new Islamist leaders have failed in dealing with their people in a democratic way. In the analysts' opinion, taking or capturing the power is one thing, and efficiently managing this power is another thing (*Annahar* 2013: 24). However, and unlike Egypt, Tunisia, Libya, Iraq, and Yemen, leaders in Morocco, and to a lesser extent in Jordan and Saudi Arabia, were more wise and efficient in dealing with uprisings in their countries, as noted by Fareed Zakaria in the *Washington Post* (cited in *Aljarida* February 3, 2013: 11).

Reelection of Obama: Reactions of Arabs

In November 2012, President Obama who raised hope as a slogan was reelected for a second term in the White House. The majority of world countries welcomed, in different degrees, Obama's re-election. Several world leaders (i.e. from Great Britain, France, Italy, Germany, Canada, European Union, UN Secretary General, Russia, India, Japan, Afghanistan, Pakistan, and South Africa) were amongst the first to express their welcome. China expressed a cautious welcome and called for mutual cooperation. In Malaysia and Indonesia, people celebrated Obama's win and expressed hope that he would help allay global conflicts and economic woes (*The Star Malaysia* 2012). As for the Arab world, leaders of Saudi Arabia, the rest of the Arab Gulf states, and Egypt expressed their welcome of the results of the election in 2012. Egyptian President Morsi said in his cable of congratulation that he looks forward to a strong friendship between Egypt and the US (*Al-Akhabar* 2012). The Arab League reflected that after the reelection of Obama, the American people's interest will be achieved if security and peace were accomplished in the Middle East. Mahmoud Abbas, the president of the Palestinian Authority expressed his hope to work with President Obama to achieve the long hoped for peace. The leaders of Hamas, Gaza Strip, called Obama to stop taking Israel's side and point of view. Moreover, the reelection of Obama for a second term has been widely received with relief and welcome among the public in the Arab and Muslim worlds (*Alrai* November 8, 2012; *Alseyassah* November 8, 2012; *Al-Ahram Weekly* November 8–14, 2012 and November 22–29, 2012).

Obama's reelection will provide Obama with the chance to protect his historic reforms concerning healthcare, Wall Street, and the Supreme Court. He will also probably look abroad as he builds his legacy but will face an immediate challenge early in 2013 and possibly have to make a decision whether to use military force to thwart Iran's nuclear program and to work more closely with his allies in solving the Syrian conflict (*The Southland Times* 2012).

E. Ibrahim wrote (*Al-Ahram Weekly*, November 8–14, 2012: 1) that Barack Obama has written another chapter in US presidential history as he wins a second term in the White House. In his victory speech, Obama told the American people, "We know in our heart that for the United States of America the best is yet to come." E. Ibrahim wonders if President Obama has the same belief about the Middle East, which represents "a moot point." The US ambassador to Saudi Arabia, James Smith announced in a celebration party in Riydah, Saudi Arabia, following the reelection of Obama that he expected real change in the US attitudes toward Syria and emphasized the necessity of working together with Russia and China and other international powers to stop the bloodshed there. He also pointed out Obama's wish to continue the Israeli-Palestinian negotiation, to strongly confront Iran, and to provide the new governments in Egypt, Tunisia, Libya, and Yemen with needed aids (*Asharq Al-Awsat*, November 8, 2012).

An article by Liz Peek in *Fiscal Times* (*Aljarida* December 10, 2012: 11) indicates that Obama's policy in the Middle East will hurt the US economy. The author states that Obama's policies contradict his promises, which he had made in Cairo in May 2009, and such policy did not follow the changes resulting from the Arab Spring, and at the same time, ignore severe problems such as unemployment in countries such as Egypt, Tunisia, Jordan, Lebanon, and even Saudi Arabia. In the author's opinion, such policies led to a significant decline in US popularity in the Middle East countries, except Turkey, and it will lead the United States to lose the Middle East as an important market for American exports.

In the same context, a report (cited in *Al-Watan* November 8, 2012: 43) indicates that Obama's win instigates a feeling of anxiety in Arab Gulf states and Middle Eastern countries due to the connection between US influence and Iran's nuclear program. A survey conducted in August 2012 in Egypt by the G. K. Rosner Research Institute (Ibid.) shows that 61% of the respondents reported that they approve of Iran's nuclear program while 30% disapproved. Also it was shown that 65% prefer (and 30% rejected) the reestablishing of diplomatic relationships between Egypt and Iran.

According to Fox News (http//www.foxnews.com/world/10/12/2012), the US administration has decided to send twenty more F-16s to Egypt, despite the turmoil in Cairo. Several Egyptian analysts and politicians considered such action as difficult to understand. A Pentagon spokesman said the United States and Egypt have an important alliance that is furthered by the transfer. Lt. Col. Wesley Miller said, "The delivery of the first set of F-16s in January 2013 reflects the U.S. commitment to supporting the Egyptian military's modernization efforts. Egyptian acquisition of F-16s will increase our militaries' interoperability, and enhance Egypt's capacity to contribute to regional mission sets." In the context, State Department official Andrew J. Shapiro explained why the administration plans to continue military support to Egypt, as he said, "I know that the uncertainty over the Egyptian transition has prompted some in Congress to propose conditioning our security assistance to Egypt." He added that the US Administration "believes that putting conditions on our assistance to Egypt is the wrong approach, and Secretary Clinton has made this point strongly. Egypt is a pivotal country in the Middle East and a long-time partner of the United States. We have continued to rely on Egypt to support and advance U.S. interests in the region, including peace with Israel, confronting Iranian ambitions, interdicting smugglers, and supporting Iraq."

The Fall of Islamist Rule in Egypt

Between June 30, 2012 and July 3, 2013, Morsi was the president of Egypt. During that time Morsi and the Muslim Brotherhood failed to achieve the required reconciliation and the hoped for social and economic reforms; rather they caused more divisions among the Egyptians who did not witness any progress in social, economic, and political fields. The threats and unsuitable language repeatedly used by Morsi and the Muslim Brotherhood upset many Egyptians. They became convinced that President Morsi was not able to run the state efficiently, and consequently started to ask for an early presidential election.

In May 2013, a group of youths established a movement called "Rebel" that was aimed at collecting signatures of Egyptians to call for early presidential elections. In less than two months, Rebel successfully managed to collect more than 22 million documented signatures, and asked all Egyptians to gather together in town squares on June 30, 2013. Sources have estimated that the protesters numbered 33 million in all of Egypt. Other analysts described the June 30 events as the largest gathering in human history and considered it as a second Egyptian revolution, representing a corrective attempt to the January 25, 2011 events (*Al-Mintor Daily Briefing* July 4, 2013).

Morsi rejected opposition calls for early presidential elections and said he would not tolerate any deviation from the constitutional order. He claimed that his early resignation would undermine the legitimacy of his successors, creating a state of endless chaos. Morsi insisted there would be "no second revolution." His rejection of calls for early elections was a pointed reminder of Mubarak's last words before being toppled: "either me or chaos" (*Al-Ahram Weekly* July 3–10, 2013).

The enormous size of the nationwide protests on June 30 wrong-footed not just Morsi and the Muslim Brotherhood leadership but also key Western governments including the Obama Administration. The mass protests were accompanied by a show of sympathy for the Armed Forces, and the demonstrators also received a sympathetic nod from both the Grand Sheikh of Al-Azhar and the patriarch of the Coptic Church.

On June 30, millions of demonstrators flocked to the presidential palace where they complained of deteriorating living conditions and attacks on their freedom of expression. At times it felt as if the entire population was on the streets. As the demonstrations were growing, Morsi insisted that protesters numbered only tens of thousands, all of them supposedly supporters of the ousted regime of Hosni Mubarak.

The leadership of the Muslim Brotherhood, which had anticipated a much smaller turnout, was left clinging to claims of legitimacy. Numbers obviously meant nothing to them.

The protesters stressed that they would remain peaceful but were seeking fulfillment of what they described as the 2011 Revolution demands—bread, freedom, and social justice—that had not been met by the "Brotherhood's rule" (*Al-Ahram Weekly* July 3–10, 2013; *Al-Mintor* July 4, 2013). In addition, the opposition alliance held President Morsi fully responsible for the acts of violence that took place across the country that Sunday. Moreover, their statement demanded that the authorities reveal the identity of those responsible for inciting violence and hold them fully accountable.

On June 23, 2013, the Egyptian Army asked all political sides for a quick reconciliation and gave them one week to accomplish it. Due to the failure of political parties and various sides to reach an acceptable reconciliation and agreement, the army gave all parties—including President Morsi and his Muslim Brotherhood—48 hours as a final alarm. On July 3, 2013, the army—supported by civil and religious leaders, i.e., the Grand Sheikh of Al-Azhar and the patriarch of the Coptic Church—outlined the ground rules for the post-Morsi transition while appointing the chairman of the Supreme Constitutional Court as an interim president of Egypt (*Al-Mintor* July 9, 2013).

Most Egyptians ran out of patience with Morsi because, rather than building a democratic state, he showed himself determined to use his time in office to reinforce the Brotherhood's grip on power and impose its strict version of Islam on Egyptians. It is likely that if the electorate had waited until 2016, Egypt would then be dominated by an entrenched Islamic oligarchy that would be very difficult to remove, as G. Essam El-Din has noticed (*Al-Ahram Weekly* July 3–10, 2013).

The Brotherhood group is likely to suffer internal rifts between young activists who want the group to be more democratic and open to the outside world and an aging elite devoted to the Qutbist ideology. The ideology, however, has been rejected by a majority of Egyptians, as they made clear after just one year of Morsi in office (*Al-Ahram Weekly* July 3–10, 2013).

As for the reactions that appeared in the Arab world and elsewhere after Morsi's ouster, the Tunisian ruling party feels the heat created by the Egyptian "Coup," while Lebanese Salafists grew frustrated by Morsi's ouster. A fuel crisis threatens the Gaza Strip after Egypt's border closure, and Hamas became much more isolated after July 3. Moreover, what happened in Egypt represents a strategic loss for the Turkish leader, Erdogan, and it shocked many in Turkey (*Al-Mintor* July 8–9, 2013). On the other hand, Saudi Arabia, United Arab Emirates, and Kuwait quickly showed very positive reactions and offered $12 billion as urgent aid to help Egypt overcome its acute economic crisis (*Al-Qabas* July 7, 8, 2013; *Al-Mintor* July 8, 2013). The European Union respects the will and the rights of Egyptian people to change its leaders. The US administration, however, took more than a week to assess what had happened in Egypt on July 3, 2013: Was it a coup or a revolution? A few days later, however, the US decided to provide Egypt with four F-16 fighter airplanes. On July 11, however, the US labelled Morsi's rule undemocratic (*Arab Times* July12, 2013: 1). In the author's opinion, the US administration faced a dilemma whether to defend democracy (according to the so-called US role in protecting democracy in the world), or support its own interests. Eventually, and after days of hesitation, the US chose the second option. A recent cover of *Time Magazine* (July 2013) clearly expressed the US standpoint toward Morsi's opponents and supporters: *World's Best Protesters, World's Worst Democracy.* The future of democracy in Egypt remains uncertain.

Conclusion

Obama has to encounter a unified Arab front to make him take heed or, at least, to offer him some advice. Of course, he must have received contradictory advice from the Arabs, and his advisors would have conveyed to him equally conflicting reports about Palestinian hopes and expectations.

Naturally, he would have heard that Arabs excel at undermining each other, instigating mutual antagonisms, and promoting their own agendas in secret while overruling efforts to achieve some kind of justice for the Palestinians. This is perhaps the major reason why Arabs should not expect promises of positive actions from any American president. They have yet to establish this promise among themselves. There is no reason why the Arabs should anticipate a change in the prevailing situation in which so many factors favor Israel when the Arabs are doing far too little to tip the scales in their direction (*Al-Ahram Weekly* 2008).

The Arabs' chief weakness is that they are disunited and fragmented, lacking a common agenda and the resolve and power to back any joint decision or action they might make. So, even when propelled by some impending crisis to meet and come up with a joint statement, they fail to back those words with concrete action (ibid.).

There are no shortcuts. The Arabs will not see change in their favor until they do what is needed to make their presence felt as a cohesive and forceful factor in the international arena. Meanwhile, as things stand, something new is needed in the United States. Sadly, there is nothing new with the Arabs (ibid.). Clearly, some in the Arab and Muslim worlds hold stereotypes and prejudices against the Americans that are just as troubling as those held by some Americans against Arabs and Muslims. These mutual stereotypes and prejudices should be changed as soon as possible. The nongovernmental organizations could play a positive and effective role in overcoming these attitudes (Tessler and Corstange 2002). Some Arab analysts (*Al-Ahram* August 19, 2012) anticipate that the following four directions/attitudes will shape the Arab policies in the foreseen future:

1. Political instability
2. The strong rise of political Islam
3. A gradual increase of the influence of public opinion
4. Economic instability resulting from political instability

Therefore, these analysts believe that the American-Arab relationships should be reorganized according to five axes/dimensions:

1. The United States should seek engagement with wider sectors in the Arab countries (such as intellectuals, leaders of different syndicates), and not only political leaders (presidents, kings, diplomats, army generals, etc.)
2. The United States should adopt a new strategy toward the rise of political Islam in the region
3. The United States should give maximum priority to political and economic reforms in the Arab countries, especially those which witnessed the Arab Spring, not only because these required reforms will fit with American values, but also because such reforms will serve the American interests in the long run
4. The United States should strongly support the social and economic reforms in the Arab countries (such as Egypt and Tunisia), which should occur along with political reform
5. In the light of the September 11, 2012, events and their consequences, the United States has to reformulate its policy toward the Arab and Muslim worlds. This policy should be based on respect for the religion, beliefs, values, and habits and norms, which are strongly rooted in the hearts and minds of the Arabs as well as so many other Muslims around the world.

References

Abou-el-Leil, K. A. 2011. *The Image of Jews in Arabic Folklore*. Cairo: The Supreme Council for Culture [in Arabic].

Ahmed, R. A. 2010. North Africa and the Middle East. In M. H. Bornstein (ed.). *Handbook of Cultural Developmental Science* (pp. 359–383). New York: Psychology Press/Taylor & Francis.

Ahmed, R. A. unpublished. *The World's Leaders as Perceived by Kuwaiti University Students.* Kuwait University, Kuwait.

Akhabar el-Youm. February 11, 2012. [Egyptian weekly newspaper in Arabic].

Al-Ahram. September 10, 2011. [Egyptian daily newspaper in Arabic].

Al-Ahram. 2012. February 10, February17, August19, December 4. [Egyptian daily newspaper in Arabic].

Al-Ahram Al-Arabi. July 7, 2012. [Egyptian weekly magazine in Arabic].

Al-Ahram Weekly. December 17–23, 2009. [Egyptian weekly newspaper].

Al-Ahram Weekly. 2010. January 14–20, June 3–9, June 17–23, September 2–9. [Egyptian weekly newspaper].

Al-Ahram Weekly. 2011. January 27–February 2, February 10–16, February 17–23, March 24–30, July 21–27. [Egyptian weekly newspaper].

Al-Ahram Weekly. 2012. February 17, March 15–21, June 7–13, June 14–20, August 2–8, August 9–15, August 16–22, August 30–September 5, September 6–12, November 8–14, November 22–29.[Egyptian weekly newspaper].

Al-Ahram Weekly. July 3–10, 2013. [Egyptian weekly newspaper].

Al-Akhabar. November 8, 2012. [Egyptian daily newspaper in Arabic].

Alanba. September 12, 2012. [Kuwaiti daily newspaper in Arabic].

Aljarida. 2012. September 11, September 23, October 7, December 10. [Kuwaiti daily newspaper in Arabic].

Aljarida. 2013. February 3, February 17, February 18. [Kuwaiti daily newspaper in Arabic].

Al-Mestkawy, T. A. 2007. *Self-Image and Others' Image: Between Arabs and Israel.* Cairo, Egypt: Human and Social Studies [in Arabic].

Al-Mintor Daily Briefing. December 3, 2012; January 9, 2013; March 15, 2013; July 4, 2013; July 8, 2013, July 9, 2013.

Al-Qabas. 2012. September 13, September 15, September 26, October 2. [Kuwaiti daily newspaper in Arabic].

Al-Qabas. 2013. January 3, January 23, February 9, February 16, February 28, March 16, March 19, July 7, July 8. [Kuwaiti daily newspaper in Arabic].

Alrai. November 8, 2012. [Kuwaiti daily newspaper in Arabic].

Alseyassah. 2012. September 13, November 8, December 3. [Kuwaiti daily newspaper in Arabic].

Al-Watan. 2012. November 8, November 26, December 7. [Kuwaiti daily newspaper in Arabic].

Annahar. September 27, 2012. [Kuwaiti daily newspaper in Arabic].

Annahar. 2013. February 13, March 18. [Kuwaiti daily newspaper in Arabic].

Arab Times. 2012. September 8, September 14, September 26, September 29. [Kuwaiti daily newspaper].

Arab Times. 2013. July 12 [Kuwaiti daily newspaper].

Asharq Al-Awsat. 2012. September 14, November 8. [Saudi daily newspaper in Arabic].

Daily Beast, The. March 28, 2011.

Esposito, J. L. 2009. *Islamic Threat: Myth or Reality.* [Arabic translation by K. A. Kasem]. Cairo: The National Center for Translation.

Ezzat, D. Obama's Extended Hand. *Al-Ahram Weekly On-line,* Issue 950, June 4–11, 2009. http://weekly.ahram.org.eg/2009/950/fr1.htm. Accessed August 2, 2009.

Financial Times. 2012. December 1, December 2.

Galal, S. 2010. *The American Mind Thinks: From Individual Freedom to Morphemes.* Cairo: The General Egyptian Book Organization [in Arabic].

Gielen, U. P. 2012. *The Shaping of Barack H. Obama Jr.'s Identity.* Paper presented at the International Congress of Psychology. Cape Town, South Africa, July 20, 2012.

Guardian, The. September 29, 2012.

Hammond, A. 2011. US President Barack Obama's speech on uprisings sweeping the Arab world show Washington is struggling to guide democratic movements that took it by surprise, Arab analysts said, threatening US regional allies. Dubai, May 20, 2011.

Hill, E. 2010. Survey: Arabs Lose Faith in Obama. Al Jazeera, August 11, 2010. http://www.aljazeera.com/focus/2010/08/201086121926345758.html. Accessed August 6, 2013.

Huntington, S. P. 2009. *Who Are We? The Decline and Renewal of American Identity.* [Arabic translation by A.M. El-Gamal]. Cairo: The National Center for Translation.

Khalil, M., and E. Bashier. (Supervisors) 2011. A report on the status of cultures' dialogue in the world: A survey on English, French, German, and Arabic newspapers and magazines. Beirut, Lebanon: Arab Thought Organization [in Arabic].

Kuwait Times. September 13, 2012. [Kuwaiti daily newspaper].

Little, D. 2009. *American Orientalism: The United States and the Middle East since 1945.* [Arabic translation by T. Al-Sheib]. Cairo: The National Center for Translation.

New York Times, The September 22, September 29, 2012.

Pew Global Attitudes Project. Released on June 13, 2012. http://www.pewglobal.org/2012/06/13/chap.

Reuters. 2012. January 18, February 14.

Sharma, D. 2011. *Barack Obama in Hawai'i and Indonesia: The Making of a Global President.* New York: Praeger.

Simons, J. 2009. Obama's Egyptian Report Card: His First 100 Days and the Cairo Speech. Arab Media & Society. No. 9, Fall 2009. http://www.arabmediasociety.com/?article=725. Accessed August 2, 2009.

Southland Times, The. November 8, 2012.

Star Malaysia, The. November 8, 2012.

Tessler, M., and D. Corstange. 2002. How Should Americans Understand Arab and Muslim Political Attitudes: Combating Stereotypes with Public Opinion Data from the Middle East. *Journal of Social Affairs* (UAE), 19(76), 13–13.

Thebat, A., and Kh. Al-Enany. 2007. *Arabs and the American Empire Tendency.* Cairo: The General Egyptian Book Organization [in Arabic].

14

OBAMA, IRAN, AND THE NEW GREAT GAME IN EURASIA: A JOURNALIST'S PERSPECTIVE

Pepe Escobar

I deeply cherish Isfahan. Isfahan is at the heart of Eurasia—roughly equidistant from Paris and Shanghai. And Eurasia is the geopolitical pivot of the world.

Iran is the ultimate crossroads at the heart of Eurasia, strategically straddling most of the globe's oil and gas reserves and a privileged hub for the distribution of energy to South Asia, Europe, and East Asia. As both China and India emerge as two of the twenty-first century big powers, Iran is the Great Prize par excellence.

My favorite place in Isfahan is inside Sheikh Lotfollah mosque, looking up at incredibly intricate-painted dome tiles progressively changing color from cream to strong pink as the day wears out and the light reflection forming the tail of a legendary painted peacock on the dome's roof also, imperceptibly, moves.

So whenever the dogs of war start barking—which is pretty much all of the time during the past few years—I time-travel back to that peacock's tail inside an Isfahani mosque, at the very center of Eurasia, and stare at the abyss; how could anyone possibly want to launch a war with unspeakable collateral damage[1] against this magical place?

In the 2012 US election's theater-of-the-absurd "foreign policy" debate in Florida, Iran came up no less than forty-seven times. Republican candidate Mitt Romney astonished America—and the world—with news that Syria is Iran's "route to the sea." Cutting through the fear and loathing—and threats and lies—permeating the preelection billionaire bipartisan contest, what was clear is that Americans were being offered virtually nothing substantial about Iran, even as Iran's (nonexistent) WMDs are relentlessly hawked as the top US national security issue.

Romney's position boiled down to "the ayatollahs" being scared into scraping their "nuclear ambitions" because of "American resolve."[2] Millions were falling for it. A late September 2012 NBC/WSJ poll had found that no less than 58% of Americans would endorse a new war if Iran continues with its (legal) nuclear program.[3] It didn't matter that "secret" talks between President Obama's special envoy Valerie Jarrett—actually born in Iran—and a special Tehran delegation had been going on in Doha, Qatar, with the (vague) possibility of an agreement between Washington and Tehran being announced before November 6, Election Day. But then the news was leaked[4] to the *New York Times*, and the White House came up with a nondenial denial—followed by a denial from Tehran.

We could all see Otto von Bismarck screaming out of his lush geopolitical grave; "Yes, fellas! Of course it's all true!" Iranian Supreme Leader Ayatollah Khamenei may have been furious[5] about the leak. But what my sources in Tehran were telling me is that the leadership does want a deal—paying particular attention to the concerns of Russia, China, and the European Union; nevertheless, that could only happen when everyone knew who was going to be part of Obama's new negotiating team.

The burning question remains: How an Obama 2.0 term would bridge the gap between the current policy—we don't want war, but there will be war if you build a bomb—and Iranian optics—we don't want a bomb (the supreme leader said so) and we want a deal, but you have to grant us some measure of respect. We should not forget that President Obama spelled it out as "*potentially* having bilateral discussions with the Iranians to *end* their nuclear program." Tehran won't "end" its (legal) nuclear program; and "potentially" is a graphic reminder of how the establishment in Washington loathes even the possibility of bilateral negotiations.

Mr. President, Tear Down this Wall

President Obama did inherit in early 2009 a tortuous, three-decade-long "Wall of Mistrust" in Iran–US relations. To his credit, only twelve minutes into the presidency he offered a hand of friendship if Tehran would "unclench" its fist. Six days into the presidency, when talking about "negative preconceptions" in the Middle East, he implied that as these remained, the Wall of Mistrust would never be torn down.

Then, in March 2009, Obama directly addressed all Iranians in a message for Nowruz, the Iranian New Year.[6] He called for "engagement that is honed and grounded in mutual respect." He even quoted the thirteenth-century Persian poet Sa'adi: "The children of Adam are limbs of one body / which God created from one essence."

Yet an undercurrent of imperial arrogance could already be detected, as in the offer of "a choice": Iran could become a part of the "community of nations" or remain an outsider. A quick examination of Iran's relations with most member-nations of the Non-Aligned Movement (NAM), as well as the BRICS group of emerging powers, would reveal already by early 2009 that Iran was not exactly an international pariah.

In his Nowruz address, Obama also stressed that a possible entente cordiale "will not be advanced by threats." Yet even as the president was delivering the message, Obama administration officials were briefing European Union diplomats—as I was told at the time by Brussels sources—that Washington's strategy actually boiled down to the "pressure" track in a "dual track" approach, according to a Wikileaks cable.[7]

Handicapped by a set of Washington misconceptions, a bipartisan consensus for an aggressive new strategy toward Iran was emerging even before Obama's inauguration. A September 2008 report by the Washington think tank Bipartisan Policy Center assumed a nuclear-weapons-capable Iran as a fact and detailed a strategy "incorporating new diplomatic, economic, and military tools in an integrated fashion."[8]

The report was drafted by Michael Rubin from the neo-con American Enterprise Institute, a think tank that unashamedly promoted the disastrous 2003 invasion and occupation of Iraq. Obama senior advisers who "unanimously approved" the report included Dennis Ross, former Senator Charles Robb, Ashton Carter (former assistant secretary for defense under Bill Clinton), Anthony Lake, Susan Rice, and Richard Clarke. The 2007 National Intelligence Estimate (NIE) by all US intelligence agencies stating that Iran had ended any nuclear weapons program in 2003 was bluntly dismissed.[9]

Mirroring the Bush administration's "all options are on the table" approach, the report proposed—what else—a military surge in the Persian Gulf, targeting "not only Iran's nuclear infrastructure, but also its conventional military infrastructure in order to suppress an Iranian response." In fact, such a surge would indeed begin before George W. Bush left office and only increase in scope in the Obama years.

The crucial point is that as tens of millions of US voters were choosing Obama because he was promising to end the war in Iraq, a very powerful cross-section of US elites were drafting the blueprint for his prosecution of US geopolitical/strategic/economic interests in what the Pentagon was still calling the "arc of instability" from the Middle East to Central Asia. And the key plank of this strategy was to create the conditions for a military strike against Iran.

Time Waits for No One

With the Obama 2.0 administration in place, the time to solve the immensely complex Iranian nuclear drama is now. But as Columbia University's Gary Sick—the key White House adviser on Iran during the Iranian Revolution and the Tehran hostage crisis—has suggested,[10] nothing will be accomplished if Washington does not start thinking beyond sanctions, now practically fossilized as "politically untouchable."

Sick proposes a sound path; private bilateral discussions; credible negotiators (on both sides); a mutually agreed agenda; and finally revamped, full-blown negotiations under the existing P5+1 framework (encompassing the five permanent members of the UN Security Council—United States, Russia, China, France, and Britain—plus Germany).

This might sound like a dream scenario. But it's impossible even to start dreaming if we don't know where we stand. So let's take a closer look at some timeline highlights since early 2009—a frantic seesawing of sanctions, threats, military surges, and colossal mutual incomprehension—to see whether a pattern of "mutual respect" actually emerges out of Washington's much-vaunted "dual track" approach.

March 2009. US Director of Intelligence Dennis Blair tells the US Senate Armed Services Committee that Iran had not decided whether to build a nuclear weapon and did not have any highly enriched uranium. Yet Blair was certain "Tehran at a minimum is keeping open the option to develop" a nuclear weapon.[11]

Admiral Mike Mullen, then chairman of the Joint Chiefs of Staff, stresses that as far as Iran is concerned, the United States and Israel are one.[12] Just to make sure, Israeli Prime Minister Benjamin "Bibi" Netanyahu sends a message to Obama: Stop Iran—or I will.[13]

April 2009. An internal Obama administration debate is raging; should we use Israel's incessant threats of a military strike to gain leverage in our negotiations with Tehran?[14] Gen. David Petraeus, then head of CENTCOM, is convinced Israel "may" decide to attack. Obama for his part does not wait for a White House meeting with Netanyahu to deliver his own message; via an official "pigeon," he forbids Israel to start a war.[15]

June 2009. The emergence of the Green Movement, the fiercely contested reelection of President Mahmoud Ahmadinejad, and the Tehran leadership's repression drive. Obama in effect calls on the Iranian government to allow protesters to control the streets of Tehran. Two years later in the United States, as the Occupy Movement emerged, local authorities would not allow protesters to control the streets of New York City.

October 2009. A suicide bomber from the shadowy Sunni group Jundallah ("Soldiers of God"), which profits from instrumental CIA help, kills at least twenty-nine people in the ultrasensitive Sistan-Balochistan province in southeastern Iran. According to Majlis (Parliament) speaker Ali Larijani—very close to Ayatollah Khamenei—"Mr. Obama has said he will extend his hand towards Iran, but with this terrorist action he has burned his hand."

January 2010. As Obama's tentative December 2009 deadline for at least some success in negotiations with Iran has expired, he seems to be losing control of his Iran policy. The US Senate passes a bill crammed with unilateral sanctions against foreign companies that export gasoline to Iran or invest in its domestic refineries. It's up to Patrick Disney, assistant policy director of the National Iranian American Council (NIAC)—in favor of engagement—to provide the context; "No president can lift the embargo [against Iran] without certifying to Congress that Iran has met a laundry list of demands that no president in his right mind will certify."[16]

It's surge time—again—in the Persian Gulf, even as Gen. Petraeus warns that a strike on Iran could lead the very nationalistic Iranians to rally behind the Tehran leadership. The neo-con echo chambers, for their part, urge the president to make a "dramatic gesture to change the public perception of him as a lightweight, bumbling ideologue"; the prescription is to bomb Iran. In this case, it would be Americans who would "presumably rally around the flag."[17]

February 2010. It's all about sanctions now. Secretary Gates: "The only path that is left to us at this point, it seems to me, is that pressure track."[18]

May 2010. The Tehran declaration fiasco. After interminably tortuous negotiations, Brazil and Turkey revive a deal almost entirely according to Washington's demands.[19] At first Secretary of State Hillary Clinton said the Brazil–Turkey mediation was bound to fail. Then the State Department said it was the "last chance" for an agreement without sanctions. And finally, less than twenty-four hours after a deal was clinched in Tehran, Clinton wins over the United Nations Security Council and announces a draft resolution for a fourth United Nations round of sanctions against Iran.[20]

Worryingly enough, this was interpreted in Tehran as Obama lying to then Brazilian President Lula and Turkey's Prime Minister Recep Tayyip Erdoğan; the White House never wanted an agreement. That, in fact, was the scenario envisaged by Obama's team of Iran advisers.

November 2010. "Engagement" seems to resurface—at least as sound advice. A seventy-seven-page report, *Engagement, Coercion, and Iran's Nuclear Challenge,* by two centrist Washington think tanks, suggests Obama should go for "strategic engagement" with Iran.[21]

December 2010. Forget about engagement. The report *Which Path to Persia* rears its head as the new Bible in terms of attacking Iran.[22]

June 2011. The NIE on Iran is updated and reinforces the key conclusion of the 2007 report: Iran halted weaponization in 2003. And whatever research there was before 2003 was directed towards Iraq, not Israel; "The public dispute over the 2007 N.I.E. led to bitter infighting within the Obama Administration and the intelligence community over this year's N.I.E. update—a discrepancy between the available intelligence and what many in the White House and Congress believed to be true. Much of the debate, which delayed the issuing of the N.I.E. for more than four months, centered on the Defense Intelligence Agency's astonishing assessment that Iran's earlier nuclear-weapons research had been targeted at its old regional enemy, Iraq, and not at Israel, the United States, or Western Europe. One retired senior intelligence official told me that the D.I.A. analysts had determined that Iran "does not have an ongoing weapons program, and all of the available intelligence shows that the program, when it did exist, was aimed at Iraq. The Iranians thought Iraq was developing a bomb."[23]

Does that matter? Of course not; absolutely no one, from the president to Secretary Clinton to every soul in Capitol Hill dares to quote the NIE conclusions.

August 2011. Engagement is seen as being drowned by threats, sanctions, and "intimidation aimed at isolating Iran, subverting its economy and overthrowing its regime." But this is something to be read in Asian, not US media.[24]

September 2011. Obama is being bombarded by Republicans, whose master narrative is that diplomacy failed, sanctions are not enough, and the only option is to bomb Iran, something Obama won't contemplate because he does not like wars.[25]

October 2011. The Fast and the Furious—or the Iranian cum Mexican cartel terror plot, which, in the words of Attorney General Eric Holder, was "directed by factions of the Iranian government to assassinate a foreign Ambassador on U.S. soil with explosives."[26] The frenzy fizzles in a matter of days. The result? More sanctions—what else?[27]

November 2011. The House Foreign Affairs Committee starts to consider a new "crippling sanctions" bill that reads like an eye-popping blueprint for war.[28] More bunker buster bombs find their way to the Persian Gulf.[29] Seymour Hersh observes that a new International Atomic Energy Agency (IAEA) report "leaves us where we've been since 2002, when George Bush declared Iran to be a member of the Axis of Evil—with lots of belligerent talk but no definitive evidence of a nuclear-weapons program."[30] The White House at least admits its strategy is not working.[31] Yet everything points to the "Iraqization" of the whole drama, as Flynt Leverett and Hillary Mann Leverett perfectly set the scene up to 2016; "American elites are gearing up for military confrontation with the Islamic Republic—and, in the process, displaying all of the cultural, intellectual, and political pathologies that produced the 2003 Iraq war. We do not believe that the United States is likely to initiate such a confrontation before the next presidential election in November 2012. But [President of the Council on Foreign Relations Richard] Haass' timetable—that is, during either an Obama second term or the first term of his Republican successor—seems on point. It will take a lot to head this one off. For those who, like us, believe that another U.S.-initiated war would be a strategic disaster—first of all, for the United States—the next 18 months will likely be the period in which either there is enough of an intellectual pushback to stop the folly, or the United States puts itself on an inexorable path toward attacking Iran."[32]

December 2011. Iran acquires the most sophisticated US stealth drone ever made nearly completely intact. Although drones flying over Iran for years have found absolutely no indication of a weapons program, Iran for its part has managed to find at least one drone.[33]

January 2012. The Obama administration launches an all-out economic war against Iran's Central Bank.[34] Obama's shadow war duly complements the economic war. A new, elite, previously secret Joint Special Operations Task Force-Gulf Cooperation Council starts to do business in the Persian Gulf, providing "highly trained personnel that excel in uncertain environments" to Washington's pet petro-monarchies.[35] And a much more powerful 30,000-pound bunker-buster bomb known as the Massive Ordnance Penetrator is also getting ready to rumble.[36]

February 2012. Expanding on the no-unilateral-strike theme, Chairman of the Joint Chiefs of Staff Gen. Martin Dempsey warns Israel that any strike must be preceded by a US green light.[37] At least Gen. Dempsey admits, "the Iranian regime is a rational actor." But the Bomb Iran crowd is not listening.[38]

"Boxed in by lobbyists and by a Congress that takes its marching orders from them," Obama's Iran policy didn't fail; it was aborted. Thus argues Trita Parsi, president of the NIAC and author of arguably the most comprehensive book so far on Obama's Iran policy: *A Single Roll of the Dice: Obama's diplomacy with Iran* (Yale University Press 2012).

According to Parsi, "Obama's intention was genuine, but his vision for diplomacy was soon undermined, for four reasons: pressure from Israel and its powerful allies in Congress, and to a lesser extent from Saudi Arabia and France, to adopt a confrontational policy; the June 2009 election mayhem in Iran and the subsequent repression and human rights abuses, which hardened the regime in Tehran and narrowed Obama's space for diplomacy; Obama's early adoption of a contradictory 'dual track' policy, combining diplomacy with escalating pressure on Tehran; and Obama's unwillingness to create more domestic political space for diplomacy by challenging a status quo in Washington that is set on enmity."[39]

Former spokesman for the Iranian nuclear negotiation team, Ambassador Hossein Mousavian, illustrates the "enmity" theme describing the IAEA visit to Iran on October 2011, led by Deputy Director General Herman Nackaerts.

According to Mousavian, "during the visit, Fereydoon Abbasi-Davani, the head of Iran's Atomic Energy Organization, offered a blank check to the IAEA, granting full transparency, openness to inspections and co-operation with the IAEA. He also informed Nackaerts of Iran's receptiveness to putting the country's nuclear program under 'full IAEA supervision,' including implementing the Additional Protocol for five years, provided that sanctions against Iran were lifted."

Washington's reaction included the Fast-and-Furious plot trying to frame Tehran for the assassination attempt on the Saudi ambassador to the US; the pressure to divert the IAEA's November 2011 report on Iran by adding a spin on a "possible" military angle to the nuclear program; the oil embargo; and the sponsoring of a UN resolution against Iran on terrorism.

A new report by the International Crisis Group, based in Brussels, virtually endorses Iran's approach as outlined by Mousavian. The result would be the recognition of Iran's right to enrich uranium up to 5% and the lifting of existing sanctions—in stages.

The report recommends the United States and the European Union follow Turkey's diplomatic way of dealing with Iran. Instead of sanctions, sabotage, and nonstop threats of war, the report stresses that "economic pressure is at best futile, at worse counter-productive," and that Tehran "ought to be presented with a realistic proposal." This is exactly what the BRICS group of emerging powers, plus Turkey, has been advocating all along.[40]

Crucially, Ayatollah Khamenei—who has repeatedly condemned a nuclear weapon as un-Islamic, even issuing a fatwa bearing his authority as Theologian-in-Chief of the Islamic Republic—tells a group of Iranian nuclear scientists, "nuclear weapons are not at all beneficial to us. . . . From an ideological and juridical perspective, we consider developing nuclear weapons unlawful. We consider using such weapons as a big sin. We also believe that keeping such weapons is futile and dangerous, and we still never go after them."[41]

March 2012. As the Obama-approved sanctions make it increasingly difficult for Iran to import wheat from the Ukraine and India, the sanctions start to be regarded across the developing world as collective punishment. The Iranian middle class may be sliding into poverty, yet the Tehran leadership keeps reaping oil/gas profits.

As for a strike, it remains "on the table"—but only with a US green light. Just in case, the US Navy launches yet another Iran surge.[42] But the two-week war game Internal Look—the pride of CENTCOM—concludes that an attack on Iran would lead to a wider regional war, deeply "troubling" Gen. James N. Mattis, commander of all US forces in the Middle East, Persian Gulf, and Southwest Asia.[43]

April 2012. Weighing Benefits and Costs of Military Action Against Iran, a fifty-seven-page bipartisan study produced by the NGO Iran Project and endorsed by a group of more than thirty former senior US officials and national security experts, including former national security advisers Brent Scowcroft and Zbigniew Brzezinski, once again concludes the obvious. An attack on Iran would "rally the Iranian population behind its current hard-line leadership and, perversely, increase Iran's motivation to build a bomb. Iran might also withdraw from the Nuclear Non-Proliferation Treaty (NPT) and end all cooperation with the International Atomic Energy Agency (IAEA)."[44]

May 2012. By 401–11, Congress passes a bill that in effect calls for bombing Iran when it obtains a hazy "nuclear weapons capability"; that could already apply not only to Iran but also to Brazil, Argentina, Japan, Germany, and the Netherlands. Col. Lawrence Wilkerson, former chief of staff for Secretary of State Colin Powell, warns, "This resolution reads like the same sheet of music that got us into the Iraq war, and could be the precursor for a war with Iran."[45]

Secretary of Defense Leon Panetta once again reminds everyone "all options are on the table"; the United States is "ready" to launch an attack and will do it as soon as President Obama says so.[46]

June 2012. The economic war ramps up.[47] And the answer to the "Iran threat" is . . . the GCC (Gulf Cooperation Council—the six petro-monarchies Bahrain, Kuwait, Oman, Qatar, Saudi Arabia, and the United Arab Emirates; I prefer to call them the Gulf Counter-Revolution Club, for their manifest aversion to any push toward democracy inherent to the true spirit of the Arab Spring). A Senate Foreign Relations Committee report—under chairman John Kerry—hails the GCC as the ideal tool to "promote regional stability" and "provide a counterweight to Iran."[48]

Translation: the Pentagon's twenty-first-century security strategy—centered on the strategic "pivot" to Asia—is as much about "rebalance toward the Asia-Pacific region" as beefing up Pentagon assets in the Middle East/Southwest Asia. Top designated "threats": Iran and China.[49]

The Obama administration has uncritically bought into the House of Saud's one-track strategy— which is to fund, train, and weaponize hardcore Sunni outfits ideologically aligned with al-Qaeda, and thus extremely anti-Shi'ite. The House of Saud's ultimate enemy is Iran—endlessly depicted as dangerous, sectarian Shi'ites (thus non-Sunnis) and Persians (thus non-Arabs), heretical unbelievers bent on infiltrating the Arab world and destabilizing Sunni states. As much as the Obama administration has carried out a selective war against Pashtuns in Af-Pak, it has also embarked on selective discrimination against Shi'ites in the Persian Gulf and Southwest Asia.

July 2012. Obama has warned that the United States will "expose any financial institution, no matter where they are located, that allows the increasingly desperate Iranian regime to retain access to the international financial system." The Tehran leadership cannot but interpret this as an economic war whose chief reason is that Iran has replaced the US dollar with yuan, rubles, Indian rupees, and even gold in its energy trade. Eventually, they reason, the US military might intervene to stop Iran from renouncing the petrodollar.

August 2012. Ambassador Hossein Mousavian, research scholar at Princeton University's Woodrow Wilson School of Public and International Affairs and former spokesperson for the Iranian nuclear negotiating team from 2003 to 2005, finally explains it all in one single phrase; "The history of Iran's nuclear program suggests that the West is inadvertently pushing Iran toward nuclear weapons."

Mousavian stresses the West was never interested in solving the nuclear issue. "Rather, the West wanted to compel Iran to forgo its enrichment program completely." This could only lead Tehran to "change its nuclear diplomacy and accelerate its enrichment program, as it sought self-sufficiency in nuclear fuel."

Flashback to February 2010. Mousavian says Tehran proposed, "keeping its enrichment activities below 5% in return for the West providing fuel rods for the Tehran reactor. The West refused this offer."

Another flashback to May 2010. "Iran reached a deal with Brazil and Turkey to swap its stockpile of LEU for research reactor fuel. The deal was based on a proposal first drafted by the Obama administration with Brazilian and Turkish officials under the impression that they had the blessing of Washington to negotiate with Iran. Regrettably, the United States trampled on their success by rejecting the plan; the UN Security Council subsequently passed additional sanctions against Iran."

Yet another flashback to September 2011. "When Iran had completely mastered 20% enrichment and had a growing stockpile, it proposed stopping its 20%-enrichment activities and accepting Western-provided fuel rods for the Tehran reactor. Once again, the West declined and made it necessary for the Iranians to move toward producing their own fuel rods."

Mousavian's conclusion mirrors any decent progressive or centrist US think tank report; if there is an attack, "Iran would be likely to withdraw from the NPT and pursue nuclear weapons."

What makes it even more absurd is that there is a solution to all this madness: "To satisfy the concerns of the West regarding Iran's 20% stockpile, a mutually acceptable solution for the long term would entail a 'zero stockpile.' Under this approach, a joint committee of the P5+1 and Iran would quantify the domestic needs of Iran for use of 20% enriched uranium, and any quantity beyond that amount would be sold in the international market or immediately converted back to an enrichment level of 3.5%. This would ensure that Iran does not possess excess 20% enriched uranium forever, satisfying the international concerns that Iran is seeking nuclear weapons. It would be a face-saving solution for all parties as it would recognize Iran's right to enrichment and would help to negate concerns that Iran is pursuing nuclear weapons."[50]

September 2012. Chairman of the Joint Chiefs of Staff, Gen. Martin Dempsey, once again exhumes the "no strike without U.S. green light" theme.[51] Crucially, Dempsey also hints that an attack would be illegal. And this as the 120 members of the NAM, gathered in Tehran of all places, issue a Tehran declaration quite different from that one in 2010. NAM not only emphasizes Iran's right to develop peaceful nuclear energy, as a subscriber to the NPT, but also acknowledges its right to enrich uranium and master the full nuclear fuel cycle. This could not but puncture the myth—widely circulated in Washington—of an "isolated" Iran, as well as plenty other nuclear Iran-related myths.[52]

The Obama administration removes the Iranian cult-cum-terrorist group Mujahedin-e Khalq (MEK) from the US list of foreign terrorist organizations. That's the result of a lavishly funded public relations campaign, which included bipartisan stars bagging five-figure fees to speak on behalf of delisting MEK.[53]

The IAEA releases yet another report. These are the two crucial quotes: (1) the IAEA is confident about "the absence of undeclared nuclear material and activities in Iran" and (2) the IAEA can "conclude that all nuclear materials in Iran is in peaceful activities."

October 2012. As much as the Obama administration—as well as the European Union—insist there is no quarrel "with the Iranian people," ultimately it is "the Iranian people" who are paying the price for the devastating sanctions package, despite government subsidies for milk, bread, rice, yogurt, and vegetables. The "crippling" sanctions cycle—which aims not only to paralyze the economy but to incite riots against the leadership in Tehran—does display overtones of collective punishment.

Yet, from the Obama administration' point of view, it's counterproductive that the urban middle class—which comprises the bulk of the reformist movement in Iran—is weakened while the ultra-conservatives keep the upper hand.

A further complicating factor is that the Obama administration's strategy conflates with the ineptitude of the Central Bank of Iran to deal with the effect of the sanctions. Tehran has been confronted with a de facto war economy. But many at the top refuse to admit it. A key nuance is that Speaker of the Iranian Parliament Ali Larijani, who is very close to Ayatollah Khamenei, swears that the drama is 80% due to the Ahmadinejad administration's mismanagement and only 20% to sanctions.

Still, as economist Djavad Salehi-Esfahani has explained, the Tehran leadership continues to manage the worst effects of the sanctions and a declining currency by using its oil wealth to subsidize essential imports.[54]

Hit the New Silk Road(s)

Even this admittedly simplified, seesaw timeline suggests the Obama administration has not exactly followed up on that initial "engagement" drive.

On the eve of the 2012 US presidential election, Iranian negotiators—and Iranian public opinion, a key Obama constituency—had already ceased to believe the president is genuinely interested in a diplomatic solution to the nuclear drama; with the nonstop accumulation of sanctions, economic war, assassination of scientists, and a military strike as a perennial option on the table, the consensus was that no US administration—even if headed by Obama—is willing to deal with the Islamic Republic on a basis of mutual respect.

Now we're back to a variant of our initial burning question: During his second term, will Obama finally admit that Washington doesn't need regime change in Tehran to improve its relationship with Iran? Only that would open the real possibility of real negotiations toward a Wall of Mistrust–blasting deal—incorporating a real détente, addressing Iran's lawful pursuit of a nuclear program, providing guarantees there won't be a nuclear weapons program, and shattering the odds of a devastating war in the Persian Gulf and the oil/gas heartlands of the Greater Middle East.

After the election of moderate Hassan Rouhani as Iran's President on June 14, 2013, conditions seem to be in place for a breakthrough. "Seem" is the operative word, though.

Rouhani is a courteous, logical diplomat who keenly respects international norms and regulations. He was nicknamed "the diplomatic Sheikh" during his term as Iran's chief nuclear negotiator, from 2003 to 2005. His administration would be more than ready for a fair deal, including all the key demands of both parties, based on the NPT, and part of a careful package to be implemented, as Russian diplomacy has insisted from the beginning, step-by-step and in mutual reciprocity.

Of course the fundamental stone for this process is direct talks with the United States, but as far as Tehran is concerned, if Washington really wants a serious discussion, demonstration should be offered through an act of goodwill. It has been endlessly proven that sanctions, threats and humiliation of Iran won't cut it; Rouhani will make it clear that everything is on the table as long as the dossier is treated in an atmosphere of mutual respect and cooperation.

Theoretically, this could also include something else: an Obama "Nixon in China" moment, a dramatic journey or gesture by the US president to decisively break the deadlock. Yet as long as a barrage of furiously misinformed Washington anti-Iran hawks, in lockstep with the Israeli government, deploy a relentless PR offensive crammed with red lines, deadlines, preemptive sabotage of the P5+1 negotiations and incendiary rhetoric, an Obama "Nixon in China" moment will remain a receding dream.

And to think this elusive "Nixon in China" moment would not even be the end of the story; rather a twist in the Big Picture. And that leads us—literally—to the heart of the action: Iran's strategic positioning in Eurasia.

Before the 2012 round of sanctions, Iran was producing 3.8 million barrels of oil a day and exporting 2.5 million of it. Production then fell to 3 million and exports to 2 million, especially directed to Asian giants China, India, and South Korea. Over 60% of Iran's export markets are in Asia. Throughout 2012, Saudi Arabia and Iraq made up for the loss of Iranian exports while Iran rearranged forms of payment with its Asian clients.

But as soon as Asian demand grows—as it will—Iran is inevitably bound to export more and keep finding ingenious ways to escape the US/EU financial blockade, such as exporting oil to China and South Korea in Iranian tankers (bought from China), covering the insurance, and accepting payment in yuan and Indian rupees.

This in itself torpedoes the Obama administration's assumption that the Tehran leadership may be irretrievably impoverished by 2014 because of a Western oil boycott.

The Tehran leadership sees it all as a Western plot not only to drive an irreconcilable schism between the Christian West and Islam, but also to accelerate *fitna* (upheaval, chaos) inside the world of Islam, especially between Sunnis and Shi'ites. Once again it's important to remember that Ayatollah Khamenei has repeatedly condemned a nuclear weapon as un-Islamic.

As for the myth of an Iranian "threat," it pales in comparison to the United States spending a whopping $1 trillion on defense annually—when foreign military aid and maintenance of its hefty nuclear arsenal is also taken into account.[55]

Iran for its part spends a maximum of $12 billion, much less than the United Arab Emirates, and only 20% of the six Persian Gulf monarchies grouped in the GCC.[56]

Moreover, the myth of a nuclear Iranian "threat" would disappear for good would the new Obama administration push for a Middle East as a nuclear-free zone. Iran and the GCC have endorsed the idea in the past. Israel—a de facto, but never officially acknowledged, nuclear power, with an arsenal of up to 200 warheads—has rejected it.

Yet, the big picture goes way beyond the United States' and Israel's strategic gaming. Iran's position as the ultimate Southwest Asia strategic crossroads conditions all that comes next in the New Great Game in Eurasia; the alliances weaved by BRICS member-nations and emerging powers China and Russia; the conflicting Silk Road scenarios—the US route and the Eurasian route; and, last but not least, the tectonic movements in the great energy chessboard I call Pipelineistan.[57]

I have argued for years that all these intertwined developments must be analyzed as a whole—and that certainly includes the new US military "pivot" strategy unveiled in early 2012 by President Obama, in which the focus of Washington's attention moves from two disastrous wars in the Greater Middle East to the Pacific—and especially China. Iran also happens to be right at the heart of the "pivot," in Southwest Asia, with all that oil heading toward energy-hungry China over waters patrolled by the US Navy.

Thus the relationship between the new Obama administration and Iran is as much about the nuclear dossier as about Pipelineistan developments; Beijing's concerted movements to prop up the yuan in relation to the US dollar—not to mention accelerate the demise of the petrodollar;[58] and last but not least, the matter of who will dominate the twenty-first century Silk Road(s).[59]

At the 2012 NAM meeting in Tehran, Iran, India and Afghanistan have started a push toward a new Southern Silk Road connecting Iran to Central and South Asia through roads, railways, and major ports. The crucial Silk Road port in this case is Chabahar, in Sistan-Balochistan province in southeast Iran. Chabahar is bound to link Iran directly to Afghanistan and India.

As much as the Obama administration is against it, for Delhi getting closer with both Kabul and Tehran is all about its own Eurasian strategy. Chabahar is crucial for the Iran–India strategic partnership not only in terms of Central Asia but also for India's commercial relations with Southwest Asia and the wider Middle East.

In this New Silk Road subplot, enters Pipelineistan—via the key Iran–Pakistan umbilical cord in the making; the $1.2 billion, 2,700 kilometer-long IP gas pipeline, from Iran's gigantic South Pars field across Balochistan and Sindh and into Punjab. One of those typically interminable Pipelineistan soap operas, IP used to be IPI (Iran-Pakistan-India), but Delhi eventually pulled out, forced by relentless pressure from the Bush and Obama administrations.

And that's where Beijing steps in, as few things would be more appetizing than turning the former IPI into IPC (extended to China). China's Minister of National Defense Liang Guanglie swears the Middle Kingdom "has no plans for Indian Ocean military bases." What does interest Beijing is to build and profit from Indian Ocean ports. This includes the Holy of the Holies, Gwadar, in southwest Balochistan in Pakistan.

Gwadar was built mostly with Chinese money—over $220 million. It was managed by Singapore. When Singapore decided to pull out, in 2012, China took over; all in line with China's extremely complex energy strategy, which essentially translates into an escape from two bottlenecks, the straits of Malacca and Hormuz.[60]

So as much as India bets on Chabahar in Iran, China bets on Gwadar in Pakistan as a key transshipment hub linking it to Central Asia and the Gulf. Both ports are key pawns in the New Great Game in Eurasia; both are at the heart of Pipelineistan; and in both cases there is virtually nothing the Obama administration can do to prevent these instances of closer Eurasian integration.

The IP pipeline will transit in Gwadar, which includes the now distinct possibility of a Chinese-built extension going north, parallel to the Karakoram highway, all the way to Xinjiang, China's Far West. And Gwadar may also become a terminal in case the perennially plagued Turkmenistan-Afghanistan-Pakistan-India (TAPI) pipeline is ever built. That's what successive US administrations since Clinton in the mid-1990s have been striving for.

Originally TAP, the $7.6 billion, 1,600-kilometer steel serpent crossing a horribly dangerous war zone has always been the invisible star of the "good" Afghan war, as President Obama defined it. Washington's plan during the Bush administration was to seduce gas republic Turkmenistan to provide energy for the Clinton-approved Baku-Tblisi-Ceyhan (BTC) pipeline, and then to TAP.

Negotiations with the Taliban until virtually the eve of 9/11 failed because of transit fees. TAP was part of a grand Washington strategy of a "Greater Central Asia" centered on Afghanistan and India—then revived by the Obama administration as the US version of the New Silk Road[61] (see Central Asia and the Transition in Afghanistan).

The problem with the Obama administration's New Silk Road—centered on Afghanistan and essentially promoting free trade with the Central Asian "stans" and South Asia via good communication networks and energy infrastructure—is its obsession in bypassing Iran at all costs. That's where it dovetails with the Clinton and Bush administration's Pipelineistan obsession in bypassing both Iran and Russia as sources of oil and gas.

The only Silk Road the Obama administration has been able to devise is war-related; the Northern Distribution Network (NDN)—a logistical/military marathon snaking across Central Asia so the United States and NATO may supply the Afghan war bypassing "unreliable" Pakistan. The NDN may also be seen as a road map illustrating Washington's desire to implant or reimplant the Empire of Bases all over the Central Asian "stans." That explains Secretary Clinton's 2012 schmoozing of both Kyrgyzstan and Uzbekistan.

Way beyond its New Silk Road dreams, it remains to be seen how successful—if at all—will be the Obama administration 2.0 in establishing a long-term military presence in Central Asia.

In Afghanistan—that notorious pawn of Big Power play—Washington is bound to keep privileging Tajiks and Uzbeks over Pashtuns while no one really knows what degree of influence the Taliban will exercise in the vast Pashtun-majority areas. In wider Central Asia, the Obama administration may exploit the fierce competition between Moscow and Beijing who in spite of their strategic alliance will keep roaming around securing top economic assets.

Moscow will do anything to prevent a long-term US/NATO presence in Central Asia. Along with Beijing, which regards Central Asia as a strategic rearguard in Pipelineistan terms but also for economic expansion, they will basically coordinate their policies via the Shanghai Cooperation

Organization (SCO). That's how Beijing plans to channel a solution for Afghanistan—securing its long-term investments in mineral exploitation.

Beijing wants a negotiated peace between all Afghan parties, including key external actors; and most of all, a neutral Afghanistan. Within the SCO, nearly all of the players surrounding Afghanistan are either members or observers (that includes Iran and China ally Pakistan, increasingly aligned with Russia as well). Both Pakistan and Iran will eventually become full SCO members. This will configure the SCO as a prime platform for Eurasian political stability.

Ultimately, both Russia and China want post-2014 Afghanistan to be stabilized by the United Nations. It's unclear whether NATO will engage in collaborating with—instead of antagonizing—Russia. In the long run, this suggests no role for NATO as peacemaker and a reduced US influence at best.

As much as the ancient Silk Road was the first globalization highway, centered on trade, China is now also pushing for a new Iron Silk Road focused on tapping into energy—oil and gas, especially in Myanmar, Iran, and Russia, by linking no less than 17 countries with more than 8,000 kilometers of high-speed rail (not to mention over 8,000 kilometers already built inside China).[62]

Beijing still suspects that Washington is bent on taking over Central Asia's energy wealth—as much as China is winning in, for instance, Turkmenistan, where successive Bush and Obama administrations' missions extracted nothing while the Chinese built a pipeline and are guaranteed a hefty supply of gas for the next thirty years. Beijing also mightily worries that in the event of a showdown Washington will be in control of the flow of energy from the Persian Gulf—and thus able to suffocate China. So we're back to arguably the number-one nightmare of Washington strategists, namely an always-evolving Tehran–Beijing axis that will keep preventing the US strategic target of isolating Iran.

In my early 2009 essay *Obama Does Globalistan* (Nimble Books), I set out to examine how the new president might deal with the Liquid War landscape he inherited—and how he would position himself in relation to an inevitably emerging multipolarity.

Today we see the SCO slowly but surely uniting China, Russia, and Central Asia with Iran and, in the long term, India; the gradual solidification of what pan-Asian energy experts have defined as the Asian Energy Security Grid; and a leading Russian role in Pipelineistan. From the Obama administration, we have had essentially the unfulfilled dream of a New Silk Road and the Pentagon aim of pivoting from the Middle East to Asia-Pacific.

So what remains of that initial Obama drive to reach out to Iran with an "engagement that is honed and grounded in mutual respect"?

A quick examination of the Obama administration's 2010 Quadrennial Defense Review, the 2010 Nuclear Posture Review, and the January 2012 strategic defense guidance report *Sustaining U.S. Global Leadership: Priorities for 21st Century Defense* doesn't leave a lot of room for "mutual respect" regarding Iran and beyond. And it must be stressed this is essentially a bipartisan consensus—calibrated by barely perceptible nuances.[63]

Key aims remain sanctions as a road map toward wrecking the Iranian economy, leading to regime change; and regime change in Syria as it is Russia's key Arab ally. In contrast, scant attention is being paid to the wildly divergent, hazy agendas of Saudi Arabia, Qatar, and Turkey.

In the long run, with pro-American political set-ups in place in both Iran and Syria, the path—in theory—should be open for total US dominance of MENA (Middle East-North Africa), arguably the crucial node in Pipelineistan.

Efforts will also be concentrated on undermining the increasingly closer economic and political cooperation between BRICS members Russia and China—even as Russia under President Putin remains adamantly opposed to NATO expansion and the US missile defense program. As for the "containment" of China, it steps up to "encirclement" levels after the Obama administration's pivot, that was announced in early 2012 at the Pentagon.

US allies in Europe and among the Persian Gulf oligarchies may interpret all this as the exercising of "global leadership." Yet many power centers in Eurasia and across the developing world will interpret it as a further refinement of the Pentagon's Full Spectrum Dominance doctrine.[64]

It didn't have to be this way. With the International Energy Agency forecasting an energy self-sufficient United States by 2020,[65] nothing would make more sense than to dump those Persian Gulf oligarchies for good. That would free Washington to concentrate on where the real economic action is—Asia; not with a clumsy, missile defense shield military offensive,[66] but rather a meaningful economic pivoting.[67]

A crucial subplot would be the recognition of Iran as a regional power—leading to substantial Pipelineistan-related consequences such as the go-ahead for the $10 billion Iran–Iraq–Syria pipeline from South Pars (the largest gas field in the world) to the Eastern Mediterranean. That's what the Chinese would typically call a win-win situation for all players involved, in the Middle East, Europe, and Asia.

It won't happen. Blame it—once again—on the Pentagon, for whom Iran will remain the number one "threat."[68]

Somebody has yet to break the news to those generals that in an increasingly multipolar geopolitical reality Eurasian powers Russia, China, and Iran simply won't subscribe to Washington scenarios. As for the New Silk Road(s) linking South Asia to Central Asia, Southwest Asia, and China—as well as most Pipelineistan networks—they will be built in Asia by Asia, not America.[69]

What the record shows, so far, is that the twenty-first as yet another "American century," as well as unipolar hegemony characterized as "American exceptionalism," have continued to be key themes under the first Obama administration as much as they were under both Bush's terms. They constitute unshakable propositions unquestionably disseminated by the powers that be, including mainstream media.

America may indeed be exceptional in innumerable aspects—as in its unbounded capacity for technological innovation. But apart from GCC petro-monarchies and a few European right-wingers, no one in a multipolar world buys political/economic/military American exceptionalism anymore. It remains to be seen whether in his new term President Obama will conclude that American exceptionalism—as a political doctrine applied to Eurasia—is all dressed up with nowhere to go.

Notes

1. http://nucleargamble.org/wordpress/wp-content/uploads/2012/09/Impact-of-Strikes.pdf.
2. http://online.wsj.com/article/SB10001424052970204224604577027921373481512.html?mod=googlenews_wsj.
3. http://www.informationclearinghouse.info/article32830.htm.
4. http://www.nytimes.com/2012/10/21/world/iran-said-ready-to-talk-to-us-about-nuclear-program.html?hp&_r=2&.
5. http://www.wnd.com/2012/10/iran-secret-deal-report-upsets-ayatollah-obama/.
6. http://www.whitehouse.gov/the_press_office/VIDEOTAPED-REMARKS-BY-THE-PRESIDENT-IN-CELEBRATION-OF-NOWRUZ.
7. http://mrzine.monthlyreview.org/2010/leverett061210p.html.
8. http://bipartisanpolicy.org/sites/default/files/us%20policy%20toward%20iranian%20nuclear%20development.pdf.
9. http://www.nytimes.com/2007/12/03/world/middleeast/03cnd-iran.html.
10. http://edition.cnn.com/2012/11/16/opinion/sick-mideast/.
11. http://www.aljazeera.com/news/americas/2009/03/200931135043573744.html.
12. http://www.israelnationalnews.com/News/News.aspx/130439#.UGkXAUIz2rc.
13. http://www.theatlantic.com/magazine/archive/2009/03/netanyahu-to-obama-stop-iran-or-i-will/307390/.
14. http://www.atimes.com/atimes/Middle_East/KD15Ak02.html.
15. http://www.haaretz.com/print-edition/news/obama-warns-netanyahu-don-t-surprise-me-with-iran-strike-1.275993.
16. http://original.antiwar.com/ali-gharib/2010/01/29/obama-losing-control-of-iran-policy/.
17. http://www.nationalreview.com/articles/229059/how-save-obama-presidency-bomb-iran/daniel-pipes.
18. http://www.atimes.com/atimes/Middle_East/LB10Ak01.html.
19. http://www.pbs.org/wgbh/pages/frontline/tehranbureau/2010/05/nuke-deal.html.
20. http://www.huffingtonpost.com/pepe-escobar/iran-sun-tzu-and-the-domi_b_585059.html.

21. http://www.usip.org/files/resources/Engagement_Coercion_and_Irans_Nuclear_Challenge.pdf.
22. http://www.brookings.edu/~/media/research/files/papers/2009/6/iran%20strategy/06_iran_strategy.pdf.
23. http://www.newyorker.com/reporting/2011/06/06/110606fa_fact_hersh?currentPage=all.
24. http://thediplomat.com/2011/08/07/how-iran-defeated-obama/.
25. http://www.salon.com/2011/09/18/gop_iran/.
26. http://www.aljazeera.com/indepth/opinion/2011/10/201110121715573693.html.
27. http://www.juancole.com/2011/10/sanctions-on-iran-will-never-produce-real-change.html.
28. http://www.informationclearinghouse.info/article29641.htm.
29. http://online.wsj.com/article/SB10001424052970204358004577030392418491690.html.
30. http://www.newyorker.com/online/blogs/comment/2011/11/iran-and-the-iaea.html.
31. http://edition.cnn.com/2011/11/22/politics/us-iran-sanctions/index.html.
32. http://www.raceforiran.com/the-iraqization-of-americas-iran-debate-mohammad-javad-larijani-and-the-mainstream-media.
33. http://www.moonofalabama.org/2011/12/here-is-the-drone.html#comments.
34. http://online.wsj.com/article/SB10001424052970204720204577132923798499772.html.
35. http://www.wired.com/dangerroom/2012/01/jsotf-gcc/?utm_source=feedburner&utm_medium=feed&utm_campaign=Feed%3A+WiredDangerRoom+%28Blog+-+Danger+Room%29.
36. http://online.wsj.com/article/SB10001424052970203363504577187420287098692.html?mod=WSJ_hp_LEFTTopStories.
37. http://www.ipsnews.net/2012/02/dempsey-told-israelis-us-wont-join-their-war-on-iran/.
38. http://globalpublicsquare.blogs.cnn.com/2012/02/17/watch-gps-martin-dempsey-on-syria-iran-and-china/.
39. http://www.huffingtonpost.com/trita-parsi/war-with-iran_b_1268534.html.
40. http://www.aljazeera.com/indepth/opinion/2012/02/2012226892751941.html.
41. http://english.khamenei.ir/index.php?option=com_content&task=view&id=1595&Itemid=4.
42. http://www.wired.com/dangerroom/2012/03/navy-persian-gulf/.
43. http://www.nytimes.com/2012/03/20/world/middleeast/united-states-war-game-sees-dire-results-of-an-israeli-attack-on-iran.html?_r=1.
44. http://www.wilsoncenter.org/sites/default/files/IranReport_091112_FINAL.pdf.
45. http://news.antiwar.com/2012/05/17/house-bill-shifting-red-line-for-war-on-iran-passes-overwhelmingly/.
46. http://thehill.com/blogs/defcon-hill/policy-and-strategy/229693-pentagon-has-military-plans-ready-to-prevent-nuclear-iran-says-panetta-.
47. http://www.atimes.com/atimes/China/NF30Ad01.html.
48. http://www.foreign.senate.gov/imo/media/doc/74603.pdf.
49. http://www.defense.gov/news/Defense_Strategic_Guidance.pdf.
50. http://www.atimes.com/atimes/Middle_East/NH22Ak06.html.
51. http://in.reuters.com/article/2012/08/31/israel-iran-pressure-idINL6E8JV1U620120831.
52. http://www.juancole.com/2012/09/top-myths-about-irans-nuclear-enrichment-program.html.
53. http://www.raceforiran.com/by-delisting-the-mek-the-obama-administration-is-taking-the-moral-and-strategic-bankruptcy-of-america's-iran-policy-to-a-new-low.
54. http://www.lobelog.com/understanding-the-rials-freefall/.
55. http://www.usfederalbudget.us/defense_budget_2012_3.html.
56. http://iranprimer.usip.org/resource/conventional-military.
57. http://www.tomdispatch.com/post/175050/pepe_escobar_welcome_to_pipelineistan.
58. http://goldswitzerland.com/the-petrodollar-is-either-dead-or-dying/.
59. http://www.tomdispatch.com/post/175490/tomgram%3A_pepe_escobar%2C_sinking_the_petrodollar_in_the_persian_gulf/#more.
60. http://www.thenation.com/article/155334/chinas-pipelineistan-war.
61. http://www.foreign.senate.gov/publications/.
62. http://qz.com/6140/the-new-silk-road-is-made-of-iron-and-stretches-from-scotland-to-singapore/.
63. http://original.antiwar.com/jack-a-smith/2012/10/05/obama-and-romney-are-the-same-on-imperial-grand-strategy/.
64. http://www.defense.gov/news/newsarticle.aspx?id=45289.
65. http://www.realclearenergy.org/charticles/2012/11/19/iea_projection_of_self-sufficiency_106777.html.
66. http://www.globalresearch.ca/no-wonder-china-is-nervous-as-obama-pivots/5312523.
67. http://www.atimes.com/atimes/Middle_East/NK22Ak02.html.
68. http://www.military.com/daily-news/2012/11/28/pentagon-still-sees-iran-as-threat-no-1.html?comp=7000023317828&rank=1.
69. http://www.aljazeera.com/indepth/opinion/2012/09/20129138245360573.html.

15

GREAT DISAPPOINTMENTS IN THE ARAB WORLD DURING OBAMA'S FIRST TERM

Mohammad Masad

Introduction

In the beginning of 2009 the new American president, Barack Obama, started his first term after decisively winning the elections two months earlier in what amounted to a rare popular mandate and a global wave of support and optimism about a new American approach to world problems. The embrace was almost universal and the support for Obama ignited the kind of optimism and adoration usually reserved for exceptional leaders. The president's messages of "hope" and "change" were not lost to people across the globe; and the Arab world was no exception. People in the Arab world, where American presidents traditionally garnered little sympathy or were systematically demonized and seen as mortal enemies, seemed to have a new positive perspective regarding this American president. The warm welcome for Obama's presidential victory among many Arabs, especially constituencies of western-minded liberals and Arab youth with whom the message and personality of the new president resonated the most, was palpable, and enthusiastic expressions of relief and optimism swept the print, electronic and social media. Some relative indifference to the US 2008 elections was observed among certain people, especially Palestinians, mostly the result of the chronic lack of confidence in a real change of American policy; yet even this lack of interest failed to eclipse the general sense of hopeful anticipation and cautious optimism the election of Obama provoked in the region as a whole.[1]

The "promise of Obama" of a different direction was sealed in several public overtures, but most importantly in the key speech, "A New Beginning," delivered at Cairo University in June 2009. In it, Obama extended a hand of friendship and cooperation to the Muslim and Arab worlds, stressing America's intention to help foster ties with Muslims and Arabs based on mutual understanding and a global partnership.[2] Regarding the Palestine–Israel conflict, Obama seemed to suggest a new direction, emphasizing the legitimate rights of the Palestinian people, including their right to an independent state of their own, and acknowledging their long suffering under Israeli military occupation. This position was already expressed two months earlier in a speech before the Turkish Parliament where Obama stressed the need for Palestinian statehood as agreed between the parties in the Roadmap for Peace (proposed by the Quartet for the Middle East in June 2002) and at the Annapolis Conference of November 2007, as well as the importance of a Palestinian state as a foreign policy goal that he will actively pursue as president.[3]

The speeches, combined with the personality and African-American origins of the president, caused a positive surge in the US global image, with some of the highest ratings recorded in the summer of 2009 for more than ten years, or since the time before Bush's first term in office. This included noticeably improved attitudes towards the United States in Arab and Islamic countries. A survey by the Pew Research Center's Global Attitudes Project conducted in May–June 2009 found that the main reason for that improvement was the global confidence in Obama's foreign policy approach.[4] For example, compared with surveys on George Bush in 2008, more Egyptians, Jordanians, Lebanese, and Palestinians favored Obama with large margins as a president who "will do the right thing in world affairs."[5] Though the change in image was modest compared to other countries in Europe and non-Muslim nations, it still marked a significant shift in the perception by the Arab peoples of the United States. But it was still a fragile shift, heavily conditioned on Obama's ability to carry out his program of change and contingent on his fulfillment of his promises.

Four years later, it is fair to say that Obama did not meet those expectations of global leadership and that much of the credit he earned at the beginning of his presidency was squandered. Despite his relative progress on the pressing issues of US military involvement in Iraq and Afghanistan, where he tried to minimize the presence of American troops without abandoning the two countries to anarchy, Obama did little, in terms of active engagement, to meet the lofty goal of harnessing a closer relationship with the Arab and Muslim worlds. While the departure from the Bush foreign policy doctrine in certain areas seemed obvious, it was less so in other cases involving America's role in the Middle East, especially the handling of the Arab Spring that erupted in early 2011 and the approach to the Palestine question. From the list of the administration's priorities articulated in the Cairo Speech, only winding down the wars in Iraq and Afghanistan and opposing Iran's nuclear program became truly actively pursued major goals.[6] As for the remaining items, including encouraging democratic change and promoting human rights in the Arab world, as well as ending the Palestinian–Israeli conflict, Obama did not fare so well.

The policy of hesitantly and selectively supporting the uprisings of the Arab Spring might have earned Obama some credit in some quarters, but did little to visibly strengthen America's standing in the Arab World. Similarly, the scarce and unsuccessful effort of the president to find an Israeli–Palestinian peace agreement or even restart and put the negotiations between the two sides on a serious footing was equally damaging and counterproductive. This setback was made worse because of the perception that Obama has gone to extremes in supporting Israel, despite the failure by Netanyahu and his government to entertain any progress towards peace or meet any of the basic demands put forth by the United States in this context, particularly on the subject of building colonies in the West Bank and East Jerusalem. Politically, the US administration was being increasingly sidelined and marginalized, sometimes by choice, and sometimes under the effects of changes on the ground. There are perhaps three factors or theaters of operation that can together explain this dramatic change of image, from the popular Obama who committed himself to oppose the Bush interventionist and aggressive foreign policy agendas, to the much less likeable Obama with his rather extra careful and somewhat conventional exercise of American power and influence abroad: the outreach to the Muslim world, the approach to the Arab Spring, and the position on the Israeli–Palestinian conflict.

On Reaching out to the Muslim World

Much of Obama's popularity around the Muslim world was the result of his bold overtures to Muslims as partners and to Islam as a great religion. This included a commitment to end the wars in Iraq and Afghanistan, closing down the Guantanamo detention center, and treating Muslims with the dignity they deserve as members of a major faith with more than a billion followers. The contrast between this attitude and that of the hawkish policies of George W. Bush made Obama all the more endearing as a leader. From early on, Obama sought to change the rhetoric used by the previous administration, especially the connection between Islam and the "war on terror," and create a new language, one tempered with reconciliation and respect. During his visit to the first large Muslim country, Turkey, he used the occasion to communicate that message. "Setting out his perspective on America's relationship with the Islamic world, Mr. Obama told the Turkish Parliament that: 'America's relationship with the Muslim community, the Muslim world, cannot and will not just be based upon opposition to terrorism,' he said. 'We seek broader engagement based upon mutual interest and mutual respect.'"[7] The punch line of his wide-ranging speech was written carefully for maximum effect: "The United States has been enriched by Muslim-Americans," he said. "Many other Americans have Muslims in their family, or have lived in a Muslim-majority country. I know," he said, "because I am one of them."[8] The thunderous applause that followed was repeated many times over during that speech and, later, in front of thrilled audiences in other Muslim countries.

The choice of Turkey to begin his tour was most likely no accident. Turkey is a Muslim-majority country but one that is also strongly secular. From this perspective, "Mr. Obama also seemed to be pushing for more acceptance of the separation of religion and the state."[9] The move was further affirmed through Obama's visit to the mausoleum of the founder of the modern secular Turkish state, Mustafa Kemal Ataturk, and by referring during his speech to the "vibrant secular democracy" that is modern Turkey as Ataturk's greatest legacy. Other positive comments regarding Turkey, included the country's role in the G-20 group, its membership in NATO, its candidacy for the European Union and even the friendly gesture of one of the Ottoman Sultans of sending a marble plaque as a tribute to the building of the Washington Monument. The challenges facing Turkey and the United States as democracies were described as similar, namely economic crisis and extremism. As a result, Obama declared:

> This much is certain: no one nation can confront these challenges alone, and all nations have a stake in overcoming them. That is why we must listen to one another, and seek common ground. That is why we must build on our mutual interests, and rise above our differences. We are stronger when we act together. That is the message that I have carried with me throughout this trip to Europe. That will be the approach of the United States of America going forward.[10]

Obama's visit to Egypt presented him with yet another opportunity to reach out to Muslims and Arabs, capitalizing on his success in Turkey; and he did that brilliantly. From the opening paragraph of his speech, Obama sounded a conciliatory and positive tone, recognizing the historic role of Egypt and its Islamic institutions in the story of human progress, and even greeting the audience in Arabic:

> I am honored to be in the timeless city of Cairo, and to be hosted by two remarkable institutions. For over a thousand years, Al-Azhar has stood as a beacon of Islamic learning, and for over a century, Cairo University has been a source of Egypt's advancement. Together, you represent the harmony between tradition and progress. I am grateful for your hospitality, and the hospitality of the people of Egypt. I am also proud to carry with me the goodwill of the American people, and a greeting of peace from Muslim communities in my country: assalaamu alaykum.[11]

Egyptians have not experienced such eloquence and charisma since the days of Nasser, notwithstanding the many differences that separate the two leaders.

Once again Obama painted a picture of a radical new approach to American policy towards Islam and Muslims. One of the lengthiest parts of the speech focused on the contribution of Islam to world civilization and the debt of humanity to Islamic learning, art, and culture, including the noble values of tolerance and coexistence. The president stressed the fact that Islam is part of the American narrative, including his own personal story, and pledged to fight against the crude stereotyping of Islam and to strengthen the notion of the common humanity between the Muslim world and the United States. He went on to say that, "[My] experience guides my conviction that partnership between America and Islam must be based on what Islam is, not what it isn't. And I consider it part of my responsibility as President of the United States to fight against negative stereotypes of Islam wherever they appear."[12] At the heart of Obama's outreach to the Islamic world was his promise to end the war in Iraq and find a solution to the Israeli–Palestinian conflict based on a two-state solution. This was two years before the Arab Spring, and therefore these issues became the two obvious barometers of the president's new approach in this area.

Obama's brave words, however, were never translated into concerted effort and concrete action, and the promised partnership failed to materialize, while the old partnerships, especially the strong relationship with Israel, continued unabated. Within two years of taking office, Obama's image among Muslims suffered a massive reversal. In the Arab world, a survey of public opinion in the summer of 2010 found out that Arabs were losing patience and hope in the Obama administration and that, "for the first time a majority of the public across the region—including a sizable minority in Saudi Arabia—believes a nuclear-armed Iran would be a positive development in the Middle East.... The poll [found] that Arabs have traded in last year's 'wait-and-see' attitude towards the new American president in favor of something much more negative, and the support for Iran is, in many ways, being seen as one part of that anger."[13]

According to one analysis of the survey, "The results of Arab Public Opinion were a devastating indictment of U.S. policies in the Middle East and showed strong disapproval of President Obama."[14] Negative views of Obama jumped from 23% in 2009 to 62%; positive views plummeted from 45% to 20%; and neutral views of the president dropped from 28% to 16%. As to people's attitudes to Obama's policies in the region, only 16% of respondents said they were "hopeful" (a drop from the 51% in 2009); 20% said they were "neutral" (28% in 2009); and 63% declared they were "discouraged" (15% in 2009). The president's handling of the Palestine–Israel conflict ranked as the most disappointing of all, with a 61% disapproval rate. In contrast, those who said they were satisfied with Obama's policy on Palestine–Israel were a mere 1%. The favorability ranking of the United States dropped from 18% to 12%, while the percentage of those who had an unfavorable opinion of the United States increased from 77% in 2009 to 85% in 2010.[15] Asked to identify the two most important factors (out of a list of nine) that they thought motivated American Middle East policy, 49% picked "protecting Israel," 44% picked "controlling oil," 33% picked "weakening the Muslim world," and another 33% picked "preserving regional and global dominance." Only 7% picked "fighting terrorism" as a driver of US policy in the Middle East. Interestingly, in a harsh objection to the perceived US regional role, 57% said they believe the Middle East will be better off if Iran acquires nuclear weapons.[16]

The poll, conducted by Shibley Telhami from the University of Maryland on behalf of Zogby International, depicted a bitter backlash in Arabs public opinion against the United States, classifying the United States next to Israel as the Arab world's worst enemies, much more so than Iran. The worsening US image ended a brief period where the United States was judged positively by a small majority of Arabs in a poll the year before, a shift described by Telhami as nothing short of "amazing" given longstanding negative Arab views of the United States. "In 2009, 51 percent of the public was 'optimistic' about the US. This year, nearly two-thirds say they are 'discouraged' about America's actions in the region."[17] The reasons for the shift as given by Telhami centered on the Arab public perception of disappointment over the lack of progress on the Israeli–Palestinian conflict, and on the US Iraq policy. According to the poll, 77% named the United States (second only to Israel) as posing the biggest threat to their country while Iran was named by 10% only.[18]

During the four years of his first term, Obama and senior members of his administration visited six Muslim countries but did little to live up to the hyped anticipation of reaching out to Muslims and Arabs. In addition to Turkey and Egypt, where Obama delivered his two outreach speeches, other Muslim countries on his itinerary included Iraq (April 2009), Afghanistan (December 2010 and May 2012), Saudi Arabia (June 2009), and Indonesia (November 2010 and November 2011). With very few exceptions, most of these visits were short excursions, either to meet with US troops (Afghanistan), briefly discuss mutual relations (Saudi Arabia), sign strategic agreements (Afghanistan), or attend an international forum (ASEAN in Jakarta in 2012). The only exception was the president's first trip to Indonesia where he visited the Istiqlal Mosque and delivered a passionate reaching out speech at the University of Indonesia. The address was received warmly, especially as the president reminisced at length about his four years of childhood spent in Jakarta in the 1960s and emphasized the shared humanity, welcoming tolerance, and the experience of unity in diversity that America and Indonesia have in common. The president reiterated his intention to have a new beginning with the Muslim world. Recalling his Cairo speech, Obama once again pointed out the challenge facing him: "We also know that relations between the United States and Muslim communities have frayed over many years. As President, I have made it a priority to begin to repair these relations.... As part of that effort, I went to Cairo last June, and I called for a new beginning between the United States and Muslims around the world—one that creates a path for us to move beyond our differences."[19]

The speech seemed to be designed to improve Obama's image and help lift his sagging reputation among Muslims as a man of broken promises. Marc Lynch talks in one article of a "well-crafted speech" that had the effect of being "a reminder of some of the early promise of [Obama's] outreach to the Muslim communities of the world." Lynch tries to defend the president's record, lamenting the lack of praise for his initiatives and listing a litany of complaints his critics, including Lynch himself, normally hold against him, including "failure to deliver on the Israeli–Palestinian peace or on Gaza, little visible follow-through in the months after the speech, the inability to close Guantanamo, escalating drone strikes, the impact of rampaging anti-Islam trends in U.S. domestic politics, and so on."[20] Lynch offers a balancing perspective, praising the president for "he has quietly made some real progress in many lower profile areas upon which the media doesn't focus," and saying that if this strategy to which the president has committed works in terms of creating durable networks of connections and mutual interests with new generations of Muslims around the world, "then we may wake up a decade from now extremely grateful for efforts which didn't seem noteworthy today."[21] For many Muslims, however, this defense of Obama, based on possible future achievements, would be hard to digest. For them, Obama was to be judged on his current policies and, as he himself asked people to do, on his actions.

Obama's outreach and engagement strategy generated much controversy and, depending on the ideological platform, became different things for different people. As Charles Kupchan points out, over a year into Obama's presidency, the debate on the merits and risks of his approach continued to rage among policymakers and scholars. For example, the possible reciprocity by the other side, whether any concessions from adversaries were the result of rapprochement or blunt force, and whether reconciliation with autocracies was possible without democratization were some of the questions debated. While many commentators seemed to either praise the president for his outreach or give him the benefit of the doubt, there were those on the other extreme who strongly disagreed with Obama's efforts in this regard and even saw it as a sign of weakness.

> Many of Obama's critics have already made up their minds on the merits of his outreach to adversaries, concluding not only that the president has little to show for his efforts but also that his pliant diplomacy demeans the United States and weakens its hand. Following Obama's September 2009 speech to the United Nations General Assembly, in which he called for "a new era of engagement based on mutual interest and mutual respect" and "new coalitions that bridge old divides," the conservative commentator Michelle Malkin charged that the president had "solidified his place in the international view as the great appeaser and the groveler in chief.[22]

In fact, despite this conservative indignation with Obama's outreach policy, perhaps the most visible form of "reaching out" of the president has been a continuation of one of the Bush administration's most controversial policies, namely the drone strikes against Muslim hardliners in Pakistan, Afghanistan, Yemen, and Somalia. In addition to a large number of militants and terrorists, the attacks also led to the killing of many innocent civilians and hardened feelings against the United States among many Muslims. According to Michael Boyle, a former Obama security advisor, the Obama approach to counter-terrorism was only different from Bush's policy in tone, but was more widespread and ruthless. Boyle says that "the US administration's growing reliance on drone technology was having 'adverse strategic effects that have not been properly weighed against the tactical gains associated with killing terrorists.'"[23] The unmanned aerial vehicles or drones program, which is run by the Pentagon and the CIA, and mostly not subject to Congress or the courts, is one of the most distinctive elements of Obama's foreign policy in the Middle East, with more than six times as many drone attacks launched during Obama's first term compared to those conducted during President Bush's eight years in office.[24] While the declaration of the president's plan to reduce American troops in Iraq and Afghanistan by the end of his first term (as announced in December 2009 and in a speech to the United Nations in September 2010) drew much support and praise globally, the drone attacks policy was and still is very problematic and seems to erode any credit Obama receives from the polices of rapprochement or military withdrawals. In terms of numbers of casualties, the Bureau of Investigative Journalism (TBIJ) has collected data showing that there were 346 drone strikes in Pakistan between June 2004 and October 2012 that resulted in a death toll of 2,570–3,337 people.[25]

The TBIJ estimates that civilian casualties account for 18%–26% in Pakistan, 16% in Yemen and between 7%–33.5% in Somalia.[26] Other unintended consequences for the drone warfare included the weakening of the governments of those countries, mostly friends of the United States, where drone strikes have been taking place. "The vast expansion of drone warfare under the Obama administration has placed enormous pressure on Pakistan for its complicity with the US, multiplied the enemies that its government faces and undermined parts of the social fabric of the country. By most measures, Pakistan is more divided and unstable after the Obama administration's decision to ramp up the tempo and scale of drone attacks than it was during the Bush administration."[27] Reactions by Pakistanis to drone attacks have been hostile and both Obama and his Pakistani clients suffered from a negative image. According to a Pew Research Center poll from June 2012, some 74% of Pakistanis classified the United States as an enemy, and only 17% were in favor of drone strikes against extremist groups in their country.[28]

Boyle notes the irony of how the drone strikes policy reinforces the dangerous stereotype of the "image of the United States—as an all-seeing, irreconcilably hostile enemy who rains down bombs and death on innocent Muslims without a second thought. . . . Even the casual anti-Americanism common in many parts of Europe, the Middle East and Asia, much of which portrays the US as cruel, domineering and indifferent to the suffering of others, is reinforced by a drones policy which involves killing foreign citizens on an almost daily basis."[29] The remote-control war against what the United States designates as "high value targets" has been the subject of controversy for years. The assassination style attacks and the frequent "collateral damage" of civilian deaths have prompted much questioning of the drone warfare and caused a certain amount of moral quandary for Obama and his advisors. One of the earliest incidents to expose the inherent dangers of drones was a mistaken attack on a funeral procession in South Waziristan on June 23, 2009, which killed eighty noncombatants. Investigating such tragic incidents and proposing ideas aiming to review the use of drones, new guidelines, or even the bizarre idea of fitting them with new software resembling a human "conscience," whether adopted or not, have not made the use of drones any less controversial.[30]

If Obama wants to stay true to the strategy of reaching out and change he espoused during his first term, then, as one analyst says, he needs to be more serious about the "new beginning" he promised in his Cairo Speech. In other words, "As he begins a second term it is clear that this new beginning needs to be reinvigorated in both style and substance. That initial speech, while poignant then, today rings hollow. If indeed President Obama and the administration are to achieve a definitive step change in relations with Muslim communities, there must be a renewed effort for honest dialogue, robust development initiatives, and tangible shifts in policy."[31]

Response to the "Arab Spring"

For many years before Obama came to office, the view of the United States and its leadership had been expressly negative. This was the case even in the country that is the largest recipient of US foreign aid after Israel, i.e., Egypt. At its most intense, this negative perception stemmed from American policies in the Middle East, including policies towards ruling regimes, the Arab–Israeli conflict and the "war on terror." Two years into Obama's first term, a report by the Princeton Anti-Americanism Group indicated a worsening situation as far as America's image is concerned; the report warned that, "The United States is often seen as hypocritical for its support of President Mubarak's oppressive regime and its limited criticisms of violations of human rights and democratic practice in Egypt. This contributes to popular anti-Americanism in Egypt, which is much more problematic today due to the diminishing health of President Mubarak, who has led a highly authoritarian regime in Egypt since 1981."[32] Quoting findings of research done by the Pew Global Attitudes Project, the disapproval rating of the United States in Egypt in 2010 reached 82%, up by 12% compared with 2009. Similarly, confidence in President Obama was quite low, a mere 31%.[33]

The policies and decisions of the Obama administration towards the Arab uprisings, known as the Arab Spring, fluctuated from confusion, to reluctance, to strong words, to bold actions in responding to the tumultuous changes the region has been going through since late 2010 when the first spark was let in Tunisia. For example, Ryan Lizza describes Obama's decisions regarding Libya and Egypt as bolder and more risky; "He [Obama] broke with Mubarak at a point when some of the older establishment advised against it. In Libya, he overruled Gates and his military advisers and pushed our allies to adopt a broad and risky intervention. It is too early to know the consequences of these decisions."[34] Though it has been more than a year since Lizza's article was published, the consequences are yet to fully materialize and be accounted for. But the first signs are not encouraging.

The rise of Islamic forces in Tunisia and Egypt, the chaotic divisions and the threat of civil war in Libya, and the violent attack against the United States consulate in Benghazi, leading to the loss of American lives, including that of the United States ambassador to Libya, Christopher Stevens, were some of the most unpleasant surprises for Obama and his advisors. And so, as the *New York Times* puts it, "Nineteen months later, Mr. Obama was at the State Department consoling some of the very officials he had overruled. As he talked to them, he tried to make sense of these events, stressing the importance of the risky work done by American diplomats abroad, as well as the need to continue 'the outreach to the Arab world, . . . even in the face of mob violence that called into question what the United States can accomplish in a turbulent region.'"[35]

The Arab Spring events came on the heels of the Iranian 2009–2010 Green Revolution, where the US administration's position was seen as less than rigorous and mostly disappointing. Obama's reactions to the events of the Arab uprisings seemed from the beginning to reflect this very cautious position that tries to balance the basic principles of supporting freedom and democracy with the impetus to maintain stability of regimes and a status quo, for years seen as part of the American strategy in the region. Afraid to upset this delicate balance, the president's reactions to the Arab uprisings, especially in the beginning, seemed often late, unsure, and inconsistent. The shift in positions went from extreme to extreme, from mild encouragement for reform, to cautious criticisms of the regimes, to calls for orderly transition, to accommodation of complete political change, to full embrace of revolutions and their demands, to public calls for the regimes' heads to quit without delay. There is no better proof for this fluctuating policy than Ryan Lizza's fascinating account of the administration's almost daily change of policy on the Egyptian uprising.[36] US administrations, with Obama's being no exception, have worked from the assumption that the stability and continuity of major Middle Eastern regimes considered US allies was a vital American interest. The nature of these regimes, none of which was democratic, and all of which had a poor rights record, was recognized as a problem, but never as one that justifies sacrificing the strategic imperative of preserving them. This meant among other things, avoiding any harsh criticism of these regimes or their autocratic rulers. According to Lizza, an Obama memorandum, "Political Reform in the Middle East and North Africa," prepared in August 2010, recognizes the potential for major trouble, referring to the regimes campaign of repression against freedom activists and the "evidence of growing citizens discontent," and the possibility of even greater repression rather than reform by US allies in the face of domestic dissent.[37] Yet, even in this memorandum, Obama's choice to balance interests and ideals meant that "the goals of reform and democracy were couched in the language of U.S. interests rather than the sharp moral language that statesmen often use in public."[38] Repression was bad mainly because it would undermine the regimes and their ability to be credible US allies looking after American regional interests, rather than because of clear moral reasons or objections rising from idealistic principles.

It is interesting in this regard to notice that in the "Guiding Principles" of American foreign policy, as posted on the official Obama whitehouse.gov site, there is no clear mention of the promotion of freedom and democracy or any other specific principles for which the US stands for, except for the vague reference to "America's values." According to the site:

> President Obama has pursued national security policies that keep the American people safe, while turning the page on a decade of war and restoring American leadership abroad. Since President Obama took office, the United States has devastated al Qaeda's leadership. Now, thanks to our extraordinary servicemen and women, we have reached a pivotal moment—we definitively ended the war in Iraq and have begun to wind down the war in Afghanistan. Meanwhile, we have refocused on a broader set of priorities around the globe that will allow the United States to be safe, strong, and prosperous in the 21st century. To advance America's national security, the President is committed to using all elements of American power, including the strength of America's values.[39]

Soon after Obama finally took the decision to abandon Mubarak and fully support the Egyptian revolution, he found himself in the middle of another crisis, this time in Libya. Qaddafi was more of a pacified enemy than an ally, and so Obama was not keen on accommodating his ruthless regime. But unlike Tunisia and Egypt where change was accomplished peacefully, the revolution here quickly turned into an armed insurrection. After one full month of quietly debating the various options facing the United States and its allies in Libya, while the French seemed to be leading the way for imposing a United Nations no-fly zone over the country, the United States pushed for a United Nations Security Council resolution authorizing military intervention. The resolution, supported by the Arab League, passed without objections and for the first time in the history of the UN authorized military action to preempt an "imminent massacre."[40] Obama's position here won him much-needed admiration and support from the Libyan people and supporters of their revolution. However, the very nature of the intervention and the NATO and US bombing runs over Libya for the next few months, culminating in the opposition routing of the regime and the killing of Qaddafi, weakened that support and raised questions about the intention behind it. Many people were not sold on the "humanitarian" reasons and were convinced that the intervention was motivated by the desire of Western countries to control the country's vast oil reserves, win rebuilding contracts and strengthen their presence in the region. Some researchers, such as Michael Chossudovsky, emphasized that the intervention in Libya was yet another NATO–US military oil war; "An invasion of Libya under a humanitarian mandate would serve the same corporate interests as the 2003 invasion and occupation of Iraq. The underlying objective is to take possession of Libya's oil reserves, destabilize the National Oil Corporation (NOC) and eventually privatize the country's oil industry, namely transfer the control and ownership of Libya's oil wealth into foreign hands."[41] The public squabbles in the aftermath of the intervention on who should benefit from oil and rebuilding contracts, with France, Britain and Italy leading the way, only seemed to confirm this suspicion.[42]

As the Arab Spring spread to new countries, other more troubling questions were being asked about Obama's commitment to supporting the protestors against authoritarian regimes in the region. The president was facing a dilemma as he tried to maneuver between the seemingly two irreconcilable goals of democracy and stability.

> In fact, Mr. Obama's staunch defense of democracy protesters in Egypt . . . drew him into an upheaval that would test his judgment, his nerve and his diplomatic skill. Even as the uprisings spread to Libya, Yemen, Bahrain and Syria, the president's sympathy for the protesters infuriated America's allies in the conservative and oil-rich Gulf states. In mid-March, the Saudis moved decisively to crush the democracy protests in Bahrain, sending a convoy of tanks and heavy artillery across the 16-mile King Fahd Causeway between the two countries.[43]

Obama's reaction to the Bahrain crackdown was to turn a blind eye. Here, clearly the stakes were high and the United States seemed to prefer to be more neutral. "[Obama's] realism and reluctance to be drawn into foreign quagmires has held sway ever since, notably in Syria, where many critics continue to call for a more aggressive American response to the brutality of Bashar al-Assad's rule."[44] The violence and uncertainty of the Syrian crisis was casting a long shadow over the chaotic transitions in the more promising of the Arab Spring countries, Tunisia, Egypt, and Yemen, and the ominous rise of Islamic forces as the clearest winners. These trends seem to have pushed Obama towards an even more cautious policy. In addition to the fact that such differences in policy reflected the differing circumstances in the Arab Spring countries themselves, the *New York Times* described that also as a symptom of two or three more realities about Obama himself; first, "the gap between the two poles of his political persona: his sense of himself as a historic bridge-builder who could redeem America's image abroad, and his more cautious adherence to long-term American interests in security and cheap oil . . . [and, second,] his impatience with old-fashioned back-room diplomacy, and his corresponding failure to build close personal relationships with foreign leaders that can, especially in the Middle East, help the White House to influence decisions made abroad."[45]

With the Arab Spring in full motion and other countries facing turmoil, including Yemen, Bahrain, Jordan, and Syria, Obama realized the need for a clarification of the American approach to these events. The opportunity was seen as a follow-up to the Cairo "New Beginning" Speech. The address was delivered by President Obama on May 19, 2011, at the US State Department. The speech was dubbed by John Esposito, professor of religion, international affairs and Islamic studies at Georgetown University, as "a good start in improving U.S.–Muslim World relations, but 'as post Cairo so today, many will now be expecting bold and decisive policies and actions that turn the administration's rhetoric into reality.'"[46]

Another perspective clearly favored American idealism over realpolitik; it criticized past US foreign policy for having been too tepid and closely linked to undemocratic Middle Eastern regimes and invited Obama to take advantage of the changing circumstances to put his full weight behind the Arab uprisings and the change it is bringing, even if sometimes it looks problematic.

> For decades, the United States undermined Arab democracy through its consistent support of Arab autocrats. But the Arab uprisings have changed that basic calculus and upended our Faustian bargains with the region's despots (well, at least with some of them). In countries like Egypt, Tunisia, and of course Libya, interests and values are not fully aligned—they never will be—but they are as closely aligned as one can hope. And that is not an opportunity that should be squandered. In all three countries, the United States is finally playing a positive, even crucial, role in supporting the economic recovery of democratically elected governments that, while deeply flawed, enjoy popular legitimacy.[47]

The writer recognizes the problem that the United States faces in improving its image, even after doing the right thing. It describes Arab attitudes towards the US as generally inflexible, regardless of what it does. US favorability ratings during the Obama years and even after withdrawing from Iraq and supporting the Libyan revolution militarily have actually been lower than they were in the final years of the Bush administration. However giving up on the Arab Spring or disengaging from the Arab world would be a "grave mistake," because that is exactly what the Salafist extremists and dictators want. "The more the United States disengages, the more room they [extremists and tyrants] will have to grow in influence and power."[48] The Obama administration has an obligation and a strategic interest to support nascent Arab democracies and nurture social and political change in the region. In doing this, Obama should not be swayed by critics at home or enemies abroad. Taking an active role in supporting the Arab Spring "has the added virtue of being not only good policy for the Arab world, but good politics back home."[49]

As Obama takes office for his second term, his administration seems no clearer about its response to the continuing Arab Spring events. Stories of divisions between Obama and his previous team about the best approach to the escalating civil war in Syria are one sign of the difficulty of finding consensus on a major foreign policy crisis and the cautious approach characterizing Obama's strategy, especially in the aftermath of the Libyan debacle. According to several sources, "Pentagon leaders have said they supported a recommendation from the US State Department and CIA to arm Syrian rebels, but Barack Obama ultimately decided against it. The Obama administration has limited its support to non-lethal aid for the rebels who, despite receiving weapons from countries such as Qatar and Saudi Arabia, are poorly armed compared with the army and loyalist militias of the Syrian president, Bashar al-Assad."[50]

While Obama has repeatedly reaffirmed his position about the need for Assad to leave power to allow for change and reform in Syria, he has so far objected to offering military aid to antigovernment forces. At the heart of this calculus is the fear that the weapons might fall into the "wrong hands," especially with the knowledge that some of the strongest fighting rebel factions on the ground are extremist groups affiliated with the Al-Qaeda; one of them at least, the Jabhat al-Nusra, has been designated by the United States as a "terrorist organization."

Similarly, American virtual silence on protests in Bahrain and Qatif in eastern Saudi Arabia by mostly Shi'a citizens against the Sunni monarchies there has been conspicuous. In one *New York Times* article, Obama's reluctance in this case is analyzed in terms of American strategic interests in the Gulf region, along with the two opposing assessments of his policy in this situation:

> The reasons for Mr. Obama's reticence were clear: Bahrain sits just off the Saudi coast, and the Saudis were never going to allow a sudden flowering of democracy next door, especially in light of the island's sectarian makeup. Bahrain's people are mostly Shiite, and they have long been seen as a cat's paw for Iranian influence by the Sunni rulers of Saudi Arabia and Bahrain. In addition, the United States maintains a naval base in Bahrain that is seen as a bulwark against Iran, crucial for maintaining the flow of oil from the region.... Some analysts credit Mr. Obama for recognizing early on that strategic priorities trumped whatever sympathy he had for the protesters. Others say the administration could have more effectively mediated between the Bahraini government and the largely Shiite protesters, and thereby avoided what has become a sectarian standoff in one of the world's most volatile places.[51]

The same worldview might explain Obama's position on the protests in Yemen, where the White House declared its support for peaceful transition to democracy, but remained mild in its call for President Ali Abdullah Saleh to quit and embraced the mediation efforts of the Gulf States that eventually resulted in a managed and limited change and not a revolutionary one. These different calculations, though justified and praised by many as realistic and pragmatic, were criticized and condemned by many activists and observers as showing what they call the double standard of the United States and other Western powers in dealing with different Arab Spring protests. Two writers in the *Guardian* for example described the approach to Bahrain as, "hypocrisy for the history book; ... Instead of condemning the Bahraini government's oppression of its citizens and backing the protesters' legitimate demand for a constitutional monarchy, the EU and the US have confined themselves to vacuous statements without taking any action proportionate to the gravity of the political crisis in Bahrain."[52] This double standard seems to be a curse that haunts Obama's and US policy in general, not only in relation to the Arab Spring, but also to other critical issues, including the position on the central question of the Israeli–Palestinian conflict.

The Approach to the Palestine Question

In his Cairo Speech, as well as other occasions, Obama has promised that helping the Palestinians and Israelis reach a peace deal would be one of his first priorities in office. The speech contained an unprecedented admission by an American president of the suffering of the Palestinians, past and present:

> [The] Palestinian people—Muslims and Christians—have suffered in pursuit of a homeland. For more than sixty years they have endured the pain of dislocation. Many wait in refugee camps in the West Bank, Gaza, and neighboring lands for a life of peace and security that they have never been able to lead. They endure the daily humiliations—large and small—that come with occupation. So let there be no doubt: the situation for the Palestinian people is intolerable. America will not turn our backs on the legitimate Palestinian aspiration for dignity, opportunity, and a state of their own.[53]

However, by the end of the first term Obama seemed as far removed from supporting Palestinian statehood as he could be. The language of sympathy all but disappeared, and the White House didn't miss a chance to show its unconditional support for Israel, militarily, politically, and diplomatically. The irony of ironies was the administration's vote, along with only seven other nations including Israel, against accepting Palestine as a nonmember state in the United Nations on November 29, 2012. This was the second objection by the Obama administration to Palestinian statehood in as many years. The year before that the United States declared publicly its opposition and readiness to veto the membership request by the Palestinians to the Security Council to join the UN; this was despite the fact that one year earlier Obama declared, and from the same UN forum, his hope to see Palestine joining the international organization as a full member the following year. In a remarkable comment, Obama told his United Nations audience: "This time we should reach for what's best within ourselves. If we do, when we come back here next year, we can have an agreement that will lead to a new member of the United Nations—an independent, sovereign state of Palestine, living in peace with Israel."[54] That never happened; neither the following year, nor the year after, as Obama's first term was approaching its end, was there any tangible progress made towards that goal. In a stunning turnaround, the Obama administration spent much energy in the following two years opposing Palestinian statehood.

Among Palestinians and Arabs, there was a definite sense of frustration and even betrayal. The political editor of the London-based Al-Majalla summed it up this way:

> The Middle East diplomacy was the source of the greatest gap between Obama's promises and his realization of those promises, and represented the greatest frustration to the President. And this is ironic, if we consider that Obama committed to achieving peace in the Middle East as his top priority from day one of taking office; but when he proved unable to fulfill his promises in resolving the Palestine question and closing down Guantanamo, the Arab street felt disappointed, and eventually turned their back on him once he switched his positions towards Israel with the approach of his reelection date.[55]

To be sure, there was not much switching of positions towards Israel at that point; unless one compares the situation with Obama's position in 2009.

Obama started his first term with a strong and principled position on Israeli settlements, asking the Netanyahu government to stop all settlement activity. One of the strongest remarks by an American official to be made on the subject then came from American Secretary of State Hillary Clinton. "Speaking of Obama, [she] said, 'He wants to see a stop to settlements—not some settlements, not outposts, not 'natural growth' exceptions. . . . That is our position. That is what we have communicated very clearly.'"[56] Israel however refused to comply and only observed a limited and conditional freeze on settlement activity the next year, which was never renewed after expiration, prompting the Palestinians to abandon the fruitless negotiations they were conducting with the Israel government. The negotiations themselves proved futile, and the United States did little to find a way out of the impasse. One Arab columnist decried Obama's weakness and the lack of seriousness by all parties: "In this situation, the negotiations have become absurd, or talks for the sake of talks . . . the Obama Administration wants them because it needs an achievement on the eve of the American half-term elections; and the Israeli government needs them to counter the international calls to delegitimize Israel as a result of its continued crimes against the Palestinians; and president Mahmoud Abbas needs them because the option of armed resistance is non-existent, and because he doesn't want to be accused that there was a Palestinian state on the negotiating table but that he missed the chance."[57] Another analyst pointed out the pointlessness of the mission of Obama's Special Envoy to the Middle East, Senator George Mitchell, who, like his bosses, failed to make any progress and eventually quit, causing the administration to start piling pressure on the Palestinian Authority's weak President, despite the culpability of Netanyahu, who was allowed to walk away scot-free.[58] The Obama administration, afraid to exert any real pressures on the Israelis, practically changed its position on the matter and adopted the view that the Palestinians should go back to negotiations regardless of the Israeli continued building of settlements.

From the beginning the American position towards Israel, though phrased firmly once or twice, lacked any clear means of pressure, and occasionally looked quite embarrassingly acquiescent in front of Israeli intransigence. Thus the announcement by Israel of its plans to build 1,600 new housing units in occupied East Jerusalem ahead of a visit by Vice President Joe Biden, though slammed by Obama's aids as "insulting," went practically unpunished. Stunned by the rare criticism, Israeli officials apologized for the timing of the announcement, but never canceled the plan itself. Another casualty of the announcement was the new "proximity talks" Biden was hoping to get restarted during his visit "between Israel and Palestinians, with the US mediating. Almost immediately, the news prompted Palestinian leaders to pull out of the new round of talks."[59]

Equally startling was Obama's lack of response to Netanyahu's repeated insults and aggressive support of his Republican opponents, including challenging the president in the US Congress and siding publicly with Mitt Romney during the presidential elections campaign. An apparent "response" came later in the form of a leaked report by journalist Jeffrey Goldberg just prior to Israeli elections in January 2013. According to the report, Obama was gravely concerned that Netanyahu's positions, including his continued settlement expansion, were pushing Israel into becoming more of a pariah state and discouraging Obama from investing any new efforts in the Middle East peace process.

> On matters related to the Palestinians, the president seems to view the prime minister as a political coward, an essentially unchallenged leader who nevertheless is unwilling to lead or spend political capital to advance the cause of compromise . . . Obama . . . has been consistent in his analysis of Israel's underlying challenge: If it doesn't disentangle itself from the lives of West Bank Palestinians, the world will one day decide it is behaving as an apartheid state. The White House did not deny the words attributed to the president.[60]

The almost personal nature of the attack reflects the bitterness Obama must have felt about the Israeli Prime Minister's transgressions against him and his policy. From the perspective of Arabs and Palestinians however, Obama's public silence on Netanyahu's persistent undermining of peace efforts and incitement against the president himself looked more appalling than Netanyahu's behavior. It is almost incomprehensible to them that the president of the United States has to bite his tongue and swallow insult after insult and let someone like Netanyahu run the show. According to one Arab journalist, by failing to respond to such insults, "[Obama's] Administration risked losing whatever prestige it had left for it in the region and the world."[61]

Obama's approach to the Palestine–Israel conflict can hardly be placed in his emerging new doctrine of leadership and foreign policy, known as "leading from behind," as dubbed by some analysts.[62] On the face of it, the administration's lack of initiatives, such as conferences, meetings, and summits, on this issue might seem to conform to the "leading from behind" or "leading from afar" kind of doctrine. However, the reality is that the US remained visibly and actively very supportive of Israel, often going to extremes to demonstrate that. This policy could be easily seen in the continued US massive aid to Israel militarily and financially and in defending it unreservedly in international forums and organizations. The early and unusual public criticisms of Israel's settlement policy and the demand to halt it as a prelude to resume negotiations between the Israelis and Palestinians were short-lived and seemed to give way to more of the old policies; namely softly criticizing settlement building, without condemnation; insisting on direct negotiations as the only way forward; expressing the US belief in the two-state solution as an ultimate objective; and affirming the strategic and historic ties and friendship between the United States and Israel. In the face of Israeli resistance to American demands to freeze the construction of Jewish colonies and criticisms of Obama by the pro-Israel lobby in the United States as abandoning Israel, it became clear at some point that Obama had retired his plans to engage actively in the Palestine question to sponsor a historic deal between the two parties, something that also eluded previous presidents.

In his *New Yorker* article, Ryan Lizza observes that, "Obama has emphasized bureaucratic efficiency over ideology, and approached foreign policy as if it were case law, deciding his response to every threat or crisis on its own merits. 'When you start applying blanket policies on the complexities of the current world situation, you're going to get yourself into trouble,' he said in a recent interview with NBC News."[63] This could not be more false than in the case of Palestine, where no matter what happens on the ground, the president's position, largely inherited from previous administrations, seems to be written in stone and is hardly subjected to any meaningful review or change. Perhaps on this one issue there is something resembling a doctrine; and not just any doctrine dictated by a careful reading of geopolitical realities and other considerations such as moral principles and values, but a hard doctrine that is essentially inexplicable, inflexible, and unassailable.

The fact that President Obama has gone out of his way to accommodate one of the most hard line and extreme governments in Israel's history speaks volumes. The ultra-pragmatist seems to have won the day over the moderately idealistic president, as Obama sought to pacify any opposition for his reelection from the strong pro-Israel lobby by offering unlimited support to Israel. So much so that during the campaign for the second term there was no question of Obama's commitment to the absolute support of Israel, despite the Republican proclamations to the contrary; and so, in the words of Stephen Walt, "As the Obama campaign repeatedly emphasized, they had been extraordinarily supportive of Israel from Day One: providing increased levels of military aid, expanding various forms of security cooperation (including joint operations against Iran), and providing diplomatic cover in the United Nations and elsewhere. Obama dropped his early insistence on a settlement freeze and eventually gave up on the peace process. The only thing that Netanyahu didn't get from Obama was a war against Iran, and plenty of top Israeli officials didn't think that was a very good idea either."[64]

In contrast, the Obama administration continued to take increasingly hostile positions towards the Palestinians. US representative in the United Nations Susan Rice consistently voted to block any resolutions that criticized Israel or intended to improve Palestinian representation in international forums. This included voting against accepting Palestine as a member of the United Nations cultural agency UNESCO in October 2011. The United States was one of a minority of fourteen nations who opposed the decision.[65] There were more such actions, culminating in the US refusal to consider the Palestinian application for full statehood at the United Nations Security Council and voting against the membership of Palestine in the General Assembly one year later, all of which were particularly damaging to Obama's image among Palestinians, Arabs, and Muslims.

In February 2011, the Obama administration used its veto power at the Security Council to block a resolution condemning Israeli settlement activity in the Occupied Territories as illegal and an obstacle to peace. "The lopsided vote in the Council, where among the 15 members only the United States voted no, as well as the more than 100 co-sponsors of the measure, underscored the isolation of the United States and Israel on the issue."[66] This was one of a series of actions and positions by the administrations that were increasingly pro-Israel and anti-Palestinian, that peaked in Obama's United Nations speech in September, which is perhaps one of the most pro-Israel speeches given by any American president.

The same thing happened in December 2012 as the Security Council stepped up to condemn Israeli plans to intensify settlement building in Jerusalem in the aftermath of the United Nations General Assembly vote in favor of accepting Palestine as a nonmember state on November 29 with a huge majority. The United States was one of the handful of countries that voted against accepting Palestine to the United Nations, and in the Security Council "all but one of the 15 members of the U.N. Security Council made statements at the United Nations opposing Israeli plans to expand Jewish settlements around Jerusalem after the United States repeatedly blocked attempts to take stronger action [against Israel]."[67] Considering all three votes, one could claim that in all these cases the United States voted against its own declared policy. It is not hard to imagine the anger and frustration felt by Palestinians and their supporters and friends at this kind of contradictory, double-faced policy. The February 2011 vote in particular was strongly criticized as absurd by several analysts, including one Middle East expert who was quoted on the Jews for Justice for Palestinians website, under the heading: "US Vetoes its own Policy at the Security Council."

> The U.S. stood alone. Ambassador Susan Rice's statement was astonishingly defensive—she went to great lengths to claim that the U.S. actually agrees with the resolution, that no one has done more than the U.S. to support a two-state solution, that the U.S. thinks settlement activity (not, we should note, the continuing existence of longstanding settlements now home to 500,000 illegal Jewish settlers in the West Bank and occupied East Jerusalem) violates Israel's international commitments and more. She tried to convince the world that "opposition to the resolution should not be misunderstood" to mean the U.S. supports settlement activity—only that the Obama administration "thinks it unwise" for the United Nations to try to stop that settlement activity.[68]

Another observer, Philip C. Wilcox Jr., president of the Foundation for Middle East Peace, chastised the Obama administration for its fruitless efforts over eighteen months to get Israel to stop settlement activity as Israel continued to defy US policy and for being disingenuous about its explanation for vetoing a proposal that wasn't contradictory to its own position. "In casting the U.S. veto of the resolution, the US representative explained that only direct negotiations will bring peace and that the resolution would have risked "hardening attitudes" and further resort to the UN. This is not persuasive. The text of the resolution called on the parties "to continue with . . . their negotiations" and was entirely consistent with this goal, and otherwise reflected U.S. policy."[69]

More criticism of the veto came from the director of Human Rights Watch who pointed out the hypocrisy of the Obama administration and the inconsistency of its messages. "President Obama wants to tell the Arab world in his speeches that he opposes settlements, but he won't let the Security Council tell Israel to stop them in a legally binding way."[70] One commentator, Professor Stephen Zunes, went on to accuse the Obama administration of showing the same disregard for international legality as previous ones: "The US veto of a mildly worded United Nations Security Council resolution supporting the Israeli–Palestinian peace process and reiterating the illegality of Israeli settlements in occupied territories leaves little doubt that, in certain critical respects, President Barack Obama shares his predecessor's contempt for international law."[71]

Before the November 2012 US vote against Palestinian United Nations membership, signs of US frustration with the Palestinian strategy of seeking international recognition and refusal to negotiate with Israel as long as it continued to build colonies were visible. This attitude was clear, for example, in a speech delivered by the president in the State Department in May 2011, in which Obama sided almost completely with Israel, offering a vision that was, even for the most accommodating Palestinians, very depressing. The discourse adopted in that speech would be a prelude for later similarly one-sided speeches, where Obama reserved all of the praise and friendly language for Israel and pointed all the criticisms at the Arabs and Palestinians.

One editor in the Palestinian daily, *Al-Hayat al-Jadeeda*, wrote that, "Obama's speech had many contradictions and empty claims, as he talked about the Arab peoples who suffered oppression and humiliation, and he mentioned among [such] peoples, Libya, Egypt, Tunisia, Yemen, Bahrain and Iran, and how they are entitled to freedom and liberty and full rights; but never uttered a word about the rights of the Palestinian people or their suffering for over sixty years. To the contrary, he said that friendship with Israel is deep-rooted and eternal and that he will stand against any criticism of Israel."[72] Raising the possibility of using the veto against Palestine, another report in the same newspaper registered the irony of Obama's unenviable situation as he finds himself doing that just one year after his public call for the creation of a Palestinian state that would be a member of the United Nations, risking the hostility of an Arab Islamic world undergoing major transformations.[73]

Perhaps sensing the negative reactions to his State Department address, Obama gave a ray of hope to the Palestinians in an interview with the BBC soon after that. In it he asked for progress to be made on territory and security, with a two-state solution to be based on the 1967 border. "The basis for negotiations will involve looking at that 1967 border, recognising that conditions on the ground have changed and there are going to need to be swaps to accommodate the interests of both sides," Obama told the BBC's Andrew Marr in an interview."[74] Israel dismissed the plan immediately and Netanyahu described the 1967 borders as "indefensible." Palestinian officials who took some heart in Obama's statement about the 1967 border mostly remained silent about their next move, but this comfort did not last very long.

Obama's pro-Israeli position reached a new height in his September 2011 speech at the United Nations. Here he made a vehement assertion of the deep bond between Israel and the United States, with unprecedented passionate language that adopted the Israeli narrative verbatim, portraying the Jewish state as the classic victim surrounded by belligerent and hostile Arabs states. Obama made a standard mention of the need for peace and the support for a Palestinian state, but failed to make any reference to the suffering of the Palestinians under Israeli occupation and the aggressive Israeli policy of colonization. It was a very biased and polemical speech that put the Israeli case better than the Israelis themselves.

Ironically, the speech coincided with the end of the time frame provided by Obama two years earlier for the creation of a Palestinian state. The Obama deal envisioned the development of the Palestinian authority and building of Palestinian economy and institutions that would form the foundation of a state to be declared at the end of negotiations with Israel around September 2011. Israeli actions and American ambivalence have largely undermined that goal. In one key passage of the speech, the president sounded like he was undoing his Cairo Speech. He started by reiterating the American goal of a two-state solution, though clearly conditional to negotiations with Israel, then quickly moved to make the case for an American–Israeli strategic relationship:

> We seek a future where Palestinians live in a sovereign state of their own, with no limit to what they can achieve. There is no question that the Palestinians have seen that vision delayed for too long. And it is precisely because we believe so strongly in the aspirations of the Palestinian people that America has invested so much time and effort in the building of a Palestinian state, and the negotiations that can achieve one. America's commitment to Israel's security is unshakeable, and our friendship with Israel is deep and enduring. And so we believe that any lasting peace must acknowledge the very real security concerns that Israel faces every single day. Let's be honest: Israel is surrounded by neighbors that have waged repeated wars against it. Israel's citizens have been killed by rockets fired at their houses and suicide bombs on their buses. Israel's children come of age knowing that throughout the region, other children are taught to hate them. Israel, a small country of less than eight million people, looks out at a world where leaders of much larger nations threaten to wipe it off of the map. The Jewish people carry the burden of centuries of exile, persecution, and the fresh memory of knowing that six million people were killed simply because of who they were. These facts cannot be denied. The Jewish people have

forged a successful state in their historic homeland. Israel deserves recognition. It deserves normal relations with its neighbors. And friends of the Palestinians do them no favors by ignoring this truth, just as friends of Israel must recognize the need to pursue a two state solution with a secure Israel next to an independent Palestine.[75]

While Israelis celebrated the speech as a milestone of American empathy and support for Israel and the Jewish people, Palestinians and Arabs were shocked and horrified. The *Guardian*'s correspondent Harriet Sherwood, for example, reported from Ramallah the sense of betrayal Palestinians felt by the US position on Palestinian statehood: "I think people here will be very surprised and disappointed that he made no mention of the borders of a Palestinian state being based on the pre-1967 lines. That will be seen as a significant retreat on Obama's 19 May speech, and an alarming indication of the US stance of the Palestinians' approach to the UN this week. I've been talking to people in the West Bank today, and they feel very let down, indeed betrayed, by Obama."[76]

One Palestinian activist, independent politician, and former Palestinian presidential candidate, Mustafa Barghouti, declared his deep disappointment with Obama's speech and his double standards. He criticized Obama for championing freedom, human rights, and justice for people in South Sudan, Tunisia, and Egypt, but not for the Palestinians. He also critiqued Obama's call to the Palestinians to return to negotiations without reference to the 1967 borders as basis for territorial settlement and without considering that 20 years of negotiations have produced nothing for the Palestinians. In Ramallah's central square, another Palestinian, shop owner Marwan Jubeh, expressed a similar disappointment: "Israel and the US are one and the same: the US is Israel, and Israel is the US. Israel doesn't want to give the Palestinians anything and Obama can't do anything without Israel because Congress is pro-Israel."[77] Obama did not even spare the UN itself, from whose podium he was delivering his speech, making a cynical reference to its obsolete role in resolving the Israeli–Palestinian conflict: "Peace will not come through statements and resolutions at the UN—if it were that easy, it would have been accomplished by now."[78] Perhaps the most cynical of all was that the speech, meant as a statement on American positions on crucial international issues and ostensibly aimed at the nations of the world, sounded very much like another domestic address to American voters to help Obama improve his flagging ratings ahead of the next election.

Conclusion

The crashing fall of the Obama image in the Arab World can clearly be linked to both Obama's breaking of the promises he had made regarding American policy in the region and his weak and inconsistent responses to the Arab Spring crises. Obama's nonchalant and hesitant positions on the upheavals in Tunisia and Egypt and his relative silence on other uprisings, especially in Bahrain, were seen in stark contrast with his obsession with moving aggressively against Iran and unconditionally supporting Israel; seemingly unruffled that the Netanyahu government was effectively undermining the two-state solution and openly challenging Obama in the American domestic politics. Even Arabs who might have welcomed Obama's tough stance against Iran, mostly from among the Sunni constituencies and the Gulf states, would still find it hard to fathom his hawkish support for Israel, sometimes at the risk of looking like a brazenly hypocritical and self-contradicting president. This blind pro-Israel position culminated in the American vote in November 2012 against the upgrading of the status of Palestine into the United Nations as a nonmember observer state, in complete departure from its European friends and pretty much the rest of the international community.

The reelection of Obama for a second term seemed to have rehabilitated his image and that of the United States in the Arab world to some extent. According to a survey of Arab public opinion in November 2012, conducted by Zogby Research Services, "favourability ratings regarding the United States had spiked in most Arab countries. More significantly, there were strong majorities in several countries that responded that the United States was making a positive contribution to peace and stability in the Arab world."[79] It seems that the decline in the reputation of the United States and the standing of Obama has been brought to a halt, if not reversed. The results stand in stark contrast with the disastrous ratings Obama and the United States earned in a poll of Arab opinion during 2010 and 2011. For example, "more than 80 per cent of Jordanians and Emiratis said they believed that 'the US is contributing to peace and stability in the Arab world'—a dramatic rise from the less than 10 per cent who held that view a year and a half ago."[80] People in other Arab countries, including Saudi Arabia, Egypt, Lebanon, and Morocco also indicated a significant rise in the positive appreciation of the US role in contributing to peace and stability. Obama was praised for his "low-key and cooperative approach" and for fulfilling his commitment to withdraw from Iraq and supporting political change in Egypt and Syria.[81]

However the US rating on the question of Palestine remained very low, as Arabs still had little confidence in the American role in resolving the Israeli–Palestinian issue. And so not surprisingly the lowest favorability rating of the United States, at 2%, came from Palestine. Yet people who were interviewed after the survey to better understand the results expressed their hope that the President will renew his efforts in his second term to push for a peaceful solution to the Israeli–Palestinian conflict. This hope is a faint echo of the euphoric support Obama received following his election in 2008 and the defeat of the Bush doctrine; but this is clearly a more contingent and less enthusiastic support; and for Obama to really earn it, he needs to follow a different path. As James Zogby puts it: "Obama begins his second term with Arab public opinion giving him a second vote of confidence. The challenge is clear: he must act. A second disappointment could be irreversible."[82]

Some Arab writers and journalists from popular media outlets didn't see a second chance coming and expressed grave doubts about Obama's readiness to rise to the expectations of Arab peoples, such as to reengage in the peace process or play a more positive role in the Syrian crisis. One journalist and Middle East expert, Abdelbari Atwan, understood Obama's second-term inaugural speech as a clear sign of resignation from Middle Eastern affairs and a shift to a more American isolationism and aversion to wars and conflicts. Commenting on Obama's virtual avoidance of mentioning the Israeli–Palestinian conflict, Atwan wrote that, "Obama has no plans to reignite the peace process or exert any pressures on the new Israeli government to stop the colonization and return to the negotiating table."[83]

As he starts his second term, President Obama is once again in the driver seat, and a fresh sense of anticipation and even hope in the Arab world is in the air, though perhaps tinged with more caution and modest expectations. One hopes that the great disappointments of the first term will be replaced with true achievements in the second, with the president tackling the most urgent global issues, including those that define the relationships between America and Arab and Muslim nations. President Obama needs to engage Arabs and Muslims in tangible ways that promote respect, reconciliation, friendship, development, and peacemaking. The more than 1 billion Muslims and 300 million Arabs deserve to be recognized, not only as a rhetorical number, or a wartime ally, but as real people with real richness, real potential, and real problems. America has an obligation to work with these nations to help them play a productive and responsible global role and also to find creative ways to confront their challenges and solve their problems.

The United States can go a long way in creating a cooperative environment and partnership with the Arab world, where American leadership can be trusted, not as a global hegemon that can defend its loyal regimes and protect its narrowly defined geopolitical interests, but as a force for cooperation, development, progress, human rights, and peace. Obama has a chance to take America to this new horizon of leadership in the Arab world, where idealism rather than fear is the motivator for action, and bilateral strategic thinking rather than crude self-interest is the shaper of the future of the region and America's place in it. Till now, the US role in the Middle East has been, unfortunately, part of the problem rather than part of the solution. This has to change. America still enjoys indisputable global leadership, which is both a privilege and a burden. Millions of Arabs will be thrilled to see Obama live up to his expectations as a global leader and deliver on his promises of reaching out to Muslims, supporting peaceful transition to democracy in the Arab world, and facilitating the just resolution of the Palestinian problem, including the creation of a sovereign Palestinian state. But this requires much more than words. Perhaps Obama needs, as one analyst observed earlier, a new "new beginning," one by which the president seriously oversees the realization of his vision and boldly proceeds to book his place in the pantheon of extraordinary world leaders.

Epilogue: The First Six Month of Obama's Second Term

On Reaching out to Muslims

In the first six months of his second term, Obama seemed more busy trying to manage the US role in relation to multiple crises in key Muslim countries, including two close allies, Egypt and Turkey, and one strategic foe, Syria, than embarking on a visible new vision of reaching out to Muslims. The first two countries were shaken by popular protests, as gigantic popular protests culminating in a military intervention toppled Morsi and the Muslim Brotherhood in Egypt, and a small environmental protest in Istanbul mushroomed into large demonstrations across Turkey, leading to violent clashes with the security forces and creating a major challenge for the Erdogan government. The events in Turkey were seen as a potential problem for Obama. According to news reports, "[Turkish] government crackdowns against protesters in Turkey could test the close ties between President Barack Obama and Turkish Prime Minister Recep Tayyip Erdogan, a strategically important U.S. ally in a tumultuous region."[84]

The Turkish experience, including the success of the government of Erdogan and his Islamist party, the Justice and Development Party, in working within parameters of democracy and secularism, was praised by Obama as a model for other Muslim nations in his speech in Ankara. However concerns were heightened as the protests and security crackdown continued, especially in Istanbul's Taksim Square, and suddenly Erdogan's model seemed more flawed than Obama had come to believe. Though both countries needed each other and coordinated closely on some fronts, such as Syria, they also differed greatly on several other critical issues, such as Israel and the ousting of President Morsi in Egypt, which Erdogan blasted bluntly as a military coup that is not legitimate. By July 2013, Obama's reaching out strategy to Muslims appeared as distant, empty rhetoric and was reduced, at least for the time being, to calls for unity, national reconciliation, democracy, and the pressing need for protestors and security forces to conduct themselves peacefully. On the other hand, there was no tangible progress on the closing down of Guantanamo, US troops were still in Afghanistan, and the drone war continued.

On the Arab Spring

Egypt

Obama's major test on the change in Egypt came later when massive popular protests against President Morsi called for by the opposition, especially the new grassroots youth movement Tamarod (Rebellion), on June 30, 2013, triggered the armed forces to step in and force him out of office. President Morsi himself was put in protective custody and dozens of cadres of his Freedom and Justice Party and its mother organization, the Muslim Brotherhood, were arrested. The decision was followed by the shutting down of all pro-Morsi media outlets. The head of the Supreme Constitutional Court, Adly Mansour, was installed as acting president to prepare for new presidential and parliamentary elections; within days he suspended the constitution and dissolved the Consultative Council, the one parliament chamber that was still functioning. In less than two weeks, he appointed a new government made mostly of civil leaders and technocrats. The change received the backing of other political parties and seemingly a majority of Egyptians, but it did not go unchallenged as large protests and street sit-ins by Morsi supporters were organized to counter what they saw as a military coup led by the defense minister and commander-in-chief of the Egyptian Armed Forces, Abdul Fatah al-Sisi, and to demand the return of the deposed president. Some of the protests turned violent and dozens of demonstrators were killed and injured in clashes, while members of the security forces were attacked by gunmen, especially in the Sinai Peninsula, and suffered casualties.[85] The standoff between the two sides seemed to be heading for more escalation as each side insisted on the legitimacy of their actions and vowed to fight to the end.

Whatever support and goodwill Obama has invested in his relations with the post-Mubarak Islamist government in Egypt had to be abandoned as the administration took notice of the popular change and decided to switch its horses. The fact that the change took place in a coup-like manner and that a democratically elected president was deposed and arrested, though discomforting, were not enough grounds for Obama to reject or condemn what happened. The White House language focused on the need to move forward to a new civilian government and elections and national reconciliation. There was mild criticism of the crackdown on the Brotherhood and the arrests of its leaders, including Morsi, but nothing that would intimidate or anger the new Egyptian leadership.

In fairness to Obama, as we are reminded by Rober Fisk, he did warn in his Cairo Speech of the dangers of elected leaders who try to exclude their opponents, and emphasized that democracy is much more than just the ballot box. "There are some," he said, "who advocate for democracy only when they are out of power; once in power, they are ruthless in suppressing the rights of others . . . you must respect the rights of minorities, and participate with a spirit of tolerance and compromise; you must place the interests of your people and the legitimate workings of the political process above your party. Without these ingredients, elections alone do not make true democracy."[86] President Morsi, according to Fisk, ignored this advice and sought to monopolize power, excluded the opposition from the political process, and showed no interest in protecting Egypt's Christian and non-Sunni Muslim minorities; in other words, he committed exactly the mistakes Obama warned against. Yet, Fisk criticizes Obama and other Western leaders for failing to call what happened in Egypt with its proper name, i.e., a military coup. "This doesn't let Obama off the hook. Those Western leaders who are gently telling us that Egypt is still on the path to 'democracy,' that this is an 'interim' period—like the 'interim' Egyptian government concocted by the military—and that millions of Egyptians support the coup that isn't a coup, have to remember that Morsi was indeed elected in a real, Western-approved election."[87]

Still, compared with the January 25 Revolution, this time around Egyptian protesters expressed much more anti-American sentiments and many accused Obama of currying favor with the Islamists and turning a blind eye to the transgressions of President Morsi and his narrow Islamist agenda. The role of the American ambassador in Egypt, Ann Patterson, which was much more visible than that of the White House, was not welcomed by the anti-Morsi forces. Young Egyptian activists made her the abominable symbol of what they perceived as the manipulative American intervention in their country's affairs. According to news reports, "Her image has been plastered on banners in Tahrir Square, crossed out with a blood-red X or distorted and smeared with insults. She is too cozy with Egypt's deposed president and the Muslim Brotherhood, the signs say, and should leave the country."[88] Similarly, protesters carried images of Obama crossed out in red in the same manner as they chanted against him and US policy.

The clearest sign of trouble for Patterson came in a speech in Cairo some two weeks earlier as anti-Morsi action was picking up pace, in which she reiterated American support for democratic change in Egypt, but also stressed that the United States still had to deal with those in power, and that "she was 'deeply skeptical' that 'street action will produce better results than elections.'"[89] Protesters saw that as a swipe at their "street legitimacy" and an indirect validation for the Brotherhood and Morsi. Obama's initial reaction to the dismissal of Morsi by the military, in which "[he] warned of the dangers of violence and tried to steer Egypt's military toward a prompt resumption of democratic rule," while avoiding describing the change as a "coup," demonstrated to many Egyptians the lack of decisiveness, as much as it signified the lack of leverage the United States has over Egypt. The whole attitude seemed to be "reviving memories of Mr. Obama's early reluctance to cut loose Mr. Mubarak, a longtime ally of the United States."[90] It must be said here that the mistrust among Egyptians towards the United States is deep seated and certainly did not start with this crisis. This view was captured for example in a poll of public opinion regarding foreign aid to Egypt conducted by Gallup in December 2011, nine months after the ousting of President Mubarak. According to the poll, 71% of Egyptians opposed US economic aid to Egypt; while 26% only supported it. In contrast, 50% of respondents supported economic aid from the IMF and 68% were in favor of such aid coming from other Arab countries.[91]

While Obama's policy seemed to be again a hands-off, wait-and-see approach, it is most likely that secretly the administration welcomed the ousting of an Islamist president who was seen as ineffective, divisive, and autocratic. This was reflected in the *New York Times* headline for July 5, which read: "Egypt Crisis Finds Washington Largely Ambivalent and Aloof."[92] However within two weeks, Obama was more openly supportive of the new direction. The White House basically recognized the legitimacy of the new leadership and the roadmap put forward by the military, as was evident in Deputy Secretary of State William Burns's visit to Cairo in mid-July and his meeting with the interim President Adly Mansour. After the meeting, Mr. Burns called for national reconciliation and unity while warning against wasting the new chance for a democratic government and the exclusion of the Islamists from the political process. However, he met none of the Brotherhood leaders, never mentioned Morsi, and did not ask for Morsi's release as the White House had done earlier.[93] Now the pro-Morsi forces, who had already criticized Obama and his administration for standing by and failing to condemn the military coup, found new evidence for their claims of an American betrayal of democratic values and even a conspiracy in collusion with the military to bring the Brotherhood's reign to an end. Obama, for the time being, seems incapable of winning either side, as his leadership on the Egyptian crisis is tested yet again.

Tunisia

While Tunisia continues to go through a transitional period, with moderate Islamists at the helm of power, the Obama administration is still cautiously optimistic that this might be a success story after all. However there are concerns at the revolutionary state's ability to survive the tests and tribulations of the tug of war between radical Islamists and liberal secularists, both of whom pose a serious challenge to the current government. The mysterious assassination of the opposition leader Chokri Belaid, head of the Democratic Patriots Movement, in February 2013; regular anti-government protest; as well as multiple attacks on security forces and soft secularist "targets" by militant Islamists have made things much more problematic. Since the Tunisian elections in 2012, secularists have accused the Islamist-led government of hijacking the revolution and criticized the cozy and even supportive attitude the Obama administration took towards the moderate Islamist party Ennahda.[94] This support was clearly not factored in when a Tunisian court issued very light sentences against twenty Islamists who attacked the US embassy in September 2012 after the release on the Internet of an American-made anti-Islam film, resulting in some deaths and injuries.[95] The two-year suspended jail sentence to all defendants can be seen as an insult to the Obama administration's expectations of a different kind of justice, especially after the repeated attacks on US embassies in countries experiencing the Arab Spring. American officials said that the White House was stunned by the verdicts, which "do not correspond appropriately to the extent and severity of the damage and violence that took place. Officials said . . . that the lenient sentences signaled to the Salafist movement that it could strike U.S. interests with impunity."[96]

These concerns were heightened by reports of a Salafist radicalization campaign targeting young Tunisians to undermine secular freedoms and rights in Tunisia, or to volunteer as jihadists to fight in Syria. Reports of the presence of hundreds of fighters from Tunisia (and other countries), as well as the free flow of arms from Libya to the jihadists there, might be a depressing confirmation of the view that the Arab Spring was at some level an awakening of jihadism as much as a revolutionary change to democratic politics, both of which represent a real test to America's role and Obama's leadership.

Libya

The White House continued to be on the defensive over the circumstances surrounding the attacks on the American consulate and a CIA annex in Benghazi on September 11, 2012, that led to the killing of four Americans, including Ambassador J. Christopher Stevens. The administration had been dogged by questions about its role in the alleged manipulation of the narrative of what happened soon after the attacks for domestic political reasons. In May 2013, two Obama officials, Thomas R. Pickering and Mike Mullen, who were on the panel that investigated the attacks, were subpoenaed to appear for a public hearing before Congress to answer questions about their panel's report regarding its exoneration of all senior State Department officials from accountability.[97] But despite the increasing questioning of the responsibility of the CIA in the tragedy in light of new revelations about its role, the political damage to the Obama administration from the "Benghazi Scandal" as the Republicans insisted on calling it, was inevitable. The roles of two top Obama officials, Susan Rice, the US Representative to the UN, and State Department's Spokesperson Victoria Nuland, in introducing changes to the "talking points" dealing with the aftermath of the deadly attacks in the midst of the 2012 presidential campaign also came under intense scrutiny. For Republicans, the developments in this case "have suggested that the Obama administration sought to play down the possibility of terrorism during the campaign and has misled the country."[98] No wonder then that Obama kept a low profile on the deteriorating security developments in Libya as the country descended further into post-revolutionary chaos. Bloody clashes in Benghazi and Tripoli in May and June 2013 between militias and army units and amongst competing militias, as well as attacks on foreign diplomats, only deepened the sense of insecurity and uncertainty in the country whose deliverance from the tyranny of the Gaddafi regime was aggressively accomplished by NATO and the Obama administration.[99]

Syria

While Obama's position on Syria was relatively clear in its insistence on the need for real change and the removal of Assad from power, it was still plagued with hesitations, reversals, and lack of an overall strategy. Two and a half years into the Syrian crisis, Obama's policy on this issue is seen as confused and indecisive, despite the stated shift in June 2013 in favor of arming the Syrian rebels (specifically the Free Syrian Army). The pressure was ratcheted up by hawkish Congress members who demanded a more aggressive Obama policy, including a US role in the toppling of President Assad by declaring a no-fly zone over Syria and providing military assistance to the rebel forces, if not even intervening in the conflict directly. A visit by Senator John McCain in May 2013 to Syrian territory under the control of the armed opposition, in which he met Syrian rebel leaders, highlighted Obama's dilemma in this regard. "The Arizona senator has been leading efforts in Congress . . . to force Barack Obama to intervene in Syria following reports of alleged chemical weapons use by forces loyal to Assad."[100] The change in policy came a few weeks later as the United States and its principal allies, the UK and France, announced their intention to arm the rebels in Syria to regain the balance of forces on the ground that was shaken after the Syrian regime's gains in certain areas.[101]

The shift in the previous policy of supporting change in Syria from the sidelines came after the tide on the battlefield started to turn in favor of the Syrian government's forces following the direct intervention of thousands of Hezbollah fighters in support of the regime, leading to the important victory in the border town of Al-Qusayr. The official rationale for the new approach was the supposed use of chemical weapons by the regime's forces, thus breaching the "red line" repeatedly announced by Obama as a situation that would require American intervention. However several questions were raised about the veracity of the evidence and the investigation, which was not carried out by a neutral body. The report also painted a picture of incomplete data, with chemical attacks that are few in number and limited in scope and casualties; not to mention the existence of counter reports of the use of chemical weapons by the rebel forces. In one such report in May 2013, UN human rights investigator Carla del Ponte accused the Syrian rebels of using sarin gas, though she stressed that this was a preliminary conclusion that requires further verification.[102]

But within a month of the announcement, and in the face of strong opposition from members of Congress and increased fears that the weapons might fall into the "wrong hands," namely the militant Islamist and terrorist groups fighting against the regime, such as the Al-Nusra Front, the administration, at least publicly, had all but reversed itself on this issue; or perhaps is still actively discussing the pros and cons of this option and the possible repercussions of this kind of active military involvement. The hesitation coincided with similar climbing down by the British and French governments from the same position. There are signs that, in addition to "nonlethal" aid that the three countries have been sending to the Syrian rebels, they might be willing to supply them with light weapons rather than the sophisticated anti-tank and anti-aircraft systems. However such weapons have been provided to the FSA and other groups in increasing quantities, but apparently from Qatar and Saudi Arabia, probably in cooperation with Turkey and with some semi-covert help by American, British, French, or NATO officers in the training of rebels in secret bases in Jordan.

Parallel to contemplating this militaristic approach, which many criticize as having the potential for lengthening the conflict and increasing the bloodshed and suffering of the Syrian people, Obama continues to speak of the need for a diplomatic solution as the only way to end the crisis, though this diplomacy is often projected as contingent on the ousting of President Assad, either as a pre-condition for the negotiations between the regime and rebels, or as an assured outcome of that process. And on this front, the White House seems to be closer to the Russian position, which has always advocated dialogue and negotiations between the parties as the only way out; in effect making the US policy more schizophrenic than that of other countries involved in the crisis. In one editorial in Bloomberg, the new policy was criticized as self-defeating and lacking in focus. The article, while admitting that all options in Syria are terrible, states, "The most convincing explanation of Obama's Syria policy is that it is designed simply to play for time in a vexed, desperate situation—arming the rebels just enough to assuage critics in Congress but not enough to run the risk of pouring fuel on the fire."[103] Whether this really is what Obama's policy on Syria amounts to in the end, only time can tell.

On the Question of Palestine

Perhaps given all the troubles Obama has been facing in other areas of foreign policy, he turned his attention again to the Palestine–Israel conflict to create some movement and a sense of achievement. After three years of frozen negotiations between Israelis and Palestinians, the US Secretary of State, John Kerry, embarked on an intensive shuttle diplomacy to break the stalemate and reconvene peace talks between the two sides. Kerry visited the region multiple times, moving between Jerusalem, Ramallah, and Amman, to work out a new framework for the negotiations. However there was a sense of déjà vu, that there was nothing radically new here, except the sense of urgency as the two-state solution looked increasingly imperiled and more unfeasible with the spike in Israeli settlement activity in the Occupied Territories. Another idea is to use economics to push for an opening in the dead-end politics. Kerry indicated at one point that "he is hoping to use the economic development of Palestinian areas on the West Bank as a means to build support for a new set of Middle East peace negotiations."[104]

With little to do in the face of an extreme nationalist and settler government in Israel, Obama ended up piling the pressures on the Palestinian side to push Abbas to agree to the negotiations with Netanyahu without seeing the fulfillment of any of the long-standing Palestinian demands, seen as unfulfilled commitments by Israel under the Oslo Accords and the Road Map plan. Most important among these is to halt Israel's continued building of colonies in the West Bank and East Jerusalem, acknowledging the borders of June 4, 1967 as the basis for the two state solution, and the release of Palestinian prisoners with long sentences from Israeli jails, especially those from the pre-Oslo Accords period.

Though the specific ideas offered by Kerry to bridge the gaps and create enough momentum to get back to the negotiations were still shrouded in secrecy, news reports indicated that the plan depends on "a broad package of economic incentives, security reassurances and political gestures in hopes of bringing the two sides to the negotiating table, the border question seems to be among the major sticking points. Mr. Abbas has for years insisted that any new talks be conducted on the basis of Israel's borders before it seized Arab territories in the 1967 war, with minor adjustments. Prime Minister Benjamin Netanyahu of Israel has just as steadfastly refused."[105]

While the personal involvement of Mr. Kerry and his extensive and persistence diplomacy is a far cry from the style of the previous Secretary of State Hillary Clinton, it is hard to imagine that it will be effective enough to bear the kinds of fruits that would lead to a resolution of the conflict and a two-state solution. Despite many Palestinian misgivings about the lack of guarantees and a shortage of trust in Netanyahu and his government, Kerry announced on July 19, 2013, that the two sides agreed to go back to direct negotiations after they "reached an agreement which establishes the basis for resuming peace talks."[106] The Palestinian leadership apparently agreed to do that after coming under tremendous pressures from the Americans, facilitated by the Arab League, which has given its backing to the Kerry plan. In addition to economic incentives, such as the transfer of more land to the Palestinian Authority and support for major economic projects that were presented to Obama in April 2013 as necessary to push-start the strangled Palestinian economy, the other factor that helped secure Palestinian agreement, according to one Palestinian official, is that Kerry himself is seen as a "well trusted" diplomat. He apparently told them that, "He does not want to get engaged in another 20 years of negotiations."[107] It is hard to believe that this would be sufficient to achieve a historic breakthrough; at least not without pressures by Obama on the Israeli side to go to the negotiations in good faith and be ready to make major concessions.

As Kerry was feverishly engaged in his shuttle diplomacy, the EU perhaps showed the way for what might be a different and potentially more productive approach towards the Israel–Palestine question by deciding to stop all EU funding to any Israeli project in the occupied West Bank and East Jerusalem. The decision will practically bring an "end to the ambiguity that has helped Israel to maintain and expand its presence beyond the old 'green line' border since the 1967 Middle East war—without incurring significant costs. The EU's 'territorial applicability clause' spells out that there can be consequences for flouting UN resolutions and international legality."[108] The decision was described as an earthquake in Israel, but warmly welcomed by Palestinians and peace-loving Israelis who have been asking for a stronger international role in resolving the conflict and have grown desperate of the lack of an effective Obama policy in this regard. Though it is practically impossible to envision a credible resolution of the question of Palestine without the contribution of the United States, perhaps in the current absence of courageous American leadership on this issue, other global actors, in this case the Europeans, will come forward to do at least part of the hard work.

Notes

1. On the reception of the 2008 US presidential election in general and Obama in particular in Palestine, see Mohammad Masad, "Palestine's View of the US 2008 Presidential Elections," In *The World Views of the US Presidential Election: 2008*, ed. Matthiass Mass (New York: Palgrave Macmillan, 2009), 151–168.

2. For a video recording and a transcript of the text of the speech, see, [Barack Obama] "President Obama's Speech in Cairo: A New Beginning," The White House, http://www.whitehouse.gov/blog/NewBeginning/ transcripts; see also, "Text: Obama's Speech in Cairo," *The New York Times*, June 2, 2009, http://www.nytimes.com/2009/06/04/us/politics/04obama.text.html?pagewanted=all&_r=0.

3. Helene Cooper, "Obama Pushes for Mideast Accord," *The New York Times*, April 7, 2009, http://www.nytimes.com/2009/04/08/world/europe/08prexy.html?_r=0.

4. "Confidence in Obama Lifts U.S. Image Around the World," Pew Research Center, July 23, 2009,http://www.pewglobal.org/2009/07/23/confidence-in-obama-lifts-us-image-around-the-world/.

5. "Confidence in Obama," 1.

6. For an interesting discussion of these priorities and a review of Obama's Middle East foreign policy in the first three years, see Ryan Lizza, "The Consequentialist: How the Arab Spring Remade Obama's Foreign Policy," *The New Yorker*, May 2 2011: 1–18, http://www.newyorker.com/reporting/2011/05/02/110502fa_fact_lizza.

7. Helene Cooper, "Obama Pushes for Mideast Accord," *The New York Times*, April 7, 2009, http://www.nytimes.com/2009/04/08/world/europe/08prexy.html?_r=0.

8. Cooper, "Obama Pushes for Mideast Accord."

9. Cooper, "Obama Pushes for Mideast Accord."

10. "Full Text of the US President's Speech at Turkish Parliament," *Hurriyet Daily News*, http://www.hurriyet.com.tr/english/domestic/11376661.asp.

11. "Text: Obama's Speech in Cairo," *The New York Times*, June 4, 2009, http://www.nytimes.com/2009/06/04/us/politics/04obama.text.html?pagewanted=all&_r=0.

12. "Text: Obama's Speech in Cairo."

13. Howard LaFranchi, "New Poll: Angry at US: Arabs Support Iran Nuclear Bomb," *The Christian Science Monitor*, August 6, 2010, http://www.csmonitor.com/USA/Foreign-Policy/2010/0806/New-poll-angry-at-US-Arabs-support-an-Iran-nuclear-bomb.

14. Shibley Telhami, "2010 Arab Public Opinion Poll," University of Maryland and Zogby International, *Politico*, August 5, 2010, http://www.politico.com/static/PPM170_100804_arabpublic.html.

15. Telhami, "2010 Arab Public Opinion."

16. Telhami, "2010 Arab Public Opinion."

17. LaFranchi, "New Poll."

18. LaFranchi, "New Poll."

19. [Barack Obama], "Remarks by the President at the University of Indonesia in Jakarta, Indonesia, November 10, 2010," The White House, Office of the Press Secretary, http://www.whitehouse.gov/the-press-office/2010/11/10/remarks-president-university-indonesia-jakarta-indonesia.

20. Marc Lynch, "In Defense of Obama's Muslim Outreach," *Foreign Policy Magazine*, November 10, 2010, http://lynch.foreignpolicy.com/posts/2010/11/10/in_defense_of_obamas_muslim_outreach.

21. Lynch, "In Defense."

22. Charles A. Kupchan, "Enemies into Friends: How the United States Can Court Its Adversaries," *Foreign Policy*, March/April 2010, http://www.foreignaffairs.com/articles/65986/charles-a-kupchan/enemies-into-friends.

23. Nick Hopkins, "US Drone Attacks 'Counter-Productive,' Former Obama Security Adviser Claims," *The Guardian*, January 7, 2013, http://www.guardian.co.uk/world/2013/jan/07/obama-adviser-criticises-drone-policy; see Boyl's full article in, Michael J. Boyle, "The Costs and Consequences of Drone Warfare," *International Affairs* 89:1 (2013): 1–29; also available at Chathamhouse, http://www.chathamhouse.org/sites/default/files/public/International%20Affairs/2013/89_1/89_1Boyle.pdf.

24. Boyle, "The Costs," 2.

25. Boyle, "The Costs," 5.

26. Boyle, "The Costs," 6.

27. Boyle, "The Costs," 16–17.

28. Boyle, "The Costs," 15–16.

29. Boyle, "The Costs," 29.

30. "Remote-Control Warfare: Droning On: How to Build Ethical Understanding into Pilotless Planes," *The Economist*, March 31, 2010, http://www.economist.com/node/15814399.

31. Taufiq Rahim, "On Day One: A New "New Beginning," *Diplomatic Courier Magazine*, January 18, 2013, http://www.diplomaticourier.com/news/regions/middle-east/1315-on-day-one-a-new-new-beginning.

32. John Caves, et al., "Anti-Americanism in the Obama Era," Woodrow Wilson School of Public and International Affairs, Princeton University, December 2010, 10, http://www.princeton.edu/~smeunier/Anti-Americanism%20Task%20Force%20Report%20FINAL.pdf.
33. John Caves, "Anti-Americanism," 10.
34. Lizza, "The Consequentialist," 18.
35. Helene Cooper and Robert F. Worth, "In Arab Spring, Obama Finds A Sharp Test," *The New York Times*, September 24, 2012, http://www.nytimes.com/2012/09/25/us/politics/arab-spring-proves-a-harsh-test-for-obamas-diplomatic-skill.html?pagewanted=all&_r=0.
36. Lizza, "The Consequentialist," 13–15.
37. Lizza, "The Consequentialist," 10.
38. Lizza, "The Consequentialist," 10.
39. Foreign Policy, Guiding Principles, The White House Obama, http://www.whitehouse.gov/issues/foreign-policy.
40. Lizza, "The Consequentialist," 17.
41. Michael Chossudovsky, "Operation Libya and the Battle for Oil: Redrawing the Map of Africa," *Global Research*, March 9, 2011, http://www.globalresearch.ca/operation-libya-and-the-battle-for-oil-redrawing-the-map-of-africa/23605.
42. David Gauthier-Villars, "Rift Over Libyan Oil Emerges Among Allies," *The Wall Street Journal*, September 2, 2011, http://online.wsj.com/article/SB10001424053111904716604576544580088946772.html.
43. Helen Cooper and Robert F. Worth, "In Arab Spring, Obama Finds a Sharp Test," *The New York Times*, September 24, 2012, http://www.nytimes.com/2012/09/25/us/politics/arab-spring-proves-a-harsh-test-for-obamas-diplomatic-skill.html?pagewanted=all&_r=0.
44. Cooper, "In Arab Spring."
45. Cooper, "In Arab Spring."
46. John Esposito, Esposito, "Obama's Middle East Speech: a Significant Step Forward But a Long Way to Go," *The Washington Post*, May 20, 2011, http://www.washingtonpost.com/blogs/on-faith/post/obamas-middle-east-speech-a-significant-step-forward-but-a-long-way-to-go/2011/05/20/AFo3zm7G_blog.html.
47. Shadi Hamid, "Don't Give Up the Arab Spring: Why Americans Did the Right Thing in Libya—and Freedom Will Eventually Win" *Foreign Policy Magazine*, September 12, 2012, http://www.foreignpolicy.com/articles/2012/09/12/dont_give_up_on_the_arab_spring?page=0,0.
48. Hamid, "Don't Give Up."
49. Hamid, "Don't Give Up."
50. Reuters in Washington, "Obama Blocked US Plan to Arm Syrian Rebels," *The Guardian*, February 8, 2013, http://www.guardian.co.uk/world/2013/feb/08/pentagon-supported-plan-syrian-rebels.
51. Lara Lee, "Bahrain and the True Face of US Foreign Policy," *The Huffington Post*, July 28, 2011, http://www.huffingtonpost.com/iara-lee/post_2239_b_911891.html.
52. Hooshang Amirahmadi and Kaveh Afrasiabi, "The West's Silence Over Bahrain Smacks of Double Standards," *The Guardian*, April, 29, 2011, http://www.guardian.co.uk/commentisfree/2011/apr/29/bahrain-saudi-arabia-iran-west.
53. "Text: Obama's Speech."
54. Barack Obama, "Remarks by the President to the United Nations General Assembly," The White House, Office of the Press Secretary, September 23, 2010, http://www.whitehouse.gov/the-press-office/2010/09/23/remarks-president-united-nations-general-assembly.
55. "Barack Obama: A Pragmatist Trying to Change the Course of History: A Statement of Account," *Al-Majalla*, September 9, 2012, http://www.majalla.com/arb/2012/07/article55236881.
56. Mark Landler, "Israeli Settlement Growth Must Stop, Clinton Says," *The New York Times*, May 27, 2009, http://www.nytimes.com/2009/05/28/world/middleeast/28mideast.html?_r=0.
57. Jihad Al-Khazen, "More Weakness and Hatchet," *Al-Hayat*, September 22, 2010, http://www.sauress.com/alhayat/183657.
58. Zuheir Quseibati, "Worse than a Palestinian Zero," *Al-Hayat*, December 9, 2010, http://www.sauress.com/alhayat/210698.
59. Daniel Nasaw, "Obama Aid Calls Israeli Settlement Announcement an "Insult" to the US," *The Guardian*, March 14, 2010, http://www.guardian.co.uk/world/2010/mar/14/israel-palestinian-territories.
60. Harriet Sherwood, "'Political Coward' Binyamin Netanyahu Sees Rift with Barack Obama Widen," *The Guardian*, January 20, 2013,http://www.guardian.co.uk/world/2013/jan/20/netanyahu-obama-rift-widens; see also, Jeffrey Balcnkfort, "A Crisis in US / Israeli Relations? Sure, but . . . Why Israel Always Prevails," *Counterpunch*, March 19–21, 2010,http://www.counterpunch.org/2010/03/19/why-israel-always-prevails/.
61. Aref Galal, "America Swallows the Israeli Insult," *Al-Bayan*, March 21, 2010, http://www.albayan.ae/opinions/1265975145837-2010-03-21-1.230986.

62. The term, now commonly accepted as denoting Obama's new style of American leadership, was the subject of an investigative best-seller book; see Richard Miniter, *Leading from Behind: The Reluctant President and the Advisors Who Decide for Him* (New York: St. Martin's Press, 2012).

63. Lizza, "The Consequentialist," 18.

64. Stephen M. Walt, "Obama and Israel Lobby: Quo Vadis?" *Foreign Policy Magazine*, November 9, 2012, http://walt.foreignpolicy.com/category/one_time_tags/obama_and_the_israel_lobby.

65. "How Unesco Countries Voted on Palestinian Membership," *The Guardian*, November 1, 2011, http://www.guardian.co.uk/world/2011/nov/01/unesco-countries-vote-palestinian-membership.

66. Neil MacFarquhar, "The US Blocks Security Council Censure of Israeli Settlements," *The New York Times*, February 18, 2011, http://www.nytimes.com/2011/02/19/world/middleeast/19nations.html?_r=0.

67. Michelle Nichols, "Israeli Settlements Leave US Odd Man Out at UN Security Council," Reuters, December 18, 2012, http://www.reuters.com/article/2012/12/19/us-palestinians-israel-usa-un-idUSBRE8BI1KF20121219.

68. Phyllis Bennis, "US Vetoes UN Resolution Condemning Illegal Israel Settlements: Will the Palestinians End up Benefiting from the Move?" *Jews for Justice for Palestine*, February 18, 2011, http://jfjfp.com/?p=21359.

69. Philip C. Wilcox Jr., *Jews for Justice for Palestine*, February 18, 2011, http://jfjfp.com/?p=21359.

70. Sarah Leah Whitson, Middle East director at Human Rights Watch, " US Veto on Settlements Undermines International Law," *Human Rights Watch*, February 18, 2011, http://www.hrw.org/news/2011/02/18/israel-us-veto-settlements-undermines-international-law.

71. Stephen Zunes, "Obama's Veto on Israeli Settlements Demonstrate Contempt for International Humanitarian Law," *The Huffington Post*, March 21, 2011, http://www.huffingtonpost.com/stephen-zunes/obamas-veto-on-israeli-se_b_838060.html.

72. Mohammed Abdulrahman: "Obama's Speech," *Al-Hayat Al-Jadeeda*, May 23, 2011, http://alhayat-j.com/newsite/details.php?opt=1&id=138930&cid=2236.

73. "The Palestinian Plan to Go to the UN Embarrasses Obama and Leaves Israel in a Quandary," *Al-Hayat Al-Jadeeda*, http://www.alhayat-j.com/newsite/details.php?opt=3&id=148091&cid=2350.

74. "Obama Says 1967 'Basis' for Israel-Palestinian Peace, "*BBC*, May 19, 2011, http://www.bbc.co.uk/news/world-us-canada-13464427.

75. Barack Obama, "Remarks by President Obama in Address to the United Nations General Assembly, *The White House, Office of the Press Secretary*, http://www.whitehouse.gov/the-press-office/2011/09/21/remarks-president-obama-address-united-nations-general-assembly," September 21, 2011.

76. Richard Adam's Blog, "Obama Speech at the UN on Palestinian statehood," *The Guardian*, September 21, 2011, http://www.guardian.co.uk/world/2011/sep/21/un-obama-speech-palestine-live.

77. Richard Adam's Blog, "Obama Speech."

78. Richard Adam's Blog, "Obama Speech."

79. James Zogby, "Obama Gets a Second Chance in Arab Public Opinion," *The National*, December 30, 2012, http://www.thenational.ae/thenationalconversation/comment/obama-gets-a-second-chance-in-arab-public-opinion.

80. Zogby, "Obama Gets a Second Chance."

81. Zogby, "Obama Gets a Second Chance."

82. Zogby, "Obama Gets a Second Chance."

83. Abdelbari Atwan, "Obama Turns His Back to the Arabs," *Al-Quds Al-Arabi*, January 21, 2013, http://www.alquds.co.uk/index.asp?fname=data%5C2013%5C01%5C01-21%5C21z999.htm&arc=data%5C2013%5C01%5C01-21%5C21z999.htm.

84. Julie Pace, "Turkey Protests Test Obama's Ties with Erdogan," Yahoo News, June 11, 2013, http://news.yahoo.com/turkey-protests-test-obamas-ties-erdogan-075345785.html.

85. Ben Hubbard, "Mayhem in Cairo as Morsi Backers Fight for Return," *The New York Times*, July 5, 2013, http://www.nytimes.com/2013/07/06/world/middleeast/egypt.html?pagewanted=all&_r=0.

86. Robert Fisk, "When Is a Military Coup not a Military Coup? When it Happens in Egypt, Apparently," *The Independent*, July 4, 2013, http://www.independent.co.uk/voices/comment/when-is-a-military-coup-not-a-military-coup-when-it-happens-in-egypt-apparently-8688000.html.

87. Fisk, "When Is a Military Coup not a Military Coup?"

88. Mark Landler, "Ambassador Becomes Focus of Egyptians' Mistrust of U.S.," *The New York Times*, July 3, 2013,http://www.nytimes.com/2013/07/04/world/middleeast/ambassador-becomes-focus-of-egyptians-mistrust-of-us.html?pagewanted=all.

89. Landler, "Ambassador Becomes Focus of Egyptians' Mistrust of U.S."

90. Landler, "Ambassador Becomes Focus of Egyptians' Mistrust of U.S."

91. "Most Egyptians Oppose U.S. Economic Aid," Gallup World, February 6, 2012, http://www.gallup.com/poll/152471/egyptians-oppose-economic-aid.aspx.

92. Peter Baker, "Egypt Crisis Finds Washington Largely Ambivalent and Aloof," *The New York Times*, July 5, 2013, http://www.nytimes.com/2013/07/06/world/middleeast/egypt-crisis-finds-washington-ambivalent-and-aloof.html?pagewanted=all.

93. David D. Kirkpatrick and Kareem Fahim, "U.S. Warns Egypt's Generals Against Jeopardizing 'Second Chance' at Democracy," *The New York Times*, July 15, 2013, http://www.nytimes.com/2013/07/16/world/middleeast/us-steps-up-public-diplomacy-in-egypt-crisis.html.

94. Michael J. Totten, "US Criticized by Tunisian Secularists for Backing Islamists," *World Affairs Journal*, March 21, 2012, http://www.worldaffairsjournal.org/blog/michael-j-totten/us-criticized-tunisian-secularists-backing-islamists.

95. "Tunisia Court 'Convicts 20' over US Embassy Attack," BBC News, May 28, 2013, http://www.bbc.co.uk/news/world-africa-22698080.

96. "US Shocked by Light Sentences for Salafists Who Attacked Embassy in Tunisia," Herald Tribune, June 2, 2013, http://www.worldtribune.com/2013/06/02/u-s-shocked-by-light-sentences-for-salafists-who-attacked-embassy-in-tunisia/.

97. Eric Schmidt, "Subpoena for Head of Benghazi Panel," *The New York Times*, May 17, 2013, http://www.nytimes.com/2013/05/18/us/subpoena-for-head-of-benghazi-panel.html?_r=0.

98. "Benghazi: State Department 'Pressed to Change' Susan Rice Talking Points," *The Guardian*, May 10, 2013, http://www.guardian.co.uk/world/2013/may/10/benghazi-state-susan-rice-talking-points

99. Chris Stephen, "Army Chief Quits after Militia Kills Dozens in Benghazi," The Guardian, June 9, 2013, http://www.guardian.co.uk/world/2013/jun/09/libya-shield-benghazi-clash-militia.

100. Dan Roberts, "John McCain Makes Surprise Visit to Rebel Leaders in Syria," The Guardian, May 27, 2013, http://www.guardian.co.uk/world/2013/may/27/john-mccain-rebel-leaders-syria.

101. Dan Roberts, "US Says It Will Arm Syrian Rebels Following Chemical Weapons Tests," *The Guardian*, February 14, 2013, http://www.guardian.co.uk/world/2013/jun/13/syria-chemical-weapons-us-confirm.

102. Damien McElroy, "UN Accuses Syrian Rebels of Chemical Weapons Use," *The Telegraph*, May 6, 2013, http://www.telegraph.co.uk/news/worldnews/middleeast/syria/10039672/UN-accuses-Syrian-rebels-of-chemical-weapons-use.html.

103. Editors, "Obama's Confused Syria Policy," Bloomberg, July 17, 2013, http://www.bloomberg.com/news/2013-07-16/obama-s-confused-syria-policy.html.

104. Michael R. Gordon, "Kerry to Focus on Palestinian Economy as Part of Peace Process," *The New York Times*, April 8, 2013, http://www.nytimes.com/2013/04/09/world/kerry-to-focus-on-palestinian-economy-as-part-of-peace-process.html.

105. Michael R. Gordon and Jodi Rudoren, "Kerry Extends Stay in Mideast to Push for Talks," *The New York Times*, July 19, 2013, http://www.nytimes.com/2013/07/20/world/middleeast/kerry-extends-stay-in-mideast-to-push-for-talks.html.

106. "Israel and Palestinians Reach Agreement to Resume Talks," BBC News, July 19, 2013, http://www.bbc.co.uk/news/world-middle-east-23386162

107. Michael Gordon, "Kerry to Focus on Palestinian Economy as Part of Peace Process," *The New York Times*, April 8, 2013, http://www.nytimes.com/2013/04/09/world/kerry-to-focus-on-palestinian-economy-as-part-of-peace-process.html?_r=0.

108. Ian Black, "EU guidelines on Israeli Settlements Send out Powerful Message," *The Guardian*, July 16, 2013, http://www.guardian.co.uk/world/2013/jul/16/eu-guidelines-israeli-settlements-message.

Part VI

ASIA-PACIFIC REGION

16

BENT BY HISTORY IN AFGHANISTAN

Arturo G. Muñoz

In his December 2009 speech to the cadets at West Point, President Barack Obama announced a troop surge of 33,000 additional US soldiers for Afghanistan, while simultaneously setting an 18-month time frame for their withdrawal.[1] This provoked a major controversy and set the parameters as to how the world sees his Afghan foreign policy. From the point of view of whether he is "bending history" in Afghanistan, the 2014 withdrawal timetable may turn out to be one of the key decisions upon which the success or failure of his policy will be judged.[2] Announcing to the Taliban beforehand when US troops will withdraw was heavily criticized as violating one of the ancient rules of war: keep the enemy guessing about one's true intentions and capabilities. Obama's West Point speech addressed this expected criticism: "There are those who oppose identifying a time-frame for our transition to Afghan responsibility. Indeed, some call for a more dramatic and open-ended escalation of our war effort—one that would commit us to a nation-building project of up to a decade. I reject this course because it sets goals that are beyond what can be achieved at a reasonable cost, and what we need to achieve to secure our interests."[3]

Currently, Afghanistan officially is in "transition" leading to full Afghan government responsibility for the war. General John Allen, at the March 2012 House Armed Service Committee Hearing, argued convincingly that this process is on track and that US forces have seriously degraded the Taliban's military capabilities.[4] However, numerous critics have expressed concerns over the pitfalls of this strategy. Barbara Stapleton's article for the *Afghan Analysts Network* provides a good example of this body of criticism:

> To succeed in reaching its objective, the transition process cannot be divorced from actual conditions on the ground with respect to security, governance and development. Implementation of the transition without these conditions being sufficiently in place, in combination with the brevity of a transition timeline that is likely to be accelerated further, increases the risk of the Afghan state's collapse and with it, the prospect of strategic failure for NATO. In the rush to get out of the quagmire that Afghanistan has become, the US and other NATO member states may be preparing the ground for more instability there, rather than less. . . . The idea that the official transition timeline can generate even minimally conducive conditions on the Afghan ground . . . is a delusion.[5]

President Obama evidently hoped that fixing a deadline would change fundamentally the relationship with our Afghan allies, fostering a sense of urgency among them to put their house in order soon and become less dependent on foreigners to get things done. In this regard, a NATO senior civilian representative described the ongoing transition process as a "forcing mechanism" to promote improvement in the performance of the Afghan civilian bureaucracy and military. In her criticism of this strategy, however, Stapleton argues that "a weak government cannot be forced into being a sufficiently strong or effective one through the rushed withdrawal of the support on which it has come to depend."[6]

Similarly, former CIA official Robert Grenier considers the self-imposed deadline for withdrawal of US troops, compounded by the language used in the 2009 speech, as signaling a lack of commitment on the part of the president to the Afghan campaign:

The US president delivered a speech which confounded almost everyone. Giving no indication that he intended a fundamental shift in strategy, the US president announced the "surge" commitment of an additional 33,000 troops, nearly all that his commanders had requested. . . . But there were also myriad indirect indications in that speech that the President's heart was no longer in it. No longer did the President promise the "defeat" of the Taliban; instead, he would "deny their ability to overthrow the government," while buying time in hopes that the Afghan National Army could be expanded at break-neck speed to pick up where the Americans left off. No longer was he promising the resources necessary for success. Instead, he firmly rejected both "open-ended escalation" and the very idea of "a nation-building" project of up to a decade.[7]

In its controversial October 8, 2012 report, *Afghanistan: The Long, Hard Road to the 2014 Transition*, the International Crisis Group (ICG) emphasized that various political and legal reforms must be implemented soon to give the Afghan government the legitimacy and popular support essential for leading the nation after 2014. Afghan officials sharply criticized the ICG for presenting a speculative, excessively pessimistic scenario in its conclusion:

The danger is that President Karzai's top priority is maintaining control, either directly or through a trusted proxy. He and other leading members of the elite may be able to cobble together a broad temporary alliance, but political competition is likely to turn violent on the heels of NATO's withdrawal. There is a genuine risk that security and political developments within the next year could induce the president to invoke a state of emergency. Such a move would not only imperil the state itself but would also undoubtedly encourage the international community's financial and political as well as further military disengagement. This would accelerate state collapse and likely precipitate the next civil war in the country. If that occurs, there would be few opportunities to reverse course in the near term. Securing the peace in Afghanistan would then remain at best a very distant hope.[8]

Looking at the same issue from a different perspective, former British foreign secretary David Miliband in a July 2013 speech admitted that his faith in Western foreign policy had been profoundly shaken. Referring to the "inordinate" human, financial, and political cost of the interventions in Iraq and Afghanistan, he criticized the international community for showing "over-reliance on military power and under-investment in politics and diplomacy." The end result in Afghanistan could well be years of civil war after the US and NATO withdrawal, "as if the Afghan people have not suffered enough."[9]

In contrast to these negative views of the future, young, educated Afghans like to point out that Afghanistan has changed profoundly during the past decade and that a powerful yearning for democracy and progress exists.[10] Some of them argue that foreign observers underestimate Afghan capacity to do what it takes to move their country forward. In the absence of foreign meddling, Afghan negotiators may be able to reach a deal on amnesty and power sharing with the Taliban that will bring them into the political system and end the war. In the countryside, a different argument for optimism can be made based on the proliferation of local uprisings against the Taliban.[11] Despite various forecasts that the Afghan army will collapse after foreign forces withdraw, their combat performance over the past year generally has been good.[12] The determination displayed by some units to confront the enemy belies the pessimism among pundits. Nonetheless, juxtaposed against these favorable reports are contrary accounts of university students who emigrate because they see no hope for the future, villagers who support the Taliban and soldiers who fight poorly. Regardless of which of these conflicting accounts one considers most representative of the overall situation, a key factor influencing the outcome of events often is ignored: American public opinion.

By seeking to avoid "open-ended escalation" in Afghanistan, President Obama is complying with the majority view in the United States. Nationwide polling indicates that Americans have grown weary of the twelve-year war in Afghanistan and increasingly question whether the blood and money being expended in that distant land is worth it. The majority of those surveyed want to end American involvement in the Afghan war. This negative view probably has been aggravated by "green-on-blue" incidents in which Afghan soldiers and policemen have murdered an increasing number of US and NATO servicemen, threatening to create a "trust deficit" between Afghan and coalition forces.[13] Undeterred by this terrorism, Obama has reaffirmed his commitment to the transition process and the strategy to end the American combat role while establishing closer working relationships with Afghans in an advisory and training capacity.[14]

The growing anti-Afghan war sentiment in the US spans political party lines. According to a June 25–26, 2011 Gallup poll, 87% of Democrats surveyed approved of Obama's timetable for withdrawing from Afghanistan, along with 74% Independents and 50% Republicans.[15] The March 2012 *New York Times/CBS News* Poll showed that more than two-thirds of those polled—69%—thought that the United States should not be at war in Afghanistan.

> The *Times/CBS News* poll was consistent with other surveys this month that showed a drop in support for the war. In a *Washington Post/ABC News* poll, 60 percent of respondents said the war in Afghanistan had not been worth the fighting, while 57 percent in a *Pew Research Center* poll said that the United States should bring home American troops as soon as possible. In a *Gallup/USA Today* poll, 50 percent of respondents said the United States should speed up the withdrawal from Afghanistan.[16]

In the April 2012 *Washington Post/ABC* poll, "for the first time, more Republicans and Republican-leaning independents opposed the war than supported it, with 55 percent saying they considered the costs of the war greater than its benefits."[17] In the most recent Washington Post/ABC poll, published July 25, 2013, only 28% of all respondents said that the war in Afghanistan has been worth fighting, "the lowest number on record and clearly below the least-popular stretches of the Iraq war." Overall support for U.S. military operations in Afghanistan dropped eleven percentage points since March 2013. "Declining support crosses demographic and party lines, with double-digit drops among men and women, whites and non-whites, Democrats, Republicans and independents."[18]

On November 29, 2012, the Senate voted overwhelmingly for an accelerated withdrawal of US forces from Afghanistan, with a strong bipartisan vote of 62–33. Thirteen Republicans backed the measure, agreeing with the declaration of the bill's sponsor, Democrat Jeff Merkley: "It is time to end this war, the longest war in United States history."[19] The extent of bipartisan support for withdrawing from Afghanistan became apparent in the debates between Obama and Mitt Romney during the presidential campaign. The Republican candidate did not attack the ongoing transition to Afghan government control, nor did he argue in favor of stopping the withdrawal of US forces. One of the often repeated "lessons of Vietnam" is that the US military should not fight a war that the US public does not support. Afghanistan has slipped into that category.

Some of Obama's critics have charged that announcing a surge constrained by a withdrawal deadline is unprecedented or highly unusual in foreign affairs. That is inaccurate. Although they may not inspire emulation, significant precedents exist. In his research for the US Army War College in Carlisle, *Making a Sandwich in Afghanistan: How to Assess a Strategic Withdrawal from a Protracted Irregular War*, Paul Rexton Kan writes that surges often precede withdrawals: "This is a common feature among the cases—national leaders have contemplated withdrawal more seriously following their nations' escalations, expansions and increased offensives. In many cases, like the US military in South Vietnam and the Red Army in Afghanistan, political leaders actually used the military as a 'final push' to add to the calculus of disengaging."[20]

In the case of Afghanistan, the Soviet leadership had decided by the mid-1980s that the invasion had been a mistake and sought a graceful exit that would preserve its equities in the region. Accordingly, they decided to launch a decisive military offensive 1986/1987 to secure as much territory as possible, cause maximum havoc among the *mujahidin*, and give the communist Afghan regime additional time to build up its armed forces and militias so that they would be able to take over combat operations when the Soviet army withdrew. The objectives of the Soviet surge were very similar to those of Obama, to include a timetable for withdrawal. "Gorbachev reportedly gave the military one more year to achieve victory, 'to prove themselves,' before he would order a withdrawal."[21] Given Obama's limited goals in Afghanistan, and the similarities with the Soviet experience, it is hard to argue that his surge and withdrawal should be seen as an attempt to bend history.

Instead of idealism, a salient feature of the 2009 West Point speech is the frank recognition of the limits of power and the historic dangers of military overextension. Engaging in this type of analytic discussion in announcing a major foreign policy decision seems highly unusual in contemporary American politics. It suggests that Obama had in mind a correlation between economic wealth and military power as articulated in Paul M. Kennedy's *The Rise and Fall of the Great Powers* and was determined to avoid imperial overreach.[22] If we compare Kennedy's thesis with the sober, cautionary language used by Obama—"our prosperity provides a foundation for our power"—it is evident that the president was using that type of academic analysis as his point of reference:

> As President, I refuse to set goals that go beyond our responsibility, our means, or our interests.... Over the past several years, we have lost that balance. We've failed to appreciate the connection between our national security and our economy. In the wake of an economic crisis ... we can't simply afford to ignore the price of these wars. All told, by the time I took office the cost of the wars in Iraq and Afghanistan approached a trillion dollars. Going forward, I am committed to addressing these costs openly and honestly. Our new approach in Afghanistan is likely to cost us roughly $30 billion for the military this year. ... Our prosperity provides a foundation for our power. It pays for our military. It underwrites our diplomacy. It taps the potential of our people, and allows investment in new industry. And it will allow us to compete in this century as successfully as we did in the last. That's why our troop commitment in Afghanistan cannot be open-ended—because the nation that I'm most interested in building is our own.

This can be interpreted as a compelling argument for limited intervention in Afghanistan, and other countries as well, but it seems to have garnered little public scrutiny, in contrast to the copious opinions expressed regarding the specific timetables for troop withdrawals. Lost in the typical politically motivated charges against Obama's foreign policies are a serious discussion of the intellectual underpinnings of this position and the view of history it represents.

The time frame for withdrawal of US and NATO forces and the ongoing transition period are closely correlated to the central mission in Afghanistan as defined by President Obama. According to the perceptive review of his foreign policy in the Brookings Institution's *Bending History,* the mission is primarily counterterrorism, not counterinsurgency.[23] This is a crucial distinction in the effort to assess the reaction to his Afghan policy and make a judgment whether it constitutes an effort to bend history. In his 2009 West Point speech, the stated goals for sending 33,000 additional troops to Afghanistan were to "disrupt, dismantle, and defeat al Qaeda in Afghanistan and Pakistan, and to prevent its capacity to threaten America and our allies in the future."[24] Furthermore, "to meet that goal, we will pursue the following objectives ... deny al Qaeda a safe haven ... reverse the Taliban's momentum and deny it the ability to overthrow the government. And we must strengthen the capacity of Afghanistan's security forces and government so that they can take lead responsibility for Afghanistan's future."[25]

On June 22, 2011, President Obama announced the beginning of the American troop withdrawal called for in 2009. He reiterated the limited counterterrorism mission: "When I announced this surge at West Point, we set clear objectives: to refocus on al Qaeda, to reverse the Taliban's momentum, and train Afghan security forces to defend their own country. I also made it clear that our commitment would not be open-ended and that we would begin to draw down our forces this July."[26] Based on Obama's own publicly stated rationale—denying terrorists a sanctuary to plan attacks on the United States—the basic justification for ramping up a military and civilian surge in Afghanistan is not that much different from the preceding Bush administration. Obama even mentioned the potential danger of al-Qa'ida acquiring nuclear weapons—the previously much publicized terrorism and weapons of mass destruction nexus. However, the 18-month timetable for beginning to withdraw troops is profoundly different. Also, Obama's signature multilateralism marks a different approach. "This burden is not ours alone to bear. This is not just America's war . . . we are joined by a broad coalition of 43 nations that recognizes the legitimacy of our action."[27]

To delve further into the nature of Obama's commitment to the Afghan war, and whether or not it can be viewed as an attempt to bend history, it is useful to delineate distinctions between counterterrorism and counterinsurgency and recapitulate key differences between terrorists and insurgents. Briefly, insurgents seek to become the government and, in pursuit of that overriding goal, they try to establish control over land and people.[28] Indicators of insurgent success in the latter endeavor include the ability to tax the population and recruit among them. This presupposes a political platform with mass appeal and the ability to gain popular support. Insurgents also must have a military capability to confront government forces. This varies with each situation, ranging from rudimentary guerrilla bands limited to hit and run ambushes, to conventional battalions with heavy artillery and tanks. Finally, insurgents sometimes receive international recognition, either as governments-in-exile or as belligerents within their own countries.[29]

In contrast, terrorists generally comprise small groups conducting ideologically or politically motivated acts of violence. They do not control land or people, have little or no military capability, usually do not collect taxes systematically, and lack widespread popular support. Although insurgents frequently practice terrorism as a tactic, terrorists per se should not be categorized as insurgents. Examples of exclusively terrorist groups are the German Bader Meinhoff gang, the Italian Red Brigades, the Japanese Red Army, and the Greek 17 November. When al-Qa'ida attacked New York City, it did so as a terrorist group, displaying no intention to gain control of people or territory, not caring that its actions would be repudiated by everyone in the city. Their objective was to terrify, not rule.

Some analysts conclude that today al-Qa'ida in certain regions has transformed itself into an insurgent movement, an assessment complicated by the fact that al-Qa'ida also has become very decentralized and its allies and surrogates enjoy considerable leeway in planning operations. In 2012, these allies established control over land and people in a vast territory in northern Mali, but the determined counteroffensive led by the French beginning in January 2013 drove their armed units out of the main population centers, a defeat facilitated by their failure to gain essential local support.[30] The Islamic radicals had erred by turning on their tribal Tuareg allies and alienating the large majority of the population by imposing a Draconian version of sharia law which clashed against centuries of local tradition. Similarly, early gains in Somalia were reversed. In contrast, al-Qa'ida and its surrogates in parts of the Afghan–Pakistan border region seem to have achieved much greater success as insurgents, reportedly transforming tribal society. To what degree all of these diverse insurgent movements can be defined as al-Qa'ida is a matter of debate. It may well be that Western politicians and analysts are too fixated on viewing al-Qa'ida as a cohesive, hierarchical organization. Instead, al-Qa'ida should be seen as a loose network bound by a radical Islamic ideology that justifies violence and has the ability to motivate and train people all over the world to engage in terrorism, without any direction from a central command.[31] Despite the increasingly amorphous nature of the threat, the distinctions between terrorism and insurgency remain relevant analytically and operationally.

In general, to destroy an exclusively terrorist group, it is sufficient to kill or capture the terrorists. When the few radicals comprising Bader Meinhoff and the Japanese Red Army were captured, for instance, those terrorist groups disappeared. President Obama's framing of the troop withdrawal from Afghanistan in "mission accomplished" terms seems premature in the light of the Benghazi consulate disaster, but it is nonetheless pegged to the inherent vulnerabilities of a terrorist group:

> We're starting this drawdown from a position of strength. Al Qaeda is under more pressure than at any time since 9/11 . . . we have taken out more than half of al Qaeda's leadership. And . . . killed Osama bin Laden . . . The information that we recovered from bin Laden's compound shows al Qaeda under enormous strain. Bin Laden expressed concern that al Qaeda had been unable to effectively replace senior terrorists that had been killed, and that al Qaeda has failed in its effort to portray America as a nation at war with Islam—thereby draining more widespread support. Al Qaeda remains dangerous, and we must be vigilant against attacks. But we have put al Qaeda on a path to defeat, and we will not relent until the job is done.[32]

In retrospect, the degree to which al-Qa'ida indeed is on the "path to defeat" is open to question. Recent research by Seth Jones, who has followed closely al-Qa'ida's trajectory since 9/11, concludes that "far from being dead and buried, the terrorist organization is now riding a resurgent tide as its affiliates engage in an increasingly violent campaign of attacks across the Middle East and North Africa . . . al Qaeda's bloody fingerprints are increasingly evident."[33] Jones argues that not only has the size of al-Qa'ida's global network dramatically expanded, but it is also carrying out an increasing number of attacks. Regardless of this assessment of a resurgent al-Qa'ida, however, insurgent groups generally possess greater resilience and human resources than exclusively terrorist groups.

A strong, well-organized insurgent group like the Colombian Revolutionary Armed Forces (FARC) can suffer devastating losses in manpower and leadership, yet continue to function, thanks to its long-established control of land and people, popular revolutionary ideology and military capabilities. Compared to terrorists, insurgent groups tend to display greater longevity. The FARC has fought the Colombian government continuously since 1964; in the Philippines, the New People's Army has been in rebellion since 1969. In contrast, a Combating Terrorism Center study concludes that the average life span of a terrorist group is eight years.[34]

Terrorist groups under pressure often break up or meld with others to form new groups under new names or disappear altogether. Algeria's Armed Islamic Group (GIA), for example, was formed in 1992 and effectively ceased to function by 2002. In 1998, a GIA dissident faction formed the Salafist Group for Preaching and Combat, which in turn melded with al-Qa'ida in 2006 to become Al-Qa'ida in the Islamic Maghreb.[35] Similarly, Egypt's al-Gama'a al-Islamiyya splintered in 1997 into rival groups over a ceasefire announcement by one faction, followed by the massacre of tourists at Luxor by the more radical faction. As of this writing, neither faction is operating in Egypt.

In the case of Afghanistan, al-Qai'da allied itself with the Taliban when it was the government between 1996 and 2001 and this continuing alliance remains the main justification for the US intervention. However, the nature of the relationship with al-Qa'ida today varies among the different factions comprising the Taliban insurgent movement. Many Taliban fighters do not interact directly with the relatively few al-Qa'ida members present in Afghanistan. Nonetheless, the Taliban movement over the years has been influenced by al-Qa'ida's ideology and has adopted some of its terrorist tactics, notably suicide bombings, which had not been seen in Afghanistan prior to 2001. Like many others throughout the world, the Afghan Taliban are insurgents who practice terrorism as a tactic.

As a general rule, applying a counterterrorist strategy to an insurgency is likely to produce only limited results. Counterterrorism is not a viable substitute for counterinsurgency. By keeping his focus on counterterrorism in Afghanistan, President Obama is limiting the scope of American intervention, but this does not promote the long-term solution to the problem of instability and violence postulated by a strategy of counterinsurgency.[36]

In his impassioned critique of Obama's Afghan foreign policy, Grenier insists that the counterinsurgency mission required in Afghanistan should not be ignored. Moreover he disputes a basic assumption of the 2011 speech that the withdrawal of US troops is taking place from a position of strength:

> Of course, the president would have US believe that the steady drawdown he plans is based on the success of the surge he launched in December 2009. Nothing, in fact, could be further from the truth. Yes, US troops have predictably made considerable inroads against the Taliban in the South; but the President also has to know that these gains cannot be maintained, as the Afghan government lacks either the military or governing capacity to sustain them. This will not matter, however: Irrespective of the conditions, the president intends to withdraw.[37]

Top of Form

In contrast, *New York Times* reporter David Sanger takes a more sympathetic view of Obama's decision-making process concerning Afghanistan:

> Mr. Obama concluded in his first year that the Bush-era dream of remaking Afghanistan was a fantasy. . . . So he narrowed the goals in Afghanistan, and narrowed them again, until he could make the case that America had achieved limited objectives in a war that was, in any traditional sense, unwinnable. . . . Mr. Obama began to question why Americans were dying to prop up a leader, President Hamid Karzai of Afghanistan, who was volatile, unreliable and willing to manipulate the ballot box. Faced with an economic crisis at home . . . he was also shocked . . . by the war's cost . . . he also began to reassess whether emerging victorious in Afghanistan was as necessary as he had once proclaimed. Ultimately, Mr. Obama agreed to double the size of the American force while training the Afghan armed forces, but famously insisted that, whether America was winning or losing, the drawdown would begin in just 18 months. "I think he hated the idea from the beginning," one of his advisers said of the surge. "He understood why we needed to try, to knock back the Taliban. But the military was "all in," as they say, and Obama wasn't.[38]

Despite his reported lack of enthusiasm, Obama did embrace counterinsurgency temporarily at the beginning of his administration.

In his 2009 West Point speech Obama made comments that fall within the scope of counterinsurgency and nation-building: "We'll support Afghan ministries, governors, and local leaders that combat corruption and deliver for the people. . . . And we will also focus our assistance in areas—such as agriculture—that can make an immediate impact in the lives of the Afghan people."[39] *Bending History* summarizes the grim situation posed by a resurgent Taliban and concludes: "Against such a backdrop, as it appeared in 2009, Obama decided that he had little choice but to try a classic counterinsurgency approach . . . he saw the stability of Afghanistan as crucial, given the potential for that country to otherwise offer safe haven to extremist groups. . . . Counterinsurgency methods were seen as needed to achieve a counterterrorism objective."[40]

By appointing General Stanley McChrystal as ISAF commander, Obama put a man in charge who was committed to a daring vision of counterinsurgency. In looking for evidence of a concrete initiative that tried to bend history, McChrystal's 2009 *ISAF Commander's Counterinsurgency Guidance* fits that criterion:

> We need to understand the people and see things through their eyes. It is their fears, frustrations and expectations we must address. We will not win simply by killing insurgents. We will help the Afghan people win by securing them, by protecting them from intimidation, violence, and abuse, and by operating in a way that respects their culture and religion. This means that we

must change the way that we think, act and operate. We must get the people involved as active participants in the success of their communities.

Every action we take must reflect this change: how we interact with people, how we drive or fly, how we patrol, how we use force, how we fund work projects and programs. This is their country and we are their guests.

An insurgency cannot be defeated by attrition; its supply of fighters, and even leadership, is effectively endless. . . . The intricate familial, clan and tribal connections of Afghan society . . . will want vengeance. . . . This is part of the reason why eight years of individually successful kinetic actions have resulted in more violence. The math works against an attrition mind-set. . . .

The will of the people is the Objective. An effective "offensive" operation in counterinsurgency, therefore, is one that takes from the insurgents what they cannot afford to lose—control of the population.[41]

This vision of counterinsurgency was not new. It was consistent with the 2006 US Army *Counterinsurgency* manual, the earlier USMC *Small Wars* manual and other many writings on the subject going back to the campaigns against communist guerrillas in various parts of the world between the 1950s and the 1980s.[42]

However, McChrystal adapted standard counterinsurgency strategy to the situation he faced in Afghanistan in an innovative manner, articulating his thinking with particularly blunt, compelling language. The 2009 *ISAF Commander's Counterinsurgency Guidance* should be required reading in the genre of counterinsurgency literature. It can be assumed that President Obama played no direct role in formulating it. Nevertheless, as commander-in-chief, he ultimately was responsible for it and its content was entirely consistent with his approach to foreign policy.

However, the announcement of a deadline for withdrawal preceded by a major drawdown of US forces posed fundamental obstacles to the implementation of the strategy proposed by McChrystal. Basically, Obama seemed to back the idea, but did not give his commander enough time or resources to implement it. In response to the political flap caused by the *Rolling Stone* article alleging inappropriate or insubordinate statements by the general's staff regarding their superiors in Washington, President Obama relieved McChrystal of his command in June 2010 and replaced him with General David Petraeus.[43] Although Petraeus had approved of McChrystal's innovative counterinsurgency, the new commander took a different approach, giving more emphasis to kinetic operations to drive the Taliban out of key areas before the 2014 deadline.

In the relatively brief period in which McChrystal could act on his own advice, he did back up his words with actions. To carry out his mandate to "get the people involved as active participants in the success of their communities," he supported the ground-breaking Local Defense Initiative (LDI). Emulating the traditional Pashtun tribal *arbakai* (community police) organized by the council of elders (*jirga*), the LDI constituted a volunteer civil defense force of local villagers against the Taliban. This is a classic counterinsurgency measure that has proven its worth all over the world, given the constant problem of insufficient troops to patrol vast areas of countryside.

Despite its high-potential value, the LDI encountered opposition from its inception, not only from within the US foreign policy establishment, but also journalists, academics, and certain sectors of the Afghan government—all fearing the revival of uncontrollable tribal militias. Strong opposition from Ambassador Eikenbery combined with the removal of General McChrystal doomed LDI.[44] It was reformulated as Village Stability Operations (VSO) under General Petraeus, who gave orders to expand the program aggressively, fusing it with the version favored by the Afghan government, the Afghan Local Police (ALP).[45] In its 2012 review of the program, the *Small Wars Journal* concludes that it is "having a positive impact on security and governance at the local level in Afghanistan."[46] In his review of the implementation of the program in a Khas Uruzgan, Major Brandon Bissell writes:

The introduction of ALP has been one of the most influential programs for us in garnering support. . . . By giving Afghans the ability to secure themselves and their own villages we have given them a real choice that they didn't have before. . . . Both Special Forces teams operating in the district over the last 12 months had understood the environment, had understood the limitations and had understood available resources. They were operating under significant constraints, but incorporating into the plan what they knew about the culture and what was important to the people of Khas Uruzgan had assisted in building the populace's confidence in their own abilities and those of their government officials. Consolidating this new belief and confidence with programs like ALP and governance systems like the Tribal Leadership Council allowed significant strides to be made. . . . By no means is the district completely secure. However, with a governing council in place that is representative of the tribes and villages, a district chief of police that is impartial and respected, and an internally developed local police force that is capable of providing a defense against insurgent operations, the people of Khas Uruzgan have made major progress in a short period of time. . . .[47]

The Taliban see local defense forces as a serious threat and are trying to weaken them by assassinating their leaders and members, sending night letters threatening retribution. At the same time, the ability and willingness of the Afghan government to take over the American support role during the ongoing transition period is in doubt.[48] Today this innovative program is at a critical juncture, aggravated by "green on blue" incidents and negative media reports about abuses by ALP members. President Obama, except for a brief mention in a speech referring favorably to the formation of local police, has taken a neutral role on this issue.[49] He remained silent when General McChrystal and Ambassador Eikenbery clashed over LDI and today is not taking a public position on VSO/ALP. Whether these civil defense forces succeed or fail, the Obama administration is letting the commanders in the field handle it. Ultimately, this may be the most prudent course of action—avoiding micromanagement from Washington—but this is not bending history.

Another hallmark of McChrystal's approach to counterinsurgency consisted of new directives regulating air strikes and the use of firepower in combat operations in populated areas—clearly intended to reduce civilian casualties. In so doing, he addressed the single biggest complaint of the Afghan population against coalition forces. Public opinion polls consistently showed that Afghans held NATO and US forces responsible for the deaths of innocent civilians killed in air strikes and combat operations.[50] President Karzai himself expressed this popular sentiment, repeatedly condemning deaths of innocent Afghan civilians caused by air strikes.

In 2011, shortly after a NATO air strike in Kunar reportedly killed sixty-two civilians by mistake, including women and children, an American helicopter crew mistook nine boys collecting firewood for Taliban guerrillas and strafed them.[51] Karzai traveled to Kunar Province to attend their funerals. Speaking to their grieving parents he declared emotionally: "I would like to ask NATO and the US . . . to stop their operations in our land. . . . We are very tolerant people but now our tolerance has run out."[52] McChrystal was unusual in that he took these complaints to heart and implemented directives changing the conduct of operations to minimize civilian casualties. Soldiers complained that they were being put at greater risk, but President Karzai greatly appreciated the new directives because they did reduce civilian casualties.[53] When the *Rolling Stone* flap broke, Karzai expressed support for the beleaguered general and made entreaties to keep him in place, to no avail.

During the controversy over air strikes, the White House proved to be ambivalent, lamenting civilian casualties while backing tactical measures that kept American men and women safer in a combat zone. Obama did not take a bold position on this politically sensitive issue. For example, in May 2009, General James Jones, the president's security adviser, responded to Karzai's public admonition that the United States would lose the "moral fight" against the Taliban if it kept killing civilians during the conduct of military operations by declaring: "We're going to take a look at trying to make sure we correct those things we can correct, but certainly to tie the hands of our commanders and say we're not going to conduct airstrikes would be imprudent. We can't fight with one hand tied behind our back."[54]

In contrast to his hands-off attitude toward local defense forces and air strikes, President Obama initially took a much more decisive stance toward development projects. In March 2009, he announced a historic "Whole of Government" interagency effort in Afghanistan.[55] The Obama administration described it as a civilian surge aimed at improving Afghan living standards, complementing the military surge approved the same year. Sixteen US government agencies, chiefly the US Department of State, the US Agency for International Development, and the US Department of Agriculture, began an ambitious program to recruit, train, and deploy US civilian development experts to work in conjunction with their US and NATO military counterparts in provincial capitals and district centers. Not since the Vietnam War's CORDS (Civil Operations and Rural Development Support) program had the United States deployed such a large number (over 1,000) of civilian "expeditionary diplomats" to work alongside the military, in essence, implementing civic action in a counterinsurgency environment.[56] By early November 2009, the first waves of civilians arrived in Afghanistan to work with Provincial Reconstruction Teams and District Support Teams. By 2013 progress has undoubtedly been achieved. Statistics from diverse sources show that Afghanistan has made great strides in education, healthcare, women's rights, economic development, and reconstruction.[57]

Nevertheless, in evaluating whether the "Whole of Government" approach and the civilian surge constituted an attempt to bend history to justice, the answer would have to be a "no" because history was bent in that direction already. Although President Obama's approach was innovative, the basic goals and methods essentially were the same as that of the preceding Bush administration. Copious literature exists on the humanitarian, development, and good governance projects implemented before President Obama's 2009 initiative. Particularly useful is Robert Kemp's 2011 *Military Review* article "Provincial Reconstructions Teams in Eastern Afghanistan: Utility as a Counterinsurgency Tool," based partly on his own experiences between 2004 and 2008 in that region.[58]

In addition, there has been such a broad-based, multinational effort involving both government agencies and nongovernmental agencies seeking to promote progress in Afghanistan that no single country or leader can take credit for it. In his opening remarks to the May 2012 conference in Chicago of foreign donors and allies to formalize accords for continuing assistance to Afghanistan after 2014, Obama praised the multinational nature of the aid effort in Afghanistan, which fits squarely with his multilateral approach to foreign policy: "The presence of so many leaders and nations illustrates once again that this is a truly international mission, and that's because the region and the world have a profound interest in an Afghanistan that is stable, that is secure, and that is not a source of attacks on other nations. . . . Our nations and the world have a vital interest in the success of this mission."[59]

In his 2009 West Point speech, President Obama addressed the Afghan public directly and stated, "We have no interest in occupying your country."[60] He reiterated that "America has no interest in fighting an endless war in Afghanistan."[61] Nonetheless, what Obama puts forth to American audiences as a pragmatic approach based on a nuanced understanding of the limits of power, many Afghans see as America reneging on its promises to help rebuild their country. The Western powers went into Afghanistan proclaiming that their intervention would suppress terrorism and bring about social and economic progress. Today terrorism is worse than ever.

Violence has spread to previously stable areas including the overwhelmingly anti-Taliban Hazara province of Bamiyan. Suicide bombers and IEDs seem unstoppable, wreaking havoc on civilians and government personnel alike throughout the country, most recently the chief of the Afghan intelligence service himself was wounded seriously by a suicide bomber who came to him as a peace envoy from the Taliban.[62] In Helmand Province, the scene of the highly successful counterinsurgency campaign carried out by the US Marines in targeted localities, the Taliban recently beheaded seventeen people who attended a wedding and violated Taliban-imposed rules against mixed gender gatherings, dancing and music.[63] In Paktika's Sar Hawza district, following the scaling back of US military patrols in August 2012, the Taliban have killed more than twenty-five local ALP members, with seven beheaded in Marzak.[64] Many more examples of worsening violence can be cited.[65]

The Afghan *Pajhwok* news agency conducted a public opinion survey in December 2011 on the US military presence.[66] The results were mixed, with some surveyed stating that the foreigners did more harm than good and should leave:

- "Foreign troops have not come to our country to help us but to destroy it." —Muhammad Saleem, Paktia Province
- "We ask people of US to put pressure on their government, to stop killing of innocent people in Afghanistan." —Burhan-ud-Din, Samangan Province
- "US should respect religion and culture of Afghans." —Naqibullah, Nimroz Province
- Afghans can provide better security. "I want to tell US, our own army is enough strong by now to secure the country and foreign forces should withdraw as they are not effective." —Gran, Aibak city

These negative views on the US presence in Afghanistan corroborate the assessment of Ahmed Rashid, a long-time observer of Afghan affairs: "The Afghan people are exhausted by a war that has gone on in one form or other since 1979. . . . Increasing numbers of Afghans would agree with what the Taliban have been arguing for almost a decade: that the western presence in Afghanistan is prolonging the war, causing misery and bloodshed. The hundreds of civilians killed already this year across the country are almost forgotten now in the aftermath of the killing of children by a *farengi*, or foreigner."[67]

Civilian casualties caused by air strikes or combat operations continue to harm coalition forces public relations with the Afghan public, a situation aggravated by the case of the apparently deranged US soldier who wandered off base at night to murder women and children in a nearby village.[68] While reaction to that massacre was relatively muted, perhaps because Afghans have become desensitized to the deaths of civilians after thirty years of war, the burning of the Qur'an by US troops was repudiated widely as an intolerable, sacrilegious act. Like the killings of civilians, the Qur'an burnings were accidental, but a decade of accidents has taken its toll on Afghan perceptions of the United States, and by extension the image of President Obama.

In his typically negative assessment of US policies in Afghanistan, Gilles Dorronsoro, currently with the Carnegie Endowment for International Peace, concludes: "Mistakes have turned public opinion against the foreign troop presence—even among Afghans who originally welcomed US troops and who remain ideologically against the Taliban."[69] In a December 7, 2012 article in the *Washington Post*, a villager from Wardak province interviewed after the Taliban bombed his town expressed intense resentment against both the Americans and the Taliban: "We have nowhere to stand. We have trouble with the government, the Americans and the Taliban too. . . . We don't even feel human. . . . I know we will suffer more when the American forces go, but we are fed up with them too. We don't expect much from the Taliban except beatings, but the Americans are supposed to bring laws and principles. What we have here now is just chaos."[70]

Nevertheless, the majority opinion expressed in the *Pajhwok* survey favors the foreign presence as beneficial, with the corollary that Americans should not withdraw until progress and security are achieved. The following comments are representative of that view point:

- "US should not leave us alone after 2014 as she had done after the war with USSR." —Muhammad Amin Azizi, a Balkh Provincial official
- "US should not leave soon as Afghan security forces are unable to bring peace in the country without their help." —Arzu Noorzad, Badakhshan Province

- "They would witness civil war and internal conflicts in the country if foreign forces withdrew." —Shah Arab Darwishi, Badakhshan Province
- "I want US to fulfill her promises, such as support for democracy, freedom of speech, women's rights and human rights which were made by them." —Farid Ihsas, Farah Province
- "If International Community especially US left Afghanistan, they would experience the situation of 1990s in the country again." —Muhammad Yaqub Maftoon, freelance reporter
- "US must not leave Afghanistan soon because I know Taliban would not join any peace process." —Farida, high school principal
- "US should help Afghans in bringing peace and stability as was promised and they must keep that promise." —Muhammad Usman, Herat Province
- The US should help Afghanistan in education, military, and economic sectors. "US should not leave Afghanistan soon." —Khan Mohammed, college student Ghor Province

Some respondents expressed intense ambivalence in the same response:

- "I am agreed with US presence but they must know their limits, not to kill innocent people. . . . My business has grown after US presence but disappointment among people is growing day by day which must be stopped. . . . US should learn a lesson from past experiences in Afghanistan and they should not offend Afghans, otherwise they will be ashamed like Russians and English." —Haji Abdul Hakim, Faryab Province
- "US should implement important and basic projects in Afghanistan but there must be transparency in it." —Farzana Qayumi, Farah Province

The mixed findings of the *Pajhwok* agency poll track with those of the 2011 Asia Foundation poll, which has been surveying Afghan public opinion since 2006. Nearly half the 6,348 Afghans surveyed in all of the country's 34 provinces said the country was moving in the right direction—a trend that has held up since 2008. The survey also showed continued high esteem for the Afghan army and growing confidence in government at the provincial and district levels.[71] Other positive results, which corroborate the biannual Defense Department report to Congress, include:

- The majority of respondents report satisfaction with the availability of most basic services.
- More people report an annual improvement across all areas of economic well-being.
- More than half of respondents say they are aware of development projects related to reconstruction/building of roads and bridges and education in their local areas.
- Overall satisfaction with the performance of the national government has remained the same as in 2010 with 73% of respondents saying the government is doing a good job.
- More than two-thirds of respondents (69%) say they are satisfied with the way democracy works in Afghanistan.[72]

The 2012 Asia Foundation poll also contains an essentially positive outlook for the future and broad recognition of the progress that has been made.[73] It should be noted, however, that the accuracy of polling in general in Afghanistan has been questioned, to include the Asia Foundation; the latter has been criticized for not polling in contested or dangerous areas and thus skewing results. Given the potential for reprisals, some critics also assume that many respondents in rural villages do not express their true opinions when questioned by strangers.

Moreover, the rosy picture presented in these national level polls clashes with various assessments presenting much more negative conclusions, particularly those written in 2012. For example, Rashid wrote in March: "Faced with an increasingly corrupt and incompetent government, Afghans are seeing fewer improvements on the ground. So-called 'nation building' has ground to a halt, simple justice and rule of law is unobtainable and a third of the population is suffering from malnutrition.

The people blame not just the Americans but equally Hamid Karzai and his inner circle, which gives him conflicting and contradictory advice, leading him to flip and flop on policy issues."[74]

In a similar vein, the 2012 Gallup poll conclusions state: "Afghans on average rate their current lives a low 3.88 showing no gains since dropping from a high of 4.76 in 2010. Afghans' outlook for their future remains near its lowest point since Gallup began asking this question in 2008."[75] In sharp contrast to the Asia Foundation results, Gallup states: "Despite more than a decade of international development efforts, Afghans' satisfaction with their standard of living has steadily deteriorated, which may partly explain their bleak outlook on their lives and their increasing worry. Average satisfaction with standard of living, at 29% remained low and flat between 2011 and 2012—much lower than the majority of Afghans who were satisfied as recently as 2009."[76]

Gallup and Asia Foundation findings coincide in describing growing concern over insecurity. In the Asia Foundation survey, "Insecurity is again the most commonly cited reason for pessimism, and again identified as the most important problem facing Afghanistan. More than half of respondents (56%) say they fear for their personal safety in their local area."[77] However, the results vary regionally: "The highest proportions of respondents who report fearing for their safety are in the Southeast, West and East. There have been significant increases in the incidence of crime and violence experienced by respondents of those same regions since 2010."[78]

The Gallup poll ties the negative perceptions of Afghan respondents regarding their future to the 2014 deadline for the withdrawal of the US and the ongoing transition process: "In the run-up to NATO's exit from Afghanistan, Afghans are also more likely to say they experience stress and worry, according to 2012 data."[79] Anxiety over the consequences of the drawdown of US and NATO forces aggravates concerns over deteriorating security and living standards:

> Afghans' increasing dissatisfaction with their standard of living likely has much to do with their bleak outlook on their lives. Residents may also have doubts about their future in a post-NATO Afghanistan as Taliban insurgency and ongoing violence continue to wrack the country. Afghans' pessimism about their future, bolstered by increased levels of stress and worry, portend a difficult road to stability and prosperity following military withdrawal. In a country where 95% of GDP consists of foreign aid, continued international support for Afghanistan's civilian infrastructure remains indispensable in ensuring that a growing humanitarian crisis doesn't envelop the country's most vulnerable citizens during what will likely be a difficult transition process.[80]

To Afghans worried about the future, the April 2012 announcement of Afghan defense minister, General Abdul Rahim Wardak, regarding the planned reduction in the size of the Afghan National Security Forces (ANSF—including army, police, and border protection forces) likely intensified their anxiety. Wardak declared that the ANSF would decline from the projected peak strength of 352,000 in 2012 to 230,000 after 2014, assuming a reduced annual budget of $4.1 billion.[81] Thus the number of Afghan soldiers needed to fight the insurgents is expected to decline, not increase, after the NATO and US withdrawal of combat forces. In a similar vein, because of disputes and delays in the US military bidding and contracting system, the Afghan Air Force will not receive needed warplanes until 2016, three years after the ANSF is scheduled to take the lead in combat operations requiring that type of air support.[82]

Stapleton's critique of the withdrawal timetable suggests that Afghan worries about the future are well-founded and that President Obama's policy does not inspire confidence:

> NATO's effective abandonment of a conditions-based approach in implementing the transition has in practice been rendered unavoidable by the brevity of the transition's timeline. But the weakness of Afghan institutions that may be subjected to additional and intense economic and political pressures linked to the transition, beyond the challenges of taking over responsibility for security makes the risk of state collapse all the greater. So far, the US and NATO member

states have shown no sign of reconsidering the viability of the transition timeline despite multiple factors, including the state of the Afghan security forces, that makes this essential. Instead, the priority of the NATO member states most prominently engaged in Afghanistan is to keep the transition timetable on track, or even speed it up.[83]

In conclusion, those Afghans opposed to the presence of foreign forces in their country are undoubtedly happy to see them leave. Although it can be assumed they support Obama's timetable for withdrawing US forces, they are not likely to give him credit for it as they do not think the surge he ordered was justified or produced long-term benefits. Ordering troops home that should never have been sent to Afghanistan in the first place is unlikely to promote a favorable view of Obama's presidency among this sector of the Afghan population.

However, the majority view among Afghans seems to favor a continuation of the foreign presence. According to this viewpoint, foreigners should be appreciated for helping to drive the oppressive Taliban from power and bringing economic and social progress. However, the job is not finished. There is still much to be done and the United States and NATO should continue to play a constructive role. Among these Afghans, the announced deadline for withdrawal of US forces and the ongoing transition process are producing intense anxiety about the future.

The Strategic Partnership Agreement signed by Afghanistan and the United States in 2012 intends to affirm the long-range commitment of the United States to Afghan security. However, the details of this commitment remain to be worked out. Per this plan, a still undetermined number of American soldiers will continue to provide advice and training and other support to the Afghan military, police, and VSO/ALP, assuming that a mutually acceptable Status of Forces agreement is reached. A small contingent of US Special Forces would still conduct raids jointly with their Afghan counterparts against terrorists. Augmenting this continuing military presence, the United States and other donor nations pledged to continue financial assistance at the Chicago conference. However, many Afghans question the reliability of these pledges.

As of this July 2013 update, the crucial negotiations over implementation of the Strategic Partnership Agreement have been suspended by Karzai ostensibly in protest over US handling of peace talks with the Taliban. The clock is ticking. If some US forces are to remain, a certain amount of lead time is needed for logistical and personnel planning. Partly in response to this unexpected and capricious suspension of talks, the White House reportedly is considering accelerating the troop withdrawal and adopting a "zero option" leaving no US forces behind after 2014.[84] US military commanders and others have warned against this possibility, saying that it would jeopardize hard-fought gains.[85] Some observers have called it a negotiating ploy, but, depending on Karzai's response, it could become a policy decision.

Prospects for resolving this impasse are not helped by recent news reporting that the Afghan government is taxing heavily every container of US military material and equipment being shipped out of the country as part of the withdrawal.[86] This will probably bolster a perception of Afghan ingratitude among American politicians and policymakers, already incensed by Karzai's public criticisms of the United States, and bolster their desire to pull out. Whatever the case may turn out to be, current publicity on the zero option likely adds to the uncertainty in Afghanistan and exacerbates anxiety among those Afghans who repudiate Karzai's outbursts and favor a continuing US presence.

According to multiple sources, the United States and NATO are giving Afghans the impression they are "beating a retreat," an impression reinforced by budget cuts that already are being felt, personnel reductions, programs being cut back, and closing of bases. Various NATO countries have accelerated their dates of departure, a point gleefully noted by Taliban propaganda, which has always painted Obama's 2014 deadline as an admission of defeat. Despite contradictions in the polling data, Afghan public opinion about the future generally is bleak. There is talk of civil war. The recent collapse of peace talks with the Taliban may be only a temporary setback, but it gives the impression that fighting will continue uninterrupted after US and NATO forces withdraw and perhaps intensify. As a key architect of this worrisome situation, Obama does not seem to enjoy much popularity among Afghans, even among those who tend to be pro-American. There is no indication that Afghans see him as having a special insight into the problems of Muslim people. They do not consider he bent history in favor of justice in their country.

On the contrary, anti-Taliban Afghans tend to feel that they are being abandoned again by the United States and are not convinced by assurances otherwise. The Afghan case suggests that, instead of multicultural or multilateral idealism, President Obama is driven by pragmatic *realpolitik* and the pursuit of US interests foremost. Although Afghans may be unhappy with his foreign policy regarding their country, it reflects the will of the American people.

Notes

1. "Remarks by the President in Address to the Nation on the Way Forward in Afghanistan and Pakistan," The White House, Office of the Press Secretary, December 1, 2009, US Military Academy at West Point, http://www.whitehouse.gov/the-press-office/remarks-president-address-nation-way-forward-afghanistan-and-pakistan.
2. "Bending history towards justice" is a theme in Obama's speeches recalling Martin Luther King's line about the long arc of history bending toward justice. In a foreign relations context the best articulation may be in Obama's Nobel Peace Prize acceptance speech: "Our actions matter and can bend history in the direction of justice"; see "Barack Obama's Nobel Peace Prize Speech," December 10, 2009," http://articles.nydailynews.com/2009-12-10/news/17942536_1_war-and-peace-norwegian-nobel-committee-norway.
3. "Remarks by the President in Address to the Nation on the Way Forward in Afghanistan and Pakistan" 2009.
4. "Transcript: Gen. John Allen says successful Afghan transition is 'linchpin' to US strategy," March 22, 2012, http://www.whatthefolly.com/2012/03/22/transcript-gen-john-allen-says-successful-afghan-transition-is-linchpin-to-u-s-strategy/.
5. Barbara Stapleton, "Beating a Retreat: Prospects for the Transition Process in Afghanistan," *Afghan Analysts Network*, May 2012, http://www.aan-afghanistan.com/uploads/20120516_ExecSum_Beating_a_Retreat.pdf.
6. Stapleton, "Beating a Retreat."
7. Robert Grenier, "What Is Obama's Afghanistan Plan? Obama's 'Way Forward' with Respect to Afghanistan Leaves Many Baffled and Questioning His Motives," July 1, 2011, http://www.aljazeera.com/indepth/opinion/2011/06/2011629113850508883.htm.
8. See http://www.crisisgroup.org/~/media/Files/asia/south-asia/afghanistan/236-afghanistan-the-long-hard-road-to-the-2014-transition.pdf.
9. http://worldnewsviews.com/2013/07/13/david-milibands-farewell-blast-at-wests-failings-in-iraq-and-afghanistan/.
10. Author interview with Afghan democracy activist employed by US NGO, October 15, 2012.
11. See http://articles.latimes.com/2013/jun/01/world/la-fg-afghanistan-uprising-20130602; http://www.nytimes.com/2013/03/21/world/asia/afghan-villages-rise-up-against-taliban.html?pagewanted=all;http://online.wsj.com/article/SB10000872396390444620104578006201295641128.html.
12. See http://www.nytimes.com/2013/06/16/world/asia/afghan-forces-taking-lead-hold-steady-in-violent-district.html?pagewanted=all&_r=0; and http://www.stripes.com/news/middle-east/ground-forces-commander-cautiously-optimistic-about-afghan-military-performance-1.229862.
13. "Trust Deficit a Risk in Afghanistan," United Press International, September 7, 2012, http://www.upi.com/Top_News/Special/2012/09/07/TrUSt-deficit-a-risk-in-Afghanistan/UPI-98791347028310/#ixzz265FiRM9F; According to *The Long War Journal* between January 1, 2008, and November 11, 2012, there have been sixty-nine "green on blue" attacks, with forty-two occurring in 2012; seehttp://www.longwarjournal.org/archives/2012/08/green-on-blue_attack.php.
14. "Obama Sticks to Afghanistan Transition Plan Despite Green-on-Blue Attacks," *The Guardian*, August 21, 2012, http://www.guardian.co.uk/world/2012/aug/21/barack-obama-afghanistan-green-on-blue.
15. http://www.gallup.com/poll/148313/americans-broadly-favor-obama-afghanistan-pullout-plan.aspx; also see http://thinkprogress.org/security/2012/04/19/467247/pew-poll-low-support-afghanistan/?mobile=nc.
16. Elisabeth Bumillerr and Allison Kopicki, "Support in US for Afghan War Drops Sharply, Poll Finds." *New York Times,* March 26, 2012, http://www.nytimes.com/2012/03/27/world/asia/support-for-afghan-war-falls-in-US-poll-finds.html.
17. Ariel Edwards-Levy, "Afghanistan Poll: Majority Of Republicans No Longer Support War," *The Huffington Post*, March 12, 2012, http://www.huffingtonpost.com/2012/04/12/afghanistan-poll-republicans-war_n_1420697.html.

18. Karen De Young and Scott Clement, "Many Americans Say Afghan War Isn't Worth Fighting," *Washington Post*, July 25, 2013, http://articles.washingtonpost.com/2013-07-25/world/40862986_1_afghan-war-total-u-s-casualties-afghanistan.

19. Donna Cassata, "Senate Backs Quicker Afghanistan Withdrawal," *Associated Press*, November 29, 2012, http://www.armytimes.com/news/2012/11/ap-senate-backs-quicker-afghanistan-withdrawal-112912/.

20. Paul Rexton Kan, *Making a Sandwich in Afghanistan: How to Assess a Strategic Withdrawal from a Protracted Irregular War*, (Carlisle, US Army War College, February 24, 2011) published by the *Small Wars Journal* at http://www.dtic.mil/dtic/tr/fulltext/u2/a546496.pdf.

21. Ibid; also see Svetlana Savranskaya, (ed.) Volume II, *Afghanistan Lessons from the Last War: The Soviet Experience in Afghanistan—Russian Documents and Memoirs* (George Washington University National Security Archive, October 9, 2001) athttp://www.gwu.edu/~nsarchiv/NSAEBB/NSAEBB57/soviet.html.

22. Paul M. Kennedy, *The Rise and Fall of the Great Powers: Economic Change and Military Conflict from 1500 to 2000* (New York: Random House, 1989).

23. Martin S. Indyk, et al., *Bending History: Barrack Obama's Foreign Policy* (Washington, DC: Brookings Institution Press, 2012), 86–99.

24. "Remarks by the President in Address to the Nation on the Way Forward in Afghanistan and Pakistan," The White House, Office of the Press Secretary, West Point, December 1, 2009, http://www.whitehoUSe.gov/the-press-office/remarks-president-address-nation-way-forward-afghanistan-and-pakistan.

25. Ibid.

26. "Remarks by the President on the Way Forward in Afghanistan." The White House, Office of the Press Secretary, June 22, 2011, http://www.whitehoUSe.gov/the-press-office/2011/06/22/remarks-president-way-forward-afghanistan.

27. "Remarks by the President in Address to the Nation on the Way Forward in Afghanistan and Pakistan," 2009.

28. The US military defines insurgency as an "organized movement aimed at the overthrow of a constituted government through the use of subversion and armed conflict (JP 1–02). Stated another way, an insurgency is an organized, protracted politico-military struggle designed to weaken the control and legitimacy of an established government, occupying power, or other political authority while increasing insurgent control. Counterinsurgency is military, paramilitary, political, economic, psychological, and civic actions taken by a government to defeat insurgency. See *Counterinsurgency, FM 3–24/ MCWP 3–33.5*, December 2006, Headquarters, Department of the Army, http://www.everyspec.com/ARMY/FM-Field-Manual/FM_3-24_15DEC2006_13424.

29. See the *Guide for the Analysis of Insurgency*, January 5, 2009, http://www.tribalanalysiscenter.com/Research%20Tools/Guide_to_the_Analysis_of_Insurgency.pdf.

30. See http://www.globalpost.com/dispatch/news/afp/130701/key-dates-french-led-mali-intervention.

31. For an excellent description of how al-Qaida indoctrinates and sometimes trains the new generation of "lone wolf" terrorists, see Seth Jones, *Hunting in the Shadows, the Pursuit of al-Qa'ida since 9/11* (New York: W.W. Norton and Company, 2012).

32. "Remarks by the President on the Way Forward in Afghanistan," 2011.

33. Seth G. Jones, "Think Again: Al Qaeda," *Foreign Policy*, May/June 2012, http://www.foreignpolicy.com/articles/2012/04/23/think_again_al_qaeda.

34. Audrey Kurth Cronin, " No Silver Bullets: Explaining Research on How Terrorism Ends," Combating Terrorism Center, April 3, 2010, http://www.ctc.usma.edu/posts/no-silver-bullets-explaining-research-on-how-terrorism-ends; also see Seth Jones and Martin Libicki, *How Terrorist Groups End: Lessons for Countering al Qa'ida* (Santa Monica, CA: RAND, 2008).

35. See http://www.cfr.org/algeria/armed-islamic-group-algeria-islamists/p9154.

36. Presently there is a revisionist wave among certain researchers, journalists, and even military personnel not only questioning the viability of counterinsurgency in Afghanistan, but the viability of the "COIN" strategy in general; see Elisabeth Bumiller, "West Point Divided on War Doctrine's Fate," *New York Times*, May 27, 2012, http://www.nytimes.com/2012/05/28/world/at-west-point-asking-if-a-war-doctrine-was-worth-it.html?pagewanted=all; see also "Officer Questions Petraeus's Strategy: Iraq War Veteran Says Focus on Counterinsurgency Hinders Ability to Fight Conventional War," *The Wall Street Journal*, April 7, 2008, http://online.wsj.com/article/SB120753402909694027.html; for a more positive assessment of counterinsurgency, see Octavian Manea and Daniel R. Green, "Reflections from the Valley's Edge: A Year with the Pashtuns in the Heartland of the Taliban," *Small Wars Journal*, May 11, 2012 athttp://smallwarsjournal.com/jrnl/art/reflections-from-the-valley%E2%80%99s-edge-a-year-with-the-pashtuns-in-the-heartland-of-the-taliban.

37. Grenier, "What Is Obama's Afghanistan Plan?"

38. David E. Sanger, "Charting Obama's Journey to a Shift on Afghanistan," *New York Times*, May 19, 2012, http://www.nytimes.com/2012/05/20/US/obamas-journey-to-reshape-afghanistan-war.html?pagewanted=all.

39. "Remarks by the President in Address to the Nation on the Way Forward in Afghanistan and Pakistan," 2009.

40. Indyk, *Bending History*, 92.
41. General Stanley McChrystal, *ISAF Commander's Counterinsurgency Guidance,* 2009, http://www.nato.int/ isaf/docu/official_texts/counterinsurgency_guidance.pdf.
42. See *Counterinsurgency, FM 3–24/ MCWP 3–33.5.*
43. "Obama said bluntly that Gen. Stanley McChrystal's scornful remarks about administration officials represent conduct that 'undermines the civilian control of the military that is at the core of our democratic system.'" "Obama relieves McChrystal of command: Gen. David Petraeus named to take over troubled Afghan war," *NBC News*, June 23, 2010,http://www.msnbc.msn.com/id/37866754/ns/US_news-military/t/ obama-relieves-mcchrystal-command/.
44. For a summary account of Eikenberry's misgivings about LDI see Mathieu Lefèvre, "Local Defence in Afghanistan: A Review of Government-Backed Initiatives," *Afghan Analysts Network*, May 2010, http://www .humansecuritygateway.com/documents/AAN_LocalDefenceAfghanistan.pdf.
45. See Scott Mann, "Shaping Coalition Forces' Strategic Narrative in Support of Village Stability Operations," March 31, 2011,http://smallwarsjournal.com/jrnl/art/shaping-coalition-forces-strategic-narrative-in-support-of-village-stability-operations.
46. Seth A. Shreckengast, "The Only Game in Town: Assessing the Effectiveness of Village Stability Operations and the Afghan Local Police," *Small Wars Journal*, March 27, 2012, http://smallwarsjournal.com/jrnl/art/ the-only-game-in-town-assessing-the-effectiveness-of-village-stability-operations-and-the-a.
47. Major Brandon Bissell, "Turning the Tide," US Army Special Operations Command, February 22, 2011, http://www.soc.mil/UNS/Releases/2011/February/110222-01.html.
48. See Maria Abi-Habib, "Seals Battle for Hearts, Minds, Paycheck," *Wall Street Journal*, August 30, 2012.
49. In his June 22, 2011, address, announcing the beginning of troop withdrawals from Afghanistan, President Obama did refer positively to the VSO/ALP: "In the face of violence and intimidation, Afghans are fighting and dying for their country, establishing local police forces, opening markets and schools, creating new opportunities for women and girls, and trying to turn the page on decades of war." "Remarks by the President on the Way Forward in Afghanistan. 2011."
50. See Arturo Muñoz, *US Military Information Operations in Afghanistan: Effectiveness of Psychological Operations 2001–2010* (Santa Monica, CA: RAND, 2012), 40–45.
51. "Afghan Officials say NATO Killed 62 Civilians," AFP, February 24, 2011, http://www.google.com/ hostednews/afp/article/ALeqM5j0kGmnp28jYehlOz9Xdo3tLX44AQ?docId=CNG.85ce9eae1aabb7ca4ece9 553e35c868a.7a1; and Joshua Partlow, "US general casts doubt on Afghan burn injuries," *The Washington Post*, February 23, 2011.
52. Yasar Hameed, "End operations in Afghanistan, Karzai tells NATO," March 12, Assadabad (AFP), http:// netmail.verizon.com/netmail/driver?nimlet=deggetemail&fn=INBOX&page=1&degMid=12201&folder Selected=INBOX&uidValidity=null&sfield=Num&sorder=descending&reqReceipt=false.
53. Mark Thompson, "McChrystal's Rules Helped Reduce Attacks, Study Says," *Time US*, July 22, 2010,http:// www.time.com/time/nation/article/0,8599,2005733,00.html.
54. http://www.nytimes.com/2009/05/11/world/asia/11karzai.html.
55. See Matthew Cordova, "A Whole of Government Approach to Stability: Civil-Military Cooperation Underpins Smart Power," *Civilian Response*, March/April 2009, No. 8, US Department of State, Coordinator for Reconstruction and Stabilization, http://www.state.gov/documents/organization/183895.pdf; and http:// www.state.gov/documents/organization/123604.pdf.
56. Melinda Hutchings participated in this surge and spent several years in Afghanistan implementing humanitarian and development projects; her March 2012 unpublished manuscript, "Bottom-Up Expeditionary Diplomacy in Instability Operations: Lessons Learned from the 2009–2011 Civilian Surge in Afghanistan," contains excellent insights on the program.
57. See the biannual Defense Department report to Congress: *Report on Progress Toward Security and Stability in Afghanistan*, April 2012, http://www.defense.gov/pubs/pdfs/Report_Final_SecDef_04_27_12.pdf.
58. See http://usacac.army.mil/CAC2/MilitaryReview/Archives/English/MilitaryReview_20111031_art007.pdf; also see Robert Kemp, "The District Delivery Program in Afghanistan: A Case Study in Organizational Challenges," *Small Wars Journal*, June 26, 2012, http://smallwarsjournal.com/author/robert-kemp.
59. "NATO Summit 2012: Obama's Speech At McCormick Place," *Huffington Post*, May 22, 2012,http:// www.huffingtonpost.com/2012/05/21/nato-summit-obama-speech_n_1533353.html.
60. "Remarks by the President in Address to the Nation on the Way Forward in Afghanistan and Pakistan," 2009.
61. Ibid.
62. "Afghan spy chief wounded in Kabul attack," December 7, 2012, http://www.aljazeera.com/news/asia/2012 /12/2012126135813500308.html.
63. "Taliban Swoop on Party and Behead 17 . . . for Dancing: Women among Victims Killed for Breaking 'law,'" *Mail Online News*," September 10, 2012, http://www.dailymail.co.uk/news/article-2194158/

Taliban-swoop-party-behead-17—dancing-Women-victims-killed-breaking-law.html?openGraphAuthor =%2Fhome%2Fsearch.html%3Fs%3D%26authornamef%3DMail%2BForeign%2BService.

64. Author interview with former translator for US military in Sar Hawza, December 11, 2012.

65. See Susan G. Chesser, "Afghanistan Casualties: Military Forces and Civilians," Congressional Research Services, December 6, 2012,http://www.fas.org/sgp/crs/natsec/R41084.pdf.

66. "Residents of Several Provinces Have Different Opinions on US Military Presence," *Pajhwok Reporter,* December 4, 2011, http://www.pajhwok.com/en/2011/12/04/residents-several-provinces-have-different-opinions-US-military-presence; see also http://www.pajhwok.com/en/2011/12/05/afghan-perception-2nd-bonn-conference.

67. Ahmed Rashid, "A Deal with the Taliban Is The Only Way Out," *Financial Times*, March 12, 2012.

68. See Matthew Rosenberg and Sangar Rahimi, "U.S. Pays Families of Afghan Victims in Massacre by Soldier," *The New York Times*, March 25, 2012, http://www.nytimes.com/2012/03/26/world/asia/us-compensates-afghan-villagers-for-soldiers-attack.html.

69. Gilles Dorronsoro, *Afghanistan: The Impossible Transition*, The Carnegie Papers, South Asia, June 2011, http://www.carnegieendowment.org/files/impossible_transition.pdf.

70. Pam Constable, "Rural Afghan Town Feels Caught between U.S. and Taliban," *Washington Post*, December 7, 2012, http://www.washingtonpost.com/world/asia_pacific/afghan-town-feels-caught-between-us-and-taliban/2012/12/07/775bf96e-3ef2-11e2-8a5c-473797be602c_story_1.html.

71. "Analyzing the Asia Foundation's Annual Survey of Afghan Public Opinion," http://afpak.foreignpolicy.com/posts/2011/11/15reflecting_on_afghan_public_opinion.

72. *Afghanistan in 2011: A Survey of the Afghan People*, The Asia Foundation at http://asiafoundation.org/resources/pdfs/KeyFindingsAGSurveyBookFinal.pdf.

73. See http://asiafoundation.org/country/afghanistan/2012-poll.php.

74. Rashid, "A Deal with the Taliban."

75. Jay Loschky, "Afghans' Outlook on Lives Remains Bleak: Unease Grows in Afghanistan as NATO Troops Continue Drawdown," August 6, 2012,http://www.gallup.com/poll/156443/afghans-outlook-lives-remains-bleak.aspx; "Gallup classifies respondents as thriving, struggling or suffering according to how they rate their current and future lives on a ladder scale with steps numbered from 0 to 10, based on the Cantril Self-Anchoring Scale, where 0 represents the worst possible life and 10 represents the best possible life."

76. Ibid. "Results are based on approximately 1,000 face-to-face interviews each year with adults conducted April 20–26, 2012 . . . one can say with 95% confidence that the maximum margin of sampling error is plus/minus 4.1 percentage points."

77. *Afghanistan in 2011*.

78. Loschky, "Afghans' Outlook." Regional and local variation in polling results is even greater on other issues. This underscores the pitfalls of aggregating this type of data and averaging results. For example, district-level polling sometimes yields results greatly at variance with the national level on key issues such as support for the Taliban; see *Afghanistan: The Relationship Gap*, International Council on Security and Development, Brussels, July 2010, http://www.icosgroup.net/modules/reports/afghanistan_relationship_gap; other cultural, security, and logistical factors also affect the reliability of polling in Afghanistan and should be kept in mind in applying Afghan public opinion survey results to political analysis; see discussion on polling and measures of effectiveness in Muñoz, *US Military Information Operations in Afghanistan*, 22–25; also see Ben Connable, *Embracing the Fog of War: Assessment and Metrics in Counterinsurgency* (Santa Monica, CA: RAND, 2012).

79. Loschky, "Afghans' Outlook."

80. Ibid.

81. Thom Shanker and Alissa J. Rubin, "Afghan Force Will Be Cut after Taking Leading Role," *New York Times*, April 10, 2012, http://www.nytimes.com/2012/04/11/world/asia/afghan-force-will-be-cut-as-nato-ends-mission-in-2014.html?_r=0.

82. Nathan Hodge, "US Builds Afghan Air Base, but Where Are the Planes?" *Wall Street Journal*, July 24, 2012, http://online.wsj.com/article/SB10001424052702303292204577517010230335018.html.

83. Stapleton, "Beating Retreat."

84. See http://www.nytimes.com/2013/07/09/world/asia/frustrated-obama-considers-full-troop-withdrawal-from-afghanistan.html?_r=0.

85. See the July 19, 2013 *Wall Street Journal* article, "U.S. Marine Corps General Joseph Dunford Calls Talk of Zero Option Unhelpful," http://online.wsj.com/article/SB10001424127887323993804578615841508669044.html.

86. See the July 19, 2013 *Washington Times* article "Afghanistan's thanks for U.S. generosity: Harsh taxes and fees for Karzai regime," https://www.google.com/search?q=harsh+taxes%20and%20fees%20on%20US%20containers%20Afghanistan.

17

BETWEEN POPULARITY AND PRAGMATISM: SOUTH KOREA'S PERSPECTIVES ON OBAMA'S FIRST TERM

Matthias M. Maass

Introduction

Was there South Korean Obamania? How did 2008 change the perception of the United States? Has the image of the United States and view of the United States changed since Obama's election in 2008, and if so how and why? What is the foreign policy record of the Obama White House? In short, "what has been the South Korean perspective on the first Obama administration?" is the guiding question for the following investigation.

The core dynamic that defines US–South Korean relations is Northeast Asian security and in particular the North Korea's nuclear weapons program. South Korea's security depends heavily on its alliance with the United States and the presence of over 28,000 US military personnel in South Korea. The dependency on America's military commitment on the one hand, and issues stemming from the presence of a major contingent of US forces in the fairly homogenous South Korean society on the other hand can create tension, ambivalence, and uncertainty in South Korean society.

Divisions exist also along party-lines. "Since 1998, when political power passed for the first time from the dictatorial ruling party to the political opposition—the United Democratic Party—successive UDP governments have steered a more independent course from Washington, sometimes leading to friction."[1] In addition, a politically relevant generation gap exists in South Korea, with a younger generation being more critical of the United States and favoring an engagement policy toward North Korea, and an older generation strongly supporting the alliance with the United States backing hardline policies toward Pyongyang. Overall, this balance appears to be shifting, and a growth in anti-American sentiment can be observed.[2]

More specifically, substantial differences on how to counter Pyongyang's extreme diplomatic moves have at times dominated not only South Korean domestic politics, but also, by extension, South Korean–US relations. Similarly, Washington and Seoul have had disagreements on how to respond to the "rise of China." In addition, the bilateral free trade agreement has created friction between the United States and South Korea from the time it was negotiated to its ratification, at least.[3]

Moreover, (in)compatibilities of personalities among the countries' leaders have also played a role in the past. When Lee Myun-bak became president of South Korea, the strained personal relationship between this predecessor Roh Moo-hyun and US President George W. Bush improved. In fact, despite the political shift in the United States in 2008, Obama and Lee have had a solid personal relationship.[4] With South Korean society remaining hierarchically oriented, the personal relations of the state's leader with his international counterparts is of particular importance.

US foreign policy is generally evaluated in South Korea in a regional context and primarily along security and economic criteria. Overall, this has remained true in the early twenty-first century. However, the aggressive foreign policies and the "War on Terror" under the administration of George W. Bush were viewed negatively in South Korea overall. Scientifically measured favorability ratings of the United States slid continuously between 2000 and 2003,[5] the periods in which Bush broke off diplomatic engagement with North Korea (2001) and declared the country to be part of the "Axis of Evil" (2002).[6] These ratings, however, recovered toward the end of Bush's second term,[7] which might have been caused by a change in South Korean foreign policy: "In 2008, President Lee hardened policy toward the North and his emphasis on complete denuclearization of North Korea has brought U.S. and Seoul's policies closer."[8] Nevertheless, by 2008 two out of three South Koreans had little or no confidence in the Bush administration.[9] And it is against this backdrop that a South Korean perception of Barack Obama evolved during the presidential election campaign in 2008. As was the strong trend globally, South Koreans, too favored candidate Obama over John McCain by a very significant margin.[10]

This chapter will first investigate the South Korean viewpoints and attitudes toward candidate Obama in 2008, before turning to the changes in his popularity and the image of the United States and American policies during his first term. Next, important determinants of these changes, Obama's foreign policy style, and his policies toward Northeast Asia will be highlighted and presented from the South Korean perspective. The chapter ends with a survey of the status quo of the US–South Korean alliance in light of Obama's reelection and the upcoming presidential election in South Korea.

The 2008 US Presidential Election and Its Aftermath: South Korea's Perspective

In South Korea, the 2008 US presidential campaign was seen mostly in light of the candidates' assumed positions on military-security and trade matters. The focus was on the candidates and their policy pronouncements, and little attention was paid to races for the legislature, changes of the electorate, etc. The exception was the racial dimension of the 2008 election. South Koreans admired candidate Obama and the breakdown of racial barriers he symbolized. In fact, in South Korean society a somewhat dated perception of a highly racist American society persisted, making Obama's achievements seem even more remarkable. More than one newspaper emphasized this extraordinary achievement and the related permissiveness of the American liberal democracy.

However, South Korean admiration for US democracy and a candidate from a racial minority were tempered by considerable nervousness over his standpoints one policy issues critical to South Korea, in particular the free trade agreement (FTA) and Obama's commitment to the US–South Korean military alliance. Regarding the former, South Korean media focused on Obama's critical remarks about the FTA during his campaign. His claims that it was too generous and that he would insist on changes were perceived as threat to the benefits South Korea had secured during the FTA negotiations. In addition, as a Democrat, Obama was assumed to be a protectionist.[11] With respect to the latter, South Korean media pointed toward Obama's strong and principled opposition to the war in Iraq. This in turn fed the fear in South Korea that under Obama, the United States might drastically reduce its overseas commitments or even return to a policy of isolationism; either way, America's commitment to its military alliance with South Korea would have to be questioned. More dramatic for South Koreans was Obama's stated willingness to meet North Korea's leader face-to-face, because it might imply uncoordinated, unilateral policy initiatives at the expense of South Korea.[12]

In spite of a heavy dose of nervousness about the implications of a possible victory of Obama, the majority of South Koreans favored him over his opponent, Senator John McCain. In this regard, South Korea's preference in the 2008 "global election" paralleled that of most countries worldwide.[13] However, the split of 56% favoring Obama and 30% favoring McCain[14] indicated that South Korea's overall approval was tempered by the reluctance to dismiss the conservative focus on the military alliance and economic growth.

In late 2008, "Obama assured the citizens of the world. And the citizens of the world assured Obama that they believed in him and in the enduring power of democracy, liberty, opportunity, and hope to lift up the downtrodden, to give voice to the ignored, and to reestablish diplomatic relations with nations spurned by" his predecessor.[15] Worldwide, the general impression was that the 2008 election had in fact been a "global event,"[16] and the key aspect was the change of leadership it generated in the United States. While President Bush had been among the least trusted statesmen during his tenure—when polls asked whether "as leader, [he would be] doing 'the right thing.'" With President-elect Obama, these polls swung toward the expectation that Obama would "do the right thing."[17]

This global show of support was mirrored in South Korea. Here, 81% expected at least some positive changes of US foreign policy under Obama.[18] In opinion polls, Koreans agreed overwhelmingly with the notion that the election outcome would be "making a difference" to South Korea. Seventy-nine percent of polled Koreans agreed with this assumption, while only 12% explicitly disagreed.[19] Also in parallel to the global trend, the majority of South Koreans had preferred candidate Obama over McCain and was thus satisfied with the election outcome in the United States. In fact, polls indicated that nationwide, the preference was about 2:1.[20] In this context, it is noteworthy that in comparison to its neighbor Japan, Korea's preference for and immediate confidence in Obama was significantly less, with Japanese pollster finding a 4:1 preference among their nationals.[21] The causes for this were not immediately clear.

When the election results were in, South Korean mass media presented the results in an almost "celebratory" fashion.[22] Mass media transported the promise for "change" and generally painted an optimistic and hopeful picture. Although the atmosphere would not last long, the initial response was in fact "obamaniaesque" in that the outcome was given epochal meaning and one major newspaper interpreting Obama's win as the rebirth of the United States.[23] At the very least, reporting was congratulatory and optimistic,[24] and positive and welcoming even in conservative newspapers.[25] The strikingly consonant tone in conservative news outlets was noted and triggered the question that might have caused a shift from critical reporting on candidate Obama to positive and optimistic commentary in conservative newspapers.[26] It seems that this change of opinion at the very least reflects pragmatism: Regardless of South Korea's preferences, the country feels strongly that regardless of who resides in the White House, at least US–South Korean security and economic relations must be managed properly.

However, soon more somber notes were struck and the discussions were anticipating the implications of Obama's personality on his statesmanship generally and on US–South Korean relations specifically. In parallel, the immediate economic (FTA) and long-term political-strategic (military alliance) effects were discussed prominently.

It also quickly became clear that the strong favorability ratings for Obama would not translate one-to-one into improvements to America's image in Korea. South Koreans distinguished between the personal and the political. And even with respect to Obama as an individual, critics began to raise their voices. For example, South Koreans should not expect that their warm welcoming of the new president would cause US foreign policies to change. The state of South Korea would not receive preferential treatment from the United States just because South Koreans had a positive attitude toward Obama.[27] In other words, Obama's White House, too, would follow the logic of Realpolitik.[28]

Moreover, questions were raised about Obama's personality: He was charged with lacking a clear understanding of the need to build and maintain strong personal relationships.[29] Two things may help putting this curious remark in perspective. To be sure, in the Korean social and cultural context, which puts high value on direct personal relationship as the basis even for purely professional interaction, the critique has considerable substance. In the end, however, Obama was able to enjoy a solid personal relationship with the South Korean President Lee.

Normalcy soon returned to the evaluation of White House policies. What mattered were the traditional core dynamics of the US–South Korean relationship, security on the Korean peninsula and South Korea's economic development. In other words, "Obamania" was quickly overcome by sober political assessments. "In Korea, the [liberal] *Joong Ang Daily* congratulated Obama but noted the great problems—both domestic and foreign—that his administration will confront. And it highlighted the top priorities for South Korea. 'For Koreans, the North Korea nuclear issue and the pending Korea-U.S. free trade agreement are of the utmost interest,' the article said. 'The U.S. should try to balance resolving the North's nuclear issue through close cooperation with South Korea while at the same time adopting a tough diplomatic stance.'"[30]

In fact, early projections of future US foreign policy in Northeast Asia under Obama were negative, with the fear that Obama would be firmer than Bush with respect to the distribution of costs and benefits in the South Korean–US partnership, for example.[31] Such pessimistic evaluations were reflected in the return of a significant degree of skepticism to South Korea's perception of its ally and trading partner the United States. Polls in South Korea indicated that major reservations about US foreign policy remained a factor, in particular in regards to American power politics. Eighty-one percent agreed that the United States "abuses its greater power," while only 17% agreed that South Korea was treated "fairly."[32] In fact, the skepticism measured in South Korea was comparatively stronger than in many other East Asian countries.[33]

In spite of the negative image of US power and power politics in the regional context, Koreans viewed US foreign policy much more favorably in the global context. Here, about two-thirds confirmed that the United States was "playing a mainly positive . . . role in the world" and by mid-2009, the US foreign policy was generally viewed as cooperative.[34] In sum, by early 2009, the US image had improved in Korea, although the gains were noticeably lower than in other regions.[35] Moreover, Koreans gave Obama high favorability ratings, but this "Obama bump" did not lift the image of the United States by the same margins.

Return to Normalcy: South Korea's Perceptions of Obama and His Foreign Policy, 2009–2012

"In 2009, we [Pew Research Center] began to document a revival of America's global image in many parts of the world reflecting confidence in its new president, Barack Obama," stated Andrew Kohut, president of the Pew Research Center.[36] During President Obama's first term in office, he remained popular outside the United States, even if a degree of sobriety set in soon after he moved to the White House. However, the changes in popularity of the person Obama and those of the image of the United States did not parallel each other fully.[37] Moreover, the effect of the president's favorability ratings on the image of the United States appears commonsensical but is hard to measure. In light of this, it is useful to investigate personal popularity and state image as separate categories as much as possible. Clearly, Obama has seen his global popularity as political capital; at the same time, he also understood that the United States needed foreign policy changes to adjust the substance and not only the perception of the United States worldwide.

During the two terms of the Bush administration in the early twenty-first century, US foreign and security policies were increasingly seen as unilateral and disjointed from international normative thinking. The United States was seen as a "bully." Thus, upon entering the White House, Obama was faced with the expectation that he would address style and process of US foreign policy in this regard.[38]

For many South Koreans, the immediate issue was the FTA. Treaty negotiations had been conducted during the second term of President Bush, and it had been signed in 2007. However, the US ratification process had stalled soon thereafter and the issue was pulled into the presidential race and its political dynamics. Both McCain and Obama supported the FTA in principle, but Obama in particular made it clear that in its present form, he considered it unfair and that it needed to be reconsidered. On the Korean side, the ratification process had proceeded initially, despite some critique. However, soon it became clear that the treaty would have to be renegotiated.

South Korea strongly favored the initial version of the treaty and feared that a revised text would be less lenient. At the same time, getting an FTA with the United States remained a high priority. Therefore, South Koreans hoped that the Obama administration would proceed with the ratification process of the original version and refrain from insisting on renegotiations. In late 2009, "Koreans would [have] like[d] to see Obama kick-start the ratification process."[39] However, it did not happen and in the end a revised treaty was agreed upon in 2010, ratified by both sides in late 2011, and came into effect in early 2012. This episode made it clear early that Obama would not feel bound by his popular image to soften US economic interests.

While there was only a small uptick on the question whether America's economic influence was bad for South Korea,[40] US favorability ratings went up in South Korea during this time period, from 58% in 2007 to 70% in 2008 and 78% in 2009.[41] The data suggest that the US image in South Korea was not negatively affected by the forced renegotiation of the FTA, and it is possible to speculate that the positive image of Obama "spilled over" and solidified the image of the United States in general.

In fact, in the year following his election, Obama enjoyed high popularity ratings in Northeast Asia, including South Korea. However, in comparison to his worldwide ratings, those in Northeast Asia were comparatively at the lower end.[42] The overall lower regional level of ratings might be in part affected by cultural dynamics. In any case, 81% of Koreans polled in 2009 confirmed that they had a lot or at least some confidence in Obama; only 12% stated that they had little confidence or none at all in him as a statesman and foreign policy decision-maker.[43]

As was the case globally, being awarded the Peace Nobel Prize did not to have a major effect on Obama's already high popularity in South Korea.[44] His promise, made on the occasion of the award ceremony, to rekindle global denuclearization process triggered only short-term interest, because it was not followed up by policy. In particular in light of North Korea's nuclear test earlier that same year and the helpless response by the United States and its regional partners did little to generate confidence on Obama's promise made in Oslo. In fact, it appeared as if even mild engagement of Pyongyang was counterproductive,[45] which reinforced the image of the Obama White House as ambitious and aspirational, but lacking a "winning formula" for stopping nuclear proliferation in Northeast Asia.

By mid-2009 already, the losses in the favorability ratings of the United States that had accumulated during the Bush administration at the beginning of the twenty-first century had largely been recovered. "In many countries opinions of the United States are now about as positive as they were at the beginning of the decade before George W. Bush took office."[46] This suggested that much of "Anti-Americanism" during these eight years had in fact been "Anti-Bushism," because with a new president in office, the image changed quickly. However, South Korea's view of the United States was neither at the top nor at the bottom when the changes in US favorability are compared globally.[47] As much as frustration during the Bush years had been held in check, excitement for Obama's United States was now bounded as well.

Still, in light of his predecessor's foreign policy record, Obama appeared to be a sounder character with better judgment to many worldwide and thus a better steward of US foreign policy: "[C]onfidence in Barack Obama's foreign policy judgments stands behind a resurgent U.S. image in many countries."[48] Such confidence was based largely on early indications of changes in US foreign policy, e.g., Obama's campaign statements, his staff selection, his Cairo speech, and extrapolated expectations.

South Koreans shared this optimistic outlook. "In Asia, optimism about Obama is almost as extensive with 85% of Japanese and 81% of South Koreans expressing confidence in the American president. . . ."[49] While in 2009 South Koreans had mixed feelings on certain issues, polls indicated an overall sense of satisfaction with the new White House's foreign policies.[50] The exception was the United States' ongoing military operation in Afghanistan. As was the case globally, South Koreans did not support this element of Obama's foreign policy, regardless of South Korea's own small military deployment to Afghanistan. In 2009, only 28% supported the US military mission in Afghanistan in 2009, 55% were explicitly against it.[51]

In sum, within a year, Obama had managed to recover much of the confidence in the United States and its leadership that had been lost under his predecessor. Obama was a well-liked US president overseas, including in South Korea. His policy coordination with Seoul starting in 2010 earned him further trust.

In 2010 and the following two years, America's generally positive image of the United States remained largely unchanged. In fact, US favorability rating moved up slightly, by 1 percentage point, to 79% in 2010.[52] These high and stable ratings most likely benefited from US regional policy. In May, the White House published its National Security, which proclaimed a renewed emphasis on multilateralism[53] and thus a shift away from the previous administration's reliance on unilateralism. In late 2010, Obama went on a four-state Asian tour that included South Korea.

Obama was also willing to follow the lead of the Blue House. In response to the sinking of the South Korean naval ship "Cheonan" by North Korea, Washington and Seoul coordinated their policies tightly.[54] In line with South Korean President Lee's hardline policy toward North Korea, the United States rejected the possibility of US–North Korean bilateral talks, insisting that Pyongyang must first agree to direct talks with Seoul.[55] "Strategic patience" was now also the Unites States' policy toward North Korea. Such "close policy coordination over how to handle North Korea"[56] shed a positive light on America's role in the alliance with South Korea.

By mid-2012, South Korean media was beginning to acknowledge the upcoming US presidential campaign. Attention focused to the two candidates, the incumbent and his challenger Mitt Romney. In South Korea, the focus was not on the domestic American issues of the campaign, but on the anticipated implications of a second Obama term or a Romney administration for South Korea specifically, and Northeast Asian matters generally.

To be sure, there was no hint of a repeat of Obamania in South Korea in 2012. His popularity in East Asia had been eroding already before. The perception of continued unilateralism of the United States in certain policy areas contributed to the downward slide as did Obama's significant expansion of so-called drones in the ongoing "War on Terror."[57] Most likely.[58]

With respect to Romney, the question was raised whether he would bring back a neoconservative foreign policy along the lines of the Bush–Cheney administration.[59] Even if this seemed unlikely, not the least in light Romney enlisting Robert Zoellick to put together a quasi-shadow cabinet,[60] the fact that this question came up hinted at the fear that a Romney presidency would be in fact signal the return of the United States to aggressive unilateralism. The presidential candidate's potential leadership style and his skills at the "art of the deal"[61] would be assets, to be sure. However, South Korean observers were critical of Romney using the issue of security on the Korean peninsula to score points in his campaign.[62]

Regarding the substance of his regional foreign policy views, Romney was in line with current official US foreign policy: He supported the Six-Party-Talks process but, as Obama and Lee, made a return to the talks conditional on verifiable progress.[63] It was already fairly clear that the US position toward North Korea would not change much, regardless of the election results. Hence, the US ambassador to Seoul could pronounce, with confidence, that the next White House would stay the course on North Korean foreign policy.[64] Moreover, South Korea was ready to work with either a Republican or a Democratic White House. While polls showed a preference for Obama, official Seoul prepared for both elections outcomes, sending envoys to Washington to be ready to get in touch immediately with the new president-elect.[65] South Korea understands its dependent security relationship with the United States and it needs a strong partner in the White House regardless of his party affiliation.

Six weeks after the US election, South Koreans would vote a new president into office themselves. Since South Korean presidents are limited to one term in office only, it was clear that some of the dynamics in the White House—Blue House relationship would change. Whether a strong personal relationship between the two presidents would evolve again and whether the new administration in Seoul would shift toward an engagement policy was unclear when Obama was reelected.[66]

Obama's Northeast Asian Policy and Changes in the South Korean Image of the United States

Having surveyed Obama's first term from the South Korean perspective, it is now becoming clear that Obama's profile as well as the substance of his foreign policy in Northeast Asia played major roles in the maintenance of his high favorability ratings and the sustained rebound of the US image in South Korea.

South Korean observers have given Obama credit for the way in which he has been conducting foreign policy in Northeast Asia. His perceived willingness to listen and to rely on diplomacy was seen as a strength over McCain in 2008 and over Romney in 2012.[67] The strong personal relationship between Obama and Lee not only helped with regards to bilateral policy coordination,[68] but also supported the US president's popularity in South Korea. The fact that from the beginning "Presidents Obama and Lee hit it off very well"[69] contrasted positively with the at time uneasy relationships between the Bush administration and its counterparts in Seoul.

More generally, Obama's statecraft was generally held in high regards. His particular skill set (communication, organizational capacity, political skill, policy vision, cognitive style, emotional intelligence[70]) was not considered much in South Korea, but his "willingness to use diplomacy rather bombast"[71] was. In fact, right after his election in 2008 and even before he had his staff in place to start developing and then implementing his Northeast Asian foreign policy, his emphasis on the diplomatic process and on policy coordination with his allies was noted approvingly.[72] Similarly, while South Korean had little confidence in Bush "doing the right thing in world affairs" by the end of his second term (30% agreed), in 2009 the untested Obama the confidence of 81% of Koreans.[73]

In South Korea, Obama did not come across as an ideologue but rather as a pragmatist.[74] That was certainly seen as a welcome change from the early, neoconservative years of his predecessor's administration. Furthermore, Obama's early foreign policy has been put in the Realist paradigm: "Obama's pragmatism is similarly rooted in a realistic, rather than idealistic, view of the complexity of challenges facing the United States."[75] In light of this claim, a significant overlap with an overall preference in South Korean security analysis for the Realist paradigm seems relevant. In short, it appears that Obama's worldview matches well with the South Korean perspective on international affairs.

In fact, the argument has been made that US foreign policy leaders have to be Realists and must not be Idealists because the assumption of American foreign policy as being a Realist is so overwhelmingly strong overseas, that idealist policies would only generate suspicion over the "real" motives behind them. "If American leaders want to lead such leaders of other countries, they have to act in the style of realists, and not in the style of idealists."[76]

Obama's diplomatic foreign policy style was conducive to his larger Asian foreign policy strategy during his first term. His Asian foreign policy agenda fell into two groups, "new initiatives" (e.g., the Asia pivot) and "'legacy issues'" (i.e., corrections to his predecessor's policies and priorities).[77]

Obama's "inheritance"[78] included a strained relationship between the White House and the Blue House. "For reasons on both sides, the South's relationship with the previous administration had been troubled."[79] For Obama, any diplomatic progress regarding the North Korean conundrum would be difficult to achieve without a strong link between the White House and the Blue House. In fact, the status quo of America's policies toward North Korea and nuclear proliferation had to be reconsidered because ". . . the mistakes that Bush made with North Korea in his first few years in office ended up haunting him for the rest of his term, leaving Obama with a far more complicated nuclear standoff." The game-changer was now that "North Korea had accumulated all the weapons fuel it needed, and did not appear about to give it up."[80] In other words, ". . . the Bush legacy is that he took a messy, dangerous problem and made it worse."[81]

During President Bush's two terms, North Korea transitioned from being conventionally armed rogue state to a "quasi-nuclear weapons state" with demonstrated nuclear capability.[82] This development might not have been avoidable by peaceful means, but a distracted White House and the administration's focus on fighting terror in Iraq did not help. Critical developments in Asia, first and foremost the advances in North Korea's nuclear weapons program, did receive insufficient attention and resources.[83]

Consequently, the experience of statesmen in Asia was that ". . . even when President Bush and the secretary of state attended major conferences or met with Asian leaders, they seemed to care mainly about terrorism and little about the economic issues worrying Asians."[84] Thus, in addition to the neglect of critical developments in the region, the Bush administration was perceived as disregarding regional priorities in favor of the "War on Terror."

In sum, Obama inherited a failed policy on North Korean denuclearization and a "mixed bag" of Asia policy.[85] While the former needed steady, patient, and well-coordinated policy, the latter would be addressed through a "pivot" of US foreign policy toward Asia.

Obama's doctrinal emphasis on carefully separating core from peripheral US interests and pursuing these then in different ways affected his policy toward the Korean peninsula. As his deputy national security advisor, Ben Rhodes stated: "'We use force directly and unilaterally against threats to the United States, the homeland or U.S. interests. When faced with threats to global security . . . we seek to act cooperatively and multilaterally.'"[86] With no immediate threat toward the United States, American foreign policy gained the flexibility needed to design a strategic policy toward North Korean nuclear proliferation.

The policy that emerged was a comprehensive approach. It had four major components: First, the cycle of "buying the same horse twice"[87] needed to be broken. In the past, Pyongyang had traded promises for economic aid and diplomatic concessions; when the promises remained unfulfilled, new concessions were demanded for virtually the same promises by North Korea. Second, Washington gave Seoul its full support in dealing with North Korea. Third, China's uncompromising support for Pyongyang was targeted. Fourth, the sanctions regime for North Korea needed to be tightened.[88] These efforts were flanked by "strategic patience," the resistance to reengage into the Six-Party-Talks unless North and South Korea had cleared the ground beforehand in bilateral negotiations and Pyongyang had implemented its previous promises.[89]

Critically, the tough position vis-à-vis Pyongyang matched well with the South Korean president's own hard line.[90] While Obama and Lee thus "forged close policy coordination over how to handle North Korea,"[91] they also agreed to expand the bilateral alliance into a broader partnership:[92] "At a 2009 summit, South Korean President Lee Myung-bak and Obama agreed to transform the alliance's purpose from primarily defending against a North Korean attack to a regional and even global alliance, in which they cooperate on issues such as climate change and terrorism."[93]

The United States–South Korea Alliance and Perceptions of Long-Term Commitment

A proposed broader South Korean–American partnership would most likely integrate with, not supersede, the decades-old military alliance. It remains to be seen whether a deeper and wider partnership will indeed emerge. With respect to the security alliance, however, both sides remain committed and in the foreseeable future the "US–ROK Mutual Defense Treaty" will remain firmly in place. However, both sides harbor suspicions about the other side's ultimate commitment.

The claim that ". . . despite its occasional convenience as a whipping boy, Korea, North and South, remains an afterthought in American foreign policy"[94] is debatable but speaks to the point that Northeast Asia has rarely been a top priority in US foreign policy. Partly as a result, US policy toward the region, the peninsula, and North Korean nuclear proliferation has been reactive, not proactive. This might in fact partly be due to US domestic politics.[95] However, from the South Korean perspective, being a low priority creates doubt about America's commitment.

In a worst case scenario, America's commitment to its South Korean ally would include the use of nuclear weapons. However, South Koreans harbor doubts if the United States would extend the so-called nuclear umbrella, in particular in cases in which it might be the target of counterstrikes.[96] Since the United States removed its nuclear arsenal from Korea, it has been using the nuclear capacities of its navy and air force to extend nuclear deterrence to South Korea.[97] Nevertheless, a degree of insecurity remains in South Korea, feeding an argument that calls for increasing South Korea's independent deterrence capabilities.[98]

In parallel to concerns over a suspected lack of unconditional US commitment, in particular if China were drawn into a military conflict,[99] South Korea remains nervous about potential "over-eagerness" on the part of Washington. The fear is that the United States might cut a deal with North Korea unilaterally and ultimately at the expense of South Korea.[100] This latent suspicion was activated when Obama, during his 2008 campaign stated explicitly that he would not be opposed to meeting the North Korean leader in direct, bilateral talks.[101] In another scenario that South Korea is wary about, coercive US policies lead to a chain reaction of sudden regime collapse in Pyongyang and immediate reunification, which might overburden South Korea's resources. Thus, South Koreans remain skeptical about its alliance partner's commitment and the overall wisdom of a Cold War–era military alliance with the United States.

In the early twenty-first century, the memory of the Korean War, 1950–1953, is fading, and with it, the traditional reminder of America's proven commitment during the Korean War and the Cold War. Younger generations in South Korea are not fully sharing the traditional consensus of America's role on the Korean peninsula, and growing numbers of South Koreans favor a complete withdrawal of US troops from South Korea.[102]

In particular with respect to America's military presence, a latent anti-American sentiment, an "ill will,"[103] characterizes the attitude toward the United States of a growing part of South Korea society. Such ill will can flare up quickly and in extreme cases lead to demonstrations of Anti-Americanism, mostly by the younger Koreans: "The most bitter [sic] expressions of anti-Americanism today come from the younger generation. Those who suffered through the war and dictatorship do not criticize the U.S. military presence on South Korean territory, but the younger generations feel humiliated by this and want a more equal partnership."[104]

At the same time, the United States and South Korea share a strong commitment to political and economic liberalism, the rule of law, and human rights.[105] In light of this and the problematic relationship with Korea's former colonizer Japan, and China's authoritarianism, the alliance with the United States remains in many ways the obvious choice. Even if the alliance has much stronger support in Seoul's foreign policy elite, the lack of easy alternatives balances the anti-American sentiment in the public discourses.

Conclusion and Epilogue: The 2012 Presidential Elections in the United States and South Korea (and China)

In the previous discussion, it has been demonstrated that Obama was seen favorably in South Korea. His popularity had two major elements. First, he followed a US president with low rankings, which multiplied Obama's attractiveness for South Koreans. Second, while his predecessor's style and policies reinforced a stereotypical negative image of the United States as a bully, arrogant, and proceeding unilaterally, Obama's personal style and his emerging policies toward the Korean peninsula were perceived within the framework of the positive cliché of America (pushing progress globally, pursuing global community goals, working multilaterally, and refraining from using its own hard power).

Furthermore, Obama's personal popularity helped with the strong recovery of the US image, as demonstrated in opinion polls conducted in South Korea. By 2011 already, US "influence" was seen as "mainly positive" by 74% in South Korea.[106] The perception of the United States, and in particular the views on its Asian and Korean policies improved in South Korea overall, although problems and areas for future conflict remain. With regard to the latter, much will depend on the outcome of the election in South Korea at the end of 2012.

US President Obama and South Korean President Lee were able to build a reliable personal working relationship and matching policies toward North Korea. Consequently, the US—South Korean alliance appeared strong and reenergized at the end of their (first) terms. In particular after the struggle over the renegotiated FTA had settled down, both leaders were comfortable talking about a broader bilateral "partnership" in the future. The well-synchronized policies toward North Korea benefited both sides, allowing the United States in particular to present itself in a supportive role and letting South Korea set policy toward Pyongyang.

However, the new South Korean president may set different policy priorities, which may in turn create friction between Washington and Seoul. It is with good reason when it is suggested that Obama needs to "prepare for the likelihood that the next ROK gov't will expand engagement with N[orth] Korea, and decide whether he would support this policy."[107] Moreover, it will be critical to "closely consult with South Korea's incoming leadership on any new game plan at an early date."[108] The expectation is that the conservative candidate would continue to pursue the current South Korean strategy, but test avenues for reengaging the North. If the opposition candidate wins the Blue House, a full-fledged policy of engaging Pyongyang has been promised. Such a change in policy would require a reorientation of US–South Korean cooperation.[109]

A strong and cooperative relationship between the United States and South Korea will remain important, regardless of the countries' leadership, because controversies loom not only over North Korean policy, but also over South Korean wartime control of its own military, the ongoing cost of US troops in Korea, transfer of military technology, the American missile defense program, and—potentially—economic issues. Nevertheless, the focus point will remain both countries' North Korea policy.

In late 2012, it appears that the Obama White House remains committed to the policy of "strategic patience" and using coercive diplomacy to manage North Korea's nuclear weapons program.[110] Depending on the new South Korean leadership and the expected change in top-level leadership in the US State Department, this policy may need to be rethought.[111] Needless to say, much will depend on North Korea's willingness to make concessions, compromise, and refrain from military provocations or "military-diplomatic campaigns."[112]

Bibliography

"Amid Upturn in Relations, Obama Visits South Korea." *Boston Globe*. http://articles.boston.com/2009-11-19/news/29259476_1_nuclear-weapons-asian-nations-trade-ties.

Bader, Jeffrey A. *Obama and China's Rise: An Insider's Account of America's Asia Strategy*. Washington, DC: Brookings Institution Press, 2012.

Baek, Sung Won. "갈루치 전 미 국무부 차관보 "오바마, 대북 접촉 적극 나서야" (Gallucci: Obama Should Actively Reach and Communicate with Nk)." VOA. http://www.voakorea.com/content/article/1544873.html.

Bajoria, Jayshree. "The China-North Korea Relationship." Council on Foreign Relations. http://www.cfr.org/publication/11097/chinanorth_korea_relationship.html.

Bajoria, Jayshree, and Youkyung Lee. "The U.S.–South Korea Alliance." Council on Foreign Relations. http://www.cfr.org/south-korea/us-south-korea-alliance/p11459.

Barnes, Julian E., and Jay Solomon. "Unusually for Democrats, Terror War Is a Talking Point, among American Voters as a Whole, Obama's Emphasis on National Security Is a Strength, Not a Weakness." *Wall Street Journal*, 2012, 12–13.

"BBC Country Rating Poll, Views of US Continue to Improve in 2011." London: BBC World Service, 2011.

Bunn, M. Elaine. "The Obama Administration's Nuclear Policy and Implications for East Asian Security." In *Major Powers' Nuclear Policies and International Order in the 21st Century*, 37–47. Tokyo: The National Institute for Defense Studies, 2010.

Choi, Hoon-gil. "조선 "오바마, 부시보다 까다로운 상대 (Obama Could Be More Picky Than Bush)." Media Today. http://www.mediatoday.co.kr/news/articleView.html?idxno=74310.

Choi, Young-hae, and Dong-yong Min. "오바마 대통령에게 있는 것과 없는 것 (What Obama Has or Doesn't Have)." Donga Ilbo. http://news.donga.com/3/all/20100328/27187635/1.

"Clinton Has No Plan to Meet N. Korean Fm in Bali." *The Korea Times*. http://www.koreatimes.co.kr/www/news/nation/2011/07/113_91147.html.

"Confidence in Obama Lifts U.S. Image around the World." Pew Research Center. http://www.pewglobal.org/2009/07/23/confidence-in-obama-lifts-us-image-around-the-world/.

Cossa, Ralph A., Brad Glosserman, Michael A. McDevitt, NIrav Patel, James Przystup, and Brad Roberts. *The United States and the Asia-Pacific Region: Security Strategy for the Obama Administration*. Washington, DC: Center for a New American Security, 2009.

Department of Defense. "National Security Strategy—2010." http://www.whitehouse.gov/sites/fefault/files/rss_viewer/nationa_securty_strategy.pdf.

Flake, L. Gordon. "Domestic Determinants of U.S. Policy toward North Korea and Ramifications for Pyongyang." In *New Challenges of North Korean Foreign Policy*, edited by Kyung-Ae Park, 173–84. New York: Palgrave-Macmillan, 2010.

French, Paul. *North Korea, the Paranoid Peninsula: A Modern History*. London: Zed Books, 2005.

Gellman, Barton. "The Mind of Mitt." *Time*, 2012, 16–26.

Glionna, John M. "Times Seoul Bureau Chief John M. Glionna Explains What Awaits President Obama Today in South Korea, President Obama Is on the Last Leg of His Asian Trip." *LA Times*. http://articles.latimes.com/2009/nov/18/world/la-fg-korea-obama-qa19-2009nov19.

"Global Opinion of Obama Slips, Drone Strikes Widely Opposed." Pew Research Center. http://pewresearch.org/pubs/2284/obama-usimage-image-abroad-global-economic-power-drone-strikes-policy-military-terrorism-china-economy.

"Global Opinion of Obama Slips, International Policies Faulted, Chapter 1. Views of the U.S. and American Foreign Policy." Pew Research Center. http://www.pewglobal.org/2012/06/13/chapter-1-views-of-the-u-s-and-american-foreign-policy-4/.

"Global Public Opinion in the Bush Years (2001–2008), America's Image—Muslims and Westerners—Global Economy—Rise of China." Pew Research Center, http://pewresearch.org/pubs/1059/global-opinion-bush-years.

"Global Public Opinion in the Bush Years (2001–2008), America's Image; Muslims and Westerners; Global Economy; Rise of China [Extended Version]." Pew Research Center, http://www.pewglobal.org/2008/12/18/global-public-opinion-in-the-bush-years-2001-2008/.

"Global Public Opinion in the Bush Years (2001–2008)." In *Pew Global Attitudes Project*, edited by Andrew Kohult and Richard Wike. Washington, DC: Pew Research Center, 2008.

Greenstein, Fred I. "Barack Obama: The Man and His Presidency at the Midterm." *Political Science and Politics* 44, no. 1 (January 2011): 7–11.

Horowitz, Juliana Menasce. "Obama Popular in Japan, China and South Korea, but Only Modest Improvements in U.S. Image." Pew Research Center. http://pewresearch.org/pubs/1409/obama-asia-trip-popular-japan-china-south-korea.

Indyk, Martin, Kenneth Lieberthal, and Michael E. O'Hanlon. *Bending History: Barack Obama's Foreign Policy*. Brookings Focus Book. Washington, DC: Brookings Institution Press, 2012.

Kennedy-Shaffer, Alan. *The Obama Revolution*. Beverly Hills, CA: Phoenix Books, 2009.

Kim, Seung-il. "세계인들 '매케인 보다 오바마가 낫다'" (People in the World Claims "Obama Is Better Than McCain). *Busan Ilbo*, http://www.busanilbo.com/news2000/html/2008/0613/050020080613.1014103756.html.

Kim, Young-hee. "미국 새로 태어나다 (The US Reborn)." *Joongang Ilbo*, http://article.joinsmsn.com/news/article/article.asp?total_id=3367997.

Kim, Young-jin. "The Ball Remains in Nk Court." *The Korea Times*, http://www.koreatimes.co.kr/www/news/nation/2012/11/116_124205.html.

Kim, Young-jin. "Seoul Envoy in Washington for Post-Election Talks on N. Korea." *The Korea Times*, http://www.koreatimes.co.kr/www/news/nation/2012/11/116_124017.html.

Klein, Joe. "Is Romney a Realist or an Idealist? The Gop Nominee Has yet to Clarify His Foreign Policy Instincts." *Time*, 2012, 15.

Klng, Kay, and Jacob Stokes. *National Security Guide to the Presidential Election*. Washington, DC: Center for a New American Security, 2012.

Kohut, Andrew. "Obama Unlikely to Find a Quick Fix for U.S. Global Image." Pew Research Center, http://pewresearch.org/pubs/1175/obama-europe-trip-bush-legacy.

Kohut, Andrew. "Restoring America's Reputation in the World." Pew Research Center, http://pewresearch.org/pubs/1512/restoring-americas-reputation-globally-gains-may-be-fragile.

"Korea's Obama Test." *Wall Street Journal*, 26 May 2009, A18.

Kurth, James. "Pillars of the Next American Century." *The American Interest* 5, no. 2 (November/December 2009).

Kwak, Sang-a. "조중동은 왜 오바마를 환영하는 걸까? (Why Do Chosun, Joongang, Donga Welcome Obama? (Op-Ed))." *Mediaus.*, http://www.mediaus.co.kr/news/articleView.html?idxno=4795.

Lee, Byong Chul. "Testing Times for U.S.-South Korean Alliance." *The Japan Times.* http://www.japantimes.co.jp/text/eo20120320a2.html.

Lee, Chi-dong. "(News Focus) Obama's 'Strategic Patience' on N. Korea at Election Juncture." http://english.yonhapnews.co.kr/northkorea/2012/11/04/82/0401000000AEN20121104001400315F.HTML.

Lee, Eun-joo. "U.S. Envoy Promises Continuity after Elections." *Joong Ang Daily.*

Lee, Ha-won. "미국, 변화를 택하다. 오바마, 첫 흑인대통령 당선…'역사의 신(新)새벽' 열어 (US Chooses Change. Obama Elected as the First African American President of the United States, Starting a New Chapter in US History)." Chosun Ilbo. http://news.chosun.com/site/data/html_dir/2008/11/06/2008110600045.html.

Lee, Ha Jung. "오바마 재선 성공…경제재건에 주력할 듯 (Re-Elected Obama…Should Reinforce Economic Reconstruction)." BBS (Buddhist Broadcasting). http://www.bbsi.co.kr/news/news_view.asp?nIdx=580921.

Lerner, Ben, and David Reaboi, eds. *Dangerous Road, the Nuclear Policies of the Obama Administration.* Washington, DC: The Center for Security Policy, 2010.

Loy, Frank. "Obama Abroad: Ambitious Realism." *World Affairs* (May/June 2011).

Maass, Matthias. "A 'Global Event' with Global Stakeholders: Obama's Election and the 'Idea' of America." In *The World Views of the U.S. Presidential Election: 2008*, edited by Matthias Maass, 253–61. New York: Palgrave Macmillan, 2009.

Maass, Matthias. "North Korea as a "Quasi-Nuclear Weapons State." *Korea Observer* 41, no. 1 (Spring 2010): 131–60.

Maass, Matthias. *The World Views of the U.S. Presidential Election : 2008.* New York: Palgrave Macmillan, 2009.

Manyin, Mark E., Emma Chanlett-Avery, and Mary Beth Nikitin. "U.S.–South Korea Relations." In *CRS Report for Congress.* Washington, DC: Congressional Research Service, 2011.

Menon, Rajan. *The End of Alliances.* Oxford and New York: Oxford University Press, 2007.

Michishita, Narushige. *North Korea's Military-Diplomatic Campaigns, 1966–2008.* Routledge Security in Asia Pacific Series. New York: Routledge, 2009.

"Most Muslim Publics Not So Easily Moved, Confidence in Obama Lifts U.S. Image around the World, 25-Nation Pew Global Attitudes Survey." In *Pew Global Attitudes Project*, edited by Andrew Kohult. Washington, DC: Pew Research Center, 2008.

Nakamura, David, and William Wan. "Obama Welcomes South Korea's Lee to White House for State Visit." *The Washington Post.* http://www.washingtonpost.com/blogs/44/post/obama-welcomes-south-koreas-lee-to-white-house-for-state-visit/2011/10/13/gIQAX4TFhL_blog.html.

"(News Focus) Obama Faces Test of Ties with S. Korea's New President." Yonhap News Agency. http://english.yonhapnews.co.kr/northkorea/2012/11/07/28/0401000000AEN20121107005600315F.HTML.

"Obama Faces Test of Ties with Korea's New President." *The Korea Times.* http://www.koreatimes.co.kr/www/news/nation/2012/11/120_124146.html.

"Obama More Popular Abroad Than at Home, Global Image of U.S. Continues to Benefit, 22-Nation Pew Global Attitudes Survey." Pew Research Center. http://pewresearch.org/pubs/1630/obama-more-popular-abroad-global-american-image-benefit-22-nation-global-survey.

"Obama Rockets to Top of Poll on Global Leaders." World Public Opinion/Program on International Policy Attitudes. http://www.worldpublicopinion.org/pipa/articles/views_on_countriesregions_bt/618.php?nid=&id=&pnt=618.

"Obama's Most Improved Bilateral Alliance, South Korea Has Quietly Become a Model American Ally. Will It Stay That Way?" *The Economist*, 2012.

"Obama's Nobel Prize." Pew Research Center. http://pewresearch.org/pubs/1376/obama-nobel-prize-global-opinion.

Park, Jae-mok. "오바마가 던질 Mb의 3가지 정책애로 ([Lee] M[Yung]B[Ak]'S Three Rocky Policies Pointed out by Obama)." Dailian. http://www.dailian.co.kr/news/news_view.htm?id=132726.

Ray, Julie. "In Developed Asia, a Clear Preference for Obama, Margin 4-to-1 in Japan, Australia and 2-to-1 in South Korea, Singapore." Gallup, Inc. http://www.gallup.com/poll/111223/developed-asia-clear-preference-obama.aspx.

Remez, Michael, and Richard Wike. "Global Media Celebrate Obama Victory—but Cautious too, a Changed View of American Democracy." Pew Research Center. http://pewresearch.org/pubs/1033/global-media-celebrate-obama-victory-but-cautious-too.

Rochau, August Ludwig von. *Grundsätze Der Realpolitik: Angewendet Auf Die Staatlichen Zustände Deutschlands.* Frankfurt (M.): Ullstein, 1972, 1853.

"Romney Attacks Obama over North." *JoongAng Daily.* http://koreajoongangdaily.joinsmsn.com/news/article/article.aspx?aid=2961247&cloc=joongangdaily|home|newslist1.

"Romney Won't Allow N. Korea to Exploit Six-Way Talks: Aide." *The Korea Herald.* http://nwww.koreaherald.com/view.php?ud=20121011000174.

Sanger, David E. *The Inheritance: The World Obama Confronts and the Challenges to American Power.* New York: Harmony Books, 2009.

Shin, Hyon-hee. "Reinvigorated Obama to Approach N.K. Afresh." *The Korea Herald.* http://nwww.koreaherald.com/view.php?ud=20121107001089.

Swain, Geoffrey, and Nigel Swain. *Eastern Europe since 1945.* 2 ed. Houndmills, UK: Palgrave, 1998.

"Though Obama Viewed Positively, Still Much Criticism of US Foreign Policy: Global Poll." World Public Opinion / Program on International Policy Attitudes, http://www.worldpublicopinion.org/pipa/articles/views_on_countriesregions_bt/623.php?nid=&id=&pnt=623.

Wike, Richard, and Michael Remez. "As Obama Takes Office, Global Press Turns to Regional Concerns." Pew Research Center, http://pewresearch.org/pubs/1088/global-press-inauguration-reaction.

"오바마 당선 (Obama Elected)." Yonhap News Agency. http://news.naver.com/main/read.nhn?mode=LSD&mid=sec&sid1=100&oid=001&aid=0002351418.

Notes

1. Jayshree Bajoria and Youkyung Lee, "The U.S.–South Korea Alliance," Council on Foreign Relations, http://www.cfr.org/south-korea/us-south-korea-alliance/p11459.
2. Ibid; "Amid Upturn in Relations, Obama Visits South Korea," *Boston Globe,* http://articles.boston.com/2009-11-19/news/29259476_1_nuclear-weapons-asian-nations-trade-ties.
3. Jayshree Bajoria, "The China-North Korea Relationship," Council on Foreign Relations, http://www.cfr.org/publication/11097/chinanorth_korea_relationship.html.
4. Bajoria and Lee, "The U.S.–South Korea Alliance."
5. "Global Public Opinion in the Bush Years (2001–2008), America's Image—Muslims and Westerners—Global Economy—Rise of China," Pew Research Center, http://pewresearch.org/pubs/1059/global-opinion-bush-years.
6. "The U.S.–South Korea Alliance."
7. "Global Public Opinion in the Bush Years (2001–2008), America's Image—Muslims and Westerners—Global Economy—Rise of China."
8. "The U.S.–South Korea Alliance."
9. "Global Public Opinion in the Bush Years (2001–2008), America's Image; Muslims and Westerners; Global Economy; Rise of China [Extended Version]," Pew Research Center, http://www.pewglobal.org/2008/12/18/global-public-opinion-in-the-bush-years-2001–2008/.
10. Seung-il Kim, "세계인들 '매케인 보다 오바마가 낫다' (People in the World Claims 'Obama Is Better Than McCain)," Busan Ilbo, http://www.busanilbo.com/news2000/html/2008/0613/050020080613.1014103756.html; Matthias Maass, *The World Views of the U.S. Presidential Election : 2008* (New York: Palgrave Macmillan, 2009).
11. Jeffrey A. Bader, *Obama and China's Rise: An Insider's Account of America's Asia Strategy* (Washington, DC: Brookings Institution Press, 2012), 4–5.
12. L. Gordon Flake, "Domestic Determinants of U.S. Policy toward North Korea and Ramifications for Pyongyang," in *New Challenges of North Korean Foreign Policy*, ed. Kyung-Ae Park (New York: Palgrave-Macmillan, 2010), 175.
13. Maass, *The World Views of the U.S. Presidential Election: 2008.*
14. Kim, "세계인들 '매케인 보다 오바마가 낫다' (People in the World Claims 'Obama Is Better Than McCain)'; Maass, *The World Views of the U.S. Presidential Election: 2008.*
15. Alan Kennedy-Shaffer, *The Obama Revolution* (Beverly Hills, CA: Phoenix Books, 2009), xiii.
16. Matthias Maass, "A "Global Event" with Global Stakeholders: Obama's Election and the "Idea" of America," in *The World Views of the U.S. Presidential Election: 2008*, ed. Matthias Maass (New York: Palgrave Macmillan, 2009).
17. "Obama Rockets to Top of Poll on Global Leaders," World Public Opinion/Program on International Policy Attitudes, http://www.worldpublicopinion.org/pipa/articles/views_on_countriesregions_bt/618.php?nid=&id=&pnt=618.

18. "Global Public Opinion in the Bush Years (2001–2008)," in *Pew Global Attitudes Project*, ed. Andrew Kohult and Richard Wike (Washington, DC: Pew Research Center, 2008).

19. Julie Ray, "In Developed Asia, a Clear Preference for Obama, Margin 4-to-1 in Japan, Australia and 2-to-1 in South Korea, Singapore," Gallup, Inc., http://www.gallup.com/poll/111223/developed-asia-clear-preference-obama.aspx.

20. Michael Remez and Richard Wike, "Global Media Celebrate Obama Victory—but Cautious too, a Changed View of American Democracy," Pew Research Center, http://pewresearch.org/pubs/1033/global-media-celebrate-obama-victory-but-cautious-too.

21. Ray, "In Developed Asia, a Clear Preference for Obama, Margin 4-to-1 in Japan, Australia and 2-to-1 in South Korea, Singapore."

22. Remez and Wike, "Global Media Celebrate Obama Victory—but Cautious too, a Changed View of American Democracy."

23. Young-hee Kim, "미국 새로 태어나다 (the US Reborn)," Joongang Ilbo, http://article.joinsmsn.com/news/article/article.asp?total_id=3367997.

24. "오바마 당선 (Obama Elected)," Yonhap News Agency, http://news.naver.com/main/read.nhn?mode=LSD&mid=sec&sid1=100&oid=001&aid=0002351418.

25. Ha-won Lee, "미국, 변화를 택하다. 오바마, 첫 흑인대통령 당선…'역사의 신(新)새벽' 열어 (US Chooses Change. Obama Elected as the First African-American President of the United States, Starting a New Chapter in US History)" Chosun Ilbo, http://news.chosun.com/site/data/html_dir/2008/11/06/2008110600045.html.

26. Sang-a Kwak, "조중동은 왜 오바마를 환영하는 걸까 (Why Do Chosun, Joongang, Donga Welcome Obama? (Op-Ed))," *Mediaus*, http://www.mediaus.co.kr/news/articleView.html?idxno=4795.

27. Jae-mok Park, "오바마가 던질 Mb의 3가지 정책애로 ([Lee] M[Yung]B[Ak]'s Three Rocky Policies Pointed out by Obama)," Dailian, http://www.dailian.co.kr/news/news_view.htm?id=132726.

28. The term is understood here in the narrow, original sense developed by Rochau. August Ludwig von Rochau, *Grundsätze Der Realpolitik: Angewendet Auf Die Staatlichen Zustände Deutschlands* (Frankfurt (M.): Ullstein, 1972).

29. Young-hae Choi and Dong-yong Min, "오바마 대통령에게 있는 것과 없는 것 (What Obama Has or Doesn't Have)," Donga Ilbo, http://news.donga.com/3/all/20100328/27187635/1.

30. Richard Wike and Michael Remez, "As Obama Takes Office, Global Press Turns to Regional Concerns," Pew Research Center, http://pewresearch.org/pubs/1088/global-press-inauguration-reaction.

31. Hoon-gil Choi, "조선 "오바마, 부시보다 까다로운 상대 (Obama Could Be More Picky Than Bush)," Media Today, http://www.mediatoday.co.kr/news/articleView.html?idxno=74310.

32. "Though Obama Viewed Positively, Still Much Criticism of US Foreign Policy: Global Poll," World Public Opinion / Program on International Policy Attitudes, http://www.worldpublicopinion.org/pipa/articles/views_on_countriesregions_bt/623.php?nid=&id=&pnt=623.

33. Ibid.

34. Ibid.

35. "Confidence in Obama Lifts U.S. Image around the World," Pew Research Center, http://www.pewglobal.org/2009/07/23/confidence-in-obama-lifts-us-image-around-the-world/; Juliana Menasce Horowitz, "Obama Popular in Japan, China and South Korea, but Only Modest Improvements in U.S. Image," Pew Research Center, http://pewresearch.org/pubs/1409/obama-asia-trip-popular-japan-china-south-korea.

36. Andrew Kohut, "Restoring America's Reputation in the World," Pew Research Center, http://pewresearch.org/pubs/1512/restoring-americas-reputation-globally-gains-may-be-fragile.

37. Horowitz, "Obama Popular in Japan, China and South Korea, but Only Modest Improvements in U.S. Image."

38. Andrew Kohut, "Obama Unlikely to Find a Quick Fix for U.S. Global Image," Pew Research Center, http://pewresearch.org/pubs/1175/obama-europe-trip-bush-legacy.

39. John M. Glionna, "Times Seoul Bureau Chief John M. Glionna Explains What Awaits President Obama Today in South Korea, President Obama Is on the Last Leg of His Asian Trip," *LA Times*, http://articles.latimes.com/2009/nov/18/world/la-fg-korea-obama-qa19-2009nov19.

40. "Confidence in Obama Lifts U.S. Image around the World."

41. Ibid; "Most Muslim Publics Not So Easily Moved, Confidence in Obama Lifts U.S. Image around the World, 25-Nation Pew Global Attitudes Survey," in *Pew Global Attitudes Project*, ed. Andrew Kohult (Washington, DC: Pew Research Center, 2008).

42. Horowitz, "Obama Popular in Japan, China and South Korea, but Only Modest Improvements in U.S. Image."

43. Ibid.

44. "Obama's Nobel Prize," Pew Research Center, http://pewresearch.org/pubs/1376/obama-nobel-prize-global-opinion.

45. "Korea's Obama Test," *Wall Street Journal*, May 26, 2009.
46. "Confidence in Obama Lifts U.S. Image around the World."
47. "Obama Popular in Japan, China and South Korea, but Only Modest Improvements in U.S. Image."
48. "Confidence in Obama Lifts U.S. Image around the World."
49. Ibid.
50. "Obama Popular in Japan, China and South Korea, but Only Modest Improvements in U.S. Image."
51. "Confidence in Obama Lifts U.S. Image around the World"; "Most Muslim Publics Not So Easily Moved, Confidence in Obama Lifts U.S. Image around the World, 25-Nation Pew Global Attitudes Survey."
52. "Obama More Popular Abroad Than at Home, Global Image of U.S. Continues to Benefit, 22-Nation Pew Global Attitudes Survey," Pew Research Center, http://pewresearch.org/pubs/1630/obama-more-popular-abroad-global-american-image-benefit-22-nation-global-survey.
53. Department of Defense, "National Security Strategy—2010," http://www.whitehouse.gov/sites/fefault/files/rss_viewer/nationa_securty_strategy.pdf.
54. Bader, *Obama and China's Rise: An Insider's Account of America's Asia Strategy*, 83–87.
55. "Clinton Has No Plan to Meet N. Korean Fm in Bali," *The Korea Times*, http://www.koreatimes.co.kr/www/news/nation/2011/07/113_91147.html.
56. "(News Focus) Obama Faces Test of Ties with S. Korea's New President," Yonhap News Agency, http://english.yonhapnews.co.kr/northkorea/2012/11/07/28/0401000000AEN20121107005600315F.HTML.
57. "Global Opinion of Obama Slips, International Policies Faulted, Chapter 1. Views of the U.S. And American Foreign Policy," Pew Research Center, http://www.pewglobal.org/2012/06/13/chapter-1-views-of-the-u-s-and-american-foreign-policy-4/; "Global Opinion of Obama Slips, Drone Strikes Widely Opposed," Pew Research Center, http://pewresearch.org/pubs/2284/obama-usimage-image-abroad-global-economic-power-drone-strikes-policy-military-terrorism-china-economy.
58. Ha Jung Lee, "오바마 재선 성공 … 경제재건에 주력할 듯 (Re-Elected Obama … Should Reinforce Economic Reconstruction)," BBS (Buddhist Broadcasting), http://www.bbsi.co.kr/news/news_view.asp?nIdx=580921.
59. Joe Klein, "Is Romney a Realist or an Idealist? The Gop Nominee Has yet to Clarify His Foreign Policy Instincts," *Time* 2012.
60. Ibid.
61. Barton Gellman, "The Mind of Mitt."
62. "Romney Attacks Obama over North," *JoongAng Daily*, http://koreajoongangdaily.joinsmsn.com/news/article/article.aspx?aid=2961247&cloc=joongangdaily|home|newslist1.
63. "Romney Won't Allow N. Korea to Exploit Six-Way Talks: Aide," *The Korea Herald*, http://nwww.koreaherald.com/view.php?ud=20121011000174.
64. Eun-joo Lee, "U.S. Envoy Promises Continuity after Elections," *Joong Ang Daily*.
65. Young-jin Kim, "Seoul Envoy in Washington for Post-Election Talks on N. Korea," *The Korea Times*, http://www.koreatimes.co.kr/www/news/nation/2012/11/116_124017.html.
66. "(News Focus) Obama Faces Test of Ties with S. Korea's New President"; Mark E. Manyin, Emma Chanlett-Avery, and Mary Beth Nikitin, "U.S.–South Korea Relations," in *CRS Report for Congress* (Washington, DC: Congressional Research Service, 2011).
67. Sung Won Baek, "갈루치 전 미 국무부 차관보 "오바마, 대북 접촉 적극 나서야" (Gallucci: Obama Should Actively Reach and Communicate with Nk)," VOA, http://www.voakorea.com/content/article/1544873.html.
68. "Obama's Most Improved Bilateral Alliance, South Korea Has Quietly Become a Model American Ally. Will It Stay That Way?" *The Economist* 2012; David Nakamura and William Wan, "Obama Welcomes South Korea's Lee to White House for State Visit," *The Washington Post*, http://www.washingtonpost.com/blogs/44/post/obama-welcomes-south-koreas-lee-to-white-house-for-state-visit/2011/10/13/gIQAX4TFhL_blog.html.
69. Bader, *Obama and China's Rise: An Insider's Account of America's Asia Strategy*, 34.
70. Fred I. Greenstein, "Barack Obama: The Man and His Presidency at the Midterm," *Political Science and Politics* 44, no. 1 (January 2011).
71. Frank Loy, "Obama Abroad: Ambitious Realism," *World Affairs*, May/June (2011).
72. Flake, "Domestic Determinants of U.S. Policy toward North Korea and Ramifications for Pyongyang," 174–75.
73. "Most Muslim Publics Not So Easily Moved, Confidence in Obama Lifts U.S. Image around the World, 25-Nation Pew Global Attitudes Survey."
74. Greenstein, "Barack Obama: The Man and His Presidency at the Midterm."
75. Loy, "Obama Abroad: Ambitious Realism."
76. James Kurth, "Pillars of the Next American Century," *The American Interest* 5, no. 2 (November/December 2009).

77. Julian E. Barnes and Jay Solomon, "Unusually for Democrats, Terror War Is a Talking Point, among American Voters as a Whole, Obama's Emphasis on National Security Is a Strength, Not a Weakness," *Wall Street Journal* 2012, 13.

78. David E. Sanger, *The Inheritance: The World Obama Confronts and the Challenges to American Power* (New York: Harmony Books, 2009).

79. Bader, *Obama and China's Rise: An Insider's Account of America's Asia Strategy*, 12.

80. Sanger, *The Inheritance: The World Obama Confronts and the Challenges to American Power*, 279.

81. Ibid., 344.

82. Matthias Maass, "North Korea as a "Quasi-Nuclear Weapons State," *Korea Observer* 41, no. 1 (Spring 2010).

83. Bader, *Obama and China's Rise: An Insider's Account of America's Asia Strategy*, 2; Sanger, *The Inheritance: The World Obama Confronts and the Challenges to American Power*, 267–344.

84. Bader, *Obama and China's Rise: An Insider's Account of America's Asia Strategy*, 2.

85. Ibid., 1.

86. Barnes and Solomon, "Unusually for Democrats, Terror War Is a Talking Point, among American Voters as a Whole, Obama's Emphasis on National Security Is a Strength, Not a Weakness," 12.

87. Flake, "Domestic Determinants of U.S. Policy toward North Korea and Ramifications for Pyongyang," 183; Bader, *Obama and China's Rise: An Insider's Account of America's Asia Strategy*, 31; Martin Indyk, Kenneth Lieberthal, and Michael E. O'Hanlon, *Bending History : Barack Obama's Foreign Policy*, Brookings Focus Book (Washington, DC: Brookings Institution Press, 2012), 218.

88. Bader, *Obama and China's Rise: An Insider's Account of America's Asia Strategy*, 91; Indyk, Lieberthal, and O'Hanlon, *Bending History: Barack Obama's Foreign Policy*, 218–19.

89. *Bending History: Barack Obama's Foreign Policy*, 218–19.

90. Bader, *Obama and China's Rise: An Insider's Account of America's Asia Strategy*, 32; Chi-dong Lee, "(News Focus) Obama's 'Strategic Patience' on N. Korea at Election Juncture," http://english.yonhapnews.co.kr/no rthkorea/2012/11/04/82/0401000000AEN20121104001400315F.HTML.

91. "(News Focus) Obama Faces Test of Ties with S. Korea's New President."

92. Ibid.

93. Ibid.

94. Paul French, *North Korea, the Paranoid Peninsula: A Modern History* (London: Zed Books, 2005), 207.

95. Ibid.

96. Ben Lerner and David Reaboi, eds., *Dangerous Road, the Nuclear Policies of the Obama Administration* (Washington, DC: The Center for Security Policy, 2010), 20.

97. M. Elaine Bunn, "The Obama Administration's Nuclear Policy and Implications for East Asian Security," in *Major Powers' Nuclear Policies and International Order in the 21st Century* (Tokyo: The National Institute for Defense Studies, 2010), 45.

98. Geoffrey Swain and Nigel Swain, *Eastern Europe since 1945*, 2 ed. (Houndmills, UK: Palgrave, 1998), 348–49.

99. Byong Chul Lee, "Testing Times for U.S.–South Korean Alliance," *The Japan Times*, http://www.japantimes.co.jp/text/eo20120320a2.html.

100. Ralph A. Cossa et al., *The United States and the Asia-Pacific Region: Security Strategy for the Obama Administration* (Washington, DC: Center for a New American Security, 2009), 42.

101. Flake, "Domestic Determinants of U.S. Policy toward North Korea and Ramifications for Pyongyang," 175.

102. Lee, "Testing Times for U.S.-South Korean Alliance."

103. Rajan Menon, *The End of Alliances* (Oxford and New York: Oxford University Press, 2007), 162–63.

104. Lee, "Testing Times for U.S.–South Korean Alliance."

105. Ibid.

106. *BBC Country Rating Poll, Views of US Continue to Improve in 2011* (London: BBC World Service, 2011), 8.

107. Kay Klng and Jacob Stokes, *National Security Guide to the Presidential Election* (Washington, DC: Center for a New American Security, 2012).

108. Lee, "(News Focus) Obama's 'Strategic Patience' on N. Korea at Election Juncture."

109. "Obama Faces Test of Ties with Korea's New President," *The Korea Times*, http://www.koreatimes.co.kr/www/news/nation/2012/11/120_124146.html.

110. Young-jin Kim, "The Ball Remains in Nk Court," *The Korea Times*, http://www.koreatimes.co.kr/www/news/nation/2012/11/116_124205.html.

111. Hyon-hee Shin, "Reinvigorated Obama to Approach N.K. Afresh," *The Korea Herald*, http://nwww.koreaherald.com/view.php?ud=20121107001089.

112. Narushige Michishita, *North Korea's Military-Diplomatic Campaigns, 1966–2008*, Routledge Security in Asia Pacific Series (Milton Park, Abingdon, Oxon; New York: Routledge, 2009).

18

THE CHINESE VIEW OF PRESIDENT OBAMA

Benjamin Shobert

Today, the Chinese view of President Obama's leadership is influenced by four factors. First, Obama is widely perceived to be a relatively weak administrator, unable to effectively motivate political opponents toward the pursuit of his policy goals. Second, it is generally believed that he relies too heavily on facilitation and compromise versus leverage and power. Third, the Chinese are increasingly suspicious that his views toward China are becoming more hawkish less because of a real change by China, and more because of American insecurities. That Obama has been unable to refocus the Beltway conversation away from China and toward America's internal structural challenges has only further eroded China's confidence in his leadership abilities. This having been said, the Chinese do largely view Obama as more accepting of a multipolar world than his Republican predecessors, a trend they feared could have been reversed had former Massachusetts Governor Romney won the general election. Fourth, Chinese perceive Obama as lacking the sort of business and economic planning experience that will be necessary for America's economy to begin growing. Some of this frustration should be best understood as Chinese not understanding the limits to American presidential power in general, as well as more specifically in the hostile political environment President Obama has had to operate within. Regardless, China largely views Obama as lacking the ability to put forward plans that hold out hope to revitalize the American economy; this criticism is not limited to President Obama, and for many Chinese it represents a weakness of the larger American form of government and its current extravagant distrust of federally planned industrial and technology development policies. For China, the sort of strong government hand Obama should embrace would reflect insights from China and its amazing economic growth over the last several decades.

If US–Sino relations will be the most important bilateral relationship and the biggest geopolitical test of the coming century, then how China views America's leadership is essential to understand. Not only to whether either average Chinese or their political leaders view the United States as a competent partner, but also whether they fear America has become a belligerent threat. This makes Chinese opinions about President Obama and his administration's policies toward China important to explore. It comes as no surprise, and provides no solace to observe, that global attitudes toward President Obama are improved over those of President George W. Bush; however, this is not to say opinions about President Obama are all positive, merely that comparing him to his predecessor makes Obama appear better thought of by the Chinese. The Pew Research Center's "Global Attitudes Project" found that while only 30% of Chinese interviewed had confidence in President Bush's leadership in 2008, by 2012 that number had settled on a small improvement at 38% for President Obama. This is markedly down from a high of 62% in 2009 during the heady days when the world's hope for President Obama were still on the rise.

Chinese views of President Obama suffer in no small part because the American form of government remains something of a mystery to the Chinese. The chaos and diversity of America's political system stands in stark contrast to the publicly homogenous nature of Chinese politics. Consequently, when the American Congress puts forward an ill-considered bill that attempts to slap duties on Chinese-made goods or to label China a currency manipulator, most in China attach the American president to these actions when in fact, most such short sighted steps have been taken without the blessing of the president. While the executive branch of the American government has long been able to successfully tamp down protectionist and more hawkish policies emanating from the legislative branch, President Obama has found himself with not only a gridlocked American system of government, but also an economy struggling to return to vitality. In the midst of America's struggles, the tendency to blame China for problems of America's own making has been an issue President Obama has not been above, in particular during the 2012 election cycle where China-bashing took on rare bipartisan support. Given both the Republicans and Democrats have found it politically expedient to go after China during the most recent election cycle, it is unlikely Chinese opinions about America's political leaders will significantly change for the better.

Five primary factors shape how the Chinese view President Obama. First, and the most positive, is their appreciation of how he established himself politically and rose to power. President Obama's ascent to power lacks the sort of nepotism and *guanxi* that accounts for the political success of too many Chinese politicians. Second, President Obama is perceived by many in China as a weak administrator, someone whose oratorical skill set is poorly matched against his ability to get things done. Given the Chinese value a colorless technocratic form of government versus America's more personality-driven political culture, the Chinese ambivalence toward President Obama in this respect is no surprise. Third, President Obama is perceived as a leader who relies too heavily on facilitation and compromise instead of leverage and power. Within most of China, President Obama's inability to get things done is not understood to be the product of political opposition dedicated to blocking his every move. Fourth, President Obama's lack of business or engineering experience is considered troubling given the emphasis on both that many of China's political class believe is necessary to successful public leadership. Fifth, the majority of Chinese believe President Obama has become more hawkish toward China since he came into office. Many in China understand this to be a product of America's own economic insecurities, but others also believe China bashing has become a necessary part of American politics, and they deeply resent being cast as villains.

These five factors all have to be understood within four contextual elements, some of which are poorly understood by the Chinese, others that simply represent different ways by which China evaluates political leadership than how America does. The first, and in many ways most important, contextual element is what China understands (or, it might be better said, misunderstands) about the political setting within which President Obama must operate. Just as the nuances to who makes it onto the Chinese Politburo's Standing Committee are not understood by the average American, so too are the nuances of how America's executive, legislative, and judicial branches work together by the average Chinese. For most in China, the three branches of America's federal political system are seen as one monolithic entity in much the same way that most in America view China's Communist Party as a vast homogenous entity with one mind. Both abstractions serve to distract from the diverse opinions in both countries. In China, this misunderstanding goes one step further: many of the more belligerent and unnecessarily provocative political actions taken by elected officials in America have not been done by the president, but rather by members of Congress. This distinction is not well understood in China. As a consequence, many times negative perceptions about the president accrue when this negativity should be directed toward other voices within America's fractious political system. This in part explains why in advance of the last attempt to pass the Fair Currency Act, the Obama administration sent a diplomatic envoy to Beijing to address fears that China was being attacked. Rather than take the risk that Beijing might see the Fair Currency Act, a product of the Congress, as something that had the president's blessing, Obama acted to privately quell these fears. This action was undoubtedly appreciated by Beijing, but it does not translate to a broader understanding across China of the distinctions between what the American Congress and president do. The two are often seen as one, many times to President Obama's detriment.

The second contextual element that shapes how China understands President Obama is a misunderstanding of what an American president can and cannot accomplish. As we are being reminded of in the 2012 Politburo Standing Committee transition, the means by which China accomplishes its political goals is hardly transparent; yet it has been enormously successful to date. Whether the model of state-sponsored capitalism that Beijing has found so powerful thus far will continue without creating problems of its own remains to be seen; however, what cannot be disputed is that the process has yielded positive results for China. In contrast to this, at least as understood by many in China, is the inability of President Obama to get meaningful work done restarting the American economy. This misunderstanding is rooted in how the Chinese Politburo, for all its failings, has the ability to make important decisions about economic and political reform at the very top, and then be perceived to act forcefully.

The latter conditional statement is necessary to add simply because while the Chinese have a heightened sense of their government's ability to act, this same government struggles mightily to get decisions that have been made at the level of the Central Government to be consistently applied at the provincial and municipal levels. Regardless of the failings of their own system, the Chinese believe their leaders can and do act with clarity, vigor, and effectiveness. When they look at America, the Chinese see President Obama struggle to move America forward. Much of this misunderstanding is because the American political system has deliberate checks and balances between the executive and legislative branches in particular. When these counterweights work well, America's system fosters compromise. When it does not, it creates chaos and gridlock. Because the United States seems mired in the latter, many in China assume this is a reflection on the president rather than on deliberate limits designed by the Founders on what any American president is capable of achieving.

The third contextual element poorly understood by Chinese relative to President Obama is that his administration took office in the midst of not only an economic crisis, but also an ideological one. Specifically, the debate between the Republican and Democratic parties as to the proper role of government in the life of its citizens. Against the backdrop of the 2008 financial crisis, the administration of Republican President George W. Bush advanced a series of measures designed to stabilize the country's financial system. As part of this and subsequent similar policies put forward by President Obama, the American federal government took on a role of increased significance within the US economy. These moves also drove up the country's debt obligations, which further unsettled many Americans who had already grown uncomfortable with the size and scope of the federal government. The ensuing political backlash has limited what President Obama has been able to pursue. Whether outsiders think this debate and the ensuing political gridlock is good or bad is beside the point; what matters is that many Chinese do not appreciate that much of what preoccupies President Obama is a need to answer domestic critics who believe he wants a stronger federal government during a period when many Americans feel government has become too large and intrusive.

While China has its own share of debate over the proper role for its own government in the nation's economy and social systems, the ideological debates visible to the Chinese public thus far occurring in the country rarely question whether the central government should play an important role in China's economic matters. Policy analysts inside and outside of China may debate over whether the Guangdong or Chongqing Model will be taken up by the next president of the country (each offers an opposing view of how heavily involved the state should be in the economy, as well as what role it should play providing social services); but these models and the questions they pose relative to China's future do not animate the average Chinese person in the same way as do political conversations in the United States relative to the proper role of government in the American economy.

The fourth and final contextual element that influences how Chinese understand President Obama is the relative insensitivity and underappreciation by most in China to those skills that most define President Obama's political success. Few anywhere would argue against the president's rhetorical capabilities; what is relevant in China is whether this matters, and not only due to differences in language. If one assumes that much of what has lifted President Obama to his current status are his oratorical skills versus his administrative competency, then it becomes easy to see how average Chinese might be deeply unimpressed by the very things that have been most integral to his success within the American political system. Obama's quick rise to power absent any large legislative achievements left many in China unsure what to make of him. As former Ambassador to China John Huntsman shared, "the Chinese were perplexed by President Obama . . . where does he come from? What does he think? He remained a bit of a cipher."

One of the many legacy issues from Mao's era that still shapes China is fear over letting personality drive politics. The ubiquitous western suits and dyed black hair of the various Politburo members serve the purpose of obscuring individual personalities within China's governing elites, and the Chinese like this. One of the many causes for Chongqing Mayor Bo Xilai's political fall from grace was that he refused to blend into the background. Rather, he wanted to be known for personal oratorical skills and political grandstanding. If political success in China relies on what is done in private and how one's administrative successes are understood by the public, then the political acumen of President Obama, whose public success has been the product of precisely those things the Chinese do not value, is not likely to impress most Chinese.

These contextual elements are essential to keep in mind when discussing the positive and negative ways the Chinese view President Obama's administration. Heading into President Obama's first term, the Chinese feared he would advocate for a subtle but noticeably more hostile stance toward China. Many of these fears were the result of views by many in China that traditionally Democratic politicians tended to pay more attention to the concerns of organized labor. Unions in America such as the powerful Teamsters, long a strong ally of the Democratic Party, have been no friend of globalization in general, or China specifically. For many years, these groups have expressed fear over the economic dislocation across America set in motion as low-cost countries such as China enter the global workforce. Republican presidential administrations have typically encouraged globalization practices not only because they believe it drives overall economic growth, but also because it weakens one of the core Democratic constituencies. China warily greeted Obama in some part due to fears that a Democratic president facing an ongoing economic malaise would finally listen to the fears and frustrations of organized labor. In addition, China believed that a Democratic administration might be more willing to press China on human rights issues and economic reforms such as China's currency policy and opening other sectors of the Chinese economy to outside investment and influence. Many in China were of the opinion that a Democratic president would be more likely to escalate trade disputes. These concerns not-withstanding, China was intrigued by candidate Obama's personal story, seeing it as emblematic of American meritocracy and its post-racist legacy. On balance, China's expectations were that the Obama administration would advocate for policies that would largely keep US–Sino relations on solid ground, with little meaningful in terms of adjustments to the historical policy of engagement. In fact, many policy makers in Beijing believed President Obama would prove to be more conciliatory toward China with respect to ways the two countries could work together. In contrast to outgoing President George W. Bush, who was perceived by many in China as insensitive to how his administration's policies were affecting the rest of the world, the incoming President Obama was hoped to be more open to working together and de-escalating a world on edge after 9/11, the invasions of Afghanistan and Iraq, and the 2008 global financial crisis.

As Obama's term has progressed, China's hopes have largely been disappointed as the two countries have had to deal with an increasingly uncertain future marked by America's ongoing economic struggles, and the broad perception in American popular and political culture over the inevitability of both China's rise and America's descent. Against the backdrop of America's internal political turmoil, China has watched two of the three branches of American government take more aggressive positions toward China, ranging from formal complaints with the World Trade Organization (WTO) to punitive duties assigned by the US Trade Representative, and politicians in both the Senate and House work toward legislation that would punish China for its currency policies. Additionally, the Obama administration has strategically repositioned America's defenses in the Pacific— something China views as being aimed at controlling its regional aspirations. The American government has been forced to comment on a variety of difficult human rights issues in China, most recently with the Chen Guangcheng situation. Many in China believe President Obama has done too little to resist, and many in China would propose he has played along with, the idea that China is becoming a strategic threat to American interests. This is unlike fears America had over Japan's economic resurgence in the 1980s. Japan's government was built on western democratic structures and ideals; its military was intentionally handicapped as a by-product of World War II. While Japan might have been an economic threat to America, it was not an ideological or military threat. For many Americans, these same things could not be said of China. China was already an economic and ideological threat because of its state-sponsored socialist/capitalist hybrid tied to an authoritarian government. And, many in America feared China's military rise. Taken together, these have all fostered mutual suspicion between America and China. Opinions about President Obama have been damaged as a result of this distrust.

The June 2012 "Global Attitudes Project" by Pew noted that public perception in China of President Obama had suffered since he took office. The report noted, "support for Obama has waned significantly in China. Since 2009, confidence in the American president has declined by 24 percentage points and approval of his policies has fallen 30 points." This decline is noteworthy on two counts: it shows the high expectations China had after what they believed to have been a disastrous eight years under President George Bush, and the decline is shocking considering what high regard many in China had of Obama's personal story. In November of 2011, the *China Daily* wrote on what President Obama's rise to power meant to Chinese in similar situations. They profiled one young man, Li Songchen, whose own work as a lawyer representing migrant workers. The paper wrote, "Amid piles of paperwork in his simple office on the outskirts of Beijing, a 28-year-old public welfare lawyer pauses to say his job is special because he feels a kinship with the most powerful man in the United States." They went on to quote Li, "I am young, passionate and dedicated to helping the poor of the community with my knowledge . . . Barack Obama at my age was doing the same thing."

In many ways, Obama's candidacy touched something important within Chinese culture. Awash in economic success, China feels disconnected from its past and from societal values grounded in its legacy of Confucianism. Graft and corruption are a given within China's political culture. Across the Pacific was America's first black president, someone who had risen to the most powerful position in the world, and whose story was not understandable unless you saw the priority he gave to those less fortunate than himself. Obama was seen by many in China as the sort of leader they wanted to see come to power in their own country. Many young people such as Li wanted to tie their political fortunes to protecting the disadvantaged and working to reform the system in ways they believed Obama had.

These hopes have largely been dashed. The Chinese, as illustrated by the Pew Global Attitudes Project, have come to distrust President Obama. This distrust is colored by a number of factors, not least of which is the frustrating inability of the president to restart America's stalled economic engine, as well as his use of China as a convenient political target. But some of the cynicism can be understood as disappointment over President Obama's inability to deliver on the sort of changes to America that many in China hoped to see. The transformative narrative of his life and his candidacy was poorly matched to the sort of transformations he has been able to achieve while in office. In many ways, the disappointment Chinese feel toward Obama echoes similar frustrations of Americans who elected him. In China, where President Obama's autobiography *Dreams from My Father* has become a best seller, the disillusionment Chinese feel toward him as a candidate in many ways follows similar disillusion they feel toward the American people at large.

If Chinese feel a general frustration toward President Obama and his inability to more directly and more positively influence America's trajectory, they are more specifically suspicious about his administrative abilities. In a culture where the success of political leaders is weighted toward those who can effectively execute against priorities spelled out by the central government in Beijing such as the 12th Five Year Plan, being an ineffective administrator is considered problematic. It equally adds to confusion by many Chinese over what explains President Obama's meteoric rise to power;

while some may appreciate his reputation as a gifted public speaker, his seeming inability to achieve meaningful legislative objectives points back to their suspicion over his ability to govern.

China's political class is constituted by two groups: princelings and technocrats. Princelings come from families who can trace their lineage back to having held roles with responsibility during Mao and Deng Xiaoping's era. Many princelings hold positions of power in today's China simply because of their bloodline, not because they have been particularly successful as leaders in government. As a consequence of this nepotism, princelings have been particularly guilty of graft and corruption. In contrast to this group are technocrats, the modern day Confucian ideal: wise stewards of the country's economy and policy-making institutions, with a mind for policy analysis and an ego satisfied by doing the job well rather than political accolades. Technocrats, as in the case of the new Chinese President Xi Jinping, can also be princelings although such an overlap has been the exception and not the rule in China's modern politics. While China today has plenty of both princelings and technocrats, it is widely believed—both inside the country and by outside analysts—that China's success must be understood in some part because of the role its technocrats have played wisely shepherding the country through the massive economic and political reforms it has made since first opening to the west.

Even somewhat cynical outsiders of China's political system such as Richard McGregor, author of *The Party: The Secret World of China's Communist Rulers*, have acknowledged that much of the success by the Beijing Model is rooted in the country's administrative skills: "Most developing countries do not have China's bureaucratic depth and tradition, nor do they have the ability to mobilize resources and control personnel in the way that China's party structure allows. Could the Democratic Republic of the Congo ever establish and manage an Organization Department? China's authoritarianism works because it has the party's resources to back it up." For all of its flaws, the Party has managed to emphasize technocratic and administrative skills while having to turn a blind eye to the corruption endemic in too many of the country's political leaders.

While western pundits may point to what they see as excess capacity being created by China's state-led growth model, thus far, the Chinese technocrats have been amazingly successful at coordinating the necessary changes to allow its people to emerge from self-induced isolation and the poverty it engendered after Mao's disastrous rule ended. The last two global financial crises—the 1997 Asian and 2008 American-led ones specifically—have not taken down China's economy, an impressive achievement the average Chinese understands to be the result of competent leadership in Beijing. In the minds of the Chinese, who are admittedly frustrated by issues such as land-takings and corruption of government officials, the country's economic success would not be possible absent the leadership of its technocrats. They have confidence in their leadership that when push comes to shove, the very top leaders are competent administrators who can get things done. As many in China see it, if a country is underdeveloped and struggling but can still have this sort of strong administrator leading its government, then America should have these leaders even more so. But as the administration of President Obama has progressed, Chinese have watched the American economy struggle to right itself, a symptom the Chinese believe can best be explained by President Obama's weak administrative skills.

Even if someone in China were to assume, as many of President Obama's political allies would propose, that his weak administrative skills are not to blame but rather the intransigence of his political opponents, Chinese are of the mind that President Obama relies too heavily on facilitation and compromise instead of leverage and power. Nowhere is this expectation on how Obama would use power perhaps more obvious than the complex ways in which many Chinese still understand Mao. While Mao's early foray into politics required facilitation and compromise, by the time he declared "the Chinese people have stood up," he was well on his way to ruling through more direct leverage and power. Seen by many across the world as China's first secular emperor, Mao used power to bring together a country torn apart by civil war and feuding regional warlords. Today, the Chinese respect Mao's ability to unify the country through what most admit were times of enormous difficulty. What Mao lacked in nuance he made up for in brute force. Among the legacies this has created is the emphasis people in China place on the ability to get policies developed and implemented, regardless of the consequences. This at times can result in decisions that circumvent individual rights in pursuit of the greater good; but the direct action Chinese politics emphasizes has tended to value this trade-off simply because the people believe that in the end such force has been necessary.

Because the American political system is marked by, and even designed to require, compromise, the Chinese approach President Obama with divergent expectations both on outcomes he should be able to deliver as well as the means by which he should be able to achieve his stated objectives. Where the American system is transparent and prone to breaking down publicly, the Chinese system is opaque, and critical decisions are made in private, the implementation of these done through brute force when necessary. While this difference may be obvious, the ways it influences how Chinese expect a political leader to act are clearer. Rather than resort of speeches and symbolism, successful politicians in China are those who can bloodlessly wield power behind closed doors, maintain unity, and deliver results that matter to the average Chinese citizen.

If the Chinese are frustrated with President Obama, he appears to be equally frustrated by them, or at least their leadership. His frustrations have not been helped by the demands of the 2012 presidential campaign when GOP nominee Mitt Romney made China a centerpiece of his plan to renew the American economy. The traditionally pro–free trade Republican Party has now determined that to market itself in swing states like Ohio and Pennsylvania where manufacturing job losses have been most acute, it must turn on classic conservative ideas about globalization that have defined conservative economics for decades. During the 2012 general election, the most experienced businessman the GOP has put forward as a presidential candidate in recent memory found it necessary to blame China for the American economic struggle. Not able to cede ground in these key states, President Obama responded in kind, increasing his own criticisms on China. His administration publicly pivoted the American military policy toward Asia with an eye on containing China's Pacific aspirations. Under Obama's leadership, the American government has filed two new WTO cases against China since June. Each of these actions have been designed to placate restless American voters who increasingly are of the opinion that China's economic gains have been at American losses.

As the campaign has advanced, voices across China have taken umbrage at being cast as the scapegoat for American insecurities. A September 2012 *Global Times* op-ed wrote, "The provocations by these presidential candidates are too much for Chinese people to bear. US politicians show an indifferent attitude toward the feelings of the Chinese people. China should not turn a blind eye to such provocations. No matter who the current president or candidate is, they should respect China. They should mind what they say." This attitude was a common frustration across China, voiced publicly and privately as Chinese wondered whether Obama's public actions were merely ploys to win an election or something more substantive that would poison US–Sino relations if Obama were to win. This is also the more general concern held by policy makers in China. Even more troubling than Obama's rhetoric toward China was that of the GOP. If the modern GOP, once the most loyal advocate of China's role in a globalized world, could turn against it, what did this suggest was in store regardless of who won the 2012 election? For many in China, it was clear that America was become more hawkish toward China less because of any meaningful changes in how China behaved domestically or internationally, but more because of America's own insecurities about her future role in a multipolar world.

Again, the *Global Times* wrote cuttingly on what they saw as the deteriorating condition of American attitudes toward China: "Once Secretary Clinton and Assistant Secretary of State [Kurt] Campbell began to lead China policy just over a year ago, U.S.-China relations have been deeply affected. They have changed the generally positive and cooperative trend of U.S.-China policy at the beginning of Obama's term. They have destroyed the atmosphere and intensified mutual distrust. After 2010, Secretary Clinton's promotion of a return-to-Asia strategy, actively approaching China's neighboring countries and adding pressure to China, and a range of inconsistent behaviors on all sides, have swiftly created a negative and suspicious atmosphere in bilateral relations. The relationship has changed from supposed cooperation to competition." The perception that, as the *Global Times* wrote, America now was less inclined to cooperate with, and instead compete against, China has negatively influenced China's view of America as a whole and President Obama specifically.

This is particularly obvious in the Pew Global Attitudes Project when Chinese were asked whether their expectations were satisfied or unmet regarding America's multilateralism. The concept of multilateralism is important to China for a number of reasons, not least of which is China remains aware of its inability to defend its interests against the United States, let alone potential rivals such as Russia or India. The more China can bend global opinion in the direction of broad multilateral action, the more it feels protected against use of force by others. In addition, multilateralism plays to long-held beliefs in Chinese culture that acting as a collective rather than as an individual is valued. This has implications not just to personal conduct, but also to how nations are supposed to behave. Because one of the main criticisms of President George W. Bush's foreign policy was its pre-emptive and unilateral nature, policy analysts largely expected that President Obama would noticeably benefit from his apparent desire to engender more international agreement before acting. Unfortunately, Chinese attitudes when asked whether the Obama administration would "cultivate international approval for military force" showed a shocking distrust even of President Obama. In 2009, 29% said he would cultivate international support before acting militarily; by 2012 only 13% said he had acted this way. What explains this drop off? At least three factors appear to have negatively influenced China's view that President Obama will act multilaterally: the Pacific Pivot, the expansion of drone strikes, and the action in Libya.

The Pacific Pivot, a November 2011 announcement by President Obama that included new military forces deployed in Australia, has been widely interpreted by China as an attempt to contain it. In late September 2012, Zhou Fangyin, an associate research fellow at the National Institute of International Strategy at the China Academy of Social Sciences, wrote for the *China Daily*, "China's influence is increasing in the Asia-Pacific region and even the rest of the world, while the US is declining. This is a relatively long-term but inevitable trend, which the US finds very uncomfortable to accept. The change in the balance of power will gradually erode the supremacy of the US and other countries' confidence in America's might. This realization seems to be giving American politicians and policymakers sleepless nights." Whatever nuanced policy toward China President Obama hoped for, in the minds of many across China, this strategy made it easier for the United States to act unilaterally against China.

Similarly, the expansion of drone strikes has hurt the positive view of President Obama in China. Poorly understood in America, drone attacks are seen by the world to be symbolically powerful events that illustrate the ability of American power to act whenever, wherever, and however it so chooses. Recent revelations over the death toll of innocent civilians killed during drone strikes has done little to further a positive image of President Obama as an agent of multilateralism. That President Obama has so increased the frequency of drone strikes is understood by many in China to be an expression of his extension of the Bush-era policies of absolute American hegemony that left the Chinese deeply dissatisfied. While no Chinese really feels personally threatened by America's drone attacks, the ability of America to act unilaterally across the globe adds to the Chinese unease over what the United States might do if it were to ever feel threated by China.

President Obama's decision to attack Libya was widely denigrated across China. One of the longest standing disagreements between China and the United States is over the limits of international power to intervene in a sovereign nation's domestic affairs. Unilateral decisions such as America's decision to invade Afghanistan and Iraq absent any real international support were received poorly in China. Beijing's fear is that should America ever perceive China to be acting with violence toward its own people then international bodies like the United Nations could be used to approve the use of force against China. In the eyes of the Party, what America did in Afghanistan, Bosnia, Iraq, and Libya could be done to China. Given how China behaved in June of 1989 when it resorted to violence to suppress the protests in Tiananmen Square, this is not an idle concern on Beijing's part. Consequently, when American power acts unilaterally as it did when President Obama authorized military intervention in Libya, how China perceives his willingness to act with multilateral support suffers.

Some in China have taken this concern a step further and argued that President Obama is guilty of being a revolutionary power bent on remaking the world in America's image. This criticism was most commonly heard in China during the Bush presidency; however, it continues to be a rich strain of dissent across China. In late September 2012, the *China Daily* published an op-ed, which shared that, "As the superpower promoting continued revolution in the name of democracy around the world, especially in the Middle East, the US has become the power promoting revolutionary change and destabilization of governments in the name of its own ideological values and standards around the world. In contrast, Russia and China have become the 21st century's powers of the 'historic right,' that is to say, on the global scene they support stability and follow values of pragmatic realism in their foreign policy and global diplomacy. China in particular favors peace and stability across the Middle East because it imports so much of its oil from the region." In an earlier op-ed from a *China Daily* senior editor, the paper wrote: "But what the US policy has yielded in the Middle East, and in Pakistan, Afghanistan, Iraq and other Muslim states is overall hatred for the West, especially the US, and led to radical Islamic elements rising to prominence and even gaining power. The development in the Muslim world exposes, and quite blatantly, the flaws in the American policy to spread its brand of democracy to the rest of the world through any means possible.

Permanent Security Council members China and Russia, and countries like India, stand vindicated for opposing the UN resolution on Libya. And time will prove that they are right in opposing any UN action to oust Bashar al-Assad from power in Syria."

China distrusts actions that violate state sovereignty because they feel one day similar rationales could be used against it. Consequently, a country like America that has shown a willingness and aptitude for leveraging international bodies of power such as the United Nations are to be distrusted. It is no surprise that given Chinese sensitivity to the sort of unilateral military actions that have continued from President Bush under President Obama, attitudes in China toward the Obama administration have continued to suffer. Taken together—the Pacific Pivot, increased drone strikes, and the war in Libya—Chinese feel that President Obama does not represent the clean break with American unilateralism they hoped for in early 2009 when he first came into office. It is small solace to note that as negative as Chinese feel toward President Obama on this matter, they felt even worse relative to President George W. Bush.

During the June 2013 meetings in California between Xi Jinping and Obama, the ongoing distrust between the two countries over cyber-security played out for the world to see. The close-lipped Xi was reluctant to speak directly on the matter, while President Obama was more direct. Obama's approach to China's cyber-sleuthing has been to publicly acknowledge that it exists, and that it represents a stumbling block to healthy US–China relations. By taking a more direct approach with China, Obama builds on his first term where he showed a surprising willingness to use power. President Obama has cannily triangulated his Republican opponents on the foreign policy front, largely taking away their ability to score political points by his administration's embrace of much of the most contentious foreign policy practices from his predecessor. While this effort may have been good for his domestic political fortunes, Obama's foreign policy practices have left many in China concerned that he will adopt increasingly assertive positions toward China during his second term.

In Washington, the approach Obama took toward China has come under increasing scrutiny. Jacqueline McLaren Miller, a member of the global think tank the EastWest Institute, captured what many in DC felt Obama was unable to get China to address during his first term: "China was slow to address concerns over its currency and industrial policies; it snubbed Obama at the Copenhagen climate discussions; it was reluctant to apply pressure on North Korea; and it adopted more assertive regional policies. There was some progress on Iran as China supported UN sanctions in 2010, but then China refused to support new sanctions designed to undermine Iran's continued progress on its nuclear program." Given Obama's approach in the first term garnered what many in Washington believe was too little in the way of adjustments by China, now that cyber-security issues have come to light, will the administration take a more assertive stance toward China? Fears over how the president might adjust his policies color much of the distrust many in China feel toward Obama specifically, and the American system more generally.

With all of these criticisms taken into account, is the disappointment Chinese feel toward President Obama really that different from how Americans also feel toward him? Both Americans and Chinese are frustrated over President Obama's inability to kick start the American economy. Whether either group adequately appreciates the extent of damage he inherited is less clear than their collective expectation that he be able to do something meaningful to remedy the problem. In the same way, both Americans and Chinese hoped President Obama would be able to push through meaningful reforms. While Chinese opinion on how this would have been accomplished relied more on leverage and power than American expectations for facilitation and compromise, the outcome thus far as seen from anyone's perspective has been too little constructive change. Where Chinese and American attitudes toward President Obama diverge are on the Obama administration's ongoing muscular unilateralism and, most critically, on how America's political institutions seem bent on blaming China for America's woes.

As the 2012 presidential election showed, America's insecurities are thus far being directed primarily inward. Political infighting and partisan rancor has reached all-time highs, leaving many moderate Americans disenfranchised. But the inward direction of American frustrations may not last, and at some point will begin to be directed outward. The most likely receptacle of American anxieties? China. In the midst of US turmoil, a new and potentially dangerous line of thinking has begun to emerge from both Democrats and Republicans: that China does not play by the rules of the game and that China's gain has been America's loss. An idea that has circled America's politics at the periphery for at least twenty years, this is becoming more central to how Americans view China, and what they expect from their leaders when they speak about, craft policy for, or act toward China. The Chinese watch this process with bewilderment and frustration. They want to believe that this is a short-term phenomenon, that once America's economy gets back on solid ground, the country will turn away from its China bashing and refocus on areas for collaboration. But this hope turns on a key factor: can America find its way? If not, the ways both countries view one another will become further toxic, making it very difficult for future American presidents to foster understanding and compromise with China.

19

RADICAL MANHOOD AND TRADITIONAL MASCULINITY: JAPANESE ACKNOWLEDGMENTS FOR LITERARY OBAMA[1]

Eijun Senaha

Introduction

Barack Obama impressed Japanese readers in 2007 with *My Dream: Autobiography of Barack Obama*, a Japanese title for his original 1995 book *Dreams from My Father: A Story of Race and Inheritance*.[2] In a gateway story, the young Obama takes the first steps of his remarkable political career with his election as the first African-American president of the *Harvard Law Review*. He succeeds in portraying himself as a man of our times to Japanese readers. The American critics had already applauded it when it was reissued in 2004 after Obama won the Democratic nomination for a seat as the US senator from Illinois. The book sold over 1 million copies, and, as the US presidential campaign reached a fevered pitch, he started to draw more attention worldwide. Then, in late 2007, the Japanese translation was published, exposing Japanese to a literary Obama. He became a popular writer indeed.

Japanese knew little about him except that he may become the first African-American president of the United States. However, thanks to such an engaging protagonist who was born to represent multiculturalism, the Japanese appreciated him while learning much about postmodern US history. Sadaaki Kato, the editor of the Japanese version, relates the risks taken to bring the translation to press:

> Obama was not known to Japanese at all when we secured translation rights. Its copyright fee was quite high due to its best seller status in the US. I was afraid we would lose money on it unless he became the president. For us, it was key that Obama win the Democratic Party presidential nomination, or at least be tapped as the vice-presidential candidate. At that point, I believed he only had a 5% chance of becoming the US president. We took the risk based on these projections.
>
> Personally, the reason I obtained the copyright was due to his speech at the 2004 Democratic Convention that I saw on *YouTube*. He was simply cool and, from a marketing point of view, embodied almost all the global issues: race, poverty, family, religion, developed/underdeveloped countries, NPO, renewal of local communities, and such. I thought, if he creates a stir, we'll have a very good chance of financial success.[3]

Kato says it sold well eventually. It underwent 7 printings for a total of 30,000 copies between December 2007 and February 2009.[4] One of the main reasons was Obama's potential influence over Japan. The Japanese readers were curious to know him, especially after he was introduced as a strong candidate to win the presidential election of November 4, 2008.

This literary success was an incredible turn around for Obama considering the mixed reviews and poor sales of the first edition in 1995. Obama was discouraged enough to claim he would not pursue a "career as an author"(vii). The reason for the initial reaction to the book was the presence of "the shadow of his father," a seemingly antimulticultural value that contradicted the image Obama was trying to establish in the book. Miraculously, however, when the book reappeared in the 2004 in the United States and was translated to Japanese in 2007, this patriarchal value actually became the secret to its success. In Japan, his paternalism appealed to Japanese and was not questioned. During the height of political frenzy as he battled against a female radical, Hillary Rodham Clinton, Obama's combination of radical manhood and traditional masculinity won the hearts of the readers as well as the so-called battle of the sexes.

Barack Obama and Postmodern Autobiography

Obama's autobiography transforms his identity from one of "ambiguity" to "hybridity." "It's in the blood" (65), says his father when ten-year-old Barack Hussein Obama Jr. finally meets him for the first time in 1971. This idea had already haunted him and, now vocalized, continues to do so throughout the telling of *Dreams from My Father: A Story of Race and Inheritance*, in which Obama records his search for self, or according to his father, a journey to "know where you belong" (114). He starts the journey as a postmodern bildungsroman hero of hybridity as he also settles for a relatively simple identity: that of his paternal heritage. As a result, his autoandrography, a life writing of a man about himself, by himself, represents a familiar story of a man who locates himself within the myth of manhood.

The term *autobiography* is the hybrid word, partly Saxon and partly Greek, *autos* (self), bios (life) and *graphe* (writing).[5] Linda Smith and Julia Watson sum up American autobiography, by saying, "In the Americas, at least, the autobiographical gesture has become endemic" (109), and it is now recognized as one of the major national literary genres in history. Starting with the European explorers of the new continent, to the New England Puritans expressing hope and fear in the new world, the slaves and slave owners of the Southern plantations justifying their identities, and those on the frontiers conveying ambitions, they recorded not only what they witnessed but also what they thought, eventually creating the myth of America. Smith and Watson continue:

> Increasingly we incorporate autobiographical genres, modes of address, and consciousness into our everyday lives. This contemporary fascination with life narrative derives in part from the power of the ideology of individualism and its cultural hold on us—Americans in particular are attracted to Horasio Alger-esque fantasies of the self-made individual. We are also witnessing, with this new outpouring of memoirs, the desire of autobiographical subjects to disassemble the monolithic categories that have culturally identified them, labels such as "woman," "gay," "black" or "disabled," and to reassemble various pieces of memory, experience, identity, embodiment, and agency into new, often hybrid, modes of subjectivity. In this pursuit, life narrative has proved remarkably flexible in adapting to new voices and assuming new shapes across media, ideology, and the differences of subjects. (109)

In academia, autobiography studies is one of the fastest growing fields. The critical climate of recent decades has favored most forms of life writing, and at the start of the new century, literary biography still remains in vogue.[6] Linda Leavell, in her 2006 introductory essay to the special issue on autobiography in *South Central Review*, refers to Hermione Lee's observation of the rising status of autobiography studies in the past five years.[7] In fact, Yale University hosted a symposium on literary biography and modernism in 2005. And, in 2008, the English Literary Society of Japan also hosted a symposium "Fiction and Faction in Life Writing."

Smith and Watson divide the history of autobiography studies into three critical periods: before the 1960s, the 1960s and 70s, and the 1980s to present. "First-wave critics were preoccupied with the 'bio' of the autobiographer because they understood autobiography as a subcategory of the biography of great lives and excluded other modes of life narrative. Truthfulness in autobiography meant consistency with the biographical facts of the life" (123). The second wave "opened up the discussion of autobiographical narrating by insisting on its status as an act of creation rather than mere transcription" (128). In other words, there was more interest in the presentation of self-fashioning "auto." The third wave responds to "the diversity of practices of subjectivity and modes of analyzing" (137). As Smith and Watson further explain it, "notions of an authoritative speaker, intentionality, truth, meaning, and generic integrity have been challenged" (137).

Dreams from My Father was re-released in 2004 following his widely acclaimed keynote address at the 2004 Democratic National Convention. His newly established fame fuels book sales, and he is perceived as being well-intentioned. The publisher, Random House, introduces enthusiastic reviews on its homepage: "Fluidly, calmly, insightfully, Obama guides us straight to the intersection of the most serious questions of identity, class, and race" (*Washington Post Book World*); and "One of the most powerful books of self-discovery I've ever read, all the more so for its illuminating insights into the problems not only of race, class, and color, but of culture and ethnicity" (Charlayne Hunter-Gault).[8] Joe Klein, another critic, enthuses that the book "may be the best-written memoir ever produced by an American politician."[9] The audio book edition was released in 2005, and it earned him the 2006 Grammy Award for Best Spoken Word Album. Japanese readers also responded positively, by saying, "You will be moved one hundred times more if you read this as the story of a future president."[10]

The reviews for the 1995 edition, however, were not that positive. R. Detweiler of *Choice* offers a lukewarm review: "Obama writes well; his account is sensitive, probing, and compelling."[11] Hazel Rochman of *Booklist* is confused: "Will the truth set you free, Obama asks? Or will it disappoint? Both, it seems. His search for himself as a black American is rooted in the particulars of his daily life; it also reads like a wry commentary about all of us" (1844). A reviewer for *New York Times Book Review* is rather puzzled by Obama's message:

> All men live in the shadow of their fathers—the more distant the father, the deeper the shadow. Barack Obama describes his confrontation with this shadow in his provocative autobiography, *Dreams From My Father*, and he also persuasively describes the phenomenon of belonging to two different worlds, and thus belonging to neither. . . . At a young age and without much experience as a writer, Barack Obama has bravely tackled the complexities of his remarkable upbringing. But what would he have us learn? That people of mixed backgrounds must choose only one culture in which to make a spiritual home? That it is not possible to be both black and white, Old World and New? If this is indeed true, as Mr. Obama tells it, then the idea of America taking pride in itself as a nation derived of many different races seems strangely mocked.[12]

As a result, the initial sales were, in Obama's words, "underwhelming." Obama says in the preface to the 2004 edition, "And after a few months, I went on with the business of my life, certain my career as an author would be short-lived" (vii).

It appears Obama's story was never fully understood. In 1995, the reader was confused and felt mocked. In 2004, the reputation of the actual Obama was so overwhelming that the contradiction of the book was never seriously examined. Most Japanese readers did not recognize its inconsistency in 2008. It was not because he was a failed first-time author unable to make himself understood, but because he was candidly faithful to the dreams of his father.

Postmodern Hybridity

Obama calls the book "an honest account of a particular province of my life" (xvii). The text is multifaceted, allowing the reader to examine his life from various perspectives. In his analysis, Takayuki Tatsumi states that "Obama attracts people because his personal history unexpectedly represents the American cultural salad bowl and the horizon of hope for the coming democracy."[13] Among fifty-two modes of life narrative introduced by Smith and Watson, Obama's autobiography belongs at least to the following five modes: Genealogy, Narrative of ethnic identity and community, Memoir, Trauma narrative, and Bildungsroman[14] with postmodern characteristics.

Genealogy

Genealogy is "a method of charting family history, genealogy locates, charts, and authenticates identity by constructing a family tree of decent.... Genealogical projects recover the recorded past, which they can verify as an official past" (Smith and Watson 195).

Obama is an only son born on August 4, 1961, to Barack Hussein Obama Sr. and Stanley Ann Dunham. Later in life, however, he learns that he is actually a descendant of great ancestors and relatives as well as a child of modern American diversity. After divorcing Barack Hussein Obama Sr., Ann married an Indonesian, Lolo, who had a daughter, Maya. At this point, Obama's family is taking on the structure of the contemporary American stepfamily. Both horizontal *and* vertical relations make the family distinctly American as well as international. The overall Obama family lineage includes African royalty and relations to American presidents, such as George Bush and Harry S. Truman.[15] He also indicates that his maternal family genealogy may include Native American ancestors as well as showing that he is distantly related to Jefferson Davis. On the paternal side, his research shows a family that goes back twelve generations. Though monogamy was the norm on the maternal side, the paternal side practiced polygamy. Obama's father was married to three women at the same time and had six sons and a daughter. Mixed marriage was, of course, also common on both sides of Obama's family, with African, White, and Asian relatives. Two religions are also represented among the family members: the paternal religion is Muslim, and the maternal Christian. The introduction of the Obama family genealogy is an encyclopedic illustration of possible marriage styles available in this contemporary world.

Narrative of Ethnic Identity and Community

Narrative of ethnic identity and community is a mode of autobiographical narrative, emergent in ethnic communities within or across nations, that negotiates ethnic identification. It may call for a revolution, other times pushing to reform ethnic subjects through autobiographical acts.[16] In Obama's book, ethnicity is a central theme. Referring to his mixed blood, Obama sublimates his ethnic identity into a universal "American." Obama's identity becomes multiethnic. He declares that the image people may have of him as a tragic "Mulatto" is actually a tragedy of all American people who suffer from the troubled heart of who they are regardless of where they come from. This narrative also appealed to Japanese. One reader says she cried for Obama's sufferings in search of self, while others who are concerned about discrimination against Korean-Japanese found the book an encouraging story for Japanese minorities.[17] He becomes nobody representing everybody.

Memoir

Memoir is a mode of life narrative that historically situates the subject in a social environment, as either observer or participant. Obama takes the form of a memoir in which, Obama as subject, looks back on both his personal and public lives.

Japanese found some connection with him in a couple of episodes: "the internment of Japanese Americans during the war" (23), the industrial pollution induced Minamata disease in the "photograph of a Japanese woman cradling a young, naked girl in a shallow tub: that was sad; the girl was sick, her legs twisted, her head fallen back against the mother's breast, the mother's face tight with grief, perhaps she blamed herself" (29), and his three-day stopover in Japan with his mother, where they "walked through bone-chilling rains to see the great Buddha at Kamakura and ate green tea ice cream on a ferry that passes through high mountain lakes" (31–32). These mosaic representations of

Japan–US history, domestic issues caused by industrialization, and its traditional culture and nature did keep Japanese readers turning the pages.

However, memory itself is fallible.[18] Therefore, the autobiography has to be recognized as a literary form of self-invention rather than an "ultimate" truth of private fact, as Obama justifies his memoir, by saying:

> There are the dangers inherent in any autobiographical work: the temptation to color events in ways favorable to the writer, the tendency to overestimate the interest one's experiences hold for the others, selective lapses of memory. (xvi)

Despite Obama's disclaimer, his vivid memories of Japan endear Japanese to him, creating a sense of intimacy. Obama seems to "know" Japan.

Trauma Narrative

It is no exaggeration to call *Dreams from My Father* a story of trauma, a mode of writing about the unspeakable. Obama's traumatic shock of his lost racial identity that overshadows Obama's life was experienced when his mother took him to the US embassy library in Indonesia, where he found a collection of *Life* magazines and came across a photograph of an older man. He describes:

> He must be terribly sick, I thought. A radiation victim, maybe, or an albino—I had seen one of those on the street a few days before, and my mother had explained about such things. Except when I read the words that went with the picture, that wasn't it at all. The man had received a chemical treatment, the article explained, to lighten his complexion. He had paid for it with his own money. He expressed some regret about trying to pass himself off as a white man, was sorry about how badly things had turned out. But the results were irreversible. There were thousands of people like him, black men and women back in America who'd undergone the same treatment in response to advertisements that promised happiness as a white person.
> I felt my face and neck get hot. My stomach knotted; the type began to blur on the page. (30)

What he experiences here is the self-hate of an African-American who, wanting to be white, tries to peel off his skin with bleaching cream. Intuitively, Obama learns this is something unspeakable, even to his mother.

Obama remembers the photograph even after he comes to Chicago over ten years later, especially when he tries to pin down the idea of self-esteem. He questions the man in the magazine, "Did you dislike yourself because of your color or because you couldn't read and couldn't get a job? Or perhaps it was because you were unloved as a child—only, were you unloved because you were too dark? Or too light?" (194).

Bildungsroman

Traditionally regarded as the novel of development and social formation of a young man, Bildungsroman recounts the youth and young manhood of a sensitive protagonist who is attempting to learn the nature of the world, discover its meaning and pattern, and acquire a philosophy of life and an "art of living."[19]

His youth at Occidental College represents a period of storm and stress. He is trapped by his race:

> I had grown tired of trying to untangle a mess that wasn't my making.
> I had learned not to care.
> I blew a few smoke rings, remembering those years. Pot had helped, and booze; maybe a little blow when you could afford it. (93–94)

The angry youngster transfers to Columbia University in 1981, and the turning point comes when he receives a letter from his father, a letter asking him to visit Kenya and get to know himself and his people. Thereafter, Obama stops getting high, runs three miles a day, fasts on Sunday, and starts keeping a journal. In 1983, after graduation, he decides to become a community organizer. The excited Obama says, "That's what I'll do, I'll organize black folks. At the grass root. For change" (133). For change, he changes. He moves to Chicago in 1985 and learns to be a successful community organizer. And then, in 1990, he becomes the first African-American president of the *Harvard Law Review*. Needless to say, he has experienced continued success since.

Examining Obama's life story through the five genres of Smith and Watson's life narratives reveals Obama's work as a hybrid postmodern autobiography. By dramatizing his life using the Bildungsroman motif Obama ensures that the memoir of family, race, and trauma is not only his anymore. As Julia Swindells says:

> The autobiography now has the potential to be the text of the oppressed and culturally displaced, forging a right to speak both for and beyond the individual. People in a position of powerlessness—women, black people, working-class people—have more than begun to insert themselves into the culture via the autobiography, via the assertion of a "personal" voice, which speaks beyond itself. (7)

Because of "graphying beyond," literary biography becomes a hybrid art in which a body of facts is crossbred with the art of narrative.

The text illustrates pictures of postmodern hybridity that weaves issues of race, ethnicity, religion, and marriage. Obama portrays his life as shared experiences with many other people and makes the pictures more universal than personal. This is why *Dreams from My Father* deserves serious literary attention as a representation of contemporary America.

Anti-Postmodern Manhood

As his "personal history" provides us with his postmodern liberal image, his conservative character captures the minds of Japanese readers. According to Bret E. Carroll and Annette Richardson, the "challenge to the conventional notion of boyhood emotional suppression gained momentum during the 1960s and 1970s, when a growing youth counterculture, and increasingly powerful feminist movement, and an emerging men's movement all questioned traditional models of masculinities" (67–68). Despite these radical changes that have occurred in postmodern gender politics, Obama admirably describes traditional masculinity.[20] He is so preoccupied with the values his father practiced that he accepts them uncritically. In the formation of Obama's identity, paternity becomes its foundation.

This may confuse the reader who has read the book as a success story of a postmodern liberal. Curiously, however, the book also portrays a man who is molded by an anti-postmodern ideology of manhood. It is particularly true for Japanese readers who were misled by the Japanese title *My Dream*, suggesting an autobiographical work rather than a paternal work, as the English title *Dreams from My Father* seems to indicate. The English title forthrightly discloses the presence of his father's shadow during Obama's sentimental journey.

Myth and Resurrection of Manhood

Obama grew up learning his father's stories from his white grandparents and mother, and his father remained a "myth" (5). However, after the "bleaching cream" photograph in *Life* magazine, his gender perspective changes and his recognition of racial differences starts to distance him from his mother and her family. And then, Obama feels closer to his father, idealizes him, and finally realizes that he is the one he can truly trust. When Obama meets his father for the first time and listens to his speech at school, the son is impressed with "the power of my father's words to transform" (106).

The conventional gender ideology arises in Obama's mind as he learns more about his father. As a member of the African-American minority, he stands for the oppressed, but as a man of the gender majority, he does not doubt the right of men to possess power over women. This attitude of his toward men and women makes him a gender essentialist, while he strongly recognizes himself as a constructionist against other social issues. Obama doesn't practice this essentialist ideology of gender, but he accepts it to accept his father.

Father Absence and Father Presence

So it was something sacred for him to visit Kenya after he read the letter from his father: "The important thing is that you know your people, and also that you know where you belong" (114). Six years after the death of his father in 1982, Obama finally makes his pilgrimage to Kenya and becomes overtly fulfilled by his father's omnipresence. Obama is not alone:

> I feel my father's presence as Auma and I walk through the busy street. I see him in the schoolboys who run past us, their lean, black legs moving like piston rods between blue shorts and oversized shoes. I hear him in the laughter of the pair of university students who sip sweet, creamed tea and eat samosas in a dimly lit teahouse. I smell him in the cigarette smoke of a businessman who covers one ear and shouts into a pay phone; . . . The Old Man's here, I think, although he doesn't say anything to me. He's here, asking me to understand. (323)

Obama now looks for something he should inherit from his father and finds a recommendation letter written for his father to take a position at an American university, which says "[G]iven Mr. Obama's desire to be of service to this country, he should be given a chance." Immediately, the son says, "This was it, I thought to myself. My inheritance" (427). Obama then concludes that this "service to this country" equates to his career as a community organizer, that he comes full circle, and inexplicably, he concludes his journey in search of his father:

> Oh, father, I cried. There was no shame in your confusion. Just as there had been no shame in your father's before you. No shame in the fear, or in the fear of his father before him. There was only shame in the silence fear had produced. It was the silence that betrayed us. (429)

Meanwhile, throughout his interior journey, Obama encounters potential "male role models" who demonstrate manhood of their own. Lolo and Rev. Wright play father figures. Lolo teaches him the importance of self-protection, and Rev. Wright becomes Obama's religious mentor. Obama's brothers, Mark and Roy, present opposing characters. Over the foundation of the homosocial networks of these brotherhoods, Obama particularly favors the one who is closer to his father, i.e., Roy Obama.

Roy is the eldest brother, and Obama's intimate response is immediate:

> Auma had been right, though; his resemblance to the Old Man was unnerving. Looking at my brother, I felt as if I were ten years old again. (263)

Therefore, when Roy decides to return to Africa, Obama praises Roy highly again. Roy now has an African name: Abono. He has decided to assert his African heritage and has converted to Islam. Obama says, "His heart is too generous and full of good humor, his attitude toward people too gentle and forgiving, to find simple solutions to the puzzle of being a black man" (442). Roy becomes an ideal figure not only for the Luo tribe but for Obama who finds him perfectly in line to inherit their father's dream. Roy becomes Obama's living father figure.

Hierarchy of Patriarchy

Dreams from My Father is a paradoxical work of postmodern hybridity with traditional gender perspective. During the stay in Kenya, Obama learns that his father was in fact abusive, an alcoholic, a racist, and a sexist after all. However, having already fantasized his father unconditionally, Obama remains uncritical of him, especially when Auma refers to his tyranny at home and his decision not to give her any education. Roy also feels that his life was ruined by his father, saying, "I don't think I really like myself. And I blame the Old Man for this" (264). Obama's faith in his father is so deeply rooted that his father's masculinity, which is anachronistic and therefore anti-postmodern, becomes a part of his (un)conscious identity inscribed to inherit.

Obama's father, whose presence appears inconsistent and contradictory in the postmodern writing, may be a rational figure for a male African-American, who could have lost both male heritage and power as a racial minority, to paradoxically believe in the tradition of manhood. Obama's strong faith in his father has created the supposition that he is above reproach, and his concern becomes more about powerful male heritage than women's struggles. Toward the end of the book, Obama tries to sum up his journey:

I felt the circle finally close. I realized that who I was, what I cared about, was no longer just a matter of intellect or obligation, no longer a construct of words. . . . *The pain I felt was my father's pain. My questions were my brothers' questions. Their struggle, my birthright* (430 Italic added).

In the epilogue, Obama rushes to conclude his story, with a masculine triumph. He introduces two of the major male missions in which he was involved. One is his own marriage with Michelle Robinson in 1992, and the other is about his father-figure brother Roy's decision to inherit their paternal calling. Obama concludes his story as "a happy ending" (442) and congratulates himself as "the luckiest man alive" (442). Patriarchy overrules other issues that Obama could have considered more seriously.

Conclusion: Impress of Autoandrography

Dreams from My Father represents postmodern male anxieties. Obama values his role as community organizer, as a person who connects people and makes them realize that they are not alone. By doing so, he can unite the people while respecting their diversity. Japanese readers are envious of his talent and competence as they compare him with Japanese politicians. One Japanese reader equals him to Abraham Lincoln.[21]

At the same time, the story can be read as an autoandrography, a life writing of a man about himself by himself. This is a male version of an autogynography, a term first proposed by Domna C. Stanton in 1984, to suggest a centrality of gendered subjectivity to the literary production of self-referential acts. According to her, "women's gendered narrative involved a different plotting and configuration of the split subject."[22] In autoandrography, a male author reveals himself as someone who is trapped by the myth of masculinity as well as the postmodern depreciation of manhood. In African-American autoandrography, gender is more comparative. Being a racial minority and gender majority, he finds himself difficult to locate in this world of diversities. The ultimate decision for Obama was to rely on what he thought to be definite: i.e., paternity. It sounds, therefore, naïve for one Japanese reader to intuitively question whether a boy can live without his father.[23]

"It must be the blood" (209), says Auma, when she connects Obama's bossy attitude to that of their father's. Obama laughs but Auma doesn't—her perception different. For Obama, his father is somebody he wishes to be, for Auma he was somebody she could hardly understand. In the postmodern presentation of Barack Obama's life story, the paradox we ultimately find is his essentialist stance toward gender that he inherits from his father. Barack Obama tells his-story with paradox of hybridity and masculinity in this autoandrography and become enraptured with the presence of his father, who persistently whispers in the son's ear, "It's in the blood." His voice also echoes in the minds of Japanese readers, not to mention their American counterparts, who (un)knowingly acknowledge the patriarchal supremacy imprinted in the postmodern performance by the literary Barack Obama.

Works Cited and Consulted

Anderson, Linda. *Autobiography*. New York: Routledge, 2001.

Benton, Michael. "Literary Biography: The Cinderella of Literary Studies." *Journal of Aesthetic Education*. 39.3 (Fall 2005): 44–57.

Blog Rev. of *Dreams from My Father*, Barack Obama. *Biiingo!!* (http://suguri-bingo.jugem.jp/?eid=283), Nov. 6, 2008.

Blog Rev. of *Dreams from My Father*, Barack Obama. Book & Cinema (http://scbookinfo.seesa.net/article/110475646.html), Dec. 1, 2008.

Blog Rev. of *Dreams from My Father*, Barack Obama. Jugem (http://jugem.jp/mono/amazon/4478003629/), Jul. 11, 2009.

Carroll, Bret E., ed. "Boyhood" *American Masculinities: A Historical Encyclopedia*. Thousand Oaks, CA: Sage, 2003.

Chow, Rey. *Ethics after Idealism: Theory—Culture—Ethnicity—Reading*. Bloomington: Indiana University Press, 1998.

Customer Rev. of *Dreams from My Father*, Barack Obama. Amazon.co.jp, Jan. 13, 2008.

Customer Rev. of *Dreams from My Father*, Barack Obama. Rakuten (http:review.rakuten.co.jp/rd/2_213310_12604992_0), Feb. 7, 2009.

Detweiler, R. Rev. of *Dreams from My Father*. Barack Obama. *Choice* 33 (Feb. 1996).

"Dreams from My Father" *Wikipedia*. http://en.wikipedia.org/wiki/Dreams_from_My_Father.

Eakin, Paul John. *Fictions in Autobiography: Studies in the Art of Self-Invention*. Princeton: Princeton University Press, 1985.

Harmon, William, and C. Hugh Holman. *A Handbook to Literature*. 7th ed. Upper Saddle River, NJ: Prentice Hall, 1996.

Holloway, Karla F. C., and Stephanie A. Demetrokopoulos. *New Dimensions of Spirituality: A Biracial and Bicultural Reading of the Novels of Toni Morrison*. Westport, CT: Greenwood, 1987.

Holmes, Richard. "Inventing the Truth." *The Art of Literary Biography*. Ed. John Batchelor. Oxford: Clarendon, 1995.

Jolly, Margaretta, ed. *Encyclopedia of Life Writing: Autobiographical and Biographical Forms*. 2 vols. Chicago: Fitzroy Dearborn, 2001.

Kimmel, Michael S., Jeff Hearn, and R. W. Connell, eds. *Handbook of Studies on Men & Masculinities*. Thousand Oak, CA: Sage, 2005.

Klein, Joe. Rev. of *Dreams from My Father*, Barack Obama. "The Fresh Face." *Time*. Oct. 15, 2006. http://www.time.com/time/magazine/article/0,9171,1546362-3,00.html.

Leavall, Linda. "Introduction." *South Central Review* 23.3 (Fall 2006): 1–4.

Lejeune, Phillipe. *On Autobiography*. Ed. Paul John Eakin. Trans. Katherine Leary. Minneapolis: University of Minnesota Press, 1989.

Miller, Nancy K. *Bequest and Betrayal: Memoirs of a Parent's Death*. New York: Oxford University Press, 1996.

Obama, Barack. *Dreams from My Father: A Story of Race and Inheritance*. 1995. New York: Crown, 2004.

Obama, Barack. *My Dream: Autobiography of Barack Obama [Mai Doriimu: Baraku Obama Jiden]*. Tokyo: Diamond, 2007.

"The Obama Family—Barack, Michelle, Malia, and Natasha. http://www.makemyfamilytree.com/articles/barack_obama_family_tree.html.

Olney, James, ed. *Autobiography: Essays Theoretical and Critical*. Princeton: Princeton University Press, 1980.

Rev. of *Dreams from My Father*. Barack Obama. https://www.randomhouse.com/catalog/ display.pperl?isbn=9780307383419&view=quotes.

Rev. of *Dreams from My Father*, Barack Obama. *New York Times Book Review* (Aug. 6, 1995): 17.

Rochman, Hazel. Rev. of *Dreams from My Father*. Barack Obama. *Booklist*. 91.21 (July 1995): 1844.

Smith, Sidonie, and Julia Watson. *Reading Autobiography: A Guide for Interpreting Life Narratives*. Minneapolis: University of Minnesota Press, 2001.

Spicer, Jakki. "The Author Is Dead, Long Live the Author: Autobiography and the Fantasy of the Individual." *Criticism* 47.3 (Summer 2005): 387–403.

Swindells, Julia. *Victorian Writing and Working Women*. Cambridge: Polity, 1995.

Tatsumi, Takayuki. Rev. of *My Dream/Audacity of Hope*. Asahi.Com Book. (http://book.asahi.com/review/TKY200802050155.html), Feb. 3, 2008.

Notes

1. This essay is a revision of "Barack Obama and His-Story: Paradox of Hybridity and Masculinity in His Autoandrography," *Journal of the Graduate School of Letter, Hokkaido University* 4 (2009): 57–67, with much additional information of Japanese responses. See also a proceeding of the NASSS 2008, *Nanzan Review of American Studies: Journal for American Studies* 30 (2008): 211–21.

2. Obama, Barack. *My Dream: Autobiography of Barack Obama* [*Mai Doriimu: Baraku Obama Jiden*]. Tokyo: Diamond, 2007. *Dreams from My Father: A Story of Race and Inheritance*. 1995. New York: Crown, 2004. All references to the text are from this English edition.

3. An email interview with Kato, May 20, 2011.

4. An email interview with Kato, May 19, 2011. Its first impression of 8,000 copies was issued on Dec. 13, 2007; 2nd of 2,000 on Feb. 15, 2008; 3rd of 3,000 on Feb. 26, 2008; 4th of 2,000 on Mar 14, 2008; 5th of 5,000 on Nov. 14, 2008; 6th of 5,000 on Dec. 12, 2008; and 7th of 5,000 on Feb. 3, 2009.

5. Smith, Sidonie, and Julia Watson. *Reading Autobiography: A Guide for Interpreting Life Narratives*. Minneapolis: University of Minnesota Press, 2001, 2.

6. Benton, Michael. "Literary Biography: The Cinderella of Literary Studies." *Journal of Aesthetic Education*. 39.3 (Fall 2005): 1 and 44.

7. Leavall, Linda. "Introduction." *South Central Review* 23.3 (Fall 2006): 2.

8. Rev. of *Dreams from My Father*. Barack Obama. https://www.randomhouse.com/catalog/display.pperl?isbn=9780307383419&view=quotes.

9. Klein, Joe. Rev. of *Dreams from My Father*, Barack Obama. "The Fresh Face." *Time*. Oct. 15, 2006, 3. http://www.time.com/time/magazine/article/0,9171,1546362-3,00.html.

10. Blog Rev. of *Dreams from My Father*, Barack Obama. *Biiingo!!* (http://suguri-bingo.jugem.jp/?eid=283), Nov. 6, 2008. This is one of about fifty book reviews, customer reviews, and personal websites that anonymously refer to Obama's book. Most Japanese responses introduced in this essay are from these anonymous but publicly available sources, unless the authors are identified.

11. Detweiler, R. Rev. of *Dreams from My Father*. Barack Obama. *Choice* 33 (Feb. 1996): 1012.

12. Rev. of *Dreams from My Father*, Barack Obama. *New York Times Book Review* 6 Aug. 1995: 17.

13. Tatsumi, Takayuki. Rev. of *My Dream/Audacity of Hope*. Asahi.Com Book. http://book.asahi.com/review/TKY200802050155.html Feb. 3, 2008.

14. Smith and Watson, 183–206.

15. The Obama Family—Barack, Michelle, Malia, and Sasha. http://www.makemyfamilytree.com/articles/barack_obama_family_tree.html.

16. Smith and Watson, 194, 107.

17. Customer Rev. of *Dreams from My Father*, Barack Obama. Amazon.co.jp, Jan. 13, 2008.

18. Holmes, Richard. "Inventing the Truth." *The Art of Literary Biography*. Ed. John Batchelor. Oxford: Clarendon, 1995, 17.

19. Harmon, William, and C. Hugh Holman. *A Handbook to Literature*. 7th ed. Upper Saddle River, NJ: Prentice Hall, 1996, 59.

20. Carroll, Bret E., and Annette Richardson. "Boyhood" *American Masculinities: A Historical Encyclopedia*. Ed. Bret E. Carroll. Thousand Oaks, CA: Sage, 2003, 67.

21. Customer Rev. of *Dreams from My Father*, Barack Obama. Rakuten (http:review.rakuten.co.jp/rd/2_213310_12604992_0), Feb. 7, 2009, and blog rev. of *Dreams from My Father*, Barack Obama. Jugem (http://jugem.jp/mono/amazon/4478003629/), Jul. 11, 2009.

22. Smith and Watson, 187.

23. Blog Rev. of *Dreams from My Father*, Barack Obama. Book & Cinema (http://scbookinfo.seesa.net/article/110475646.html), Dec. 1, 2008.

Part VII

CONCLUSION

20

A VIEW FROM ISRAEL: A CRITICAL COMMENTARY ON OBAMA'S LEADERSHIP STYLE

Dovid Efune

As Jews in this country and around the world celebrated the Jewish New Year, Rosh Hashanah, just fifty days prior to the US presidential elections, they were all concerned about the candidates. Traditionally, it is a time of introspection about decisions made in the past and of considered resolutions for the future. For many Jews, especially the undecided, it may also have been a time to answer the question of which candidate would best serve the community, and reflect Jewish values, earning the congregational vote.

Typically, discussion over a candidate's reflection of Jewish values, and thereby worthiness of Jewish support has revolved around the Mishnaic *tikkun olam* (repairing the world) concept. Largely co-opted by the Democratic Party, and interpreted in practice to relate to social justice–inspired initiatives, the term is referenced on the Obama campaign's website and is a prominent theme in the literature of the National Jewish Democratic Council. On Dec 16, 2011, the president himself referenced the rabbinic dictum in a speech before members of the Union of Reform Judaism. "American Jews have helped make our union more perfect. . . . They pursued tikkun olam, the hard work of repairing the world," he said.

Recently, a strong case was made by former George W. Bush speechwriter Noam Neusner, in an article for the Jewish Daily Forward, that in fact Mitt Romney was the real *tikkun olam* candidate. He wrote, "[Mitt Romney] has shown through his own example of voluminous giving of charity . . . that prosperity and success breed far more *tikkun olam* than can be achieved through the taxing power of the state." The insinuation earned him a rebuke from liberal Jewish columnist Bradley Burston, who was of course eager to retain the treasured *tikkun olam* crown for the liberal camp.

However, whilst perhaps the most highly publicized Jewish tenet, the truth is that students of Jewish law and tradition will be well aware that there is a hierarchy in the precedence of principles, and there is one above all that in all cases, save three, overrides the others, including *tikkun olam*.

The concept of *pikuach nefesh* (saving a life) is inferred from the biblical verse in Leviticus 18:5, which states, "You shall therefore keep my statutes and my rules; if a person does them, he shall live by them." The preservation of life is granted such dominance in Jewish law, that even if there is minimal reason to believe that one's life may be endangered, such Jewish fundamentals as eating kosher or observing the Sabbath are readily discarded.

Living as we are today in perilous times, surely a candidate's *tikkun olam* credentials shouldn't serve as the primary Judaic principle guiding the Jewish vote. In the days since Obama has led this country, Jews have witnessed unspeakable horrors in places like Toulose, Burgas, and Itamar, among others. Syrians are being slaughtered daily, and the threat of a nuclear armed Iran carries with it the Ayatollah's promise of Israel's attempted annihilation. Shouldn't pikuach nefesh be the first consideration?

It is true that there are some limitations to the application of the law, which usually must be applied to a specific individual as opposed to an abstract beneficiary, but some of the greatest rabbinic authorities of modern times have applied the concept in a grander, geopolitical context.

The Rabbinical Congress for Peace, which represents more than 350 prominent Israeli rabbis, calls itself the pikuach nefesh committee, and issues recommendations to the Israeli government on the basis of rulings resulting from the application of the law.

Rabbi Menachem Schneerson, the late leader of the highly successful Chabad movement, which was described by *Newsweek* as "sprawling and influential," routinely applied the principle to Israeli political decisions. "I am completely and unequivocally opposed to the surrender of any of the liberated areas currently under negotiation, such as Judea and Samaria," he wrote in a letter to former United Kingdom Chief Rabbi, Immanuel Jakobovits in the 1980s. He continued, "I have repeatedly emphasized that this ruling has nothing to do with the sanctity of Israel . . . but solely with the rule of *pikuach nefesh*."

As Jews stand wrapped in prayer shawls absorbing the piercing sounds of the shofar blasts, it may be time to consider, "Who was the *pikuach nefesh* candidate?"

Obama, Bibi, and Iran: The Compounded Risk Equation

Amid the din of self-congratulatory pronouncements regarding his administration's relationship with Israel, the most significant line conveyed by President Obama to an audience of 13,000 at AIPAC's annual policy conference on March 4, 2012, was: "Israel must always have the ability to defend itself, by itself, against any threat." Although not said specifically in the context of the Iranian issue, the truth is, that for Israeli Prime Minister Benjamin Netanyahu it was the understanding of this fundamental reality that he was seeking to assert as the single most significant product of his trip to the United States.

Unfortunately for Israel, the president's subsequent words and further statements at a press conference two days following were hardly supportive of this pronouncement.

Some pundits heralded the speech as further indication of the president's shifting position on Israel that they say began in the fall of 2011. It is clear, however, that with his reelection the president has motive to temporarily modify his Israel position, as such, the one thing that is certain is that none can be sure of where he stands.

So much so, that the *Washington Post* ran an article on the home page of its website on Sunday titled "Obama Allies, Foes Speculate on a Big—and Hypothetical—Second-Term Agenda." The article highlighted the widespread uncertainty from friends and enemies alike over where Obama stands on a number of key issues saying, "Even after three years in office, Obama remains a political Rorschach test. His friends still project their brightest hopes on him. His enemies still project their deepest nightmares."

This may have been the idea behind Senate Republican Leader Mitch McConnell's suggestion at AIPAC that he may introduce new legislation that would force Obama on Iran. He said, "If the administration can't articulate an effective policy then Congress will do it for them." Congress could remove doubt over Obama's Iran policies by creating a well-defined framework and a timeline that would be mandated by law, leaving no room for Iranian or Israeli uncertainty over the position of the United States.

In the absence of such measures however, the bottom line is this: For Israel, dealing with Iran is fraught with risk and doubt at every turn, and kowtowing to Obama in any shape or form would significantly compound that risk.

What Israel needs from America, from its "friend," right now, at this challenging juncture for its safety and security, is the exact opposite: the articulation or implementation of any measures that would reduce the risk factor for the Jewish State. For example, at the very minimum, a statement along these lines: "Whilst the United States has articulated its independently held sovereign position, we support the right of our ally Israel to defend itself against any and all threats that it faces and will stand behind Israel and support any security decisions made by its democratically elected government."

To their credit, statements made on March 6, 2012 by Republican presidential candidates to AIPAC, generally appeared to strike this tone.

Israel doesn't know for certain how effective an Iran strike would be; she doesn't know how Iran will respond or how Hamas, Hezbollah, and the international community will respond. Additionally Iran's status as a "rational actor" is a subject of discussion. How best to conduct a strike? How potent are Iran's air defenses?

If Israel then had to add reliance on President Obama to that equation, then Bibi is right, the very purpose of Zionism will be lost. The Jews may as well pack up their bags, disperse themselves among the nations and subject themselves to the whims of their host countries as in the last two millennia of Jewish history.

For now, at the very minimum, because of the looming elections, Netanyahu can bundle considerations over President Obama into Israel's general evaluation of "international responses" to any Iran actions. For the future he should be sure to do little to encourage American Jews to support the president in November as there is a strong case to be made that journalist Ari Shavit of *Haaretz* was right when he said, "If Obama is re-elected there will immediately be a very strong attack and Israel will find itself in a very sharp crisis, because right now, Netanyahu has succeeded in restricting Obama, Obama is now like a lion in a cage."

For Israel, a Second Term from Hell

Within days, Hurricane Sandy and all its devastation was featured less prominently on front page headlines, to be replaced by a rapid countdown to the next week's presidential election.

There was no consensus over who was slated to win. Even reliable polls were largely out of sync with each other. Unexpected events and the three debates have never failed to bring continued new elements to the table.

For the president, the hurricane was a political blessing, as Americans tend to unite around their sitting leaders during times of crisis. More importantly, the graphic imagery of wholesale devastation has forced the emerging and ever-evolving debacle, over the administration's handling of the September 11, 2012, terror attack in Benghazi, Libya, from national focus.

For many around the world, there has been continued concern over President Obama's attitude towards Israel, which at times has been overtly hostile. *Haaretz* journalist Ari Shavit described it thusly in an interview on Israeli TV last year: "The rage that Barack Obama expresses towards Binyamin Netanyahu and the State of Israel is a raging fury."

I have no doubt that Shavit is right when he says that "If Barack Obama is elected . . . There will immediately be a very strong attack and Israel will find itself in a very sharp crisis. Because right now . . . Obama is . . . like a lion in a cage."

To estimate the steps that Obama might take toward Israel, with his last election behind him, his intent must be judged based on his past actions and sentiments expressed. The president has been clear about his opinion on a number of matters relating to Israel, and his current muted stance on the eve of Election Day, surely has no postelection staying power.

1. Obama believes that Israel is engaged in an illegal occupation and that building anywhere beyond the 1948 armistice line is against international law.
2. He believes that the claims of Palestinian Arabs against Israel are generally legitimate.
3. He believes that the establishment of a Palestinian Arab state is necessary and important.
4. He believes that the term pro-Israel can be applied in a prescriptive fashion. What Israelis think is in their interests is not necessarily pro-Israel.
5. Obama believes that the pro-Israel community can be bought off by sending financial aid to Israel.
6. Obama believes in the power of public opinion and words, "daylight," to steer public sentiment in favor of his policies.

When it comes to unrestricted sitting duck policy, these ideals can find damaging manifestation in a number of areas. For example, in a second term, Obama is likely to further the cause of Israel's delegitimizers like none other before him, by aggressively and publicly slamming any and all construction outside of pre-1967 Israel. It is unlikely that he would condemn anti-Israel resolutions at the United Nations and I believe that he will not veto Palestinian Arab attempts at the UN towards a unilateral declaration of statehood.

On the whole, since 1974, once coming to the understanding that Israel could not easily be vanquished militarily, the Jewish state's enemies have waged a war of accusation, seeking to isolate and diplomatically weaken the country to the extent that it is forced to significantly compromise its security.

A second Obama term would go a long way in furthering that agenda.

But in truth, the extent to which the sitting US president can impact affairs on the ground in Israel was significantly altered on January 22 when Israelis went to the polls. Israelis view the state of the US–Israel relationship as vitally important, and typically prime ministers who are viewed as having jeopardized that relationship have difficulty staying in power.

When President Obama was reelected, and Israeli voters had veered leftward, Zionism would have fall into regression.

The new Lieberman–Netanyahu coalition marked significant gains, and the country has entered a troublesome adolescent stage in its relationship with the US. Perhaps Israel the adult will emerge and embark on an independent new path.

What Do Glenn Beck and President Obama Have in Common?

Nothing, you say? Not quite.

In the way by which they address Jews, they both seem to define Jewish identity through the lens of victimhood.

I have been present on three occasions in the last twelve months where Beck was addressing a Jewish audience and each time I came away with the same impression; Beck views himself as some sort of guardian and "savior" of the Jewish people.

I noted in a previous column that in a letter on Beck's website posted Aug 11, 2011, that introduced his "Rumors of War" documentary, he explained his support for Israel, opening with the words "never forget," referring to the Holocaust. He then continued, "As the world spirals into financial chaos and conditions continue to worsen, fingers are already being pointed to determine a scapegoat. The nation dubbed 'Little Satan' is one obvious candidate to be on the receiving end of the blame."

President Obama's interactions with the Jewish community have of course been broader and more multidimensional, but following his visit on April 23, 2012, to the Holocaust Museum in Washington, DC, I couldn't help but notice a trend. Politics aside, when he addresses the Jewish community, it is through the lens of the Holocaust, and the Jewish icon that he has most publicly attached himself to—outside of a political setting—is Elie Wiesel.

Throughout his presidency, Obama has presided over about ten public addresses to the US Jewish community and some additional off-the-record meetings with communal leaders. Of those that were public, the two Jewish American Heritage Month events, two Rosh Hashanah phone calls with American Rabbis and various video messages for Jewish holidays were relatively insubstantial.

The speeches that were of most significance included the following: two that were delivered before an AIPAC audience that focused on international politics specifically addressing Israel's challenges with Iran and other belligerent neighbors. These speeches were essentially addressed to the entire pro-Israel community in the United States as well.

The president also spoke before the Union of Reform Judaism focusing on domestic politics and policies in working to energize his shrinking American Jewish liberal base.

The two remaining times that his message was directed towards the Jewish people exclusive of specific political motive were almost entirely Holocaust-centric.

The first was in 2009. On Obama's journey back from addressing the Arab world in Cairo, where he referenced Jewish suffering as the root of "aspiration for a Jewish homeland," he stopped in Buchenwald. His speech there, amounting to an extended tribute to Jewish victimhood, transitioned to reference Israel by saying, "They could not have known how the nation of Israel would rise out of the destruction of the Holocaust." The world's most famous survivor Elie Wiesel was by his side.

Monday's message followed the same pattern. Much was said of the sorry history of Jewish suffering and the need to prevent further atrocities against other minorities. Again, Wiesel accompanied him.

In no way do I wish to diminish the importance of this recognition and remembrance, but I know that not so far below the surface, America's Jews would like to see the president connect to another dimension of the Jewish message to mankind as well.

On the very same day that Obama visited Buchenwald, *The Algemeiner* published an interview with Britain's Chief Rabbi Jonathan Sacks, where he said, "If you tell a young generation of Jewish teenagers, we want you to know about Jewish history come to Auschwitz, Bergen Belsen and Treblinka and you'll know what it is to be a Jew, then they will have 2 or 10 thoughts before marrying another Jew and having Jewish children. Who wants to confer the status of victimhood onto their children and grandchildren?"

He continued, "We have failed to connect with the positives and we have failed to connect with the message of Jews to humankind 'through you will all the families of the earth be blessed.'"

The next time a President of the United States addresses the Jewish people, I have one request; let him stand beside a figure that represents the Jewish future, and pick a venue that highlights the gifts that our people have bestowed upon the nations of the world, a prestigious Jewish house of worship or of study, a museum documenting our illustrious history, or better yet, the Knesset.

References

Beck, G. (2011, August 11). FREE documentary—Rumors of War 2: The Last Days? *Glenn Blog*. http://www.glennbeck.com/content/blog/glenn/rumorsofwar.

Burston, B. (2012, August 30). GOP Jews and Chutzpah: Rebranding Romney-Ryan as the "Tikkun Olam" Ticket. *Haaretz*. http://www.haaretz.com/blogs/a-special-place-in-hell/gop-jews-and-chutzpah-rebranding-romney-ryan-as-the-tikkun-olam-ticket-1.461737?block=true.

Eckman, J. (2012, July 28). President Obama's failure with Israel. *Issues in Perspective*. http://graceuniversity.edu/iip/2012/07/12-07-28-1/.

Efune, D. (2009, June 5). The Jewish Response to the Economic Collapse: Exclusive Algemeiner Interview with Britain's Chief Rabbi Lord Jonathan Sacks. *The Algemeiner*. http://www.algemeiner.com/2009/06/05/the-jewish-response-to-the-economic-collapse-exclusive-algemeiner-interview-with-britain%E2%80%99s-chief-rabbi-lord-jonathan-sacks/.

Fahrenthold, D. A., and Wallsten, P. (2012, March 4). Obama Allies, Foes Speculate on a Big—and Hypothetical—Second-Term Agenda. *The Washington Post*. http://articles.washingtonpost.com/2012-03-04/politics/35449210_1_ben-la-bolt-obama-agenda-obama-campaign-spokesman.

Lucas, F. (2012, March 5). Netanyahu to Obama: "Israel must have the ability to defend itself." *CNS News*. http://cnsnews.com/news/article/netanyahu-obama-israel-must-have-ability-defend-itself.

Neusner, N. (2012, August 29). Mitt Romney Is Real tikkun olam Candidate. *The Jewish Daily Forward*. http://forward.com/articles/161869/mitt-romney-is-real-tikkun-olam-candidate/?p=all.

Obama, B. (2011, December 16). Remarks by the President at the 71st General Assembly of the Union for Reform Judaism. *The White House Office of the Press Secretary*. http://www.whitehouse.gov/the-press-office/2011/12/16/remarks-president-71st-general-assembly-union-reform-judaism.

Puschett, B. (2012, July 13). Tikkun-Olam. *Faces of the Campaign Blog*. http://www.barackobama.com/news/entry/nm-tikkun-olam.

Shavit, A. (2011, December 9). If Obama Reelected, Israel Will Face Crisis. *Weekend News Magazine*. http://www.disclose.tv/action/viewvideo/84648/Ari_Shavit____Haaretz___If_Obama_reelected_Israel_will_face_crisis_wmv/#ixzz2NvmHa7Eg.

Streeter, D. (2012, August 30). Burston: When American Jews Vote for Tikkun Olam, It Will Still Mean Obama. NJDC Blog. http://www.njdc.org/blog/post/burston083012.

21

A COMMENTARY FROM SOUTH AFRICA

Saths Cooper

"There is little doubt as to which candidate most of the world wanted to win the US presidential election." (The Independent 2012). While Barack Obama "may have disappointed the higher hopes of many of his supporters abroad, as he has at home" it is "also because we still harbour the hope that he could yet change the world for the better." (Ibid.) This global optimism that something better can still come out of the Obama administration is perplexing as it patently gives the benefit of the doubt to the US president, who most people want to succeed in making a difference as to how the United States is perceived and how it acts in the rest of the world.

When Malik Obama, 54, Barack Obama's brother, announced that he "will run for president of Kenya if he first wins a local governors' poll in March" (The Times 2013), he stated that "he would not be seeking a direct endorsement from the US President" (Ibid.) Whilst acknowledging that they "are cut from the same cloth" (Ibid.), the older brother appeared cautious about any premature marketing of the obvious blood connection with his well-known younger brother. This may not have been the case if the clock were turned back some five years ago, during the heady and historic multimedia and social networking blitz that catapulted the name, image, and words of Barack Obama to most electronically connected households the world over. Even if Malik Obama were to rely on his lineage with the president, there are other better-connected and locally relevant politicians, like Oburu Odinga, brother of Kenyan Prime Minister Raila Odinga, who are contesting the gubernatorial post.

Barack Obama is one of the few world leaders who can claim multiple nationality through immediate lineage, adding to the mystique and racial fascination that he holds for most people. Hawaiian-born of a white American mother, reared in Indonesia and having Kenyan fatherhood (and other nationalities through his maternal grandparents), he has excited outpourings of support from different parts of the world, leading to the Nobel Committee perhaps precipitously awarding him the symbolic Nobel Peace Prize. This probably got more credit and coverage outside the United States than it did in the often parochial US media, feeding as it does into the inward-looking and narcissistic localism that tends to signify the average Mr. Joe Soap and Ms. Jane Soap in the United States. This racial and cultural amalgam, resident in the White House, is the allure that defied the odds in 2008 and again in 2012.

In South Africa, he was roundly ignored by the political elite in the early stages of the primary campaign to become the Democratic Party's candidate and was not feted as he was in Kenya. Of course, there was the subsequent expectation that he would return to South Africa and Kenya and visit other African countries. But he "made only one, cursory trip to sub-Saharan Africa during his first term, and at the time made it fairly clear that he would not be smothering the continent with attention" (Harding 2012). He correctly declared in Ghana that "Africa's future is up to Africans" in a speech "that quietly acknowledged the limitations of American influence" (Harding 2012) in Africa. That Africa does more trade with China than it does with the United States clearly has to do more with the Obama administration's lack of interest in Africa than it does with Mark Okoth Obama Ndesandjo (another Kenyan sibling) being a successful businessman living in China since 2002.[1]

Professor Matthew Baum, at Harvard's Kennedy School of Government states that "The joke is that US presidents suddenly discover Africa in their second term" and that "Obama will look to less politically contentious places like sub-Saharan Africa to achieve concrete goals" (Philp 2012). But the *al-Qaeda* presence in countries like Mali in the west to Somalia in the east and Libya and Algeria in the north, as well as the Lord's Resistance Army in central Africa, continue to pose problems for the United States, which has never managed to fully appreciate the complexities of a postcolonial Africa that is caught up in a problematic quest for democracy, aided and abetted by multinational companies that take advantage of the continent's patent vulnerabilities. The labeling as "Islamist" does little to help one understand the history and emergence of raw religious primal reaction that is excited by most things American, and ironically aided and abetted by erstwhile US policy, which has not appreciably changed since the cataclysmic events of 9/11. Certainly not during the first Obama term of office.

President Obama can enjoin US and other multinational corporations to engage in Africa on precisely the same basis that they do in their western home countries, where they reap the enormous profits that they rake in from their African operations. But will he, especially when many of these corporations were probably Tea Party supporters? He can usher in a new meaningful era in US–Africa relations that can result in a serious difference to the material conditions of many on the continent. But will he, when he continues to be attacked for being Kenyan and a Muslim and for being soft on certain issues? The stilling footage of a sitting US president witnessing the assassination of bin Laden demonstrates that he patently is not soft. He is quintessentially American, yet he has a deeper appreciation of human foibles that needs to be translated into a lasting legacy at home and abroad to usher in a more peaceful and equitable future in global relations.

References

Harding, A. (2012, November 7). "Obama Second Term: What It Means for Africa." http://www.bbc.co.uk/news/world-africa-20236007.

Philp, R. (2012, November 11). "Obama to Focus More on Africa." *Sunday Times*, Johannesburg.

The Independent. (2012). "Four Years Later, Hope Still Lingers." Reprinted in *The Star*, Johannesburg, November 8, 2012.

The Times. (2013, January 17). "Obama's Brother Eyes Top Kenya Job."

Note

1. Obama's June 2013 visit to Senegal, South Africa, and Tanzania had the expected impact and promise of renewed interest and investment in Africa.

22

OBAMA'S LEADERSHIP PARADIGM IN INDIA: A PERSONAL REFLECTION

Surat Singh

I will attempt to decode my Harvard friend President Obama's paradigm of leadership, and in the second part, I will work out its implications for Indian leadership. The paradigm of President Obama's leadership is a key theme of his life (and that of his equally magnificent wife): to empower yourself and empower others.

I will briefly narrate his journey of self-empowerment during his Harvard Law School years in August 1988–91. I was his contemporary at Harvard Law School from August 1988 until April 1990. When Obama entered in 1988, his basic question was: "Where do I belong?" Three years of Harvard Law School provided him the answer.

The *Harvard Law Review* only invites the top scorers to be the editors of this prestigious journal, and Obama, along with 70 or so others, were chosen for the role. In 1990, they elected him to be the president of this most prestigious law journal. So Harvard Law School provided the answer to the question "Where do I belong?" The answer was "you belong to the TOP."

This experience in 1990 was a defining moment of his life. He did not have to prove to himself whether he was as good as any other. He proved it beyond any doubt that he was more than his peers.

After earning this self-empowerment in 1991, he had offers from top law firms in front of him, but he chose to honor his deepest aspiration, and that is to help others in discovering their empowerment. He joined a civil rights group in the South Side of Chicago and helped voters to register their votes so that their voices could be counted. As he had discovered his own voice, he wanted to help others to find theirs.

In 1998, Obama successfully contested for State Senate and made his voice heard in the state-level legislature. However, the lowest period of his life occurred when he lost the election for House of Representative, but from his past successes, he had learned that temporary defeat will not come in the way of his long-term success. In 2004, he contested as a senator from Illinois and was elected. In 2004, he made his mark by delivering a remarkable speech at the Democratic Convention in Boston. He articulated the vision of the *United* States of America—a nation not divided into Red States and Blue States.

He is a quick learner. In Washington, DC, he soon discovered that the greatest challenge of any human institution was the widening gap between its declared purposes and concrete end results. He found that when we establish an institution, we often start with a very desirable purpose. To achieve that purpose, we create a structure and develop standard operating procedures to achieve that purpose. But more often than not, during the course of its journey, that institution develops its own agenda, its own subpurposes, and its own vested interests.

The net result is that instead of serving the stated initial goals, the institution starts serving its own subgoals at the cost of fulfilling the stated goals. He noticed a big gap between the stated purpose and the actual action by elected representatives in Washington, DC, and he declared his goal to set Washington straight by bridging the gap between stated goals and delivered results.

He decided to contest for the presidency of the United States of America by reminding the American people of the basic decency and the aspirational goal of the American Constitution to form "a more perfect Union."

But after four years in office as president, President Obama realized that there *are* Red States and Blue States in America; the aspiration to be the *United* States has not been achieved. Unity of political parties around common goals is a worthy goal, but it has to be achieved; it is not given, and it can't be taken for granted. Despite all of the good will that President Obama showered upon the Republicans—both in the Senate and in the House of Representatives—Republican Senator Leader McConnell did not hesitate to exhort the Republican Party that the main goal of Republicans was to see that Obama did not get elected to a second term. Kindly note that the stated goal of the US Congress is to make laws for the United States that are good for the American public. [Nowhere does it state that the main goal of members of the House of Representatives and those of the Senate is to stop an incumbent president from getting a second term.] But Republicans—like any other political party—put party interests above the interests of the nation.

So Obama got chastened in his first term and learned from his naive assumptions of 2004 the realities of Washington politics. But one of the characteristics of Obama, as I have observed since our student days at Harvard Law School (1988–90), is that he gains strength by facing challenges. Challenges do not dampen his spirits for long. He has great resilience. He learns lessons from difficult challenges and emerges stronger after overcoming them.

The lesson Obama learned in his first term as president of the United States of America was that laudable objectives in the Declaration of American Independence might be "self-evident" but they are not *self-executing*. The Declaration says that we take these truths to be self-evident that all men are created equal. Yes, but it takes a lot of efforts to make it so.

Similarly, the need for a stronger union of the United States of America is self-evident but it is not self-executing. Ideally, there should be a *United* States of America and not Red States and Blue States but America is not united. America is divided into many things, as parties composed of Red States and of Blue States.

Another remarkable quality of a good leader, as President Obama demonstrates, is that he goes to the *heart* of things—he tries to catch the "essentials of a situation" quickly.

He realized that his real power came not from the Senate or House of Representatives but from the people, for the people of America are the fountainhead of his power. So he started approaching people *directly* by sending mass emails. He is the first Internet president of America, and he uses this technology with great effectiveness. Tell your senator, tell your representative — Obama would send in his emails to the people — what does passing or not passing this legislation mean to you. For example, in December 2012, without renewal by Congress, tax liability would go up to $2,000 for a middle class American who makes up to $200,000 per annum. Tell your representative — Obama would write — what $2,000 means to you, to your family. He collected real stories about how $2,000 would affect real people. He encouraged people to write to their chosen legislators to vote for his proposals. Hence overcoming vested interests of legislature institutions and his office bearers, he went directly to the source of the power—the people.

So Obama's formula to discover your own greatness is by learning and doing and helping others in discovering theirs.

He discovered his own power and confidence to change things and he is teaching people, "You have the power to set this country's course."

Thus Obama's formula of leadership is: learn, do, teach, and multiply (as shown in his example as the Internet President). To conclude, the paradigm of Obama's leadership can be summarized in two sentences:

> Discover your own power, and empower yourself by constant learning and doing things with an open mind.

and

> After learning by doing, empower others to discover their power to set things right. In other words, Obama's code is: Have faith in yourself and have faith in the potential greatness of America.

But this faith alone is not enough. You have to work very hard and in a sustained manner with a clear focus on your vision while realizing what we have and what we need. My friend Obama has done well in his first term as president, and he is engaging himself and others to do the unfinished work in his second term.

Implications of Obama's Model of Leadership for India

Obama's model of leadership of discovering your own greatness and helping others in discovering theirs has huge implications for Indian leadership.

Like America, India is a great democracy. In 1776, America declared itself free from Great Britain and started a long and successful experiment to create and realize the dream of liberty, equality, prosperity, and justice for all. America has succeeded in achieving many of its goals and served as a beacon of light for the aspiring democracies. But President Obama keeps on reminding American people that all these ideals are self-evident but not self-executing. A lot of hard work, with clear vision and sustained execution, is required to keep the American promise alive. The same goes for India. In fact, Indian Constitution was drafted and adopted in 1950 with a lot of idealism. Its preamble says:

> WE THE PEOPLE OF INDIA, having solemnly resolved to constitute India into a [SOVEREIGN SOCIALIST SECULAR DEMOCRATIC REPUBLIC] and to secure to all its citizens.
> JUSTICE, social, economic and political;
> LIBERTY of thought, expression, belief, faith and worship;
> EQUALITY of status and of opportunity;
> and to promote among them all
> FRATERNITY assuring the dignity of the individual and the [unity and integrity of the Nation]

In fact, the first prime minister of India, Pt. Jawaharlal Nehru, told members of the Constituent Assembly at the time of drafting of the Constitution:

> The first task of this assembly is to free India through a new constitution, to feed the starving people, and to clothe the naked masses, and to give every Indian the fullest opportunity to develop himself according to his capacity.

But these were merely goals and aspirations. They do not execute themselves. They require a lot of planning, strategies, structures procedures, personnel, coordinated efforts, and vast resources to make them reality. But like President Obama, Pt. Jawaharlal Nehru reminded the Indian people in his famous speech "Tryst with Destiny" on the eve of independence in 1947 that "the dream of the greatest man of our time was to wipe every tear from every eye. That may be beyond us but as long as there are tears in the eyes, our task will not be over."

There is a remarkable similarity between the tone of Prime Minister Nehru's 1947 speech and the State of Union address of President Obama on February 12, 2013, where President Obama focused on the unfinished task and the unfinished journey in his second term.

So Indian politicians can learn from President Obama what they could have easily learned from their first prime minister, Pt. Jawaharlal Nehru. In fact, there are striking similarities between President Obama and Pt. Jawaharlal Nehru.: Both received the benefit of the finest education of their time; both cared about the welfare of their country more than their individual egos; both made considerable sacrifices for the sake of their nation. Incidentally, another fact (in which I personally rejoice) is that both were trained as lawyers.

In fact, there is another similarity between President Obama and Pt. Jawaharlal Nehru: Obama takes his inspiration from the great civil rights leader and visionary Dr. Martin Luther King Jr., and Dr. Martin Luther King Jr. took his inspiration from Mahatma Gandhi of India. Thus Gandhi was the guru of Jawaharlal Nehru, and Gandhi is Obama's guru's guru. Gandhi had always wanted people to have the power to shape their own destiny. For Gandhi, democracy was nothing less than a people having the power to make those decisions that shape their destiny. Both Jawaharlal Nehru and Obama are preaching the same message, i.e., people have the power to change the course of their country. Thus Indian leaders can get the inspiration from the model of leadership of President Obama.

But inspiration alone is not enough. In fact, President Obama himself has highlighted that three qualities are needed in a leader:

(i) CLEAR VISION

A leader must know where his country is and where he wants to take it. So a clear distinction is needed between what we have and what we need and an audacity of hope to take it to its desired destination.

(ii) POWER OF JUDGMENT TO PRIORITIZE

A leader is chosen to see the big picture and to set the agenda for the nation. Because there are so many issues before a nation, a leader has to clearly prioritize how much value is to be attached to what. What is the order of priorities?

(iii) POWER OF CHARACTER TO SEE THE EXECUTION THROUGH

In the journey of execution of these priorities, there would be a lot of obstacles, oppositions, and temporary setbacks. A leader should have the character to see the execution of his key priorities through, despite heavy odds. Leadership is not made either for the chicken - hearted or for the timid souls. It requires a certain robustness of character to remain focused on key priorities despite compiling distractions. As President Bill Clinton has rightly pointed out in his autobiography that the task of a leader is to keep the nation focused on those things that are really important for the nation—again and again. I would add one more quality to these three qualities of leadership: connectivity.

President Obama has not highlighted it in his list of leadership qualities, but it is implicit in his actions. Leadership is not about you; it is about the common goals that are to be achieved with the participation of all stakeholders. So connectivity with the stakeholders—right from the stage of formulation of goals to devising strategies and through execution—is crucial for the success or failure of leadership. Leadership is a team sport and not a solo role. Building a consensus around the core issues for a nation is a hallmark of great leadership.

Related Issue: Who Is Obama for India?

India has a great tradition of producing great leaders like Gandhi, Jawaharlal Nehru, and Sardar Patel. As mentioned, there are a lot of striking similarities between Jawaharlal Nehru and Barack Obama. But the present question is—where is the Obama for India?

Many aspirants in political leadership try to present themselves as the future Obama. But show me a person who possesses all four qualities that Obama represents, namely the vision for India, a clear set of priorities, a character to execute them until completion, and a connectivity with the people.

There are many aspirants that have the right kind of training and correction to be potential candidates. For example, Rahul Gandhi is a future hope of the Congress Party to lead the country, but what are his claims to greatness?

Though he is dedicated to youth power, the first thing Obama represents is that greatness is not dependent on the circumstances of your birth. Any American-born can hope to reach the highest position in the land, as exemplified by Obama himself. Rahul Gandhi's basic identity is dynastic and not based on his individual achievements. How does he make sure that the leadership of the country is not dependent on the accident of birth that he represents? The accident of birth should neither count as a trump card nor a deadly liability for a leader in a democracy. One has to go beyond circumstances of birth to achieve one's greatness. For that purpose, Rahul Gandhi will have to achieve greatness in his own right. Can he do that?

For example, let us look at Prime Minister Dr. Manmohan Singh. He was a great finance minister under the prime ministership of Mr. Narasimha Rao. He initiated economic reforms and liberalization process from 1993 onward. But now, despite being the prime minister, he is under the tutelage of Congress President Sonia Gandhi. I have no doubt that Sonia Gandhi is the most patriotic leader of India. Despite her Italian birth, her commitment to India is beyond doubt. Furthermore, there is no doubt that Gandhi and the Nehrus have contributed tremendously to the successful journey of India, but the nation is far richer, far more diverse, and far greater than any great individual family. Can the Gandhi family put India above their family identities?

Please remember that Obama's model of leadership is to empower yourself and to empower others. Can the able persons outside the Gandhi family be found and empowered to lead the country? One good example is Rattan Tata, who made a thorough search outside the Tata family to find his successor for the Tata empire. Can Congress transcend its old habit of placing loyalty to family above ability, and instead put the country's interests over family interests?

The answer to this question will be the answer to the question whether Congress can produce an Obama. In the leading opposition party, Bhartiya Janta Party (BJP), Mr. Narendra Modi is presented as the next Obama. In fact, in Gujarat there were videos made during his recent election projecting him as greater than Obama. That may be understandable for political reasons, but let us examine the reality. In his recent lecture, before a leading business education college of India (Shri Ram College of Commerce), Mr. Narendra Modi, three-times elected as chief minister of Gujarat, tried to project himself as the future national leader. He presented his vision of development of India based on the pattern he has adopted in his state Gujarat. Can he be the next Obama?

It is interesting that in the same week when his news of a development agenda for India was published in a newspaper, other news also made headlines, i.e., that his government objected to the central government's scheme of giving scholarships to minority students. It is true that Gujarat High Court rejected his objections and upheld the federal government scheme of providing scholarships to minority children. But this kind of attitude makes him a sectarian leader and not a national leader. India is too vast and too diverse to be represented by a single community—Hindus or Muslims. It is a pluralistic society. So India's leadership, like America's leadership, will require both the temperament and the talent for coordinating various communities together in the service of the nation. Can Mr. Narendra Modi get his limited and prejudiced vision of the world corrected and make it more inclusive, which is needed for national leadership? Or is it too hard for an old dog to learn the new tricks?

In fact, it is not even a question of learning tricks; it is a question of basic temperament. How will he develop tolerant, inclusive, truly democratic temperament that respects differences of opinion in a democratic set up?

In addition, the BJP looks for the greatness of India in the past and not in the present and future. They are looking at the world in a rearview glass. India was great in the past, but now its greatness lies in the future. Can BJP liberate itself from a past-focused vision of India? Can it focus its efforts on building temples of learning and research rather than building temples on top of dilapidated structures in the name of recovering self-identity or self-respect?

The third important claimant who is presented as Obama for India is the young chief minister of the largest state of India, Uttar Pradesh, Mr. Akhilesh Yadav. I will ask the same question to Mr. Akhilesh Yadav as I have asked of Rahul Gandhi. What is his claim to greatness apart from his family roots? Even in terms of time, Yadav's dynasty is far too recent to be established at par with older dynasties like the Gandhi's. What are the remarkable things Mr. Akhilesh Yadav has done so far in Uttar Pradesh so as to claim to be a worthy candidate for national leadership? Only his party can reflect on this question and give an honest answer. My message for Mr. Akhilesh Yadav would be that you first prove yourself as a great chief minister of the largest state of India and then you stake your claim for national leadership.

There is another leader who has tried to present herself as the next Obama of India, the former chief minister of Uttar Pradesh Ms. Mayawati. What is her claim to greatness?

She says that because she comes from the lower class of India she represents the equivalent of the blacks of India. But she must realize that leadership is much more than identity politics. President Obama was elected president of the United States of America, not as a reward for his being black but in recognition of his vision as to what he can do for America. Let Mayawati answer the question about what she can do for India before she displays her card of being the black leader of India. Great leaders are chosen for their potential contribution to their countries rather than as a compensation for past wrongs. Let her think about what she can do for India as a leader and persuade Indian people that she would be best for India. Only then she should stake her claim for Indian leadership.

I realize that judging the present leaders of India by President Obama's standards is based on a very high benchmark. But kindly do not forget that India has produced leaders like Gandhi and Nehru who are sources of inspiration—even for the guru of President Obama, namely Dr. Martin Luther King Jr. If we can produce Obama's guru's guru, we can definitely produce an Obama for India. But we have to look long and hard without fear or favor, without affection or ill will, beyond a single family, looking beyond the prejudiced past with an open, fearless, but hopeful eye, keeping our small egos under control and focusing our eyes on the single most important question: who has the vision, judgment, character, and connectivity to continue India as a success story and to keep the Indian dream alive as Obama is trying to keep the American dream alive?

23

PRESIDENT OBAMA: A COMMENTARY FROM RUSSIA

Evgeny Osin

The Audacity of Hope

On the day when the Gulf War ended, in February 1991, we used to live in a totally different world. Internet virtually did not exist, just like my country, Russia, which was still the heart of the Soviet Empire. Shelves were empty in Moscow stores, food was sold in exchange for ration cards, and currency had shortly been changed to the new ruble in three days. I was at primary school, where we still had Lenin stories in our textbooks. But I remember an intense feeling of joy as we celebrated the end of the war, and hoped for a new, peaceful world brought by the international news.

The reality turned out to be more complex. The world had yet to face many conflicts in the coming years, and Russia became a ship in the ocean of economic and political turmoil of the 1990s. It was the time when many people here lost their hope for the triumph of justice, equality, and human values. And it took seventeen years for us to experience a glimpse of that hope again. It happened in November 2008, when Barack Obama was elected for the first time.

This event was important in Russia for two reasons. First, even though President Bush was initially presented as Putin's friend who had a "sense of his soul," the assertive external policy of his administration amplified by an increasing anti-American stance of the Russian state-controlled media had created a negative image of the United States. In 2008, only 4% of Russian believed that the United States played a positive role in the world[1] (a drastic change from 27% in 2001[2]), compared to 67% holding a contrary opinion. There was hope that the coming of a new president would change the situation.

But there was another reason why the election of Barack Obama would mark the end of an old era. Many Russians (at least, those aged thirty and up at the time) had grown up with an idea that the United States was a country where African-Americans were being oppressed. This idea was particularly dear to old Soviet propaganda that did its best to find the worst in capitalist countries. The election of an African-American president would finally show that the world has changed, and that the United States has become a country of equal opportunities.

This hope was not unique to Russia. The decision of the Nobel committee to award the 2009 Peace Prize to President Obama as a "call to action"[3], not only supporting his efforts for international cooperation and nuclear disarmament, but also emphasizing the importance of politics guided by human values rather than pure pragmatism. This award was an expression of hope that Obama's vision of "a just peace based on the inherent rights and dignity of every individual" would help people "reach for the world that ought to be"[4], eventually bringing the vision closer to reality.

The Tedium of Reality

When the Russians are asked about their feelings for Barack Obama, the predominant answer is indifference (40% in 2012), followed by respect, liking, and hope (between 10% and 20%)[5]. Even though Obama was supported by 48% of Russians during his second campaign (up from 38% in

2008), many Russians said they would simply ignore the elections even if they had a chance to vote (34%), and most believed that his second presidentship would bring no serious change in the US–Russia relations (65%). The Russians' interest in Barack Obama (based on the number of Google searches) at the peak in 2012 was only about 15% of that in 2008 compared to 50% in the United States. There was remarkably little interest in Obama in Russia throughout the final three years of his first term[6], see Fig. 23.1, and the number of Russians who put a lot or some confidence in his doing the right thing in world affairs has remained nearly the same as the number of those who put not too much confidence or no confidence at all[7].

Why is the interest for Obama so low in Russia? The explanation seems simple: Russia is not one of the top foreign-policy priorities for the United States, and vice versa. The recent isolationist trend taken by the Putin administration can be summarized as "no one has the right to tell us what is the right thing to do," thereby refusing the role of a world leader or moral authority to the United States or any international entity. This trend was evident in the disproportionate Russian government reaction to the Magnitsky Act in December 2012, when international adoptions to the United States were banned with a law infamously nicknamed "Herod's law"[8].

And the Obama administration does not seem very eager to tell Russia what it should do either. The cautious and pragmatic approach taken by the United States after the symbolic "reset" of Russian–American relations in 2009 resulted in a rather mild version of the Magnitsky Act being signed by President Obama, despite the criticism of his "unseemly efforts"[9] to avoid offending Vladimir Putin. In response to this, the Russian journalist Yulia Latynina characterized Obama's external policy as "attempts of a respectable gentleman riding on a bus to apologize to a drunken hooligan who knowingly stepped on the gentleman's foot in search for self-affirmation"[10]. However, the Magnitsky Act can be seen as a statement about the value of human rights the United States made while trying to avoid confrontation with Russia that could spoil the cooperation of both countries in other areas, and this approach seems to be in line with the nonviolent policy values proclaimed by Barack Obama at the beginning of his presidency.

Time is needed to see whether the Magnitsky Act and the ensuing inadequate legal response coupled with anti-American hysteria in Russian state-controlled media have really changed the

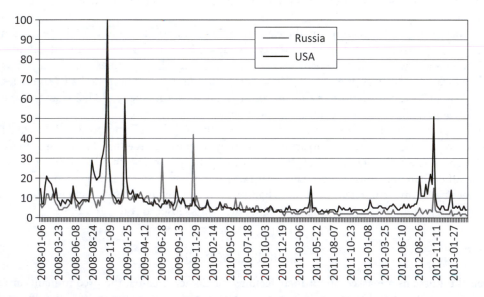

Figure 23.1 Weekly numbers of search for "Obama" in Google in the United States and in Russia in 2008–2013, in percentages of the relative maximum in November 2008. [6]

Russian–American relations. According to the 2013 public opinion polls, the number of Russians with a positive attitude about the United States did not change compared to 2012 (55%), but the Russian–American relations are evaluated as more chilly (35%) and tense (17%)[11]. Quite alarmingly, the number of Russians supporting the adoption ban is increasing[12], and May 2013 data from the Levada-Centre shows that this year the USA has topped the list of Russia's enemies for the first time since 2005, when this poll was first conducted[13].

The recent Snowden affair only makes the situation between the two countries more complicated. As of early July 2013, while this text is being written and while the controversial exposer is still remaining in the transit zone of Sheremetyevo airport, the Russians are more inclined to think of him as a hero[14] but do not see the data he disclosed as a big deal, since wiretapping does not surprise most Russians (only 6% are sure their own phone calls are not being wiretapped)[15]. Though opinions differ on the problem of asylum, Russians tend to see Snowden as a problem for the USA that Russia would better not meddle with, and it seems that both the Obama and Putin administrations are attempting to avoid confronting one another on this issue.

The Magnitsky Act seems to be the first and so far the only step taken by the United States since the 2009 "fresh start" that directly targets Russia. Before it happened, Russians believed that Obama's presidency has made either no change or only a little positive change in the relations between the two countries[16] and expected no change after his reelection[5], in line with the overall indifference discussed earlier. Time will show whether they were right and whether the two countries can avoid dealing with issues in earnest for the next three years. With time, it might become more and more challenging for Obama, in the light of such coming events as the absurd trial started by Russia against Magnitsky posthumously in 2013, counter to both the country's law and to common sense. But instead of prognoses, I will propose a psychological explanation for the surprising indifference of Russians toward the current president of the USA.

The Pain of Contrast

After Barack Obama's inauguration in November 2012, Russian social network users were sharing a series of pictures that showed its amazing differences from the inauguration of Vladimir Putin that took place a few months earlier, in May. On one side of the screen, a square by the Capitol in Washington, DC, full of people cheering the new president; on the other side, a completely empty Red Square that was cleaned up and closed off by security services as were many streets in the center of Moscow to prevent potential protesters from gathering on the inauguration day. On one side, happy Michelle Obama congratulating her husband; on the other side, Lyudmila Putina, despondent and aloof, standing by her husband with tears in her eyes during the inauguration ceremony, which turned out to be her last public appearance until the couple announced their divorce a year later. In one photo, Obama hugging a random boy from the audience, in another one, Putin shaking a little boy's hand in the company of three sullen security guards, two of them holding the boy's arm and one more holding his neck, as if it the boy were a little member of Al-Qaeda.

The political life in the two countries presents no less of a contrast. The US presidential election debates received very little media coverage in Russia, apparently because Putin has repeatedly refused to participate in any public debates during his presidential campaigns. While there is often disagreement in the US Congress, the Russian parliament is "not a place for political battles," as its speaker Boris Gryzlov once blurted out, passing ambiguous laws so quickly and unanimously that it was nicknamed "a printer gone mad" by Dmitry Gudkov, one of the handful of its opposition members. According to the president of one country, the Dixie Chicks "are free to speak their minds"[17], whereas the president of the other country states that Pussy Riot "were arrested correctly, and the court has made the right decision" jailing the female singers for two years[18]. Obama supports LGBT in his inaugural speech, while Putin signs a law against "propaganda of homosexuality" that sets a $3,000 fine for writing things like "gay is ok" in one's blog, and another law banning adoption of Russian children by citizens of any country where same-sex marriage is legal[19]. This list of striking differences could take many pages.

The political systems in Russia and in the United States are very different. On paper, Russia is a democracy, just like the USA. In reality, Russia is a very different country where the legal system is repressive and state-dependent, political activity is only permitted to loyalists, and freedom of press is restricted to a few select media outlets with very limited audience, resulting in the absence of public control over corruption which thrives at all levels. Any information suggesting that this situation is not universal and not normal produces a painful dissonance with reality in the minds of the people who have to live in it. And the easiest way to cope is to suppress the undesirable information, resulting in overall ignorance about and indifference toward the United States in general.

A choice of other defense mechanisms are also available in psychology textbooks. Denial has lead to a gradual decrease in the percentage of Russians who believe that American society is more just than Russian [1], although they still prevail over those holding a contrary opinion. Projection reveals itself in delirious public speeches by parliament members saying literally that Americans buy Russian orphans as living goods for organ donations[20]. Rationalization leads to moral nihilism, such as an idea that human rights only exist as a disguise for private and political interests; this was expressed by the president in his recent speeches about the nongovernmental organizations[21]. The alternatives for a conscious approach are fewer, in line with the old Soviet menu: emigration, dissent, and organized protest or becoming a part of the corrupt system to change it from within.

Like the rest of the world, most Russians had hoped that the arrival of Barack Obama would change the situation on a global scale, and some, more audacious ones, may have even hoped that it would change things in Russia. Apparently, a positive change is much easier to proclaim and to hope for than to achieve. It requires "fundamental faith in human progress"[4], patience, and hard work of each person on his or her own behalf. The Moscow street protests of 2012 and increased volunteer activism in many spheres indicate that the number of people in Russia who endorse the agenda proclaimed by Obama is growing, increasing the hope that the dream of Martin Luther King can one day become reality in Russia.

Notes

1. "Myths about the USA Are Going from Russians' Consciousness, Experts Say." RIA News. February 19, 2013. http://ria.ru/society/20130219/923731098.html (in Russian).
2. "On the Role of the USA in the Contemporary World." FOM. April 1, 2004. http://bd.fom.ru/report/map/of041208 (in Russian).
3. "The Nobel Peace Prize 2009—Presentation Speech." Nobelprize.org. May 4, 2013, http://www.nobelprize.org/nobel_prizes/peace/laureates/2009/presentation-speech.html.
4. "Barack H. Obama—Nobel Lecture: A Just and Lasting Peace." Nobelprize.org. May 4, 2013, http://www.nobelprize.org/nobel_prizes/peace/laureates/2009/obama-lecture_en.html.
5. "USA Election Outcomes: Every Second Russian Supported Obama." WCIOM.ru. November 15, 2012. http://wciom.ru/index.php?id=459&uid=113378 (in Russian).
6. Google Search Trends.
7. "Pew Global Attitudes Project Question Database." Pew Research Global Attitudes Project. Retrieved on July 12, 2013. http://www.pewglobal.org/question-search/?qid=724&cntIDs=&stdIDs=.
8. "Herod's Law." The Economist. January 5, 2013. http://www.economist.com/news/europe/21569079-russian-civil-society-outraged-law-bans-russian-orphans-being-adopted.
9. "Russia Fumes as U.S. Senate Passes Magnitsky Law Aimed at Human Rights." The Washington Post. December 6, 2012. http://www.washingtonpost.com/world/europe/us-passes-magnitsky-bill-aimed-at-russia/2012/12/06/262a5bba-3fd5-11e2-bca3-aadc9b7e29c5_story.html.
10. "Instead of Accepting the American Compromise, Kremlin Starts Shouting Like a Hooligan Sensing Hesitation of a Bespectacled Intellectual." Novaya Gazeta. April 19, 2013. http://www.novayagazeta.ru/columns/57772.html?p=3(in Russian).

11. "Russia and the USA: A Monitoring of Relations." Russian Public Opinion Research Center (VCIOM). February 25, 2013. http://wciom.ru/index.php?id=459&uid=113677 (in Russian).
12. "Do Not Give Away the Orphans Abroad." Russian Public Opinion Research Center (VCIOM). April 09, 2013. http://wciom.ru/index.php?id=269&uid=113840 (in Russian).
13. "External Enemies and Friends of Russia." Levada-Center. June 18, 2013. http://www.levada.ru/18-06-2013/vneshnepoliticheskie-vragi-i-druzya-rossii (in Russian).
14. "Snowden Is a Hero, 44% Internet Users Say: A Regnum Poll." Regnum. July 5, 2013. http://www.regnum.ru/news/1680515.html (in Russian).
15. "New Secret Snowden Data Do Not Surprise 2/3 of Russians." RBC-Rating. July 7, 2013. http://rating.rbc.ru/news.shtml?2013/07/07/33982964 (in Russian).
16. "The Presidency of Barack Obama: Russians Are Summing Up." Russian Public Opinion Research Center (VCIOM). September 20, 2011. http://wciom.ru/index.php?id=459&uid=111983 (in Russian).
17. "Full Text of Brokaw's Interview With Bush." The New York Times. April 25, 2003. http://www.nytimes.com/2003/04/25/international/worldspecial/25BUSH-TEXT.html?pagewanted=all.
18. "Putin on Air at NTV." October 7, 2012. http://www.gazeta.ru/politics/news/2012/10/07/n_2560857.shtml (in Russian).
19. "Putin Signs Law Banning Gay Couples from Adopting." Russia Today, July 3, 2013. http://rt.com/news/putin-ban-gay-adoption-636/.
20. "Parliament Members Suspect that Russian Children Are Used for Organ Donations in the USA." NTV. February 22, 2013. http://www.ntv.ru/novosti/474898/ (in Russian).
21. "Putin Pushes NGO Foreign Agent Law." The Washington Post. April 15, 2013. http://www.washingtonpost.com/world/europe/putin-pushes-ngo-foreign-agent-law/2013/04/15/d9509ec2-a37e-11e2-9c03-6952ff305f35_story_1.html.

24

AMERICA'S ASIAN CENTURY: A MIRAGE OR REALITY?

Dinesh Sharma

"What do I think of Western civilization? I think it would be a very good idea."
—Mahatma Gandhi

"The future of politics will be decided in Asia, not Afghanistan or Iraq, and the United States will be right at the center of the action."
—Hillary Clinton

"Development is about transforming the lives of people, not just transforming economies."
—Joseph Stiglitz

A new epoch in international relations seems to have kicked-off with the new Chinese premier Xi Jinping's inaugural visit to Russia and then to the meeting of the BRIC economies in Africa. Both trips confirm China's growing influence in the world. First, the trip to Russia renews ties with an old cold war ally. Next, the trip to Africa with the emerging economies confirms a multipolar world is taking shape before our eyes. In an interview, Xi Jinping said, "The economy of these countries play an important role in contributing to the joint development, countering international financial crises and stimulating the global economic growth. This corresponds to the modern tendencies of peace, development and cooperation."[1]

During Obama's first term much of the world suffered through a severe economic crisis. However, if during that period you were among the 14 million persons residing in the larger metropolitan area of Chengdu, the capital of Sichuan Province in Southwest China, you would have seen none of that. Indeed, Chengdu's foreign trade volume tripled from $15.34 billion in 2008 to $47.54 billion in 2012 (Liy and Chao 2013).[2] Thanks in part to a new Comprehensive Bonded Zone that was established as recently as 2010, 40 multinational high-tech enterprises such as Intel, Foxconn, and Dell have settled down in Chengdu and are rapidly turning it into one of the world's most important manufacturing bases for electronics. By 2015, so the projections go, some 100 million computers and 200 million tablets will be produced in that city. What is most astonishing about these developments is the lightning speed with which they are occurring. At the same time, they tell us something essential about the evolving twenty-first century: Asia is ascendant, and the United States better adjust—or it will be left behind. This is apparently what America's first Pacific president, Barack Obama, had already concluded some years ago, and his actions during his second presidential term will shape the coming decades.

According to the Asian Development Bank, approximately 3 billion people will enter the middle class in the coming decades as part of Asia's transformation and enjoy life standards similar to those of Europeans and Americans today. This singular development "could account for over half of global output by the middle of this century." The report titled, "Asia 2050: Realizing the Asian Century," outlines a potentially promising future which may be realized, but it is not etched in stone.[3]

Nonetheless, Australia has seen the writing on the wall and undertook its own comprehensive study. It released a white paper titled, "Australia in the Asian Century," which anticipates some of the landmark changes underway.[4] The report states that Australia and Australians can navigate the Asian century, taking advantage of great opportunities and leading to a more prosperous and resilient Australia. The report envisions fully integrated Australia as part of the Asian region, identifying 25 objectives with policy pathways to be achieved by 2025.

The report highlights "a wealth of opportunities" in mining, tourism, sports, education, manufacturing, services and sustainability, where Australia is a reliable partner in the development of the Asia-Pacific region. Thus, it was not surprising when the United States announced a pivot toward the Asian economies: it was first made public at the Pentagon, at the APEC meeting in Hawai'i in 2011, and then most importantly in Darwin, Australia.

The office of the US National Intelligence Council predicts that Asia will exercise more global influence than the United States and NATO allies combined by 2030. According to the report, it was released to coincide with Obama's second term, designed to promote strategic thinking. The report suggests that China will not become "a superpower like the US." China will probably have the largest economy in the world, while the economies of Europe, Japan, and Russia will slowly decline. Instead, the report anticipates China will not emerge as a superpower akin to the United States and not forge coalitions to take on international issues.[5]

A study by Price Waterhouse Coopers (PwC) suggests, the big seven Asian economies will eclipse G-7 economies in size as the world's biggest emerging markets within two decades. When matched for combined gross domestic product, China, India, Brazil, Russia, Mexico, Indonesia, and Turkey will be around 30% higher by 2030 than that of the United States, Japan, Germany, France, United Kingdom, Italy, and Canada, according to John Hawksworth of PwC's London-based macroeconomics group.[6]

Not surprisingly, Hillary Clinton, the former secretary of state has suggested an expanded vision of the United States in the coming century: "We are also expanding our alliance with Australia from a Pacific partnership to an Indo-Pacific one, and indeed a global partnership. From cyber security to Afghanistan to the Arab Awakening to strengthening regional architecture in the Asia-Pacific, Australia's counsel and commitment have been indispensable."[7]

When the president released his defense review in January 2012, he struck a similar tone: "Our nation is at a moment of transition. Thanks to the extraordinary sacrifices of our men and women in uniform, we have responsibly ended the war in Iraq, put al-Qaida on the path to defeat—including delivering justice to Osama bin Laden—and made significant progress in Afghanistan, allowing us to begin the transition to Afghan responsibility. . . . Indeed, as we end today's wars, we will focus on a broader range of challenges and opportunities, including the security and prosperity of the Asia-Pacific."[8]

An analysis in *The Guardian* went so far as to state that the pivot was the main foreign-policy achievement of the Obama administration's first term in office. Obama's first term, the newspaper suggested, included the significant pivot to Asia, minor tweaks to Latin America, where India got charm but little substance from the US president's foreign policy, while Europe was mostly exasperated.[9]

When I interviewed Christine Fair, a South Asia expert at Georgetown University, she explained that the pivot toward Asia was a long time in the making, started during the first Clinton administration but stalled due to the testing of the nuclear capability by India in 1998 and completely thrown off-track by the events of September 11, 2001. Now, ten years after the war on terror the pivot is finally coming into focus as China's rise is imminent.

An especially interesting witness to the dramatic changes in China is Mark Okoth Obama Ndesandjo, the president's half-brother who has resided in China during the past ten years. In an interview, confirming China's recent and ongoing rise, he described to me: "From a layman's perspective, without being a sinologist, or representing anybody other than myself, I believe that from the point of view of GDP China will likely lead the world in the first half of the twenty-second century. However, if one defines power from the point of view of per capita income and diplomatic clout, it is unlikely to do so. In general, a multipolar century will focus on three spheres of influence: NAFTA, Japan and Oceania on the one hand, the EU, and China. India and several Asian countries are likely to gravitate away from China as long as China is unable to temper its nationalism, as forming alliances will be quite difficult. There is an old Chinese strategy of war: 远交近攻, yuan jiao jin gong.

"Basically, cultivate alliances with anyone other than your immediate neighbor. Many of China's neighbors are following this strategy vis-a-vis China and the United States. Unless one has lived here, it is easy to underestimate the ordinary Chinese. They have maintained strong opinions in private, an unbreakable work ethic, and a strong sense of family during centuries of privations and glory. They also have an aching need and passion for freedoms that Americans have long taken for granted. They are slowly but surely realizing that such freedoms are not "granted" but "inalienable," without requiring permission. How China balances these conflicting demands from the top and bottom will be the great epic of the new millennium.

"The biggest issues China will confront going forward are resolving internal dissension resulting from the widening gap between rich and poor, meeting the environmental and quality of life demands of a growing middle class (whose rise in just thirty years is itself a remarkable achievement). From a foreign policy viewpoint, China will set the agenda vis-a-vis its management of energy resources and territorial ambitions."

Arturo Muñoz, political scientist at RAND, who is featured in this book earlier on the Afghan policy, has suggested that the pivot is partly determined by the regional needs. The smaller nations in the Pacific feel they need the American presence to "rebalance" America's foreign policy that has been heavily focused on the Middle East and the two long wars in Iraq and Afghanistan. In other words, the US allies in the Pacific need the Americans to balance the growing military and economic power of China, he said.

Pepe Escobar, who has been writing about Central Asia for more than a decade, believes that the pivot toward Asia, if it is to have any chance of success, by default has to go through Iran and the tearing down of the "wall of distrust" that has existed between Tehran and DC.[10] Without any real change in the US–Iranian stalemate on the nuclear issue, the Asian pivot will always be drawn back to the Mideast peace process and the Israeli–Palestinian conflict. While Escobar has been urging the president to "tear down this wall," the president and his team have been busy nation-building at home.

Leading from behind or Nation-Building at Home?

Approaching it from a neoconservative perspective, Robert Kagan has made a similar observation when he claimed, "United States can't pivot away from Middle East," arguing instead for a concerted engagement with the traditional allies. At a meeting of diplomats in Abu Dhabi in November 2012, he noted "No one was suggesting the United States could or ought to have all the answers, but among this gathering of Arab, North African, South Asian and European diplomats and international civil servants, the overwhelming consensus was that the superpower is AWOL. The only question was whether the absence is temporary or permanent."[11] Kagan concluded by urging the Obama administration to reengage. America can pivot, suggested Kagan, but it can't leave. America's role in the Middle East is just as pivotal as it is in the Pacific. The world cannot afford America to be missing in action in the most turbulent region in the world.

Other critics of the president have been even more strident in their attack on his leadership style. They have argued that the president has been "leading from behind" in the Middle East and North Africa, a strategy first described by one of the State Department aids to describe the actions in Libya. Richard Miniter (2012), author of *Leading from Behind*, states that the president's leadership style suffers from several deficits, all centering around his solitary, aloof, and almost lonely—"brooding isolation" and "paralyzing cautious"—leadership style.

"Obama's solitary style shows up during the workday, too. Even West Wing staffers—people who in any other presidency are the president's "inner circle"—say the president rarely makes a decision in their presence. . . . Instead, he prefers to retreat to a makeshift private office on the White House's third floor—the Treaty Room, near the Lincoln Bedroom—where, at a paper-stacked antique table, with ESPN droning from the television near the fireplace, he ponders and weighs. He does his best thinking after he has had dinner with his wife and daughters. Usually, he is there at night, when no moving traffic is visible in the ornate window frame. He is, almost always, alone." Taking a psychological approach to Obama's "habits of mind," Miniter notes, "Obama's mother herself was often described as 'solitary and bookish.' He is very much his mother's son" (Miniter 2012: 5).[12]

P. J. Crowley, a former State Department spokesman to Hillary Clinton, when asked about Obama's style, told Miniter that it's "very corporate." Much less relaxed than the Clinton White House, final decisions rest with the executive, not much is shared with the staffers about the decision-making process. "Pushed a bit, Crowley conceded that once decisions reach the president's desk, no one knows what happens. Aides are consulted, memos scribbled on, questions asked, but in the end Obama decides alone, in an upper room where even the West Wing staffers dare not intrude," according to Miniter (p. 6).

I have described his decision-making style in my earlier book as studied, premeditated, and measured; he is not someone who shoots from the hip (Sharma 2012).[13] Based on interviews with his elementary school teachers, homeroom teachers, and high school teachers, the Obama we know is not an impulsive decision maker; he usually relies on in-depth processing of layers of information.

Highlighting the socialization involved in the transmission of globalization, Maya Soetoro-Ng, the president's half-sister described to me in an interview the role of cross-cultural and cooperative learning in the acquisition of global competence:

> Our mother felt uncomfortable with argument but at the same time saw conflict as a potential catalyst for growth. That's why she must have worked so hard to emphasize interdependence at the local and global levels, and why she looked for ways to transform conflict and seek long-term solutions. She taught us to build resources within any setting for constructively responding to conflict and helped us develop the capacity to see problems complexly. In order to do this, we needed to expand our sense of kinship and see ourselves as part of a larger community and, because she was our teacher, we changed the way that we learned history, current events, and philosophy—using these subjects as a vehicle for emotional empathy and intellectual exchange.
>
> As a teacher, our mother made use of cooperative learning commons and nonformal and informal spaces of learning. We were also taught the value of civic engagement, leadership, and service. My brother, our President, took these lessons to heart. He strives to maximize participation of people in decisions that affect their lives. He is genuinely committed to finding the greatest good for the greatest number, and he is prepared to engage in the negotiation, bargaining and compromise, which are so important in good politics. And I strive to teach in a way that honors personal reflection, public dialogue, and broad international service.

Sarlito Wirawan Sarwono, a well-known psychologist in Jakarta, who attended Obama's talk at the University of Indonesia in 2009, made a similar point to me in an interview:

> The point is that Obama is indeed encouraging proficiency. Of all crises facing Indonesia, Obama could have raised positive things about democracy, for example. When many Indonesian people themselves are tired with the way democracy is in place, and instead want to retreat to the era in which the government is in control again, Obama said that we cannot retreat anymore. The strength of Indonesia and India, he said, precisely is in its democracy. While Demokrasilah (including freedom of the press) is sometimes annoying, it will provide opportunities to various

sectors to develop, in particular economic sectors. America also experienced a fall, but America will not retreat from democracy. Indonesia, too, should not retreat, said Obama. It was evident a lot of people were stunned at Obama and his style full of enthusiasm in welcoming the problems in the future. This is what I think has been heartbreaking American people in 2008.

Clearly, Obama is a unique leader, partly due to his upbringing and socialization in the Pacific, his life experiences in some of America's inner cities, his biracial family background and marriage, and his historic rise to the presidency. Is he a "great man of history" or a great president? History will be the judge. Does his decision-making style reflect a pragmatist at the core, yet an idealist in his vision, oratory, and speech-making? While he may be a Rorschach test in the populist sense of the term, his second inaugural speech made clear that he is an unreconstructed progressive at heart.

Internationally, the president has been a champion of American values and ideals, yet he has also been hawkish on security, trying to extend America's geopolitical and military presence in the Asia-Pacific region, one of his strongest policy moves yet. As a champion of American exceptionalism, he has been supporting the soft power of American cultural experience. Moreover, the effect of his policies and many other global initiatives will be felt in the years to come. While he has tackled many significant leadership challenges in his first term, several global issues remain unsolved and new challenges emerge regularly, such as, the Syrian crisis and the use of chemical weapons:

- Tackling ongoing challenges of the Syrian civil war, including the use of chemical weapons, and the threat of spillover effects into neighboring countries
- Successfully confronting Iran's nuclear challenge
- Dealing with the challenges of Mideast peace
- Reforming America's immigration system with a special focus on Latin American and Asian American immigrants
- Dealing with the ongoing and long-term threat of climate change

At the time of editing this book, the Syrian crisis in many ways represents "the perfect storm" that has challenged Obama's leadership style and grasp of the Middle East, our national security interests, and the spread of chemical weapons. If the Obama administration is able to solve these challenges convincingly for the foreseeable future, it will potentially carve out a history-making record on foreign policy while securing his legacy. On the downside, a failure on any of these key issues will be seen as a negative for his second term and historical opportunity. Without a crystal ball, we can only assess the effect of his actions based on the evidence. We know that Obama's political rise, when combined with the difficult fiscal conditions, gave rise to the Tea Party; it remains to be seen whether the Tea Party will become part of the Republican Party or a stand-alone third party. In 2012, it had certainly brought the government to a standstill in terms of the fight over the budget, deficits, and spending (Maxwell and Parent 2012).[14]

While the Obama administration's foreign policy has changed over time, the spending on foreign aid has not increased, remaining proportionally similar to that during the Bush years (Gibler and Miller 2012).[15] Not having a majority in the House, it has not been easy for the president to get his legislative agenda passed, and he faced persistent obstructions on many of his domestic and international policies.

George C. Edwards, presidential historian at Texas A&M has stated that attempts based on persuasion will ultimately not work. The president has made many efforts at bipartisanship, to reach across the aisle and try to create policy change. He has tried to gain Republican support to pass legislation and to buy political cover for his sweeping legislations. His team has tried to build support for healthcare, budget, and fiscal issues, including debt and deficit. "He and his top aides spent many hours meeting with Republicans in large groups and consulting with individual Republicans, especially senators, such as Olympia Snowe, Susan Collins, and Charles Grassley. Despite consistent rebuffs, Obama kept trying. My theory of leadership leads one to predict that governing strategies dependent on persuasion will fail," said Edwards (2012).[16]

On the foreign policy side where he has had a free reign without much obstruction from the opposition, he has arguably been more successful. Regarding its response to the Arab Spring, some of the emerging evidence suggests that the Obama administration did show calculated leadership. Morey et al. (2012), however, have claimed "though we find some evidence pointing toward leadership, the bulk of our evidence indicates that Obama was largely either an active spectator or a follower during the uprisings. . . . We conclude that, at best, Obama showed weak evidence of leadership during the Arab Spring uprisings."[17] In this book, Ahmed and Masad also express this view from Kuwait and UAE, respectively.

A report by Brookings claims otherwise. The United States will benefit in the long run from policies that are willing to prevent humanitarian disasters, are aware of limits on its power, recognize what can be achieved by coalition-building, accept the legitimizing role of the UN and other international bodies, offer economic support, and can earn the respect and support of the governments and the peoples. Only policies that are modulated to all of these elements can have lasting influence and win the admiration of the new generations (Dervis 2011).[18]

Due to the polarized politics in the Senate, the president has not been able to pass many international treaties during his first term, as noted by several news stories (Bellinger 2012).[19] When we examine the president's use of international treaties to advance his foreign policy agenda we find that "while President Obama uses executive agreements at similar levels as previous presidents, he has used the treaty mechanism far less often." Peake et al. (2012) note partisan polarization has substantially constrained his ability to conduct diplomacy through treaties.[20] Thus, a recent attempt by the White House to initiate a large trade deal with the European Union has been well received.

Despite the recent upsurge of trade with China, the European Union still remains a strong partner of the United States. According to a report by Brookings, this longstanding historical trend cannot be reversed easily nor is it wise to do so (Galston 2013).[21] The United States and Europe prefer each other as economic partners overwhelmingly for foreign direct investments. For the past decade, 56% of the total FDI from the United States to Europe has remained constant, while Europe's investment in the United States represents a high 71%. The growth of Asia—especially, the Chinese and Indian economies—has not fundamentally changed this ratio. The United States has invested 14 times as much in the Netherlands as in China for the past decade, and 11 times as much in the United Kingdom, clearly aligning with the developed economies.

While the president's rhetoric around the world has broad appeal, the widespread change he has sought requires negotiation, collaboration, and long-term strategy. When obstructed by Congress or even by those within his own party, he has often resorted to the State of the Union address (SUA) to speak directly to his supporters. When we examine his addresses using content analysis, we find that he has deployed credit claiming, position taking, and symbolism to report to the Congress. In his first term, he used credit taking about 17% of the time, made about 35 large-scale legislative requests, and relied on both historical and biographical symbolism to appeal to the American Dream. The evidence suggests that 45% of his legislative requests have been fully or partially met, a percentage that is slightly higher than the median rate established by previous presidents going back to 1965 (Hoffman and Howard 2012).[22]

The investigators of the study concluded: "Obama's rhetorical choices in the SUA portray him as an unusual chief legislator in many ways. He is deferential to Congress on legislative detail, tending to focus his SUA requests on large-scale items and leaving the details of legislation to Congress. If Congress failed to act, he occasionally sought to accomplish his policy goals through executive actions if he could. He was then able to use the rhetoric of the SUA to portray himself as an active and effective president, something that would aid his reelection and legacy goals. Furthermore, Obama often had to confront unreasonably high expectations, and this strategy helped him position himself against the unpopular institution of Congress as he sought reelection" (p. 1316).

Obama's symbolic power has carried a lot of weight with several key segments of the population, leading to the increase of black optimism and investment in the American Dream and arguably around the world, as pointed out by Mazrui earlier in this book. Independent of the economic realities, several surveys conducted between 1987 and 2010 have documented higher levels of optimism among blacks in spite of the tougher economic conditions (Stout and Le 2012).[23] These findings clearly suggest that the closing of the gap in positive symbolism has greater weight for key segments of the American population and the southern hemisphere of the globe. Certainly, they don't believe Obama is leading from behind—be it domestically or internationally.

Objectively, when we examine Obama's judicial appointments, it seems evident that he has nominated more women and minorities to the bench. "Using data from 1993 to 2012 provided by the American Constitution Society for Law and Policy," investigators Kimel and Randazzo have confirmed, "President Obama has nominated more women and minorities to the federal bench than either of his two immediate predecessors." Obama's nominees appear more moderate in their ideological stance than those appointed by presidents Clinton and Bush, suggesting that the president is more concerned with race and gender diversity than any ideological position. "Therefore, President Obama's claims of pragmatism and his desire to nominate individuals who reflect American society, often doubted by both political supporters and detractors, appear supported by the available data," conclude the authors (Kimel and Randazzo 2012: 1243).[24]

The tension between Obama's transformational rhetoric and pragmatic record seems to be part and parcel of his personality—as a grassroots organizer, he likes to inspire people to action, but structural change is incremental and generational. When we code the president's political speeches, undertaking a textual study—using frames for transactional and transformational categories—we find that the President Obama deploys transformational leadership but more often employs rational persuasion rather than inspirational appeals. "The informal powers of the presidency do include the power to inspire" argue political scientists Engbers and Fucilla (2012), "but for President Obama this power is secondary to appeals to reason."[25] Based on the official White House memoranda and an examination of presidential signing statements, Kelley (2012) argues that the president "has governed very much like his predecessors, where acting unilaterally is concerned" (p. 1146).[26]

Similarly, Rockman (2012) while examining the Obama record has suggested that the president has been very sensitive to "contextual opportunities," seizing them when possible, but he has been constrained by limits on his powers. "The notion of transformational leadership, and the rhetoric that accompanies it, is massively asymmetric" argues Rockman while real "leadership takes place when strategic opportunities arise, and these more frequently than not are rare."[27] In fact, the skills required to be elected are not the same set of skills needed to run the country once in office. Most presidents generally go through a change in rhetoric between campaigning and governing. However, when we look at Obama's rhetoric we see a consistency between campaigning and managing the country, suggesting that he has used the same strategies to campaign and to build a base of support to govern. "We find no statistical difference in the level of certainty or inclusiveness that he used before or after taking office. We conclude that most differences between presidential campaign rhetoric and governing rhetoric, at least in the case of Barack Obama, seem to be caused by the specifics of the political environment," concluded Olson et al. (2012).[28] This may be due to the highly polarized political environment, with 24–7 media and cable news cycle, and the supply of money needed to run large campaigns.

In an interconnected world, it is mighty difficult to argue that what happens domestically does not affect the global challenges the United States faces. Thus, the fiscal and political constraints at home affect Obama's policies in the Middle East and on the climate debate. While the war on terror under a toned-down rhetoric has been successful, the issues related to Middle East peace, the nuclear stalemate with Iran, and the exacting toll of events related to global warming have been allowed to fester without any meaningful solutions.

In his first term, the president focused heavily on the economy and jobs, healthcare, education, and defense or security, based on an objective analysis of his speeches (Engbers and Fucilla 2012); he has been nation-building at home rather than trying to lead from behind. Since his reelection, Obama has mostly focused on the economy, the national debt, and the budget including its looming deficit. Thus, while he gets moderately high marks in Europe, developed and developing Asia and Latin America, his ratings in the Middle East, North Africa (except Sub-Saharan Africa), and parts of South Asia remain disappointingly low; these societies are also high on in-group collectivism.

Societies with high in-group collectivism, such as in the Middle East, Africa, South Asia, and Latin America, who related to Obama as "one of their own" with high expectations—due to his biography, skin color, Arabic-sounding name, or his global rhetoric—tended to rate Obama much more harshly for implementing policies that are pro-American and pro-Western. In the Arab world and Pakistan, they are disappointed at the discovery that like other American presidents—and constrained by his role, national interest, and cultural history—he has not been willing to take their side in an argument. In Sub-Saharan Africa, in particular, many expected Obama to show a more humane orientation to their problems.

Europeans, although not high on collectivism, wanted to reelect Obama for his rhetoric of global cooperation and multilateralism. French value participative leadership the most; Germans value performance, assertiveness, future orientation, and uncertainty avoidance. Unlike central European countries, Eastern Europeans are higher on in-group collectivism and family traditions and long for leaders who speak to these needs. Thus, the European response to Obama, while remaining positive, is a reflection of these cultural attitudes.

In Southeast Asia, China, and South Korea, Obama is admired for his charismatic leadership, team-orientation, and humane skills but may seem a bit of an enigma to many because of his young age, race, and inexperience. Thus, he is valued for his bold approach toward Asia even though he is looked at with a bit of skepticism. Yet, there is no doubt that in a highly globalized world, Obama's leadership style and traits evoke a response filtered through the highly competitive environment for scarce resources and markets, where emerging economies are chasing the American dream at turbo speed.

Not surprisingly, after almost four of years of unrelenting obstruction from the opposition on the domestic front, the toll of the drawdown of the wars in Iraq and Afghanistan, and the great global economic recession, the US approval around the world has slumped, according to the latest report by Gallup Polls (Ray 2013).[29]

After the high point of the 2008 election, Obama's advisors expected that his approval might decline precipitously. Back then, you might have thought that Barack Obama was made of kryptonite or that he was a Superman and a Jedi warrior. Today, people have a more realistic view of his powers in office and a better understanding of the formidable powers of persuasion he possesses as a global leader.

In June 2012, Pew Global Poll stated that "while many still hold Obama in high regard, general confidence in his foreign policy leadership has slipped by six percentage points or more in most countries since 2009."[30] While Obama received higher approval ratings than Bush Jr., the overall confidence in him and the US global leadership has slipped. While traditional allies remain confident throughout Europe, Asia, and Africa, the US approval ratings have slipped. . . . in part because of tough policy decisions.

According to Gallup world poll released on March 13, 2012, the image of US global leadership has seen better days. Gallup results are based on face-to-face and telephone interviews with approximately 1,000 adults, aged 15 and older, conducted throughout 136 countries in 2011 and 130 countries in 2012.

The recent poll shows that Obama's global leadership was the weakest during his fourth year heading into the reelection—"Median approval of U.S. leadership across 130 countries stood at 41% in 2012, down measurably from 49% approval in Obama's first year," according to Julie Ray of Gallup Polls. Despite the decline in approval ratings, they were higher than at the end of the last Bush administration. Given President Obama still won reelection, it seems that global opinion matters but not very much in determining election results.

The poll does not suggest what were the causes of the decline in approval—whether it was the drone strikes, the Benghazi events, protests on the streets of Cairo or a general discomfort with the US image abroad. However, the decline in approval does suggest that the president and the new secretary of state may find it a little harder to sell their message of "development and democracy" around the world.

It appears the world is a bit more critical of the United States four years after Obama's landmark election. However, the image of US leadership remained very strong in Africa in 2012, "bolstered by strong majority approval in sub-Saharan Africa." US leadership remains far less popular in North Africa—Morocco, Algeria, Tunisia, and Egypt, where only approximately one-third approved and ratings remained mostly flat. According to the survey, Libyans (54%) surveyed before the attack in Benghazi approved of US leadership in 2012.

In the Americas, the US leadership seems to have stabilized around a 40% approval rating. "The free fall in U.S. approval in the Americas that began after Obama's first year in office ended in his fourth year," stated Julie Ray of Gallup Polls. While there were no major declines in Latin America or the Caribbean nations, Mexico, one the closest allies, showed a significant increase in approval for the US leadership, perhaps, due to the visit by President-elect Enrique Pena Nieto to the White House in late November 2012. Clearly, more can be done to bolster support for American policies in the Americas.

In the Eurozone, the median approval of the United States slumped by 11 points. During Obama's first year in office, US approval was twice as high as during the Bush years. The crisis in the Eurozone is partly responsible for the decline in approval, according to Gallup Polls, where "the U.S. was likely shouldering some of the blame for the ongoing financial crisis in Europe." The median approval declined to 36% in 2012 from 42% in 2011.

The US approval has remained high in Kosovo, Albania, Ireland, the United Kingdom, the Netherlands, and Italy. It has declined in France, Spain, and Sweden. In countries hit by the financial crisis—Hungary, Croatia, Macedonia, and Austria—US approval suffered significant losses. In Russia, US leadership has the lowest approval among all the Eastern European countries (13%).

Despite the pivot to Asia, or may be due to America's heavy shift in policy, Gallup's surveys observed that the approval ratings in the Asian countries have been heading in a negative direction in 2012. What is not clear is whether this is mostly due to the downward trend in Pakistan, Afghanistan, and neighboring countries or also due to the shift in policy toward the Pacific nations.

In the Philippines, Japan, South Korea, Thailand, Cambodia, and Australia, US approval remains strong. Ratings in Asia tended to be more positive than negative, except for the Middle East and parts of South Asia. Nevertheless, the 37% median approval in Asian countries in 2012 was still higher than any rating during the Bush years.

The highest disapproval ratings were in the Middle East and South Asia, perhaps due to the Palestinian crisis and the drone strikes, respectively. "More than three in four residents in Pakistan (79%) and the Palestinian Territories (77%) disapproved of U.S. leadership in 2012," according to the Gallup report. These findings are consistent with the views presented in the papers in this volume.

In those countries suffering from social upheaval and conflict in Africa, South Asia, and Central Asia, US approval took significant losses. However, in other countries such as Bangladesh, Thailand, and Chad with better than expected performance, US approval has gained ground.

According to Gallup, "U.S. leadership faces increasing challenges as it attempts to build engagement worldwide, and in many places, this job may be even tougher than it has been in the past. U.S. leadership thus far has been unable to recoup the favor it lost among audiences in key countries in 2011 and has continued to lose support in many places."

According to the similar poll by Pew Research in June 2012, the expectations were clearly very high. Many around the world thought in 2009 that the Obama administration would bring enlightened leadership such as trying to resolve the conflict between the Israelis and Palestinians fairly and making climate change a priority.

Many around the world feel their hopes have been dashed. Obama gathers high marks, however, for addressing the global economy and the crisis in the Eurozone. With his reelection, however, hope springs eternal. While the general mood has tempered, the dream endures. Populations around the world hope the Obama administration will be able to take on the global challenges it could not tackle in the first term.

Globalization's Discontents or the New Economy?

According to the US Competitiveness Project, the American economy has been suffering from several long-term deficits. Prior to the 2012 election, I hosted a panel at the Harvard Club in New York City of business leaders and entrepreneurs to discuss some of these issues. These are hardly partisan issues, since they are based on findings generated by the Harvard Business School study, led by the same group of business leaders who have trained many Republican business-friendly "job creators." According to Michael Porter and Jan Rivkin, "We should have been worried before the Great Recession" (HBS 2012).[31] Indeed, something very different is taking place within the US economy, according to those business experts, which does not resemble any other previous transitions. The 2008–2012 recession has been masking stagnant wages, low productivity, and real lack of competitiveness in the US job market. These latter phenomena clearly point to long-term issues that have been escalating since the end of the Cold War, the beginning of automation, and supply-chain or inventory management.

President Obama has claimed he does not want to double down on trickle down policies of the previous Bush and Reagan administrations. The economic trends under his watch are in the right direction, even though job growth may be sluggish. His plan has created significantly more jobs in the past thirty months, and the economy is gradually coming out of the recession.

According to the Center for Budget and Policy Priorities, the "economic activity as measured by real (inflation-adjusted) gross domestic product (GDP) was contracting sharply when policymakers enacted the financial stabilization bill (TARP) and the American Recovery and Reinvestment Act. The economy has been growing for 12 straight quarters, but the pace of recovery has been modest" (CBPP 2012).[32]

The unemployment rate has been hovering around 7.3%, and, according to Bloomberg, consumer confidence has been rising. The Thomson Reuters/University of Michigan final sentiment index rose to 81.4 in August 2013.

According to Willy C. Shih, former executive at Kodak and now a business professor, there was no way to produce and go to market in the United States, while trying to innovate digital camera technology. Advanced digital capabilities had been outsourced, which weakened the production capability and innovation in manufacturing digital cameras. "Part of the problem is that people don't think of manufacturing as knowledge work," said Shih.[33]

The two political parties have outlined different paths to retain manufacturing in the United States, while bashing Chinese manufacturing. President Obama believes in American workers, in American industry, and in the American auto industry. Obama has blamed the Republicans for outsourcing jobs overseas. Republicans have been attacking China and Obama for being co-conspirators: "We face another continuing challenge in a rising China. . . . It is in our mutual interest for China to be a partner for a stable and secure world, and we welcome its participation in trade. But the cheating must finally be brought to a stop. President Obama hasn't done it and won't do it. I will," said Romney during his failed election campaign.

Obama, however, championed the auto industry: "You know, four years ago we went through the worst financial crisis since the Great Depression. Millions of jobs were lost, the auto industry was on the brink of collapse. The financial system had frozen up. And because of the resilience and the determination of the American people, we've begun to fight our way back. Over the last 30 months, we've seen 5 million jobs in the private sector created. The auto industry has come roaring back. And housing has begun to rise. But we all know that we've still got a lot of work to do. And so the question here tonight is not where we've been, but where we're going."[34] On manufacturing, the president's plan seems to be working and may need to be applied to other industries.

"The twin crises of modern American capitalism . . . can be traced in part to the proliferation of these very high-powered incentive contracts," said Mihir A. Desai at Harvard Business School.[35]

Clearly, the economic gap between 1%, 99%, and 47% has been widening. During the past three decades, Desai claims, American capitalism has been radically altered by the idea that financial markets can objectively measure performance and compensation. Compensations for high-powered contracts in investment banks have dramatically changed the incentives structures on both sides of the capital market.

"Unfortunately, the idea of compensation based on financial markets is both remarkably alluring and deeply flawed: It seems to link pay more closely to performance, but it actually rewards luck and can incentivize dangerous risk taking," according to Desai. This compensation system has led to the crisis of American capitalism, where failure of governance among US managers and investors contributed to the financial collapse of 2008 and exacerbated rising income inequality. These structural flaws, if they can be fixed at all, have to be corrected for building a strong middle class.

The financial editor, Chrystia Freeland, makes this claim even more forcefully when she describes the rise of the superrich, the global elites, or "the plutocrats." She claims "Forget the 1 percent.... [I]t is the wealthiest 0.1 percent who are outpacing the rest of us at break-neck speed. What's changed is more than numbers. Today, most colossal fortunes are new, not inherited—amassed by perceptive businessmen who see themselves as deserving victors in a cut-throat international competition."[36] The new tribe of transglobal class of money managers see themselves as self-made oligarchs, who have more in common with their peers than with their family of origin and countrymen; the new class knows no national boundaries.

She takes us back to the Gilded Age to look forward—the era dominated by the "robber barons," such as the Carnegies and the Rockefellers. It was a similar historical period as now, where new technologies collided with the new markets to produce unprecedented wealth for the few at the top, while the masses in the middle and lower rungs simply managed to get along. The wealthy few did exceptionally well and shaped our world in incalculable ways with unchecked power and influence. Today, the same process is operating in many more countries, including the BRIC economies, which are in turn influencing the Western societies and economies.

According to Thomas Kocham, a management professor at MIT, "All of the other things we used to think about as a social contract" have eroded.[37] The main problem may be that the American economy has mainly become a financially driven economy. American corporations, while they value their workers as the most important assets, have somehow slipped in creating the jobs of the twenty-first century. They need to retool and rebuild the jobs for the next century. This is partly a solution to the manufacturing crisis as well.

Republicans too have been making the same claims, highlighting the dynamism of the American workforce as the country's greatest renewable natural resource. American workers need to update and retool their skills to unleash their potential. "One of the troubling features of the American economy today is the mismatch between the skill set of the American workforce and the requirements of the employment market. The gap between the two lies at the heart of our jobs crisis," said Romney during the debates. High-tech jobs are not filled fast enough by the existing labor pool.

During the debate, Obama championed the education plan—"Race to the Top"—and the investment in junior or trade colleges. Republicans lurched toward the center and tried to agree with many of the initiatives already begun by education secretary Arne Duncan, while at the same time attacking the anemic job growth.

Has America become complacent about its assets? Does America need more business ecosystems like the Silicon Valley tech start-ups around the country? Clearly, this is one way out of the recession, which has been exacerbated by the politics of the moment and gridlock in the Congress. The political gridlock has been well documented as an indication of the president's leadership style locking horns with the dysfunction that pervades the government.

Former Vice President Al Gore, a Noble Laureate, has released a book, *The Future: Six Drivers of Global Change*, which reboots his "futuristic" vision.[38] In a densely packed vision of the world— something he has been refining for almost a decade, Gore claims we are in the midst of a tectonic shift. While the megatrends described in the book are not really "futuristic," the reader might feel deluged by the rapid succession with which Gore conjures up new frames of reality when, for instance, he talks about the "global mind" from the billions of social media connections that now constitute our daily interactions or the effect of the policies he helped put in place for stem-cell research and genomics when he was in office. Other readers may be somewhat disheartened by the sheer onslaught of the dehumanizing effects of markets and technology.

The future is now, literally, because many of Gore's prophecies have already come true and many more will come true in the not so distant future. Gore deals with six interlocking trends or predictions about an emerging future very different from anything we have seen before.

Due to outsourcing and robo-sourcing of jobs, globalization has led to new economic formations—"integrated holistic entity with a new and different relationship to capital, labor, consumer markets, and national governments than in the past."

The nature of money and markets has become fluid; the nature of labor and work has become migratory and moveable; while national economies have not disappeared, they have become more open and porous to influences from outside. While national borders have not vanished, they seem less relevant today than fifty years ago to international trade, to the flow of capital, goods, and natural resources.

This has led to the "crisis of capitalism" and some of the largest wage gaps in the developed and the developing world, where the few, the rich and powerful, the so-called 1% or the "global jet-setters," park their money and assets around the world while the middle classes in the local cultures are left holding the bag, for example, in the latest housing crisis. We need "sustainable capitalism," argues Gore, which is not focused on the short-term gains, also known as "quarterly capitalism."

Just as fast as technology and the Internet had connected the world, humans—the innately social creatures that they are—had started to form online communities to work and play. This has led to emergent forms of global consciousness, unprecedented in human history, where people can communicate, organize, and challenge power structures—a nascent form of "human technogenesis"[39] that links "the thoughts and feelings of billions of people and connects intelligent machines, robots, ubiquitous sensors, and databases."

There is a "convergence" of minds in East and West in thoughts, feelings, and aspirations, as Kishore Mabhubani recently said at a talk at Asia Society. Across diverse cultures and societies, increasingly people are aiming for universal aspirations, democratic values, and "the common good."[40]

However, Gore is only cautiously optimistic. He urges Americans to restore both democracy and capitalism that have been "hacked." "The results are palpably obvious in the suffocating control of policy decisions by elites, the ever increasing inequalities of income and growing concentrations of wealth." Yet, the rise of the Global Mind is challenging the established order, where new emergent centers of influence not controlled by elites are challenging established behaviors.

Al Gore has walked the corridors of power. He understands better than most what is at stake—a global shift in power is taking place, unlike anything we have seen in our lifetimes or in many generations. "The balance of global political, economic, and military power is shifting more profoundly than at any time in the last five hundred years—from a U.S.-centered system to one with multiple emerging centers of power, from nation-states to private actors, and from political systems to markets."

International relations experts have called this the "multipolar world," evident in new global formations, such as, the G-20. The State Department has called it the "Pacific Pivot" to reorient and manage the dynamism of the Asia Pacific region, or what Mabhubani has called the "irresistible shift of global power to the East."

The march of civilization and progress, now joined by the teeming masses in the developed and the least developed countries, has led to an imbalance in the earth's atmosphere, the so-called "climate crisis." This is a reframing of Gore's original thesis about reclaiming the "earth in the balance." "A deeply flawed economic compass is leading us to unsustainable growth in consumption, pollution flows, and depletion of the planet's strategic resources of topsoil, freshwater, and living species," argues Gore. While experts debate the planet is becoming "flat, hot and crowded."

One of the clearest evidence is the correlation between carbon emissions and the rising sea levels, predicted to continue to rise with "potentially catastrophic difficulties for shore-based communities in the next centuries." There is also evidence that Americans may be finally waking up to the climate debate. According to a recent poll by Think Progress, superstorm Sandy has been associated with climate change by 69% of New Yorkers, including 73% of independents.[41]

In the final analysis, Gore takes on the potential solutions to the energy crisis as a way to solve the climate debate, both scientifically and politically. There are no easy solutions to the crisis we face, he says; the US political system has been hijacked by the special interest, which has partly led to the impasse on the climate debate. US democracy is broken, yet the world still expects the United States to lead.

"There has been a radical disruption of the relationship between human beings and the earth's ecosystems, along with the beginning of a revolutionary transformation of energy systems, agriculture, transportation, and construction worldwide," says Gore. Whatever your political orientation, you must contend with the issues described in this book by one of the leading minds kicking around today, who has been a very successful politician, visionary entrepreneur, and a big-picture thinker. The conundrums raised by Al Gore will affect not only your future, but also the future of your children and grandchildren.

In the end, Gore is poetic (Samuel Taylor Coleridge), when he urges us to take meaningful action for "a sustainable future":

> "So often do the spirits
> Of great events stride on before the events,
> And in today already walks tomorrow."

The Pacific Century or America's Asian Dream?

While foreign policy experts are searching for the Obama doctrine that will define his legacy, there is no doubt that the "pivot" or "rebalancing" toward Asia-Pacific will be one of its key features. America's involvement in Asia is not new, argues historian Warren I. Cohen, but the pivot will certainly lead to an intensification of the "Americanization of Asia" and the "Asianization of America" that has been underway for several decades now.[42] Ronald Takaki, the founder of Asian Studies on American campuses, also noted this trend when he observed in an op-ed that Obama had given his Swahili-sounding name an American flavor and his multicultural Hawaiian upbringing an American hue. As his longtime friend and colleague, Lawrence Friedman, told me in an interview Takaki's big contribution to our understanding of history was that American destiny was multiracial and multicultural at the core. America's rise as global power, after the British Empire, was propelled by managing both theaters of war in the Atlantic and the Pacific. Can America rise to the opportunity again in the twenty-first century?

The Obama administration has faced down the challenge of "ensuring that cascading crises do not crowd out the development of long-term strategies to deal with transcendent challenges and opportunities," said Tom Donilon, a key national security advisor.[43] The State Department set out to identify the key national security interests. The assessment resulted in a set of key determinations. Evidently, there was an imbalance in the projection and focus of US power. "It was the President's judgment that we were over-weighted in some areas and regions, including our military actions in the Middle East. At the same time, we were underweighted in other regions, such as the Asia-Pacific. Indeed, we believed this was our key geographic imbalance," explained Donilon at a recent meeting.

As a Pacific power, the United States has played a critical role in the stabilization of Asia and its growth and development through the cold war years. As Asia rises, the United States looks to play an active role in the region. Over the next decade, nearly half of all growth outside the United States may be projected from Asia, according to most estimates. By mid-century, this growth will fundamentally reshape the region—China leading the pack, followed by resilient Japan, globalizing Korea, "an eastward-looking India," and a network of Southeast Asian tigers wealthier and more prosperous. The rebalancing seems to be a two-way dynamic, signaled by the leaders and publics in the Asia-Pacific region, yet initiated by the United States. The demand "for U.S. leadership, economic engagement, sustained attention to regional institutions and defense of international rules and norms" is high, according to Donilon.

Obama gave a full-throated endorsement of America as the Pacific power in Canberra in front of the Australian parliament in 2011. "Our new focus on this region reflects a fundamental truth—the United States has been, and always will be, a Pacific nation. Asian immigrants helped build America, and millions of American families, including my own, cherish our ties to this region. From the bombing of Darwin to the liberation of Pacific islands, from the rice paddies of Southeast Asia to a cold Korean Peninsula, generations of Americans have served here, and died here—so democracies could take root; so economic miracles could lift hundreds of millions to prosperity. Americans have bled with you for this progress, and we will not allow it—we will never allow it to be reversed."[44] While the Atlantic theater was the more important theater for staging the war in Europe and it remained central to the global economy, the Pacific theater reshaped the Asian hemisphere and is now resurgent.

To fully pursue this vision, the United States is enacting a multidimensional strategy consisting of strengthening alliances; deepening partnerships with emerging powers; building a stable, productive, and constructive relationship with China; empowering regional institutions; and helping to build a regional economic architecture that can sustain shared prosperity. The act of rebalancing is not simply to contain China, dictate to smaller Asian countries, or display military might. This is an effort that harnesses military, political, trade and investment, development and values. The president has committed to attending the ASEAN meetings annually, a first for an American president, and has met all of the heads of Asian states in the region on multiple occasions.

Existing alliances with Japan, South Korea, and Australia remain the cornerstone of regional security. Renewed ties with Thailand and Philippines on counterterrorism, humanitarian assistance, and disaster relief have been established. Despite defense cuts, the United States has shifted resources to the Asia-Pacific region: "Sixty percent of our naval fleet will be based in the Pacific by 2020. Our Air Force is also shifting its weight to the Pacific over the next five years. We are adding capacity from both the Army and the Marines." The Pacific Command is being refurbished with modern capabilities—new submarines, Fifth-Generation Fighters such as F-22s and F-35s, and reconnaissance platforms—while making rapid progress in expanding radar and missile defense systems to protect against the most immediate threat, the dangerous, destabilizing behavior of North Korea, according to the State Department.

With North Korea, the United States maintains the same tough stance, while supporting its allies in the region, including the Japanese and South Koreans. Recent evidence from Burma is a perfect example of what the North Korean regime needs to do to comply with international demands for nuclear inspections and peaceful cohabitation of the Korean peninsula, according to officials. "Burma has already received billions in debt forgiveness, large-scale development assistance, and an influx of new investment. While the work of reform is ongoing, Burma has already broken out of isolation and opened the door to a far better future for its people in partnership with its neighbors and with the United States. And, as President Obama said in his speech to the people of Burma, we will continue to stand with those who continue to support rights, democracy and reform. So I urge North Korea's leaders to reflect on Burma's experience," said Donilon.[45]

In terms of supporting emerging powers, the United States is keenly focused on deepening ties with India, Indonesia, and Brunei. "To that end, the President considers U.S. relations with India—the world's largest democracy—to be 'one of the defining partnerships of the twenty-first century.'

From Prime Minister Singh's visit in 2009 to the President's trip to India in 2010, the United States has made clear at every turn that we don't just accept India's rise, we fervently support it," said Donilon. Likewise with Indonesia, the United States is working on several multilateral deals to advance sustainable development.

The relationship with China is the other big pillar of the US strategy. There are few global challenges that can be addressed without China's input. Whether its "diplomatic, economic or security challenges," increasingly China is an indispensable nation in Asia. "As China completes its leadership transition, the Administration is well positioned to build on our existing relationships with Xi Jinping, Li Keqiang and other top Chinese leaders. Taken together, China's leadership transition and the President's re-election mark a new phase in U.S.-China relations—with new opportunities," according to the State Department.

Of course, the US–China relationship has and will continue to have elements of both cooperation and competition. As the president has made clear, the United States speaks up for universal values because history shows that nations that uphold the rights of their people are ultimately more successful, more prosperous and more stable. "The United States welcomes the rise of a peaceful, prosperous China," said Donilon, "as we do not want our relationship to become defined by rivalry and confrontation."

The officials in the State Department disagree with the premise put forward by some historians and theorists that a rising power and an established power are somehow destined for confrontation. There is nothing preordained about such an outcome. It is not physical law, but strategic decisions made by leaders, which draw great power confrontation. Containment of China is also not a viable option. A better outcome is possible, which requires both sides—the United States and China—to build a new model of bilateral relations. Chinese premier Xi Jinping and President Obama have both endorsed this strategic goal.

To build this new model, the United States and China must keep improving the channels of communication and demonstrate practical cooperation on issues that matter to both sides. A deeper US–China military-to-military dialogue is seen as central to addressing many of the sources of insecurity and potential competition. This remains a necessary component of the new model, and it is a critical deficiency in the current relationship. The Chinese military is modernizing its capabilities and expanding its presence in Asia. Here the issue of cybersecurity is also paramount, which has become a growing challenge on the American side. Economies as large as the United States and China have a tremendous shared stake in ensuring that the Internet remains open, interoperable, secure, reliable, and stable. Both countries face risks when it comes to protecting personal data and communications, financial transactions, critical infrastructure, or the intellectual property and trade secrets that are so vital to innovation and economic growth.

The American dream and the Asian dream seem to be converging, as argued by Kishore Mabhubani, aiming toward universal values and goals. With the recent upsurge of the growing Asian-American population in the United States, arguably the American dream has become America's Asian dream, especially, as the US businesses align themselves with the growth in China, India, and the larger Pacific region. The prize of America's Asian dream, according to some estimates, is around $10 trillion and growing, if you take into account the consumer markets in India and China alone, notwithstanding the other smaller economies.[46]

You may have heard of the burgeoning consumer markets in China and India that are driving the world economy. But did you know there will likely be 1 million middle-class consumers in China and India within the next 10 years? More than 135 million Chinese and Indians will graduate from college in this timeframe, compared to just 30 million in the United States. By 2020, 68% of Chinese households and 57% of Indian households will be in the middle and upper classes. The number of billionaires in China has grown from 1 to 115 in the past decade alone. Clearly, the Obama administration gets credit for pivoting American foreign and economic policy toward the Asia-Pacific region.

This leads to the fourth pillar of the US strategy—strengthening regional institutions—which also reflects Asia's urgent need for economic-, diplomatic-, and security-related rules and understandings. There is no underestimating the strategic significance of this region. The ten ASEAN countries, stretching across the Indian and Pacific Oceans, have a population of well over 600 million. Impressive growth rates in countries like Thailand—and a 25% increase in international investment in 2011—suggest that ASEAN nations are only going to become more important, politically and economically.

Finally, the United States will continue to pursue the fifth column of the strategy: expanding the economic architecture that allows the people of the Asia-Pacific—including the American people—to reap the rewards of greater trade and growth. It is the US view that the economic order that will deliver the next phase of broad-based growth that the region needs is one that rests on economies that are open and transparent and trade and investment that are free, fair, and environmentally sustainable. US economic vitality also depends on tapping into new markets and customers beyond our borders, especially in the world's fastest-growing region.

America's Asian pivot has drawn a lot of attention and debate. Chandran Nair, author of *Consumptionomics* and founder of Global Institute for Tomorrow, for instance, has argued that the shifting of economic and political power eastward means the West must wake up to the fact that promoting consumption-led growth to Asia is not a viable option when natural resources are being so rapidly exhausted. He outlines how Asia should abandon Western-style economic practices to achieve a sustainably prosperous future on its own terms.[47]

There are deniers of the Asian century who claim this is a highly flawed concept. Asia is not a country; it's a highly diverse region, with competing interests, often clashing, where the American presence has kept the peace. China cannot emulate this role as it rises to become a regional power and an international power, certainly not in the near future, argues David Shambaugh in his book *China Goes Global*.[48]

Devin Stewart of the Carnegie Council agrees with this claim, believing that the China hype is just that: a hyperbolic claim.[49] The Asian hemisphere, Stewart states, lacks a singular vision of the state founded in principled ideas and philosophy; there are Asian values, to be sure, but can these values unite a diverse region teeming with ethnic rivalries and national conflicts? Will Asia always need a policeman to mediate disputes in addition to regional alliances? Is the United States still an indispensable nation—extending the rise of America's Asian century—while expanding its military presence in the Pacific?

"Not a week passes, it seems, without a big-picture thinker releasing a big-picture book or giving a big-picture sermon describing the gradual eclipse of American hegemony in Asia," states John Lee, an international security expert in Australia. He suggests that for the most part the proclamation of the end of the American century in the Pacific ring hollow. While it is true that American power will decline somewhat in relative terms as Asian giants such as China and India rise, the United States was never a hegemon in Asia. "Only some American post–Cold War triumphalists thought it was," argues Lee. American power in the Pacific region was always subtle and clever, and as India and China rise, it could find itself in a stronger position rather than at a disadvantage.[50]

While the rate at which the Chinese and Indian economies have been growing suggests that Asia will eclipse the United States and Europe in the next decade, as confirmed by several intelligence reports, it is far from certain this will be a smooth process. Asia may display greater diversity and division on the path to democracy and development. Asian democracies tend to more hierarchical than the European or Western societies. Asian leaders are more interested in keeping traditional hierarchies in place rather than replacing them. This may not easily transition to democratic institution building or justice, freedom and equality for all. Instead, we may arrive at multipolar centers of power in Asia as democracies mature and vie for greater international clout, in need of greater security infrastructure and mediation or conflict management.

"Despite the fact that America spends more on defense than the next ten powers combined, it has never been a regional hegemon because it actually relies on the cooperation of other states to remain predominant. Without cooperation from allies such as Japan, South Korea, Singapore, and the Philippines, the US could not retain its forward military positions in the West Pacific. Likewise, the US needs the cooperation of Indonesia, Malaysia, and Thailand to host its critical radar infrastructure," according to Lee.

To remain relevant and needed, America relies on other key states and regional groupings, such as ASEAN and APEC, to maintain security and economic relationships. In other words, there are agreed-upon arrangements of US ties with major regional powers (Japan, South Korea, and Australia), as well as emerging powers (Philippines, Singapore, Thailand, and India). These bilateral relationships are based in widespread support from national and international agencies. When "combined with the raw military capacity that the US brings to the table, this means that America is powerful enough to enforce the peace and provide stability for commerce to thrive." America's presence and bilateral partnerships are complementary to Asian states' postcolonial preoccupation with counter-dominance, nonalignment and noninterference in the region.

Why can't Pax Americana, which has held sway in Europe, balance Asia and facilitate growth? "This dynamic 'liberal order'—largely fair, flexible, and open enough to welcome new entrants as they rise—will continue to serve Asia well. For example, even China has been a major beneficiary of the public goods provided by the US-led hierarchical system" argues Lee.

This interdependence means that the United States is not a sole superpower in the world. In other words, bilateral relationships compel the United States to not ignore the wishes of regional powers. What is an apparent weakness may actually turn out to be strength in diplomacy. America does not have absolute dominion, authority, and power over any Asian nation; thus, its power has to be distributed. In a world where America is multipolar, Asian democracies can balance each other while remaining on the path to growth and institution-building. China can be balanced by other regional powers even as Japan declines and India rises.

In Asia, "any balancing tends to take place in order to *preserve* the hierarchy, not to replace or supersede it. Other states tend to resist bids by any Asian power—be it Japan, China or India—to rise to the top of the pyramid." Given America is a foreign-based power it needs the cooperation and goodwill of Asian partners. This keeps its ambitions in check. If China were to rise to the top, it would threaten other regional powers. It would not rely on regional cooperation for security. Ideally, rising China and India will balance Japan. Even as they check each other, their reliance on the United States that one nation does not dominate the other. "If China makes a bid for regional hegemony, it will find it difficult to resist the structural constraints placed on it within this hierarchy," suggests Lee.

US power may be in relative decline, but within the larger multipolar world this is not such a negative outcome. The need for interdependence, generated by geopolitical vulnerability, has always been the driver to successful US leadership globally and particularly in the Asia-Pacific region. Thus, as the United States becomes a more diverse nation at home, especially on the back of the new wave of immigrants, it can certainly dream of leading the Asian century to a more democratic future. Thus, it is only fitting that Americans elected the first Pacific president, Barack Obama, to lead the oldest representative democracy into what many are predicting will be the Asian century.

Imagining the Asian-American Century

America's confidence in the Asian hemisphere has been buoyed by the long history of involvement with the Asia-Pacific region and the growth of the Asian-American population at home.

As President Obama pointed out in his speech on the sixtieth anniversary of the Korean War:

> Korea taught us that, as a people, we are stronger when we stand as one. On President Truman's orders, our troops served together in integrated units. And the heroism of African Americans in

Korea—and Latinos and Asian Americans and Native Americans—advanced the idea: If these Americans could live and work together over there, surely we could do the same thing here at home.

While many pundits and policy makers are predicting that the twenty-first century will be the "Asian Century," it is also likely that "there is another alternative or parallel scenario by which migration of highly skilled Asians to the economically punch-drunk America rejuvenates that economy, and launches it off on a new Asian-driven America century," according to a report by the Asian Century Institute.

After all, America's excursions into Asia for geopolitical, economic, and cultural exchange stretch back to when American marines landed in the Sino-Japanese war in 1894–1895. According to Alfred T. Mahan, considered by many the greatest American military strategist of the previous two centuries, if America could not control the sea lanes in the Pacific it would cease to be a significant power with the rise of the Asian countries; this remains true even today. Thus, US naval forces expanded in the North Pacific and took control of Hawai'i and the Philippines, putting an end to peaceful Chinese expansion and Japanese militarism. According to Warren I. Cohen, in his book "The Asian American Century," through the occupation of Philippines, wars in Korea and Vietnam, and World War II, the US presence although strongly supported by the Atlantic partners has kept the peace and helped expand the Asian dream of self-governance and free economy. Yet, the struggle for dominance in Southeast Asia continues as we reconsider "the Asian Century" hypothesis for the twenty-first century.

As the fastest growing region of the world for the past half-century, while most of the developed economies in OECD have been in economic decline, with the exceptions of Canada and Australia, Asia's dynamic growth even with the reduced forecasts for China and India is expected to be the engine of the global economy. However, another Asian Century is also in the making, an American Asian Century, as claimed by a recent report by Pew Research, "The Rise of Asian Americans." The report suggests that the growth and dynamism of the US economy has been built on the backs of the successive waves of immigration. Today, Asian Americans are the fastest-growing racial group in the United States, with high levels of income and education, perhaps best matched to the new information economy that increasingly relies on highly skilled workers.

While the rise of Asian Americans may be a historically recent phenomenon, they are not new to the history of immigration, stretching back to more than a century on the West coast. Prior to the Immigration Act of 1963, the Asian-American share of the US population was less than 1 percentage point, effectively suppressed by a century of race-based exclusionary policies. During the mid-1960s, the US government opened the gates to immigration, allowing people from all parts of the world to come to the United States. As a result, Asian Americans now represent 18.2 million or 5.8% of the US population.

Over the past decade, Asian Americans have comprised the largest group of new immigrants, surpassing even the new Hispanic immigrant population. By mid-century 2050, the Asian-American population will triple in size to 41 million, accounting for close to 10% of the US population. According to the Pew report, Asian Americans are a diverse group by country of origin: Chinese Americans (4.0 million or 23% of Asian Americans), Filipino Americans (3.4 million or 20%), Indian Americans (3.2 million or 18%), Vietnamese Americans (1.7 million or 10%), Korean Americans (1.7 million or 10%) and Japanese Americans (1.3 million or 8%). Together these six groups make up 83% of the total Asian population in the US, well positioned to conduct cultural diplomacy with the rising Asian hemisphere.

The new immigrants from Asia are increasingly more skilled and educated, nearly twice as likely as those who came three decades ago to have a college degree, and many go into high-paying fields such as science, engineering, medicine and finance. This dramatic rise of Asian Americans is significant as the US deals with the worst economic crisis since the great depression and as Asian economies rise. The highly skilled and educated Asian-American population offers a competitive advantage in weathering the economic storm at home and in reaching out to the emerging economies abroad. Thus, "the high levels of immigration from Asia will become an even more important driver of the US economy," according to a report from Asian Century Institute.

As the US economy begins to return to normal levels of growth, the Asian-American population will be poised to make a major contribution to the US economy—and perhaps result in America's Asian Century. According to the Nobel Prize-winning economist Joseph E. Stiglitz, there are several key lessons to be learned from the rise of Asian economies that can be instrumental here in the US.

At Asia Society recently, Stiglitz claimed that the US has become one of the most unequal countries in the developed world, contrary to many Americans' self-perception based on the historical record. According to him, "all new wealth generated in the past two decades has gone to the top tier of earners, and one-fifth of American children live in poverty."

He believes that lack of opportunity, rent-seeking by vested interests, instability and lack of public investment are driving the vicious circle of income inequality. So why do Americans tolerate this? Americans have been sold a bill of goods—inaccurate messaging and packaging—which suggests that equality sacrifices growth. When asked in a behavioural experiment which income distribution they view as most fair, most Americans prefer the Swedish model. Yet, the political discourse and ideas marketed in the media, Stiglitz suggested, are responsible for creating the perceptual gap between what Americans believe about themselves and what the everyday economic reality is.

Stiglitz argued that we need to look at the Asian models of success, such as in Korea, Taiwan and other "tiger" economies where a lot of effort has been made to ensure that economic development remains egalitarian. The rise of the Asian economies has proven their continued success. According to Stiglitz, both stagnant Japan and growing China would do well to heed this advice as well.

The Asian model may not be the right one for America, but Stiglitz's convincing argument is that the current US model has created more inequality. While there's "no magic bullet," this problem has to be corrected for America to grow again. Otherwise, average Americans in the coming century may be left behind by their counterparts in Asia and other emerging economies.

Notes

1. Jiping, Xi. 2013. BRICS Economies Help Strengthen Global Peace—Xi Jinping, http://www.itar-tass.com/en/c154/681933.html.
2. Yu, Li, and Chao Peng. 2013. Chengdu Special: Foreign Trade Continues to Drive the Economy, http://usa.chinadaily.com.cn/epaper/2013-03/14/content_16308695.htm.
3. Asian Development Bank. 2012. Asia 2050: Realizing the Asian Century, http://www.adb.org/publications/asia-2050-realizing-asian-century.
4. Australian Government. 2012. Australia in the Asian Century, http://asiancentury.dpmc.gov.au/white-paper.
5. US Intelligence Council. 2012. Global Trends 2030, http://globaltrends2030.files.wordpress.com/2012/11/global-trends-2030-november2012.pdf.
6. Price Waterhouse Cooper. 2013. World in 2050, http://www.pwc.com/en_GX/gx/world-2050/pdf/world-in-2050-jan-2011.pdf.
7. Clinton, Hillary. 2011. America's Pacific Century, Foreign Policy, November 2011, http://www.foreignpolicy.com/articles/2011/10/11/americas_pacific_century.
8. Obama, Barack. 2012. Remarks by the President on the Defense Strategic Review, January 5, 2012, http://www.whitehouse.gov/the-press-office/2012/01/05/remarks-president-defense-strategic-review.
9. Branigan, Tania. 2012. Obama's First Term. The Guardian, October 21, 2012, http://www.guardian.co.uk/world/2012/oct/21/obama-foreign-policy-pivots-asia.
10. Escobar, Pepe. 2012. Obama in Tehran? Tom's Dispatch, December 6, 2012, http://www.tomdispatch.com/post/175625/tomgram%3A_pepe_escobar,_obama_in_tehran/.
11. Kagan, Robert. 2012. US Cannot Pivot Away from the Middle East, Washington Post, November 20, 2012, http://articles.washingtonpost.com/2012-11-20/opinions/35510489_1_obama-administration-middle-east-obama-campaign.
12. Miniter, Richard. 2012. Leading from Behind, New York: MacMillan. http://www.amazon.com/Leading-Behind-Reluctant-President-Advisors/dp/125001610X.

13. Sharma, Dinesh. 2012. *Barack Obama in Hawai'i and Indonesia: The Making of a Global President*. New York: Praeger.

14. Maxwell, A., and T. W. Parent. 2012. The Obama Trigger: Presidential Approval and Tea Party Membership, *Social Science Quarterly*, 93, 5, December, 1384–1401.

15. Gibler, D.M., and S. V. Miller. 2012. Comparing the Foreign Aid Policies of Presidents Bush and Obama, *Social Science Quarterly*, 93, 5, December, 1203–1217.

16. Edwards, G.C. 2012. Creating Opportunities? Bipartisanship in the Early Obama Presidency, *Social Science Quarterly*, 93, 5, December, 1080–1100.

17. Morey, D.S., C. Thyne, S. Hayden, and M. Senters. 2012. Leader, Follower, or Spectator? The Role of President Obama in the Arab Spring Uprisings, *Social Science Quarterly*, 93, 5, December, 1186–1201.

18. Dervis, K. 2011. The Obama Administration and the Arab Spring, http://www.brookings.edu/research/opinions/2011/04/01-obama-arab-spring-dervis.

19. Bellinger, J. 2012. Obama's Weakness on Treatise, *New York Times*, December 18, http://www.nytimes.com/2012/12/19/opinion/obamas-weakness-on-treaties.html?_r=0.

20. Peake, J., G. Krutz, and T. Hughes. 2012. President Obama, the Senate, and the Polarized Politics of Treaty Making, *Social Science Quarterly*, 93, 5, December, 1295–1315.

21. Galston, W. 2013. Obama's Pivot to Europe: Forget China. An EU Trade Deal Would Be the Real Game-Changer. http://www.brookings.edu/research/opinions/2013/02/20-obama-pivot-europe-galston.

22. Hoffman, D., and A. Howard. 2012. Obama in Words and Deeds, *Social Science Quarterly*, 93, 5, December, 1316–1337.

23. Stout, C., and D. Le. 2012. Living the Dream: Barack Obama and Blacks' Changing Perceptions of the American Dream, *Social Science Quarterly*, 93, 5, December, 1338–1359.

24. Kimel, T., and K. Randazzo. 2012. Shaping the Federal Courts: The Obama Nominees, *Social Science Quarterly*, 93, 5, December, 1243–1250.

25. Engbers, T., and L. Fucilla. 2012. Transforming Leadership and the Obama Presidency, *Social Science Quarterly*, 93, 5, December, 1127–1145.

26. Kelley, C. 2012. Rhetoric and Reality? Unilateralism and the Obama Administration, *Social Science Quarterly*, 93, 5, December, 1146–1160.

27. Rockman, B. 2012. The Obama Presidency: Hope, Change, and Reality, *Social Science Quarterly*, 93, 5, December, 1065–1080.

28. Olson, J., Y. Ouyang, J. Poe, A. Trantham, and R. Waterman. 2012. The Teleprompter Presidency: Comparing Obama's Campaign and Governing Rhetoric, *Social Science Quarterly*, 93, 5, December, 1402–1423.

29. Ray, J. 2013. U.S. Leadership Earning Lower Marks Worldwide, Gallup Polls, March 13, 2013, http://www.gallup.com/poll/161201/leadership-earning-lower-marks-worldwide.aspx.

30. Pew Global Poll. 2012. Global Opinion of Obama Slips, http://www.pewglobal.org/2012/06/13/global-opinion-of-obama-slips-international-policies-faulted/.

31. Harvard Business School. 2012. US Competiveness at Risk, September 20, 2012, http://hbswk.hbs.edu/item/7094.html.

32. CBPP. 2012. Chart Book: The Legacy of the Great Recession, http://www.cbpp.org/cms/index.cfm?fa=view&id=3252.

33. Shih, W. 2012. Manufacturing. *Harvard Magazine*, September–October 2012, http://harvardmagazine.com/2012/09/manufacturing.

34. http://www.cnn.com/2012/10/03/politics/debate-transcript.

35. Desai, M. 2012. The Incentive Bubble. *Harvard Business Review*, March 2012, http://hbr.org/2012/03/the-incentive-bubble/ar/1.

36. Freeland, C. 2012. *Plutocrats: The Rise of the New Global Super-Rich and the Fall of Everyone Else*. New York: Penguin.

37. Kochan, T. 2012. Workforce. *Harvard Magazine*, September–October 2012, http://harvardmagazine.com/2012/09/the-workforce.

38. Gore, A. 2013. *The Future: Six Drivers of Global Change*. New York: Random House.

39. Sharma, D. 2004. *Human Technogenesis*. New York: John Wiley.

40. Mabhubhani, K. 2012. *The Great Convergence: Asia, the West, and the Logic of One World*. New York: Public Affairs.

41. Allen, W. 2012. Superstorm Sandy Linked to Climate Change, Think Progress, December 4, 2012, http://thinkprogress.org/climate/2012/12/04/1275841/poll-69-percent-of-new-yorkers-link-superstorm-sandy-with-climate-change/.

42. Cohen, W. 2002. *The Asian American Century (Edwin O Reischauer Lectures)*. Cambridge, MA: Harvard University Press.

43. Donilon, T. 2013. Remarks By Tom Donilon, National Security Advisory to the President: "The United States and the Asia-Pacific in 2013" http://www.whitehouse.gov/the-press-office/2013/03/11/remarks-tom-donilon-national-security-advisory-president-united-states-a.

44. Obama, B. 2011. Address to the Australian Parliament, November 27, http://www.theaustralian.com.au/national-affairs/obama-in-australia/obamas-speech-to-parliament/story-fnb0o39u-1226197973237.
45. Donilon, T. 2013. Remarks By Tom Donilon, National Security Advisory to the President: "The United States and the Asia-Pacific in 2013", http://www.whitehouse.gov/the-press-office/2013/03/11/remarks-tom-donilon-national-security-advisory-president-united-states-a.
46. Silverstein, M., A. Singhi, A. Liao, and D. Michael. 2012. *The $10 Trillion Prize: Captivating the Newly Affluent in China and India*. Cambridge, MA: Harvard Business Press.
47. Nair, C. 2011. *Consumptionomics: Asia's Role in Reshaping Capitalism and Saving the Planet*. New York: Wiley.
48. Shambaugh, D. 2013. *China Goes Global: The Partial Power*. New York: Oxford Press.
49. Stewart, D. 2012. The Asian Century Crumbles, *Huff Post*, December 23, 2012, http://www.huffingtonpost.com/devin-stewart/the-asian-century-crumble_b_2352088.html.
50. Lee, J. 2009. Why America Will Lead the Asian Century. Project Syndicate, August 14, 2009, http://www.project-syndicate.org/commentary/why-america-will-lead-the—asian-century.

INDEX

The annotation of an italicized "f" indicates a reference to a figure on the specified page.

Taylor & Francis

eBooks

FOR LIBRARIES

ORDER YOUR
FREE 30 DAY
INSTITUTIONAL
TRIAL TODAY!

Over 22,000 eBook titles in the Humanities,
Social Sciences, STM and Law from some of the
world's leading imprints.

Choose from a range of subject packages or create your own!

Benefits for
you

▶ Free MARC records

▶ COUNTER-compliant usage statistics

▶ Flexible purchase and pricing options

Benefits
for your
user

▶ Off-site, anytime access via Athens or referring URL

▶ Print or copy pages or chapters

▶ Full content search

▶ Bookmark, highlight and annotate text

▶ Access to thousands of pages of quality research
at the click of a button

For more information, pricing enquiries or to order
a free trial, contact your local online sales team.

UK and Rest of World: **online.sales@tandf.co.uk**

US, Canada and Latin America:
e-reference@taylorandfrancis.com

www.ebooksubscriptions.com

ALPSP Award for
BEST eBOOK
PUBLISHER
2009 Finalist
sponsored by

Taylor & Francis eBooks
Taylor & Francis Group

A flexible and dynamic resource for teaching, learning and research.